Shadow-Makers

Shadow-Makers

A Cultural History of Shadows in Architecture

Stephen Kite

Bloomsbury Academic
An imprint of Bloomsbury Publishing Plc

B L O O M S B U R Y
LONDON · OXFORD · NEW YORK · NEW DELHI · SYDNEY

Bloomsbury Academic

An imprint of Bloomsbury Publishing Plc

50 Bedford Square	1385 Broadway
London	New York
WC1B 3DP	NY 10018
UK	USA

www.bloomsbury.com

BLOOMSBURY and the Diana logo are trademarks of Bloomsbury Publishing Plc

First published 2017

© Stephen Kite, 2017

Stephen Kite has asserted his right under the Copyright, Designs and Patents Act, 1988, to be identified as Author of this work.

All rights reserved. No part of this publication may be reproduced or transmitted in any form or by any means, electronic or mechanical, including photocopying, recording, or any information storage or retrieval system, without prior permission in writing from the publishers.

No responsibility for loss caused to any individual or organization acting on or refraining from action as a result of the material in this publication can be accepted by Bloomsbury or the author.

British Library Cataloguing-in-Publication Data
A catalogue record for this book is available from the British Library.

ISBN:	HB:	978-1-4725-8810-4
	PB:	978-1-4725-8809-8
	ePDF:	978-1-4725-8812-8
	ePub:	978-1-4725-8811-1

Library of Congress Cataloging-in-Publication Data
A catalogue record for this book is available from the Library of Congress.

Cover design by Eleanor Rose

Cover photo: Detail of Louis Kahn looking at his tetrahedral ceiling in the Yale University Art Gallery, by photographer Lionel Freedman, American, 1919–2003, © Lionel Freedman/Yale University Archives

Typeset by Integra Software Services Pvt. Ltd.
Printed and bound in India

*Everything Time ever brings out of earth into light
Time also buries, however splendid it is,
And takes back into the shade* (Horace)

To the fond memory of family members taken
back into the shade

CONTENTS

Figures viii
Acknowledgements xxiii

1   Shadow Beginnings 1
2   Primordial Shadows 13
3   'The art of Shaddowes' 35
4   Shadows of the Sublime 81
5   Gothic 'Gloomth' 125
6   John Ruskin and Shadows of Power 151
7   Shadow Carpets 181
8   Shadows of the Unconscious 199
9   Louis Kahn and the 'Treasury of Shadows' 225
10 Shadow Futures 283

Bibliography 307
Index 317

FIGURES

1.1 St Peter's interior with Antonius T-cross. Drawing, Stephen Kite 3

2.1 Iron Age roundhouse reconstruction, St Fagans National History Museum. Drawing, Stephen Kite 15

2.2 Cruck-framed hall, Hendre'r-ywydd Uchaf farmhouse, from Llangynhafal, in Denbighshire, Wales, St Fagans National History Museum. Drawing, Stephen Kite 17

2.3 Claudine Bouzonnet Stella, *La veillée à la ferme pendant l'hiver*, engraving, 1661–7. Bibliothèque Nationale de France 18

2.4 Fireplace nook, Llainfadyn Cottage, 1762. St Fagans National History Museum. Drawing, Stephen Kite 20

2.5 Frank Lloyd Wright, William R. Heath House, 1904–5, Buffalo. Drawing, Stephen Kite 22

2.6 Utagawa Toyoharu (1735–1814), *Festivities in a mansion on the first Rat Day of the year*, Middle Edo, c. 1770. Purchased from the Frank Lloyd Wright Collection, UCLA Grunwald Center for the Graphic Arts, Hammer Museum 24

2.7 'Great sea' courtyard, Daisen-in sub-temple, Kyoto. Drawing, Stephen Kite 26

2.8 Koto-in Temple, Kyoto. Schematic space and transition plan, Stephen Kite. *Key*: 1. Main Gateway. 2. Dark

'Space Tunnel'. 3. *Hojo* Gateway. 4. Gateway to Secondary Entrance. 5. Secondary Entrance. 6. *Hojo*. 7. *Shoin*. 8. Zen Moss Garden. 9. Shoko-Ken Teahouse 27

2.9 Koto-in Temple, Kyoto. Dark space tunnel entrance. Photograph, Stephen Kite 27

2.10 Koto-in Temple, Kyoto. Moss garden. Photograph, Stephen Kite 28

2.11 Koto-in Temple, Kyoto. Shoko-ken teahouse. Photograph, Stephen Kite 29

3.1 Great towers and lofty steeples: Hawksmoor's Christ Church, Spitalfields, seen from Brushfield Street. Photograph, Edwin Smith, 1957, RIBA Library Photographs Collection 39

3.2 Interior of Leon Battista Alberti's, Sant' Andrea, Mantua. Drawing by Stephen Kite 41

3.3 Nicholas Hawksmoor, prospect of Nottingham, sketchbook c. 1680–3, p. 7, RIBA Library Drawings and Archives Collections 43

3.4 Nicholas Hawksmoor, 'Chapell Barr' Nottingham, sketchbook c. 1680–3, p. 9, RIBA Library Drawings and Archives Collections 44

3.5 Nicholas Hawksmoor, Bath Abbey, sketchbook c. 1680–3, p. 31, RIBA Library Drawings and Archives Collections 45

3.6 Nicholas Hawksmoor, study of All Saint's Church, Northampton, sketchbook c. 1680–3, p. 53, RIBA Library Drawings and Archives Collections 46

3.7 Keystones to crypt openings. Drawing by Stephen Kite 49

3.8 Interior, St George's Bloomsbury. Photograph, Stephen Kite 51

3.9 North façade, St George's Bloomsbury. Drawing by Stephen Kite 52

3.10 St George's Bloomsbury, close-up of tower and corner of portico. Photograph, Edwin Smith, 1970, RIBA Library Photographs Collection 55

3.11 Nicholas Hawksmoor, view of St Mary's Warwick. Warden and Fellows of All Souls College, Oxford 57

3.12 Nicholas Hawksmoor, preliminary design for the west towers of St Paul's Cathedral, c. 1699, pen, pencil and grey wash. The Chapter of St Paul's Cathedral 58

3.13 Nicholas Hawksmoor, elevation study of Christ Church, Spitalfields. The British Library Board, K. Top. 23. 11. t 60

3.14 Sir Christopher Wren and Nicholas Hawksmoor, Wren's project for Whitehall Palace, 1698. Warden and Fellows of All Souls College, Oxford 62

3.15 Sir John Vanbrugh, sketch plan and elevation, Sir William Saunderson's House, Greenwich, c. 1718–20. Victoria and Albert Museum, London 63

3.16 Nicholas Hawksmoor (with Sir Christopher Wren), study of St Augustine, Watling St. Warden and Fellows of All Souls College, Oxford 65

3.17 Nicholas Hawksmoor, preliminary elevation drawing of façade of St Anne's Limehouse. The British Library Board, K. Top. 28. 11. d 66

3.18 Nicholas Hawksmoor, preliminary elevation drawing for the west façade of St George-in-the-East. The British Library Board, K. Top. 23. 21. 2. h 68

3.19 Nicholas Hawksmoor, preliminary elevation drawing for the west tower of St Anne's Limehouse, with fluted trumpet-bell cap. Victoria and Albert Museum, London 69

3.20 Nicholas Hawksmoor, preliminary elevation drawing for the west tower of St Anne's Limehouse, with 'Tower of the Winds' upper stage. The British Library Board, K. Top. 28. 11. g 71

3.21 Nicholas Hawksmoor, elevation drawing for the west tower of St Anne's Limehouse, of near-final upper stage. The British Library Board, K. Top. 28. 11. c 72

3.22 Nicholas Hawksmoor, west tower of St Anne's Limehouse. Photograph, Stephen Kite 73

4.1 Joseph Wright of Derby (1734–97), *The Prisoner*, 1787–90. Yale Center for British Art, Paul Mellon Collection 83

4.2 George Dance the Younger, Newgate Prison, 1768–78. Photograph by Francis Stewart, c. 1890. © Museum of London 85

4.3 Giovanni Battista Piranesi, *Study for Différentes vue de Pesto ...*, Plate VI. The Basilica looking west with the *pronaos* in the foreground and the Temple of Neptune to the right, c. 1777–8. By courtesy of the Trustees of Sir John Soane's Museum 91

4.4 Sir John Soane, competition design for a male penitentiary, 1782. By courtesy of the Trustees of Sir John Soane's Museum 92

4.5 Drawing by Joseph Michael Gandy, interior perspective of the Breakfast Room, Pitzhanger Manor, looking towards the Library (1802–3). By courtesy of the Trustees of Sir John Soane's Museum 96

4.6 Sir John Soane, preliminary design and working drawing for the Breakfast Room, Pitzhanger Manor, 2 August 1801. SM (192) 31/4/24. By courtesy of the Trustees of Sir John Soane's Museum 97

4.7 Sir John Soane, Tyringham, Buckinghamshire, the gateway. Detail of shadow groove 'capital' and springing of arch. Photograph, Stephen Kite 101

4.8 Sir John Soane, Pitzhanger Manor, Breakfast Room. Working drawing for ceiling, 1802, office drawing made by pupil W. E. Rolfe. SM (201) 31/4/12. By courtesy of the Trustees of Sir John Soane's Museum 102

4.9 Sir John Soane, the Breakfast Room in No. 13 Lincoln's Inn Fields. Photograph, Derry Moore. By courtesy of the Trustees of Sir John Soane's Museum 103

4.10 Plan of the ground floor of the museum, from *Description* (1835) 105

4.11 Section of the dome area and Breakfast Room looking east, drawn by Frank Copland, 1818. SM Vol. 83, 1. By courtesy of the Trustees of Sir John Soane's Museum 107

4.12 A portion of the upper part of the Breakfast Room (showing top lighting and pendentives) drawn by Charles James Richardson, 7 November 1825. SM Vol. 82, 27. By courtesy of the Trustees of Sir John Soane's Museum 108

4.13 *View of part of the Collection of Antiquities....*, view of the Sepulchral Chamber and the sarcophagus of Seti I, drawn by Charles James Richardson, 9 September 1825. SM Vol. 82, 47. By courtesy of the Trustees of Sir John Soane's Museum 114

4.14 Detailed view of the dome and artefacts. Drawing, Stephen Kite 115

4.15 View of the dome area by lamplight looking southeast, drawn by Joseph Michael Gandy, 1811. SM 14/6/5. By courtesy of the Trustees of Sir John Soane's Museum 116

4.16 Perspectives of eight designs for churches, with plan, 1824: variations for Holy Trinity, Marylebone; an Ionic design for St. Peter, Walworth and the 1,800 design for the Sepulchral Chapel for Tyringham, drawn by Joseph Gandy. SM 15/4/8. By courtesy of the Trustees of Sir John Soane's Museum 118

5.1 Sir John Soane, the Monk's Parlour in No. 13 Lincoln's Inn Fields. Photograph, Derry Moore. By courtesy of the Trustees of Sir John Soane's Museum 126

5.2 Perspective of the hall and staircase at Strawberry Hill, R. Bentley. Courtesy of the Lewis Walpole Library, Yale University 128

5.3 Frontispiece to *Elegy Written in a Country Churchyard*, R. Bentley, 1753. Courtesy of the Lewis Walpole Library, Yale University 131

5.4 View of Tintern Abbey from Gilpin, *Observations on the River Wye* 133

5.5 P. Van Lerberghe, *Interior View of Tintern Abbey, in South Wales*, c. 1801–5. © The British Library Board, Maps K. Top.31.16.f 135

5.6 *Castle of Otranto, Isabella making her Escape from the Castle*, 1800, transparency, etching and mezzotint with some hand-colouring. © The Trustees of the British Museum 137

5.7 *Plan of the Grounds of Piercefield and the Peninsular of Lancaut*, from William Coxe, *An Historical Tour in Monmouthshire*, 1801 138

5.8 Entrance to Giant's Cave, Piercefield, from the Wye viewpoint. Drawing, Stephen Kite 140

5.9 Ruins of The Grotto, Piercefield. Drawing, Stephen Kite 142

5.10 Study of a man sketching, holding a Claude Glass, drawing by Thomas Gainsborough, c. 1750–55. © The Trustees of the British Museum 144

5.11 James Wyatt, *Projected Design for Fonthill Abbey, Wiltshire*, watercolour possibly by J. M. W. Turner, 1798. Yale Center for British Art, Paul Mellon Collection 146

6.1 John Ruskin, 'Sketchbook 4, 1846', pp. 41–42. Courtesy The Ruskin Museum, Coniston, Cumbria (CONRM 1990.381) 153

6.2 Plate 19, 'The Picturesque of Windmills', John Ruskin, *Modern Painters, vol. 4* 155

6.3 John Ruskin, *The Palazzo Contarini-Fasan, Venice*, graphite, watercolour and bodycolour on grey paper, 1841. © Ashmolean Museum, University of Oxford 157

6.4   John Ruskin, *Interior of San Frediano, Lucca*, watercolour, brown ink and pencil on paper, 1845, Manchester Art Gallery, UK/Bridgeman Images 158

6.5   Joseph Mallord William Turner, *The Crypt of Kirkstall Abbey, from the Liber Studiorum*, etching with mezzotint, 1812. © The Fitzwilliam Museum, Cambridge 158

6.6   John Ruskin, *Part of the Façade of the 'destroyed' Church of San Michele in Foro, Lucca, as it appeared in 1845*, watercolour and bodycolour over graphite on grey wove paper, 1845. © Ashmolean Museum, University of Oxford 160

6.7   John Ruskin, *Part of the Façade of the 'destroyed' Church of San Michele in Foro, Lucca, sketched in colour*, watercolour over graphite on wove paper, 1846. © Ashmolean Museum, University of Oxford 161

6.8   *The Seven Lamps of Architecture, Plate 6*, detail of San Michele, Lucca 162

6.9   John Ruskin, Figure 30, *Modern Painters, vol. 4* 165

6.10 John Ruskin, *Study of Portal and Carved Pinnacles, Cathedral of St Lô, Normandy*, 1848, graphite, brown ink and brown wash on cream wove paper. Harvard Art Museums/Fogg Museum, Gift of Samuel Sachs. Photo: Imaging Department © President and Fellows of Harvard College 166

6.11 Frank Furness, Pennsylvania Academy of the Fine Arts (1872–6), detail of façade. Drawing by Stephen Kite 169

6.12 Adler and Sullivan, The Chicago Auditorium (1887–9). Photograph by John Szarkowski. Pace/MacGill Gallery, New York; The Estate of John Szarkowski 171

6.13 John Ruskin, 'The Acanthus of Torcello', *Stones of Venice, volume 2, plate 2* 175

6.14 Sullivan, Guaranty Building, Buffalo, capital detail. Photograph, Stephen Kite 176

7.1 The lesson circle of the 'one-tree' Quranic school. Drawing by Stephen Kite 183

7.2 Sketch plan of *shawi* tree, Wadi al Hawasinah, Oman. Survey and drawing, Stephen Kite 184

7.3 *Shawi* tree, Wadi al Ma'awil, Oman. Photograph, Stephen Kite 184

7.4 Mosque Muslimat, Oman. Drawing by Stephen Kite 185

7.5 Aerial survey, Iran, Erich Schmidt, *Isfahan, the Masjid-Jumah or Friday Mosque.* Courtesy of the Oriental Institute of the University of Chicago 187

7.6 Aerial survey, Iran, Erich Schmidt, *Isfahan, Capital of the Safavid Kingdom, The Mosque of the Shah [Imam] in the foreground. From altitude of 200 metres on 6 July 1937.* Courtesy of the Oriental Institute of the University of Chicago 187

7.7 Entrance to bazar from *Maydan Imam*. Drawing by Stephen Kite 188

7.8 Qaysariyyih, bazar Esfahan. Drawing by Stephen Kite 189

7.9 1919 Map of Esfahan showing the shade-system of the bazar leading from the open space of the *Maydan*

Imam at centre, north-eastwards to the Friday Mosque at the heart of the older city (from Cantacuzino, Sherban, 'Can Isfahan Survive', *The Architectural Review*, vol. 159, no. 951 (May 1976), pp. 292–300, p. 299) 190

7.10 *Bunbast passage*. Drawing by Stephen Kite 191

7.11 Small community bazar (*bazarchih*), Dardasht, Esfahan. Drawing by Stephen Kite 193

7.12 Plans of courtyard houses, Dardasht. Survey and drawing, Stephen Kite 194

7.13 Section through courtyard house and *bunbast* approach. Survey and drawing, Stephen Kite 194

7.14 Alison and Peter Smithson, axonometric of area immediately outside Damascus Gate, Jerusalem. Courtesy of the Frances Loeb Library, Harvard University Graduate School of Design 196

7.15 Alison and Peter Smithson, perspective of Damascus Gate project. Courtesy of the Frances Loeb Library, Harvard University Graduate School of Design 197

8.1 A house, seventeenth century, from Adrian Stokes, *Venice* (1945), Plate 17. © Estate of Adrian Stokes 203

8.2 Santa Maria dei Miracoli, south side, from Adrian Stokes, *Venice* (1945), Plate 12. © Estate of Adrian Stokes 205

8.3 Aldo Rossi, *Composition with Teatro del Mondo and buildings in Venice* (between 1979 and 1980). Aldo Rossi fonds, Collection Centre Canadien d'Architecture/Canadian Centre for Architecture,

	Montréal, © Eredi Aldo Rossi, courtesy Fondazione Aldo Rossi 209
8.4	Aldo Rossi, *'Analogous' composition, with the entrance gate for the Architectural Exhibition at the Venice Biennale, the Teatro del Mondo, and a project for a hotel in Cannaregio-West, Venice, Italy. 1981.* Aldo Rossi fonds, Collection Centre Canadien d'Architecture/Canadian Centre for Architecture, Montréal, © Eredi Aldo Rossi, courtesy Fondazione Aldo Rossi 210
8.5	Aldo Rossi, Gianni Braghieri, *Cimitero di San Cataldo, Modena, Italy: Plan* (between 1971 and 1978). Aldo Rossi fonds, Collection Centre Canadien d'Architecture/Canadian Centre for Architecture, Montréal, © Eredi Aldo Rossi, courtesy Fondazione Aldo Rossi 212
8.6	Gallaratese housing, north Milan, 1969–70. Photograph Stephen Kite 213
8.7	Detail of clock tower, St Mark's Piazza, Venice, from Adrian Stokes, *Venice* (1945), Plate 9. © Estate of Adrian Stokes 218
8.8	Stoa, New Cemetery of San Cataldo, Modena, 1971–8. Photograph, Stephen Kite 219
9.1	George Cruikshank, *Jeanie, I say, Jeanie, woman*, etching from Walter Scott, *Waverley Novels, 48 vols.*, vol. 11 (London: Fisher and Son, 1836–9), facing p. 322 232
9.2	Louis I. Kahn, introductory letter, p. 3, to Richard Saul Wurman and Eugene Feldman, *The Notebooks*

and *Drawings of Louis I. Kahn* (1973). Louis I. Kahn Collection, The University of Pennsylvania and the Pennsylvania Historical and Museum Commission 234

9.3 Louis I. Kahn, Luxor, 1951, plate 8 in Richard Saul Wurman and Eugene Feldman, *The Notebooks and Drawings of Louis I. Kahn* (1973). Louis I. Kahn Collection, The University of Pennsylvania and the Pennsylvania Historical and Museum Commission 235

9.4 Louis I. Kahn, Carcassonne study, 1959. Louis I. Kahn Collection, The University of Pennsylvania and the Pennsylvania Historical and Museum Commission 237

9.5 Louis I. Kahn, interior of Yale University Art Gallery. Photograph, Lionel Freedman. Louis I. Kahn Collection, The University of Pennsylvania and the Pennsylvania Historical and Museum Commission 239

9.6 Louis I. Kahn, Trenton Bath House, mosaic at entrance. Photograph, Stephen Kite 241

9.7 Detail of library study carrels, Biology Building, University of Pennsylvania, Philadelphia. Drawing by Stephen Kite 244

9.8 Louis I. Kahn, interior sketch of Le Corbusier's Ronchamp Chapel, 1959. Louis I. Kahn Collection, The University of Pennsylvania and the Pennsylvania Historical and Museum Commission 245

9.9 Louis I. Kahn, perspective view of Margaret Esherick House, Chestnut Hill, Philadelphia (1959–62), c. May 1960. Louis I. Kahn Collection, The University of Pennsylvania and the Pennsylvania Historical and Museum Commission 247

9.10 Louis I. Kahn, early design study of north elevation of the Tribune Review Building, with semi-circular and triangular 'keyhole-window' options. Louis I. Kahn Collection, The University of Pennsylvania and the Pennsylvania Historical and Museum Commission 248

9.11 Louis I. Kahn, south façade detail of the Tribune Review Building. Photograph, John Ebstel. Courtesy Keith de Lellis Gallery, New York 249

9.12 Louis I. Kahn, ground floor office space of the Tribune Review Building. Photograph, John Ebstel. Courtesy Keith de Lellis Gallery, New York 250

9.13 Follower of Rembrandt, *A man seated reading*, 1628–30. © The National Gallery, London 251

9.14 Rochester, First Unitarian Church, 'Final Plan', c. 1961 (prior to community spaces extension, designed 1965). First Unitarian Church Collection, The Architectural Archives, University of Pennsylvania 252

9.15 Rochester, First Unitarian Church, interior of the sanctuary. Drawing by Stephen Kite 253

9.16 Rochester, First Unitarian Church, section drawing of intermediate four-column and umbrella-roof design. First Unitarian Church Collection, The Architectural Archives, University of Pennsylvania 255

9.17 Rochester, First Unitarian Church, detail of keel vault and column supports. Photograph, Stephen Kite 257

9.18 Rochester, First Unitarian Church, exterior view from south-east. Photograph, Stephen Kite 259

9.19 Rochester, First Unitarian Church, study of entrance (north) elevation. Louis I. Kahn Collection, The

University of Pennsylvania and the Pennsylvania Historical and Museum Commission 260

9.20 Rochester, First Unitarian Church, north elevation. © The Museum of Modern Art (MoMA), New York/ Scala, Florence 260

9.21 Rochester, First Unitarian Church, classroom window seat. Photograph, Stephen Kite 261

9.22 Isamu Noguchi, *Constellation (for Louis Kahn)*, 1980–3, Kimbell Art Museum, standing stone basalt monolith. Photograph, Stephen Kite 263

9.23 Pronaos and shadow grove, Kimbell Art Museum. Drawing by Stephen Kite 264

9.24 Louis I. Kahn, *Kimbell Art Museum. Perspective view from south-west*, 22 September, 1967. Louis I. Kahn Collection, The University of Pennsylvania and the Pennsylvania Historical and Museum Commission 266

9.25 Shadow play of the portico and vault, Kimbell Art Museum. Photograph, Stephen Kite 267

9.26 'Green' north courtyard, and coloured shadows, Kimbell Art Museum. Photograph, Stephen Kite 269

9.27 'Graduating silver, light to darkness', north-west gallery spaces, Kimbell Art Museum. Drawing by Stephen Kite 270

9.28 Louis I. Kahn, *Kimbell Art Museum. Schematic section of galleries*, 22 September 1967. Louis I. Kahn Collection, The University of Pennsylvania and the Pennsylvania Historical and Museum Commission 271

9.29 Louis I. Kahn, *Kimbell Art Museum. Schematic elevations of vault ends, detail of travertine panels*,

August 1969. Louis I. Kahn Collection, The University of Pennsylvania and the Pennsylvania Historical and Museum Commission 272

10.1 Dom van der Laan, St Benedictusberg Abbey, Vaals, Netherlands. The church. Photograph, Stephen Kite 286

10.2 Dom van der Laan, St Benedictusberg Abbey, Vaals, Netherlands. Cloister. Photograph, Stephen Kite 287

10.3 Peter Zumthor, 'Bruder Klaus' Chapel, Wachendorf, Cologne. Field setting. Photograph, Stephen Kite 289

10.4 Peter Zumthor, 'Bruder Klaus' Chapel. Interior looking up to tear-drop aperture. Drawing by Stephen Kite 290

10.5 Peter Zumthor, Kolumba Diocesan Museum, Cologne. Ruin hall. Drawing by Stephen Kite 293

10.6 O' Donnell and Tuomey, Student Centre for the London School of Economics. Photograph, Stephen Kite 295

10.7 Hugh Ferriss, Imaginary drawings. Zoning ordinances. Crude Clay for Architects, 1922–4, charcoal pencil on board. Avery Architectural and Fine Arts Library, Columbia University 296

10.8 Ashton Raggatt McDougall (ARM), Melbourne Theatre Company, 2008. Photograph, Stephen Kite 298

10.9 LAB Architecture Studio, Federation Square, 1997–2001. Photograph, Stephen Kite 300

10.10 Claesson, Kovisto Rune, Sfera Building, Kyoto, 2003. Photograph, Stephen Kite 303

ACKNOWLEDGEMENTS

Time is among the most precious resources in extended research of this kind, and I am especially indebted for the award of a Cardiff University Research Leave Fellowship from October 2013 to October 2014 which advanced the writing and enabled key parts of the fieldwork, particularly that relating to the United States. My own department within Cardiff University, the Welsh School of Architecture (and its Head of School, Chris Tweed), has matched this backing, provided support throughout and has also contributed towards the image costs. I am grateful to the Paul Mellon Centre for Studies in British Art, whose funding enabled research in London in the collections of The British Library, RIBA Library Drawings and Archives Collection, Sir John Soane's Museum and the Victoria and Albert Museum. Among the many archival sources, I wish to express individual appreciation for the guidance of William Whitacker and Nancy Thorne (Louis I. Kahn Collection, University of Pennsylvania), Stephen Astley, Susan Palmer, Bellina Adjei (Sir John Soane's Museum), Jonathan Makepeace (RIBA Library Drawings and Archives Collection), Vicky Slowe (Ruskin Museum, Coniston, Cumbria), Stephen Wildman, Rebecca Patterson, Diane Tyler, Jen Shepherd (Ruskin Library, Lancaster University), Richard Edwards (St Fagans: National History Museum, Cardiff), Ian Angus and Telfer Stokes (Estate of Adrian Stokes) and Anne Rainsbury (Chepstow Museum). I also express my appreciation to David Leatherbarrow and Mark Crinson, who have been warm advocates of the project idea from its inception, to Chris Smith for his insights into the Australian context and to Alice Brownfield, Kristian Hyde, Peter Salter, Simon Unwin and Richard Weston for their shadow conversations.

Presentations and international conferences have developed and tested key arguments of the book at inter alia Chicago, Austin, Texas (Society of Architectural Historians), Royal Academy of Arts, London, Lancaster University, Tate Britain London, University of Kent, Manchester School of Architecture, and Edinburgh School of Architecture and Landscape Architecture. I am grateful for these opportunities and the many conversations that have resulted, including those with Desley Luscombe, Andrew Benjamin, John Hendrix, Lorens Holm, Owen Hopkins, Jeremy Melvin, Stephen Wildman, Paul Tucker, David Carrier, Timothy Brittain-Catlin, Albena Yaneva and Mark Dorrian. Interim published outcomes from these sorties into the specific topic areas of the book have been a chapter on the Venetian shadows of Adrian Stokes and Aldo Rossi (J. S. Henrix and L. E. Holm, eds., *Architecture and the Unconscious*, 2016) and on Ruskin's shadow (T. Brittain-Catlin, J. De Maeyer, M. Bressani, eds., *Gothic Revival Worldwide: AWN Pugin's Global Influence*, 2016). Internal seminars and debates in the Welsh School of Architecture have also fostered the writing and I would like to thank these many friends and colleagues, especially those in the Architectural History and Theory Group. Earlier fieldwork in Iran and the Sultanate of Oman benefited from the wisdom and encouragement of Nasrine Faghih, Paolo Costa and Germana Costa. The potential of shadow-making has also been explored by the students in my Design Units at both BSc Architectural Studies (Year 3) and Masters in Architecture level; they have taught me much about the rich architecture that results in making shadow a central subject in design thinking.

At Bloomsbury Academic, James Thompson has been an enthusiastic and constructive supporter of the book from the first proposal, with the editorial advice and support of Claire Constable, Frances Arnold, Sophie Tann and, initially, Molly Beck. On the production side, thanks are due to Ken Bruce, Manikandan Kuppan and Smita Nair. I am also grateful for the encouragingly productive comments of the anonymous readers of the initial proposal and the developed manuscript.

I thank my friends and family for indulging my shadow obsessions with generosity and patience. Foremost are my now far-flung children – Edwin was a driver and companion on some of the US field trips and Catherine introduced me to the shadows of Australia – and my wife Máire, who has supported me in everything through over thirty-five years of kindness and love.

1

Shadow Beginnings

All great and beautiful work has come of first gazing without shrinking into the darkness. (John Ruskin, 'The Lance of Pallas', Modern Painters, *vol. 5)*[1]

Nordic Prelude – St Peter's Klippan

It barely looks like a building at all in any expected figural sense of a church – ancient or modern. The height of the belfry scarcely exceeds that of the body of the main structure, and is squat even for this land of thickset church towers. Its hunched, monolithic forms might be a group of erratic boulders, or megalithic remains, discovered here in the low undulating region of Skåne in south-west Sweden. This is the church of St Peter's Klippan (meaning 'the rock on the rock'), built from 1963 to 1966, in rough sombre purple-brown brick, as the last major work of Sigurd Lewerentz (1885–1975) which he began at the age of seventy-eight. It is one of the most potent examples of shadow-making in later twentieth-century architecture, built by a master of sacred architecture who 'by an architectural alchemy of great intensity ... fused the simple elements of construction into metaphors of brooding mystery'.[2] The church group crouches at the western apex of a small park which lies to the east of the small town centre. Signalled by the belfry above the sacristy, the entrance sequence begins by the road on the dark north side. The churchgoer enters a passage barely three metres wide, like one towards a tomb chamber, or akin to a cleft in those strange glacial 'split stones' the Swedes call *kluven sten*.[3] The passage slopes down to a door of domestic scale discovered to the right in the depth of the wall – the start of a steady descent that will only end at the altar.

The door opens into the arresting shadows of the vestibule of the Andreas Chapel, whose interior Lewerentz carves with his dark brick, both in the walls and in the double jack-arch vaults borne on steel beams. Though ancient in feeling here, these are a form of construction that needs the span capacity of iron or steel and originates in the pragmatics of fireproof construction in the textile mills of the early machine age.[4] Here Lewerentz mimics the cave or catacomb, as also evoked in his Resurrection Chapel (1921–5) at the Woodland cemetery and crematorium, Stockholm.[5] Lewerentz intensifies these primitive echoes by placing a brick altar in the Andreas Chapel, thus respecting an ancient custom of altars in church porches dating back to the fourth century. In the following pages we shall often find shadow linked to chthonic forces, and memories of the cave, as in Nicholas Hawksmoor's recall of catacomb worship in his churches (Chapter 3). The northern of the two vaults is low, but the southern one springs boldly upwards anticipating the scale of the main congregational space. A tomb-opening metaphor may also be indicated in how Lewerentz sets the springing emphatically back over the lower vault – like a lid set back – while a light chimney admits a shaft of light through this higher vault. This is the only source of natural light in the chapel apart from a vertical slot window onto the entrance passage. In these ways Lewerentz's works call us to challenging pilgrimages through spaces of creative spiritual darkness, invoking intense themes of death, rebirth and resurrection. At Stockholm, to reach the portico of his Chapel of the Resurrection (1921–5), one must pass through dark forest along the narrow 'Way of the Seven Wells'.[6]

Another turn to the left brings the worshipper into the branching shadow world of the eighteen metre-square Lutheran hall of *circumstantes* – that is, a non-axial place that allows a gathering-around at the altar. Adapting further to the dimness, the eyes discover a diagonal that links the baptismal zone, the off-centre Antonius T-cross of steel bearing the roof vaults, and the lectern and altar area (Figure 1.1). Though Lewerentz had played with the idea of Ronchamp-like window arrays, he fixed upon just four wall openings about one metre square.[7] Light from the two in the West wall aids the cautious tread on entry; it catches the off-white seashell of the font and casts the shadows of its supporting armature onto the sloping brick floor. The glare from the other two apertures piercing the south wall does nothing to dispel the gloom, but only intensifies the darkness of the attached shadows of the wall's uncut bricks and rough mortar. Two light slots in the vaults show the route from sacristy to sanctuary and complete the church's only natural sources of light. There are also suspended cylindrical lights – reminiscent of the lamps in the mosques of Istanbul – whose low horizon of illumination serves, as in those Islamic sacred spaces, to intensify the mystery of the vaults above, while modelling and shading their curved forms.

The three key terms used earlier – 'cast shadow', 'attached shadow' and 'shading' – derive from Leonardo da Vinci, but point up the 'confusing vagueness of differentiation in the current ordinary terms for shadow'.[8] Klippan also places the worshipper deeply in shadow as that 'indistinct form of darkness' that the English language defines separately as 'shade', whereas Italian and French use the same word – *ombra, ombre*. We can

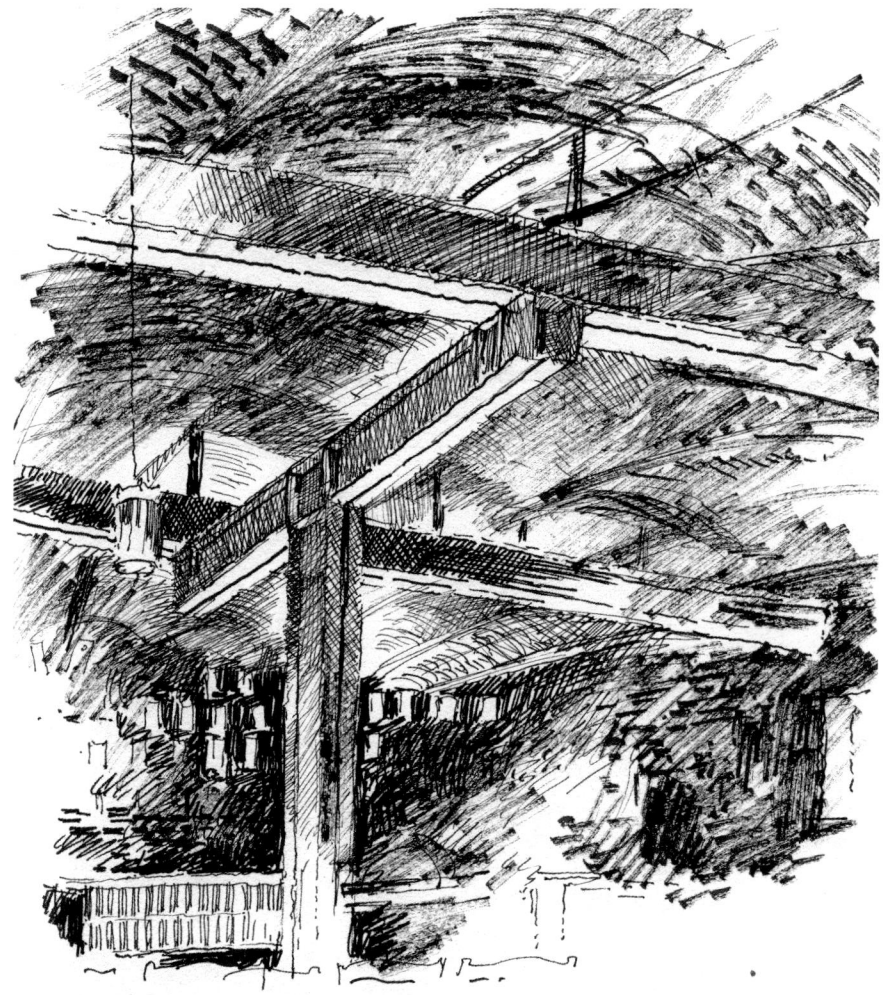

FIGURE 1.1 St Peter's interior with Antonius T-cross. Drawing, Stephen Kite.

number cast shadows, but we use a partitive such as '*some* shade' for this absence of light which is phenomenally very present, but without the distinct spatial organization of cast shadows.[9] As here at Klippan, *shadow-makers* powerfully interrelate all these forms of shadow and shade.

Colin St John Wilson finds the steel T-cross at the centre of the church space 'pregnant with symbolic meaning...almost as if the ancient legend of the Discovery of the True Cross had happened here'.[10] Unquestionably, he has in mind here the great cycle at Arezzo in whose final fresco – depicting the *Restitution of the Cross to Jerusalem* – Piero della Francesca pairs the cross of redemption of the New Testament, with the tree of knowledge of the Old. Of this lunette Roberto Longhi describes how 'these inhabitants of Jerusalem rest against the broad background...and wide expanses of the dark-shadowed wall' of the city.[11] Certainly the bifurcation of Lewerentz's Antonius cross – against the dark-shadowed walls of *his* earthy Jerusalem – suggests some such pairing. Then there is also the great ash-tree Yggdrassil of the Nordic *Eddas*, the wide-branching tree of life on which Odin crucified himself in the search for wisdom, and near whose roots springs the fountain of wisdom where Odin also gave an eye to drink of its knowledge.[12] Below the font at Klippan the paving swells to a rift that exposes a dark pool, symbolic perhaps both of such pagan places and the baptismal springs of Christianity.[13]

So with this archetype of the cave linked to shadow-making, we shall also find that of the primitive hut in the following pages, as in these atavistic memories of trees and timber construction. On the face of it nothing could be more totally stereotomic (masonry-tectonic) than this heavy brick cavern; yet, the transpositions from timber construction are arguably more evident than just in the steel cross and beams. In *Nightlands*, his study of *Nordic Building*, Christian Norberg-Schulz contrasts the traditional half-timbered tectonic skeleton of nearby Denmark – just across the Øresund Strait – with the log construction and massivity of Swedish building:

> Its basic element is not the transverse frame but an embracive rectangle of stacked timbers. The Swedish word for this construction, *knut-timring* reveals that this method acts like a 'knot-ring' around the space.... If we designate log construction as massive, it is because it functions as bearing wall: each element is equally important. This means that openings must be cut out, in contrast to half-timbering, which is potentially open over all. Holes in bearing walls have a limited size because they tend to weaken the construction.... A cavernous space results.... With this, gestalt quality is interpreted as a whole, which 'forgets' its constructive origins.[14]

Norberg-Schulz also stresses the Swedish tendency to 'elementary volumes, continuous surfaces, and sporadic openings that are glazed close to the outer edge';[15] so even Klippan's apparently radical face-glazing is strongly rooted in folk building. Whether half-timbered or log coursed in origin, Nordic buildings can be generally characterized as 'the creation of a cavelike interior that corresponds to [an] exterior clearing'[16] in the dark forest: 'In the North we are bound to a world of forces, because we inhabit the realm of the night. As sunlight fades, things lose their eidos, their identity.... Thus we are trapped in the web, the thicket, to which the forest belongs.'[17] So at Klippan, in Wilson's intense description:

> We are invited into the dark. Enveloped in that heart of darkness that calls on all the senses to measure its limits, we are compelled to pause. In a rare moment of explanation, Lewerentz stated that subdued light

was enriching precisely in the degree to which the nature of the space has to be reached for, emerging only in response to exploration. This slow taking possession of space (the way in which it gradually becomes yours) promotes that fusion of privacy in the sharing of common ritual that is the essence of the numinous. And it is only in such darkness that light begins to take on a figurative quality – the living light of the candle flame.[18]

The following chapters are also an invitation into the dark in their affirmation of the cultural significance of shadow as a shaping factor in architecture – as powerfully manifest at Klippan. Neither exhaustive nor continuous, these tracings of shadow – as an active but repressed category in the way we think about and make architecture – ask: What does the story of architecture look like when shadow itself is made the subject of thought? When shadow becomes the figure, and not merely the servant ground to light's pre-eminence. So, the book takes a global perspective – grounded to some extent in British visual culture – to analyse cultural moments where shadow has been a distinctive factor in the making of architecture. In bringing shadows, themselves out of the shadows, it reveals their expressive power, and cultural potential, in the creation of spaces for refuge, devotion, awe, political and theatrical display, mystery, power, coolness, psychological fantasies and so on. A lot can be learned in the translation from drawing to building, not least in seeing in the studies examined here how shadow-makers visualize their creations, and how architectural shadow forms have been presented in various cultural representations.

Defining shadow

Whereas this book, as a whole, attempts to define shadow in its consequences for architecture's cultural histories, it is worth appending to the Klippan overture some shadow stories and some further preliminary points on shadow definition. In his seminal study of *Shadows and Enlightenment*, Michael Baxandall quotes the eighteenth-century scientist Claude-Nicholas Lecat's (1767) definition of shadows as 'holes in light' – they are absences which originate in 'a local and relative deficiency of light'.[19] As noted at Klippan, Leonardo da Vinci characterized these deficiencies into three kinds: *cast* shadow, *attached* shadow and *shading*. These he illustrated by a diagram showing rays of light falling from above on the profile of a face. The *cast* shadows are those thrown onto the surfaces beneath by a projection blocking the light, such as the protrusion of the nose or chin. The *attached* (or 'self-shadows' as they are sometimes termed) are those belonging to surfaces that face away from the light, such as the underside of the nose. *Shading* describes the infinitesimal gradations of light between the full light hitting the forehead, for example, as compared to the receding parts of the head. In the human profile, as in the parts and spaces of architecture, all these kinds of shadow are phenomenally interrelated. Equally, there will always be stray photons invading the absences of shadow owing to reflection, refraction or filtration. In the kinds of experience with which this study is preoccupied, we shall be qualitatively engaged with all these kinds of shadow, with shading, with shade and with deeply filtered light.

One of the most famous early shadow stories begins with painting – not specifically architecture – and Pliny the Elder's (first century AD) statement that 'all agree that painting began with the outlining of a man's shadow'. A young woman of Corinth 'was in love with a young man; and she, when he was going abroad, drew in outline on the wall the shadow of his face thrown by a lamp'.[20] The absence, that is shadow, presages the imminent absence of the youth. It is an important myth of origin for fine art that has inspired innumerable representations, but how might it be reclaimed for architecture? One thing to point out is that in many of these images a strong domestic interior is already implied; so, in Joseph-Benoit Suvée's *The Invention of Drawing* (c. 1791) the wall the maid draws upon is clearly that of an interior with brackets supporting shelves of pots and domestic ware. From this do we conclude that the fine arts (drawing, painting, low-relief, sculpture) are born – from shadow – on the walls of an already-well-developed *pre-existing* architecture?

Then, in his *Invention of Drawing* (1573) on the wall of the Sala delle Arti in the Casa Vasari, Florence, Giorgio Vasari frescoed a rather different version of the myth that, as Deanna Petherbridge has noted, elides any feminine contribution: a male artist is engaged in the tricky narcissistic task of drawing his own muscular shadow.[21] As theorized in Vasari's *Lives of the Artists*, he is practising the art of *disegno*, which is not only the origin of all the arts, but the philosophical and technical foundation of sculpture, architecture and painting. *Disegno* gives the artist, architect and sculptor the conceptual ability to abstract the three-dimensional complexity of the world as profiles (*profili*).[22] Even Pliny's tale is completed by male intervention when the maid's father Butades goes on to invent the plastic arts; for, he 'pressed clay [on the outline of her lover] and made a relief, which he hardened by exposure to fire with the rest of his pottery'.[23] Butades, Pliny goes on to tell us, 'first placed masks as fronts to the outer gutter tiles on roofs.... It was from them that the ornaments on the pediments of temples originated. Because of Butades modellers get their Greek name of *plastae*'.[24] In Genesis, God forms man from clay, 'from the dust of the ground' – the Divine Architect of medieval imagery, and as also described by Vasari. So if there are contradictions in these narratives as to agency (female, male or both?), and as to whether architecture is already there to receive the cast shadow – or derives from it through *disegno* – the inventive potency of shadow is nonetheless patent in these narratives.

Love, memory, *disegno* and creativity are all properties which evidence shadow at its most benign; in Psalm 27 of the Bible, 'the Lord is my light and my salvation', and in extremity, 'in the day of evil; he will hide me in the *shadow* of his tabernacle'. And the Acts of the Apostles (5:12–15) relates how 'they even carried out the sick into the streets, and laid them on cots and mats, in order that Peter's shadow might fall on some of them as he came by'. Masaccio's fresco of *St Peter Healing the Sick* (1427–80, Brancacci Chapel, Florence) is a landmark representation of shadows in art that also enacts their beneficent effects in a fully realized perspectival urban situation of rusticated *palazzi*, and stuccoed dwellings.[25] A 'good' shadow, like that cast by St Peter, necessarily connects origin (the sun or the Holy Spirit), the cause of the shadow and its effects. While this study explores shadow as positive figure and real presence – not merely as light's servant – it is also true that when shadow appears to assume too much of an independent life, separate from light and its object, then it becomes fearfully characterized as 'bad', uncanny or sinister.

Shadow has had a 'bad' press – older than Pliny's productively 'good' shadow – ever since Plato's simile of the cave in *The Republic* (427–347 BCE), wherein the shackled prisoners, their heads held rigid, are condemned to the illusory reality of a flat and colourless shadow theatre projected before them from the light of a burning fire above and behind. Or consider the shadow of the concealed statue that stalks the steeply angled perspective of Giorgio de Chirico's canvas, *The Mystery and Melancholy of a Street* (1914), which is both embodied presence and uncannily disembodied from its hidden source around the corner. Whatever they unnervingly portend, the shadows of de Chirico's Italian streetscapes are clearly not the healing ones of Masaccio's *St Peter*.

So, The Cave may certainly be regarded as one of the great archetypes of shadow, but the story of shadow and architecture would be limited if humanity had remained in its seductive embrace; Norwegian architect, Sverre Fehn, has made some beautiful observations on shadow: 'The cave-dweller is unable to free himself from the mass, but lives in his own shadow as a token of place.'[26] In this undefined darkness, 'the opening remains the only respite. Outside, the tree fractures the horizon.... The tree mobilizes light and casts its shadow on earth, a realization of place. You are part of another's shadow, and you are no longer alone'.[27] The tree's mobile shadows tempt the cave dwellers to emerge and to 'move the mass', so making their own shadows, by raising menhirs, for example – a second great shadow archetype: 'The stone's precise placement on earth carried a message. Man could wander between arranged masses.... The stone and its place were a point on earth that conveyed a mass inhabited by spirit'.[28] And, 'each material has its own shadow', contends Fehn, 'the shadow of stone is not the same as that of a brittle autumn leaf. The shadow penetrates the material and radiates its message'.[29]

Shadow studies

It is widely the case that, given the physicality of architecture, shadow is commonly taken to mean the *cast* shadow of Pliny the Elder's story. This narrow view of shadow is reinforced by all those meticulous Beaux-Arts renderings of bases and capitals found in textbooks such as Henry McGoodwin's *Architectural Shades and Shadows* of 1904.[30] Though a fascinating aspect of architectural shadow-making, *Shadow-Makers* is not intended per se as a study of the perspectival rendering of shadow projection sometimes described as 'skiagraphy'; indeed, Henry McGoodwin himself wished to restore the following fuller meaning of shades and shadows to his pupils:

> The student should realize at the outset that in casting shadows on architectural drawings he is dealing with the materials of art rather than with the materials of mathematics. The shades and shadows of architectural objects are architectural things, not mathematical things. They are architectural entities, having form, mass and proportion just as have other architectural entities. Consequently these masses and shapes of dark must be as carefully considered in the study of design as are columns or entablatures, or other masses.[31]

Together with this phenomenal sense of shadows as living architectural entities, shadow-makers are characterized by a similar insistence on defining the spaces and forms of shadows as passionately as any of their other architectonic forms and volumes. Given that shades and shadows are such basic bodies to the making of architecture, it might be expected that there are many studies in the field examining their properties, and their experiential and cultural import? Not so. To find parallels to this kind of enquiry, it is necessary to look to art historical-cultural studies such as Michael Baxandall's *Shadows and Enlightenment* (1995), to E. H. Gombrich's *Shadows* (1995), Victor Stoichita's *A Short History of the Shadow* (1997) or Craig Koslofsky's *Evening's Empire: a History of the Night in Early Modern Europe* (2011). These are important studies in beginning to establish the historical importance of shadows in visual culture, but architecture is not at the centre of their arguments. In architectural history specifically, the special issue of the journal *VIA 11* devoted to *Architecture and Shadow* (David Murray, ed., 1990) is a notable collection of essays on the topic, but it is naturally not book length or a connected narrative. In a similar vein there is the German-English catalogue *The Secret of the Shadow. Light and Shadow in Architecture* – the outcome of a 2002 exhibition at the Deutsches Architektur Museum. A notable specific cultural contribution is the short poetic book on Japanese shadows by the novelist Junichiro Tanizaki, *In Praise of Shadows* (1991). Other general works on shadow of a scientific-philosophical character – but again lacking the architectural focus – include Roberto Casati's *Shadows* (2003) and Roy Sorensen's *Seeing Dark Things: The Philosophy of Shadows* (2008). Nonetheless, such publications do point to an evolving discourse on shadow, to which the focused architectural character of *Shadow-Makers* aims to contribute. Finally, shadow receives some discussion in architecture in the field of lighting and environmental design, as in Dean Hawkes's *The Environmental Imagination* (2008) or in Corrodi and Spechtenhauser's *Illuminating* (2008), though the latter, as the title implies, is mostly concerned with the environmental planning of natural light. And of course, there are scores of books on light and architecture in which shadow will be merely 'cast' in a supporting role.

* * * * *

The episodes of the book are broadly organized by the chronology of shadow as subject, as we enter in Chapter 2 with an examination of the primordial echt shadows cast about the medieval hearth. Chapter 3 sets out to understand how – within Baroque culture – shadow becomes a manageable instrument for spaces of devotion, drama and display in the context of the gradual conquest of the night in the early modern period. Chapters 4, 5 and 6 follow the arc of shadow-making onwards, as it shapes variously the domestic sublime of Sir John Soane, the 'Gloomths' of Horace Walpole and the picturesque, and John Ruskin's 'Lamp of Power'. With some survey of the significance of shadows to Islamic architecture and the city in Chapter 7, the overall chronology is rejoined in Chapter 8 at the cultural moment when shadow becomes psychologized through discourses of the unconscious. If we enter with the primordial shadows of room and hearth, we exit there too, in Chapter 9, with Louis Kahn's rediscovery of the primacy of the room space and its revenant treasuries of shadow. The final chapter, Chapter 10, is a necessarily open-ended one, in its speculations on present and future shadow possibilities.

Notes

1 Cook, E. T., and Wedderburn, Alexander (eds), *The Works of John Ruskin* (London: George Allen, 1904–13), vol. 7, *Modern Painters*, vol. 5, p. 271. Subsequent Ruskin references in the form: *Works*, 7: 271, *Modern Painters*, vol. 5.
2 Wilson, Colin St John, *Architectural Reflections. Studies in the Philosophy and Practice of Architecture* (Manchester: Manchester University Press, 2000, 2nd ed.), p. 112.
3 There is a striking cleft stone at Glemminge to the east of Malmö.
4 See Saint, Andrew, *Architect and Engineer. A Study in Sibling Rivalry* (New Haven, CT and London: Yale University Press, 2007), pp. 75–8, and his

discussion of the Ditherington flax mill, Shrewsbury, 1796–7 constructed in iron and brick.

5   See Hart, Vaughan, 'Sigurd Lewerentz and the "Half-Open Door"', *Architectural History*, vol. 39 (1996), pp. 181–96, 188–9.

6   See discussion of these themes in Hart, 'Lewerentz and the "Half-Open" Door'; see also Wilson, *Architectural Reflections*, Chapter 8, *passim*.

7   See original drawings in Wang, Wilfred (ed.), *O'Neil Ford Monograph 2: Saint Petri Church: Klippan 1962–66* (Austin, TA: University of Texas; Tübingen, Berlin: Ernst Wasmuth Verlag, 2009), p. 55 etc. See also images in Dymling, Claes (ed.), *Architect Sigurd Lewerentz. Vol. 1 Photographs of the Work* (Stockholm: Byggförlaget, 1997), pp. 164–75.

8   Baxandall, Michael, *Shadows and Enlightenment* (New Haven, CT and London: Yale University Press, 1995), p. 3.

9   Casati, Roberto, *Shadows. Unlocking Their Secrets, from Plato to Our Time* (New York: Vintage Books, 2003), p. 44.

10 Wilson, *Architectural Reflections*, p. 120.

11 Longhi, Roberto, *Piero della Francesca*, D. Tabbat (trans.) (Riverdale-on-Hudson, NY: Sheep Meadow Press, 2002), translation of the 1963 third edition of Longhi's work, originally published in 1927, p. 49.

12 See Donnington, Robert, *Wagner's 'Ring' and Its Symbols. The Music and the Myth* (London: Faber and Faber, 1974), p. 69.

13 On baptism imagery, see Temple, Nicholas, 'Baptism and Sacrifice: Cosmogony as Private Ontology', *Architectural Research Quarterly*, vol. 8, no. 1 (March 2004), pp. 47–60.

14 Norberg-Schulz, Christian, *Nightlands. Nordic Building*, T. McQuillan (trans.) (Cambridge, MA: MIT Press, 1996), pp. 59–60. Other tectonic aspects are also revealing, such as the way in which 'Lewerentz takes bricks across the head of an opening apparently unsupported', Blundell Jones, Peter, 'Sigurd Lewerentz: Church of St Peter, Klippan, 1963–66', *Architectural Research Quarterly*, vol. 6, no. 2 (2002), pp. 159–73, p. 171.

15 Norberg-Schulz, *Nightlands*, p. 62.

16 Norberg-Schulz, *Nightlands*, p. 17.

17 Norberg-Schulz, *Nightlands*, p. 6.

18 Wilson, *Architectural Reflections*, p. 124.

19 See Baxandall, *Shadows and Enlightenment*, pp. 1–4, 156, note 1.

20 Pliny, *Natural History with English Translation in Ten Volumes*, H. Rackham (trans.) (Cambridge, MA: Harvard University Press, 1961), p. 372.

21 Petherbridge, Deanna, *The Primacy of Drawing. Histories and Theories of Practice* (New Haven, CT and London: Yale University Press, 2010), p. 20.

22 Jacobs, Fredrika H., 'Vasari's Vision of the History of Painting: Frescoes in the Casa Vasari, Florence', *The Art Bulletin*, vol. 66, no. 3 (September 1984), pp. 399–416.

23 Pliny, *Natural History*, p. 372.

24 Pliny, *Natural History*, p. 373.

25 See the discussion in Stoichita, Victor I., *A Short History of the Shadow* (London: Reaktion Books, 1997), pp. 54–5, and also Gombrich, E. H., *Shadows. The Depiction of Cast Shadows in Western Art* (London: National Gallery Publications, 1995), pp. 21–2.
26 Fehn, Sverre, and Fjeld, Per Olave, 'Has a Doll Life', *Perspecta*, vol. 24 (1988), pp. 40–9, p. 43.
27 Fehn and Fjeld, 'Has a Doll Life', p. 43.
28 Fehn and Fjeld, 'Has a Doll Life', p. 44.
29 Fehn and Fjeld, 'Has a Doll Life', p. 47.
30 McGoodwin, Henry, *Architectural Shades and Shadows* (Washington, DC: The American Institute of Architects Press, 1989, original work published 1904).
31 McGoodwin, *Architectural Shades and Shadows*, p. 1.

2

Primordial Shadows

Primordial dwelling

Consider the primordial shadows of architecture's medieval night, when darkness was a ruling force relieved only by the hearth, the candle and the oil lamp. Defining this 'primordial presence' of shadow will enable a better understanding of the gradual conquest of the night (nocturnalization) of the early modern and Baroque period examined in the following chapter. This chapter is also 'primordial' in stressing the existential nature of shadow embedded in such archetypes as the 'shadows of the hearth' and the primitive hut. According to Craig Koslofsky, the 'nocturnalization' which

> reshaped daily life for a significant minority of seventeenth-century Europeans separated darkness from the night as never before in Western culture. Darkness was slowly transformed from a primordial presence to a more manageable aspect of life, acquiring in the process new associations with mysticism and popular devotion, political display, respectable sociability, and learned exchange.[1]

In these complex processes – encompassing both a conquest of darkness and a conscious manipulation of it – shadow emerges as a positive figure, and shadow-making as culturally operative in the shaping of architectural space and form. When attention is drawn to it, this primordial envelopment of darkness and shadow seems startling. Nowadays, it is rarely experienced as sublime thrill (Chapters 4 and 5), or temporary inconvenience, than existential fact – when camping, in power cuts, or in remote holiday retreats minus electricity. Such as the Landmark Trust's 'Tibbetts', isolated at the top of the already-far-flung island of Lundy in the approaches to the Bristol Channel; within the pale granite walls of this former admiralty watch station, there is only the light of the stove, and a pair of flickering gas mantles, to stave off the threat of total darkness and Atlantic gales. Accordingly this chapter begins by examining the primordial nature of the dwelling and these shadows cast and gathered between hearth and aperture.

Shadows of the hearth

In his *Architecture of the Well-Tempered Environment* (1969), Reyner Banham tells a parable of a 'savage tribe' arriving at a campsite 'well supplied with fallen timber' as evening falls. According to 'ancestral cultural disposition', he suggests that they have only two choices: those habituated to sturdy building will use the timber to make a strong shelter. Against this

> societies who do not build substantial structures tend to group their activities around some central focus – a water hole, a shade tree, a fire, a great teacher – and inhabit a space whose external boundaries are vague, adjustable, according to functional need, and rarely regular. The output of heat and light from a camp-fire is effectively zoned in concentric rings, brightest and hottest close to the fire, coolest and darkest away from it, so that sleeping is an outer-ring activity, and pursuits requiring vision belong to the inner rings.[2]

In Banham's adjoining diagram of 'environmental conditions', his 'savage' wandering tribe can be imagined pressed around the 'zone of radiant heat and light' of the splendid fire they have made from all the fallen timber as the shades of the night draw in. Perhaps the blaze casts their shadows upon the bodies of some early sleepers who have withdrawn to the penumbra zone between the hearth and the engulfing darkness. Naturally, Banham uses this parable to urge his well-known thesis against architecture as the conscious art 'of creating...massive and perdurable structures', but in truth, even for nomadic cultures, there is rarely a stark choice between having to build and having to make a fire. Whether in myths of origin, in the psychologies of experience, or in paradigmatic texts such as Vitruvius's *De Architectura* or Alberti's *De Re Aedificatoria*, 'the primitive hut and the primitive fire [and the shadows it casts and dispels] are revealed to be inseparable'.[3] Among many early dwellings that concretize Banham's environmental zone of hearth and dwelling circle are the Iron Age roundhouses. These structures range in diameter from less than seven metres to up to twenty; within their steep conical roofs of wet thatch, the only light came from the fire itself and the single doorway – when open. Thickening the darkness the smoke hung as a horizon in the tall roof space, usefully retaining heat energy, pitching the thatch against insects and curing joints of meat hung from the rafters. In the smaller open-plan dwellings, the family dwelt, cooked and ate around the hearth and slept in the obscurity of the periphery, matching the sixth-century BCE philosopher Eumenides' description of the family as 'those warmed by the same hearth' (Figure 2.1).[4]

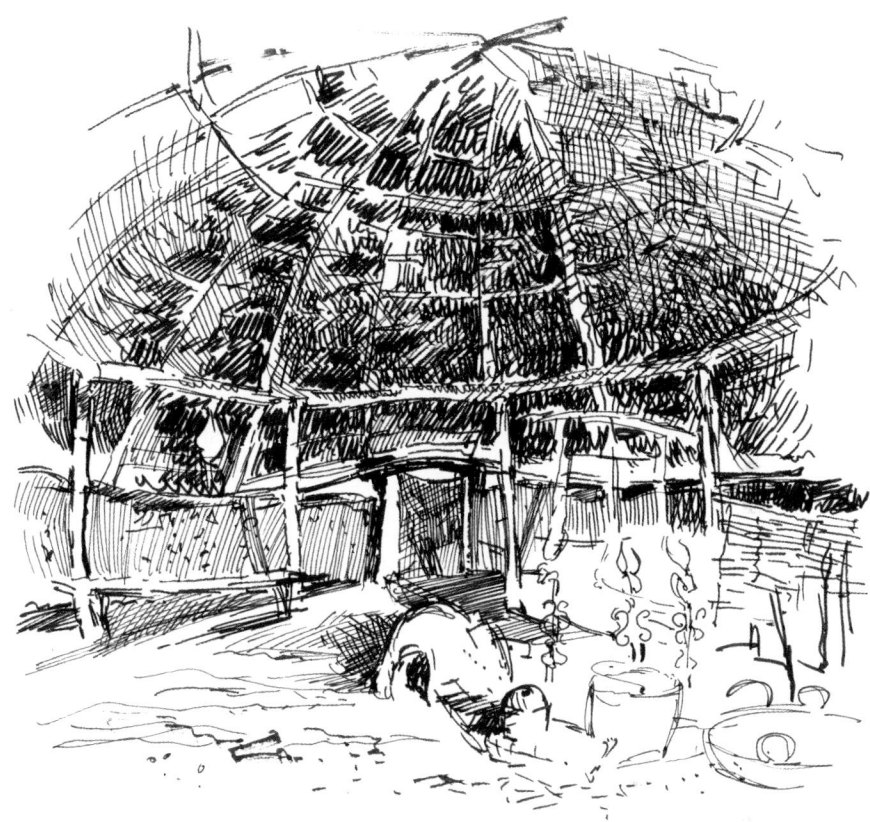

FIGURE 2.1 Iron Age roundhouse reconstruction, St Fagans National History Museum. Drawing, Stephen Kite.

Larger roundhouses might be partitioned, with animals occupying the periphery, intensifying that elemental 'joy of dwelling' in the shadows – in kinship with the beasts – which Gaston Bachelard captures when he approvingly quotes Vlaminck: 'The well being I feel, seated in front of my fire, while bad weather rages out-of-doors, is entirely animal. A rat in its hole, a rabbit in its burrow, cows in the stable, must all feel the contentment that I feel.'[5] Psychologists of dwelling like Olivier Marc tell the familiar, but still compelling, story (as also told by Fehn, Chapter 1) of humankind prompted to leave the natural shelters of caves and grottoes – caves which 'represented the womb in which an embryonic "humanity" was gradually taking form under the pressure of a consciousness soon to be born into history'.[6] Imagined as cave substitutes, the Iron Age roundhouses are also quite literal symbols of the darkly protecting uterus: 'To build a house is to create an area of peace, calm and security, a replica of our own mother's womb, where we can leave the world and listen to our own rhythm.'[7] In his

Poetics of Space Gaston Bachelard urges that the home should allow those imaginative dreams which produce the 'oneiric house' – that 'crypt of the house that we were born in'. Such a primeval house, 'apprehended in its dream potentiality', also 'becomes as nest in the world'.[8] Probing the etymology of such deep-felt homeliness (Wohnlichkeit) the phenomenological philosopher Otto Friedrich Bollnow (1903–91) discovers how the word 'behaglich' (cosy) comprises the concepts of 'hag' (a hedge) and 'hegen', 'umhegen' (protect or cherish), that is, of protection by means of a nest-like enclosing hedge.[9] And in making the first of nine points to isolate this 'entire nature of homeliness' he foregrounds its enshadowed character:

> If it is the task of the house to provide a refuge from the outside world, this must also find expression in the nature of the dwelling space. One cannot comfortably spend time in an entrance hall. Over-large windows, and walls made entirely of glass, which open the space to the outside world, suppress the homeliness of the space. The enthusiasm with which many currents of the new architecture adopted modern technical possibilities was at the expense of a house which would give the effect of protective enclosure and rest. While much was justified at the time in the battle against the degeneration of a bygone time, one must not, out of a fear of a false 'bourgeois' cosiness, destroy the true task of the dwelling, which is to be a space devoted to rest and peace. Even the window curtains which close off the space, above all at night, have a meaningful function here.[10]

In the British Isles, the womb nest of the roundhouse underwent a transformation to the 'newfangled rectangle', wherein rectangularity and Romanization are linked in aspirations to the more urban culture of the Roman Britain of the years 43 CE to 410 CE.[11] Even in the long dwelling of a quite wealthy farmer as late as circa 1500, the hearth – with its great fireplace stone [*pentanfaen*] and firedogs – remains in the centre (Figure 2.2). The cruck-framed hall of the Hendre'r-ywydd Uchaf farmhouse, from Llangynhafal, in Denbighshire, Wales, was lit by just two small opposing windows. Its roof lining of closely wattled saplings became blackened by thick deposits of soot, for there was no chimney or roof vent; smoke either seeped into the thatch or sought its way out through the four-square mullions of the unglazed apertures.[12] Even this quite prosperous house was experientially probably not much different to those of the Iron Age. Lower down the social scale, the precarious lives of short-lived generations were conducted around the cooking trivets of the 'dark, damp and malodorous internal spaces' of rickety hovels.[13] The nobility could enjoy some brightness through the luxury of glass, and at night plentiful wax candles or oil torches, as compared to the 'gloomy interiors of the almost windowless peasant's home, which relied on glass substitutes, such as wooden shutters, canvas, or linen treated with alum and made translucent and weatherproof with

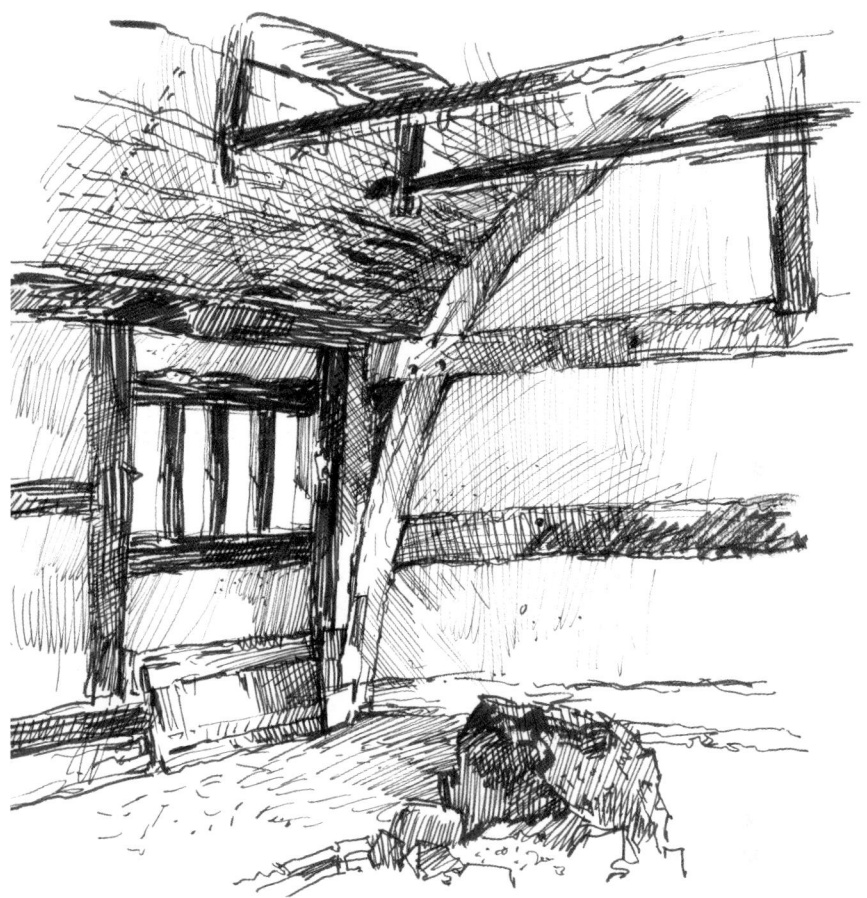

FIGURE 2.2 Cruck-framed hall, Hendre'r-ywydd Uchaf farmhouse, from Llangynhafal, in Denbighshire, Wales, St Fagans National History Museum. Drawing, Stephen Kite.

animal fat, before being stretched over a latticed wooden frame called a *fenestral*.[14] 'Ful sooty was hir bour [bower] and eek hir halle,/In which she eet ful many a sklendre [slender] meel', as Chaucer described the fourteenth-century home of the poor old widow in *The Nun's Priest's Tale*; conditions of a wretchedly medieval kind were not uncommon deep into the nineteenth century, as found in 1893 by the secretary of the Royal Commission examining the homes of the agricultural worker in Wales:

> There are still … many old-fashioned cottages and even farm-houses, which present a wretched appearance, being often built of mud and wattling, and thatched with rushes or heather.… A tapering aperture in the roof serves for a chimney, but quite as often as not the smoke

escapes by the door or oozes through the partitions after mellowing every article of furniture.... Many of the older houses of this type have their fires of peat on the floor in the centre of the dwelling, and owing to the corresponding position of the chimney they were formerly known as 'ink-bottle houses'.[15]

As counter to these desperate scenes more affirmative pictures of common life within the shadows of the hearth can be found, as in accounts of the spinning bees which animated the long winter nights in many parts of later medieval and early-modern Europe, legitimizing sociability and courtship.[16] One typical seventeenth-century engraving shows the spatiality of this nocturnal life of the peasant home. At centre-right the door stands open to the night's absolute blackness, but most of the image presents various zones of shadow mediated between the hearth, and the women's flax-working group on the left, and the candle glow from the centre of the men's drinking circle on the right. Between blaze and candle lie many zones of dim intimacy, such as that shadowy nook between fireplace and stair where the only standing couple exchange searching gazes (Figure 2.3).

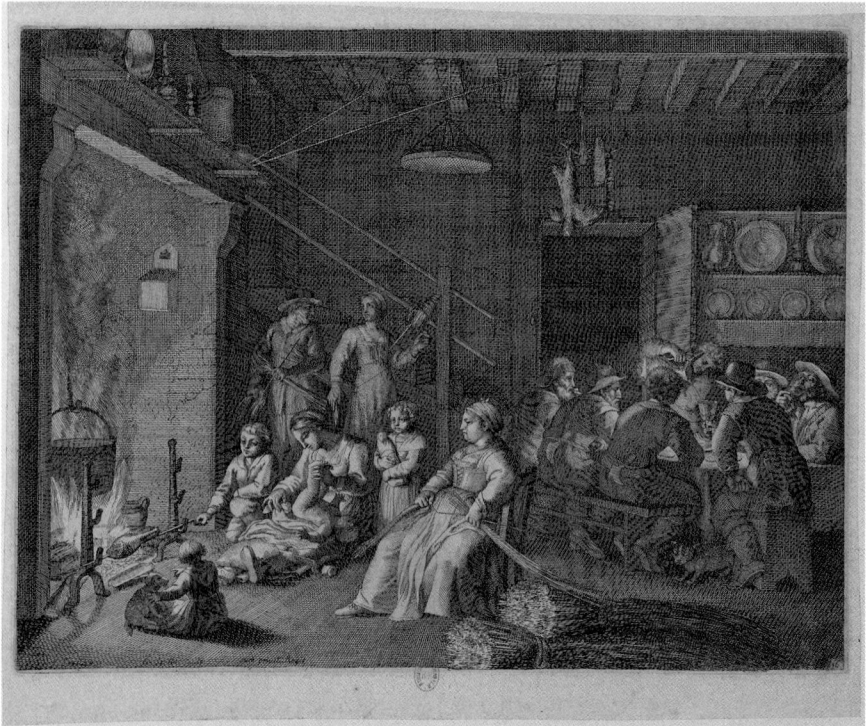

FIGURE 2.3 Claudine Bouzonnet Stella, *La veillée à la ferme pendant l'hiver*, engraving, 1661–7. Bibliothèque Nationale de France.

Bachelard: Walls of impalpable shadow

Bachelard was attracted by the outlines of such engravings of simple dwelling, for they illustrate how real poetic images become engraved upon our memories. In his chapter on 'Corners' in *Poetics of Space* he claims 'that a house in an engraving may well incite a desire to live in it. We feel that we should like to live there, between the very lines of the engraved drawing'.[17] Later, Louis Kahn's capacity to live within the lines of a fireside engraving of George Cruikshank's will be examined as a crucial lesson for him in shadow-making (Chapter 9). For Bachelard the imagination functions to create 'the essence of the nature of home', wherever 'the human being has found the slightest shelter: we shall see the imagination build "walls" of impalpable shadows, comfort itself with the illusion of protection'.[18] Bachelard calls his rigorous psychological research into the locales of our intimate lives *topoanalysis*. Topoanalysis asks for a house that 'is a bit elaborate', not in the way of a palace, but akin to the simple home of the engraving, with 'a cellar and a garret, nooks and corridors', these physical refuges foster memory and daydreaming, whereas in a palace, as Baudelaire stated, 'there is no place for intimacy'.[19] As the scholar of place, Edward Casey explains:

> Topanalysis tries to convince us that *the house is a world*. It is a place-world, a world of places. Here, Bachelard rejoins Heidegger's early description of the 'sunny' and 'shady' sides of the house as locales (*Plätze*) that orient the division and arrangement of a house into rooms (*Räume*). But topoanalysis deepens this description by exploring the intimacy of a house *room by room*, that is to say, place by place.[20]

Bachelard psychologizes the dwelling on a human-like vertical axis between the 'polarity of cellar and attic', opposing 'the rationality of the roof to the irrationality of the cellar' which is 'first and foremost the *dark entity* of the house'; here 'darkness prevails both day and night, and even when we are carrying a lighted candle, we see shadows dancing on the dark walls'.[21] 'The oneirically definitive house, must retain its shadows',[22] insists Bachelard, and in chapters such as 'Drawers, Chests and Wardrobes', and 'Corners', he examines the 'subtle shadings' that populate the oneiric home between the poles of bright garret and black basement:

> The related problems are many if we want to determine the profound reality of all the subtle shadings of our attachment for a chosen spot. For a phenomenologist, these shadings must be taken as the first rough outlines of a psychological phenomenon. The shading is not an additional, superficial colouring. We should therefore have to say how we inhabit our vital space, in accord with all the dialectics of life, how we take root,

day after day, in a 'corner of the world'.[23]

The shadings of 'corners' can be examined in another superlative example of Welsh cottage building. Llainfadyn was the moorland home of a slate quarryman from the Rhostryfan area of north-west Wales.[24] Though timeless, it bears the date of 1762 on the twisted fireplace beam and was constructed from mighty glacial boulders gathered nearby. Unconsciously, it packs into its one-room 8.5 × 6.0 metre footprint some of the aesthetic force later to be associated with the cyclopean lithic design of the nineteenth-century US architect Henry Hobson Richardson (Chapter 6). Some of these huge stones run the full one-metre thickness of the walls which, as these are kept roughly flush within, project vigorously externally. The main room is open to the roof as in the medieval Hendre'r-ywydd Uchaf mentioned earlier, but in the intervening centuries the fire has moved from the central hearth

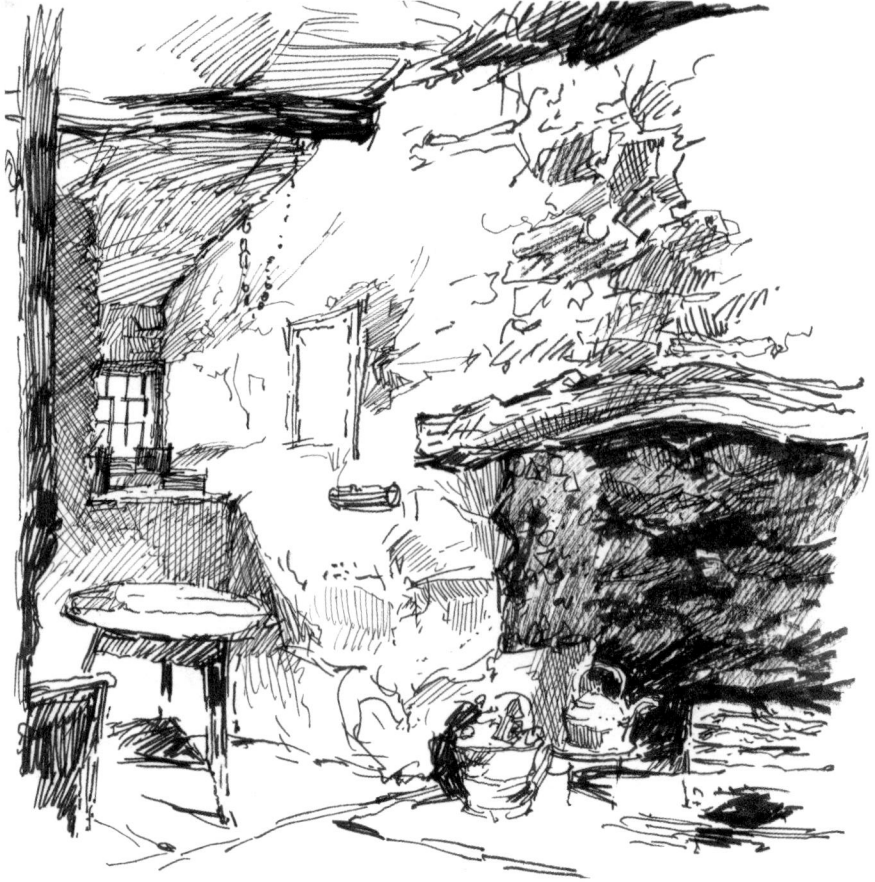

FIGURE 2.4 Fireplace nook, Llainfadyn Cottage, 1762. St Fagans National History Museum. Drawing, Stephen Kite.

and brazier, to the fireplace and chimney wall, thereby 'multiplying the shades of being that characterize the corner dweller', as in the spinning bee etching, or as in a character of the Lithuanian poet, O. V. de Milosz – noted by Bachelard – who 'leads a fervent existence, setting aside certain corners to which he often repairs. As ... "That little dark corner between the fireplace and the oak chest, where you used to hide"'.[25] Llainfadyn makes one such dreaming corner, barely two metres wide, between entrance and fire, with a draught-excluding partition of a single slab of slate. This nook is lit by one of the three small windows that, through deep splayed reveals, throw a dim light into this rock-built cave. With just space enough for a seat and small table, it is – with its 'subtle shadings' – the heart of the house (Figure 2.4).[26]

Shadows without corners: Wright and Japan

What Frank Lloyd Wright wished to achieve through his daring reconfiguration of spatial reality was the abolition of the corner along with its lingering shadows, as in a 'Conversation' broadcast in May 1953:

> The corner window is indicative of an idea conceived early in my work, that the box is a Fascist symbol, and the architecture of freedom and democracy needed something basically better than the box. So I started out to destroy the box as a building.... The light now came in where it had never come in before and vision went out. You had screens for walls instead of box walls – here the walls vanished as walls, the box vanished as a box.[27]

Corners can still be found aplenty in Wright's architecture nonetheless. The modernity of his 'liberation of space' and aspiration to 'a radical change in the idea of a building'[28] is firmly grounded in the primordial archetypes of hearth – of 'the *integral* fireplace ... a fire burning deep in the masonry of the house itself'[29] – and of shelter, and is rich in the play of shadows as Robert McCarter underscores:

> Wright utilized roofs as shadow makers and defined the place of inhabitation as the space made by shadows on the earth. Wright's domestic interiors were relatively dimly lit, not flooded with light. In his houses there are large amounts of glass, but the shadows cast by overhanging roofs and deep-set piers allow an increase in openness without simultaneous increase in light level.[30]

Under the shadows of the cantilevered roofs of the William R. Heath House, Buffalo – built in 1904–5 for a lawyer who became vice president of the Larkin Company – Wright defined openly protected places of habitation, on a long narrow site, by placing the substantial dark-red brick dwelling

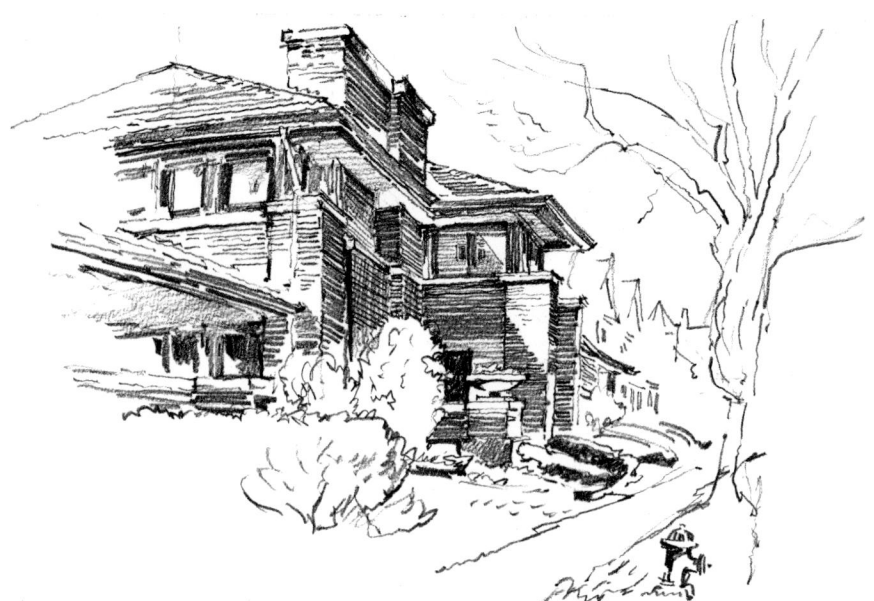

FIGURE 2.5 Frank Lloyd Wright, William R. Heath House, 1904–5, Buffalo. Drawing, Stephen Kite.

hard to the pavement of Bird Street and concealing the entrance against a broad anchoring chimney (Figure 2.5). The Heath House's siting and linear configuration makes it a significant precursor to the Robie House, Chicago, of 1908–9 – the culminating masterpiece of this early period of Wright's development. In his study of 'Pattern and Meaning' in Wright's houses, Grant Hildebrand finds the Robie 'an exquisite platform for prospect...meticulously managed [in section] to provide refuge from a busy thoroughfare', if weaker in its capacity for smaller refuge spaces with its half-inglenook fireplace somewhat islanded in the sweep of the living-dining volumes – at least as compared to the 'cave-refuge' hearth zone of the 1907 Avery Coolney House, Springfield, related to the 'grove-refuge' of its tent-like living volume. And to capture Wright's 'mood of refuge,' he invokes Bachelard on 'the spectacle of the family sitting-room, [where] to listen to the stove roaring in the evening stillness, while an icy wind blows against the house, [is] to know that at the house's centre, in the circle of light shed by the lamp, he is living in the round house, the primitive hut, of prehistoric man'.[31] Hildebrand's rich readings of Wright's place-making draw on the behavioural aesthetics of Jay Appleton's *The Experience of Landscape* (1975, rev. 1996), which recognizes the interaction between two primary human needs and the habitat, a *prospect* space – the 'foraging-ground' – to supply food, and a *refuge* 'nesting-place' wherein to raise a family.[32] Although these are opposites in that *refuge* is intimate and dark, while *prospect* is expansive and luminous, Appleton stresses the importance in architecture of the permeability of what he calls 'the indoors-outdoors interface'. For although 'the walls of a castle, can communicate the idea of an effective protective screen' and an absolute sense of refuge, they are *too* impermeable and damage 'opportunities for passing easily between outdoors and indoors' – to secure food or refuge – or to occupy the dappled in-between shadows of the forest-edge equivalent. Accordingly he encourages such devices as the following:

> Arcades, porticoes, verandas, balconies, overhanging eaves, exterior staircases and recesses of all kinds [which] render the separation of indoors and outdoors to some degree less absolute. If they do no more than cast shadows they will have begun to suggest a zone of transition between the bright light of the open air, the zone of exposure, and the subdued light of the interior, the zone of concealment.[33]

At the Heath House, the Robie House or Wright's own home of Taliesin, Spring Green, Wisconsin – explicitly built in 1911 as 'a kind of refuge for me and mine at the time'[34] – the cast shadows of the deeply overhanging eaves, the recessed bands of glinting windows and the cave-like anchoring chimney masses, all denote invitation to the subdued light of sanctuary. Everyone agrees that at least some of this atmosphere of subdued light, marked shadow and spaces delimited by screen-like planes – further defined by dark timber grids – can be traced to the architecture of Japan in general and to Wright's passion for the Japanese print in particular. To the kind of architecture shown, for example, in a late eighteenth-century print by Utagawa Toyoharu, from Wright's collection, of dancers performing in the interior of a Shoin style mansion – one he included in his 1912 book *The Japanese Print: An Interpretation* (Figure 2.6).[35] Such images helped Wright to abstract the traditional moulding as a 'horizontal and vertical mesh' that marks a key low horizon at screen door height, equated to the traditional *nageshi* frieze rail band.[36] Above these float upper planes, softly illumined by eave-shaded clerestories, while below this datum, space is pushed and pulled into Appleton's 'recesses of all kinds' – alternately glowing or gloomy. Thus, for David Van Zanten, 'Wright's cross sections are all right-angled, making the mouldings read as mere boards attached to the surface, while he plays with the deep shadows that result to make their planes seem to float in an indefinite relationship to one another.'[37] Wright must have already assimilated key aspects of Japanese spatiality early on from publications and prints, and from the cult of 'Japonisme', for McCarter finds this sophisticated level of volumetric manipulation even in the relatively simple volumes of the first phases of the Wright home at Oak Park, Chicago, of 1889–95. Initially, that is to say, before his direct experience of seeing the Japanese Ho-o-den Temple at the Columbian World's Fair of 1893, and well before his first trip to Japan in 1905. In his autobiography (1932), Wright

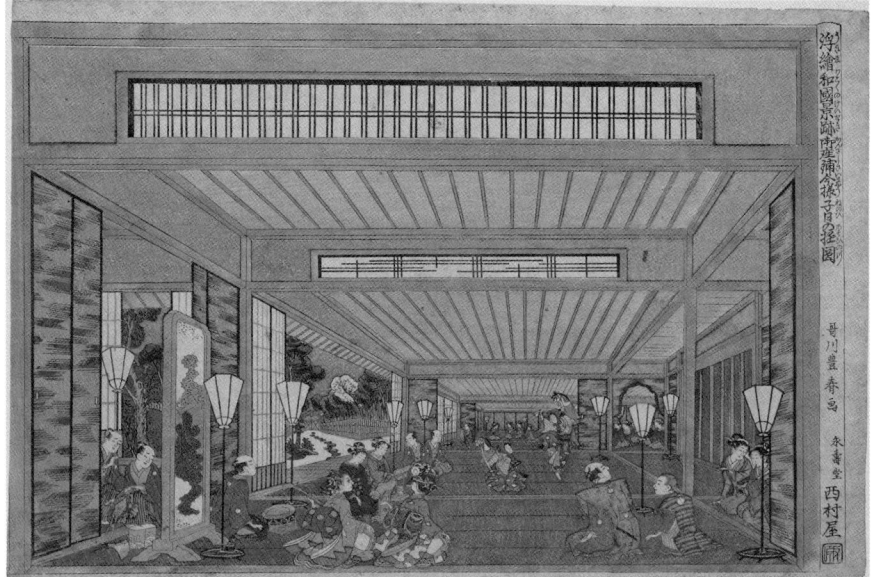

FIGURE 2.6 Utagawa Toyoharu (1735–1814), *Festivities in a mansion on the first Rat Day of the year*, Middle Edo, c. 1770. Purchased from the Frank Lloyd Wright Collection, UCLA Grunwald Center for the Graphic Arts, Hammer Museum.

wrote how 'during the years at the Oak Park workshop, Japanese prints intrigued me and taught me much'.[38] Pre-eminent among the openings and recesses that unfold below the door-height trim is the inglenook fire cave; here – over the semi-circular brick arch – Wright had carved: 'Truth is Life. Good friend, around these hearth stones speak no evil word of any creature.'[39]

So it may not surprise that the only twentieth-century building for which the Japanese novelist Junichiro Tanizaki (1886–1965) finds guarded praise, in his celebrated aesthetic essay *In Praise of Shadows* (1933–4), is Wright's Imperial Hotel, Tokyo (1922–67) which, 'with its indirect lighting, is on the whole a pleasant place, but in summer even it might be a bit darker'.[40] When translated into English in 1977, Tanizaki's essay came, as architect and educator Charles Moore has written, 'with the thrill of a slap for us then to hear praise of shadows and darkness…. Thus darkness illuminates for us a culture very different from our own; but at the same time it helps us to look deep into ourselves to our own inhabitation of the world.'[41] 'In making for ourselves a place to live, we first spread a parasol to throw a shadow on the earth, and in the pale light of the shadow we put together a house',[42] says Tanizaki, and accuses 'the roof of a Western house [as being] no more than a cap', and 'built to create as few shadows as possible' – in contrast to the generous parasols of his homeland.[43] As for Wright's roofs, there can be little doubt that they are real shadow-making canopies. Though

Tanizaki claimed to 'possess no specialized knowledge of architecture' in his passion for the beauty of shadows, he conveys this:

> In the temples of Japan...a roof of heavy tiles is first laid out, and in the deep, spacious shadows created by the eaves the rest of the structure is built. Nor is this true only of temples; in the palaces of the nobility and the houses of the common people, what first strikes the eye is the massive roof of tile or thatch and the heavy darkness that hangs beneath the eaves. Even at midday cavernous darkness spreads over all beneath the roof's edge, making entryway, doors, walls, and pillars all but invisible. The grand temples of Kyoto...and the farmhouses of the remote countryside are alike in this respect.[44]

As example, one of these great temple complexes of Kyoto will serve to intimate the Japanese qualities of shadow-making. Daitoku-ji, in the northern part of the city, is one of Kyoto's largest Zen temple precincts and its twenty-three sub-temples hold some of the finest Zen spaces and gardens. The Daisen-in sub-temple, founded in 1509 at the height of Zen Buddhism, exhibits a remarkable homology between its dry landscape garden (akin to that of the more famous Ryoanji), and the monochrome ink landscape paintings of their inspiration, as both the landscape paintings that adorn the temple's sliding doors, and a collaborative role in the garden design, are attributed to the same figure – the Noh artist Soami (1445–1525).[45] The gardens can be scanned like a scroll wherein sand simulates a stream moving through a rocky landscape to the calmer courtyards of the 'middle sea' (Chûkai) – with an island mountain-rock group – and the 'great sea' (Taikai) where just two white sand cones break the raked extent of white sand (Figure 2.7). Here, where the same Zen monk was both painter and garden-maker, painted screens and dry-gardens show a reciprocal monochromaticism: real stones and plants resemble the same muted brush strokes that abstract the essence of mountains and foliage.[46] In this context Henry Plummer writes of shadows as 'overlaid washes [that] are thin and blurred, recalling the unhurried brushwork of *sumiye* [ink] painting...eluding all exact definition in black-and-white tones that are wet and moist'.[47] Similarly, the architect Kisho Kurokawa speaks of a Japanese 'culture of greys'; if the Mediterranean culture of the West is about 'the strong southern sun and the deep dark shadows it creates', then 'Kyoto, representative of traditional Japanese beauty, is even more beautiful on a rainy day, or at dusk, the time of the intermediary zone between light and darkness'.[48] And he goes on to say, 'The shadow that Tanizaki praises is not a shadow etched out by light, but a dimness that envelops the entire space. It is a grey space, a symbiosis of light and darkness.' All the elements of Japanese architecture work to blur the dualism of light and shadow: the verandah (*engawa*), the sliding paper screens (*shoji*) and the dark post and beam structure itself. Tanizaki extols the 'absolute harmony' between a 'blurred old painting and the dark

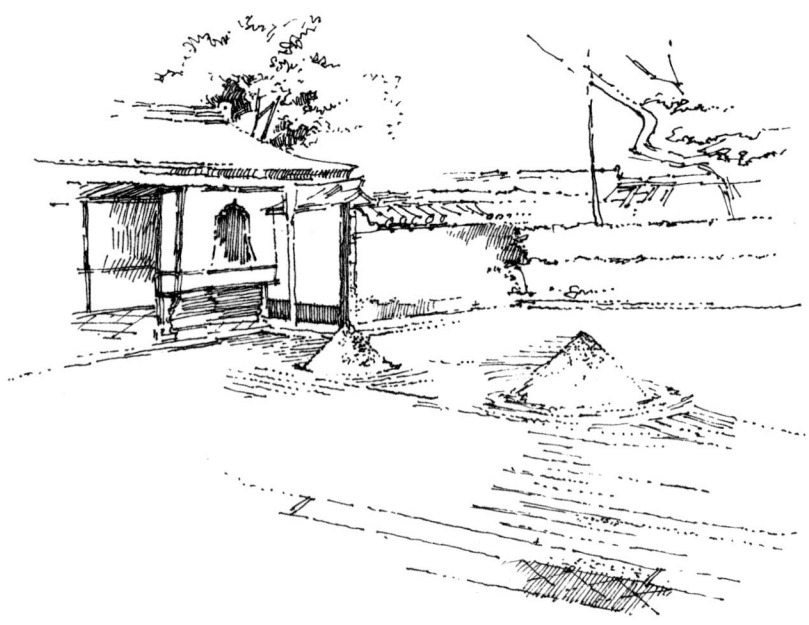

FIGURE 2.7 'Great sea' courtyard, Daisen-in sub-temple, Kyoto. Drawing, Stephen Kite.

alcove', and also likens a Japanese room to 'an inkwash painting, the paper-panelled shoji being the expanse where the ink is thinnest, and the alcove where it is darkest', marvelling at the Japanese 'comprehension of the secrets of shadows, our sensitive use of shadow and light'.[49] These are secrets best understood in journeyings, whether vicariously as in unrolling the painted travelogue of a hand-scroll or in scanning the 'stream-course' of the Daisen-in rock garden from the abbot's *shoin* (study), or best of all in experiencing the subtle choreography of darkness and space in the transition into another of the sub-temples, such as the seventeenth-century Koto-in, located in the south-western part of Daitoku-ji.

The whole Daitoku-ji complex is organized through transitions from formal, through semi-formal to informal in the compositional system known as *shin-gyo-so*.[50] To arrive at the entrance to Koto-in, the visitor must make four key right-angle turns (Figure 2.8). The first is a left turn the path makes to confront the main gateway, within a small, clay-walled entry forecourt that opens off one of Daitoku-ji's main avenues, belonging to the *garan* – the public and formal part of the wider precinct. On passing through the gate, the path immediately makes a right turn to reveal a mysterious narrow route over thirty metres long, bordered with moss and dappled with the shade of maple trees (Figure 2.9). To follow this 'dark space tunnel'[51] pattern of temple design – in cautious progress along the damp, uneven stones of the bamboo-railed pathway – is to experience a certain monotony, and a

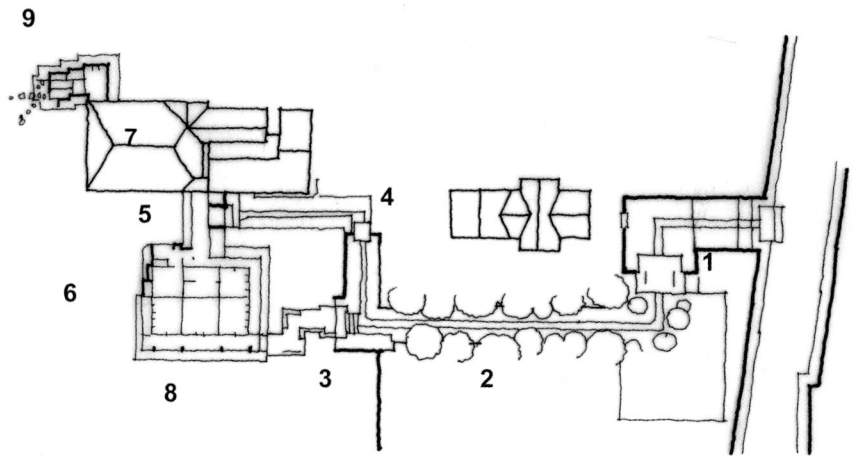

FIGURE 2.8 Koto-in Temple, Kyoto. Schematic space and transition plan, Stephen Kite. *Key*: 1. Main Gateway. 2. Dark 'Space Tunnel'. 3. *Hojo* Gateway. 4. Gateway to Secondary Entrance. 5. Secondary Entrance. 6. *Hojo*. 7. *Shoin*. 8. Zen Moss Garden. 9. Shoko-Ken Teahouse.

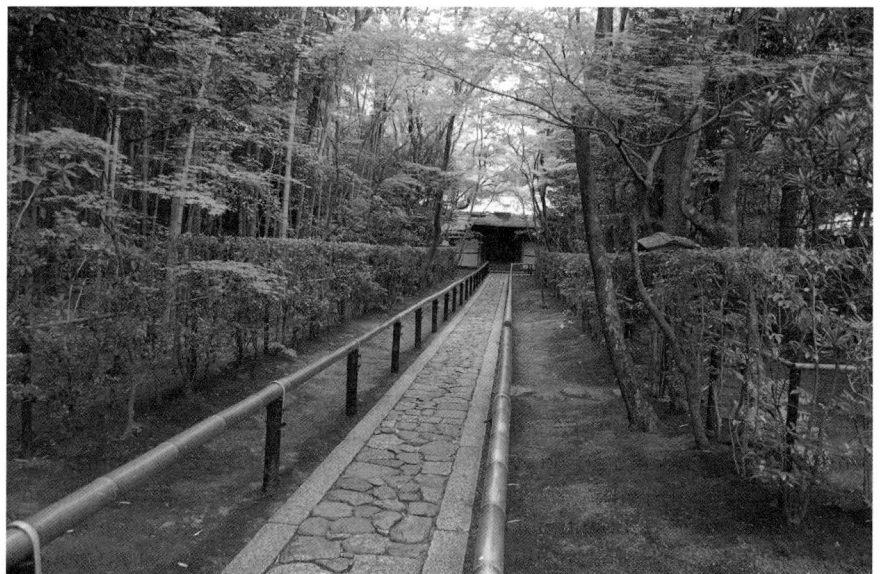

FIGURE 2.9 Koto-in Temple, Kyoto. Dark space tunnel entrance. Photograph, Stephen Kite.

further withdrawal even from the world-within-a-world of the main temple precinct. At the end of this shadowy semi-formal tunnel, the dark-doored, moss-roofed gateway of the *Hojo* (Abbot's quarters) mysteriously invites, within the field of a bright tile-capped wall. But on closer approach the invitation is declined, and this largely symbolic gateway remains firmly closed, and a second right turn must be made to pass through a lowlier gateway leading to the commonly used secondary entrance. This entry is finally attained along a fifteen-metre path, after the fourth of the key turns – to the left. The place of arrival – the verandah that links the *Hojo* and the *Shoin* of the temple – is also an in-between semi-dark 'grey space', which offers the immediate prospect of an intimate garden and a choice of direction to left or right. A spatial pattern, in fact, like that of Wright's early Taliesin, Spring Green, where the visitor – having arrived under the darkness of the entry porch and having drunk in the prospect therefrom of Wright's ancestral valley – could turn either left into the *shoin* of Wright's studio or right into the *hojo* of the master's main dwelling.[52] A turn left at Koto-in brings the visitor, by further dimmer turns, to the deep shade of the main *engawa* of the *Hojo*, where the outlook is onto a rare Zen garden – not dry – but a covert of maples hovering above a softly rumpled carpet of luminously dark moss, accentuated by a single stone lantern (Figure 2.10).

Koto-in was established in 1601 by a famous samurai, Hosokawa Tadaoki (1563–1645), who in later life devoted himself to the study of Zen under the Daitoku-ji abbot, Seigan, achieving notability as a distinguished disciple of the tea master Sen no Rikyu (1522–91), and building the

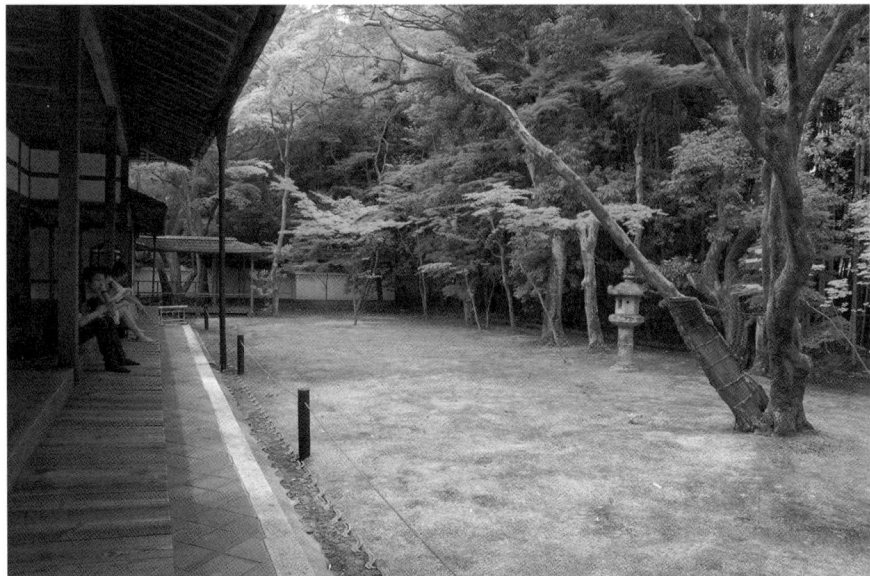

FIGURE 2.10 Koto-in Temple, Kyoto. Moss garden. Photograph, Stephen Kite.

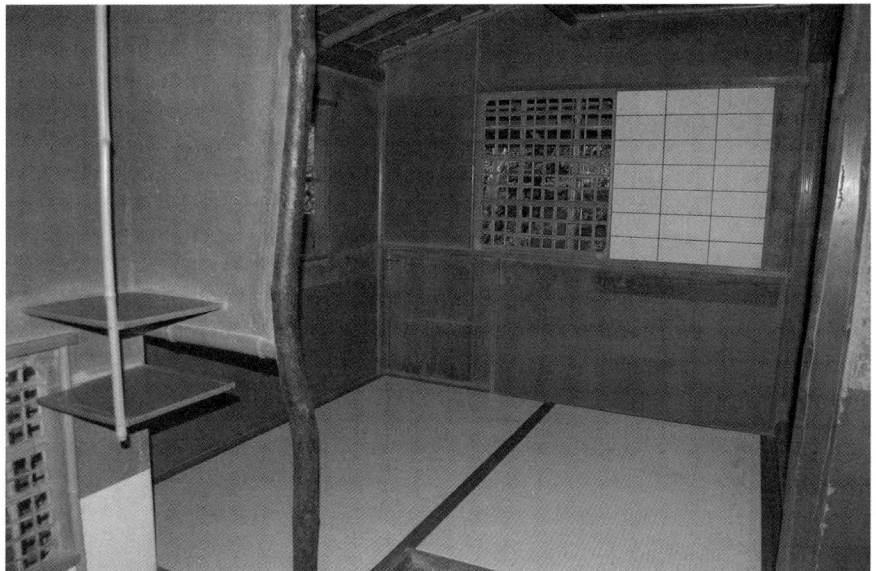

FIGURE 2.11 Koto-in Temple, Kyoto. Shoko-ken teahouse. Photograph, Stephen Kite.

tiny, two and three-quarter tatami mat, Shoko-ken teahouse at the end of the *Shoin* wing within his foundation (Figure 2.11). Built in the early Edo period in 1628 it is a rare and generic example of the *wabi* (refined poverty) *roji-soan* (dewed-path, informal-style) teahouse of the great Rikyu.[53] During this period we have the oldest *daime* style of the teahouse, distinctive for its central roughly hewn post structure marking a hierarchy between host and guests and for 'the attention given to the *tokonama* alcove and the spatial composition of these often darkened and solitude oriented tea-room spaces', intended, with the rough earthen texture of its clay walls, to suggest the humble poverty and semi-darkness of an old and remote farmhouse, somewhat in contrast to the 'open, courtly and elegant *sukiya*' teahouses associated with the Katsura Palace for example.[54] In the subdued light of a tiny tearoom such a natural, irregular column has the suggestive power to evoke a spirit of desolation, and human and material frailty.[55] At Shoko-ken the natural ochre of the lath plaster, applied to the wall surfaces between the structural members, was darkened with charcoal to intensify the rustic (*sabi*) atmosphere; this darkness is intensified by the dark green paper lining applied to the base of the plastered walls of the guests' seating areas.[56]

Associated with this twilight atmosphere of the tea cult is the ash-dyed neutral hue that came to be known as Rikyu grey (Rikyu *nezumi*) as first mentioned in a passage from the *Choando Ki* (the tea writings of Choando, 1571–1640):

[Rikyu's] distaste for colourful show achieved a widespread following, as did his verses advocating *wabi* austerity. [Practitioners were instructed to] wear cotton kimono dyed with ash to a neutral hue.... From then on, the colour grey enjoyed great popularity.[57]

Kurokawa links this cult of Rikyu grey to his aforementioned praise of Kyoto in the rain, or in the 'greying light of dusk', when 'there is a fusing of perspective as the slate-coloured tiles and white plaster walls dissolve into grey, flattening all sense of distance and volume; a drama of transition from three-dimensions down to two'.[58] This planarity is key to the architectonic character of the varied apertures and related garden views, to the strange juxtapositions of rough and smooth, within the dimness of the teahouse and to the aperspectival scenes that successively unroll – like the travelogue of a scroll – in journeyings into, and pauses within, a temple such as Koto-in. It is in the autumnal mood of this poem by Fujiwara no Teika (d. 1241):

Casting wide my gaze,
Neither blossoms
Nor scarlet leaves;
From the rush-thatched seaside hut,
Only the autumn dusk.[59]

So this chapter on ur-shadow ends in the autumnal shades of the consciously 'primitive hut' of Tadaoki's teahouse. But it is not only greyness and *wabi* poverty that defines Japan, and Kurokawa also stresses the overblown and gaudy sides of Japanese culture. Yet even these glittery things are made to be seen in the shadows, as Tanizaki understood:

And surely you have seen, in the darkness of the innermost rooms of these huge buildings, to which sunlight never penetrates, how the gold leaf of a sliding door or screen will pick up a distant glimmer from the garden, then suddenly send forth an ethereal glow, a faint golden light cast into the enveloping darkness, like the glow upon the horizon at sunset. In no other setting is gold quite so exquisitely beautiful.[60]

Kurokawa even discovers affinities between Rikyu's grey and Western Baroque, neatly hinging Japan's primordial shadows to the next chapter's theme of Baroque shadows. For Kurokawa, Rikyu's grey aesthetic can be equated in formal terms to a teahouse neo-Baroque of 'interactive coexistence of motion and suspended stillness, straight lines and curves... [in] intricate balance'.[61] And he parallels the grey culture's suggestive chromatics of shadow and twilight, to those informing the sacred spaces of the Baroque – 'one time in the West when the rational and irrational were allowed to coexist, and when religion took a turn towards nondualism'.[62] These scenarios of Enlightenment and shadows shape the following chapter.

Notes

1. Koslofsky, Craig, *Evening's Empire. A History of the Night in Early Modern Europe* (Cambridge: Cambridge University Press, 2011), p. 278.
2. Banham, Reyner, *The Architecture of the Well-Tempered Environment* (London: Architectural Press, 1969), p. 20.
3. See Fernández-Galiano, Luis, *Fire and Memory: On Architecture and Energy*, G. Cariño (trans) (Cambridge, MA: MIT Press, 2000), Chapter 1, 'Architecture discovers fire'.
4. Denison, Edward, and Ren, Guang Yu, *The Life of the British Home. An Architectural History* (Chichester: John Wiley, 2012), p. 25.
5. Quoted in Bollnow, O. F., *Human Space*, C. Shuttleworth (trans), J. Kohlmaier (ed) (London: Hyphen Press, 2011), p. 128.
6. Marc, Olivier, *Psychology of the House* (London: Thames and Hudson, 1977), p. 12.
7. Marc, *Psychology of the House*, p. 14.
8. Quoted in Bollnow, *Human Space*, p. 127.
9. Quoted in Bollnow, *Human Space*, p. 142.
10. Quoted in Bollnow, *Human Space*, p. 143.
11. See Denison and Ren, *Life of the British Home*, pp. 36, 37.
12. Peate, Iorwerth C., 'Hendre'r-ywydd Uchaf, Llangynhafal, Denbighshire. A Late Fifteenth-Century House', *Transactions of the Denbighshire Society*, vol. 11 (1962) (reprinted as a Welsh Folk Museum booklet). This building was re-erected at St Fagans National History Museum (The National Museum of Wales), near Cardiff, in 1962.
13. Denison and Ren, *Life of the British Home*, p. 72.
14. Denison and Ren, *Life of the British Home*, p. 91.
15. William, Eurwyn, *The Welsh Cottage. Building Traditions of the Rural Poor, 1750–1900* (Aberystwyth: Royal Commission on the Ancient and Historical Monuments of Wales, 2011), p. 13.
16. Koslofsky, *Evening's Empire*, p. 206.
17. Bachelard, Gaston, *The Poetics of Space*, M. Jolas (trans) (New York: Penguin Books, 2014, original work published as *la poetique de l'espace*, 1957), p. 164.
18. Bachelard, *Poetics of Space*, p. 27.
19. Bachelard, *Poetics of Space*, p. 50.
20. Casey, Edward S., *The Fate of Place: A Philosophical History* (Berkeley and Los Angeles, CA: University of California Press, 1998), p. 291.
21. Bachelard, *Poetics of Space*, pp. 39, 40.

22 Bachelard, *Poetics of Space*, p. 34.
23 Bachelard, *Poetics of Space*, p. 26.
24 This building was re-erected at St Fagans National History Museum (The National Museum of Wales), near Cardiff, in 1962.
25 Bachelard, *Poetics of Space*, pp. 158, 159.
26 See also the subtle analysis of this cottage in Unwin, Simon, *Analysing Architecture* (4th ed) (Abingdon, Oxon: Routledge, 2014), pp. 261–4.
27 Wright, Frank Lloyd, *The Future of Architecture* (New York: The New American Library, 1970, original work published 1953), p. 29.
28 Wright, *Future of Architecture*, p. 29.
29 Quoted in Fernández-Galiano, *Fire and Memory*, p. 28.
30 McCarter, Robert, 'The Integrated Ideal: Ordering Principles in Wright's Architecture', in R. McCarter (ed), *On and By Frank Lloyd Wright: A Primer of Architectural Principles* (London: Phaidon, 2011), pp. 286–337, 331–2.
31 Hildenbrand, Grant, *The Wright Space: Pattern and Meaning in Frank Lloyd Wright's Houses* (Seattle: University of Washington Press, 1991), p. 53.
32 Appleton, Jay, 'Landscape and Architecture', in B. Farmer and H. Louw (eds), *Companion to Contemporary Architectural Thought* (London: Routledge, 1993), pp. 74–81, 74.
33 Appleton, 'Landscape and Architecture', pp. 74–5.
34 Wright, *Future of Architecture*, p. 18.
35 See also McCarter, 'Integrated Ideal', p. 312.
36 Meech, Julia, *Frank Lloyd Wright and the Art of Japan: The Architect's Other Passion* (New York: Japan Society and Harry N. Abrams, 2001), p. 52.
37 Van Zanten, David, 'Schooling the Prairie School: Wright's Early Style as a Communicable System', in McCarter (ed), *On and By Frank Lloyd Wright*, pp. 116–23, 121.
38 Meech, *Wright and the Art of Japan*, p. 34.
39 This is an early example of a Wright-ian pattern evident a fortiori in the Darwin Martin House, Buffalo, New York (1904), whereby the 'indoors-outdoors interface' transforms between sitting and standing. Sitting on the benches by Wright's home hearth, refuge is complete; but upon standing eye-level apertures allow a surprising cross-vista between inglenook, dining room and the study area (of the 1895 remodelling).
40 Tanizaki, Junichoro, *In Praise of Shadows*, T. J. Harper and E. G. Seidensticker (trans) (London: Vintage, 2001, original work published 1933–4), p. 58.
41 Quoted in Tanizaki, *Praise of Shadows*, p. 2.
42 Tanizaki, *Praise of Shadows*, p. 28.
43 Tanizaki, *Praise of Shadows*, p. 29.
44 Tanizaki, *Praise of Shadows*, p. 28.
45 Bring, Mitchell and Wayembergh, Josse, *Japanese Gardens: Design and Meaning* (New York: Mc-Graw Hill, 1981), p. 71.

46 Bring and Wayembergh, *Japanese Gardens*, p. 173.
47 Plummer, Henry, *Light in Japanese Architecture* (Tokyo: Architecture and Urbanism Publishing, 1995), p. 102.
48 Kurokawa, Kisho, 'Shadows, Symbiosis, and a Culture of Wood', in David Murray (ed), *Via 11. Architecture and Shadow. The Journal of the Graduate School of Fine Arts, University of Pennsylvania* (1990), pp. 26–31, 30.
49 Tanizaki, *Praise of Shadows*, p. 32.
50 Nitschke, Günter, '"Ma" The Japanese Sense of Place in Old and New Architecture and Planning', *Architectural Design*, vol. 36 (1966), pp. 116–55, 147.
51 Nitschke, Günter, *From Shinto to Ando: Studies in Architectural Anthropology in Japan* (London: Academy Editions, 1993), p. 39.
52 Hildebrand, Grant, *The Wright Space: Pattern and Meaning in Frank Lloyd Wright's Houses* (Seattle: University of Washington Press, 1991), pp. 64–70.
53 Walker, Robin Noel, *Shoko-Ken. A Late Medieval Daime Sukiya Style Japanese Tea House* (Abingdon, Oxon: Routledge, 2002), p. 5.
54 Walker, *Shoko-Ken*, 5; see also Engel, Heinrich, *The Japanese House: A Tradition for Contemporary Architecture* (Rutland, VT; Tokyo: Charles E. Tuttle, 1964), pp. 283–90.
55 Engel, *Japanese House*, p. 289.
56 See Walker, *Shoko-Ken*, p. 181.
57 Quoted in Kurokawa, Kisho, *Rediscovering Japanese Space* (New York: Weatherhill, 1988), p. 61.
58 Kurokawa, *Rediscovering Japanese Space*, p. 62.
59 Kurokawa, *Rediscovering Japanese Space*, p. 63.
60 Tanizaki, *Praise of Shadows*, p. 35.
61 Tanizaki, *Praise of Shadows*, p. 68.
62 Kurokawa, *Rediscovering Japanese Space*, p. 69.

3

'The art of Shaddowes'
The Baroque of Hawksmoor and Vanbrugh

'Baroque' only emerges as a term in art criticism in the 1750s, to label something regarded as strange or weird.[1] Contemporary critics of the English Baroque architects Nicholas Hawksmoor (1661–1736) and Sir John Vanbrugh (1664–1726) described their buildings as 'unreasoned', 'licentious' and 'bizarre', or more positively as 'ingenious' or 'gotico'. Interpretations of Hawksmoor's buildings today are inevitably shaded by the dark imaginings of Iain Sinclair and Peter Ackroyd.[2] On the first pages of Ackroyd's novel *Hawksmoor*, Dyer (his fictional Hawksmoor) teaches his assistant this:

> And now we come to the Heart of our Designe: the art of Shaddowes you must know well, Walter, and you must be instructed how to Cast them with due Care. It is only the Darknesse that can give trew Forme to our Work and trew Perspective to our Fabrick, for there is no Light without Darknesse and no Substance without Shaddowe.[3]

We do not need to follow the novelist's fantasy of Dyer the Satanist to agree that Ackroyd has grasped a central characteristic of Hawksmoor's architecture, in thus placing the 'art of Shaddowes' at the 'Heart of [his] Designe'. Hawksmoor's work is also a dark presence in T. S. Eliot's poem *The Waste Land* (1922) – as the downhearted commuters flow down King William Street 'To where [Hawksmoor's] Saint Mary Woolnoth kept the hours/With a dead sound on the final stroke of nine'.[4] A building, like those in Eliot's *The Love Song of J. Alfred Prufrock*, which 'Let[s] fall upon its back the soot that falls from chimneys',[5] dramatizing a surrogate chiaroscuro of black stains and bleached Portland stone in the pale London light. As a result of handling these stones in the sooty city over decades Hawksmoor must surely have anticipated such effects. As Dyer/Hawksmoor reminds his draughtsman: 'From what Purse are we building these Churches, Walter? From the Imposicion on Coles. And are the Coles not the blackest Element, which with their Smoak hide the Sunne?'[6] Sir Christopher Wren's St Paul's Cathedral (1675–1711) had been built from a tax on sea coal. Ackroyd characterizes London, in his *Biography* of the capital, as 'always...a shadowy city', one 'packed to blackness' whose inhabitants always felt the soot up their nostrils, and found the furnishings of their chambers, as John Evelyn complained in the seventeenth century, 'evenly covered with a black thin soot'.[7]

Commentators on Ackroyd's *Hawksmoor* expose a tension between shadows and Enlightenment in the spatialities of London and its churches, the latter signified by Sir Christopher Wren's rationalism and luminosity and the former by Dyer/Hawksmoor's darker metaphysics.[8] This dualism is encompassed within a complex discovery of the night in early modern Europe that is necessarily coequal with a conquest of darkness in the city, through street lighting and a growing nocturnal culture of coffee houses, theatres and so forth. In Chapter 2, Koslofsky's *History of the Night in Early Modern Europe* was cited to show how 'darkness was slowly transformed from a primordial presence to a more manageable aspect of life' spiritually, politically and socially, with profound consequences for the handling of shadow in the spaces and forms of the church.[9] While some voices pointed to the retreating shadows as evidence of the triumph of reason, others became intrigued by these manageable darknesses as tools to explore realms of the spirit and the psyche. Hawksmoor's architecture participates strongly in this creative discovery of 'active darkness'.[10]

The roles light and 'active darkness' play in English church architecture between the mid-sixteenth century and the early eighteenth century are deeply interwoven in fiercely contested arenas of reformation and counter-reformation. The iconoclasm of Edward VI was followed by the *via media* settlement of Elizabeth I; then the ascendancy of the Anglican counter-reformation under the influence of Archbishop Laud in the 1630s overturns this austerity. These reformers sought a 'beauty of holiness' (Psalm 96:9) and an environment of reverence, ceremonial and imagery (as advocated in influential texts such as the 1638 *De Templis* of the anonymous 'R. T.'), creating a 'Gothic Survival' of mysteriously layered, shadowy spaces.

The Puritan counter-revolution was brutal and swift when it came in 1640–1, but the restoration of the monarchy (1660), and Wren's rebuilding of the London churches in the 1670s and 1680s, produced a new church model that retained the magnificence of the railed Laudian altar within spaces that were essentially rectangular, evenly lit 'auditories' focused on the pulpit.[11]

The 'Fifty' new churches

The work of the Fifty New Churches Commission, appointed by Parliament in 1711, must be seen against the above background. London had grown enormously since the Great Fire, and by the early 1720s Daniel Defoe could refer to the city 'in the modern acceptance' as

> all that vast mass of buildings, reaching from Black-Wall in the east, to Tot-Hill fields in the west...and all the new buildings by, and beyond, Hannover Square, by which the city of London...is extended to Hyde Park Corner...and almost to Maribone in the Acton Road, and how much farther it may spread, who knows?...nothing in the world does, or ever did, equal it, except old Rome in Trajan's time.[12]

In the face of this phenomenal growth the need for new places of worship was recognized by even the most disputatious divines and, among members of the established church, there was fear that unmet spiritual needs would be fed by the easily established meeting houses of the dissenters or by proselytizing Papists. The final impetus to action was given by the Tory victory in the general election of 1710 and a renewed resolve to confront the problem of what churches were needed both for the new suburbs and to replace decrepit ones in the older quarters. To pay for the new places of worship, a bill was passed imposing an additional duty on coals brought into the Port of London, and the Commission began its business on 28 September 1711 – it would sit until 1734. Given the recent electoral triumph, its membership was dominated by Tories and High Anglicans. While the battles between the Laudians and the Puritans had been resolved to some extent in the Wren church model, the Commission aspired for grander steepled and porticoed buildings of stone, which were ordered around stricter High Church rules embodied in the experience of early Christianity as it was then understood.

As the principal officers of the Royal Works appointed to the Commission, Sir Christopher Wren and John Vanbrugh were prompt in providing advice on the form of the churches – Hawksmoor was appointed as a salaried surveyor along with another Wren pupil, William Dickinson (c. 1671–1725). The ideal for both Wren and Vanbrugh was for the churches to be as freestanding as possible to enhance the city and to be further dignified with porticoes and steeples. Here is Wren:

> As to the Situation of the Churches, I should propose they be brought as forward into the larger and more open Streets, not in obscure lanes.... Such Fronts as shall happen to lie most open in View should be adorned with Porticoes, both for Beauty and Convenience, which, together with handsome Spires, or Lanterns, rising in good Proportion

above the neighbouring houses…may be of sufficient Ornament to the Town.[13]

And here is Vanbrugh:

First. That their Situations may ever be Insulate [i.e. isolated]. This do's…give them that Respectfull Distinction & Dignity which Churches Always ought to have….That they may be all Accomodated and Adorn'd with Portico's, no part in Publick Edifices being of greater use, nor no production in Architecture so solemnly Magnificent….That for the Ornament of the Towne, and to shew at a distance what regard there is in it to Religious Worship; every Church…may have a Tower, but to Answer these endes, they shou'd be all of Stone or Brick; High and Bold Structures; and so form'd as not to be subject to Ruin by fire, but of such Solidity and Strength, that nothing but Time, and scarce that, shou'd destroy them.[14]

Vanbrugh's vision – influenced by, and shared with, Hawksmoor – though ostensibly similar to Wren's is markedly different in intent and language. Wren's portico is an element of 'Beauty', but essentially 'convenient' – something to keep off the rain as you step into the building, whereas Vanbrugh's portico offers scope for the 'art of Shaddowes' in its solemn magnificence. Wren certainly desires 'Spires or Lanterns' (but warns against 'great Towers, and lofty Steeples, [which] are sometimes more than half the Charge of the Church'), whereas Vanbrugh and Hawksmoor seek a *real* tower, a mighty structure rich in plastic potential (Figure 3.1). Wren's materiality is also modest: 'In Windows and Doors *Portland* Stone may be used, with good Bricks' for the body of the fabric 'and stone Quoyns', all on the model of one of his finest churches, St James's Piccadilly, as mentioned in his 'Letter'.[15] Vanbrugh espoused 'the utmost duration both in respect of the material, the Solidity of their Walls, and the Manner of their Construction'[16] and in their 'Rules for the Fifty New Churches' of 11 July 1712, the Commissioners decreed, for magnificence, 'that, the Churches be all built with Stone on the Outside'.[17] Yet more stark is the contrast in conception between Wren and Vanbrugh as to the 'Insides' of these churches. Plentiful fenestration pours light into the transverse vaults and barrel-vaulted nave of Wrens' St James. Like his city churches 'fitted for Auditories', it is conceived as a modestly scaled single room, yet able 'to hold above 2000 Persons, and all to hear the Service, and both to hear distinctly; and to see the Preacher'. 'The *Romanists*, indeed', mutters Wren, 'may build larger Churches, it is enough if they hear the Murmur of the Mass, and see the Elevation of the Host'.[18] What Vanbrugh wished to achieve – in contrast to Wren's stress on audibility and visibility – if not 'Romanist', was certainly more Laudian and High Church in its aspiration to shadowly evocative sacred spaces:

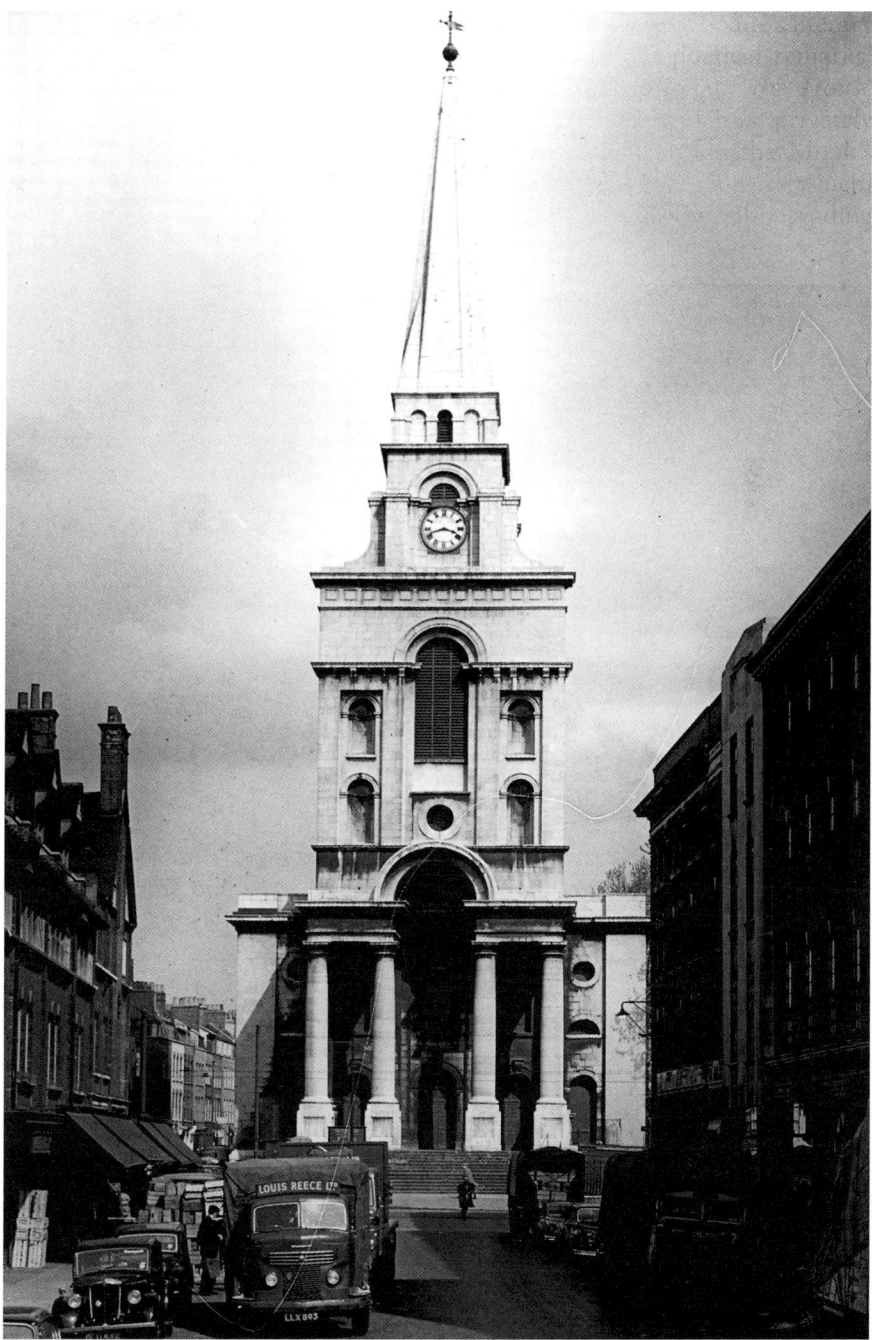

FIGURE 3.1 Great towers and lofty steeples: Hawksmoor's Christ Church, Spitalfields, seen from Brushfield Street. Photograph, Edwin Smith, 1957, RIBA Library Photographs Collection.

That for the Lights, there may be no more than what are necessary for meer use; many Windows making a Church cold in Winter, hot in Summer, and being very disagreeable and hurtful to the sight. They likewise take off very much, both from the Appearance & reality of strength in the Fabrick; giving it more the Air of a Gay Lanthorn to be set on the Top of a Temple, than the Reverend look of a Temple it self; which shou'd ever have the most Solemn and Awfull Appearance both without and within, that is possible.[19]

Evidently Vanbrugh's proposals are also strongly influenced by Leon Battista Alberti's (1404–72) *On the Art of Building in Ten Books*. In Book Seven on 'Ornament to Sacred Buildings', Alberti advises:

The window openings of a temple should have modest dimensions and should be placed high up, where they have a view of nothing but the sky, which will not divert the minds of celebrant or supplicant from divine matters. The awe that is naturally generated by darkness encourages a sense of veneration in the mind; and there is always some austerity about majesty. What is more, the flame, which should burn in a temple, and which is the most divine ornament of religious worship, looks faint in too much light. For this reason, surely, the ancients were usually content with a doorway as the only opening. But, for my part, I would prefer to make the entrance to a temple thoroughly well lit, and the interior and nave not too gloomy. I would place the altar, however, in a place of majesty rather than of elegance.[20]

Alberti invokes a sombre and shadowed space, as in his own attempt at the primitive, the 'Etruscan shrine' of his barrel-vaulted Sant' Andrea, Mantua (Figure 3.2).

A middle way is represented by Reverend George Hickes (a well-regarded biblical and Anglo-Saxon scholar), who submitted to the Commission his 'Observations on Mr. Vanbruggs Proposals About Buildinge the New Churches'. 'As for lights', he observed, 'they ought not to be too many, or too wide: so I think they ought not to be too few, or too narrow, because, it would make the air of a church too like that of a cave, or grotto.'[21] Hickes's wish to emulate primitive Christian architecture impacted greatly on the Commissioners' thinking, and consequently on Hawksmoor's architecture – at the same time reinforcing the architect's innate preference for the primitive:[22]

The plans of the most primitive of churches, as described in Eusebius's history may be seen, not to mention other Authors in the third vol. of Mr. Bingham's Ecclesiastical Antiquities and there it will appear that the old way of building churches is capable of most if not all the state, and graces of Architecture, and as that way of building was the most ancient: so it is

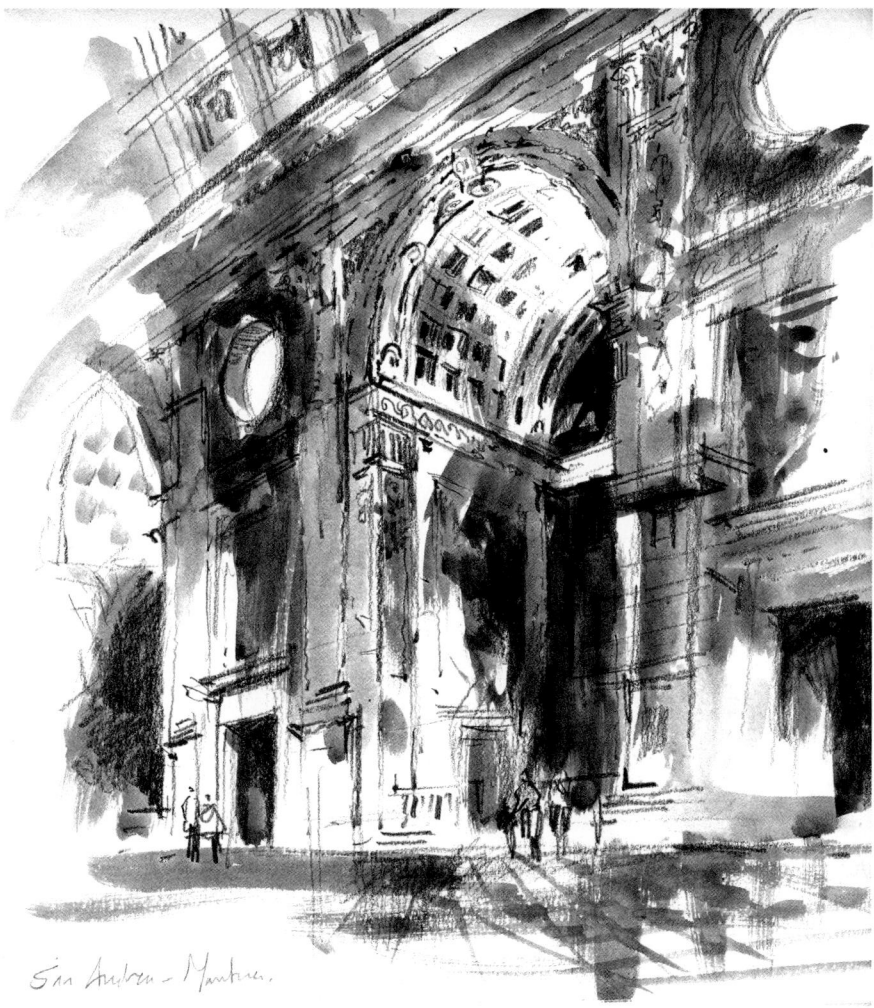

FIGURE 3.2 Interior of Leon Battista Alberti's, Sant' Andrea, Mantua. Drawing by Stephen Kite.

most fit to be imitated, and the same modelle will serve for building little, as well as great churches.[23]

As Joseph Rykwert explains:

The apparent primitivism of Eastern Christianity was to exercise a permanent fascination on Western churchmen: the very use of the Greek language, the language of the New Testament, was a direct link to the primitive gospel and to a sacred antiquity which obsessed ecclesiastics as well as church builders in the seventeenth and eighteenth centuries without respecting distinction of nationality or denomination. It was, moreover, a link to a remoter, sacred antiquity, whose documents were almost all known in their Greek form, and in which Plato and Zoroaster could figure as foreshadows of Christ.[24]

The significant figure who connects Hickes to the aforementioned Eusebius is a young clergyman, Reverend George Wheler (1650–1723). He had studied under Hickes, who inspired him to travel to the Levant to study the early Christian churches there.[25] In 1689, he published *An Account of the Churches, or Places of Assembly of the Primitive Christians, from the Churches of Tyre, Jerusalem and Constantinople Described by Eusebius, and Ocular Observation of Several Very Ancient Edifices of Churches Yet Extant in Those Parts; with a Reasonable Application*. Eusebius Pamphilius – the fourth-century bishop of Caesarea – had described these early churches in his *Ecclesisatical History* and his *Life of Constantine*. Wheler's engraving of the Prospect and 'Plane of the Primitive Churches' interprets Byzantine-Greek Orthodox forms to produce a building of domed, cross-in-square plan, entered through an octostyle Corinthian portico; the edifice stands isolated in a protective outer courtyard of the kind Eusebius had described in a church at Tyre.

It is within this primitivizing matrix of ideas and images that Hawksmoor's contribution to the form of the new churches needs to be understood, namely his remarkable plan for 'The Basilica after the Primitive Christians', also inscribed 'Manner of Building the Church as it was in ye fourth Century in ye purest times of Christianity'.[26] As a surveyor, Hawksmoor was tasked by the Commission with producing plans and buildings, not speculative ideas or theories; his Basilica plan of circa November 1711–July 1712 (now in Lambeth Palace Library) was an unrealized proposal, for a site at Hare Field in the hamlet of Bethnal Green. Fusing his own predilection for blocky forms (capable of producing strong shadows) with these primitive prescriptions, Hawksmoor produced a highly articulated church composition (most unlike a Wren preaching box) nested in a protective enclosure – as Wheler had shown – demarcated at its corners by houses for church functionaries. Conspicuous elements are the baptistery entrance to the building at the west (spacious enough for the immersion of adult persons as urged by Hickes), the eastern apse, and the 'Stairs to ye Womens Gallerys' which anchor the central body of the plan and closely foreshadow the prominent stair turrets he would build at Saint George-in-the-East.[27] From sources such as Guillaume-Joseph Grelot's *A Late Voyage to Constantinople* (1683), Wren and Hawksmoor also knew how these elements, of projecting stairs serving upper galleries, buttress the composition of Hagia Sophia.

There is no need to look as far as the Near East for precedents for blocky composition; in *The Englishness of English Art*, Nikolaus Pevsner describes the 'compartmented English plan', as at Salisbury Cathedral, and an 'English ideal of the square block' most intensely evident in the Perpendicular

England of square-topped towers and expressive verticals and horizontals, forms that continue in Elizabethan works like Hardwick Hall and Wollaton Hall, in Hawksmoor's own piled up masses, and even the cubic ensembles of Palladian country houses.[28]

Hawksmoor thought Wollaton Hall displayed 'some true stroakes of architecture'[29] and a 19 cm × 15.5 cm (portrait format) sketchbook of 1680–3 shows a real empathy for Gothic building for a young man in his early twenties (given the accepted date of his birth to be around 1661). As a would-be palazzo, built in the latest Italian style, he studied the just-completed Nottingham Castle (1679) delicately in line elevation. Its aristocratic designer, the Duke of Newcastle, had lived in exile in Rubens's house in Antwerp and knew enough of Continental Baroque to produce an animated essay of columns, pilasters and bold modillioned cornice, layered on the rusticated limestone mass of the mansion.[30] The castle appears again at the right of Hawksmoor's 'prospectus occidenta' of the town, shown on its dark sandstone crag; shadows track across the whole foreground of the image, coarse cross-hatchings of pen and brown ink for crag and hills, and more subtle vertical striations for the medieval houses pressing around the sooty stump of St Peter's steeple, made more prominent in its darkness than the greater church of St Mary's (Figure 3.3). The medieval town gate of 'Chapell Barr' (demolished 1743) is a prominent element, and in a strongly awkward hand Hawksmoor closes in to record

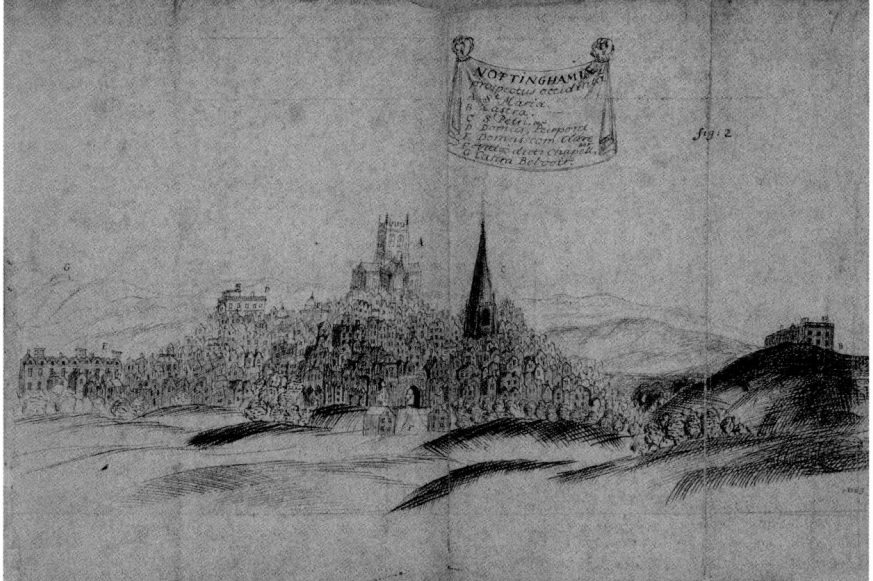

FIGURE 3.3 Nicholas Hawksmoor, prospect of Nottingham, sketchbook c. 1680–3, p. 7, RIBA Library Drawings and Archives Collections.

its frontal solidity of wall and half-cylinder turrets, penetrated by the deep-hatched shadows of the angular-arched gateway which opens beyond to a brighter receding street (Figure 3.4). Frontality and perspective are also fused in a sketch of the late perpendicular west front of Bath Abbey; this captures some detail such as the famous angels ascending the ladders of the pinnacles, but forceful cross-hatching blackens the building mostly into silhouette, so enhancing the brighter perspectives of nave and aisles glimpsed through the doorways (Figure 3.5). Context is given by outlines of

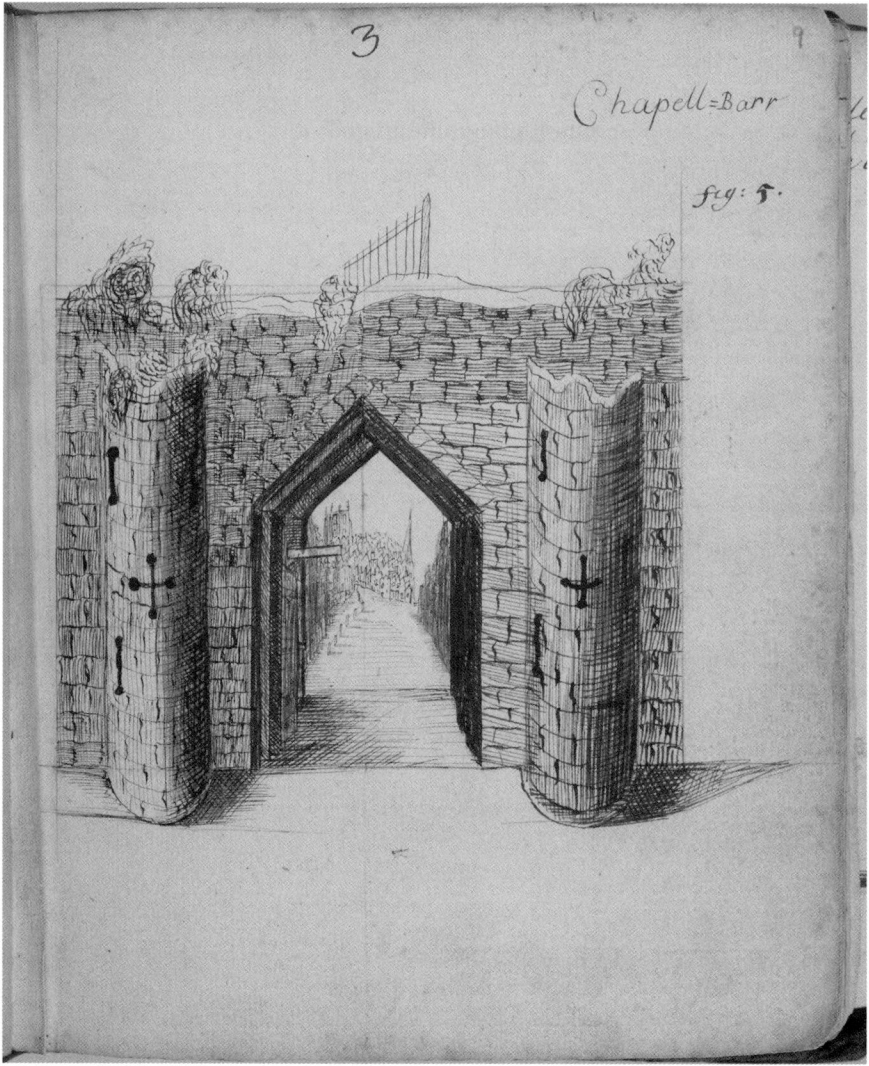

FIGURE 3.4 Nicholas Hawksmoor, 'Chapell Barr' Nottingham, sketchbook c. 1680–3, p. 9, RIBA Library Drawings and Archives Collections.

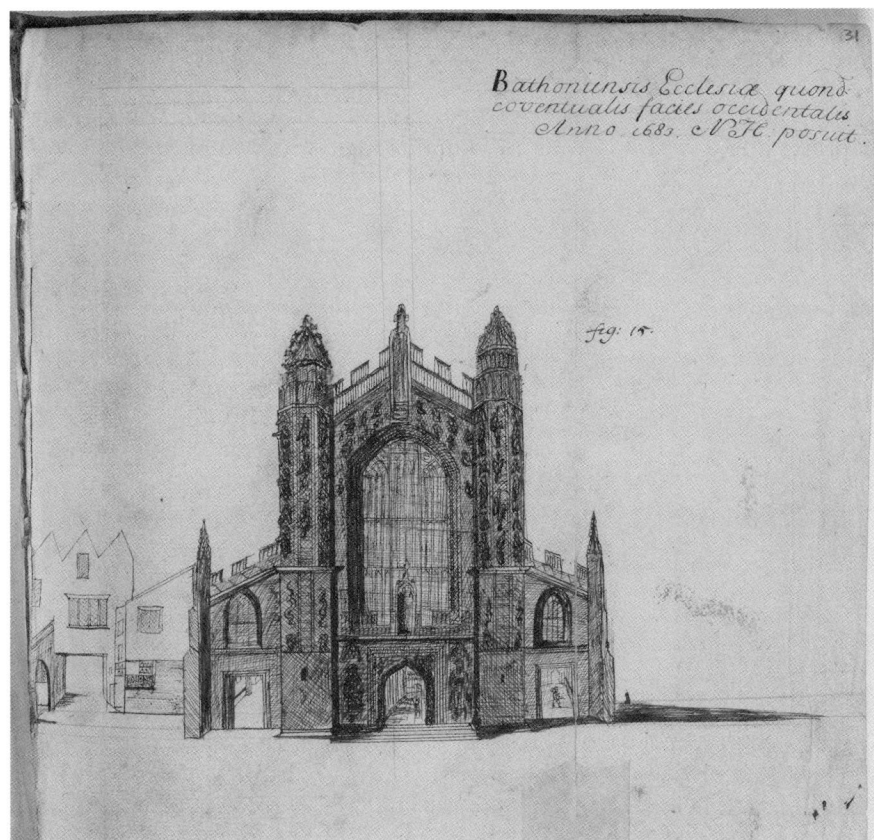

FIGURE 3.5 Nicholas Hawksmoor, Bath Abbey, sketchbook c. 1680–3, p. 31, RIBA Library Drawings and Archives Collections.

the congested Wade's passage dwellings built against the north side of the abbey (only cleared in 1825–35), balanced by a long spike of shadow, curiously thrown on the south side of the building. Other panoramas of Bath, Coventry, a 'Northe prospect of Warwick', Oxford, and Northampton, like – or possibly from – topographical prints, confirm an affection for those medieval groupings of turret and steeple which some of his church designs attempt to capture in a single building. Another sketch of a contemporary building shows All Saint's Church, Northampton, completed in Wren style in 1680 after a town fire of 1675 had destroyed the medieval church. Hawksmoor drew the rebuilt church, looking from the south in a steep perspective (roughly set up on graphite lines drawn to a vanishing point) that emphasizes the blocky engaged volumes and pronounced shadows of the Greek cross plan (Figure 3.6). But there are puzzles here; Hawksmoor's drawing shows Corinthian columns and scrolls flanking the tower, while the realized building has an ionic order and no scrolls, leading to

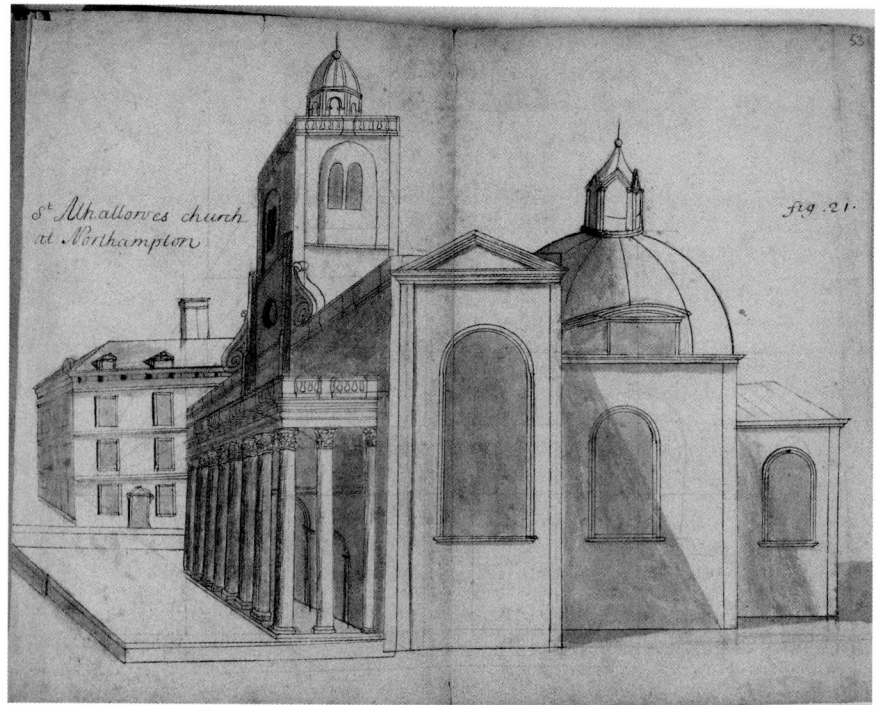

FIGURE 3.6 Nicholas Hawksmoor, study of All Saint's Church, Northampton, sketchbook c. 1680–3, p. 53, RIBA Library Drawings and Archives Collections.

speculation that the drawing may indicate some project involvement of his with the portico design (completed c. 1696) – his first building perhaps?[31]

Hawksmoor had been taken on as Surveyor General Sir Christopher Wren's personal clerk around 1679–80 at the age of eighteen, coming to London from a modest yeoman farming background in East Drayton, Nottinghamshire. Under Wren, at the Office of Works, Hawksmoor acquired a rigorous on-the-job training – one unlike that of a gentleman-architect such as Vanbrugh, who would not have possessed Hawksmoor's surviving pocket 'building notebook' which is full of practical on-site data, sketches of building construction, notes of inspections, materials and rates of work. Thus, 'it records that a mason can work 30 foot of Oxford Stone or make a baluster of a certain length in a day'.[32] It opens with the statement: 'Arcana Mecha/in/Re Adificattora/nec non/altri scientiis', which translates as, 'secret (or abstruse) artisanship (or skill) in building and other branches of knowledge';[33] these are secrets gained, not from 'learned' treatises, but from watching tradesmen and from intimate acquaintance with the construction site. Juhani Pallasmaa describes this as 'embodied wisdom',[34] and Hawksmoor's art of shadows demonstrates this connection between conception and idea, and the physical realities of matter and making. If any of this might suggest Hawskmoor as an inspired technician, the evidence of his brilliantly individual buildings, and the catalogue of his library (sold off four years after his death at his house in Millbank on 25 March 1736 from 'gout in the stomach') also verifies the fuller learned man portrait of his obituary[35]:

> He was perfectly skilld in the history of Architecture and could give an exact account of all the famous buildings, both antient & modern in every part of the World.... Nor was Architecture the only Science he was master of, he was bred a scholar, and knew as well the learned as the modern tongues – he was a very Skillfull mathematician geographer and geometrician, and in drawing which he practiced to the last ... few excelld him.[36]

Though incomplete (the catalogue is also confusingly mixed with the effects of another person), it proves that Hawksmoor had editions of Vitruvius, Serlio, Palladio and Alberti; many later theoretical works such as Blondel's *Cours d'Architecture*; works on geometry and perspective by Langley, Moxon and Pozzo; classics of English architecture such as *Vitruvius Britannicus*; and a large collection of works on topography and travel.

De Templis – mystical darkness

The earlier-noted studies of the early modern night describe the emergence of a nocturnalization that could be manipulated to mystic effect – with potent consequences for the shadowy realms of architecture. The approach to the divine in the seventeenth century is transformed by John of the Cross's (1542–91) engagement with darkness and his discovery of the *Dark Night of the Soul* (1582–85). These are the ascetic shadows of George de la Tour's (1593–1652) *The Magdalene with the Smoking Flame* (1638–40), or Henry Vaughan's poem 'The Night': 'There is in God – some say -/A deep, but dazzling darkness .../O for that Night! where I in Him/Might live invisible and dim'.[37] Primitive shadows enthuse the anonymous 'R. T.', author of *De Templis, A Treatise of Temples: Wherein Is discovered the Ancient manner of Building, Consecrating, and Adorning of Churches* (1638), he was friend to the Laudians, and acquainted with Roman Catholic practices.[38] Like Hawksmoor's 'Basilica after the Primitive Christians', R. T.'s ideal church is tripartite, 'built with three parts, after the fashion of Salomons Temple': 'portch', nave or 'the ship or body of the Church' and 'quire or Chancell';[39] the last must be higher 'divided from the body of the Church, by an ascent of steps'.[40] The vaults that support this higher chancel are more than functional:

> It has been an ancient custome ever since *Constantines* time, that vaults should be built under the Quire which were called *Cryptae*, in

remembrance of those vaults, caves, and secret places, underground, where the Christians, in times of persecution, were wont to assemble to serve God.[41]

The massive keystones guarding the black openings to Hawksmoor's undercrofts commemorate these catacombs – as in St George's Bloomsbury (Figure 3.7). Following observations on the lighting of the dark main body of the church, R. T. returns to this point about these mystically obscure crypts where Christianity originated:

> Over [the 'Capitals' and 'Architrave freeze'] let the windoores be placed, which because they stand high differ more from profane buildings, keep our thoughts from wandring abroad, whilst our eyes have nothing but Heaven, and heavenly objects to behold....The number of windoores ought to observe the grace of the whole structure, which if they be not of common glasse, but pained, adorne the Church with a glorious light, and moderate that bright light, which is a hinderance to devotion. The Utopian Temples saith St *T: More*, were *sub obscura*; somewhat... For devotion requires collected spirits, which light diffuses, as Sir *H: Wotton* seems to interpret him in his Elements of Architecture. And we find it by experience, that in our light Churches, did not wee close our eyes, wee could hardly keepe our thoughts from distractions till the end of a short collect. And I verily believe that the holy fervour of devotion was more intense in the primitive Christians dark obscure vaults, than hath ever beene in our lightsome churches.[42]

In *The Elements of Architecture* (1624), that R. T. cites, Sir Henry Wotton (1568–1639) aimed to influence aristocratic patrons and their architects directly, whereas *De Templis's* stimulus to architecture was via an audience of divines. Wotton writes: 'And indeed I must confesse that a Franke Light, can misbecome noe *Aedifice* whatsoever, *Temples* onely excepted; which were anciently darke, as they are likewise at this day in some Proportion. *Devotion more requiring collected then defused Spirits.*' And a Latin printed marginal note reinforces this stating: 'Light spreads out itself and other things' – i.e. light distracts.[43]

These shadows, which attend the emergence of the early modern subject in the Baroque period, create scopic regimes as powerful in their own way as those that evolve in the Romantic period around 1810 to 1840. Some commentators, such as Alberto Pérez-Gómez, argue for the continuities in visual culture between these early modern and more modern observers[44], whereas Jonathan Crary stresses a disjunction from the passive spectator of the classical period, whose paradigm Crary locates in the incorporeal relationships of the architectural enclosure of the camera obscura. Within its darkness the observer 'confronts a unified space of order, unmodified by his or her own sensory and physiological experience, on which the

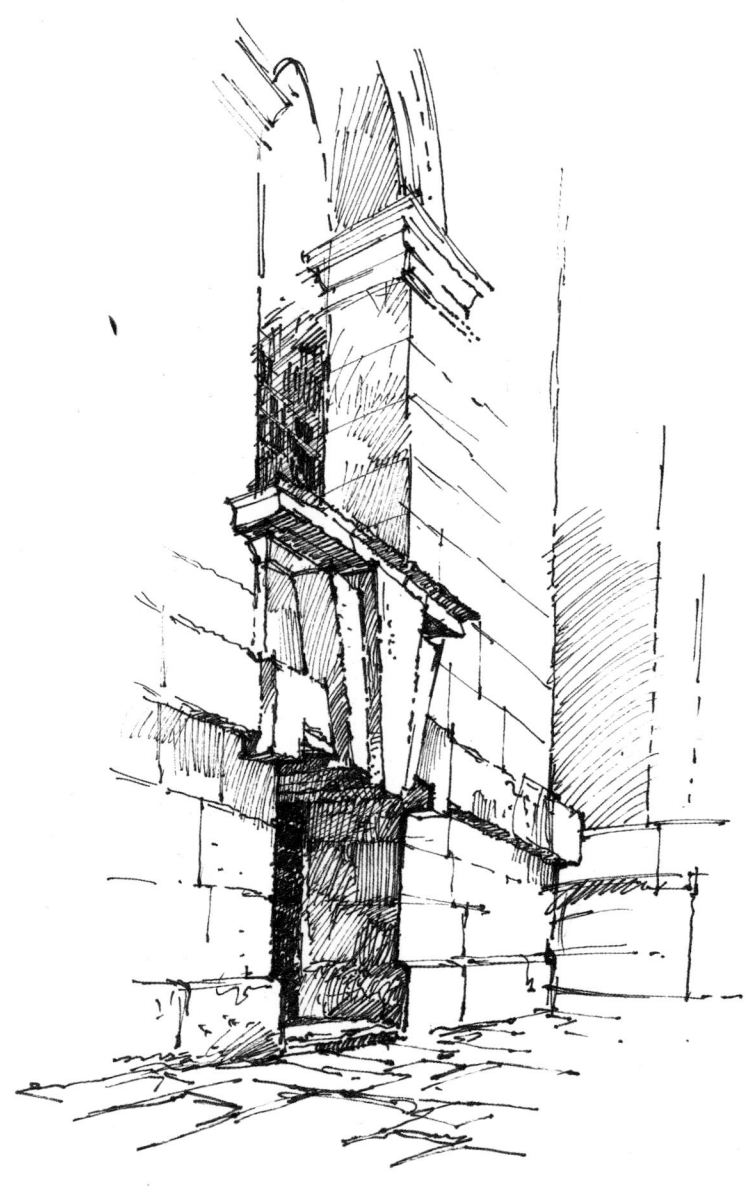

FIGURE 3.7 Keystones to crypt openings. Drawing by Stephen Kite.

contents of the world can be studied and compared, known in terms of a multitude of relationships'.[45] For Crary, it is only in the early 1800s that vision is 'taken out of the incorporeal relations of the camera obscura and relocated in the human body'; once vision is truly constituted in the body of the observer, it becomes psychological, social, aesthetic and so on – all that we recognize as modern. But Crary's detached classical observer seems cold and most unlike what we know of the Baroque. I agree with the more nuanced standpoint of Pérez-Gómez, who points out: 'The observer in the camera obscura did not occupy the locus of an illusion but rather witnessed an apparition independent of her – or himself. Although this popular device evidenced an external geometric reality, it would be wrong to infer that painters and philosophers believed that it demonstrated a reality in which the subject is absent'[46] – so we still have an embodied viewer. For this subject of shadows the camera obscura is a deeply fascinating construction as imaged in Locke's *Essay Concerning Human Understanding* (1690):

> External and internal sensations are the only passages that I can find of knowledge to the understanding. These alone, as far as I can discover, are the windows by which light is let into this *dark room*. For, methinks, the understanding is not much unlike a closet wholly shut from light, with only some little opening left... to let in external visible resemblances, or some idea of things without.[47]

Here is a cerebral interiority to be read in parallel to the mystical ones of St John of the Cross, as portrayed in Vermeer's paintings of *The Astronomer* (1668) and *The Geographer* (c. 1668–89).[48]

Shadow theatres – St George's Bloomsbury

Restored in 2008 to its original arrangement of galleries and dual orientation, St George's Bloomsbury (1716–31) restages the full Baroque complexity of a Hawksmoor interior space.[49] I say 'restage' here to reinforce the coexistence of theatrical representations in the Baroque world view in both secular and sacred settings. For Arnaud Maillet the Baroque 'opened passageways between the space of the spectator and that of the work, but in a mode quite different from that of Romanticism.... In Romanticism this opening tends to occur through the erasure of the frame, whereas in the Baroque the frame itself is redoubled and exceeded'.[50] This multiplication of frames calls to mind those seventeenth- and eighteenth-century Italian School stage sets of columnar framing wing flats – rarely fewer than six, and often as many as twenty.[51]

St George's employs a similar redoubling of receding frames: entering through the sombre hexastyle Corinthian portico, and beneath the south gallery the north wall of Hawksmoor's nave presents a Serliana of segmental arch and entablature, carried on coupled Corinthian columns, aligned on the west-east axis, all evenly lit from the square lantern over. The Serliana repeats in the shadowy zone that defines the (reinstated) north gallery, but now as a *coupled* arch borne on a north-south aligned pair of columns – thus making three theatrically receding arches in close succession. Beyond the original Parish Room zone, the dark plane of the north wall, pierced by three round-arched windows, sets off this trio of arches (Figure 3.8). Externally, to complete the theatre analogies, this references the Theatre of Marcellus and the Colosseum with its tiers of Corinthian pilasters and columns (Figure 3.9). Between 1782 and 2008 the altar piece closed this perspective, relocated from the eastern apse in a reordering that destroyed Hawksmoor's plays of ambiguity between the north-south processional axis – as dictated by the confined site – and the liturgical east-west one. To find the altar (returned now to its original place in the eastern apse) Hawksmoor compels the viewer to turn from the north-south alignment of retreating arches and to grasp the whole space in its rich three-quarter aspect, in a move that reflects Ferdinando Bibiena's introduction in the 1700s of the two-point perspective, or *scena per angolo* in stage design, and the abandonment of the central axis.[52] Hawksmoor's library contained works such as John James's translation of the great Jesuit illusionist Andrea Pozzo's *Perspectiva pictorum et architectorum* (1693); so we know he was well aware of the potential of Baroque perspectivity.[53] At the heart of St George's, Kerry Downes finds 'a considered and deliberate ambiguity.... Whichever way you enter, what you see is unexpected, disorienting, but calculated'.[54]

FIGURE 3.8 Interior, St George's Bloomsbury. Photograph, Stephen Kite.

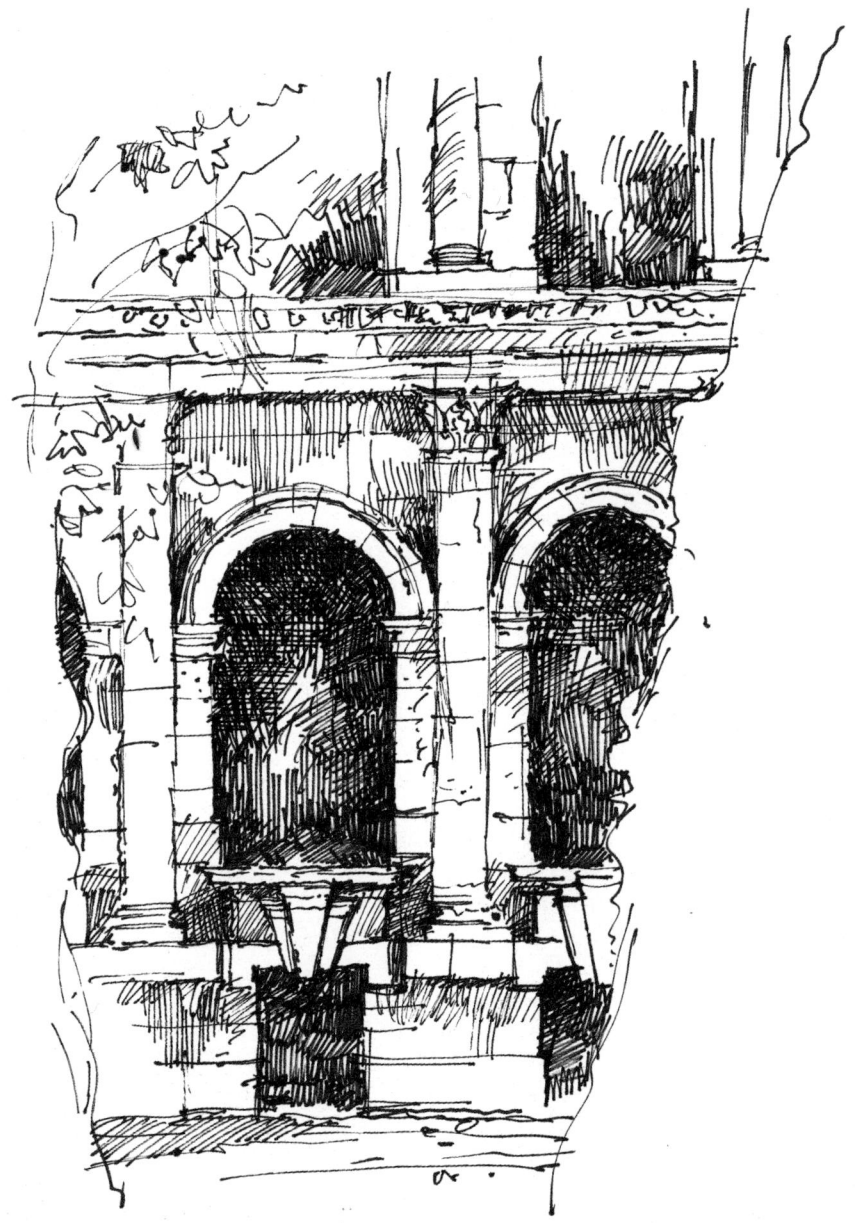

FIGURE 3.9 North façade, St George's Bloomsbury. Drawing by Stephen Kite.

Koslofsky concludes that nocturnalization was indeed a revolution:

> Princes and urban oligarchs alike projected their glory onto the night with illuminations and fireworks displays, while purpose-built baroque theatres could be fully darkened, day or night, to enable the complex 'special effects' and illusions of baroque opera or theatre. These practices reveal a new willingness to deploy and manipulate darkness and the night.[55]

These illusionist possibilities of darkness became part of the architect's armoury in the seventeenth and eighteenth centuries. At St George's, Hawksmoor – as in all his sacred and secular interiors – shows profound awareness of the dramatic potential of shade and light. Though dimmer than a Wren 'auditory' St George's is not extremely dark, and with what remains of the Clayton and Bell glass of the 1871–2 Victorian intrusions, it is still dimmer than Hawksmoor intended. In actuality the mood of the interior derives from the interplay between the top light of the clerestory – square in plan but equivocally coffered to read in two directions – and the subdued illumination filtering through the Serlianas from the arched windows cut into St George's hemmed-in walls.

These are sensations calculated for that individual subject who begins to be identified in Locke's aforementioned *camera obscura* (1690). Within these new territories of the eye David Cast describes the buildings of Vanbrugh and Hawksmoor as 'an architecture of effect', for they devolve upon the individual spectator the task of working from the 'effects', that both architects spoke of, to the concept and structure of the building.[56] Through Locke and his followers this means that philosophically architecture is increasingly validated not by the authority of classical precedent and rules of proportion, but by the pleasure it gives as judged by the individual.[57] Joseph Addison disseminated and popularized these ideas in his series of *Spectator* articles 'On the Pleasures of the Imagination' of 1712 (nos. 411–21). 'Paper 5' (26 June 1712) examines how architecture 'affects the imagination', sharing Hawksmoor's enthusiasms for 'the greatness of bulk in the ancient oriental buildings' such as the Tower of Babel, Babylon's Hanging Gardens and the Pyramids. Wonders like these, or the Classical Pantheon in Rome, 'open the mind to vast conceptions, and fit it to converse with the divinity of the place. For every thing that is majestic imprints an awfulness and reverence on the mind of the beholder, and strikes in with the natural greatness of the soul'.[58] Another crucial term in this discourse is the notion of 'Association' deriving from Locke. In his following, sixth *Spectator* article, Addison writes of the 'Affinity of Ideas', for along with the pleasure we take from that which is 'actually before our Eyes', there is the 'Secondary Pleasure of the Imagination [which] proceeds from that Action of the Mind, which compares the Ideas arising from the Original Objects, with the Ideas we receive from a Statue, Picture, Description, or Sound that represents them'.⁵⁹ The spectators of a Hawksmoor building have to work hard for their pleasures, as Cast describes the act of observing St Mary Woolnoth, for example: 'The eye is kept engaged, crossing from part to part, making similitudes, so too is the mind, the historical mind, equally exercised, thinking of the past and the present, caught in ... meditation.'⁶⁰

St George's interior provokes and stimulates an engaged eye and mind for it defies expectations. Outside it also challengingly appeals to the 'primary' and 'secondary' Imaginations: 'We are obliged to devotion for the noblest buildings that have adorned the several countries of the world', said Addison, and here Hawksmoor collages memories of the Mausoleum of Halicarnassus (to crown his tower), a Baalbek-Pantheon portico, and the Colosseum (of the north façade) (Figure 3.10). Fiddly detail undoes Antique greatness of breadth and mass, as Addison warns quoting Fréart's *A Parallel of the Ancient Architecture with the Modern*:

> To introduce into architecture this grandeur of manner, we ought so to proceed, that the division of the principal members of the order may consist but of few parts, that they be all great, and of a bold and ample rilievo and swelling; and that the eye, beholding nothing little and mean, the imagination may be more vigorously touched and affected with the work that stands before it. For example in a cornice ... if we see none of that ordinary confusion, which is the result of those little cavities, quarter rounds of the astragal, and I know not how many other intermingled particulars, which produce no effect in great and massy works ... it is most certain that this manner will appear solemn and great.⁶¹

Hawksmoor owned the 1664 and 1707 editions of Fréarts *Parallel* (translated from the French by John Evelyn), and his work takes to heart this principle of solemnity, in whole and part, of broad surfaces and distinct masses.⁶² The shadow strokes of a cyma-bracketed block cornice – borrowed from the great drum of Rome's Pantheon – binds together Bloomsbury's disparate quotations from the antique: its boldness most evident where it collides with the delicate modillions of the Corinthian portico. While down at plinth level, giant triple keystones docked into inverted 'U' lintols, guard the shadows of the crypt openings like so many tomb capstones, recalling as noted R. T.'s 'primitive Christian's dark obscure vaults'.

Representing the Baroque shadow

In drawing to building, how did Hawksmoor's draughtsmanship serve his personal dramatic genius and his 'art of shaddowes'? To this point only the topographical sketchbook he made on his 1679–80 travels, at the time of entering Wren's office, has been examined in any detail – though even these juvenilia revealed much. Through his drawings, Anthony Geraghty

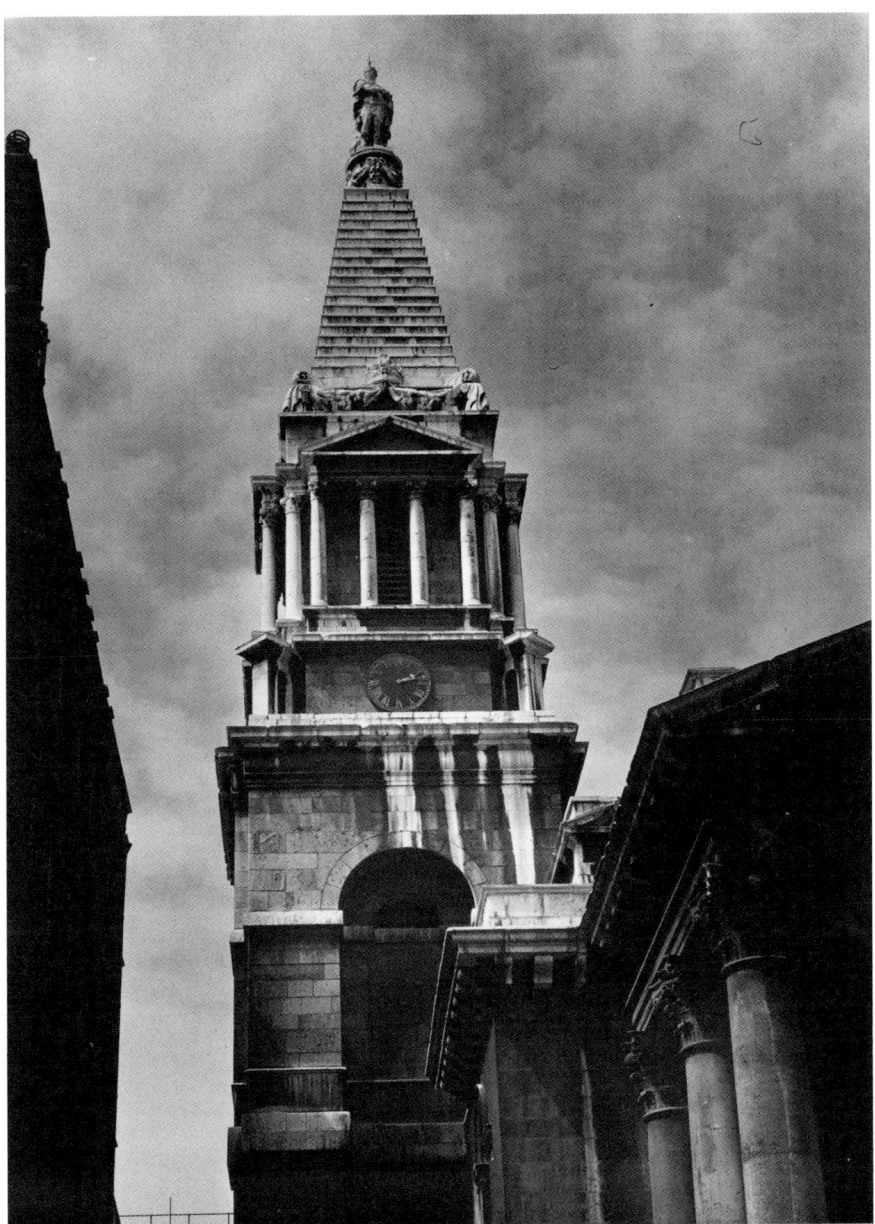

FIGURE 3.10 St George's Bloomsbury, close-up of tower and corner of portico. Photograph, Edwin Smith, 1970, RIBA Library Photographs Collection.

has charted Hawksmoor's development from junior assistant, to Wren's personal clerk, to an individual architectural persona. Early on, and uniquely in the Wren office, he 'developed an intermediary category of drawing in which the design is assembled and finalized to scale in pencil'.[63] The early presentation drawings are less individual, 'controlled and tight, similar in appearance...to Wren's presentation drawings of the 1670s. The designs are extensively set out with a scoring implement; drawn in pen and ink with a fine, delicate line; and intensely shaded with grey and (occasionally) blue washes, with strong, diagonally cast shadows'.[64] From 1689 Hawksmoor abandons the scoring implement, producing rapid elevations based on pencil under-drawing, sheets that reflect both fluency in technique and a need for haste in production. Then:

> In the mid-1690s Hawksmoor developed a new type of drawing, the wash sketch, in which he dispensed with pen and ink outline altogether and expressed the designs by means of pencil and wash shading. The massing of the designs is thereby emphasized, and their sculptural quality is miraculously conjured up before our eyes.[65]

In the same period he starts the hybrid practice of introducing perspectival elements within the convention of orthogonal elevation drawings, something he will readily do when evolving the towers of his London churches. The story of Hawksmoor's development shifts to a new gear at this point; Wren still calls the tune in his office but we now register a distinctive mind who designs *with* shadow and a plastic feeling for mass. One celebrated birds-eye perspective, in pencil and grey wash (c. 1695–7), returns to Warwick (whose 'Northe prospect' he had drawn in his sketchbook) to present an unrealized Gothic scheme for the church of St Mary (Figure 3.11). Here, Downes captures a fundamentally abstract imagination, one that shapes architecture as astylar volumes and shadows:

> [The St Mary's designs] include a perspective which reduces to essentials both the medieval work and his own design for tower, nave and transepts. The grey wash which is the greater part of the drawing describes a building [of]...large masses boldly defined by horizontal and vertical lines, and made fully plastic by the selective emphasis of highlights and shadows. The linear patterns and complexities of Gothic architecture did not concern him. Yet because he conceived all buildings in terms of masses and cavities and observed the way light falls and casts shadows on them, he came nearer to the nature of Gothic than most of the eighteenth century gothicisers.[66]

Most breathtaking is a monochromatic wash sketch for a Bramante's Tempietto-like version of the north-west tower of St Paul's cathedral (Figure 3.12):

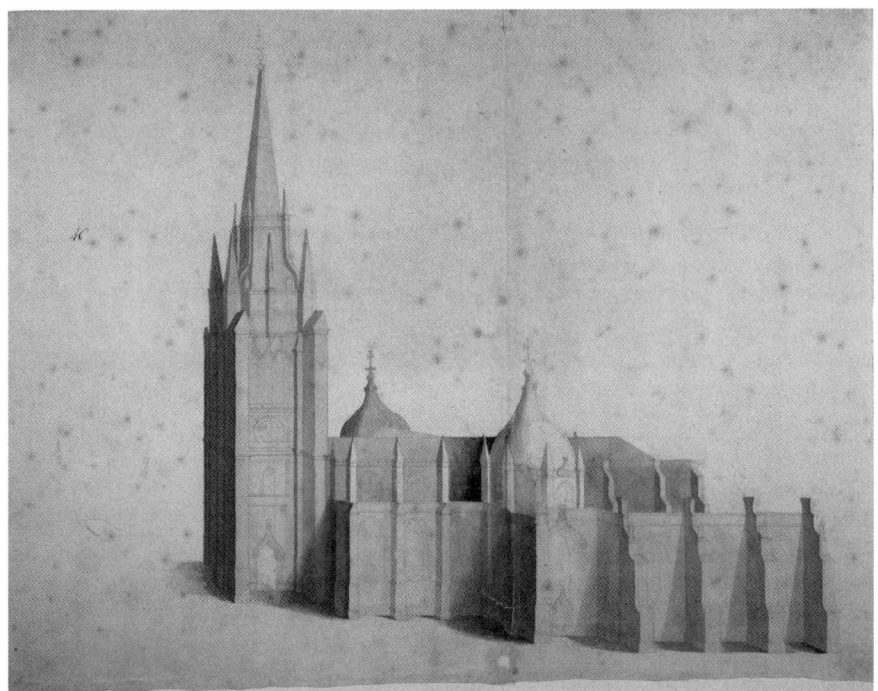

FIGURE 3.11 Nicholas Hawksmoor, view of St Mary's Warwick. Warden and Fellows of All Souls College, Oxford.

What little outline there is, is executed in pencil, lightly and inconspicuously. The falling light is crisp and clear, casting strong shadows across the design, thereby revealing, with extraordinary power, the cylindrical geometry of the tower and the solids and voids of the colonnade. Pools of darkness reside in the upper reaches of the peristyle.[67]

The peristyle is drawn strictly orthogonally, whereas the chamfered base and cupola are suggested in perspective; the sketch is all the more striking in being pasted onto a straightforward pen line drawing of the upper part of the north-west elevation. From the seventeenth century, the improvisatory medium of the sketch is crucial to the creation of a Baroque culture which emphasizes the parts at the expense of the whole: fragments which emerge from the shadows of subconscious gestation, from the memory palaces of antiquity, from the insights of the contemplative, or the hells and paradises enacted on the stage.[68] When Heinrich Wölfflin first theorized the Baroque in his *Renaissance und Barock* (Renaissance and Baroque) of 1888, he identified the sketch-like and painterly (*malerisch*) as a leading characteristic along with a fascination with the *chiaroscuro* of strong light and shade – often with shadow becoming the positive figure:

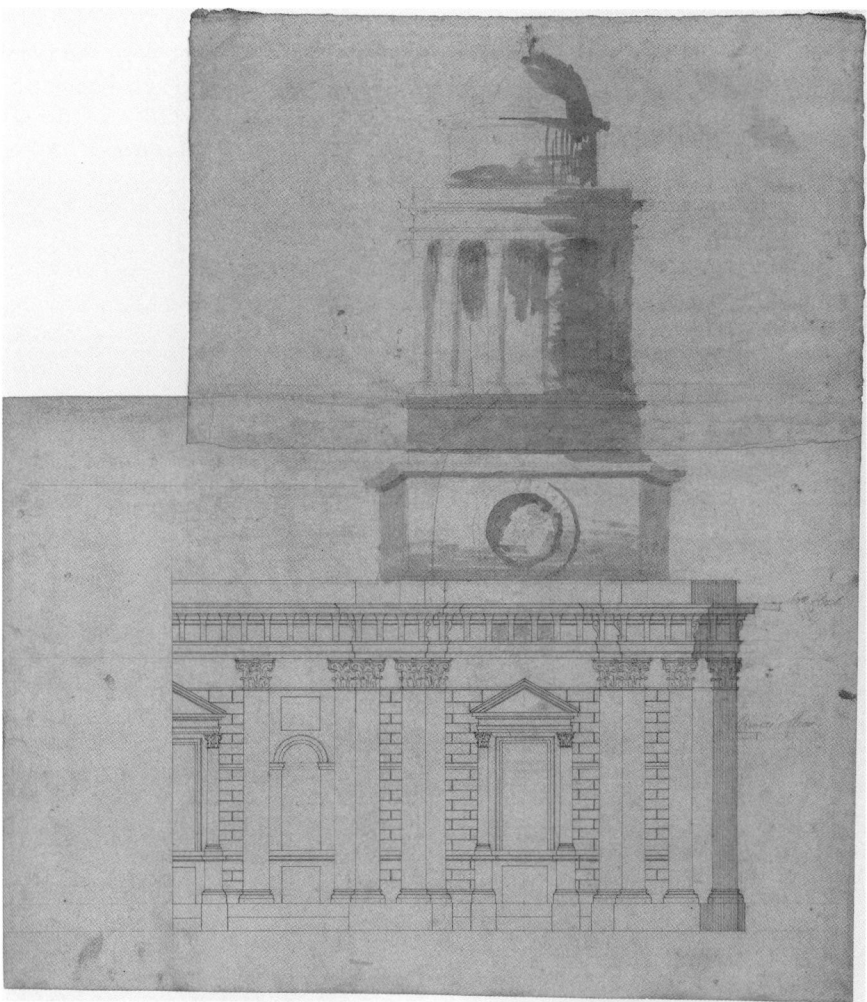

FIGURE 3.12 Nicholas Hawksmoor, preliminary design for the west towers of St Paul's Cathedral, c. 1699, pen, pencil and grey wash. The Chapter of St Paul's Cathedral.

> The aim of the painterly style is to create an illusion of movement; its first element is composition in terms of areas of light and shade; its second is what I should call the *dissolution of the regular*.... The third element may be called *elusiveness*, the lack of definition.[69]

By *malerisch* Wölfflin does not want us to think architecture merely imitates painting, so he adds 'massiveness' to 'movement' as the key principles of Baroque architecture: 'The baroque required broad, heavy, massive forms. Elegant proportions disappeared and buildings tended to become weightier until sometimes the forms were almost crushed by the pressure.'[70] At the same time there is 'a totally new conception of *matter*, that is of the ideal aspect of matter which gives expression to the inner vitality and behaviour of the members'.[71] As Wölfflin's study ends in Rome around 1630, historians would now call the façades he studies, such as Il Gesù, 'Mannerist' rather than 'Baroque'. As a consequence his readings, which miss out the plastic extremes of Continental Baroque, aid in the interpretation of Hawksmoor's proto-Mannerism. For Robert Harbison:

> The vocabulary is classical, but the content is secretly Romantic. That division explains the disquieting effect that Vanbrugh's and Hawksmoor's buildings almost always produce. They conceal passionate narratives which classicism cannot comfortably contain. The severe forms do not always look Baroque, but the powerful underlying tensions make dynamic imbalance out of rectilinearity and stolid symmetry.[72]

Massiveness and movement are qualities absent from the linear French-Baroque walls of St Paul's Cathedral which 'wears a decorative relief skin'[73] that fails to convey the 'inner vitality' Wölfflin describes. As collaborators, Vanbrugh and Hawksmoor clothed the palaces of Blenheim and Castle Howard with similar skins – albeit more intense than those of Wren, whereas Hawksmoor's independent building is consistently massive, plain and astylar. For Downes:

> Hawksmoor was concerned with the wall as a plastic medium capable of exploration, development or sculptural treatment, and we may even become metaphorical and call it, for him, an organic medium with its own life, in which individual forms grow out of the wall or grow together to compose it. We may say on the contrary that for the Palladians the wall is dead, inert, a medium on to which forms may be fixed but which is not developed in itself.[74]

Let us then take a Hawksmoor wall and see how he conceives it. One of the Hawksmoor sheets in the British Library is an early study – in brown ink and wash on graphite under-drawing – of the body of Christ Church, Spitalfields (1714–29); it focuses on the wide central bay of the long south elevation (Figure 3.13). (The key elements are close to the realized eighteenth-century building, albeit lacking the central entrance and the arches and windows of the end bays). From the plinth some forty feet of sheer Portland stone rises to the great cornice, broken halfway by the moulded impost of a range of five recesses cut boldly, without mouldings, into the wall plane.[75] The shadow projections of Hawksmoor's drawing catch the drama of these incisions against the sheerness of the main wall. The impost continues as the springing of the concentric unmoulded arches of the windows to the aisles, represented as deep pools of shadow (the two tiers of windows shown on

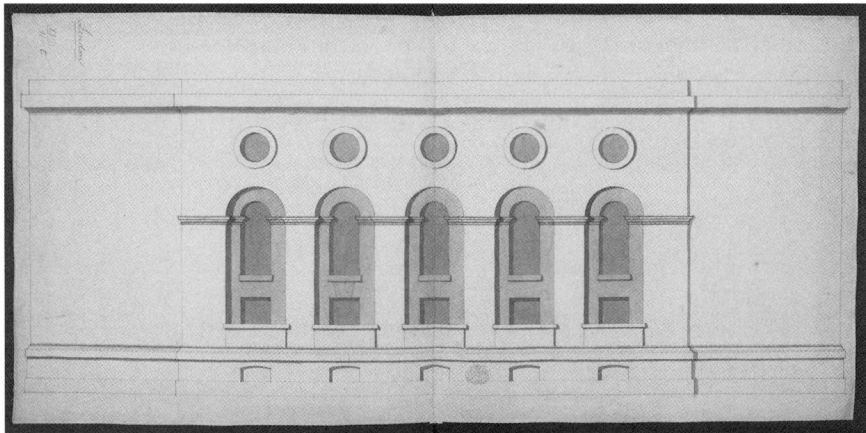

FIGURE 3.13 Nicholas Hawksmoor, elevation study of Christ Church, Spitalfields. The British Library Board, K. Top. 23. 11. t.

the drawing were later telescoped into one in 1866 when the galleries were removed, and the lower central openings reduced to slots).[76] Aligned above – interchanging this handling – Hawksmoor drills five deep black portholes ringed by plain *projecting* bands that throw shadow onto the main wall. Hawksmoor's arches thus dramatize the mass of the wall by his favourite device of carving into it, plane by unmoulded plane. Externally it echoes that theatrical multiplication of frames seen within Bloomsbury (and also inside Christ Church in the succeeding barrel vaults of the aisles): shadow deepens layer by layer – by two or even three offsets – to the ultimate darkness of door or aperture.

'Carving' is used intentionally here to describe Hawksmoor's handling of the wall plane in light of the significance with which the twentieth-century art writer Adrian Stokes (1902–72) endowed the term, when in *Stones of Rimini* (1934) he contrasts 'carving' to 'modelling':

> Briefly, the difference between carving approach and modelling approach in sculptural art can be illustrated as follows. Whatever its plastic value, a figure carved in stone is fine carving when one feels that not the figure, but the stone through the medium of the figure, has come to life. Plastic conception on the other hand, is uppermost when the material with which, or from which, a figure has been made, appears no more than so much suitable stuff for this creation.[77]

'Carving' as a stance to the inherent life of material therefore applies as much to the painter's approach to the canvas, or the architect's to the substance of building. Hawksmoor is a carver because he feels the stone alive to a depth inaccessible to Wren before, or the Palladians after – and he also feels the shadow alive. These readings can be taken further in the parallels many have noted between Hawksmoor's long Christ Church walls and Alberti's aqueduct-like flanks to the Tempio Malatestiano in Rimini (c. 1450).[78] Indeed, Stokes's whole architectonic was founded on a visceral response to the mass effect of Alberti's Tempio which he first encountered in 1925. From his knowledge of the ruins of Classical Rome, Alberti captured – for the first time in the Renaissance – a true *all'antica* greatness which eluded Brunelleschi. As Stokes writes in *Art and Science* (1949):

> He was the only major artist of his time who was likely to *contemplate* as well as measure the grandeur [of Rome]; to permit those giant ruins, arches and embossments...to mould his mind in a sense deeper than the seeking out from the rubble a lore of engineering feats.... The dominant image, perhaps, was in a convergence of the surveying and sightseeing expeditions themselves, of the mass of traversed rubble, the jagged ruined brickwork and the incorruptible face of the stone capital or carved stone aperture.[79]

Stokes finds a passionate intensity in Alberti's Tempio encasement at Rimini, that is 'foreign...to Brunelleschi and his school.'[80] To an extraordinary extent for someone who never left British shores, Hawksmoor's constructions also evoke the grandeur, sheerness and mass effect of the walls of ancient Rome, and with more conviction than the work of most other architects who had actually completed the Grand Tour.

Deeply felt and strongly delineated as they are, these drawn masses and shadows nonetheless follow more or less recognizable conventions of projection in use up to the present time; though it should also be stressed that at this time shadows are worked out with a mix of intuition and geometry as found in the works of G. B. Vignola, Philibert Delorme, Bertotti Scamozzi and John Shute. The exact, mechanical skiagraphy of the later eighteenth and nineteenth centuries only comes in with the descriptive geometry of the engineer and scientist Gaspard Monge, co-founder in 1795 of the École Polytechnique in Paris.[81]

The light in the Christ Church elevation comes from the upper-left and the cast shadow accurately conveys the depth of recess or projection. But notice how Hawksmoor also shades the whole plane of the recess with a mid-tone to signify that it lies beyond the main wall plane. In a related study of the whole elevation (which includes the tower in its early diminutive form), Hawksmoor again tones the whole recessed plane, and the entirety of the setback tower elevation.[82] Unintentionally, this shading captures well the surrogate chiaroscuro of bleached stone and sooty stains that Hawksmoor would have anticipated as he composed his volumes in grimy London. Though his London churches have been scrubbed to a sepulchral whiteness in recent years, historic photographs of this Spitalfields façade display exactly the effect of the drawing; the main wall washed fairly clean by London's downpours, against arched recesses smudged to a smutty gloom.[83]

Geraghty indicates that Hawksmoor began to apply this shading convention in the Wren office, concurrent with his other wash sketch manner, and the appearance of perspectival projection within otherwise orthogonal drawings. Hawksmoor's renderings of the Royal Palace schemes strongly demonstrate this representational code. Thus, in the river frontage of the Whitehall Palace drawings of 1698, the grey shading of the recessed centrepiece (a remodelling of Inigo Jones's Banqueting House) materializes a moody composition of drum, dome and giant portico (Figure 3.14).[84] Left to themselves the cast shadows of the projecting wings communicate recession weakly, whereas the grey wash introduces an effect of aerial perspective appropriate to the perception of such solemn masses in the smoky mists of seventeenth-century London.

Notwithstanding Hawksmoor's typically imaginative use of this method, in fact both he and Wren learnt this convention of toning recessed parts of a building, in progressively darker shades, from French architectural drawing and engraving; here it was common from the 1660s, but rare in Britain prior to the eighteenth century.[85] Through Charles II, Wren had access to the original drawings of Jules Hardouin-Mansart's Les Invalides in Paris, which used this grey pen and wash technique as was standard practice in the Service des Bâtiment du Roi. John Harris has also shown the continuation of 'the grey wash style' into the eighteenth century within the Palladian office of the King's Works.[86]

It is revealing to follow the story of the 'grey wash style' a little further in the drawings of Vanbrugh, with whom of course Hawksmoor worked and collaborated on many significant projects, especially at Castle Howard and Blenheim Palace. As might be expected, the convention is used on many ruled, study and presentation, elevations from Vanbrugh's office. But, in the context of the Baroque sketch, we see the convention thoroughly assimilated even on Vanbrugh's most personal and rapid studies. There are many examples in 'The Vanbrugh Album' from Elton Hall at the Victoria and Albert Museum. Take the related plan and elevation in Vanbrugh's proposal for a small cruciform house for Sir William Saunderson (c. 1718–20); if built, this would have joined the Vanbrugh family's romantic colony of castellar dwellings on Greenwich Hill (Figure 3.15).[87] Vanbrugh's

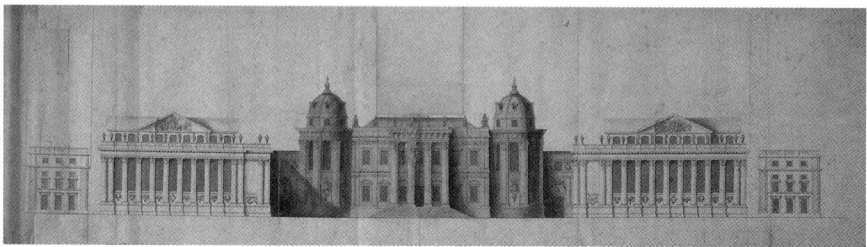

FIGURE 3.14 Sir Christopher Wren and Nicholas Hawksmoor, Wren's project for Whitehall Palace, 1698. Warden and Fellows of All Souls College, Oxford.

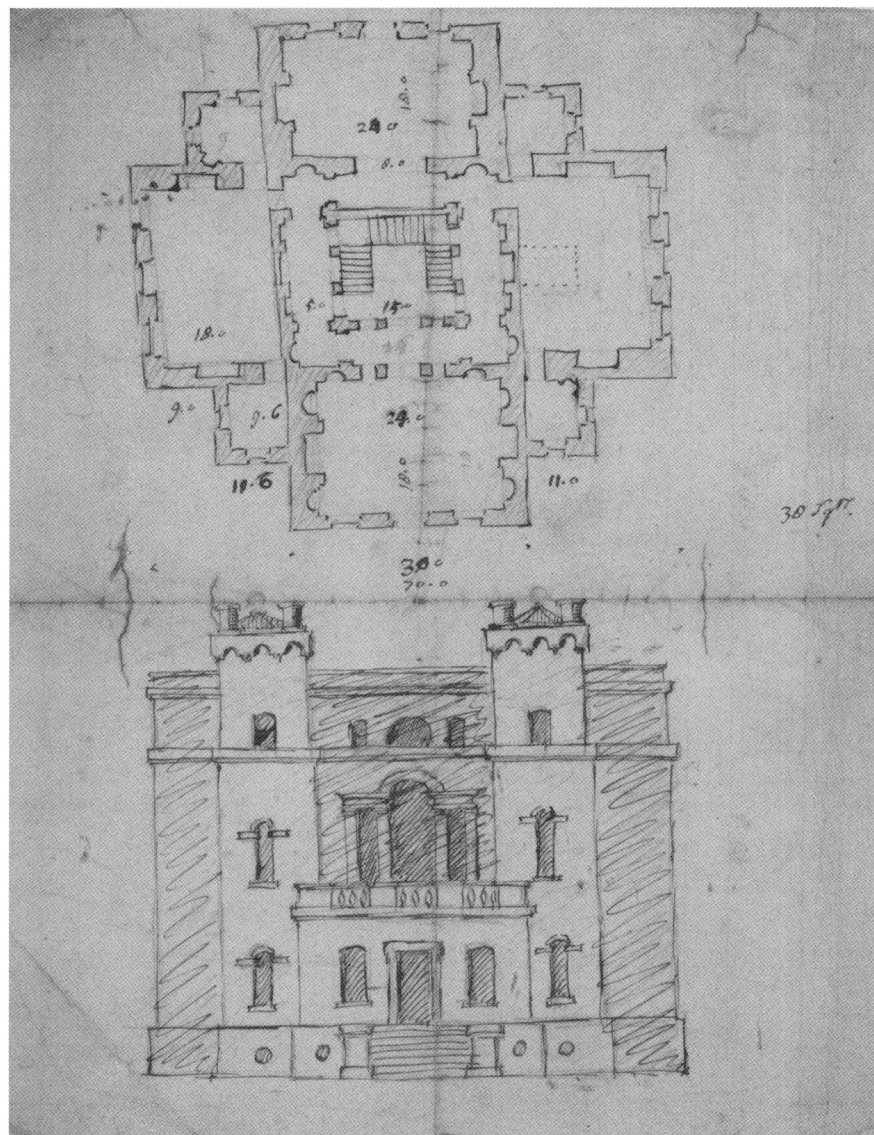

FIGURE 3.15 Sir John Vanbrugh, sketch plan and elevation, Sir William Saunderson's House, Greenwich, c. 1718–20. Victoria and Albert Museum, London.

scheme clasps four rather Romanesque towers – capped by a corbel table and cylindrical chimneys – within the arms of a Greek Cross footprint. On the upper two floors of the entrance front, two of these turrets frame the exposed core rectangle of the staircase volume, pierced by a Palladian window. On this, as on many of the album sheets, only a brown ink line is used to capture the push and pull of the planes. There are basically two codes in the linear economy here.[88] Close horizontal, vertical or diagonal hatchings denote the realistic self-shadows of, for example, the chimneys and – in the usual semi-realistic convention – the dark openings, windows and entrances: and more open vigorous continuous diagonal strokes which connote – in the grey wash manner – the conceptual scheme of the planes and volumes. No cast shadows are shown on this sketch of the Saunderson dwelling, although similar other sheets in the album do include them, while others also use a swift wash to indicate recession. Accepting that shadow is more conceptual than actual in the grey wash technique, as pointed out at Whitehall and Spitalfields, it does reflect perceptual experiences linked to aerial perspective, the accelerated weathering of recessed surfaces and the cumulative effects in setback parts of a façade of the actual cast shadows.

Towers and 'piramidall forms'

St Anne's, Limehouse and St George-in-the-East

Given the intense plastic conception of the body of Christ Church, Spitalfields, the original idea of a plain box-like tower with a pert octagonal hat, is a surprise – a tower whose whole upper stage does not even amount to the height of the nave. This is especially so, given the knowledge in hindsight of the tremendous pile of cavernous Serliana porch, triumphal arch bell stage and Gothic broach spire, Hawksmoor ultimately realized from 1723–4 (Figure 3.1). The process so demonstrated shows how Hawksmoor's towers to the 'Fifty New Churches' take on an autonomous design life – one fascinating to study in terms of the 'art of shaddowes'.

To return for a moment to Hawksmoor's schooling in Wren's office; the Tempietto study for the West Front of St Pauls was among many opportunities he had there to explore the tower and steeple as semi-independent sculptural forms: sometimes serving as Wren's draughtsman, sometimes contributing more as has been recognized at St Augustine, Watling Street, conceived in his fluent preliminary design drawing of c.1695 (Figure 3.16).[89] Though small, this leaded steeple plays a crucial compositional role in its adjacency to the dome of St Pauls. With economy of means Hawksmoor's washes set the overall silvery tone of the leadwork, and accent the strong shadows of openings and the doubled scrolls. He compares pinnacles: an obelisk type on the left – as realized – with a Rococo-like flaming urn on the right, setting the shadows with just three suggestively calligraphic ink marks. To reiterate the important points on technique, conceiving the steeple as a play of shade and light Hawksmoor makes this drawing in pencil, wash and ink line, in that order – unlike Wren, who tended to use wash as a descriptive adjunct to line.[90] Wren's office gave Hawksmoor a formative decade-and-a-half of work on the City Church steeples – a thorough apprenticeship in raising abstract forms against the sky.

FIGURE 3.16 Nicholas Hawksmoor (with Sir Christopher Wren), study of St Augustine, Watling St. Warden and Fellows of All Souls College, Oxford.

Christ Church, Spitalfields, one of Hawksmoor's three Stepney churches, which began in 1714 and was built concurrently with St George-in-the-East in Wapping and St Anne's, Limehouse. He seems to have conceived these last two together, whereas Christ Church is somewhat different in its ideas and evolution.[91] Hawksmoor's final design decision on the tower of St Anne's (1714–30) was to crown its pinnacles with pyramids, replacing the urns of the penultimate scheme – perhaps in mourning for the giant pyramids (modelled on the tomb of Gaius Cestius on the Aurelian Wall in Rome) which, in some drawings, were to crown the now-bare attics of the east end. In one line elevation – in his aforementioned hybrid manner – he introduces shading and the third dimension to examine the perspectival impact of these pyramidal masses, as seen together (Figure 3.17).[92]

Hawksmoor was an early builder of pyramids, as in the later Renaissance the form only truly came into its own in the neoclassical period; one notable English example is James Wyatt's Pelham mausoleum at Brocklesby Park, Lincolnshire (1787–94). In his study of *Death and Architecture*, James Stevens Curl finds the second half of the eighteenth century 'a new

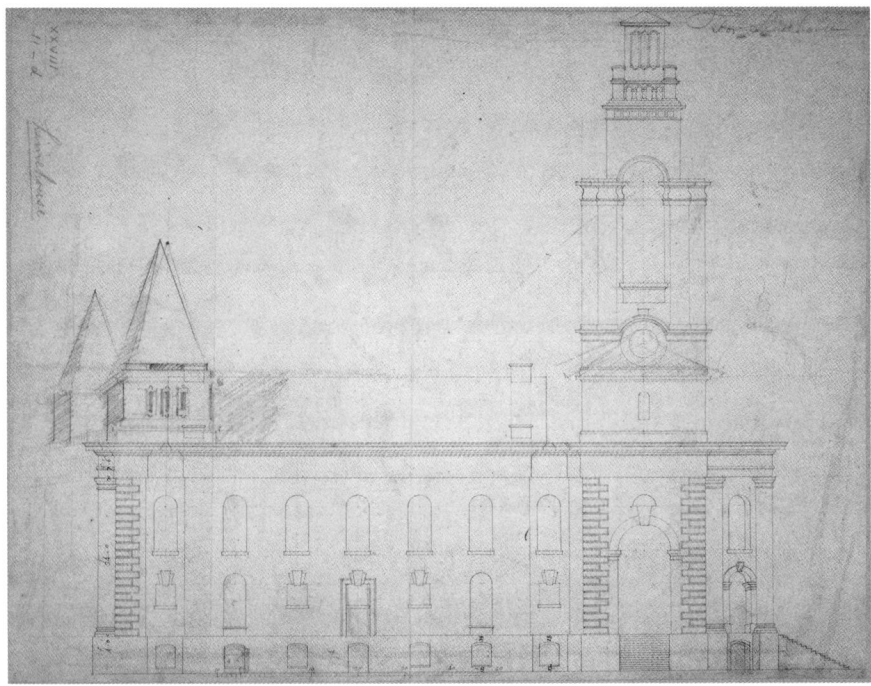

FIGURE 3.17 Nicholas Hawksmoor, preliminary elevation drawing of façade of St Anne's Limehouse. The British Library Board, K. Top. 28. 11. d.

golden age of mausolea, for the architects of the period were obsessed by Antique elements and by romantic, semi-gloomy spaces, fired by Piranesian example'[93] – as the following chapter on 'Sublime Shadows' will examine. The Frenchman Étienne-Louis Boullée (1728–99) envisioned vast pyramids such as a truncated one for a cenotaph, while another makes a funerary triumphant arch. His gloomy, melancholy art asserted the bare unadorned surface 'absolutely stripped of detail, its decoration consisting of a play of shadows, outlined by still deeper shadows'.[94] Undeniably this puts us a few decades ahead of ourselves in the reading of architectural theory, at the same time Hawksmoor's and Vanbrugh's moody compositions of 'effect' and 'association' stand in a recognized line of subjectivity that does lead to this *architecture parlante*, and on to full-blooded romanticism. Sir John Soane (see Chapter 4) clearly sensed this ancestry when he said approvingly of Vanbrugh: 'His works are full of character, and his outlines rich and varied.'[95] And, remembering that in R. T.'s *De Templis*, '*Cryptae*' are encouraged in remembrance of Christian catacombs, then in Hawksmoor's compacted compositions it is possible to triangulate the pyramid, with the crypt, and the sacrificial altar, as three kinds of forms particularly associated with such primitive memorials. Fantastical as is Sinclair's psycho-geography in *Lud Heat*, it nonetheless evokes the pyramidal presences of St Anne's:

Hawksmoor was obsessed/possessed by pyramids – continually working them into his draft sketches – the cubical lanterns at the eastern corners of St Anne's, in the 1716 version, are crowned by tall pyramids – which the masons omitted.... The constant drag of day-to-day reality/practical considerations blunts the overt statement of high ritual, the claim of kinship. So that the more obvious symbols, the elevated pyramids, are excluded – while the arcane & disguised, the subversive sentences get through, and are still operational.[96]

An extreme moment in Hawksmoor's pyramid obsession is represented by his proposal to crown the nave of St George-in-the-East with a stepped pyramid of nine stages which, internally, would have cradled a dark shallow dome. As he notes on the bottom-right of this early plan: 'The Roofe is intended in a piramidall forme and to have a Hemisphere in ye Middle.'[97] A sketch half-section, on the plan sheet, indicates a timber structure to all of this, so presumably the pyramid would have been formed upon this in leadwork. In a south elevation, stair-towers buttress the pyramid visually; as previously noted, these echo the plan of the 'Basilica after the Primitive Christians'. At this stage Hawksmoor considered topping the stair volumes with small turrets, whose distinctly Byzantine character is reinforced by the Greek cross finial shown on a related west elevation drawing dated August 1714. Du Prey describes this sheet as 'a messy but wonderfully vigorous example of Hawksmoor's draughtsmanship, with plenty of the bold hatching and cavernous areas of shading so characteristic of him' (Figure 3.18).[98] In Hawksmoor's insistent diagonal strokes, shadows leak from the crypt lunettes, and ascend via the arched openings, and a sinuous snake-like volute, to the shrouded profiles of turret and pyramid. When Hawksmoor was asked in 1728 to build a memorial at Castle Howard to Lord William Howard, he built a pyramid as the most ancient funereal form.[99] At St George-in-the-East, the pyramid and crepuscular dome would have made the entire church a sarcophagus. In this respect those shades of catacomb and crypt – always threatening to leak upward from under their giant keystones – would have claimed the whole space: even for Hawksmoor this was probably a step too far and a simpler roof was realized.

For Vaughan Hart, Hawksmoor's skylines, with their 'antique funereal iconography – statues and pyramids, obelisks and pillars, mausoleums and stelae, altars and terms, and pineapples and urns' amounts to no less than a 'monumental rooftop "garden of remembrance"'.[100] All of which apparatus reaches its climax with the towers – as in the pyramids of St Anne's, and the crown of eight Roman sacrificial altars at St George-in-the-East. I want to return now to Limehouse to examine his shadow thinking in the shaping of the tower of St Anne's. As at Christ Church, we find at St Anne's no exception to a process of restless iterations into tower form, leading ultimately to a final conception rich in memory, dramatic form and chiaroscuro. So, at

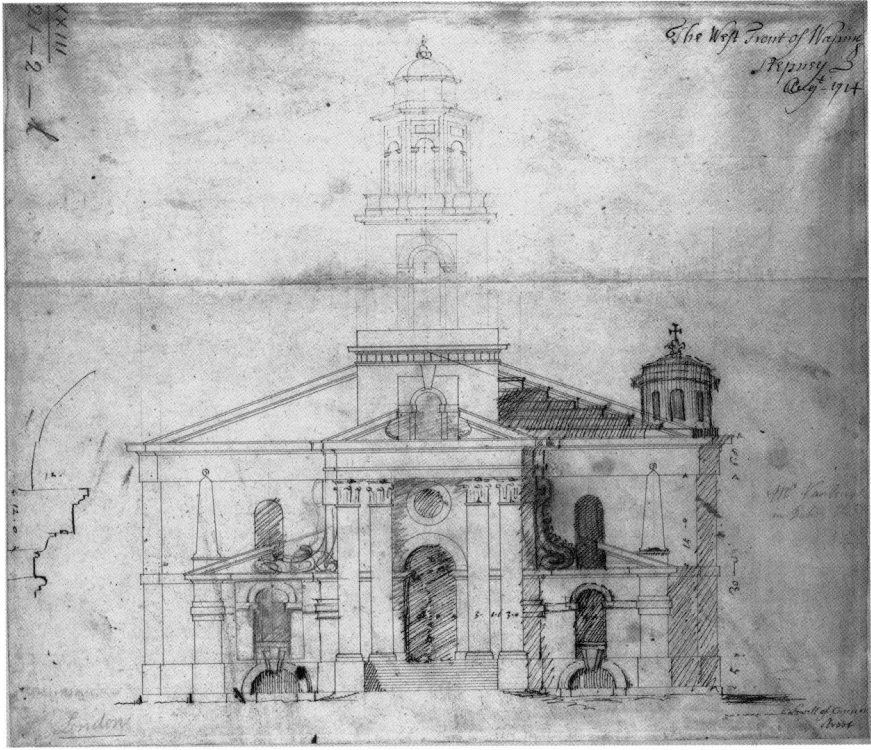

FIGURE 3.18 Nicholas Hawksmoor, preliminary elevation drawing for the west façade of St George-in-the-East. The British Library Board, K. Top. 23. 21. 2. h.

St Anne's the four identifiable key phases show stage by stage, increasing potential for the play of shadows.

The north elevation of the fated attic pyramids scheme is balanced at the west end by an apsidal Baptistery-like porch, similar to the powerful one actually constructed, made yet more imposing by the later idea of a leaded half-dome. In 'The Basilica after the Primitive Christians' this is also the first major element we encounter, here of rectangular form, and a large enough space for baptism by immersion: as Hawksmoor notes for this part 'B': 'The place for the font for ye Converts which was in ye Porch-& to be immers'd.'[101] But the circular *Baptisterium* form of early Christian churches, to which Hawksmoor alludes, was also known through sources such as the plans in Joseph Bingham's *Origines Ecclesiasticae*.[102] The tower associated with this scheme rises in three blocky stages to a heavy lantern wedged between drum altar-like forms, faced with decorative interlacing bands, and completed with a low hipped cap – the whole outline is rather reminiscent of a Victorian water tower.

A drawing in the Victoria and Albert Museum introduces the half-dome to the baptistery-like porch and develops the belfry stage in sepia ink, but the pencilled top stage is a curiously complicated affair (Figure 3.19).[103] On a cube, faced with pediments (with lunette, niche and crowning urn), Hawksmoor places a fluted cap of trumpet-bell outline, finished off with

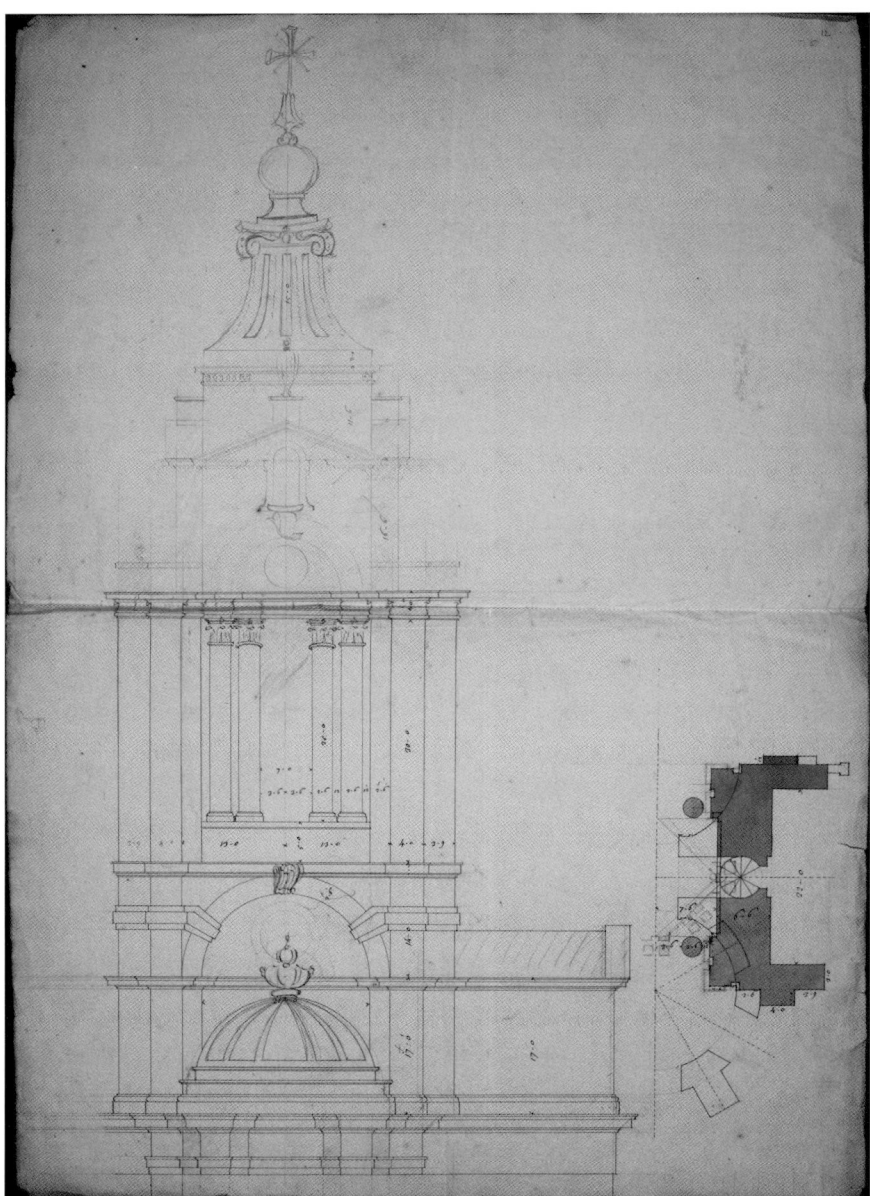

FIGURE 3.19 Nicholas Hawksmoor, preliminary elevation drawing for the west tower of St Anne's Limehouse, with fluted trumpet-bell cap. Victoria and Albert Museum, London.

ionic volutes and a ball and cross – all very much at odds with the primary volumes of the rest of St Anne's. Equally, it is a good example of the sketch-like jocularity with which he flicked in the urns on the design for St Augustine's: as Harbison writes of the Baroque: 'Sketches in architecture can mean something different, more unmistakeable holiday or license.'[104] So forceful is the rough, *Till Eulenspiegel*-like play, of Hawksmoor's primary and secondary volumes, that it can literally overshadow the license he normally contains to a tertiary, decorative level of detail – to volutes, swags, cartouches, panels and the like. In shadow drawing it is the 'holiday or license' squiggles of the pen, the lighter cross-strokes and calligraphic flicks of the brush that accent the stronger hatching and broader washes. Nevertheless, it would be a much diminished architecture that was composed only of blocky masses, lacking such adroitly animated tertiary glyphs. The St Anne's volute and trumpet-bell is a not-isolated example where this sketch-like bizarreness of Hawksmoor's, normally curbed to a detail level, establishes the character of more major forms. Hawksmoor also used a crowning volute on a similarly weird example – the exaggeratedly tapered steeple column of St John, Horsleydown, since demolished (a late 'Fifty New Churches' of 1727).[105]

In the endgame of this process, c. 1717–18, Hawksmoor returned initially to a clear two-stage octagonal form based on the Tower of the Winds in Athens (Figure 3.20). The main stage is quite richly modelled with paired Corinthian pilasters and, if executed, would have been a sufficiently strong but rather conventional climax to the building. But the seeds of a much more interesting resolution are already lightly pencilled in on the half-plan to the right of the sheet – namely, an outriding diagonal cluster of paired pilasters, much richer in the potential for silhouette and animated shadow and light.

To fix the near-final form, Hawksmoor pasted a sheet onto the upper part of a detail line elevation and part-section of the Belfry stage (Figure 3.21). In its sense of shadow as a shaping force it is as stirring as his Tempietto study for the west towers of St Pauls; except now Hawksmoor is of course his own master, and working at the height of his powers. He establishes the form almost entirely in bold grey washes adding just a few accents in ink: some lightly hatched secondary shadows, the grooved pilaster capitals and a dentilled cornice to link to the stage below. The built form has the pyramid pinnacles – in lieu of urns – as discussed; also the octagon immediately below is plain, whereas this penultimate design hints at the Romanesque with its paired arches and corbel table of small semicircles (Figure 3.22). Hawksmoor's brush strokes relish the syncopations of shadow his articulation produces: light – fine shadow (between the pilasters), shadow-light-shadow, fine shadow (between the next pair of pilasters); shadow-light-shadow, and then the culminating strong shadow of the right-most diagonal cluster.

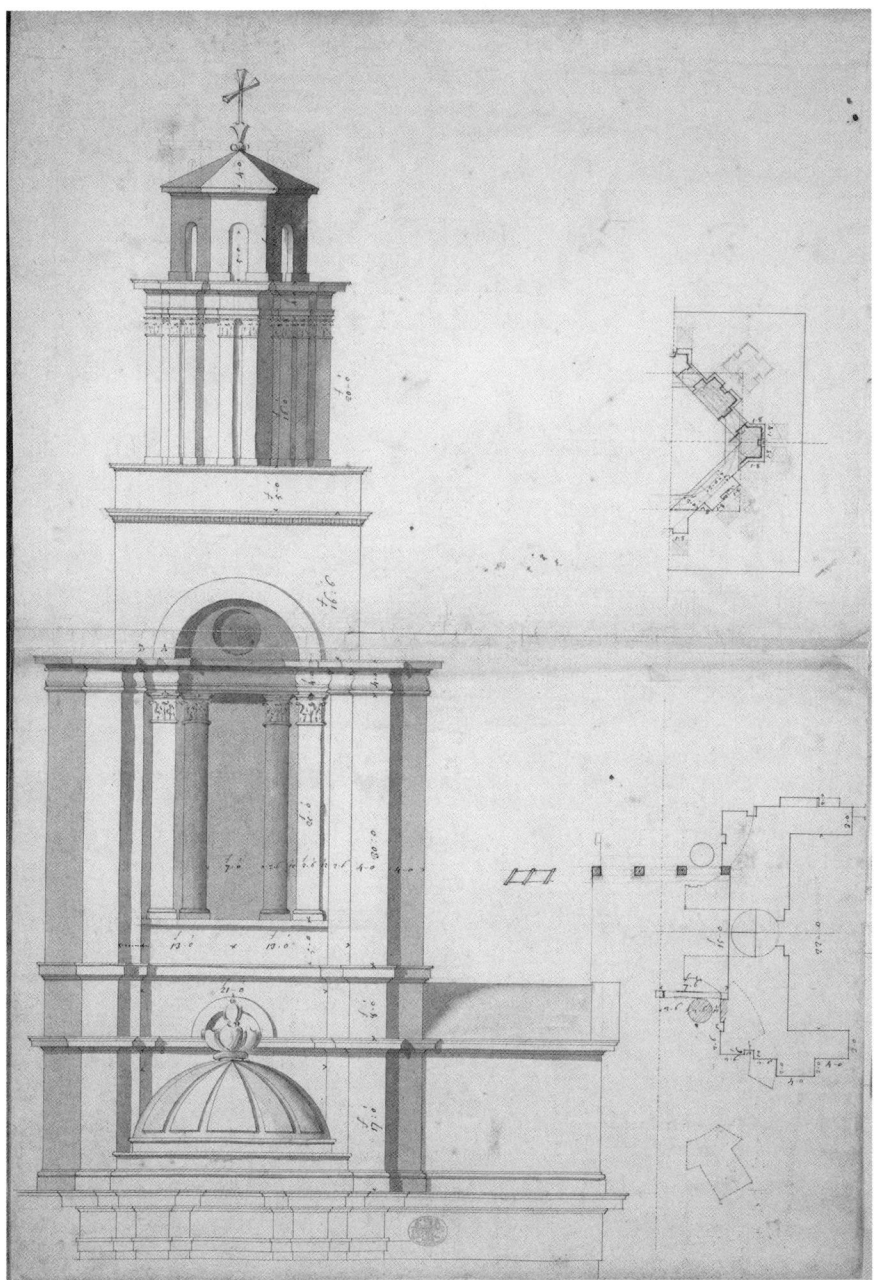

FIGURE 3.20 Nicholas Hawksmoor, preliminary elevation drawing for the west tower of St Anne's Limehouse, with 'Tower of the Winds' upper stage. The British Library Board, K. Top. 28. 11. g.

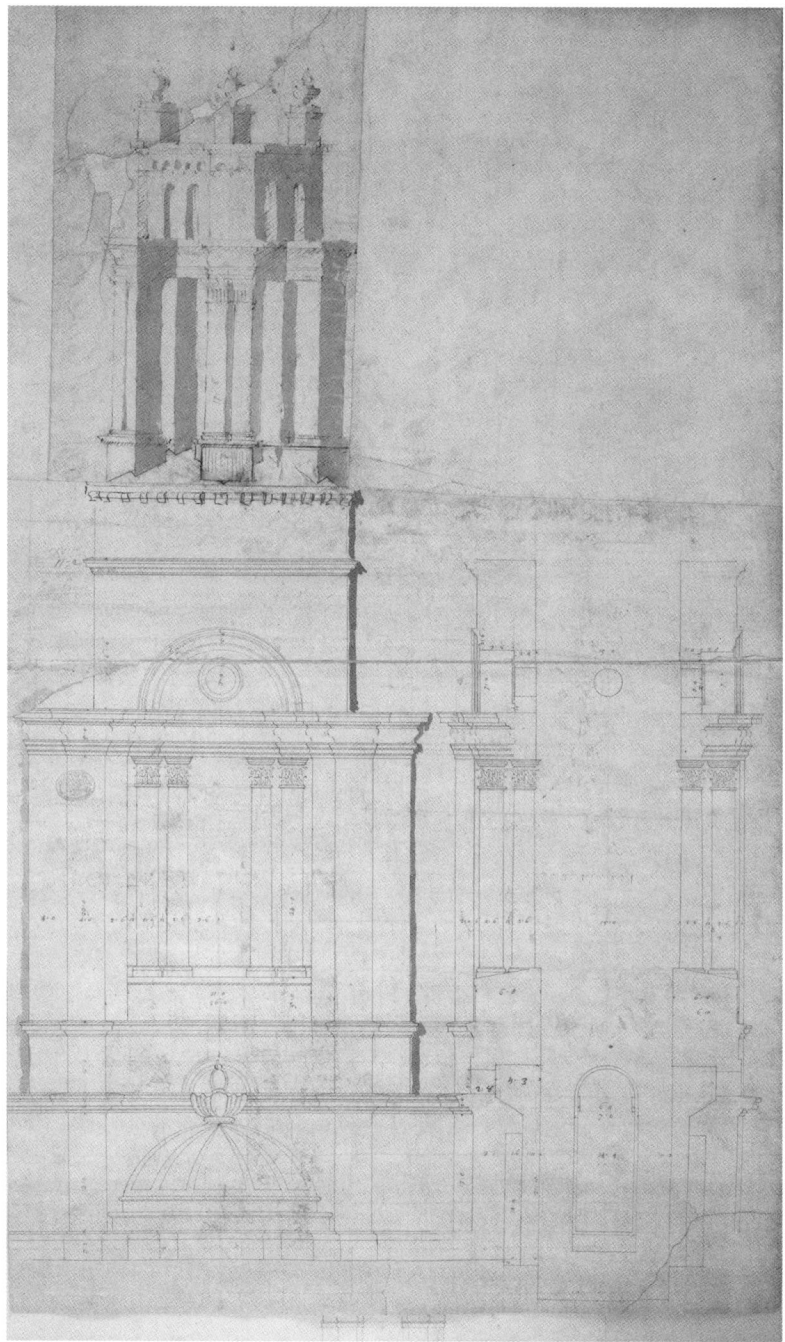

FIGURE 3.21 Nicholas Hawksmoor, elevation drawing for the west tower of St Anne's Limehouse, of near-final upper stage. The British Library Board, K. Top. 28. 11. c.

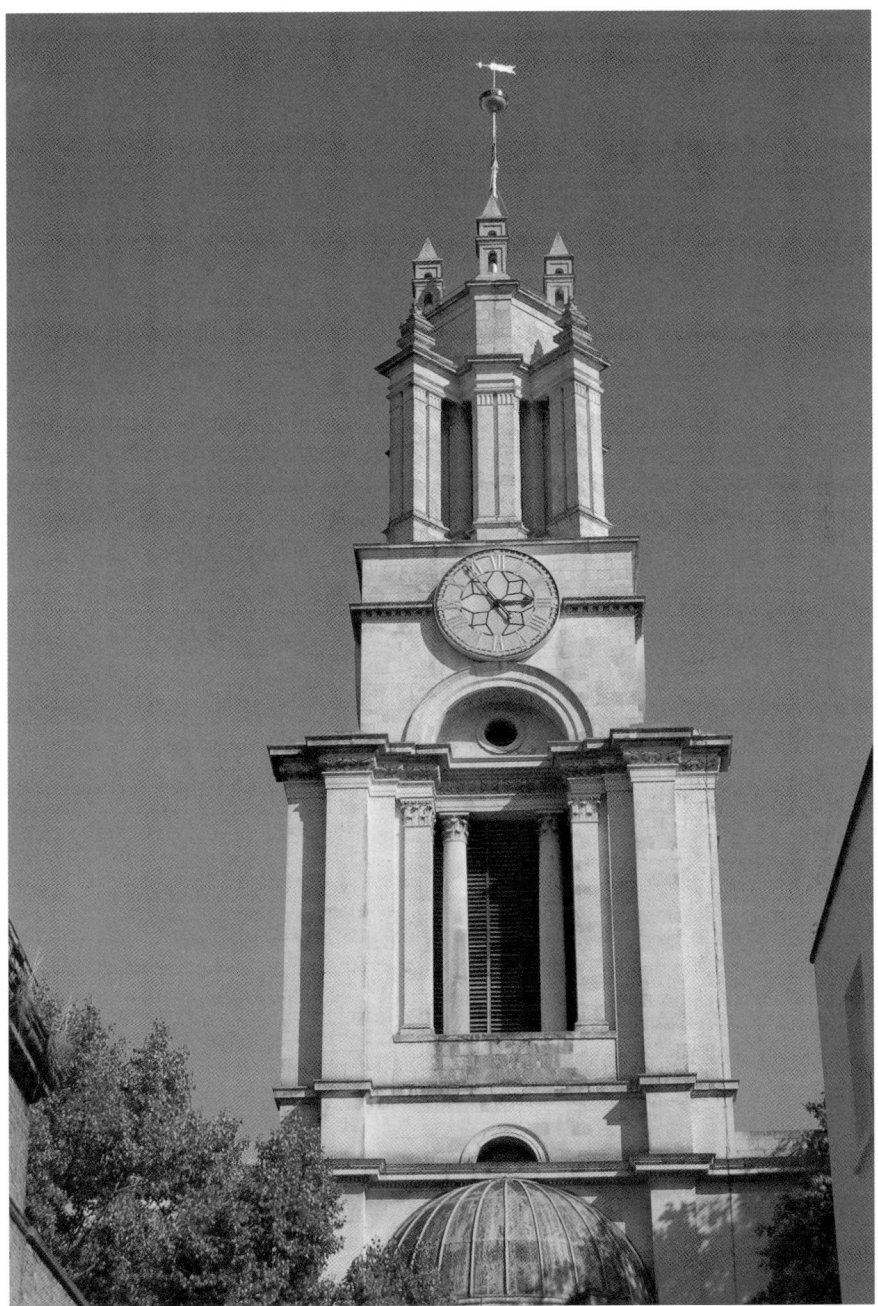

FIGURE 3.22 Nicholas Hawksmoor, west tower of St Anne's Limehouse. Photograph, Stephen Kite.

In the bust made of him by Sir Henry Cheere at the end of his life (1736), Hawksmoor looks as craggy and moody as his buildings. And if Ackroyd reads *his* Hawksmoor through a lens darkened by later 'Gothic' visualizations, the architecture itself can be as profoundly disturbing as the eponymous novel describes. The buildings speak in a language that Hawksmoor's contemporaries could only feebly describe as bizarre, ingenious or 'gotico'. In his later years Hawksmoor was already being marginalized by the new bookishly stiff fashion of neo-Palladianism – a manner with little feeling for shadow-making. Though – like Vanbrugh – Hawksmoor could play the new games too, as when he incorporates a 'Palladian window', of the new taste, into the east end of his Christ Church, Spitalfields. But then the mood of Christ Church is proleptic of a generation beyond the neo-Palladians; in its darkness, vastness of scale and sudden articulations, it anticipates that discourse of the Burkean Sublime to which we now turn.

Notes

1. On the etymology and history of the term 'baroque', see Hills, Helen, 'The Baroque: The Grit in the Oyster of Art History', in Helen Hills (ed), *Rethinking the Baroque* (Farnham, Surrey: Ashgate, 2011), pp. 11–36.
2. Sinclair, Iain, *Lud Heat. A Book of the Dead Hamlets – May 1974 to April 1975* (Cheltenham, Gloucestershire: Skylight Press, 2012, first published 1975); Ackroyd, Peter, *Hawksmoor* (London: Penguin Books, 2010, first published 1985).
3. Ackroyd, *Hawksmoor*, pp. 1, 2.
4. Eliot, T. S., *Collected Poems* (London: Faber and Faber, 1963), p. 65.
5. Eliot, *Poems*, p. 13.
6. Ackroyd, *Hawksmoor*, pp. 3, 4.
7. See Ackroyd, Peter, *London. The Biography* (London: Vintage, 2001), Chapter 9, 'Packed to Blackness', pp. 109–11.
8. See, for example, Link, Alex, '"The Capitol of Darkness": Gothic Spatialities in the London of Peter Ackroyd's *Hawksmoor*', *Contemporary Literature*, vol. 45, no. 3 (Autumn 2004), pp. 516–37; Baxandall, Michael, *Shadows and Enlightenment* (New Haven, CT and London: Yale University Press, 1995), *passim*.
9. Koslofsky, Craig, *Evening's Empire. A History of the Night in Early Modern Europe* (Cambridge: Cambridge University Press, 2011), p. 278.
10. Maria Rzepinska's term, quoted in Koslofsky, *Evening's Empire*, p. 46.
11. See Parry, Graham, *The Arts of the Anglican Counter-Reformation: Glory, Laud and Honour* (Woodbridge: Boydell Press, 2006), and Fincham, Kenneth and Tyacke, Nicholas, *Altar's Restored. The Changing Face of English Religious Worship, 1547–c. 1700* (Oxford: Oxford University Press, 2007).

12 Quoted in www.british-history.ac.uk 'Introduction', *The Commissions for Building Fifty New Churches: The Minute Books, 1711–27* (accessed October 2012). For further background to the Commission, see Du Prey, Pierre de la Ruffinière, *Hawksmoor's London Churches. Architecture and Theology* (Chicago and London: University of Chicago Press, 2000), Chapter 2, 'Hawksmoor and the Divines'.

13 Wren, Christopher, 'Letter of Recommendation to a Friend on the Commission for Building Fifty New Churches' (1711), in Caroline van Eck (ed), *British Architectural Theory 1540–1750* (Aldershot, Hants.: Ashgate, 2003), pp. 131–5, p. 132.

14 Vanbrugh, John, 'Mr Van-Brugg's Proposals about Building ye New Churches' (1712), in Caroline van Eck (ed), *British Architectural Theory 1540–1750*, pp. 136–8, pp. 137–8.

15 Wren, 'Letter of Recommendation', pp. 133–4.

16 Vanbrugh, 'Mr Van-Brugg's Proposals', p. 137.

17 Du Prey, *Hawksmoor's London Churches*, p. 143.

18 Wren, 'Letter of Recommendation', pp. 133–4.

19 Vanbrugh, 'Mr Van-Brugg's Proposals', p. 138.

20 Alberti, Leon Battista, *On the Art of Building in Ten Books*, J. Rykwert, N. Leach, R. Tavernor (trans) (Cambridge, MA: MIT Press, 1988), p. 223. See also Lang, S., 'Vanbrugh's Theory and Hawksmoor's Buildings', *Journal of the Society of Architectural Historians*, vol. 24, no. 2 (May 1965), pp. 127–51.

21 See Du Prey, *Hawksmoor's London Churches*, Appendix 3, pp. 139–42, 56–9.

22 Du Prey, *Hawksmoor's London Churches*, Appendix 3, pp. 139–42, 56–9.

23 Du Prey, *Hawksmoor's London Churches*, p. 139.

24 Rykwert, Joseph, *The First Moderns. The Architects of the Eighteenth Century* (Cambridge, MA: MIT Press, 1980), p. 266.

25 See Du Prey, Pierre de la Ruffinière, 'Hawksmoor's "Basilica after the Primitive Christians": Architecture and Theology', *Journal of the Society of Architectural Historians*, vol. 48, no. 1 (March 1989), p. 44 and *passim*.

26 Du Prey, 'Hawksmoor's Basilica', p. 38, Fig. 1, p. 39.

27 See also Downes, Kerry, *Hawksmoor. An Exhibition Selected by Kerry Downes* (London: Whitechapel Art Gallery, 1977), pp. 20, 22.

28 Pevsner, Nikolaus, *The Englishness of English Art* (Harmondsworth, Middlesex: Penguin Books, 1964, original work published 1956), pp. 91, 122. Chapter 4 'Perpendicular England'.

29 Quoted in Girouard, Mark, *Elizabethan Architecture* (New Haven, CT and London: Yale University Press, 2009), p. 457.

30 See Harwood, Elain, *Nottingham. Pevsner Architectural Guides* (New Haven, CT and London: Yale University Press, 2008), pp. 42–5.

31 See Hart, Vaughan, *Nicholas Hawksmoor. Rebuilding Ancient Wonders* (New Haven, CT and London: Yale University Press, 2002), p. 20, and Cruickshank, Dan, 'Hawksmoor's First Building? The Portico of All Saints Church, Northampton', *The British Art Journal*, vol. 1, no. 1 (1999), pp. 20–2.
32 Campbell, James W. P., 'Nicholas Hawksmoor's Building Notebook', *Construction History*, vol. 20 (2004), pp. 21–44, p. 25.
33 Campbell, 'Building Notebook', pp. 27, 41.
34 Pallasmaa, Juhani, *The Thinking Hand. Existential and Embodied Wisdom in Architecture* (Chichester: Wiley, 2009).
35 Watkin, D. J. (ed), *Sale Catalogues of Libraries of Eminent Persons. Volume 4. Architects* (London: Mansell, 1972), p. 45.
36 Quoted in Downes, Kerry, 'Hawksmoor's Sale Catalogue', *The Burlington Magazine*, vol. 95, no. 607 (October 1953), pp. 332–5, 333.
37 See Koslofsky, *Evening's Empire*, Chap. 3.
38 See Parry, *Glory, Laud and Honour*, p. 25.
39 R. T., *De Templis, A Treatise of Temples Wherein Is Discovered the Ancient Manner of Building, Consecrating, and Adorning of Churches* (London: R. Bishop, Thomas Alchorn, 1638; EEBO Eds., facsimile), p. 50.
40 R. T., *De Templis*, pp. 50, 51.
41 R. T., *De Templis*, pp. 190, 191.
42 R. T., *De Templis*, pp. 195–8.
43 Wotton, Henry, *The Elements of Architecture. A Facsimile Reprint of the First Edition (London, 1624)* (Charlottesville: University Press of Virginia, 1968), pp. 55, 131.
44 Pérez-Gómez, Alberto, and Pelletier, Louise, *Architectural Representation and the Perspective Hinge* (Cambridge, MA: MIT Press, 2000).
45 Crary, Jonathan, *Techniques of the Observer. On Vision and Modernity in the Nineteenth Century* (Cambridge, MA: MIT Press, 1992), p. 55.
46 Pérez-Gómez, *Perspective Hinge*, p. 65.
47 Quoted in Crary, *Techniques of the Observer*, pp. 41, 42.
48 In these paintings Crary stresses again the Cartesian nature of the camera obscura, pointing out the globes and charts lit clearly by the apertures and thereby made available for intellectual enquiry – yet adds: 'The sombre isolation of these meditative scholars within their walled interiors is not in the least an obstacle to apprehending the world outside, for the division between interiorized subject and exterior world is a pre-given condition of knowledge about the latter', Crary, *Techniques of the Observer*, p. 46.
49 Downes, Kerry; Amery, Colin; Stamp, Gavin, *St George's Bloomsbury. A Hawksmoor Masterpiece Restored* (London: Scala, 2008).
50 Maillet, Arnaud, *The Claude Glass. Use and Meaning of the Black Mirror in Western Art* (New York: Zone Books, 2009), p. 182.
51 Jeudwine, Wynne, *Stage Designs* (London: RIBA, 1968), p. 31.
52 Jeudwine, *Stage Designs*, p. 44; see also Pérez-Gómez, *Perspective Hinge*, p. 75.

53 Hart, *Hawksmoor*, pp. 27, 127; Watkin, *Sale Catalogues*, p. 103.
54 Downes et al., *St George's Bloomsbury*, p. 18.
55 Koslofsky, *Evening's Empire*, p. 276.
56 Cast, David, 'Seeing Vanbrugh and Hawksmoor', *Journal of the Society of Architectural Historians*, vol. 43, (December 1984), pp. 310–27, p. 314.
57 See Forty, Adrian, *Words and Buildings. A Vocabulary of Modern Architecture* (New York: Thames and Hudson, 2000), 'Memory', pp. 206–19.
58 Addison, Joseph, 'Papers V and VI. On the Pleasures of the Imagination', *The Spectator*, Thursday 26 June, Friday 27 June (1712), Paper V.
59 Addison, 'Pleasure of the Imagination', Paper VI.
60 Cast, 'Seeing Vanbrugh and Hawksmoor', p. 318.
61 Addison, 'Pleasures of the Imagination', Paper V; Fréart de Chambray, Roland, *A Parallel of the Ancient Architecture with the Modern*, John Evelyn (trans) (London: J. Walthoe et al., 4th ed.), pp. 14–15.
62 Watkin, *Sale Catalogues*, pp. 103, 104. See also Hart, *Hawksmoor*, p. 20 and for other references to Hawksmoor's use of Fréart.
63 Geraghty, Anthony, *The Architectural Drawings of Sir Christopher Wren at All Souls College, Oxford: A Complete Catalogue* (London: Lund Humphries, 2007), p. 11.
64 Geraghty, *All Souls College*, p. 11.
65 Geraghty, *All Souls College*, p. 13.
66 Downes, *Hawksmoor*, pp. 28, 29; see also Geraghty, *All Souls College*, fig. 166, p. 115.
67 Geraghty, Anthony, 'Nicholas Hawksmoor's Drawing Technique of the 1690s and John Locke's *Essay Concerning Human Understanding*', in Hills (ed), *Rethinking the Baroque*, pp. 125–41, 129, Colour Plate 12; see also Geraghty, Anthony, 'Nicholas Hawksmoor and the Wren City Church Steeples', *The Georgian Group Journal*, vol. 10 (2000), pp. 1–14, p. 5; Downes, Kerry, *Sir Christopher Wren. The Design of St Paul's Cathedral* (London: Trefoil Publications, 1988), pp. 140, 141.
68 See Harbison, Robert, *Reflections on Baroque* (London: Reaktion, 2000), pp. 40–4.
69 Wölfflin, Heinrich, *Renaissance and Baroque*, K. Simon (trans) (London: Collins, 1964), pp. 32, 33. See also Payne, Alina, 'On Sculptural Relief: *Malerisch*, the Autonomy of Artistic Media and the Beginnings of Baroque Studies', in Hills (ed), *Rethinking the Baroque*, pp. 39–64.
70 Wölfflin, *Renaissance and Baroque*, p. 44.
71 Wölfflin, *Renaissance and Baroque*, p. 46.
72 Harbison, *Reflections on Baroque*, p. 125.
73 Downes, *Hawksmoor. An Exhibition*, p. 8.
74 Downes, *Hawksmoor*, p. 148.
75 See Sheppard, F. H. W. (ed) *Survey of London: Vol. 27: Spitalfields and Mile End New Town. Christ Church Architectural Description* (London: English

Heritage, 1957) [www.british-history.ac.uk/report.aspx?comped=50166; accessed 23 September 2013].

76 Downes, Kerry, 'The Evolution of Hawksmoor's Design', *Architectural Design*, vol. 49, no. 7 (1979), p. 5. (*AD Profiles 22: Christ Church Spitalfields*); in 1866 'Ewan Christian dismantled the side galleries, lengthened the main windows downwards and (except in the endy bays) virtually stifled the lower square windows'.

77 Quoted in Kite, Stephen, *Adrian Stokes: An Architectonic Eye* (London: Legenda, MHRA, Maney, 2009), p. 147.

78 See Downes, *Hawksmoor*, pp. 156–7.

79 Quoted in Kite, *Adrian Stokes*, p. 104.

80 Quoted in Kite, *Adrian Stokes*, p. 104.

81 See Evans, Robin, 'Architectural Projection', in Murray (ed), *VIA 11, Architecture and Shadow* (Philadelphia, PA: University of Pennsylvania, 1990), pp. 134–9.

82 See Downes, *Hawksmoor*, p. 143, fig. 134.

83 See images in Chitham, R. W., 'Some Problems of Restoration', *Architectural Design*, vol. 49, no. 7 (1979), pp. 10–31. (*AD Profiles 22: Christ Church Spitalfields*), pp. 13, 31.

84 See Geraghty, *All Souls College*, p. 183.

85 See Higgott, Gordon, 'The Revised Design for St Paul's Cathedral, 1685–90: Wren, Hawksmoor and Les Invalides', *The Burlington Magazine*, vol. 146, no. 1217 (August 2004), pp. 534–47, 541, 542.

86 Harris, John, 'The Grey Wash Style of the Palladian Office of Works', *The Georgian Group Journal*, vol. 12 (2002), pp. 48–57.

87 Victoria and Albert Museum, Elton Hall 'Vanbrugh Album': E. 2124: 95–1992; 'Sketch plan and elevation, Sir William Saunderson's House, Greenwich, c. 1718–20'. For the Vanbrugh Greenwich estate, see Downes, Kerry, *Vanbrugh* (London: Zwemmer, 1977), Chapter 6 'Castles and Landscapes', and Hart, Vaughan, *Sir John Vanbrugh. Storyteller in Stone* (New Haven, CT and London: Yale University Press, 2008), pp. 217–31.

88 See Petherbridge, *Primacy of Drawing*, 'Part Two. The Linear Economy'.

89 Geraghty, 'Hawksmoor and the Wren City Church Steeples', p. 4, Fig. 2. See Amery, Colin, *Wren's London* (Luton, Beds.: Lennard Publishing, 1988) for pre-Blitz photographs of St Augustine's, pp. 62, 63.

90 See Geraghty, 'Hawksmoor and the Wren City Church Steeples', p. 3.

91 See Downes, *Hawksmoor*, p. 117.

92 (BL: K Top XXVIII II d).

93 Curl, James Stevens, *Death and Architecture* (Stroud, Gloucestershire: Sutton Publishing, 2002), p. 180.

94 Quoted in Curl, *Death and Architecture*, p. 191.

95 Quoted in Forty, *Words and Buildings*, p. 126.

96 Sinclair, *Lud Heat*, p. 32.

97 The plan is (BL, King's Maps, K. Top. XXIII-21-2-a), south elevation of the pyramid and turret scheme (BL, King's Maps, K. Top. XXIII-21-2-e), see also Du Prey, *Hawksmoor's London Churches*, pp. 83–90.
98 Du Prey, *Hawksmoor's London Churches*, p. 85. (BL, King's Maps, K. Top. XXIII-21-2-h).
99 See Hart, *Hawksmoor*, p. 151.
100 Hart, *Hawksmoor*, pp. 153–54.
101 Quoted in Du Prey, *Hawksmoor's London Churches*, p. 63.
102 See Du Prey, *Hawksmoor's London Churches*, p. 67.
103 Victoria and Albert Museum: E. 417–1951.
104 Harbison, *Reflections on Baroque*, p. 42.
105 See Downes, *Hawksmoor*, pp. 189–90.

4

Shadows of the Sublime

Prisons, Piranesi and Soane

'Sublime' has significant architectural aspects to its etymology, in its derivation from the conjunction of the preposition *sub*, which means 'below' or 'up to', and the noun *limen*, which means 'limit', 'boundary' or 'threshold'. But *limen* also means the 'lintel' that bears the weight of a wall above an opening, thereby invoking the important sublime 'sense of striving or pushing upwards against an overbearing force'.[1] The sublime experience thus entails approaching and crossing physical and psychological limits or horizons which might be read as 'upward' in a supernatural, metaphysical sense or – since *sub* also means 'below' – as 'downward' into physical internal worlds and/or subconscious realms of experience.[2] A Greek text of the first century AD by the anonymous author called 'Longinus' – entitled *Peri Hypsous* (On the Sublime) – is concerned with the rhetorical aspects of the sublime and the capacity of language to move us to strong feelings and emotions. Longinus was read by Edmund Burke (1729–97), who is a key figure for our shadow stories as we move into the later eighteenth and nineteenth centuries. The ideology of his *A Philosophical Enquiry into the Origins of Our Ideas of the Sublime and Beautiful* (published 1757) conjures 'DARKNESS terrible in its own nature' against 'Mr Locke's opinion that darkness is not naturally an idea of terror' – those enlightenment shades of the camera obscura, as described in the last chapter.[3] As well as refuting Locke, Burke transformed the associative aesthetics of Addison's *Spectator* articles (see Chapter 3) into powerfully coherent patterns. Addison described mild feelings of 'pleasing astonishment' on seeing dramatic natural features such as mountains or oceans, but did not associate them with sensations of terror or horror in the observer. But for Burke 'terror is in all cases whatsoever, either more openly or latently the ruling principle of the sublime' experience of such places.[4] Equally, his interpretation of the term 'Astonishment' is much more darkly dramatic than that of other theorists: 'Astonishment is that state of the soul in which all its motions are suspended, with some degree of horror. In this case the mind is so entirely filled with its object, that it cannot entertain any other.'[5] As suggested by the title of his *Philosophical Enquiry into the Sublime and Beautiful*, Burke identifies the sublime in contrast to beauty, and through the psychological impact on the perceiving subject of 'ideas of a very different nature, [the sublime] being founded on pain, [beauty] on pleasure':[6]

> Sublime objects are vast in their dimensions, beautiful ones comparatively small; beauty should be smooth, and polished; the great, rugged and negligent; beauty should shun the right line, yet deviate from it insensibly; the great in many cases loves the right line, and when it deviates, it often makes a strong deviation; beauty should not be obscure; the great ought to be dark and gloomy; beauty should be light and delicate; the great ought to be solid, and even massive.[7]

To sum up: of the seven key attributes of the sublime, Burke identifies in Part 2 of his *Enquiry* – darkness, obscurity, privation, vastness, magnificence, loudness, suddenness – darkness and obscurity are crucial to this sense of the terrible, as here when he invokes the 'gloomy pomp' of Milton's description of death, from the encounter of Satan, sin and death in Book 2 of *Paradise Lost*:

> The other shape,
> If shape it might be called that shape had none
> Distinguishable, in member, joint, or limb;
> Or substance might be called that shadow seemed,
> For each seemed either; black he stood as night;
> Fierce as ten furies; terrible as hell;
> And shook a deadly dart. What seemed his head
> The likeness of a kingly crown had on.

'In this description', writes Burke, 'all is dark, uncertain, confused, terrible, and sublime to the last degree';[8] and his section on the sublime of 'Light in BUILDING' is in fact all about its absence:

> As the management of light is a matter of importance in architecture, it is worth enquiring, how far this remark is applicable to building. I think then, that all edifices calculated to produce an idea of the sublime, ought rather to be dark and gloomy, and this for two reasons; the first is, that darkness itself on other occasions is known by experience to have a greater effect on the passions than light. The second is, that to make an object very striking, we should make it as different as possible from the objects with which we have been immediately conversant; when therefore you enter a building, you cannot pass into a greater light than you had in the

open air; to go into one some few degrees less luminous, can only make a trifling change; but to make the transition thoroughly striking, you ought to pass from the greatest light, to as much darkness as is consistent with the uses of architecture.⁹

So, to be a sublime experience the act of passing the *limen* (read as both threshold and lintel) to enter a building, must be attended by a dramatic intensification of darkness. If Baroque shadows are not without their sinister aspects – *pace* Ackroyd's later readings (Chapter 3) – much of a positive character was found in the manipulation of the shadows of that era; in the creation, for example, of spaces for mysticism and communal devotion, and for political and theatrical display. Enlightened figures in shadowy interiors attend the birth of the Early Modern subject – such as Vermeer's aforementioned *Astronomer* and *Geographer* – whereas in stark contrast nothing could be found more terribly abject, a few decades later, than Joseph Wright of Derby's *The Prisoner* (c. 1787–90), whose bent body lies slumped in the feeble light pool of a barred and shuttered opening, that only dramatizes the shadowy enormity of his groin-vaulted dungeon (Figure 4.1).¹⁰ In this scene there is darkness, obscurity, privation and

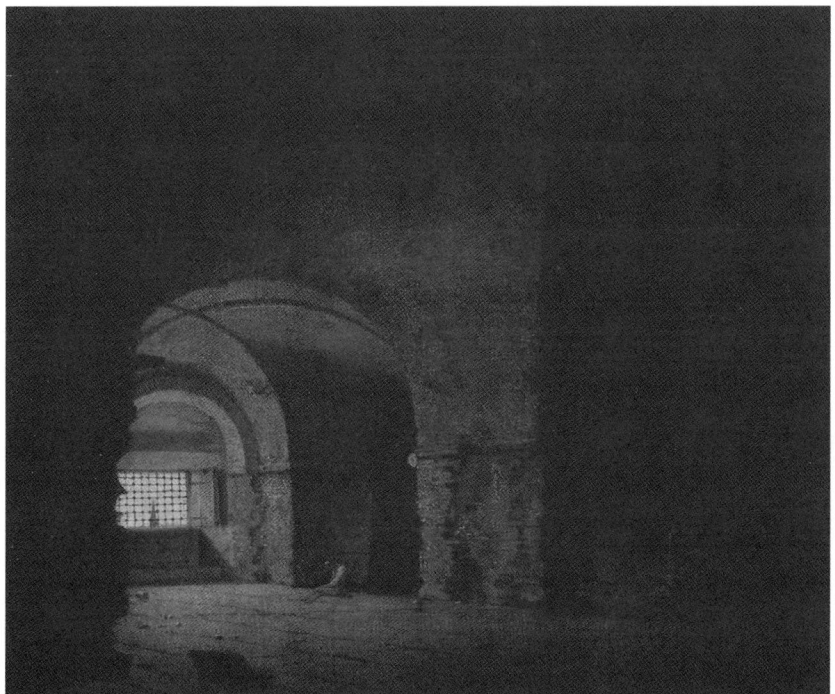

FIGURE 4.1 Joseph Wright of Derby (1734–97), *The Prisoner*, 1787–90. Yale Center for British Art, Paul Mellon Collection.

vastness to the last degree, and a compulsion to identify with the figure's pain and terror.[11] The first part of this chapter examines the prison theme as key to unlocking the architecture of the sublime and its shadows. Following an initial examination of Sir John Soane's (1753–1837) own prison projects, it then explores the extraordinary deployment of sublime shadows in his domestic architecture.

New Newgate and the *Carceri*

Within this sublime aesthetic of dark privation is an earlier Wright of Derby painting, *The Captive, from Sterne* (c. 1775–7), which portrays a celebrated passage from Laurence Sterne's *A Sentimental Journey* (1768):

> He was sitting upon the ground upon a little straw, in the furthest corner of his dungeon, which was alternately his chair and bed: a little calendar of small sticks were laid at the head notch'd all over with the dismal days and nights he had pass'd there…. As I darkened the little light he had, he lifted up a hopeless eye towards the door, then cast it down.[12]

For John Bender, the 'crushing rustications' that encase the captive in Wright's sombre painting, though 'standard to imaginary prison architecture, [in] their programmatic use here recall the actuality of [George] Dance's *architecture parlante* in New Newgate'.[13] In its darkly terrifying magnificence, George Dance the Younger's Newgate Prison (1768–78) is a central monument of the sublime which is important to examine, both in its own terms and in its links to Soane's own prison projects – Soane was a pupil in Dance's office when Newgate was under design.[14] The old Newgate prison had stood at one of the two gates by which the eighteenth-century traveller from the west entered central London; the other was Ludgate. Its inmates 'lived in abominable conditions amid filth and vermin' crowded as many as thirty to a room.[15] In April 1750, this monstrous darkness escaped its confines in the form of typhus, spreading to the adjoining sessions house where it killed sixty, including the Lord Mayor and two judges. This contagion provoked calls for a new prison which, after many setbacks, only began on site in 1769 to George Dance the Younger's design. As with Hawksmoor's churches, here again a shadowy architecture was funded by the black gold of a tax on coals.[16]

And it is out of the sooty smogs of London that its scary masses materialize in those later nineteenth-century photographs that record the final decades of the prison before its demolition in 1902 for the building of the Central Criminal Court, Old Bailey (Figure 4.2). Dance created a small piazza for his new Newgate by removing a wedge of buildings that separated Great Old Bailey and Little Old Bailey; this, together with 'the downhill slope of Great Old Bailey assisted the illusion of a plunging perspective',[17] exposing

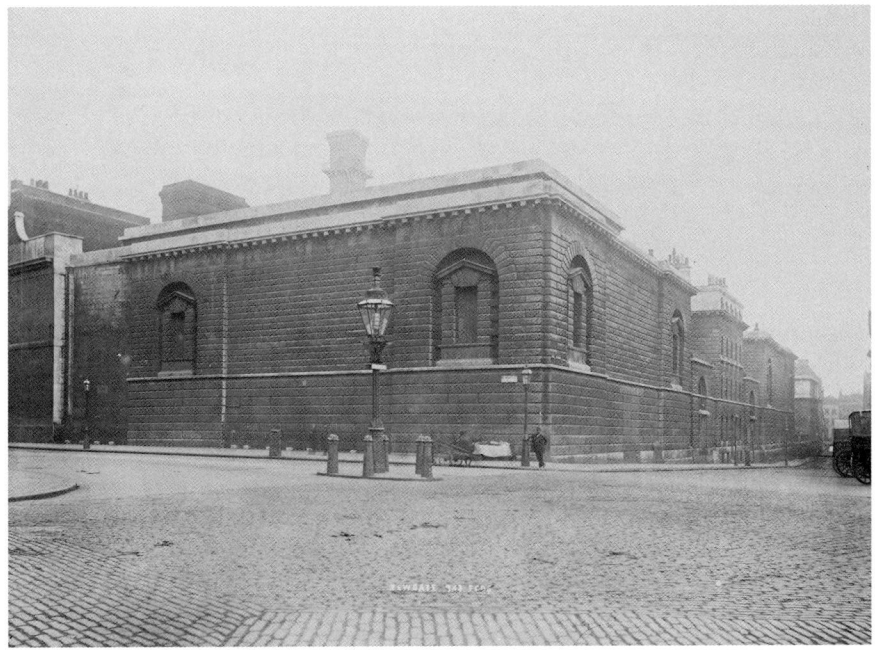

FIGURE 4.2 George Dance the Younger, Newgate Prison, 1768–78. Photograph by Francis Stewart, c. 1890. © Museum of London.

the full drama of its cubic masses to three-quarter view – a scenography very like Giovanni Battista Piranesi's *Veduta degli Avanza del Foro di Nerva* (c. 1750). Dance had known Piranesi in his time in Rome (1759–65) and would naturally have studied his *Vedute di Roma* and the imaginary prison scenes of the *Carceri* series. Piranesi's first *Carceri* series of 1749–50 is of a somewhat lighter *capriccio* character than the more heavily worked plates of 1761, but their dark power is already adumbrated in Plate X of the 1749–50 edition.[18] Here, a boldly voussoired arch opens upon a terrible and richly shadowed scene. Upon a jutting bridge fragment to the left, Piranesi has captives of Michelangelesque musculature, cruelly bound to iron spikes and bollards. Rock-faced, rusticated piers support further arches, and timber catwalks, thrown laterally across the immeasurable voids. Other elements, such as the severe portals with exaggerated keystones, the pulleys and barred grilles, accord with the brooding mood, and indeed many of the details of Dance's Newgate, down to the real iron fetters that make macabre swags over the Debtors' and Felons' doors. The Cinquecento Mannerism of Giulio Romano, or the bolder Palladio of the Palazzo Thiene in Vicenza, inspired Dance's muscular detail. He also looked at the English Baroque of Wren and Hawksmoor; from such sources derive the striking blind aedicules, within rusticated arches, of the prison's quadrangle blocks.[19]

For Harold Kalman, Dance's 'overwhelming bulk of blank rusticated wall [which] provides and expresses impenetrability' articulates 'a design remarkable for its lucid and functional plan'.[20] To the centre is the keeper's house with the chapel behind placed over a vaulted common room; then, on either side are separated entrances for debtors and felons. The classes of prisoners were kept apart, only gathering together in the chapel in distinct areas, via segregated circulation. The felons slept in large wards. All these elements of the composition, that is, 'the side quadrangles, keeper's house and entrances are seen as independent, self contained masses, set apart by deep gulfs of shadow in the spaces between them'.[21] With its practical plan expressed in a formidably didactic encasement, Newgate made prison architecture in Britain a distinct typology. But it would soon be outdated by the ideals and examples of the great prison reformer John Howard (1726–90), as laid out in his books *The State of the Prisons in England and Wales* (1777), *Appendix to The State of the Prisons* (1788) and *An Account of the Principal Lazarettos in Europe* (1789). A particularly influential example, illustrated by Howard, was the Maison de Force at Ackerghem, near Ghent (1772–5) as the first case 'in which a number of long narrow blocks were arranged radially about a common centre...to increase light, air, security and visual control over the separate blocks'.[22] Many radial and polycentric schemes flowed from this, such as William Blackburn's Liverpool Borough Gaol (1795–89), and also those of Soane as will presently be seen.

Captive shadows

Jeremy Bentham's much interpreted Panopticon designs of 1787–91 took surveillance to its ruthless extreme and suspended 'inmates in a transparent medium dominated by a hidden omniscient authority'.[23] Individual cells formed the perimeter of a circular plan open at all times internally, via full-width grilles, to the gaze of the central 'Inspector's Lodge'. As Bentham wrote, 'It is the most important point, that the persons to be inspected should always feel themselves under inspection.' He added, 'What is also of importance is that for the greatest of time possible, each man, should actually *be* under inspection.'[24] Extreme utilitarian principles of economy of time and material drive the Panopticon projects with notions of architectural expression being very much secondary.[25] 'Were *Newgate* upon this plan', writes Bentham, 'all Newgate might be inspected by a quarter of an hour's visit'.[26] The desire to maximize economy in construction time and cost made the *Panopticon* 'the first English document in which the large-scale and systematic use of iron [was] proposed' for the main columns, the roof and the inspection tower.[27] Although the perimeter walls of the second design of 1791 were of masonry, it was Bentham's aim that 'the windows in the cells...should be as large as the strength of the building...will permit'.[28] In 1797, the trajectory of this dematerializing logic produced a dodecagonal 'crystal-palace' poorhouse or 'Industry-House Establishment' for 2,000 persons, with a fully glazed iron façade.[29] Bentham enthused over the '*Lightsomeness* of the whole building'.[30] One consequence was that the darkest presences within all this 'lightsomeness' were the prisoners themselves, as Michel Foucault points out in *Discipline and Punish*:

> By the effect of backlighting, one can observe from the tower, standing out precisely against the light, *the small captive shadows* in the cells of the periphery.... It reverses the principle of the dungeon; or rather of its three functions – to enclose, to deprive of light and to hide – it preserves only the first and eliminates the other two.... Visibility is a trap.[31]

The inmates are made visible to the inspectors by their own self-shadows as seen against the light of the large perimeter cell windows. This paradox reminded Bentham of Psalm 139: 'If I say, peradventure the darkness shall cover me: then shall my night be turned into day';[32] if 'in the allegory of the cave Plato compares his shadow-making to the performances of puppeteers, [then] Bentham's design turns prisoners into shadow puppets'.[33] In this hygienic rotunda, self-exposure by one's own shadow is as terrifying as the cloaking darkness of Wright of Derby's depictions – as the Guantanomo cages of present times have proved. Foucault opines that the effect is 'to induce in the inmate a state of conscious and permanent visibility that assures the automatic functioning of power'.[34]

The sublime's fascination with shadows expresses a collective psychic repression, extrapolated from the Enlightenment project's fear of the darkness in humanity, and desire to banish it absolutely. Following Foucault, Anthony Vidler suggests: 'It was this very fear of the dark that led, in the late eighteenth century, to the fascination with those same shadowy areas.... The moment that saw the creation of ... spaces based on scientific concepts of light and infinity also saw, and within the same epistemology, the invention of a spatial phenomenology of darkness.'[35] Foucault describes this fear of the dark in 'The Eye of Power', in a passage worth quoting at length as it sets cultural scenarios both for this, and the next chapter:

> A fear haunted the latter half of the eighteenth century: the fear of darkened spaces, of the pall of gloom which prevents the full visibility of things, men and truths. It sought to break up the patches of darkness that blocked the light, demolish the unlit chambers where arbitrary political acts ... and the illusions of ignorance were fomented.... The new political and moral order could not be established until these places were eradicated. During the Revolutionary period the Gothic novels develop a whole fantasy-world of stone walls, darkness, hideouts, and dungeons which harbour, in significant complicity, brigands and aristocrats, monks and traitors. The landscapes of Ann Radcliffe's novels are composed of mountains and forests, caves, ruined castles, and terrifyingly dark and

silent convents. *Now these imaginary spaces are like the negative of the transparency and visibility which it aimed to establish.* This reign of 'opinion' so often invoked at this time represents a mode of operation through which power will be exercised by virtue of the mere fact of things being known and people seen in a sort of immediate, collective and anonymous gaze. If Bentham's project aroused interest, this was because it provided a formula applicable to many domains, the formula of 'power through transparency', subjection by 'illumination'. In the Panopticon, there is used a form close to that of the castle – a keep surrounded by walls – to paradoxically create a space of exact legibility.[36]

Soane's penitentiaries – 'gloom is the characteristic mark of a prison'

While the Panopticon might be seen as a kind of castle keep, as Foucault suggests, it has been observed that Bentham also sought to dissolve his external walls (as in the poorhouse scheme) – but reasons both practical and psychological dictated mass. As Bender explains:

> The solution, historically, was to build transparent structures within peripheral walls breached only by massive portals intended to communicate horror to the passerby. Within such walls, penitentiary structures from the 1780s onwards follow a pattern in which a maximum of light and visibility is sought inside through the use of galleries on slender supports, and a maximum of inside-outside penetration is provided through the use of glass on a scale unheard of in the old prisons. The ideal of transparency is, in other words, fully embodied up to the technical limits posed by the need to confine.[37]

When the only internal darkness is the prisoners' self-shadows, these confining penitentiary walls grow doubly dark as they accumulate all the repressed darkness forced out from the interiors, while projecting outwards that *architecture terrible* demanded by authority and society at large. Rather than Burke's transition to a greater *inner* darkness, here it is in the passage across the *limen* outwards – from the pervasive luminosity within – that the sublime prison façade must register 'as much darkness as is consistent with the uses of architecture'.[38] In turning to Soane's contribution to the narrative of shadow – initially through his contribution to prison design – it is necessary to examine further that *architecture parlante* so grimly evident in the fetters over the portals of Newgate. The whole notion of 'Character' was first introduced in eighteenth-century theory, the *Livre d'Architecture* (1745), of the French architect and writer Germain Boffrand; the idea derives from poetry, drama and rhetoric, so often the initial source of architectural theory. In an analogy from Horace's *Ars Poetica,* Boffrand argues that 'different buildings, by their arrangement, by their construction, and by the way they are decorated, should tell the spectator their purpose; and if they do not, they offend against the rules of expression'.[39] The French architect and teacher, Jacques-François Blondel (1705–74), systematically developed Boffrand's idea to produce no less than thirty-eight possible characters in architecture – sublime, noble, free, male firm, virile and so on – all limited, however, by their dry basis on literary models. Adrian Forty sees a key step forward in the contribution of Julien-David LeRoy, who broke from these textual modes of thinking by linking architectural character to the vivid experience of nature in his *Histoire de la Disposition et des forms différents que les chrétiens ont données à leurs temple depuis le règne de Constantin le Grand à nos jours* (1764).[40] The key declaration of LeRoy's nature-aesthetic is the Burke-like passage on the sublimity of peristyles (those ranges of columns surrounding a temple, as also published in the second edition of his *Ruines des plus monuments de la Grèce*) which Soane translated as follows:

> All grand spectacles impose on man: the immensity of the sky, the vast extent of the earth or of the sea, which we discover from the tops of mountains or from the middle of the ocean, seems to raise our minds, and to enlarge our ideas. Our great works make likewise on us impressions of the same nature. We feel at their sight strong sensations, very superior to those which are only agreeable and which are the only ones which small edifices can give us.[41]

David Watkin finds these emotions echoed in Goethe's account of moving among the peristyles of Paestum in 1787: 'Only when one moves around them, through them, does one really communicate life to them; one feels the life out of them again that the architect intended, yes, that he created into them.'[42] Again in Soane's translation, LeRoy contrasts the dullness of a pilastered façade with a fully columnar one which has 'this peculiar quality of multiplying the sensations'[43] which he likens to those aperspectival effects, and rich shade patterns experienced when we see rows of trees planted at a distinct distance from a wall. LeRoy's account of the peristyle of Perrault's east façade of the Louvre (1667–70) – 'the finest piece of architecture in Europe' – is striking in its foregrounding of shadow in describing the sensations produced by the coupled Corinthian columns of this 600-feet-long masterpiece:

> Let us seize the moment when the sun produces the most striking effects by making some parts to show themselves with great éclat whilst others covered with shadow, makes them ressortir ['come out again'].[44]

A superabundance of such neoclassical peristyles cloak the unbuilt works of Soane, as they pile up the craggy mountain slopes of Joseph Gandy's painting of 1820; on a foreground slab this prospect of professional disappointments is inscribed: '*ARCHITECTURAL/Visions of early fancy./ IN the gay morning of youth./And dreams in the even.g/of life*'.[45] 'All are dull, commonplace designs showing scant understanding of the power of classical composition', according to Robin Middleton, who values Soane's handling of internal space as his great achievement.[46] As collocated in Gandy's rendering, these projects do look ponderous, but there is no doubt that Soane loved the shadow play produced by these infinite colonnades. From his Royal Academy student, gold medal–winning design for a Triumphal Bridge (1776) onwards, he yearned to build them as an architect of major public buildings. A better way of putting it might be to say that his exterior spatial thinking cannot be fundamentally separated from his interiors, and that Soane translated the aperspectival shadow effects he learnt from his peristyle imaginings into those aspects of his interiors that are most admired. Informed by notions of the ruin, anyhow his interiors seem to be expecting that moment when, in due course, they also shall become exteriors.

In Piranesi's etchings and drawings Soane had a great tutor in the dramatic potential of peristyles; he met the celebrated Venetian in Rome in 1778 just before his death. In the same year Piranesi's etchings of the temples at Paestum were published (completed by his son Francesco). Soane first visited and studied these Greek colonial sanctuaries of 560–440 BCE in 1779 which were to be so crucial to debates surrounding neoclassicism and the cult of the primitive. And in 1817, along with his comprehensive sets of the etched works, Soane acquired fifteen of the seventeen surviving extraordinary Piranesi preparatory drawings for the Paestum plates; Soane was using them in his Royal Institution lectures by 1819.[47] Aware of his mortality Piranesi fully declared his intentions for the etchings on these drawings which are a '*tour de force* in evoking the full atmospheric effect of these heroic structures', and are built up like the biting etching process itself in ever denser layers of brown and Indian ink washes on black chalk outlines.[48] In view of Soane's language of layered space, the most suggestive plates and drawings are those several that place the observer immediately among the columnar forest. In the 'Study for *Différentes vues de Pesto* ..., Plate VI' we directly confront three of the great *pronaos* columns of the so-called 'Basilica' Temple (Temple of Hera I, c. 550–530 BCE); their archaic contours of pronounced entasis, broad-spreading capitals and giant lintels are deeply washed in black-and-brown ink to form a proscenium to the bewildering enfilades of columns seen through them, interwoven further with the colonnades of the adjoining Temple of Neptune to the right (Figure 4.3). In one lecture note Soane compares the aperspectival qualities of Vanbrugh at Blenheim Palace – the 'constant variety of outline that pleases from whatever point it is viewed (as are viewed ancient temples)' – with the 'great temple at Paestum' where to 'keep up the first impression there must be the same character observed in every part externally and internally'.[49] Such intense drawing, and overdrawing, of shadowy ungraspable enframings embody two key Burkean

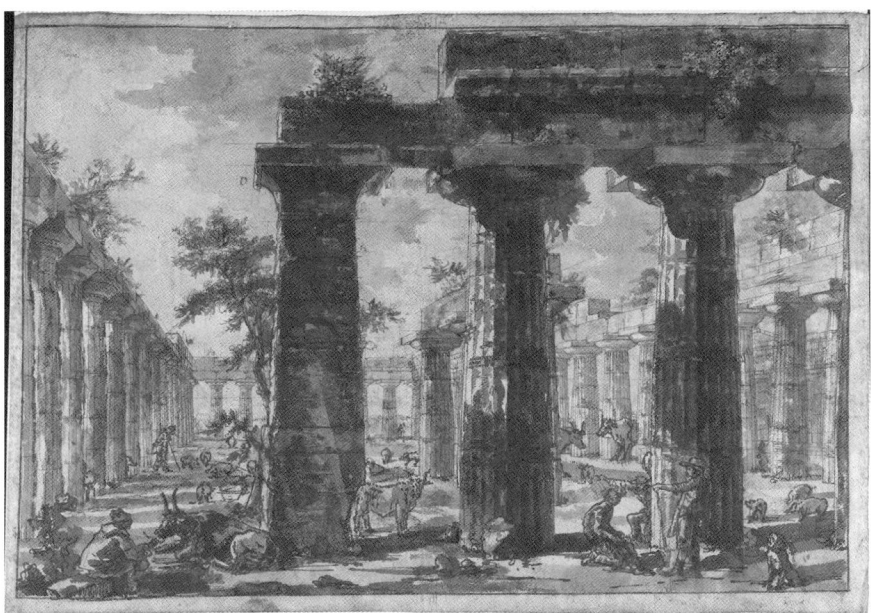

FIGURE 4.3 Giovanni Battista Piranesi, *Study for Différentes vue de Pesto ...*, Plate VI. The Basilica looking west with the *pronaos* in the foreground and the Temple of Neptune to the right, c. 1777–8. By courtesy of the Trustees of Sir John Soane's Museum.

sublime qualities of indeterminancy and infinitude. In a section that opposes 'obscurity' to 'clearness', Burke maintains that in art, as in 'nature dark, confused, uncertain images have a greater power on the fancy to form the grander passions than those have which are more clear and determinate'.[50] Burke also praises the 'principles of succession and uniformity' which inform 'the grand appearance of the ancient heathen temples, which were generally oblong forms, with a range of uniform pillars on every side'; sublimity in building requires such a sense of greatness and 'artificial infinity'.[51] Piranesi's compositions are skilful in fusing indeterminate interlocking forms with the infinity of unbroken extent, as in this same 'Basilica' Temple view which also shows the unbroken length of the south colonnade. As was the case with Hawksmoor's catacomb crypts, when shadows become active in architectural imaginings, they are often attended by archetypes of the primitive. For many, this Hera I temple – with its central colonnade dividing the cella in half to support the ridge-beam – was a more powerfully archaic image than the soon-to-be-famous 'primitive hut' of Laugier's *Essai sur l'architecture* of 1753.[52]

Piranesi presented Soane with four of his *Vedute di Roma* series of etchings when they met in the summer of 1778. One of these, showing the giant circular *Tomb of Cecilia Metella* (c. 1764–5) on the Via Appia as a formidable drum dovetailed with gloomy arches, seems to have been seminal in the imagery of the unsuccessful design Soane submitted in 1782 for a 'Male Penitentiary' for six hundred convicts in the competition for a male and female penitentiary that arose from the reforming Penitentiary Act of 1779. Soane's ambitious submission included an aerial view of the complex, outlined in a demi-octagonal fortress wall thirty feet high, and set down in a sublime landscape of lakes and craggy headlands – most unlike the actual 82 acre site at Wandsworth Fields. Robin Evans praises Soane's male and female penitentiary projects as 'fine essays in composition, effortlessly combining the detailed demands of the brief into coherent and symmetrical geometries'.[53] 'The crystalline triangular configurations' of the plans derive from the tripartite division of the prisoners who progressed in their reformation through three distinct regimes of work and confinement. These radial designs only anticipate Bentham's Panopticon principle (1791) in a metaphysical sense, with the chapel at the hub keeping a divine eye over the moral improvement of the inmates; thus, in the male penitentiary three identical Greek cross elements, for each class of prisoners, are disposed around the central chapel. The cell wings of each cross dock into a cluster of four stair towers – each almost half the diameter of the ninety-four feet Cecilia Metalla Tomb – bound together by 'bridge-of-sighs' links carried on arches thirty-five feet high. The drama of this conception comes out most in the cross section which, in cutting through the tower and bridge clusters, shows the shadow play produced by the concocting of Piranesian Rome with a Vanbrugh-ian medieval – evident especially in details like the cylindrical chimney pot clusters linked by arches that top the towers (Figure 4.4).[54] There is a sublime gigantism too in the drawings themselves – this section sheet is over ten feet long. The entrance 'Elevation next the Road' presents an infinitely long blank wall, marked by piers, leading to a central Newgate-like rusticated gateway where Soane – anachronistically for a reform-era penitentiary – also repeats the grisly Newgate ornament of manacles above the door. Soane followed Boffrand and Blondel in stressing 'character, character, character'[55] as the distinctive constituent of beauty in architectural composition:

> I think it impossible, for any contemplative mind at least, to look on the front of Newgate without shuddering at the gloomy aspect of that masterpiece of art. Gloom is the characteristic mark of a prison and what every artist would wish to stamp on his work.[56]

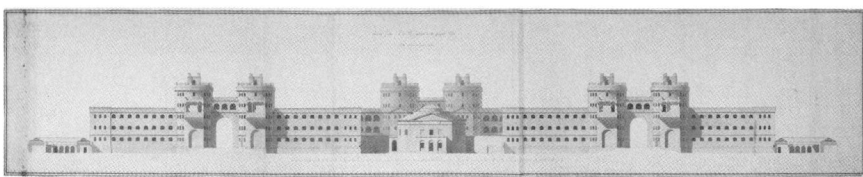

FIGURE 4.4 Sir John Soane, competition design for a male penitentiary, 1782. By courtesy of the Trustees of Sir John Soane's Museum.

But, along with these associations, Soane's scheme is already conspicuous in its directly abstract language of primary astylar volumes, of pure cylinders and cubic masses, cut into by unmoulded arches, anticipating the geometric primitivist aspects of his later work so admired by modernist critics. His reading made him deeply familiar in that eighteenth-century search for essentials 'rooted in the conception of nature as an essential first principle'.[57] Hence, Soane responded to the poetry of the work of Claude-Nicolas Ledoux (1735–1806), the reigning genius of French architecture of the later eighteenth century, and foremost in translating character into intense sensation through pared-down forms – taken to extremes in the fiercely warning cuboid of his prison at Aix of the 1780s.[58]

Etienne-Louis Boullée (1728–99) was foremost in applying 'the newly outlined precepts of the Burkean sublime to the design of public institutions',[59] through the manipulation of bold masses and shadows, as summated by his biographer Villar:

> Boullée proves that, in all the arts, *beauty* derives from nature, and nowhere depends on the caprice of men. He discovered new sources in poetry and philosophy, above all *in the architecture of shadows* (*l'architecture des ombres*) of which he declared himself the inventor.[60]

The terror of absolute darkness is displayed in the cells of his 'The Palace of Justice', described in his 'Essai sur l'Art' as an opposition between the 'brilliant light' of Justice and the shadows of the cells:

> I decided that I could incorporate the Poetry of architecture by placing the entrance to the prisons underneath the Palace. It seemed to me that if I placed this august Palace above the shadowy lair of crime, I should not only show to advantage the nobility of the architecture on account of the resulting contrast, but I should also have an impressive metaphorical image of Vice overwhelmed by the weight of Justice.... I decided I would place the entrance to the prisons at ground level, as if they were the precarious tomb of criminals. Since it is a fact that the noble majesty of architecture derives from the simplicity of masses, I did not accept any division in the Palace façade.[61]

Boullée's meditations on death, the tomb and the tragic grandeur of Nature and its 'thick woods and gloomy forests' predictably reach their greatest intensity in his account of the 'Funerary Monument'; this section of the 'Essai sur l'Art' also contains his experience of the discovery of the architecture of shadows in the mid-1790s, at a time when he had withdrawn from public life in fear of the very present Terror of Robespierre's 'political sublime':[62]

> I was in the country, on the edge of a wood in the moonlight. My shadow produced by the light caught my eye.... Because of my particular mood,

the image seemed to me of an extreme melancholy. The shadows of the trees etched on the ground made a most profound impression on me. My imagination exaggerated the scene, and thus I had a glimpse of all that is most sombre in nature.... Nature offered itself to my gaze in mourning. I was struck by the sensations I was experiencing and immediately began to wonder how to apply this especially to architecture. I tried to find a composition made up of the effect of shadows.[63]

For a funerary monument Boullée could not 'conceive of anything more melancholy than a monument consisting of a flat surface, bare and unadorned, made of a light-absorbent material, absolutely stripped of detail, its decoration consisting of a play of shadows, outlined by still deeper shadows'.[64] Though Soane cannot have known Boullée's text (only published in 1953) it sums up in extremis that enlightenment obsession with tombs, death and sensations of mystery and melancholy, which Soane fully shared. In his essay 'Sir John Soane and the Furniture of Death', John Summerson 'emphasized how eighteenth-century architects found the mausoleum an ideal subject for the untrammelled exercise of the imagination since the dead do not need light or air. Also, the forms of the typical mausoleum such as cylinder or pyramid appealed to the love of elemental geometry which characterized the generation of "neoclassical" architects'.[65] Summerson identifies four phases in Soane's mausoleum fixation: youthful studies; the archaeological phase marked by tomb chamber rooms such as the Breakfast Rooms at Lincoln's Inn Fields and Pitzhanger Manor; actual places of burial as at Dulwich Picture Gallery; and final archaeological acts such as the installation of the Belzoni sarcophagus at Lincoln's Inn Fields.[66] The second part of this chapter will examine these domestic tomb shadows.

Pitzhanger Manor – Evolving a domestic sublime

At the Soanes's first Lincoln's Fields House at No. 12 (where they moved in 1794), Summerson finds even the starfish 'low, vaulted ceiling' of the breakfast parlour 'like a Roman tomb-chamber', despite the charming representations of convolvulus-hung trellis in its curved cells.[67] But it is at Pitzhanger Manor, Ealing (Soane's country house, which he bought and rebuilt from 1800 to 1804), where he first evolved his sepulchral domestic language, one which layers a growing collection of antique artefacts within settings of mysterious gloom, filtered by amber light of a pronounced funereal cast – thereby evolving a domestic sublime. For Burke's sublime, though more naturally associated with 'vastness' and 'magnitude in building', belongs also to smaller spaces, as in the dark confinement of Wright of Derby's *Prisoner* above, or in that 'magnificence' which, for Burke, owes its 'sublimity to a richness and profusion of images',⁶⁸ such as that concentrated excess of antique fragments we encounter in the Soane-ian interior allied to indistinct illumination and a sketch-like incompleteness.

At Pitzhanger a triumphal-arch entrance front – inspired by Robert Adam's Constantine Arch south front at Kedleston Hall – opens to a barrel-vaulted vestibule of equally Roman gravitas; after a short ascent the visitor is bathed in a dim golden light descending from a vertical shaft whose crown is, for Summerson, 'like an urn lid, turned inside out'.⁶⁹ This top light signals the main staircase cross-axis and a turn to the right into the most important interiors – those of the east-facing Breakfast Room, and the interlinked library – which together make a sequence of: shallow incised circular vault, short intermediary segmental vault and starfish cross-vault.

From 1798 Soane would increasingly share his passion for sepulchral architecture with Joseph Gandy (1771–1843), who entered his office in that year. Between 1797 and 1804 Gandy exhibited no fewer than five works in the Royal Academy depicting severe funerary chambers, in images influenced by the continental scenography of French artists, such as Louis-Jean Desprez's *Tomb of Agamemnon* (1787).⁷⁰ Although Soane's language was defined in its essentials by this point, Gandy's brilliant draughtsmanship catalysed the architect's poetics of shadow and light in a symbiotic relationship that went far beyond a mere dramatic representation of his work.⁷¹ Gandy's travel diaries particularly note the caves of Gibraltar and the Roman catacombs, and it is a cavernous image, as Summerson notes, that 'comes constantly into the drawings, where...it is mysteriously illuminated'.⁷² The idea of the origins of architecture in the dark cavern or hut is one that always had appeal for Soane; in his first Royal Academy lecture, he writes that 'Egypt abounds with natural Excavations, from which the Egyptians seem to have taken their taste as well as the first ideas of their building....The Cavern is perpetually the type of their architecture';⁷³ and in 1806 he bought John Mack Gregory's strange *An Account of the Sepulchers of the Antients* (1712), noting from it that 'the first and most antient buildings are grottoes or caves....There are two sorts of grottoes or caves, great, that were dwelling places for the living, and small burial places for the dead'.⁷⁴ In Soane's intense studies of the space – from mid-1801 to its final painting in late 1802 to early 1803 – the Pitzhanger Breakfast Room translated from an intellectual's neoclassical library to indeed something very like a 'small burial place for the dead'.

Around late 1802 or early 1803, and in close consultation with Soane, Gandy spent twenty-nine days preparing an exhibition watercolour of the Breakfast Room as viewed from the east through a proscenium arch of deep subaqueous blue curtains (Figure 4.5).⁷⁵ On the right the Greek fret-patterned chimney piece is flanked by columbaria filled with cinerary urns; these face the pride of his collection at the time, the great Cawdor Vase (an ancient Apulian vessel of the late fourth century BC)⁷⁶ which stands on its own pedestal against the south wall. Caryatids in mourning support the low

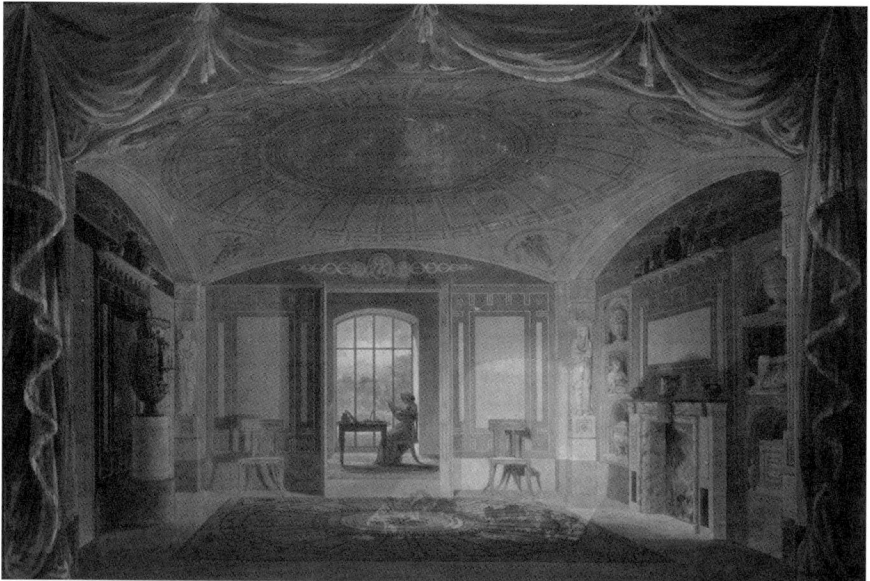

FIGURE 4.5 Drawing by Joseph Michael Gandy, interior perspective of the Breakfast Room, Pitzhanger Manor, looking towards the Library (1802–3). By courtesy of the Trustees of Sir John Soane's Museum.

vault canopy and complete, for Summerson, 'the feeling of a tomb chamber. With the great store of urns still in place the sense of present death must have been suffocating'.[77] Using all his sepulchral rendering skills Gandy solemnifies this small domestic space; a low shaft of morning sun penetrates deep into the north-west corner of the room creating a mysterious halo-like light source, more like the lamps in his tomb chamber scenes, or those of the stage, than real natural light. From this spectral aureole originate the theatrical shadows cast by the chimney mantels, the urns, the great vase itself and the open doors to the library where Mrs Soane is seated. The canopy is a hovering ochre penumbra, borne upwards by the winged victories in its spandrels, whose dim cirque echoes the corona of light. Gandy's teacher of perspective at the Royal Academy, Edward Edwards, had encouraged student architects to exploit such scenographic effects in their architectural imaginings.[78]

Gandy's is a highly dramatized representation, but it shows the intensity with which Soane collaboratively imagined the atmosphere of his interiors, working from that subdued level of luminosity (which under the influence of Le Camus de Mézières he will go on to fully develop into the *la lumière mystérieuse* of Lincoln's Inn Fields) down through all nuances of shades and shadows to the pitchest black of the grave. Soane was as aware as Gandy of the world of the theatre, but he works not as some set-designer manqué but as one of the most advanced architects of his time in his environmental control of 'warming', light, tectonics and surface, to define the character of his spaces.⁷⁹ Pitzhanger allows us to watch his growing mastery of these mysterious effects within his personal domestic realm.

The vault was there from the beginning as in a brown ink study by Soane of 2 August 1801 of the plan (with reflected ceiling plan showing a preliminary vault grooving pattern) and the south wall fitted out in its first conception as a library (Figure 4.6). Bianca de Divitiis describes how 'the sepulchral atmosphere...emerged only after an extended phase of work' with the caryatids making their appearance in December 1801 and the *columbaria* 'one of the most significant features in lending a catacomb-like atmosphere to the room' before 2 June 1802 a year after work began on this interior.⁸⁰ Thomas Hope was an undoubted influence here, and Soane seems to have been well aware from an early stage of this polymath's celebrated museum house in Duchess Street. Completed by 1801, Hope's property had no less than four vase rooms whose display he describes in his influential *Household Furniture and Interior Decoration* of 1807:

> As these vases were all found in tombs, some especially of the smaller sort, have been placed in recesses, imitating the ancient Columbaria, or receptacles of Cinerary urns. As they relate chiefly to the Bacchanalian rites, which were partly connected with the representations of mystic death and regeneration, others, of a larger size, have been situated in compartments, divided by terms, surmounted with heads of the Indian or bearded Bacchus.⁸¹

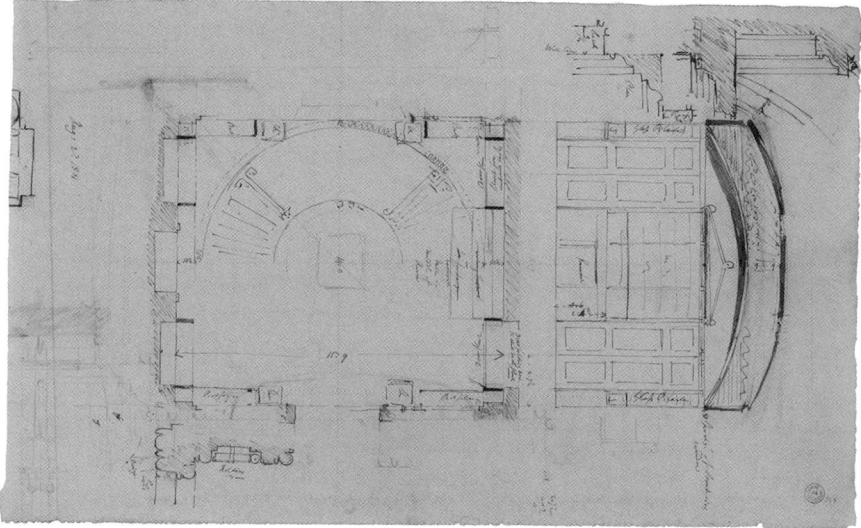

FIGURE 4.6 Sir John Soane, preliminary design and working drawing for the Breakfast Room, Pitzhanger Manor, 2 August 1801. SM (192) 31/4/24. By courtesy of the Trustees of Sir John Soane's Museum.

One passage in *Household Furniture and Interior Decoration* adumbrates the irrational accumulation of fragments Soane would layer at Lincoln's Inn Fields – one that is more than hinted at in Pitzhanger – when Hope extols

> that prodigious variety of details and of embellishments, which, under the various characters and denominations of imitative and symbolic personages, of attributes and of insignia of gods and of men, of instruments and of trophies, of terms, caryatides, griffins, chimaeras, scenic masks, sacrificial implements, civic and military emblems, & c [that gave diversity and expression to Greek and Roman design].[82]

But only gradually did the Breakfast Room acquire the intense archaeological character of Gandy's perspective. In August 1802, all the separately studied elements were brought together in a very careful drawing with reflected ceiling plan and laid-out elevations showing the room close to its realized form.[83] The colouring scheme is very important to the final atmosphere which reflects the find of an antique room near the Villa Negroni at Rome in 1777 as Ian Bristow points out in his study of *Architectural Colour in British Interiors*. In the room only the chimney piece has real jasper and yellow marble, the rest is in painted marbling as became fashionable in this period of the late eighteenth and early nineteenth century. In the final scheme, carried out at the end of 1802 and beginning of 1803, this antique scheme of red, yellow and blue was densified:

> The walls either side of the doors [are] occupied by a panel of dark green marbling within an outer margin imitating blue-grey *bardiglio*. The two were separated by a two-inch band of black.... *Bardiglio* was also used for the arches above the chimneypiece and opposite flank wall; the bronzed caryatids emerged from fluted blocks painted black; porphyry was used for the plinth, pilasters against which the bronzed caryatids stand, and segmental areas beneath the ceiling.[84]

This deepening of tonality produced a 'final result...of great intensity' even as compared to Gandy's view, striking in key details such as the bronzing of the caryatids on their black-framed bases, all working to strengthen the sombre character of this claustrophobic chamber with its oculus open to the sky and its allusions to Piranesi etchings such as those of the interiors of Hadrian's Villa or the Tempio della Tosse.[85] Originating from his discoveries here, Soane would take forward this experimental use of colour and surface techniques at Lincoln's Inn Fields.

The shadowy sublimity of the Breakfast Room is presented here as central to Soane's imaginings, but as the entry to it from the Adamesque triumphal arch shows, it forms part of a well-orchestrated journey also involving picturesque discontinuities and continuities of space. As

Gillian Darley describes, 'The picturesque interplay between the exterior and interior was continual', between, for example, the 'sternly classical' Breakfast Room and the lighter Library 'thrown open as if under a shady pergola at Pompeii', or outside again to Soane's 'final master-stroke, a miniature ruined forum, half-buried as if excavations had scarcely begun'.[86] The difference between the shadowed Breakfast Room and the light pergola library is that intensity of 'effect' Burke describes of 'a quick transition from light to darkness, or from darkness to light', immediately adding: 'But darkness is more productive of sublime ideas than light.'[87] As in the case of Pitzhanger's triumphal arch façade, Soane works here as an admiring student of Robert Adam, in this art of spatial sequencing through shadow to light.[88] Adam was in dialogue with his Scottish compatriot Henry Home (Lord Kames, 1698–1782) whose *Elements of Criticism* (1762) was the major work of philosophical criticism in the eighteenth-century Britain, and took Locke's ideas into the arena of architectural and landscape space with the vibrant notion that 'we all experience a train of ideas in the mind' related to each other by 'order and connection' and/or 'uniformity and variety':

> The world we inhabit is replete with things no less remarkable for their variety than for their number: these, unfolded by the wonderful mechanism of external sense, furnish the mind with many perceptions; which joined with ideas of memory, of imagination, and of reflection, form a complete train that has not a gap or interval.[89]

Though Soane only bought and annotated Kames's book in 1813, he had earlier absorbed this major theme of later eighteenth-century aesthetics, one which sequentially related the direct perception of objects to memory and the imagination. It reasserted the importance of changing mood and the aforesaid 'character' within his spatial practice of contrived and surprising connectivities.

Shadow grooves

Among the many ways in which Soane organized his shadow worlds, it is important to also examine his use at Pitzhanger of 'the grooves and incisions into plaster and wood that increasingly served him as interior mouldings'.[90] Thus, in his Rotunda at the Bank of England in the 1790s he developed a highly individual language that carries into the interior the naked, Ledoux-like, volumes of the exteriors of his 1782 penitentiaries, fused with the innovative use of negative detail, specifically a shadow groove reduction of 'ornamentation to the reverse of the moulding, using sunken motifs in the plaster' which goes a step beyond the bas-relief language of his earlier banking halls.[91] Eva Schumann-Bacia points to this negative working into the surface – extending the linear tradition established by the Adams' brothers – as the hallmark of 'a distinctly personal style'.[92] Gandy's *View of the Bank of England Rotunda as Built* (1798) shows an elemental cylinder and dome whose boldly shaded surfaces are described and vitalized by linear patterns of dark engraved incisions terminating in a Greek key pattern. Contemporaries certainly recognized Soane's invention, but only to mock it, as when the anonymous author of *The Modern Goth* (1796) satirized his 'pilasters scor'd like loins of pork'.[93] Compare the Rotunda to the already-striking handling of the gateway and bridge to Tyringham, Buckinghamshire – Soane's first mature work of 1792–7 – which Pevsner assesses 'in spite of its small scale, [as] a monument of European importance':

> What is remarkable about it is that it is entirely independent of period precedent, a sign of a daring only matched at that moment by what Ledoux was designing in France and Gilly in Germany.... It consists of a segmental arch on heavy, square, completely unmoulded pillars. The arch is carved out of a big, massive slab, again unmoulded.... The segmental arch is coffered inside, and a band of incised lines marks its edge. Another such band of lines runs along the place on the pillars where one would expect a capital or an abacus.[94]

The Tyringham gateway's incised shadow lines give geometric definition to the coplanar elements in an excitingly proto-modernist manner that meets the 1960s definition of the modern reveal as a 'shadow-gap', or recessed gap between surfaces, as defined for example in John Piles's *Dictionary of Twentieth Century Design* as 'a groove or slot separating two elements... applied to a recess between elements that creates a shadow line emphasizing the meeting point... in place of a moulding.... The shadow line it creates makes the joint crisp and emphatic without requiring an additional strip of moulding or trim' (Figure 4.7).[95] Writing of the architectural lineage of the modern shadow joint, Marcia Feuerstein locates its origins in the traditional reveal as 'a space to pause in shadow' – that shadowed recess between a door or window and the inner face of a wall that also 'reveals' the depth of the wall.[96] Only when we ponder upon the now commonplace shadow joint do we realize how strange it is; 'It casts no shadow beyond itself, yet is shadow. Its shadow is a space of absence between materials. It is defined through its distinctive air – filled with air, shadow, shade and mystery'.[97] At Tyringham the two square-cut shadow grooves that accentuate the arc of the arch flow into a single fine groove at the top of the sturdy piers; this definition is reinforced by the abstracted annulets of three stronger square-cut grooves below, which together hint at a capital zone. Thus defined, and with its flush voussoirs, the arch and its frame reads together as one great tomb-like capstone.

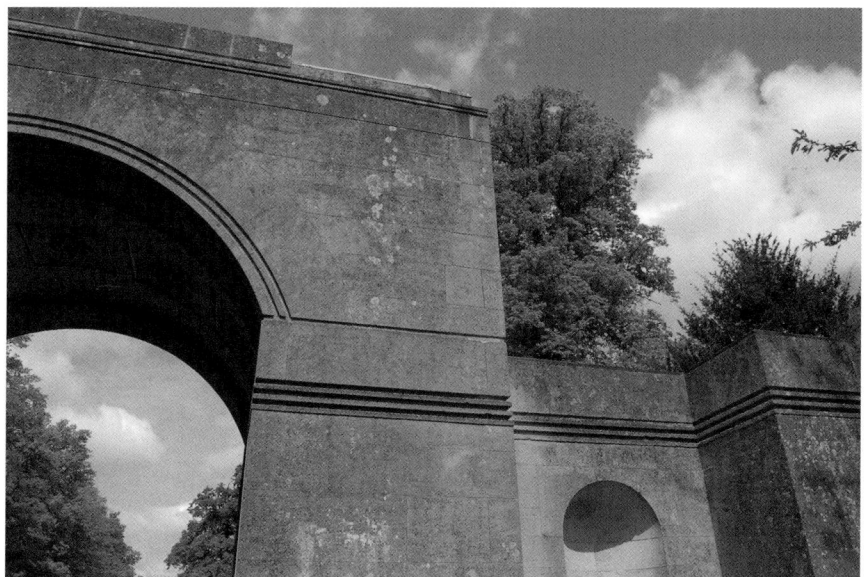

FIGURE 4.7 Sir John Soane, Tyringham, Buckinghamshire, the gateway. Detail of shadow groove 'capital' and springing of arch. Photograph, Stephen Kite.

The annulet grooves continue on, binding together the geometrically primitivist composition of intermediate niches and lodge pavilions with Doric columns *in antis*.

At Pitzhanger reversed detailing is also involved in the design of the Breakfast Room's saucer dome, broadly akin to that of the Bank of England Rotonda, but naturally at a vastly reduced scale. Again square-cut incisions – ending in Greek keys – describe the curves without disturbing the tension of the velarium-like membrane. An office sheet made in the final stages of design in 2–4 August 1802 shows the 'Section of Fret Work full size' and a plan of the 'Fret Work full size' drawn in brown ink with strong sepia washes that indicate the depth of shadow required from the decisive half-inch wide by half-inch deep grooves (Figure 4.8). These channels are edged by a quarter-inch-wide fillet, which sits one-eighth inch proud of the dome's surface, and produces its own soft shadow. Finally, to dramatize the bright painted sky seen beyond his sepulchral interior, Soane rimmed his oculus with a richly dark surround composed from two scales of roll moulding. In his eleventh Royal Academy lecture, Soane pressed the point that 'too much attention cannot be given to produce a distinct character in every building, not only in the great features but in the minor details likewise: even a moulding, however diminutive, contributes to increase or lessen the character of the assemblage of which it forms a part'.[98]

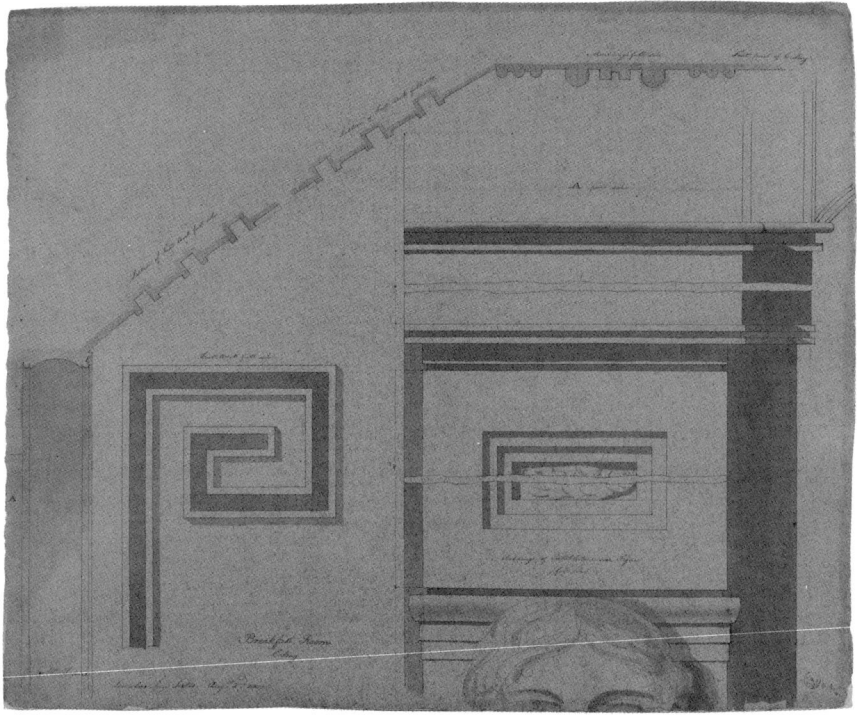

FIGURE 4.8 Sir John Soane, Pitzhanger Manor, Breakfast Room. Working drawing for ceiling, 1802, office drawing made by pupil W. E. Rolfe. SM (201) 31/4/12. By courtesy of the Trustees of Sir John Soane's Museum.

'Light subdued, not exhausted' – Lincoln's Inn Fields

Soane took the negative detailing and the sepulchral air of his Pitzhanger explorations forward to the more famous Breakfast Room at 13 Lincoln's Inn Fields. Indeed, Summerson reads number 13's Breakfast Room canopy, and contemporary tomb projects by Soane, such as the Philippe Jacques de Loutherbourg monument at Chiswick (1812–13), as no less than introversions and extroversions of the same cinerary urn lid motif.[99] Soane had put Pitzhanger on the market in the summer of 1809 while already embarked on ambitious plans at Lincoln's Inn Fields, buying the freehold next door at number 13 and building a museum and offices behind numbers 12–13 from July 1808 to the end of 1809. Pitzhanger sold in 1810, thus stimulating Soane to the rebuilding of the main house at number 13 which was complete by 1813. At 13 Lincoln's Inn, the Breakfast Room's cinerary saucer dome hovers at the nexus of a miraculously complex layering of spaces within a 'light subdued, not exhausted' – taking the phrase of Soane's literary friend Barbara Hofland (Figure 4.9). Her 'pictorial and poetical remarks' are embodied in the third edition of Soane's *Description of the House and Museum on the North Side of Lincoln's Inn Fields* which he privately printed in 1835. Though writing at this point specifically on the Monk's Parlour, Hofland's account of 'the richly tinted light descending... [which] bestows on every object that mellow lustre which aids the all-pervading

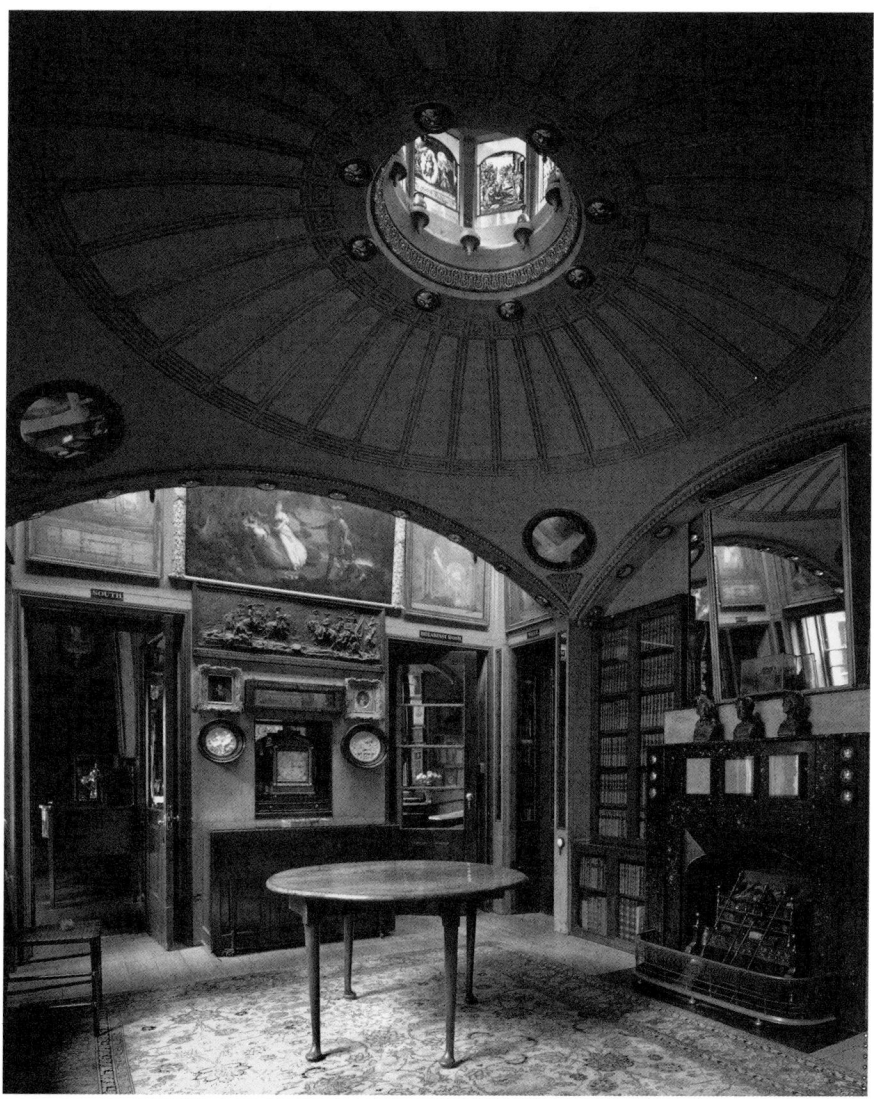

FIGURE 4.9 Sir John Soane, the Breakfast Room in No. 13 Lincoln's Inn Fields. Photograph, Derry Moore. By courtesy of the Trustees of Sir John Soane's Museum.

sentiment: it is light subdued, not exhausted – an autumnal, not a wintry and waning ray ...'[100] captures the penumbra-like mid-tone which establishes the pervasive mood of the house. This indistinctness deepens further within the gloomy recesses of the Monk's Parlour fireplace, gathering to 'deep masses of shadow' in the Egyptian Crypt, the Catacomb and the passages leading to the Sepulchral Chamber where, Hofland suggests, 'we become sensible of the value of a long unbroken vista as a source of the sublime and picturesque, and feel that we are treading "a long drawn aisle", where the "pealing organ" might be heard to advantage'.[101] The specular effects of the many mirrors and of the polished surfaces of bookcases and marbled walls glint through the prevailing obscurity; on occasion brighter shafts of sunlight penetrate the haze – as they break the grey London skies – sent down from the numerous ingeniously contrived top lights.

In Soane's *Description* the Breakfast Room is the just climax of the first and main circuit of the ground and lower levels of this house-cum-museum, which takes the visitor from the Entrance Hall, into the Dining Room and Library, then through Soane's Study and Dressing Room – formed as a passage between the Monument Court and the Monk's Yard – to the Picture Room (Figure 4.10). Next the sightseer descends to the funereal world of the Monk's Parlour, the Egyptian Crypt, and the Sepulchral Chamber where Soane installed the magnificent ancient Egyptian sarcophagus of King Seti I, which he secured for his collection in 1824. Reascending to the upper Museum levels the visitor arrives at the Breakfast Room via the passages surrounding the dome. From this vantage point in the *Description* Soane pauses to take some satisfaction in the wizardry of what he has created:

> The views from this room into the Monument Court and into the Museum, the mirrors in the ceiling, and the looking-glasses, combined with the variety of outline and general arrangement in the design and decoration of this limited space, present a succession of those fanciful effects which constitute the poetry of Architecture.[102]

As the *Description* often conveys, important ingredients of this 'poetry of Architecture' consist in endlessly diverse modulations of shadows and light. Just as the prison as building type dominated the earlier pages of this exploration of shadows and the sublime, so now the museum typology becomes important to understanding Soane's house-museum, disclosing thereby similar ambiguities between the desire to obtain knowledge through transparency and a concurrent fascination with shadow's presence. It is possible to trace the history of the museum as a 'progression from obscuranticism to light' in works such as Hubert Robert's *Project for the Transformation of the Grand Galerie of the Louvre* (1796) which proposed the introduction of great skylights while maintaining the sublimity of the Grand Galerie's infinite vista: in Bataille's analysis the museum thus becomes 'the colossal mirror in which man contemplates himself from

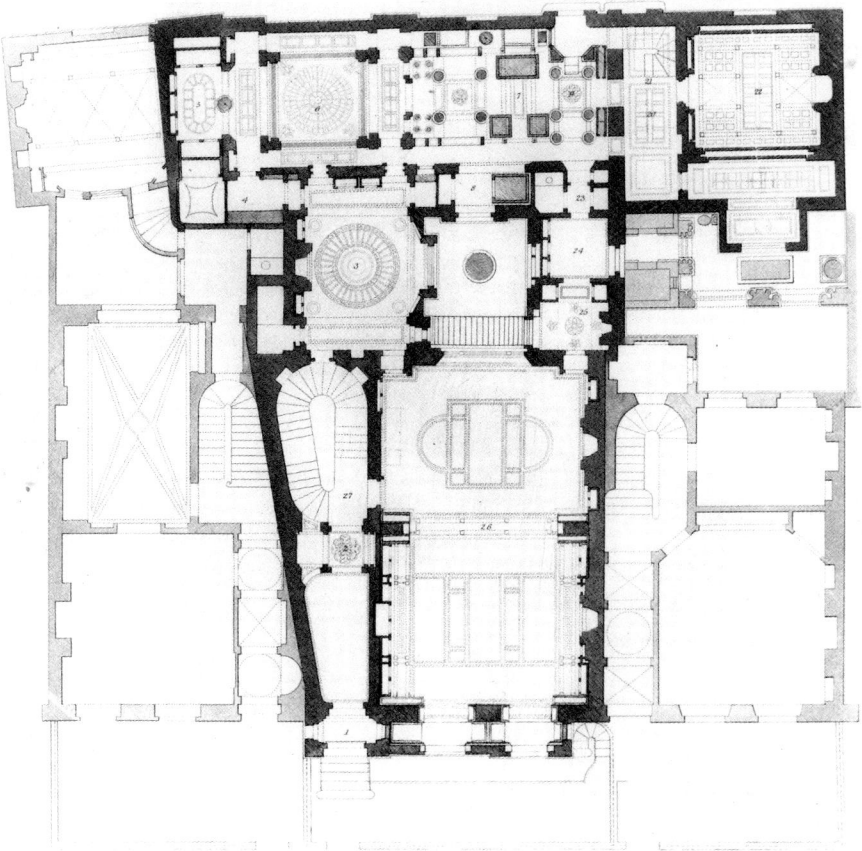

FIGURE 4.10 Plan of the ground floor of the museum, from *Description* (1835).

all sides'.[103] But, as with the prison-as-type, Georges Teyssot and Jessica Levine's arguments show that the museum's story is likewise no one-way-street to transparency. At the end of the eighteenth and the beginning of the nineteenth centuries, there were also many sensitive to the 'nocturnal' as well as the 'diurnal' who wanted 'to compose the building with shadows and light'. Those 'artists, "ruinist" painters or architects of the paintbrush [who] opened the walls to the *lumière mystérieuse* that so fascinated John Soane; they played with atmospheres, vaporized constructive elements, and raised stormy clouds up to the vaults. They formed an aesthetic of imperceptible architecture'.[104]

Middleton traces the origins of this phrase, '*lumière mystérieuse*', to Soane's interest in the ideas of the French architect and theorist, Nicolas Le Camus de Mézières (1721–89) and his work *The Genius of Architecture; or, The Analogy of That Art with Our Sensations* of 1780. Soane translated the first section of the book when preparing his lectures for the Royal Academy in 1807. Camus 'greatly enlarged architectural understanding' in his concern 'for almost the first time in an architectural treatise with movement through a sequence of spaces' within a *tout ensemble* that stimulates all the senses through the manipulation of form and space, light and shade, colour and touch.[105] Soane's empathy with related ideas in Kames's *Elements of Criticism* (1762) has been noted. Soane was particularly struck by those passages in Le Camus dealing with light and shade, such as the following:

> Light and shade artfully disposed in an architectural composition reinforce the desired impression and determine the effect.
> A building that is well lit and well aired, when all the rest is perfectly treated, becomes agreeable and cheerful. Less open, more sheltered, it offers a serious character; with the light still more intercepted, it becomes mysterious or gloomy.[106]

In his eighth Royal Academy lecture – without directly mentioning Le Camus – Soane spoke directly on this 'mysterious or gloomy' light:

> The '*lumière mystérieuse*', so successfully practised by the French artists, is a most powerful agent in the hands of a man of genius, and its power cannot be too fully understood, nor too highly appreciated. It is, however, little attended to in our architecture, and for this obvious reason, that we do not sufficiently feel the importance of character in our buildings, to which the mode of admitting light contributes in no small degree.[107]

Immediately preceding this passage Soane praises the device whereby 'light is often introduced very advantageously above the cornice, so that the window is not seen from below: by this contrivance a pleasing kind of demi-tint is thrown over the whole surface of the ceiling'.[108] The striking advance on Pitzhanger at number 13's Breakfast Room is exactly this contrivance of concealed top lighting as seen in a 'Section of the Museum (Dome) and Breakfast Room' drawn by Frank Copland in 1818 (Figure 4.11).[109] Here the Classical casts displayed in the dome stand out in cool ivory against sombre indigos, in contrast to the muted golden lights and warm shadows of the Breakfast Room's domesticity. By placing the square plan of the saucer dome within a north-south-orientated rectangle, Soane utilized the remaining slots as linear skylights whose yellow-tinted glass washes the grained yellow walls with the 'pleasing kind of demi-tint' he desired.[110] Pitzhanger's painted oculus converts here to a small real lantern, while the pendentives go through an interesting history of their own which reflects – quite literally – wider changes in the house. They start off conventionally as Pitzhanger-type winged victories, but by 1825 Soane had pierced circles in them through to the light shafts, presumably to mediate the strong contrast between these areas and the shadowy dome by admitting more of the golden *lumière mystérieuse* into the core of the space (these complicated

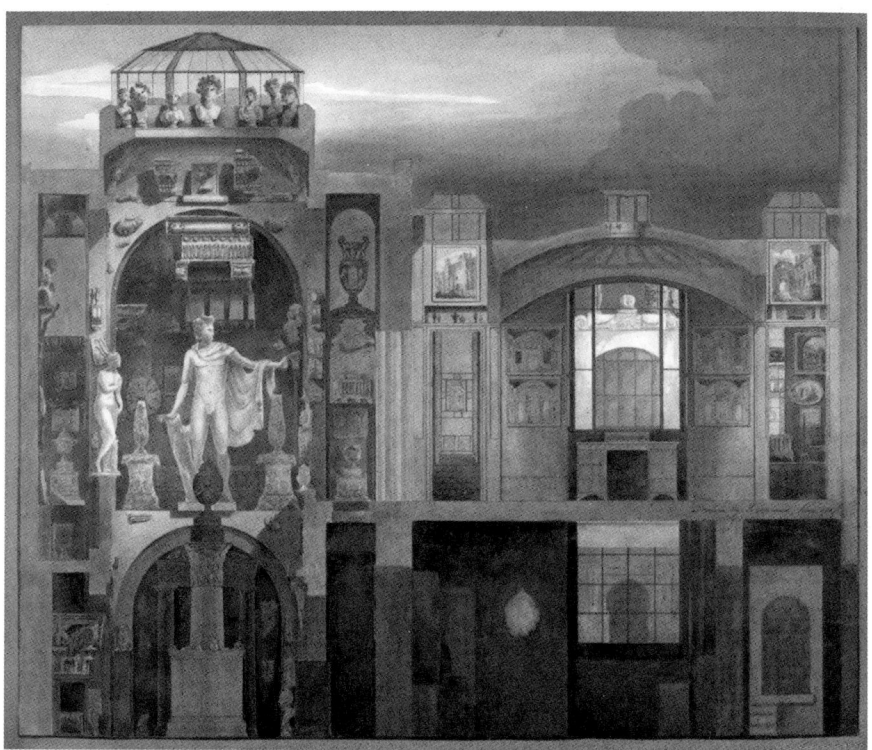

FIGURE 4.11 Section of the dome area and Breakfast Room looking east, drawn by Frank Copland, 1818. SM Vol. 83, 1. By courtesy of the Trustees of Sir John Soane's Museum.

piercings can be seen in Charles James Richardson's record watercolours dated November 1825) (Figure 4.12). By the time of Soane's death these openings had been supplanted, in turn, by large convex mirrors, together with other smaller ones dotting the intrados of the segmental dome arches. All were part of the growing specular character of the house arising in part from the desire to 'multiply the level of illumination from the inadequate sources of natural daylight and candlelight, and to compensate for ageing and failing eyesight, [by] introducing light into the furthest reaches of these complex interiors through reflections and refractions'.[111] From 1815 Soane had begun to complain of those problems with his eyes which required an operation by 1825.

Light subdued, *lumière mystérieuse*, gloom, penumbras and so forth are analogies for sensations but not a rigorous explanation for them, and in a study of shadow-makers it might be asked to what extent are we experiencing shade and shadow at all in this Breakfast Room? As a philosopher of shadows Roy Sorensen is quite strict in his definitions: even if we were to progressively darken Soane's yellow-glass top lights to the strongest of

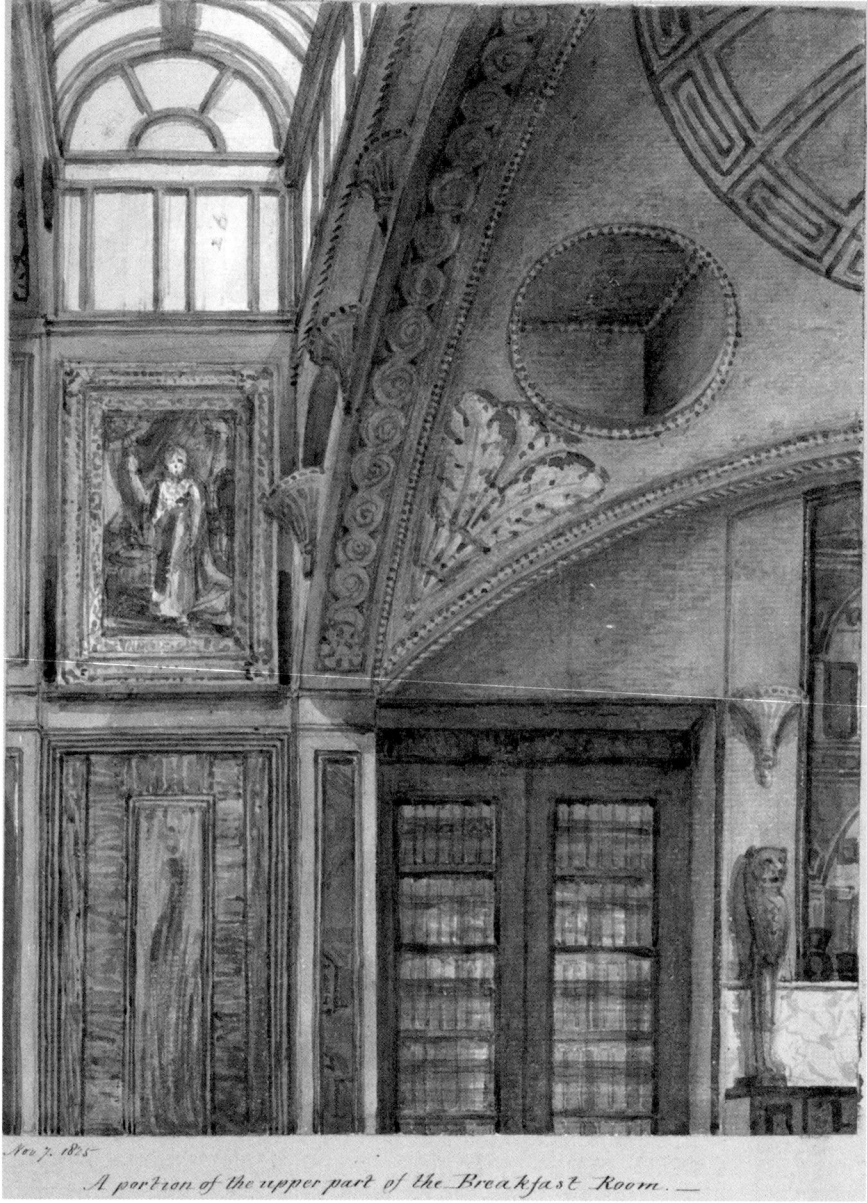

FIGURE 4.12 A portion of the upper part of the Breakfast Room (showing top lighting and pendentives) drawn by Charles James Richardson, 7 November 1825. SM Vol. 82, 27. By courtesy of the Trustees of Sir John Soane's Museum.

greys we would still not be dealing with true shadow for, Sorensen insists, a 'dark grey filter only produces a "filtow": a body of filtered light. No body of light is a shadow; therefore, no filtow is a shadow'.[112] Comparing light filters to sink-strainers and plugs Sorensen insists 'as filters let less and less through, they approach being plugs.... [But] all shadow casters are plugs. None are mere filters'.[113] But cosmic rays will still pass a plug, and Sorensen confesses that shadows to experience are the absence of only that portion of the electromagnetic spectrum visible to the human eye. So in the Breakfast Room, as in many other spaces, a lot of what we loosely describe as shadow and shade is rich with photons from filtered light, reflection and penumbras – even the last are also 'filtows' as only the true 'umbra of a shadow is actually a shadow'.[114] Confronted with these elementary definitions we have no alternative but to probably conclude that even in many apparently 'shadowy' situations we would be left with very little true shadow at all. Though important to recognize, none of this is probably crucial to the phenomenology of light dealt with here; but we are often in dusky zones at number 13, and Sorensen is surely philosophically correct to guard against 'the twilight fallacy of inferring that there is no difference between night and day because there are cases that are borderline between day and night'.[115] If Casati seems more open to the potential shadowy character of filtered light, after some subtle experiments with the shadows cast by coloured light, he also concludes that 'shadows and coloured light are false friends'.[116] Despite the delusions of experience, true shadow is always and only an absence and there is no real propagation of energy. When in around 1490 Leonardo da Vinci worked on shadow, he correctly defined shadow as 'the lack of light'; he wrote of the 'original shadows' attached to the far side of a body from the light source, but then he went on to surmise the existence of 'shadowy rays [which] come from these original shadows' to strike a plane and produce the cast shadow we see – the cast shadow he vividly called the *sbattimento*, or 'hit'.[117] Although we now know it makes no scientific sense, personal experience from childhood, and the cultural histories of shadow presented here, support a phenomenology of 'shadowy rays' in the sense that it is nigh on impossible not to feel shadow as a propagated presence, rather than a mere absence of photons.

'the golden orient or the amber coloured ether'

In his use of the filtered autumnal *lumière mystérieuse*, Soane also shows his admiration of poets such as James Thomson, whose *The Seasons* praised the luminosity and beauty of the golden light of yellow.[118] The poem was also a deep influence on the artist J. M. W. Turner, whom Soane had befriended around 1802. The two men shared humble origins, a love of fishing and strong aesthetic interests in poetry and the poetics of light, shadow and colour. In his fifth Royal Academy lecture Soane opined how it was 'impossible not to admire the beauties, and almost magical effects, in the architectural drawings of a Clérisseau, a Gandy or a Turner'.[119] From his profound study of the art of Claude Lorraine – of works such as the sunrise *Seaport with the Embarkation of the Queen of Sheba*, 1648 – the soft unifying golden light of morning haze or approaching dusk became an inextricable part of Turner's sublime vision of antiquity.[120] Turner wrote that he found in Claude 'the golden orient or the amber coloured ether ... harmonious, true and clear, replete with all the aerial qualities of distance, aerial lights, aerial colour'.[121] Consider Turner's canvas *Forum Romanum, for Mr Soane's Museum*, which he carefully calibrated for its eponymous setting.[122] With its framing segmental arch opening onto a litter of architectural fragments, it alludes to views from the Breakfast Room into the dome – but Soane rejected it; perhaps it was simply the wrong size for his hang, or too golden in tone even for him. When Turner exhibited this canvas at the Royal Academy in 1826, one critic attacked 'the same intolerable yellow hue pervading everything ... all is yellow, yellow, nothing but yellow, violently contrasted with blue'.[123]

Soane's work has been described as 'the architectural analogy to Turner's poetic blend of light and matter'. Their respective built and painted spaces are often 'rounded and dilated' and infiltrated by mysterious lights and both architect and artist 'delighted in subverting the boundaries between forms and the atmosphere that enveloped them'.[124] This dematerialization is the architectural equivalent to the painter's *sfumato*; a term stemming from the Italian *fumo* for smoke which refers to veils of smoke-like shadows that blur the contours of form, or other ungraspable transitions at the meeting of light and shadow. Since its invention by Giorgione and Leonardo, this had been a somewhat secondary counter-practice to the dominant geometrical optics, but Crary makes the case that in the progression of Turner's art it becomes 'suddenly and overwhelmingly triumphant':

> Nowhere else is the breakdown of the perceptual model of the camera obscura more decisively evident than in the late work of Turner. Seemingly out of nowhere, his paintings of the late 1830s and 1840s signals the irrevocable loss of a fixed source of light, the dissolution of a cone of light rays, and the collapse of the distance separating an observer from the site of optical experience. Instead of the immediate and unitary apprehension of an image, our experience of a Turner painting is lodged amidst an inescapable temporality.[125]

Equally, there are passages in Le Camus that strongly encourage a painterly approach to architecture:

> In a building ... the shadows must temper the light, and the light must temper the shadows .... Like the skilful Painter, [the architect] must learn

to take advantage of light and shade, to control his tints, his shadings, his nuances, and to impart a true harmony to the whole. The general tone must be proper and fitting; he must have foreseen the effects and be as careful in considering all the parts as if he had to show a picture of them.[126]

The general 'amber coloured ether' tonality of the *lumière mystérieuse* places us partly in filtered light, partly in penumbra and partly in true shadow, and often in that uncertain light of early morning, or gathering dusk, of a canvas by Claude or Turner. Any cast shadows are long; the shades – whether dispersing or thickening – are near, and a master-architect, with a painterly vision, can readily lead us up to the light or down 'one of those Carcerian dark Staircases represented in some of Piranesi's ingenious dreams for prisons'[127] – as Soane penned in 1812, in his strangely obsessive manuscript 'Crude Hints Towards an History of my House in L[incoln's] I [nn] Fields'.

'the Crypt resign'd to gloom': The Belzoni sarcophagus by lamp light

Soane's first published description of 13 Lincoln's Inn Fields was entrusted to his friend, the antiquary John Britton (1771–1857). Within his folio volume *The Union of Architecture, Sculpture, and Painting* (1827) Britton praises Soane's use of coloured glass 'to rival the amber hue of a warm evening atmosphere', and the picturesque effects he obtains through the use of concealed skylights. Confirming the painterly atmosphere of Soane's buildings, Britton emphasizes Soane's skill as a painter-architect (*pittor-architetto*) confident in chiaroscuro:

> Among the numerous circumstances that demand an architect's attention, one of the most essential, though unfortunately not generally considered as such, is the study of *chiaro-scuro*; especially if he aims, as we conceive he ought to do, at picturesque effect, – if he aspires to the title of *pittor-architetto*. Bold contrasts of light and shade will often produce more than ornament. It is this that gives a spirit and energy to architecture, without which the most elegant forms and the most beautiful proportions affect us but feebly.[128]

Britton also applauds Soane's exploitation of chiaroscuro within the constricted footprint of a typical London townhouse: 'The light and shade is so artfully arranged to produce the most piquant contrasts, that what has been primarily adopted from necessity, appears to have been the result of study and luxurious refinement. Parts thrown into shade, serve to set off more forcibly the brilliancy of others.'[129] I would argue, however, that none of this talk of *pittor-architetto* disturbs the foregrounding here of Soane as an Enlightenment admirer of the Burkean sublime, and his central passion – as extolled in his Fifth Royal Academy lecture – for the 'great and solemn effects...of the sublime exertions of Roman and Grecian talent', of 'the simple grandeur of the temples at Paestum, the sublime and imposing effect of the remains of the Temple of Minerva at Athens'[130] and so on. In its literal origins *pittoresco* means 'as in or like a picture'; however, the pictures composed in Soane's architecture aspire more to the Turnerian sublime than the lower picturesque. Naturally he was not uninfluenced by this evolving late eighteenth-century aesthetic category as it took its place between Burke's 'sublime' and 'beautiful' with qualities often shading into both (Chapters 5, 6); he learnt from it ways of placing his buildings in the landscape, for example. But his notes also criticize the irrational eclectic tendencies of the manner: 'Many objects which we call picturesque certainly are not beautiful since they may be void of symmetry, neatness, cleanness, etc....Let us therefore be cautious not to be surprised and take that for beautiful which is only picturesque.'[131] The dismissal of the 'only picturesque' is significant when Soane already had the choice of the sublime on the one hand and beauty on the other. In this passing identification with the idea of painter-architect it is also important to stress, once more, Soane's practical and tectonic understanding as the complete professional, who insisted – in his final twelfth Royal Academy lecture – on a 'thorough knowledge of construction, and of the nature and quality of the different materials applicable in the formation of buildings of different descriptions, together with the most durable, substantial, and economical modes of applying them'.[132]

Having examined the domestic sublime of the tomb shadows of the Breakfast Rooms at Pitzhanger and 13 Lincoln's Inn, we descend now to the last of Summerson's four phases in Soane's 'furniture of death' – namely the 'return to archaeology'.[133] In his acquisition, installation and display of the Belzoni sarcophagus of the Pharoah Seti I in the Sepulchral Chamber of the dome at number 13, Soane achieves a climax in the sublimity of his chiaroscuro effects.

In the 1835 *Description of the House and Museum*, Soane gives Giovanni Belzoni's narrative of entering the tomb of Pharoah Seti I in Egypt's Valley of the Kings in October 1817. Within, in a chamber he called the 'Hall of Pillars', he found 'a sarcophagus of the finest Oriental alabaster, [which] is transparent when a light is placed on the inside of it. It is minutely sculptured within and without with several hundred figures'.[134] The transparency will be crucial to Soane's theatre of display. Soane was magnetized by this magnificent object which he probably saw for the first time in 1822 when displayed in the British Museum. But when the British Museum trustees balked at the asking price of £2,000, Soane stepped in and bought it for the same figure on 12 May 1824.[135] It is as if Soane's Museum had been awaiting this dramatic centrepiece, with the darkly atmospheric spaces of the Egyptian Crypt (a former wine cellar), the gloomy linking passages and the Catacombs with their columbaria derived from the Pitzhanger Breakfast Room – intended to re-create the sepulchral vaults in which the objects had originally been found – all leading to the top-lit tribunes of the dome.[136] For Britton, 'the effect of entering the sarcophagus room, from the gloomy corridor, is particularly impressive; nor is it without feelings partaking of awe, that the visitor approaches the truly venerable relic of primeval art'.[137] The detailed watercolour that Charles James Richardson made in September 1825 seizes this awesome impression of suddenly coming upon the sarcophagus – rendered here in dark umber shadows – within framing arches that ascend in packed tiers of marble and plaster reliefs, and didactic architectural fragments, to a dome glazed in bars of coloured glass to wash the whole assemblage in the looked-for *lumière mystérieuse* (later changed by Soane to a clearer glass, thereby making a stronger contrast with the yellow-glazed sidelights which bathe the lateral walls) (Figures 4.13 and 4.14). The impact of the alabaster coffin would, of course, have been much greater before it received its protective glass casing in 1866.[138]

Six months before the making of this record watercolour Soane had invited 890 guests to view 'The Belzoni Sarcophagus and other antiquities... by lamp light' on the three evenings of 23, 26 and 30 March 1825.[139] In this highly orchestrated spectacle – involving the hire of 108 cunningly sited lamps, chandeliers and candelabra – the coup de théâtre was to place lamps within the sarcophagus itself so that it glowed through its translucent alabaster with a thrilling reddish hue. Here the stage can be left to Hofland's ecstatic account of the Crypt as 'viewed by lamplight':

> Seen by this medium, every surrounding object, however admirable in itself, becomes subservient to the sarchophagus – the ancient, the splendid, the wonderful sarcophagus is before us, and all else are but accessories to its dignity and grandeur: a mingled sense of awe, admiration, and delight, pervades our faculties, and is even oppressive in its intensity, yet endearing in its associations; for sweet and tender memories unite us to the grave.
>
> Deep masses of shadow, faint gleams that rise like ignes fatui from the adjoining crypt, lights that shine like lustrous halos round marble heads, others more vague and indistinct, yet beautiful in their revealings, present appearances beheld as in a dream of the poet's Elysium; and without enlarging the objects, the scene itself, under this artificial illumination, appears considerably expanded. By degrees this space becomes peopled – figure after figure emerges from the crypt and corridors, where they had loitered in the gloom: they assemble around the sarcophagus, which sheds from within a pale, unearthly light upon the silent awe-struck beings that surround it.... Pensive is every countenance, and soft is every falling footstep; yet in gentle accents many a voice breathes thanks to him who hath rolled back the current of time to show them glorious visions of the past, yet taught them to feel, even in the hour of pleasure itself, that
> 'The paths of glory lead but to the grave'.[140]

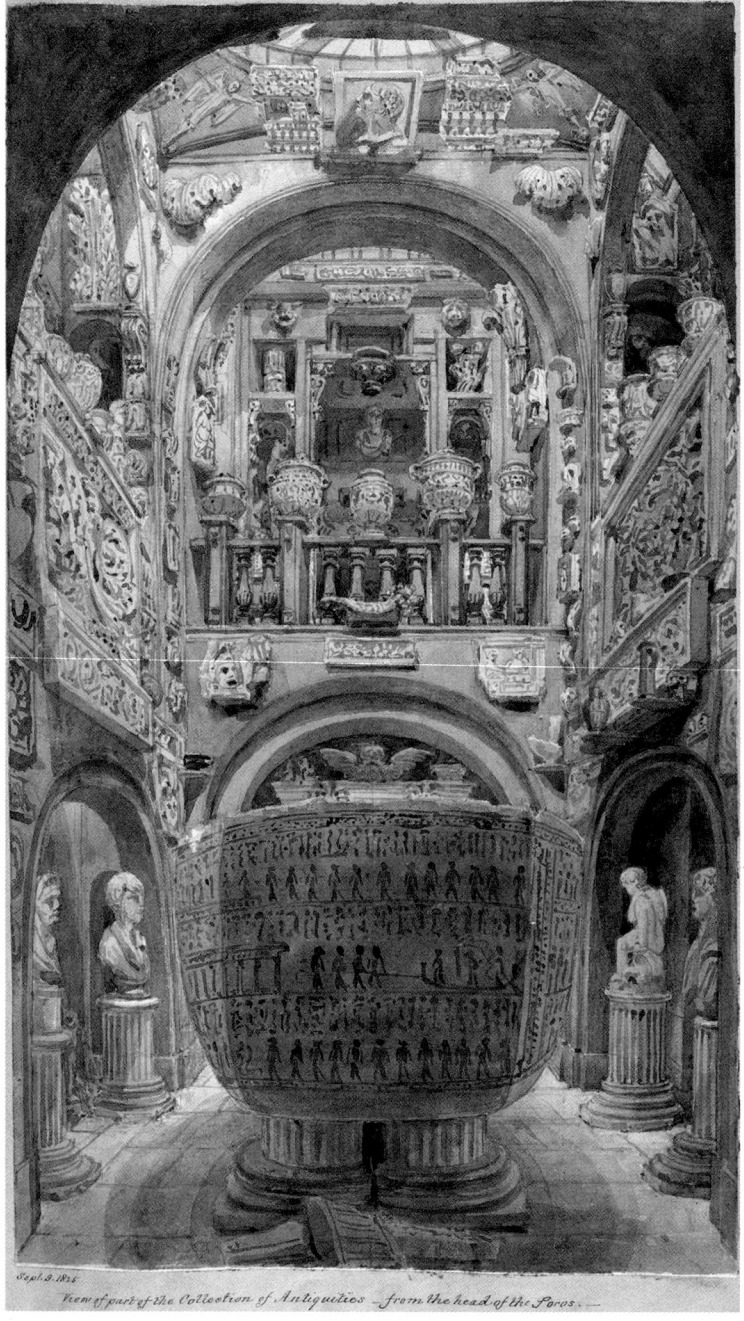

FIGURE 4.13 *View of part of the Collection of Antiquities ...*, view of the Sepulchral Chamber and the sarcophagus of Seti I, drawn by Charles James Richardson, 9 September 1825. SM Vol. 82, 47. By courtesy of the Trustees of Sir John Soane's Museum.

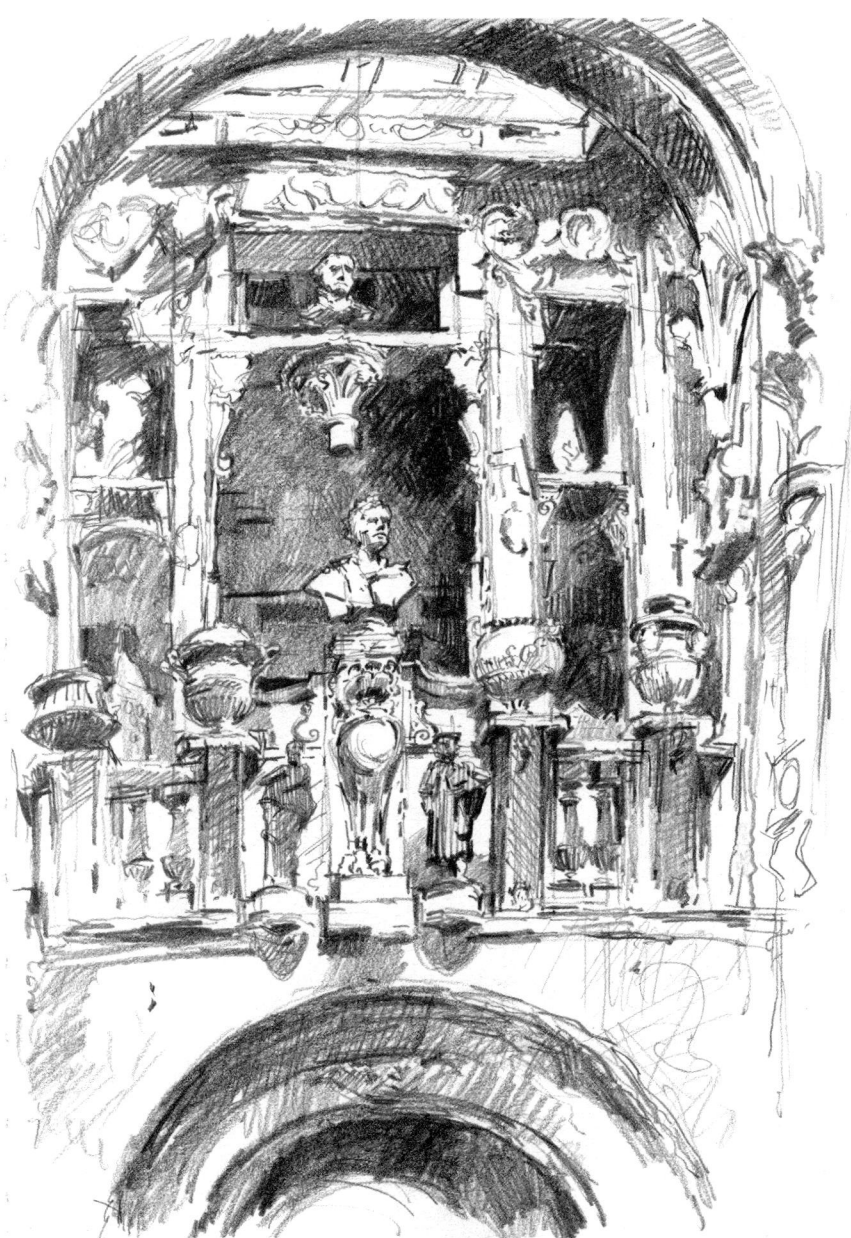

FIGURE 4.14 Detailed view of the dome and artefacts. Drawing, Stephen Kite.

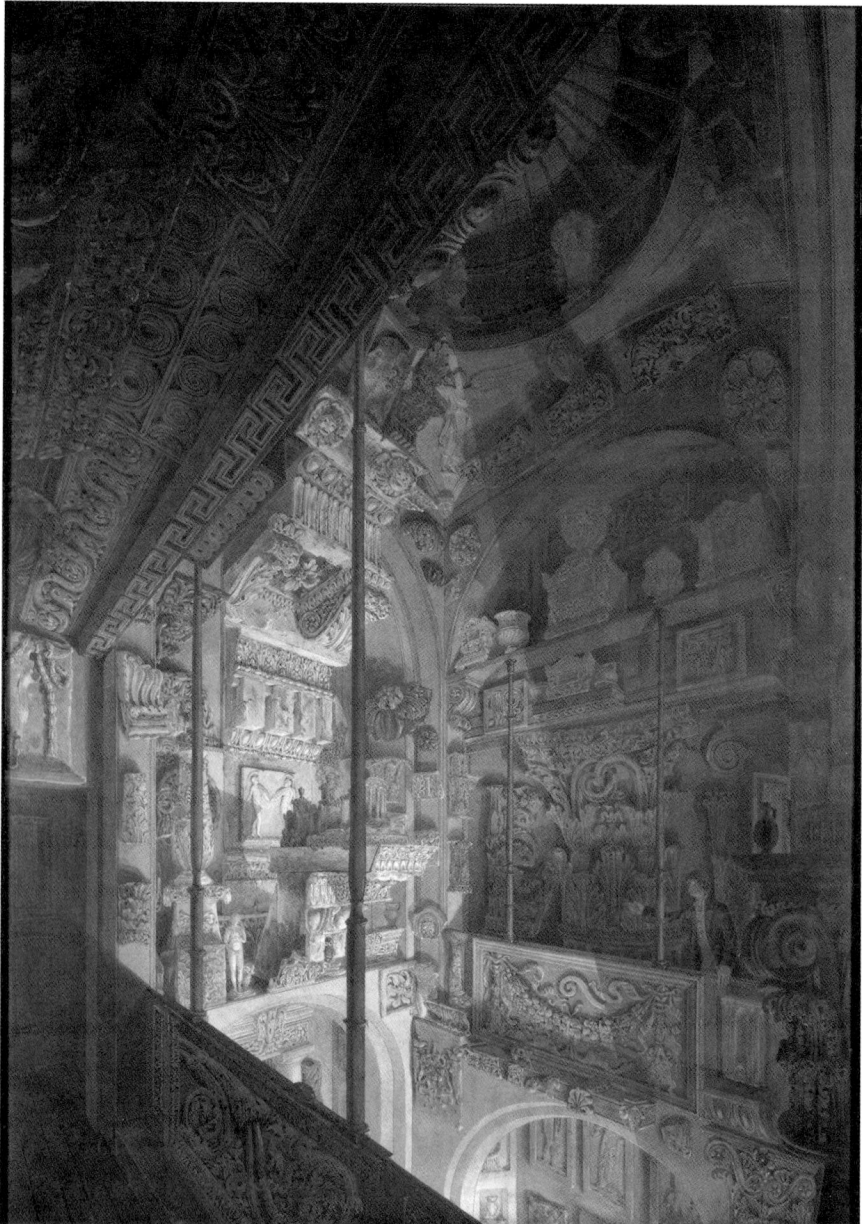

FIGURE 4.15 View of the dome area by lamplight looking south-east, drawn by Joseph Michael Gandy, 1811. SM 14/6/5. By courtesy of the Trustees of Sir John Soane's Museum.

A spectacular watercolour perspective of Gandy's of 1811, showing an earlier stage of the museum display, proves that Soane envisaged the presentation of his collection as a regular nocturnal experience – not just a special event; his view of the dome area by lamplight (1811) looks south-east across the dome void from the galleries (Figure 4.15). An upward rake of light – akin to the rays that later emanated from Seti I's coffin – probes the deep indigo realms of arches and midnight dome, projecting shadows upward from the jutting casts, provoking the imagination as does the foot lighting of the stage. At this period in the evolution of the dome area, spindly columns, inspired by Pompeian wall paintings, gave intermediate support to display beams borne on consoles at the springing level of the arches; their further layering drew filaments of light and dark across the major passages of chiaroscuro (the consoles remain, but redundantly carry only small urns). Night brings dramatic reversals of normal illumination when we see shadows cast from below, yet how more strange it must have been to see a coffin lit from within. In a further example of the fertile transactions between the febrile minds of the two men, Soane's coup de théâtre seems to be strangely anticipated nine years earlier in yet another Gandy image, *The Tomb of Merlin* (1815) which the artist had offered to Soane 'as a mark of my esteem and gratitude'.[141] Gandy paints Merlin's pearly tomb glowing from within, in a deeply shadowed setting of Romanesque chevrons, spirals, and groined vaults. For Lukacher, Gandy's image, in its 'eerie conceit of internal lighting' and of a 'lamp-like tomb lurking within a deep pocket of shadow', is a syncretism of a vast world of allusion and experience encompassing Merlin legends, neo-Platonic symbolism, and a 'late Georgian visual culture of eidophusikons, illuminated transparencies, and phantasmagoric theatres'.[142]

So why has this journey around Lincoln's Inn Fields passed one of the most obviously shadowy parts of the house-museum – The Monk's Parlour – with so little comment? There was also a monk's dining room at Pitzhanger. It is a question of emphasis. Darley is correct to say that 'Soane was no Beckford, nor a Walpole'[143] (see Chapter 5), and if the stress has been placed on the sublime in Soane's shadow world that is exactly because he is fundamentally an Enlightenment figure. His Monk's Parlour and Monk's Yard are good jokes, but they do not represent his core classical motivations. When Gandy made a perspective for Soane showing Romanesque, Gothic and Classical variants for the architect's Holy Trinity, Marylebone (1825), he spotlighted only the one with the Greek Doric portico and opened up its plan for inspection in the foreground (Figure 4.16). Though Soane admired much in Gothic architecture, it was only 'the magic circle of Grecian and Roman art' that he found irresistible.[144]

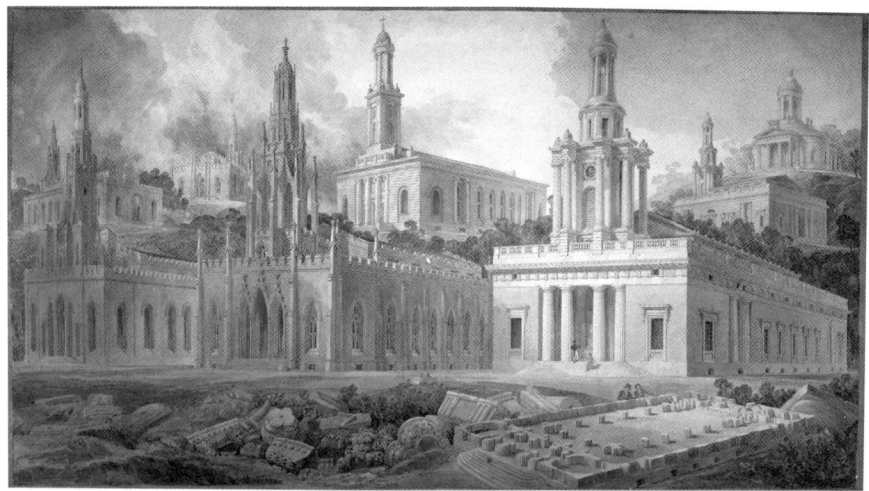

FIGURE 4.16 Perspectives of eight designs for churches, with plan, 1824: variations for Holy Trinity, Marylebone; an Ionic design for St. Peter, Walworth and the 1,800 design for the Sepulchral Chapel for Tyringham, drawn by Joseph Gandy. SM 15/4/8. By courtesy of the Trustees of Sir John Soane's Museum.

Notes

1 See Riding, Christine, and Llewellyn, Nigel, 'British Art and the Sublime', in Nigel Llewellyn and Christine Riding (eds), *The Art of the Sublime*, January 2013, http://www.tate.org.uk/art/research-publications/the-sublime/christine-riding-and-nigel-llewellyn-british-art-and-the-sublime-r1109418 (accessed 11 November 2013), pp. 1–4.

2 Twitchell, James, *Romantic Horizons. Aspects of the Sublime in English Poetry and Painting, 1770–1850* (Columbia: University of Missouri Press, 1983), p. 3.

3 Burke, Edmund, *A Philosophical Enquiry into the Sublime and Beautiful*, D. Womersley (ed) (London: Penguin Books, 2004, original work published 1757, 2nd ed. 1759), p. 173, Part IV, Section XV; pp. 171–2; Part IV, Section XIV.

4 Burke, *Sublime and Beautiful*, p. 102, Part II, Section II. See also Landow, George P., *The Aesthetic and Critical Theories of John Ruskin* (Princeton, NJ: Princeton University Press, 1971), pp. 194–5.

5 Burke, *Sublime and Beautiful*, p. 101, Part II, Section I.

6 Burke, *Sublime and Beautiful*, p. 157, Part III, Section XXVII.

7 Burke, *Sublime and Beautiful*, p. 157, Part III, Section XXVII.

8 Burke, *Sublime and Beautiful*, p. 103, Part II, Section III.

9 Burke, *Sublime and Beautiful*, p. 122, Part II, Section XIV.

10 See also Bender, John, *Imagining the Penitentiary. Fiction and the Architecture of Mind in Eighteenth Century England* (Chicago: University of Chicago Press, 1987), p. 237.
11 Similar images also haunted George Romney (1734–1802), who obsessively filled sketchbooks with confused and tenebrous images of *Prison Scenes*; see Petherbridge, Deanna, *The Primacy of Drawing. Histories and Theories of Practice* (New Haven, CT, and London: Yale University Press, 2010), p. 35.
12 Quoted in Bender, *Imagining the Penitentiary*, p. 235.
13 Bender, *Imagining the Penitentiary*, p. 236.
14 See Du Prey, Pierre de la Ruffinière, *John Soane. The Making of an Architect* (Chicago and London: University of Chicago Press, 1982), p. 216.
15 Kalman, Harold D., 'Newgate Prison', *Architectural History*, vol. 12 (1969), pp. 50–61, 108–12, p. 50.
16 See Kalman, 'Newgate Prison', pp. 50–1.
17 Bender, *Imagining the Penitentiary*, p. 245.
18 See Campbell, Malcolm, 'Chiaroscuro and *Non-Finito* in Piranesi's *Prisons*', in David Murray (ed), *VIA 11, Architecture and Shadow* (Philadelphia, PA: University of Pennsylvania, 1990), pp. 90–101.
19 See Kalman, 'Newgate Prison', pp. 54–5.
20 Kalman, 'Newgate Prison', p. 53.
21 Kalman, 'Newgate Prison', p. 54.
22 Markus, Thomas A., 'Pattern of the Law', *The Architectural Review*, vol. 116, no. 694 (October 1954), pp. 251–6, p. 252.
23 Bender, *Imagining the Penitentiary*, p. 23.
24 Bowring, John, *The Works of Jeremy Bentham*, vol. 4 (11 vols., Edinburgh: William Tait, 1838–43), p. 44.
25 Blamires, Cyprian, *The French Revolution and the Creation of Benthamism* (Basingstoke, Hampshire: Palgrave Macmillan, 2008), p. 39.
26 Bowring, *Works of Jeremy Bentham*, vol. 4, p. 45.
27 Markus, 'Pattern of the Law', p. 254.
28 Bowring, *Works of Jeremy Bentham*, vol. 4, p. 41.
29 Bowring, *Works of Jeremy Bentham*, vol. 4. See also Markus, 'Pattern of the Law', p. 254.
30 Bowring, *Works of Jeremy Bentham*, vol. 8, p. 375.
31 Foucault, Michel, *Discipline and Punish. The Birth of the Prison*, A. Sheridan (trans) (New York: Vintage Books, 1995, original work published 1975), p. 200, Kite's emphasis.
32 Quoted in Reed, Arden, 'Signifying Shadows', in Murray (ed), *Via 11. Architecture and Shadow*, pp. 12–25, p. 21.
33 Reed, 'Signifying Shadows', p. 21.
34 Foucault, *Discipline and Punish*, p. 201.

35 Vidler, Anthony, *The Architectural Uncanny. Essays in the Modern Unhomely* (Cambridge, MA: MIT Press, 1992), p. 169.
36 Foucault, Michel, 'The Eye of Power', in Colin Gordon (ed), *Power/ Knowledge: Selected Interviews and Other Writings 1972–1977* (New York: Pantheon Books, 1980), pp. 153–4, Kite's emphasis.
37 Bender, *Imagining the Penitentiary*, p. 216.
38 Burke, *Sublime and Beautiful*, p. 122, Part II, Section XIV.
39 Quoted in Forty, Adrian, *Words and Buildings. A Vocabulary of Modern Architecture* (New York: Thames and Hudson, 2000), p. 121, see chapter on 'Character' pp. 120ff. See also Watkin, David, *Sir John Soane. Enlightenment Thought and the Royal Academy Lectures* (Cambridge: Cambridge University Press, 1996), Chapter 4, 'The architecture of character and sensation'.
40 Forty, *Words and Buildings*, p. 123.
41 Quoted in Watkin, *Soane. Royal Academy Lectures*, p. 201.
42 Quoted in Watkin, *Soane. Royal Academy Lectures*, p. 201.
43 Watkin, *Soane. Royal Academy Lectures*, p. 202.
44 Watkin, *Soane. Royal Academy Lectures*, p. 203.
45 Richardson, Margaret, and Stevens, Mary Anne (eds) *John Soane Architect* (London: Royal Academy of Arts, 1999), catalogue 211, pp. 280–1.
46 Middleton, Robin, 'Soane's Spaces and the Matter of Fragmentation', in Margaret Richardson and Mary Anne Stevens (eds.) *John Soane Architect* (London: Royal Academy of Arts, 1999), p. 26.
47 Wilton-Ely, John, *Piranesi, Paestum and Soane* (Munich, London, New York: Prestel, 2013), p. 23.
48 Wilton-Ely, *Piranesi, Paestum and Soane*, p. 31.
49 Watkin, *Soane. Royal Academy Lectures*, pp. 372–3.
50 Burke, *Sublime and Beautiful*, p. 106, Part II, Section IV.
51 Burke, *Sublime and Beautiful*, p. 116, Part II, Section IX.
52 In 1758, LeRoy described 'the novelty of the spectacle produced by these columns arranged at regular intervals in the interior of temples, which heated the imagination of the inventors of the peristyle', quoted in Armstrong, Christopher Drew, *Julien-David Leroy and the Making of Architectural History* (Abingdon, Oxon: Routledge, 2012), p. 124. While in his Royal Academy lectures, Soane paraphrased LeRoy, to note how Hera's axial colonnades 'gave the idea of those beautiful peristyles in Grecian and Roman buildings', quoted in Armstrong, *Leroy and the Making of Architectural History*, p. 124.
53 Evans, Robin, *The Fabrication of Virtue. English Prison Architecture 1750– 1840* (Cambridge: Cambridge University Press, 1982), p. 121.
54 A detail pointed out by Du Prey, *John Soane*, pp. 211–12.
55 Watkin, *Soane. Royal Academy Lectures*, p. 339.
56 Watkin, *Soane. Royal Academy Lectures*, p. 339.
57 See Watkin, *Soane. Royal Academy Lectures*, p. 410.

58 Just two ranges of slits penetrate the external walls, and the corner pillbox towers, heavily lidded with abstract pediments; the equally foreboding porticoes lead, however, to more humanely reformist interiors formed around courts with trees and fountains. See Braham, Allan, *The Architecture of the French Enlightenment* (London: Thames and Hudson, 1980), pp. 199–201.
59 See Vidler, *Architectural Uncanny*, p. 169.
60 Quoted in Braham, *Architecture of the French Enlightenment*, p. 115.
61 Boullée, Etienne-Louis, 'Architecture, Essay on Art' (c. 1790), in H. Rosenau (ed), *Boullée and Visionary Architecture* (London: Academy Editions, 1976), pp. 81–116, 98–9.
62 See Vidler, *Architectural Uncanny*, p. 169.
63 Boullée, 'Architecture, Essay on Art', p. 106.
64 Boullée, 'Architecture, Essay on Art', p. 106.
65 Summerson quoted in Watkin, David, 'Monuments and Mausolea in the Age of Enlightenment', in Giles Waterfield (ed), *Soane and Death. The Tombs and Monuments of Sir John Soane* (London: Dulwich Picture Gallery, 1996), pp. 9–25, p. 10.
66 See Watkin, 'Monuments and Mausolea', pp. 10–11.
67 Summerson, John, 'Sir John Soane and the Furniture of Death', in Summerson, John, *The Unromantic Castle and Other Essays* (London: Thames and Hudson, 1990), pp. 121–42, p. 124. Originally published in *Architectural Review*, vol. 163, no. 973 (1978), pp. 147–55.
68 Burke, *Sublime and Beautiful*, p. 119.
69 Summerson, 'Soane and the Furniture of Death', p. 126.
70 See Lukacher, Brian, *Joseph Gandy. An Architectural Visionary in Georgian England* (London: Thames and Hudson, 2006), pp. 32–6.
71 See Lukacher, *Joseph Gandy*, pp. 134–45; Darley, Gillian, *John Soane. An Accidental Romantic* (New Haven, CT and London: Yale University Press, 1999), p. 145.
72 Summerson, John, 'The Vision of J. M. Gandy', in J. Summerson (ed), *Heavenly Mansions and Other Essays on Architecture* (London: Cresset Press, 1949), pp. 111–34, p. 128.
73 Watkin, *Soane. Royal Academy Lectures*, p. 178.
74 Quoted in Watkin, *Soane. Royal Academy Lectures*, p. 339.
75 But less than the forty-nine days he spent working on the Pitzhanger Library perspective, see Divitiis, Bianca de, 'New Drawings for the Interiors of the Breakfast Room and Library at Pitzhanger Manor', *Architectural History*, vol. 48 (2005), pp. 163–72, p. 168.
76 See Knox, Tim, *Sir John Soane's Museum London* (London: Merrell, 2008, photography by Derry Moore), p. 58.
77 Summerson, 'Soane and the Furniture of Death', p. 127.
78 See Lukacher, *Joseph Gandy*, p. 36.

79 An aspect explored by Hawkes, Dean, *The Environmental Imagination: Technics and Poetics of the Architectural Environment* (Abingdon, Oxon.: Routledge, 2008), pp. 4–12.
80 Divitiis, 'Interiors of the Breakfast Room and Library', pp. 163–4.
81 Hope, Thomas, *Household Furniture and Interior Decoration Executed from Designs by Thomas Hope* (London: Longman, Hurst, Rees, and Orme, 1807), pp. 22–3.
82 Hope, *Household Furniture*, p. 7.
83 SM (203) 31/4/26. See also Divitiis, 'Interiors of the Breakfast Room and Library', p. 165.
84 Bristow, Ian C., *Architectural Colour in British Interiors 1615–1840* (New Haven, CT and London: Yale University Press, 1996), p. 177.
85 See, for example, Richardson, *John Soane Architect*, p. 101.
86 Darley, *Soane, Accidental Romantic*, pp. 158–9.
87 Burke, *Sublime and Beautiful*, p. 121, Part II, Section XIV.
88 Emphasizing the Adam influence on Soane, Robin Middleton points out the most celebrated case of Adam's art of dynamically related space as the view within Derby House, London, from the third drawing room to the Countess of Derby's dressing room as recorded in the second volume of his *Works in Architecture* (1779); a view 'unparalleled in contemporary architectural publications', dramatically 'depicted in all its richness of light and shade'. Middleton, 'Soane's Spaces', pp. 26–37 ('In 1833 Soane purchased the bulk of the drawings from the Adam estate, almost nine thousand in all', p. 32).
89 Kames, Henry Home, Lord, *Elements of Criticism*, vol. 1, Peter Jones (ed) (Indianapolis, IN: Liberty Fund, 6th ed, 2005, originally published 1785), p. 216; see also Forty, *Words and Buildings*, p. 209.
90 Darley, *Soane, Accidental Romantic*, pp. 154.
91 Schumann-Bacia, Eva, *John Soane and The Bank of England* (London and New York: Longman, 1991), p. 64.
92 Schumann-Bacia, *John Soane and The Bank of England*, p. 64.
93 Quoted in Schumann-Bacia, *John Soane and The Bank of England*, p. 90.
94 Pevsner, Nikolaus, *The Buildings of England. Buckinghamshire* (Harmondsworth, Middlesex: Penguin Books, 1960), p. 272.
95 Quoted in Feuerstein, Marcia F., 'Illuminating Quality in Architectural Reveals', *Architectural Research Quarterly*, vol. 29, no. 3–4 (2009), pp. 231–9, p. 235. This is a fascinating study of the modern 'reveal' or 'shadow joint' but does not discuss Soane as an antecedent.
96 Feuerstein, 'Architectural Reveals', p. 234.
97 Feuerstein, 'Architectural Reveals', p. 232.
98 Watkin, *Soane. Royal Academy Lectures*, p. 648.
99 Summerson, 'Soane and the Furniture of Death', pp. 135–6. See also Stroud, Dorothy, *Sir John Soane Architect* (London: Giles de la Mare, 1996), pp. 272–3.

100 Soane, Sir John, *Description of the House and Museum on the North Side of Lincoln's Inn Fields, the Residence of Sir John Soane* (London: privately printed by Levey, Robson and Franklyn, 1835) (incorporating descriptions by Barbara Hofland), pp. 27–8.
101 Soane, *Description*, p. 36.
102 Soane, *Description*, p. 54.
103 Quoted in Teyssot, Georges, and Levine, Jessica, '"The Simple Day and the Light of the Sun": Lights and Shadows in the Museum', *Assemblage*, no. 12 (August 1990), pp. 58–83, p. 77.
104 Teyssot and Levine, 'Lights and Shadows in the Museum', p. 78.
105 Le Camus de Mezières, Nicolas, *The Genius of Architecture, or, The Analogy of That Art with Our Sensations*, Robin Middleton (introduction), D. Britt (trans) (Santa Monica, CA: Getty Center for the History of Art and the Humanities, 1992, original work published 1780), p. 56.
106 Le Camus de Mezières, *The Genius of Architecture*, p. 88.
107 Watkin, *Soane. Royal Academy Lectures*, p. 598.
108 Watkin, *Soane. Royal Academy Lectures*, p. 599.
109 SJSM, Vol. 83, 1. See also Richardson and Stevens, *John Soane Architect*, catalogue 76, p. 167.
110 On the wall finish, see Bristow, *Architectural Colour*, p. 208, and SM Vol. 82, 25.
111 Furján, Helene, *Glorious Visions. John Soane's Spectacular Theater* (London and New York: Routledge, 2011), pp. 56–7.
112 Sorensen, Roy, *Seeing Dark Things. The Philosophy of Shadows* (Oxford: Oxford University Press, 2008), pp. 168–9.
113 Sorensen, *Seeing Dark Things*, p. 169.
114 Sorensen, *Seeing Dark Things*, p. 179.
115 Sorensen, *Seeing Dark Things*, p. 172.
116 Casati, Roberto, *Shadows. Unlocking Their Secrets, from Plato to Our Time* (New York: Vintage Books, 2003), p. 171.
117 Leonardo da Vinci quoted in Casati, *Shadows*, pp. 168–9.
118 See Watkin, *Soane. Royal Academy Lectures*, p. 415.
119 Watkin, *Soane. Royal Academy Lectures*, p. 561.
120 See Nicholson, Kathleen, 'Turner, Claude and the Essence of Landscape', in D. Solkin (ed), *Turner and the Masters* (London: Tate Publishing, 2009), pp. 56–71.
121 Quoted in Solkin (ed), *Turner and the Masters*, p. 217.
122 See Wilton, Andrew, *Turner in His Time* (London: Thames and Hudson, 1987), p. 147.
123 Quoted in Wilton, *Turner in His Time*, p. 146.
124 Sidlauskas, Susan, 'Immortality: Turner, Soane, and the Great Chain of Being', *Art Journal*, vol. 52, no. 2 (Summer 1993), pp. 59–65, p. 60.

125 Crary, Jonathan, *Techniques of the Observer. On Vision and Modernity in the Nineteenth Century* (Cambridge, MA: MIT Press, 1992), p. 138.
126 Le Camus de Mezières, *The Genius of Architecture*, p. 95.
127 Soane, Sir John, 'Crude Hints Towards an History of my House in L[incoln's] I[nn] Fields', in *Visions of Ruin. Architectural Fantasies and Designs for Garden Follies with Crude Hints Towards a History of My House by John Soane* (London: Sir John Soane's Museum, 1999), p. 63.
128 Britton, John, *The Union of Architecture, Sculpture and Painting, Exemplified by a Series of Illustrations with Descriptive Accounts of the House and Galleries of John Soane* (London: Longman, 1827), p. 10.
129 Britton, *Union of Architecture*, pp. 13–14.
130 Watkin, *Soane. Royal Academy Lectures*, p. 557.
131 Quoted in Watkin, *Soane. Royal Academy Lectures*, p. 240.
132 Watkin, *Soane. Royal Academy Lectures*, p. 652.
133 Summerson, 'Soane and the Furniture of Death', pp. 141–2.
134 Soane, *Description*, p. 33. See also Dorey, Helen, 'Sir John Soane's Acquistion of the Sarcophagus of Seti I', *Georgian Group Journal*, vol. 1 (1991), pp. 26–35, p. 26, and *passim*. Dorey provides a full account of the display based in part on detailed household accounts of beverages, food and the hire of the all-important lamps and chandeliers.
135 For full background to his purchase, see Dorey, 'Sarcophagus of Seti I', pp. 26–8.
136 Feinberg, Susan G., 'The Genesis of Sir John Soane's Museum Idea: 1801–1810', *Journal of the Society of Architectural Historians*, vol. 43, no. 3 (October 1984), pp. 225–37, p. 234, n. 24, who notes that 'Soane's museum catacombs derive directly from Pitzhanger [Breakfast Room]'.
137 Britton, *Union of Architecture*, p. 43.
138 See Thornton, Peter, and Dorey, Helen, *A Miscellany of Objects from Sir John Soane's Museum Consisting of Paintings, Architectural Drawings and Other Curiosities from the Collection of Sir John Soane* (London: Laurence King, 1992), pp. 59–68 for the Crypt and descriptions of some of its artefacts.
139 Dorey, 'Sarcohagus of Seti I', p. 29.
140 Soane, *Description*, pp. 38–9.
141 Summerson, 'The Vision of J. M. Gandy', p. 141.
142 Lukacher, *Joseph Gandy*, p. 121–5.
143 Darley, *Soane, Accidental Romantic*, p. 159.
144 Watkin, *Soane. Royal Academy Lectures*, p. 557.

5

Gothic 'Gloomth'

In concluding the last chapter it was accepted that 'Soane was no Beckford, nor a Walpole', and that the Monk's Parlours he created at Pitzhanger Manor and Lincoln's Inn Fields were essentially mordant jokes in no way core to his fundamental classical sensibility. With bitter wit Soane created the semi-autobiographical solacing persona of Padre Giovanni to inhabit the retreat from an abrasive world of his Monk's Parlour whose accoutrements, Soane confesses, fall 'far short of the princely luxuries of the Prince of Alcobaça described with such inimitable humour by [William Beckford] the author of "Vatheck"'.[1] These include the apparatus of the 'gloomy scenery' of the 1835 *Description of the House and Museum*, of 'the mouldering ruins of [the Monk's] once noble monastery', fragments of a 'rich canopy and other decorations' all calculated to produce 'the most powerful sensations in the mind',[2] and all glimmering in the aforementioned 'light subdued, not exhausted' (Figure 5.1). Soane uses 'parloir' in its meaning of a space in a monastery for converse with visitors, and in knowing allusion to an eremitical tradition, allied to the cult of melancholy, which originated in Britain with the first secular hermitage built by Thomas Bushell in 1621. On his small estate at Enstone in Oxfordshire he built a grotto and hermitage complex whose cell was hung with black cloths to intensify its sense of sad withdrawal.[3] There are many overlaps between these cave-like archetypes of the grotto and the hermitage in the landscapes of the eighteenth and nineteenth centuries.

As Soane mocks the author of *Vatheck*, others would also mock the dilettante aspects of the 'Gothick', and its subsequent middle-class mores, as Thomas Rowlandson did in his satirical *Tour of Dr. Syntax in Search of the Picturesque* (1812). To unpack some of the shadow stories lurking under the rubric of Gothick 'gloomth,' this chapter will follow Dr Syntax's *Tour* along the Wye Valley engaging with a famed landscape which, ironically, centres on the derelict shell of Soane's country house to the Piercefield estate, above Chepstow (designed 1785). But to begin where the cult all began, with Horace Walpole and the first Gothic novel *The Castle of Otranto* (1765),

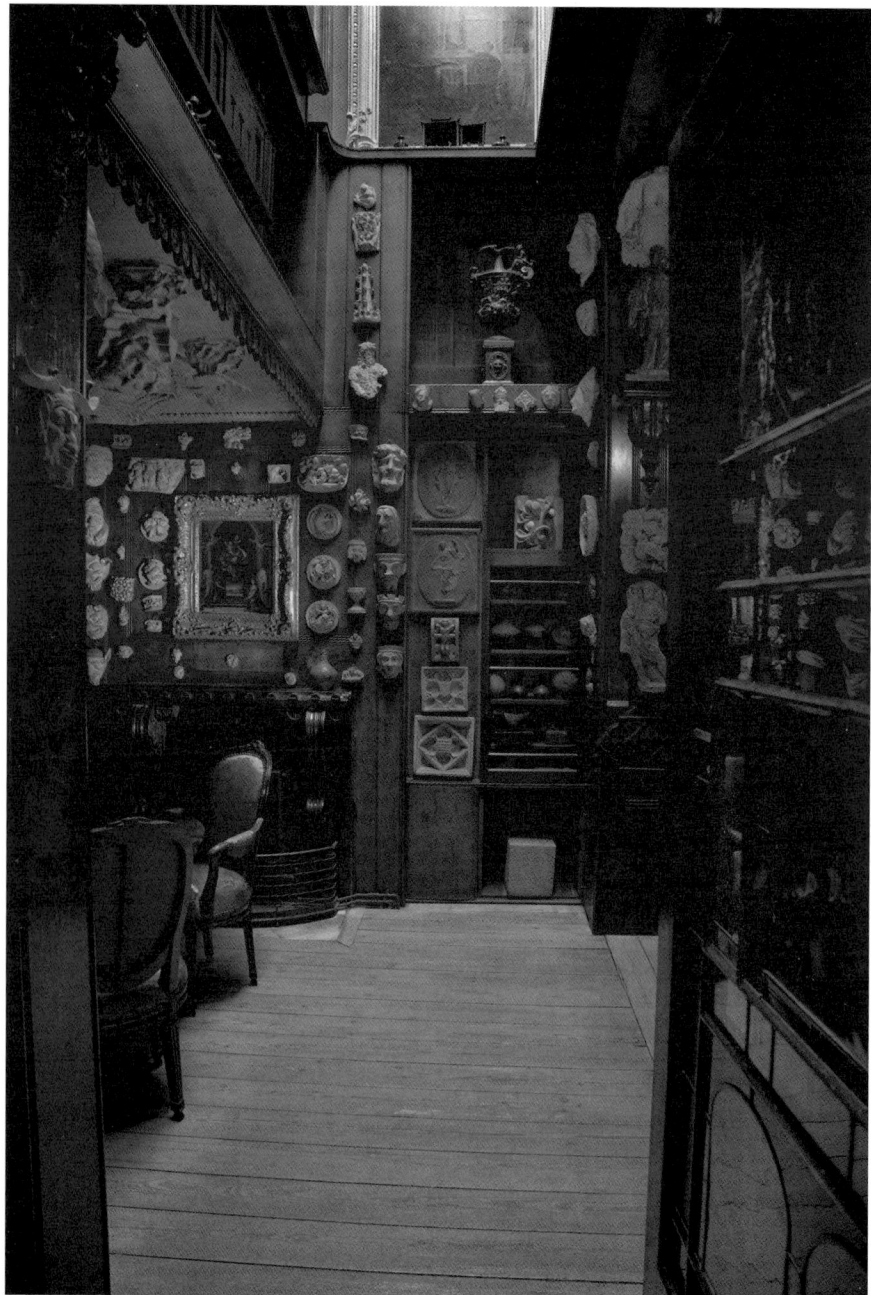

FIGURE 5.1 Sir John Soane, the Monk's Parlour in No. 13 Lincoln's Inn Fields. Photograph, Derry Moore. By courtesy of the Trustees of Sir John Soane's Museum.

from which proliferated other texts that fantasized creatures and doings, of shadows and of the night, such as Beckford's *Vathek* (1786) and Mary Shelley's *Frankenstein* (1818). Through Foucault, in the preceding chapter, these shadows were recognized as the counter-forms of Enlightenment rationalism, but soon they are also a replication of reason's collapse into the very real darkness and terror (1793–4) of the French Revolution. For Foucault in his account of the asylum in *Madness and Civilization*, 'the fortresses of confinement functioned as a great, long silent memory; they maintained in the shadows an iconographic power that men might have thought was exorcized; created by the new classical order, they preserved against it and against time, forbidden figures that could thus be transmitted intact from the sixteenth to the nineteenth centuries'. On the other hand, says Foucault, 'the images liberated at the end of the eighteenth century were not identical at all points with those the seventeenth century had tried to eliminate', as 'something had happened in the darkness, which detached them from that secret world where the Renaissance, after the Middle Ages, had found them' producing further murky mazes of ambiguity, some of which this chapter aims to address.[4] Thus, in 1764 Walpole experienced the strange unearthly dream which was the origin of his *Castle of Otranto* romance:

> I waked one morning in the beginning of last June from a dream....I had thought myself in an ancient castle (a very natural dream for a head filled like mine with Gothic story) and that on the uppermost bannister of a great staircase I saw a gigantic hand in armour. In the evening I sat down and began to write, without knowing in the least what I intended to say or relate. The work grew on my hands, and I grew fond of it....In short I was so engrossed with my tale [that] I completed [it] in less than two months.[5]

The cultural shadow-making consequences of this dream were stupendous, and the dream itself can be directly related to one of the equally germinal spaces of the Gothic imagination, the pivotal hall and staircase of Walpole's villa at Strawberry Hill, Twickenham, which he created and extended between 1753 and 1776 from the kernel of an undistinguished house (Chopp'd Straw Hall) near the River Thames (Figure 5.2). This core he first Gothicized in that style of ornamental Gothic-with-a-k (Gothick) – forever christened by his eponymous dwelling – and then considerably extended in the same vein with a Long Gallery, Cabinet of Curiosities and stocky Round Tower.

The armour that prompted Walpole's dream (possibly laudanum enhanced) was a magnificent suit designed for Francis 1, placed loomingly in a niche on the stair-flight approach to his Library, which he entered through a Gothic loggia formed on the landing. Walpole's *Description* of his villa at Strawberry-Hill tells how you first enter a small gloomy hall with hexagon tiles.... This hall is united with the staircase, and both are hung with gothic paper... from the screen of prince Arthur's tomb in the cathedral of Worcester.... In the well of the staircase, by a cord of black and yellow, hangs a gothic lanthorn of tin japanned... and filled with painted glass.[6]

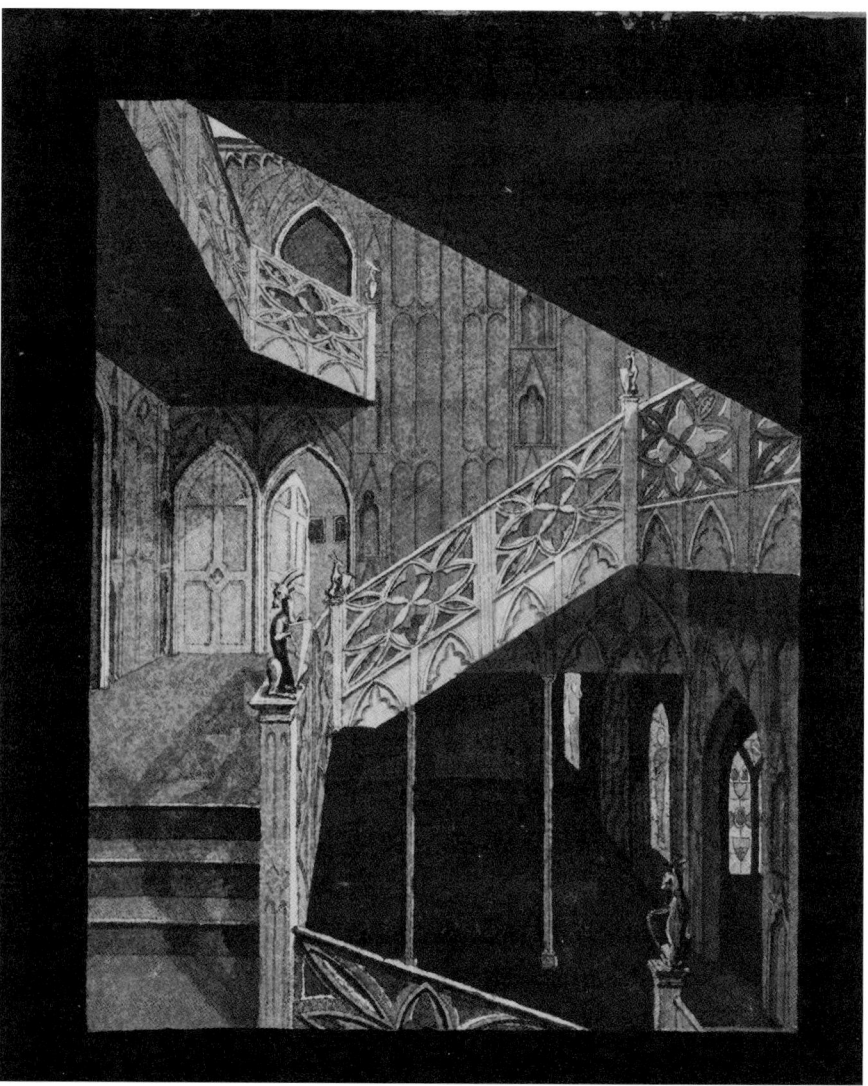

FIGURE 5.2 Perspective of the hall and staircase at Strawberry Hill, R. Bentley. Courtesy of the Lewis Walpole Library, Yale University.

Throughout the Hall, Staircase and Great Parlour the extensive use of a sober stone-colour paint produced a pervasive dark grey tone intended to 'reject rather than reflect light',[7] such little as percolates down through the quatrefoil openings in the cells of the staircase vault, or glimmers from the single candle of the black-japanned 'lanthorn'. In a letter to his friend Horace Mann (British envoy to the Court of Tuscany) of April 1753, Walpole wrote of his 'satisfaction in imprinting the gloomth of abbeys and cathedrals on one's house'.[8] The term 'gloomth' as coined here by Walpole has its background in Addison's theory of association, as encountered in the preceding two chapters. In a document explaining the experiential *Effects at Strawberry Hill* (1772) Walpole explains how 'great effects may be produced by the disposition of a House, & by studying lights and shades, and by attending to a harmony of colours. I have practised all these rules in my house at Strawberry Hill'.[9] Appealing again to the themes of abbey and hermitage, he opines elsewhere that 'gloom and well applied obscurity are better friends to devotion than wealth! A dark landscape, savage with rocks and precipices, by Salvator Rosa, may be preferred to a serene sunshine of Claude'.[10]

Later, more serious Gothic Revivalists would mock the dubious immateriality of Strawberry Hill, with its papier-mâché fan-vaulted gallery, or these staircase balustrades painted to imitate stone. But one surprise in mounting the stair – as it cleverly shuffles between the levels of the old hall and the new northern extensions – is that the most solid-seeming thing, in fact, is that 'gothic paper' from Prince Arthur's chantry tomb in Worcester. Walpole wrote to a friend to 'imagine the walls covered with...paper painted in perspective to represent Gothic fretwork'.[11] His paper-stainer's skilful use of half-lights and bold shadows gives – in *trompe l'oeil* 'gloomth' – the convincing effect of the dark niches, well-modelled traceries and finials of medieval tombs, in a manner that adumbrates the archaeological approach of nineteenth-century Gothicists.

The dark stone greyness of the stair was also intended to approximate the gravitas of an external courtyard, so making the first real interior that the visitor would encounter on the first floor the Blue Breakfast Room: in the first phase of remodelling Walpole formed this space with a bay window, over the Little Parlour below, to make the most of its pastoral view towards the River Thames, as it curved away to the south-east. To his correspondent Thomas Mann, in 1753, Walpole described this as:

The room where we always live, hung with blue and white paper...and with a bow window commanding the prospect, and gloomed with limes that shade half each window, already darkened with painted glass in chiaroscuro, set in deep blue glass.[12]

Notwithstanding the intense blue colouring of this domestic space – in contrast to the greyness of the 'external' stair approach – there remains a noteworthy stress here, in the cumulative impact of the shading limes, the deep-toned walls and the dark-painted glass, on 'gloomth' as the pervading mood associated with this place of private retreat and contemplation.

Ruinenlust

At the 1753 stage, Walpole thought the hall and staircase 'the most particular and chief beauty of the castle',[13] its balustrade inspired by the library staircase of Rouen Cathedral, its lanthorn, and chantry 'gothic paper' were all designed by Richard Bentley, a significant member of the 'Committee' who advised Walpole on the conception and taste of his evolving 'castle'. As here, Bentley made a more intense and atmospheric contribution to the interiors, furniture and decoration than the antiquarian John Chute, who was also important in shaping much of the early building; other friends who played a role included the major poet Thomas Gray (1716–71).

As an able illustrator Bentley also collaborated with Gray in providing the images to the 1753 edition of the poet's *Elegy Written in a Country Churchyard*. Bentley's *Frontispiece* conflates many of the themes under scrutiny here: gloomth; the fascination with Gothic ruins and monastic retreat; and the melancholic 'graveyard school' of literature with its excess of nocturnal associations, its 'tolling bells, night falling, owls hooting, the incarceration of the grave and the despair of forgotten and unfulfilled dreams' (Figure 5.3).[14] A ruined Gothic archway to the country churchyard has the resting-place of Gray's 'mute inglorious Milton' as centrepiece. With one foot poised on the lower kerb of the grave, a graceful youth leans on his fashionable cane, intimating the mortality he shares with his humble forbear, as the declining sun casts his shadow the length of the burial. From behind the gravestone his companion points out the famous 'Epitaph' with which Gray ends his *Elegy* to that 'Youth to Fortune and to Fame unknown' whom Melancholy had 'mark'd...for her own'. Half of the arch's architecture survives as a fragment, displaying the attenuated, decorative Gothic[k] of Strawberry Hill; its meagre shafts and ribs gain some relief from the strong shadows cast by the late evening sun. Half the arch is just the structural carcase of brick, exposing the tectonic thinness of the other half; mantled above in foliage and below in a cornucopia of country ware and fruits – tools, a barrel, baskets and sheaves. Bentley's plate synthesizes many aspects of that craving for ruins, as has been examined around Piranesi (one of its key originators) in the context of Soanes's Sublime (see Chapter 4); that passion the Germans called *Ruinenlust* in the term recast by Rose Macaulay in her *Pleasure of Ruins* (1953).[15]

We now travel westwards from Twickenham – initially to the ruins of Tintern Abbey on the River Wye, Wales – to follow after the shadows of gloomth in the language of the 'Picturesque'. This new aesthetic category, between Burke's Beautiful and the Sublime, was codified there by William

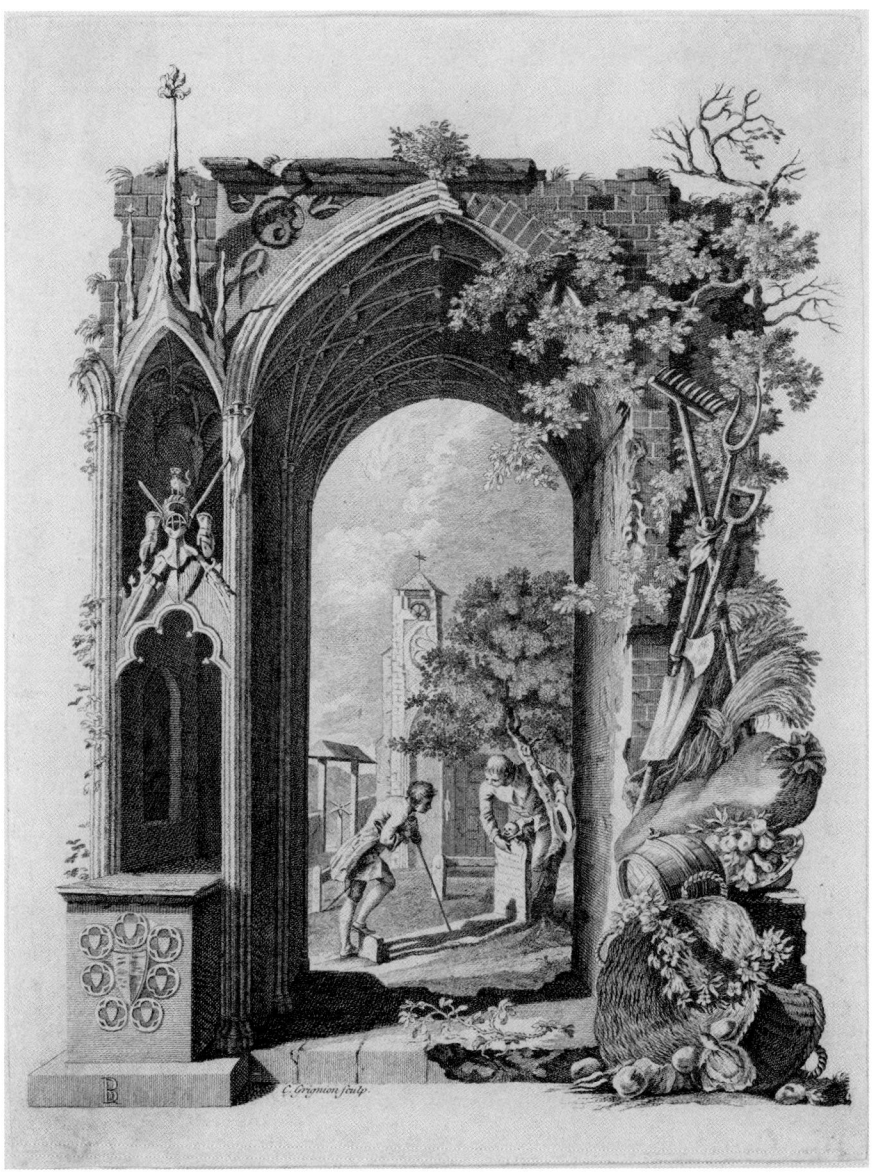

FIGURE 5.3 Frontispiece to *Elegy Written in a Country Church-yard*, R. Bentley, 1753. Courtesy of the Lewis Walpole Library, Yale University.

Gilpin, 'the venerable founder and master of the Picturesque School',[16] in his first tour-book *Observations on the River Wye* (1782). Founded in 1131 for monks of the Cistercian order, Tintern Abbey has become one of the most iconic monastic ruins in the world. As a sight it was a climactic moment of architectural poetry for travellers, as their boats followed the Wye southward to its junction with the River Severn, on a tour which had already been popular for around a quarter of a century before Gilpin's own epoch-making journey. In his *Observations* Gilpin proposed a 'new object' of travel, that of 'examining the face of a country *by the rules of picturesque beauty*'.[17] Many travellers would embark at Ross-on-Wye, just above the point where the river leaves its meanders across the broad Herefordshire plain, to loop dramatically through a succession of deeply incised valleys and gorges all the way down to Chepstow.[18] Soon they would navigate one of the Wye's 'boldest sweeps'[19] around the first great sight of Goodrich Castle on its brownstone bluff, and pass the limestone promontories at Symonds Yat; then, at the iron forge at New Weir, the Picturesque translates suddenly to the industrial Sublime. Here, in his *Observations on Modern Gardening* (1770), Thomas Whateley paints a scene of gloomy darkness, fusing the works of man and nature, and antedating the spectacles of Philip Jacques de Loutherbourg's *Eidophusikon* and his famous painting of the forges of *Coalbrookdale by Night* (1801):

> It is a chasm between two high ranges of hill, which rise almost perpendicular from the water; the rocks on the sides are mostly heavy masses: large trees frequently force their way amongst them; and many of them stand far back in the covert, where their natural dusky hue is deepened by the shadow which overhangs them. The river too, as it retires, loses itself in woods which close immediately above, then rise thick and high, and darken the water. In the midst of all this gloom is an iron forge, covered with a black cloud of smoak, and surrounded by half burned ore, with coal and with cinders.[20]

After some opening out of the landscape past Monmouth, the tourists' boat would re-enter deep sinous valleys, cut now through sandstone, to arrive at the reaches of Tintern, 'esteemed, with its appendages, the most beautiful and picturesque view on the river'.[21] At Tintern Richard Humphreys finds the following 'defining passage which best encapsulates Gilpin's general outlook'[22]:

> A more pleasing retreat could not easily be found. The woods and glades intermixed; the winding of the river; the variety of the ground; the splendid ruin, contrasted with the objects of nature; and the elegant line formed by the summits of the hills which include the whole, make all together a very enchanting piece of scenery. Every thing around bears an air so calm and tranquil, so sequestered from the commerce of life, that it is easy to conceive, a man of warm imagination, in monkish times, might have been allured by such a scene to become an inhabitant of it.[23]

Once again, the key to the 'enchantment' is the melancholy image of monastic withdrawal. Irritatingly, Nature often failed to live up to

Picturesque expectations and had to be 'improved' by the artist or landscape architect. But, for Gilpin, the attraction of the Wye was that every turn of its majestic sinuous course invariably offered 'the most perfect river-views...composed of four grand parts: the area, which is the river itself; the two *side-screens*, which are the opposite banks, and lead the perspective; and the *front-screen*, which points out the winding of the river'.[24] Struggling to find an illustrative process that captured the mood of his pen and wash drawings, Gilpin was finally satisfied with the aquatinting of the second edition.[25] In a letter of 1782, he commended 'the process of working in aqua-tinta' as 'a very beautiful mode of multiplying drawings; [it] certainly comes nearer than any other to the softness of the pencil [i.e. brush]. It may indeed literally be called *drawing*; as it washes in the shades'.[26] The oval format and deep shades of Gilpin's aquatints perhaps literally reflect the use of the darkened convex mirror as an aid to drawing; known as the Claude Mirror (after the artist), this device was available in a number of shapes, including the oval.[27] The emotional tenor of the self-immolating hermit pervades Gilpin's image of Tintern, as it does his description (Figure 5.4). As in many of his *Observations on the River Wye*, Gilpin's *side-screens* slide in spookily, enfolding, occluding and pulling down the eye to a humble and imbosked station at water level. In *The Search for the Picturesque*, Michael Andrews underscores the 'anti-georgic' nature of the Picturesque eye which rejects the elevated 'prospect' of the preceding optimistic age.[28] Instead of the looking-forward that 'prospect' means, there is a looking-back to the wildness preceding the elegant country seats, together with an iconoclastic urge to defile the beauty of elegant classical architecture. Here, maintains Gilpin, 'should we wish to give it picturesque beauty, we must beat down

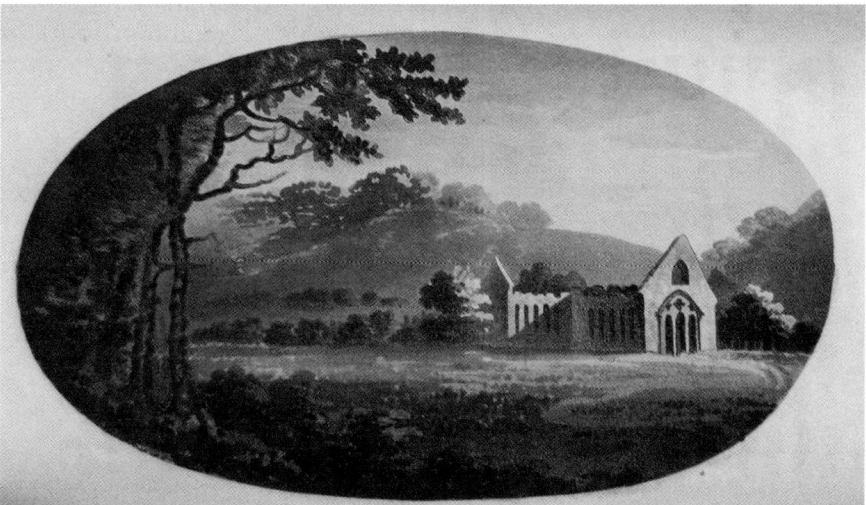

FIGURE 5.4 View of Tintern Abbey from Gilpin, *Observations on the River Wye*.

one half of it, deface the other, and throw the mutilated members around in heaps. In short, from a *smooth* building we must turn it into a *rough* ruin'.[29] This is exactly what the misfortunes of time have exacted on Soane's once-elegant Piercefield mansion overlooking the Wye.

Judged from the angle of environmental behaviour, we saw such enclosed and dark places of concealment, nesting and security as a fundamental human need; what Appleton called the *refuge*, in contrast to those extended areas of 'information-laden shadows', where we can hunt and forage, he named the *prospect* (Chapter 2).[30] In *The Experience of Landscape* (wherein he defines his *refuge-prospect* idea), Appleton examines the contrast Richard Payne Knight illustrates in his didactic poem 'The Landscape' (1794) between a park in the manner of 'Capability' Brown and one transformed according to Picturesque principles: 'The panoramic basis of the "Brown" design is narrowed in the "picturesque" version into a more vistal form which allows the refuge symbols to obtrude more effectively and introduces something of a *coulisse* effect' – the *coulisse* is a stage side-screen, akin to Gilpin's natural *side-screens*. Consequently, 'the massing of the vegetation in the foreground converts an exposed, unprotected vantage-point into a little haven of seclusion from which the prospect may be observed'.[31] In Knight's Picturesque view the architecture of the mansion has also transmogrified, from a Palladian box, into an irregular complex of shady recesses, and outward-looking bays, into a composition that allows for the interpenetration of dwelling and landscape. Even so, a lot of this is foreshadowed in the earlier emblematic 'poetic garden' of the first half of the eighteenth century. Writing in the 1730s Robert Morris already sought a garden composed 'of agreeable *Disorder*, or *artful Confusion*'.[32] And in Ronald Paulson's examination of *Emblem and Expression* in this period, the meanings disclosed by 'the effect of the different textures and shades of green', in a 'poetic garden' such as those of Castle Howard or Stowe, 'was essentially one of chiaroscuro, to define by shadow and light, but not to distract by colour'.[33] Along with prospects, landscapes of this earlier era also offered a multitude of juxtaposed, paratactic and intimate experiences where the 'general feeling is of *going down into*, of *being in* and *moving through*'.[34] Since his visit to the Wye during a tour of July 1798, its most renowned visitor has been William Wordsworth. His "Lines Written a Few Miles Above Tintern Abbey" is also haunted by the wildness of the 'deep and gloomy wood', by an instinct for shadowed seclusion, and by an empathy with the 'hermit's cave, where by his fire/The hermit sits alone'.

When true darkness descended at Tintern, Wye voyagers deepened their experiences of picturesque gloom, spiced with frissons of Sublime terror, by entering the ruins to view them by moonlight or torchlight, a *lumière* without the *son* (whereas at Piercefield they could have the *son* without the former, as we shall hear). Thus, they maintained the nocturnal traditions of *ruinenlust* where sensing the Colosseum's decay, by the shadows of moon or torch, was part of the tourist round at Rome.[35] In P. Van Lerberghe's watercolour of Tintern by moonlight (c.1801–5), servants brandish torches among the pillars and up in the heights of the abbey's triforium, provoking awe in the onlookers at this spectacle of flaring brands among the moon shadows (Figure 5.5).[36] Walpole's *The Castle of Otranto* had set in train a linking in the imagination of picturesque gloom and 'psychological terror

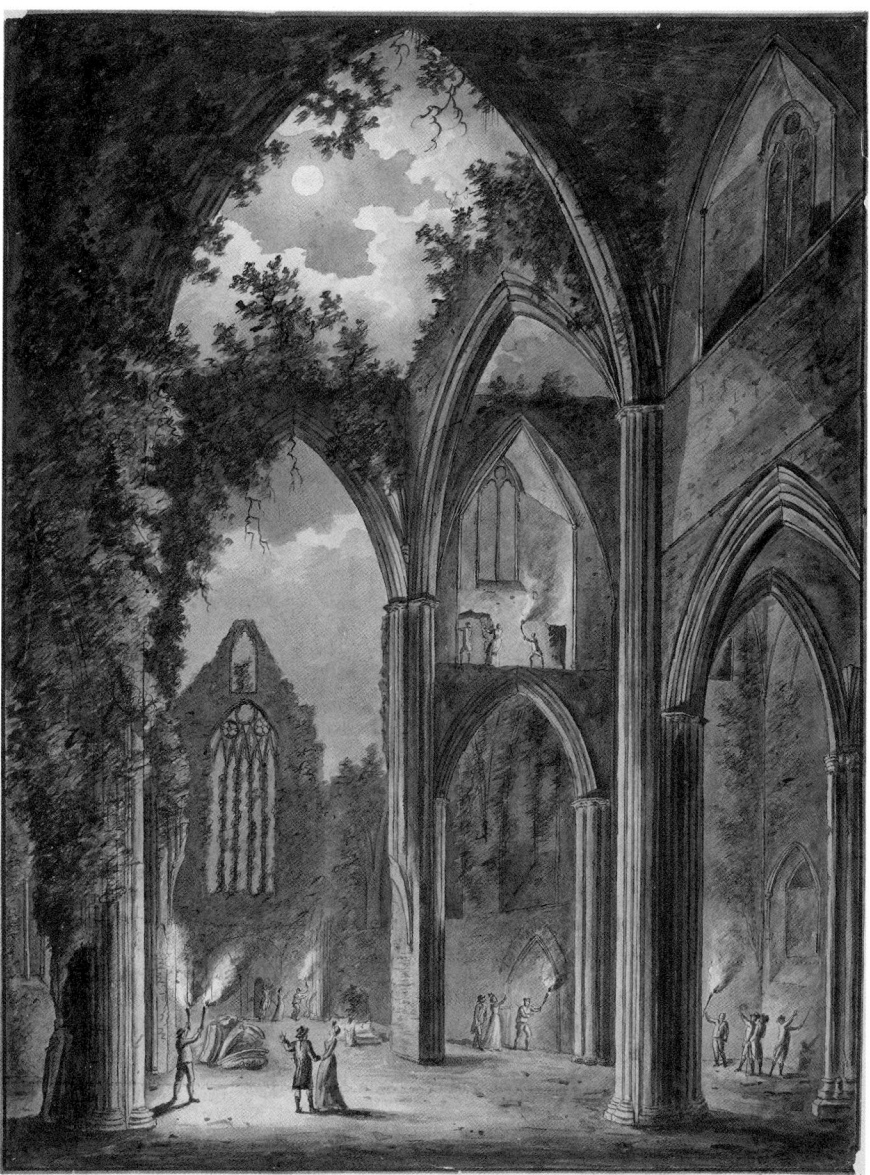

FIGURE 5.5 P. Van Lerberghe, *Interior View of Tintern Abbey, in South Wales*, c. 1801–5. © The British Library Board, Maps K. Top.31.16.f.

with architectural space'.³⁷ Tintern's nocturnal spectacles concretized the imaginings of this Gothic writing, or the excitements of those early transparencies (1800) illustrating the novel which were designed to be viewed in the dark against a flickering candlelight. One such transparency shows Isabella's desperate retreat into 'the lower part of the castle [which] was hollowed into several intricate cloysters' (Figure 5.6)³⁸:

> An awful silence reigned throughout those subterraneous regions, except now and then some blasts of wind that shook the doors she had passed, and which grating on the rusty hinges were re-echoed through that long labyrinth of darkness. Every murmur struck her with new terror.³⁹

In linkage to the last chapter, there are many passages 'leading from the *Carceri* into the strangely echoing vaults of the English Gothic novels'.⁴⁰ Walpole was enthused by 'the sublime dream of Piranesi…[who] has imagined scenes that would startle geometry, and exhaust the Indies to realize. He piles palaces on bridges, and temples on palaces, and scales Heaven with mountains of edifices'.⁴¹ These visions contributed to the architectonics of the *Castle of Otranto* and perhaps its originating dream, and are known to have haunted the ruins of Istakar in William Beckfords's *Vathek*; as Charles Rosen says in his speculations on ruins and the fragment: 'In the ruins of Piranesi…architecture begins to recede into the landscape, to merge with the process of growth'.⁴²

The 'situation of Persfield is noble'

In his *Historical Tour in Monmouthshire* (1801), the experienced traveller William Coxe cautions the visitor that 'from Tintern the Wy [*sic*] assumes the character of a tide river; the water is no longer transparent, and except at high tide the banks are covered with slime'. He urges the traveller to 'seize the moment in which [the tide] begins to ebb, when the height and fullness of the river, aided by the picturesque scenery, compensates for the discoloured appearance of the stream'.⁴³ And in farewell to Tintern he muses on how 'the impressions of pleasing melancholy, which I received from contemplating the venerable ruins, were increased by the deep solitude and romantic grandeur of the woods and rocks overhanging the river, and heightened by the gloom of a clouded atmosphere'.⁴⁴ Gilpin, in continuing his descent of the river after Tintern, entered these tidal reaches of the lower Wye to view Valentine Morris's (1727–89) famous 'improvements at Persfield'. Between 1752 and 1772, Morris had made a romantic walk that clings to the western edge of the gorge between Wyndcliffe and Chepstow, with its cliff-top castle (Figure 5.7).⁴⁵ Gilpin agrees that the elevated 'situation of Persfield is noble' but insists that 'we cannot, however, call these views picturesque. They are

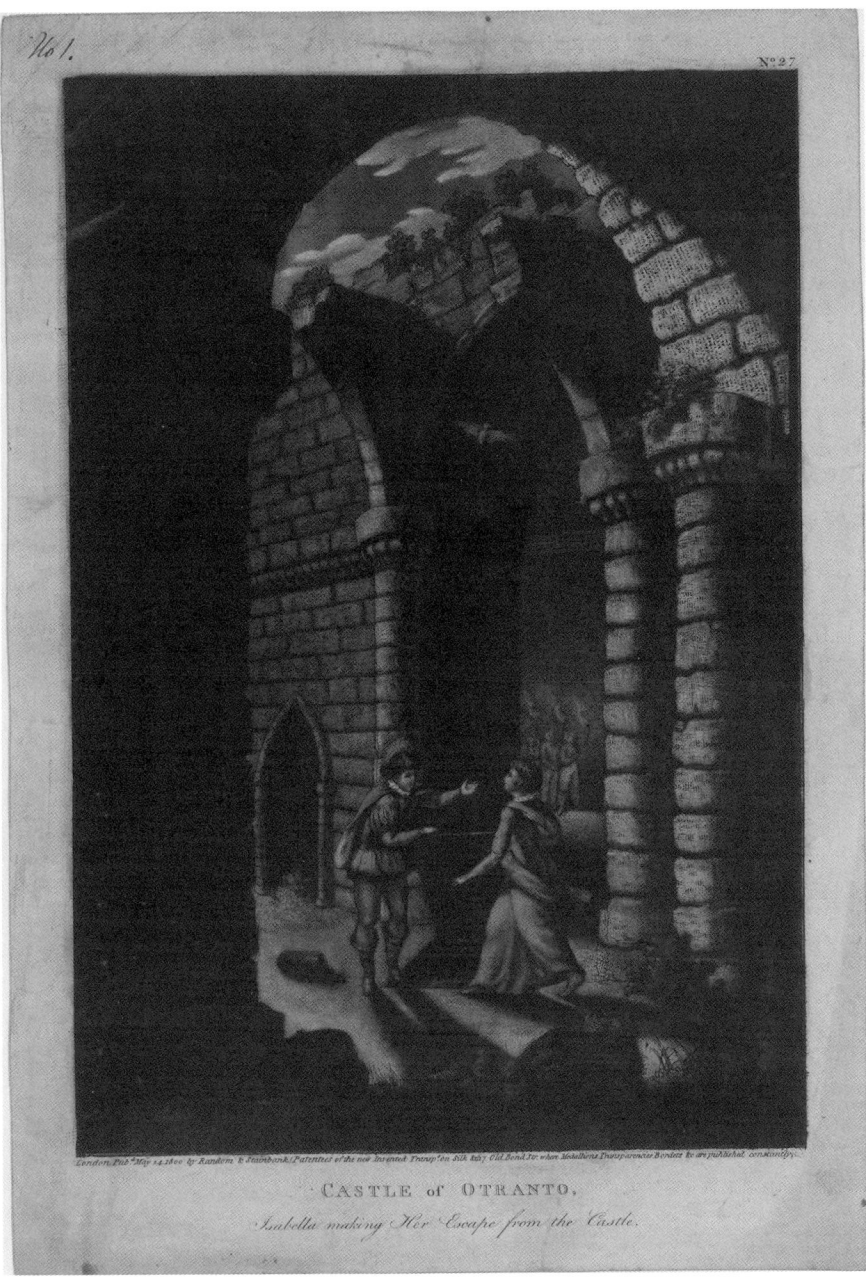

FIGURE 5.6 *Castle of Otranto, Isabella making her Escape from the Castle*, 1800, transparency, etching and mezzotint with some hand-colouring. © The Trustees of the British Museum.

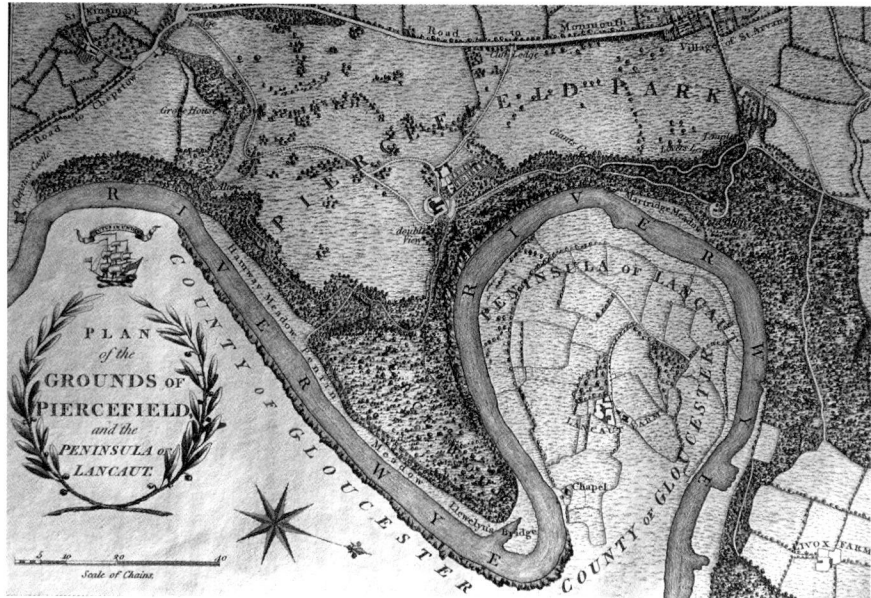

FIGURE 5.7 *Plan of the Grounds of Piercefield and the Peninsular of Lancaut*, from William Coxe, *An Historical Tour in Monmouthshire*, 1801.

either presented from too high a point, or they have little to mark them as characteristic; or they do not fall into such composition as would appear to advantage on a canvas'.[46] Though intended as 'Picturesque', for Gilpin they unfortunately present an excess of elevated prospect conditions, lacking envelopment, side-screens and shadowy imboskement. Gilpin's complaints notwithstanding, Piercefield is a remarkable example of a landscape conceived in the picturesque mode. Valentine Morris was the son of Colonel Valentine Morris, whose wealth was based on slaves and cattle from his Antigua plantations; in itself, the 'black gold' of slavery is the darkly imbosked basis to the wealth that produced many of these picturesque landscapes.[47] Working opportunistically with the superlative givens of his estate's situation, Morris provided 'a linked series of contrasting views, some expansive, some no more than peeps, of the magnificent natural scenery of this stretch of the Wye valley'[48]; it became an immediate tourist attraction, and an integral part of the Wye tour. Coxe lyrically evokes 'the dizzy heights and abrupt precipices... softened by woods' of these parts, whose darkly wild naturalisms are no 'meagre plantations placed by art, but a tract of forests scattered by the hand of nature'[49]:

> In one place they expand into open groves of large oak, elm, and beech; in another form a shade of timber trees, copses, and underwood, hiding all external objects, and wholly impervious to the rays of the sun... bringing to recollection Milton's description of the border

Of Eden, where delicious paradise,
Now nearer, crowns with her inclosure green,
As with a rural mound, the champain head
Of a steep wilderness, whose hairy sides
With thicket overgrown, grotesque and wild,
Access deny'd, and over head up grew
Insuperable height of loftiest shade.[50]

Architecture has receded into the landscape in earnest at Piercefield, which has indeed sunk under the weight of vegetation; once open prospects are now obscured by trees; buildings stand in ruin that were never intended as such (as is the case with the central Soane mansion), though there has also been some recent effective conservation and clearing. This invasion of nature has only intensified the 'pleasure of ruins' in a landscape that must now be entered in the spirit of the explorer and the archaeologist. The entry point for the main walk began from the north, through a point in the park wall on the Chepstow-Monmouth road, below the highpoint of the Wyndcliffe. Passing a number of viewing stations – such as the 'Temple' and the 'Lover's Leap' – visitors soon arrived at one of the Walk's most dramatic moments in its intense fusion of envelopment and release, the 'Giant's Cave'. Descending a steep path from the north they entered the blackness of the cave through a fissure; the cave is actually artificially formed as a tunnel, some thirteen metres long, cut through a natural bluff with its interior hollowed out (Figure 5.8).[51] In 1801 Charles Heath described it as:

> a most romantic cavern...hewn out of the solid rock, but its attractions are of secondary moment, when compared with the *View* presented before the entrance. The bold point of rock on which we stand rises perpendicular from the edge of the river, which makes another of its fine sweeps, shewing, to great advantage, on the right, the whole range of the Apostles Rocks, its left screen rising in grandeur, by presenting the correspondent Windcliff.[52]

The 'awe of the unwary traveller' was intensified by a 'Herculean figure' lodged in a cavity on top of the rock 'who held in his hands an enormous stone, which with full force he [appeared] about to hurl on the head of the passing visitor, as the latter surveyed his Throne'.[53] Here was *son* to match the aforementioned *lumière* of Tintern as 'some swivel guns were here placed, which, when discharged; produced a surprising echo in these rocky regions'. Though it is a commonplace *Observation* to liken rocks to ruins, for Whateley (1770) no ruin was ever equal to the enormity of the rock-faces hereabouts, appearing the 'remains of a city',[54] while the woods 'all of a dark colour...concur with the rocks to render the scenes of Persfield romantic'.[55] Trusting that Morris's walks posed no real threats, gentlefolk in pursuit of romantic adventure enjoyed that thrill in the control of danger

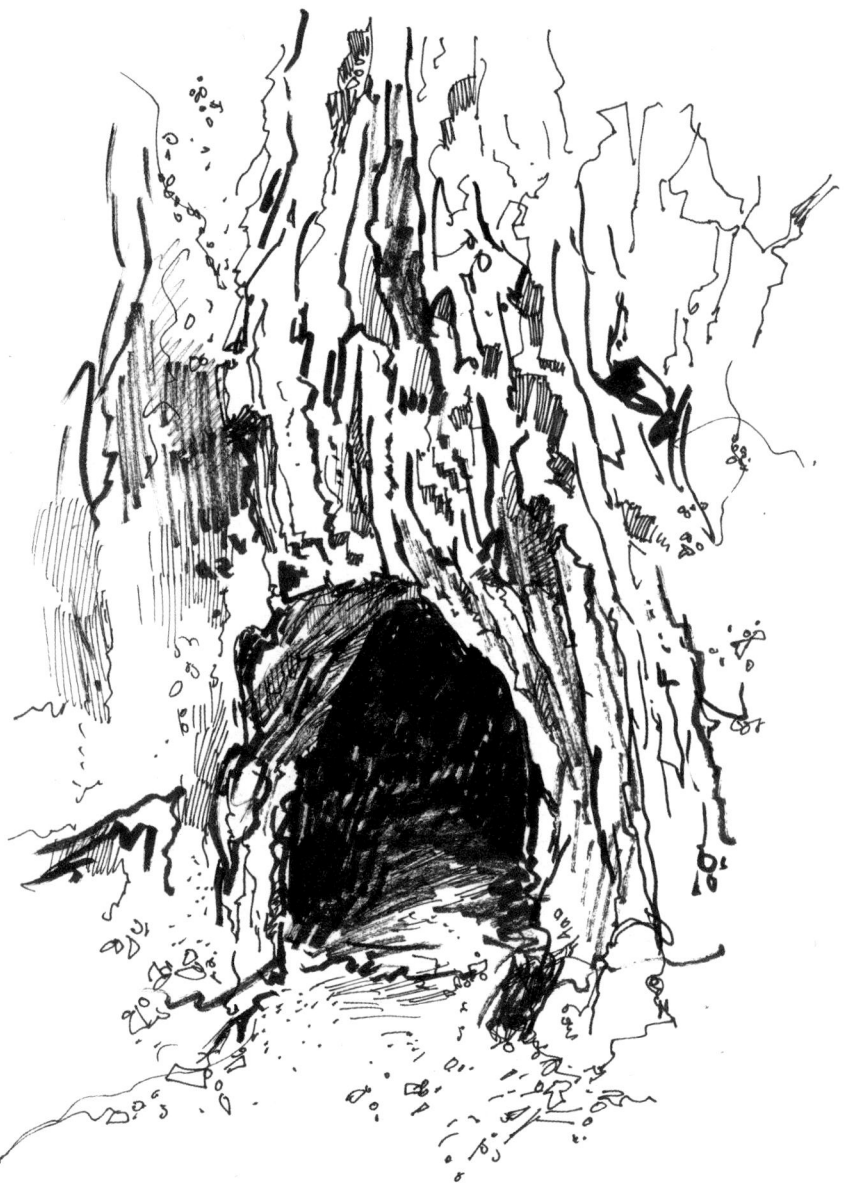

FIGURE 5.8 Entrance to Giant's Cave, Piercefield, from the Wye viewpoint. Drawing, Stephen Kite.

which Appleton describes as 'hazard'. Shadow–light sequences are integral to the enticement to hazard as in the cavern experience vividly painted by Heath: the inducement into the refuge darkness of the cleft in the rock, followed by the rebirth through a low vaginal opening into exhilarating light and prospect, but also to perils of a different kind, the fear of falling from the 'bold point of rock on which we stand' rising sheer from the Wye far below.[56] Says Appleton: 'Just as light is conducive to seeing, so deprivation of light is conducive to not being seen.... There is therefore a very direct functional association between darkness and concealment and a *prime facie* case for symbolically equating darkness with the refuge as light with the prospect.'[57]

As shadowed refuge places, the cave, the grotto and the hermitage are often imbricated in conceptions of the Picturesque landscape. Piercefield had The Grotto as well as the Giant's Cave, which the visitor reached by walking south-east, following the Wye's curve around the Lancaut Peninsular, and passing a 'Druid's Circle', and other lookouts, such as the Double View. Coxe again underlines the shrouded character of 'the walk which is carried through a thick mantle of forests, with occasional openings, which seem not the result of art or design, but the effect of chance or nature'; he quotes from James Thomson's *The Seasons*:

... [This] bowr'y walk
Of covert close, where scarce a speck of day
Falls on the lengthen'd gloom[58]

Just the infrastructure remains of The Grotto's small hemi-cycle (a metre high and three metres in diameter) embedded in the earthworks of an Iron Age fort; its seat has long gone, and its sparkly 'lining of pebbles, "alabastrine stone" or spar, copper ore and iron slag' must be imagined (Figure 5.9).[59] In Heath's account 'among the seats in these enchanting regions', this was the '*most charming* of them all':

A point of view exquisitely beautiful. It is a small cave in the rock, stuck with stones of various kinds; copper and iron cinders &c. You look down from the seat in it immediately down a steep slope on to a hollow of wood, bounded in front by the craggy rocks, which seem to part you from the [River] Severn in breaks; beyond which is seen a large part of Gloucestershire ... forming a landscape as truly picturesque as any in the world.[60]

With affinities to Soane's crepuscular Breakfast Room (Chapter 4), The Grotto makes a peculiarly specular and glinting kind of shadow cave. Two other cases are worth pointing out here, one antecedent and one a modern realization in a picturesque landscape. For the immediate ancestor we must return to Twickenham and to the famous Grotto Alexander Pope created

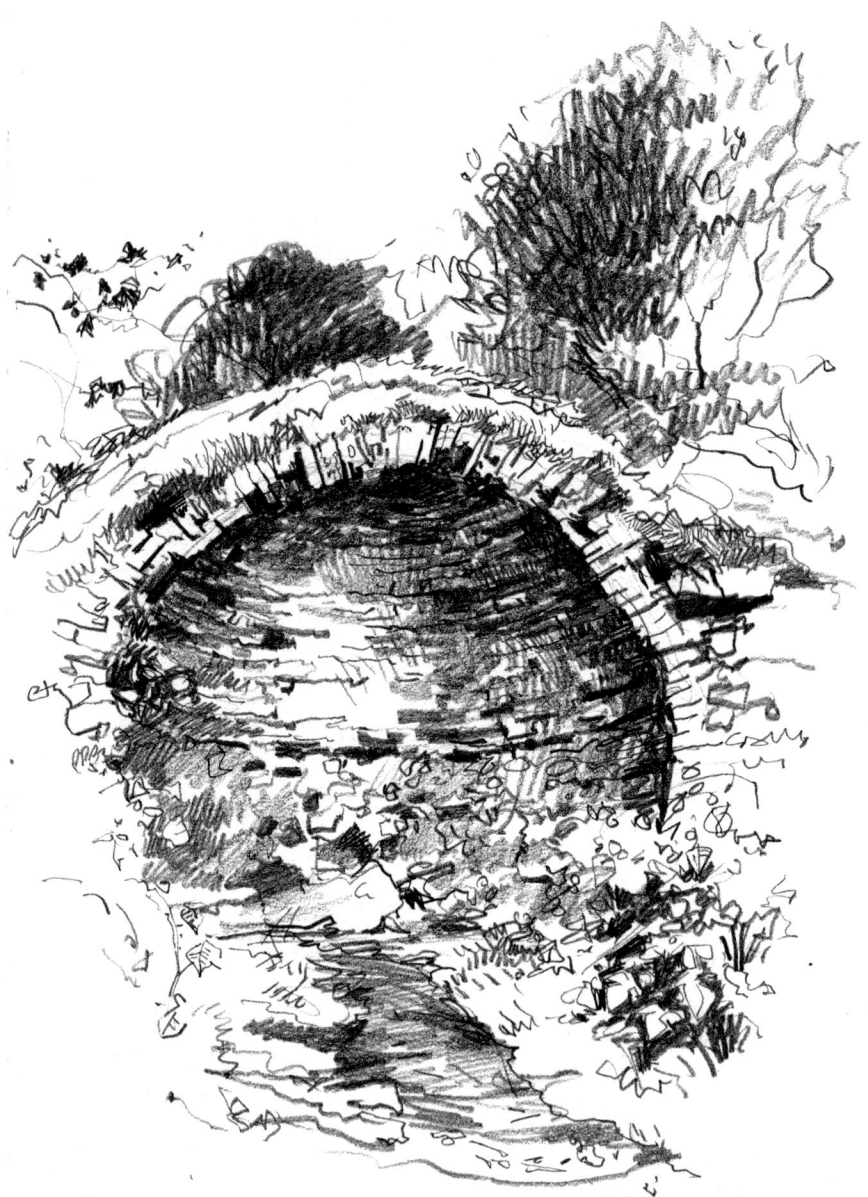

FIGURE 5.9 Ruins of The Grotto, Piercefield. Drawing, Stephen Kite.

at his villa and landscape there, the earliest account of which is found in a letter written by the poet in June 1725:

> From the River *Thames* you see thro' my Arch up a Walk of the Wilderness to a kind of open Temple, wholly compos'd of Shells in the Rustic Manner.... When you shut the Doors of the Grotto, it becomes on the instant, from a luminous room, a *Camera obscura*; on the Walls of which the objects of the River, Hills, Woods, and Boats, are forming a moving picture in their visible Radiations.... It is finished with Shells interspersed with Pieces of Looking-glass in angular forms.[61]

There are distinct analogies here to Locke's 'dark room' of the understanding, to Plato's cave and to the Cave of Poetry and Cave of Truth of Pope's own verses.

A kind of modern grotto has resulted from the relocation (in the eighteenth-century landscape of Yorkshire Sculpture Park, near Wakefield) of Roger Hiorns's crystalline *Seizure* (2008/13), protected within the glooms of a classically reticent precast concrete enclosure provided by Adam Khan architects. *Seizure* originated far from the aristocratic setting of the Park within a flat on a failed 1960s housing estate in south London.[62] Artist Hiorns tanked and filled the apartment with 75,000 litres of copper sulphate, yielding after two weeks a phenomenal scintillating surface of blue crystals. In conceiving the enclosure, for the transposed installation, architect Khan sought 'a peculiar quality of filtering and amplifying. The darkness, the thin slivers of light and air through quite massive stones'.[63] He thinks *Seizure* still 'has the potential to be just as critical in its new situation. It has that potential for the sublime here – entailing menace and fear and awe of nature as well as the political critique that the original eighteenth-century grottos had'.[64]

Seeing through a Glass, darkly

Continuing on from The Grotto, the walks ended with two more viewpoints: the now-enshrouded 'Platform' and the still-climactic prospect from the 'The Alcove', before the descent to the inns at Chepstow. From The Alcove, Piercefield captures the castle into its landscape as an immediate presence, so near says Whateley, that 'little circumstances in it may be discerned', and praising it as 'a noble ruin of great extent; advanced to the very edge of a perpendicular rock, and so immediately rivetted into it, that from the top of the battlements, down to the river seems but one precipice'.[65] While 'on the left', in Heath's account, 'is seen a fine bend of the river, the opposite shore of wild wood, with the rock appearing at places in rising cliffs, and further on to the termination of the view that way, the vast wall of rocks at Lancaut, which are here seen in length and have a stupendous effect'.[66]

Many tourists carried the aforementioned small black convex mirror known as the Claude Glass, as an aid to sketching, or to momentarily capture these ideally presented viewpoints, as sightseers now do more permanently with a camera (Figure 5.10). As you stood with your back to the view, with your Black Mirror angled over your shoulder, the vastness of the scene would be enframed, its dazzle gathered into a subdued tonality,

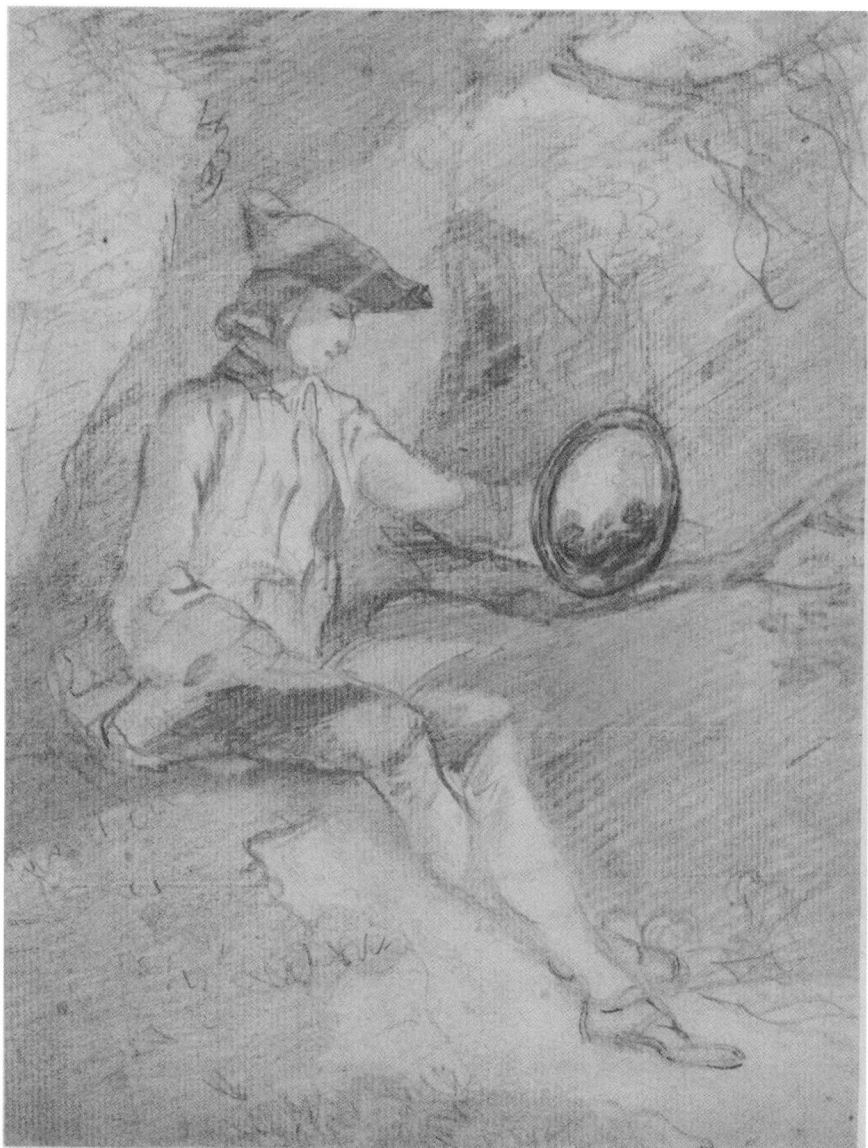

FIGURE 5.10 Study of a man sketching, holding a Claude Glass, drawing by Thomas Gainsborough, c. 1750–55. © The Trustees of the British Museum.

even as the distortion of the convex surface emphasized the foreground and its side-screens.⁶⁷ Thus, in his study of *The Claude Glass*, Arnaud Maillet calls it an 'idealizing mirror' as an instrument that enabled the slippage in Picturesque culture, between the construction of nature in the image of the landscape painter, and in seeing landscape as illustrable by painting. The mirror allowed the hunter of prospects, from viewing station to viewing station – such as those of the Cave, Grotto and Alcove at Piercefield – to 'reduce local colours to a scale of tonal gradations, from mellow brown to a pale blue, in order to give an impression of depth'; to find 'foregrounds with a warm brown tone and the distant backgrounds with the light silvery blue of the landscape painters'; and to counter the 'rawness of natural light [which] constituted…an anti-aesthetic effect, disagreeable to the very organ of sight, sometimes cruel to the point of engendering ocular maladies or madness'.⁶⁸ In his *The Practice of Drawing and Painting from Nature, in Water Colours* (1823), the artist Francis Nicholson explains how

> considerable help may be derived from the use of the blackened convex mirror, in discovering what is proper for the pencil, as it takes in as much, or nearly so, as should come into the picture: many subjects, particularly those that are near and strongly illuminated, will by this means be found to possess great beauty, and such picturesque effect, as a person of little practice would overlook. The effects of objects seen in the mirror will be like that in the camera obscura.⁶⁹

As for Gilpin, even as a child he sought this 'evening grey' of a unifying dull tint: 'I used to make little drawings, I was never pleased with them till I had given them a brownish tint. And, as I knew no other method, I used to hold them over smoke till they had assumed such a tint as satisfied my eye.'⁷⁰ For Maillet this is a smoking, not merely of an image, but of 'the rawness of this flesh, the cruelty of the real'.⁷¹

The landscape could also be viewed through coloured filters, confusingly also called the 'Claude Lorraine Glass', making it sometimes hard in texts to know whether the author is referring to a filter, or a mirror type, of instrument. One such 'Glass' was advertised as consisting of 'a variety of different coloured glasses, about one inch in diameter, mounted in horn frame and turning on one centre, for producing a great variety of colours….; it also will be found both pleasing and useful for viewing eclipses, clouds, landscapes, &c'.⁷² With a toy like this the tourist could change the scene in a moment; make a glowing golden Claude afternoon, a sunrise or sunset rose, or a moonlight gloomth. The ground of Gilpin's aquatints of Tintern is the pale pink of evening, while that of Chepstow Castle and bridge has a pronounced sunset intensity.

The sunset of the sensibility of Gothic 'gloomth' itself has been linked to the third and final collapse of William Beckford's Fonthill Abbey in 1825, its soaring 300 feet tower barely more substantial than the wallpaper on

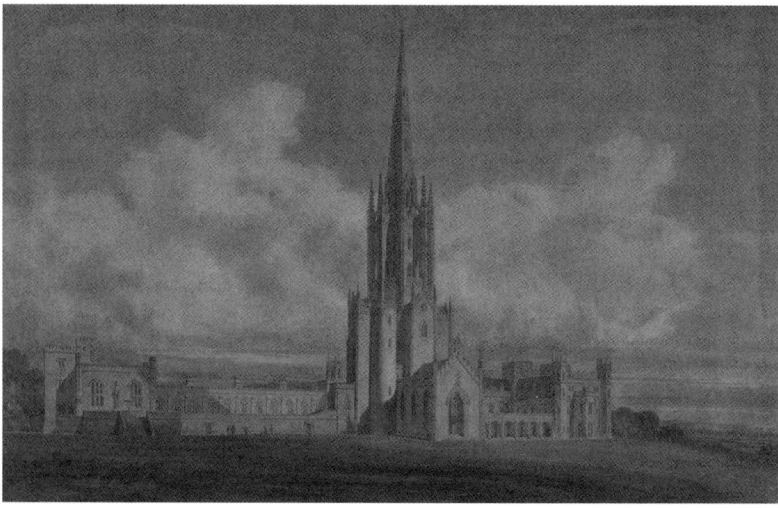

FIGURE 5.11 James Wyatt, *Projected Design for Fonthill Abbey, Wiltshire*, watercolour possibly by J. M. W. Turner, 1798. Yale Center for British Art, Paul Mellon Collection.

Walpole's staircase (Figure 5.11). Despite the stage-set aspect of Gothic[k] architecture, and regardless of all the genteel fussing with mirrors and lenses at the edge of well-protected precipices, the fact remains that the shadows we have been dealing with here are real and persistent emanations of the psyche, as demonstrated by the vital cultural ramifications of the Gothic genre to our own day. But shadow-making in architecture needed to become more tectonic, more ethical, more realistic and more political. In short, it needed the impact of John Ruskin (1819–1900), wherein shadow itself becomes, yet more intensely, a subject of thought.

Notes

1 Soane, Sir John, *Description of the House and Museum on the North Side of Lincoln's Inn Fields, the Residence of Sir John Soane* (London: Privately printed by Levey, Robson and Franklyn, 1835), p. 28.
2 Soane, *Description*, p. 26.
3 Campbell, Gordon, *The Hermit in the Garden. From Imperial Rome to Ornamental Gnome* (Oxford: Oxford University Press, 2013), p. 19.
4 Quoted in Palmer, Bryan D., *Cultures of Darkness. Night Travels in the Histories of Transgression (from Medieval to Modern)* (New York: Monthly Review Press, 2000), p. 118.
5 Quoted in Chalcraft, Anna and Viscardi, Judith, *Strawberry Hill. Horace Walpole's Gothic Castle* (London: Frances Lincoln, 2007), p. 40.

6   Walpole, Horace, *Description of the Villa of Mr Horace Walpole at Strawberry-Hill Near Twickenham, Middlesex*, third edition as part of *The Works of Horatio Walpole*, London 1798 (London: Pallas Athene, 2010), p. 401.
7   Chalcraft and Viscardi, *Strawberry Hill*, p. 150.
8   Quoted in Chalcraft and Viscardi, *Strawberry Hill*, p. 13.
9   Quoted in Harney, Marion, *Place-Making for the Imagination: Horace Walpole and Strawberry Hill* (Farnham, Surrey: Ashgate, 2013), p. 160.
10 Quoted in Harney, *Place-Making for the Imagination*, p. 84.
11 Quoted in Chalcraft and Viscardi, *Strawberry Hill*, p. 35.
12 Chalcraft and Viscardi, *Strawberry Hill*, p. 53.
13 Quoted in Chalcraft and Viscardi, *Strawberry Hill*, p. 35.
14 Groom, Nick, 'Gothic Antiquity: From the Sack of Rome to *The Castle of Otranto*', in D. Townshend (ed), *Terror and Wonder: The Gothic Imagination* (London: The British Library, 2014), pp. 38–67, p. 61.
15 Dillon, Brian, *Ruin Lust. Artists' Fascination with Ruins, from Turner to the Present* (London: Tate Publishing, 2014), pp. 5, 6; Macaulay, Rose, *Roloff Beny Interprets in Photographs Pleasure of Ruins*, C. B. Smith (ed) (London: Thames and Hudson, Book Club Associates, 1977, revised ed.).
16 *Monthly Review*, quoted in Andrews, Malcolm, *The Search for the Picturesque. Landscape Aesthetics and Tourism in Britain, 1760–1800* (Aldershot: Scolar Press, 1989), p. 56.
17 Gilpin, William, *Observations on the River Wye and Several Parts of South Wales, & c. Relative Chiefly to Picturesque Beauty: Made in the Summer of the Year 1770* (London: Pallas Athene, 2005, first published 1782–3, this edition based on revised fifth edition of 1800), p. 17.
18 See 'The Lower Wye Landscape' in Peterken, Susan, *Landscapes of the Wye Tour* (Glasgow: Logaston Press, 2008), pp. 27–38.
19 Gilpin, *Observations on the River Wye*, p. 33.
20 Whateley, Thomas, *Observations on Modern Gardening* (London: T. Payne, 1770, 2nd ed), p. 109.
21 Gilpin, *Observations on the River Wye*, p. 40.
22 'Introduction' to Gilpin, *Observations on the River Wye*, p. 10.
23 Gilpin, *Observations on the River Wye*, p. 40, 42.
24 Gilpin, *Observations on the River Wye*, p. 25.
25 See Andrews, *Search for the Picturesque*, p. 86.
26 Gilpin, *Observations on the River Wye*, p. 15.
27 One such oval 'Claude Mirror' (Private Collection) was suggestively displayed next to a Gilpin aquatint in the exhibition *Sites of Inspiration, Tintern Abbey*, Chepstow Museum, May–September 2014.
28 Andrews, *Search for the Picturesque*, p. 64.
29 Quoted in Andrews, *Search for the Picturesque*, p. 58.

30 Hildenbrand, Grant, *Origins of Architectural Pleasure* (Berkeley: University of California Press, 1999), pp. 21, 22.
31 Appleton, Jay, *The Experience of Landscape* (Chichester: John Wiley, 1996, revised edition), p. 199.
32 Quoted in Paulson, Ronald, *Emblem and Expression. Meaning in English Art of the Eighteenth Century* (London: Thames and Hudson, 1975), p. 21.
33 Paulson, *Emblem and Expression*, p. 21.
34 Paulson, *Emblem and Expression*, p. 22.
35 See Oechslin, Werner, 'How the Architect Emerged from the Shadows of the Painter', in H. Binet et al. (eds), *The Secret of the Shadow. Light and Shadow in Architecture* (Berlin: Ernst Wasmuth Verlag Tübingen, 2002), pp. 78–83, p. 81.
36 See Mitchell, Julian, *The Wye Tour and Its Artists* (Little Logaston, Herefordshire: Logaston Press, 2010), p. 119.
37 Wright, Angela, 'Gothic, 1764–1820', in Townshend (ed), *Terror and Wonder: The Gothic Imagination*, pp. 68–93, p. 75.
38 Walpole, Horace, *The Castle of Otranto. A Gothic Story* (London: J. Edwards, 1791, 6th ed.), p. 26.
39 Walpole, *Castle of Otranto*, p. 26.
40 Jørgen Andersen quoted in Praz, Mario, 'Introductory Essay', in P. Fairclough (ed), *Three Gothic Novels: The Castle of Otranto* (Horace Walpole), *Vathek* (William Beckford), *Frankenstein* (Mary Shelley) (Harmondsworth, Middlesex: Penguin Books, 1968), p. 16.
41 Walpole quoted in Praz, 'Introductory Essay', pp. 16, 17.
42 Rosen, Charles, *The Romantic Generation* (Cambridge, MA: Harvard University Press, 1995), p. 93.
43 Coxe, William, *An Historical Tour in Monmouthshire Illustrated with Views by Sir R. C. Hoare, Bart.*, 2 vols. (London: T. Cadell, jun. and W. Davies, 1801), p. 355.
44 Coxe, *Historical Tour in Monmouthshire*, p. 355.
45 See Whittle, Elisabeth, '"All These Inchanting Scenes": Piercefield in the Wye Valley', *Garden History*, vol. 24, no. 1 (Summer 1996), pp. 148–61, p. 148, *passim*.
46 Gilpin, *Observations on the River Wye*, p. 46.
47 Morris had also helped to build those good turnpike roads that conveyed fashionable visitors from important centres such as Bath and Bristol, to enjoy Piercefield and the Wye; part of the infrastructure, linked to trade and the West Indies, which had shifted the cultural and economic geography of the British Isles westwards. See Perry, Victoria, 'Slavery and the Sublime: The Atlantic Trade, Landscape Aesthetics and Tourism', in M. Dresser and A. Hann (eds), *Slavery and the British Country House* (Swindon: English Heritage, 2013), pp. 98–105.
48 Whittle, 'Piercefield in the Wye Valley', p. 149.

49 Coxe, *Historical Tour in Monmouthshire*, pp. 399–400.
50 Quoted in Coxe, *Historical Tour in Monmouthshire*, p. 400.
51 See Murphy, K., *The Piercefield Walks and Associated Picturesque Landscape Features: An Archaeological Survey*, Report No. 2004/32 (Llandeilo, Carmarthenshire: Cambria Archaeology, 2005).
52 Heath, Charles, *Historical and Descriptive Accounts of the Ancient and Present State of Chepstow Castle Including Persfield* (Monmouth, NJ: C. Heath, 1801), unpaginated.
53 Heath, *Ancient and Present State of Chepstow Castle Including Persfield*, unpaginated.
54 Whateley, *Observations on Modern Gardening*, p. 238.
55 Whateley, *Observations on Modern Gardening*, p. 240.
56 See Hildenbrand on peril and hazard, *Origins of Architectural Pleasure*, pp. 55–80.
57 Appleton, *Experience of Landscape*, p. 100.
58 Coxe, *Historical Tour in Monmouthshire*, p. 401.
59 Whittle, 'Piercefield in the Wye Valley', p. 159.
60 Heath, *Ancient and Present State of Chepstow Castle Including Persfield*, unpaginated.
61 Quoted in Mack, Maynard, *The Garden and the City. Retirement and Politics in the Later Poetry of Pope 1731–1743* (Toronto and Buffalo: University of Toronto Press; London: Oxford University Press, 1969), p. 44. As a translator of Homer, Pope also came under the influence of the classical *locus amoenus*, that pleasant shaded place which 'usually consisted of a grove, a spring, sometimes a meadow, and more often than not, an overhanging rock or cave like the one inhabited by Calypso in the fifth book of the *Odyssey*', Mack, *The Garden and the City*, p. 51. Although Pope sometime styled himself 'the hermit of Twickenham', his Grotto seems to have been, not so much a retreat from the world, as a numinous stimulus to the fertility of his muse, its murmuring rills and sparkling surfaces, inducing mental states of undifferentiated access to the unconscious (see the discussion of shadows of the unconscious in Chapter 8).
62 See Roberts, Dominic, 'Seizure Enclosure: Adam Khan Architects at Yorkshire Sculpture Park', *Architecture Today*, no. 244 (January 2014), pp. 39–44.
63 Quoted in Robson, Faye (ed.), *Roger Hiorns: Seizure 2008/13* (London: Hayward Publishing, 2013), p. 32.
64 Quoted in Robson, *Roger Hiorns: Seizure 2008/13*, p. 36.
65 Whateley, *Observations on Modern Gardening*, p. 239.
66 Heath, *Ancient and Present State of Chepstow Castle Including Persfield*, unpaginated.
67 Peterken, *Landscapes of the Wye Tour*, p. 54.
68 Maillet, Arnaud, *The Claude Glass. Use and Meaning of the Black Mirror in Western Art* (New York: Zone Books, 2009), p. 139.

69 Nicholson, Francis, *The Practice of Drawing and Painting Landscape from Nature, in Water Colours* (London: John Murray, 1823, 2nd ed), pp. 21–2.
70 Maillet, *Claude Glass*, p. 112.
71 Maillet, *Claude Glass*, p. 116.
72 Maillet, *Claude Glass*, p. 33.

6

John Ruskin and Shadows of Power

In his appendix to *The Stones of Venice* on 'Romanist Modern Art', the prominent English art critic John Ruskin (1819–1900) assaulted the architecture of the Gothic Revival pioneer, Augustus Welby Pugin (1812–52), for the 'parsimony' of its 'paltry pinnacles' and 'eruption of diseased crockets' and for its 'belfry fools' caps with the mimicry of dormer windows'.[1] Elsewhere, he described Charles Barry and Pugin's new Houses of Parliament, London (1840–) as 'the absurdest and emptiest piece of filigree ... eternal foolscape in freestone'.[2] Among other things, these trenchant comments express disappointment at the lack of mass and shadow in this architecture. In *The Seven Lamps of Architecture* (1849), Ruskin made a distinction between the Greek sculpture of the Parthenon where shadow is simply used to explain line and form and Gothic sculpture wherein 'the shadow becomes itself a subject of thought'.[3] Here Alexandra Warwick sees a crucial distinction between Victorian Gothic and the lighter Gothick of the eighteenth century, or the transitional Gothic Revival represented by Pugin's parsimonious pinnacles:

> This is, in the simplest terms, a definition of the Victorian Gothic; here the shadow becomes the subject of thought. Again we can see that it is not a crude opposition of black and white, or a reactive turn against the light, but rather that the shadow is an integral part of the whole, requiring a shift of perspective to see that which is more usually left unseen.[4]

Yet it was Pugin himself who had first moved beyond the rather brittle spaces of his early work and drawings to anticipate Ruskin's emphasis on mass and shadow; the school he built at Whitwick, Leicestershire, in 1842, is daringly 'rubble built, its presence made dramatic by one or two massive blocks laid into small walls'.[5] Ruskin's vehement rejection of Pugin's influence derives in part from his dislike, as an Evangelical, of the latter's

Catholicism, but he clearly learnt something from Pugin's material and constructional honesty. Ruskin was only seven years his younger, but by the mid-nineteenth century Pugin had arguably reached the limits of his range and influence, and it was the very different cast of Ruskin's language and aesthetics that would speak to the second half of the century and beyond. So, texts such as Ruskin's 'The Lamp of Power' (from *The Seven Lamps of Architecture*) were salient points in establishing, from the 1850s onwards, Gothic Revival concepts of primitivity, mass, abstract form and – as will be the focus in this chapter – the potential of 'energetic shadow' as a shaping factor in architecture.

Ruskin's sensibility to shadow as a positive figure in architecture evolved out of what he called his *watching* of architecture, especially the Romanesque and Gothic of Italy.[6] So this story of shadow begins with an example of Ruskin's shadow hunting in Venice, establishing the importance of two of Ruskin's key mentors in architectural representation, Samuel Prout (1783–1852), and, most importantly, J. M. W. Turner (1775–1851). This stage climaxes in 1845 at Lucca where, in Ruskin's readings of the churches of San Frediano and San Michele, shadow approaches the Sublime. It attains a new independence in relation to form, and many overtones of meaning, as presented in the text and vigorous etchings of *The Seven Lamps of Architecture*. Shadow forms presented with such abstract force, both here and in the following *Stones of Venice* (1851–3), had wide influence on architectural form-making, both in Europe and America.

Venetian shadow hunting

In the fourth volume of *Modern Painters* – in the context of an analysis of 'Turner-ian Mystery' – Ruskin writes of the practice of 'shadow hunting', of the 'singular importance of cast shadows' and of their 'sometimes gaining supremacy over even the things that cast them'.[7] So, to begin with an example of such 'shadow hunting' from Ruskin's pocket 'Sketchbook 4. 1846' (The Ruskin Museum, Coniston, Cumbria). The example is from Venice, where Ruskin was working from 16 to 27 May (Figure 6.1). It is a good year to start this enquiry into shadow-as-subject as it follows the epochal year of 1845 when Ruskin made his first continental journey without his parents as described in a reflective letter to his father written from Venice on 15 February 1852: 'In 1845 came a total change: I ... bought Turner's *Liber Studiorum*. I went into Italy with a new perception of the words drawing and chiaroscuro. My first attempts with my new perception were those of the stone pines at Sestri now in your bedroom.' After describing other studies made on this tour he concludes this section of the letter: '[The drawings] cost me great labour, but from that time I understood the meaning of the words "light and shade", and have never since had any occasion to alter my views respecting them.'[8] The confidence of his architectural shadow

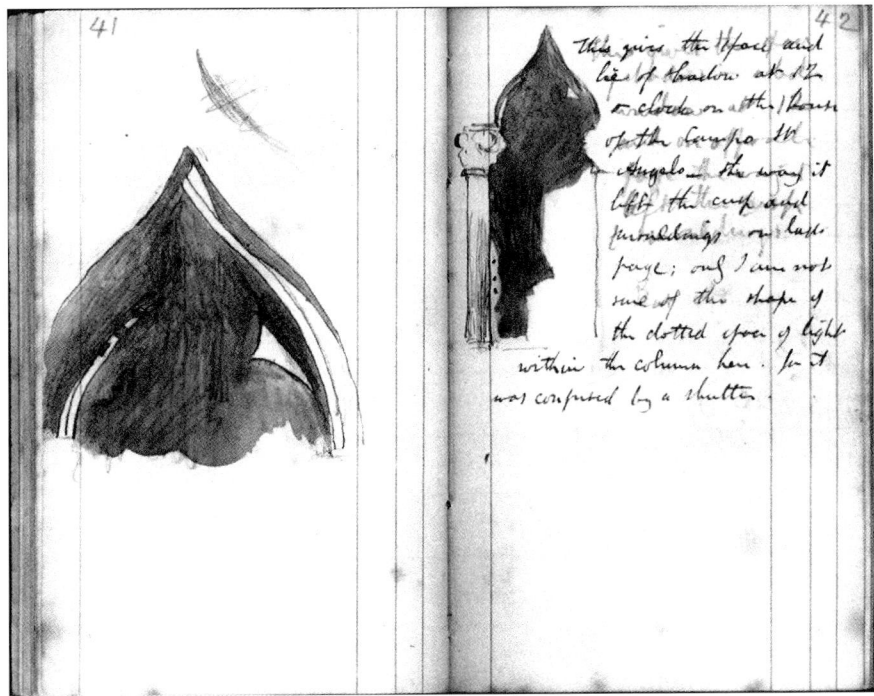

FIGURE 6.1 John Ruskin, 'Sketchbook 4, 1846', pp. 41–42. Courtesy The Ruskin Museum, Coniston, Cumbria (CONRM 1990.381).

watching is evident in the forceful chiaroscuro of his drawing of part of the façade of San Michele, Lucca also made in 1846, in June-July. At the same time this work precedes those deeply influential published accounts and images of shadow of *The Seven Lamps of Architecture* of 1849, and the arduous fieldwork he undertook for *Stones of Venice* in the years 1849–51.

Here then is the Ruskin of 1846 examining two 'houses' on the Campo St Angelo in the heart of Venice (the *sestiere* of San Marco) which show windows of that particular form (a trefoil within an ogee archivolt) which in *Stones of Venice* he will come to define as the 'Fifth Order' of Venetian Gothic. The Campo St Angelo window studies in graphite, brown ink and brown wash, occupy pages 38 to 42 of his 'Sketchbook 4'. As he notes on page 38: 'In two houses in the Campo St Angelo [this window type] occurs in grand development forming a range of four windows with grand pluming pineapple tops, and columns with exceptionally rich [Palazzo] Foscari like capitals.'[9] Evidently, he is already working towards that typology of Venetian arches which will not reach its final classification until three years later in November 1849. These 'two houses' are in fact the notable Palazzo's Gritti (on the north side of the Campo) and the Palazzo Duodo, which faces it on the south. Both are fifteenth century and, not uncharacteristically, mix the 'Fifth Order', as noted, of the *piano nobile* with arrays of Ruskin's trefoiled 'Fourth Order' on the floor above. The shadow watching of the 'Fifth Order' ogee windows of the Palazzo Gritti is recorded on the facing pages 41 and 42; on page 41 he drew a detail of the arched head of the window and on page 42 shadow notes of a whole window with a column and capital. The notes beside the latter sketch read: 'This gives the space and lie of shadow at 12 o clock on the house of the Campo S Angelo – the way it left the cusp and mouldings on last page.'

At this time the azimuth of the sun is due south, but as the Palazzo Gritti faces the Campo south-south-east this produces a definite shadow from the left of the apertures. In mid-May in Venice, the sun is already at an elevation of some 65 degrees; thus the whole of the arch zone is thrown into shadow. As the sun tracks across this imposing façade with its grand portal, Ruskin is struck, as noted, by 'the way [the shadow] left the cusp', which is picked out as a tiny glint of light in the field of shadow of the smaller right-hand sketch, and yet more clearly in the left-hand detail. In fact there is no 'detail' recorded here, for – apart from a few lines of the contour of the arch – this study is entirely a tender record of 'shadow hunting'; only the shadow is carefully washed in as it falls across the mouldings of this particular window, at this particular midday, of mid-May 1846. On the preceding page 40 he draws the trefoiled 'Fourth Order' of the uppermost range of windows noting: 'But on the top of this house & of the one opposite – the moulding instead of leaving the cusp follows it – and we have the type No 2, only the concave of the moulding is increased which I consider inferior because in sunshine it has not the little point of light on the cusp. vide over page.'

This is naturally owing to the fact that in this 'Fourth Order' the mouldings tightly follow the tri-lobate form of the arch, allowing no field of play for shadow and little opportunity for sunlight to linger on the cusp itself. At the Palazzo Gritti, the tiny flickers of sunshine which catch the cusps of the *piano nobile* order energize the shifting zones of shadow.[10] It is a detail that always delights Ruskin; in *Stones of Venice* – in describing an engraving of the 'Fifth Order' windows of the Palazzo Priuli in the Castello quarter – Ruskin remarks upon 'the penetration of the cusp, leaving only a silver thread of stone traced on the darkness of the window. I need not say that, in this condition, the cusp ceases to have any constructive use, and is merely decorative, but often exceedingly beautiful'.[11] This acute visualization of shadow demands often precarious, physical engagement with the architecture, as Ruskin described when defending the rough immediacy of his 'much-abused' etchings for *The Seven Lamps of Architecture*.

Lower and noble picturesques

To outline how Ruskin reached this level of shadow hunting, some system of thought is needed within which to frame his notions of shadow. It comes down to the familiar eighteenth-century categories of Beauty and the Sublime (see Chapter 5) with the Picturesque lying in-between, where Uvedale Price had placed it. Initially, as in the first volume of *Modern Painters*, Ruskin had argued that 'sublimity is not a specific term', but by the second volume of *Modern Painters* he had essentially accepted the generally received notion of the Beautiful and the Sublime as distinct aesthetic categories.[12]

But these are broad aesthetic categories with many nuances. Lars Spuybroek suggests that Ruskin proposed a 'warmer, livelier form of beauty and a smaller, more manageable form of the sublime, with the two categories coming so close together that they could almost touch, and in some cases actually did'.[13] At times perhaps, but in much architectural production and criticism the picturesque remains a large field of activity between the difficult-to-attain ideal of beauty (not much of a nineteenth-, and certainly not a twentieth-century ambition, anyway) and a sublime, which is always at the horizon or beyond, given that humanity can never build to the scale of the mountain abyss, or to oceanic immensity. Hence the many gradations found in Ruskin: there is 'typical beauty' and 'vital beauty'; there is the sentiment of that linear or 'surface-picturesque' stimulated by the topographer Samuel Prout; and there is a more noble and tectonic picturesque, much influenced by Turner, and characterized by the sublime emotions produced by the 'age-mark' upon a building. This is forcibly illustrated in the fourth volume of *Modern Painters* by a plate that contrasts – 'the first master of the lower picturesque' – Clarkson Stanfield's depiction of a decrepit windmill (that kind of representation that for Ruskin 'fills ordinary drawing-books and scrap-books') with the noble picturesque of the uprightly functional windmill from Turner's *Liber Studiorum* (Figure 6.2).[14] This is related to the 'extraneous Sublimity' of Ruskin's Parasitical Picturesque, as discussed later in the chapter. What

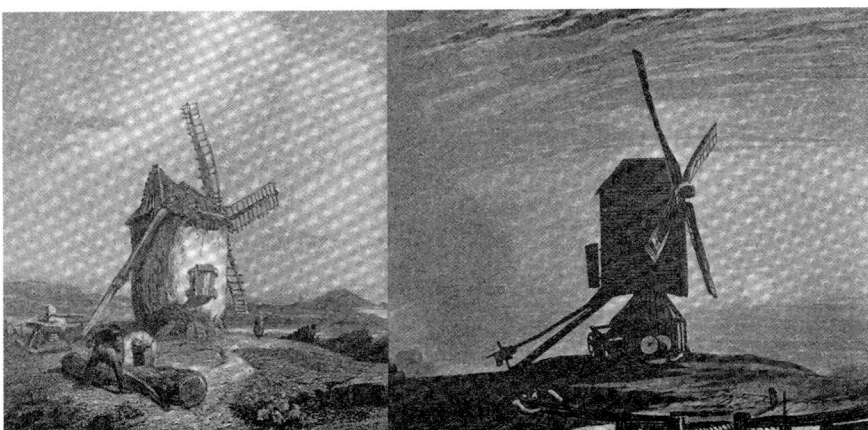

FIGURE 6.2 Plate 19, 'The Picturesque of Windmills', John Ruskin, *Modern Painters*, vol. 4.

is important to watch here is that as we move along the scale towards the sublime, the figure-ground of light and shadow interchanges, and shadow becomes much more the positive figure, serving now not merely to reveal light, but as an architectural shaping factor of its own. As the opening Palazzo Gritti example already shows, the interest here lies in what Ruskin called 'masses of energetic shadow'.[15] On the topic of 'Turnerian Mystery' and 'wayward umbrae', in the fourth volume of *Modern Painters*, Ruskin enlarges:

> on the singular importance of cast shadows, and the chances of their sometimes gaining supremacy in visibility over even the things that cast them. Now a cast shadow is a much more curious thing than we usually suppose. The strange shapes it gets into, – the manner in which it stumbles over everything that comes in its way, and frets itself into all manner of fantastic schism, taking neither the shape of the thing that casts it, nor of that it is cast upon, but an extraordinary, stretched, flattened, fractured, ill-jointed anatomy of its own, – cannot be imagined until one is actually engaged in shadow-hunting.[16]

Shadow histories

Up to the moment of these 1846 shadow studies in the Campo St Angelo, Ruskin's discovery of shadow can be summated as a move from the linear surface-picturesque manner he developed under the influence of the topographer Samuel Prout, towards the dramatic chiaroscuro he learnt from Turner. The former manner is exemplified in Ruskin's very Prout-ian study of the Ca' Contarini-Fasan, Venice, of May 1841 (Figure 6.3). Paul Walton describes drawings like this as the 'last refinement' of Ruskin's 'Oxford style' of delineation developed in his undergraduate days at Christ Church.[17] Then, drawn into the vortex of Turner's imagination, in the winter of 1844–5 he took up the study of the *Liber Studiorum* and, as he recalls, 'mastered its principles, practised its method, and by spring-time in 1845 was able to study from nature accurately in full chiaroscuro, with a good frank power over the sepia tinting'.[18]

Compare the Contarini-Fasan drawing to the forms of shadow in the cross-vista view of San Frediano, Lucca, of 1845 to see what this means for architectural understanding; and then parallel this to the tonal drama of Turner's *The Crypt of Kirkstall Abbey* (1795, published 1812) (Figures 6.4 and 6.5). *San Frediano* and *Kirkstall* both use cross-vista compositions, and both skilfully interchange the light and shadow of the architectural elements of columns and vaults, to maximally convey material presence and space. Only at Lucca in 1845 did Ruskin claim he really '*began* the study of architecture' when he saw buildings, as if for the first time, not as subjects of a sentimental picture-making gaze, but as real material constructs:

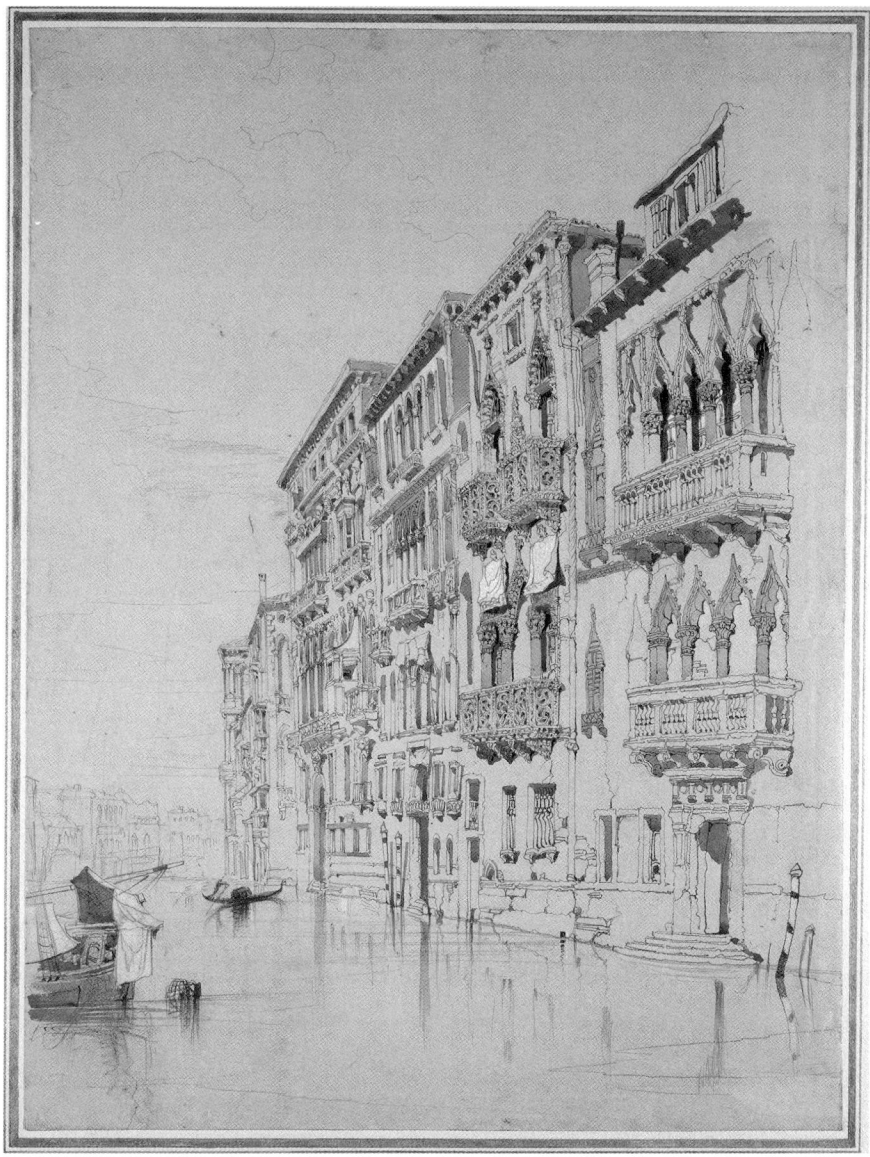

FIGURE 6.3 John Ruskin, *The Palazzo Contarini-Fasan, Venice*, graphite, watercolour and bodycolour on grey paper, 1841. © Ashmolean Museum, University of Oxford.

> Hitherto, all architecture...had depended with me for its delight on being partly in decay. I revered the sentiment of its age.... This looking for cranny and joint was mixed with the love of the rough stones themselves.... Here in Lucca I found myself suddenly in the presence of

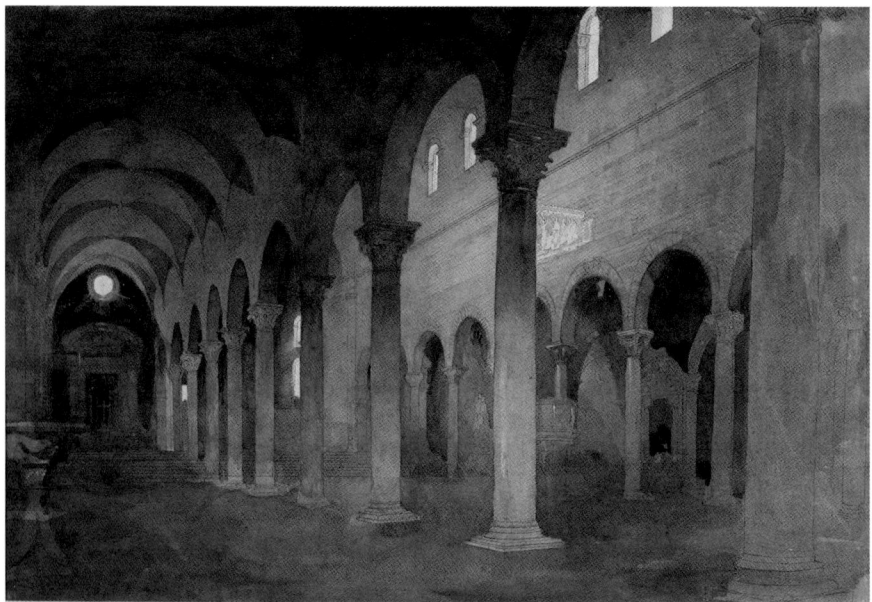

FIGURE 6.4 John Ruskin, *Interior of San Frediano, Lucca*, watercolour, brown ink and pencil on paper, 1845, Manchester Art Gallery, UK/Bridgeman Images.

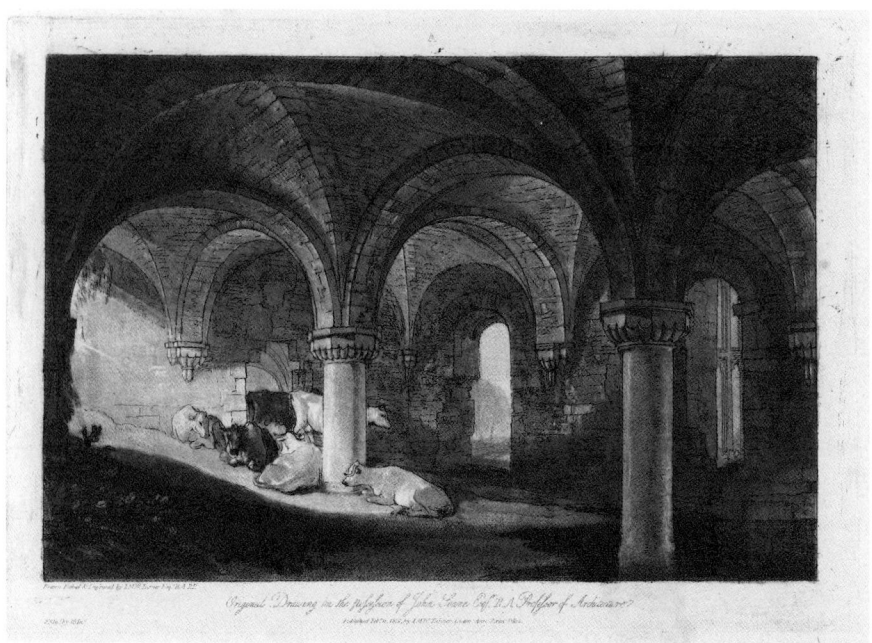

FIGURE 6.5 Joseph Mallord William Turner, *The Crypt of Kirkstall Abbey, from the Liber Studiorum*, etching with mezzotint, 1812. © The Fitzwilliam Museum, Cambridge.

twelfth-century buildings, originally set in such balance of masonry that they could all stand without mortar, and in material so incorruptible, that after six hundred years of sunshine and rain, a lancet could not now be put between their joints. Absolutely for the first time I now saw what medieval builders were, and what they meant. I took the simplest of facades for analysis, that of Santa Maria Foris-Portam, and thereon literally *began* the study of architecture.[19]

Studying these austere Luccan Romanesque churches – such as Santa Maria Foris-Portam, San Michele and San Frediano – Ruskin moves from a linear, surface picturesque of sentiment towards a much more Noble, tectonically aware, Picturesque that feels towards the Sublime. Interestingly, Prout had also drawn the same Kirkstall Abbey motif (c. 1814–8), and later Ruskin contrasted Prout's depiction, conveying 'narrow sentiment fastening only on the picturesqueness of ruined masonry',[20] with Turner's depth of feeling for the same subject, for the message of 'fate and life' told by the sturdy remains, the 'stagnant pool' and the sombre piers.[21]

Forms of Shadow

These Lucca experiences enforced a long pause in the *Modern Painters* project and confirmed Ruskin's turn to the criticism of architecture and to the astonishingly intense fieldwork that produced the *Seven Lamps* and *Stones of Venice*. Early examples are the important drawings of San Michele (Figures 6.6 and 6.7). As Ruskin accepts, the first study of the façade of 1845 is 'somewhat more delicately'[22] drawn than either the vigorous dark umber washes of the drawing of 1846 or the closer cropped arch motif published as Plate 6 of *The Seven Lamps of Architecture*, showing 'how the wall surface...became a subject of peculiar interest to the Christian architects. Its broad flat lights could only be made valuable by points or masses of energetic shadow, which were obtained by the Romanesque architect by means of ranges of recessed arcade' (Figure 6.8).[23] In an appendix to *Stones of Venice, volume 1*, Ruskin defended the veracity of these etchings against reviewers like that of the *Morning Herald* who found them 'so very rudely executed as to be actually repulsive'.[24] Ruskin admits: 'They are black, they are overbitten, they are hastily drawn, they are disagreeable.'

> But their truth is carried to an extent never before attempted in architectural drawing. It does not in the least follow that because a drawing is delicate, or looks careful, it has been drawn carefully from the thing represented; in nine instances out of ten, careful and delicate drawings are made at home. It is not so easy as the reader, perhaps, imagines, to finish a drawing altogether on the spot, especially of details

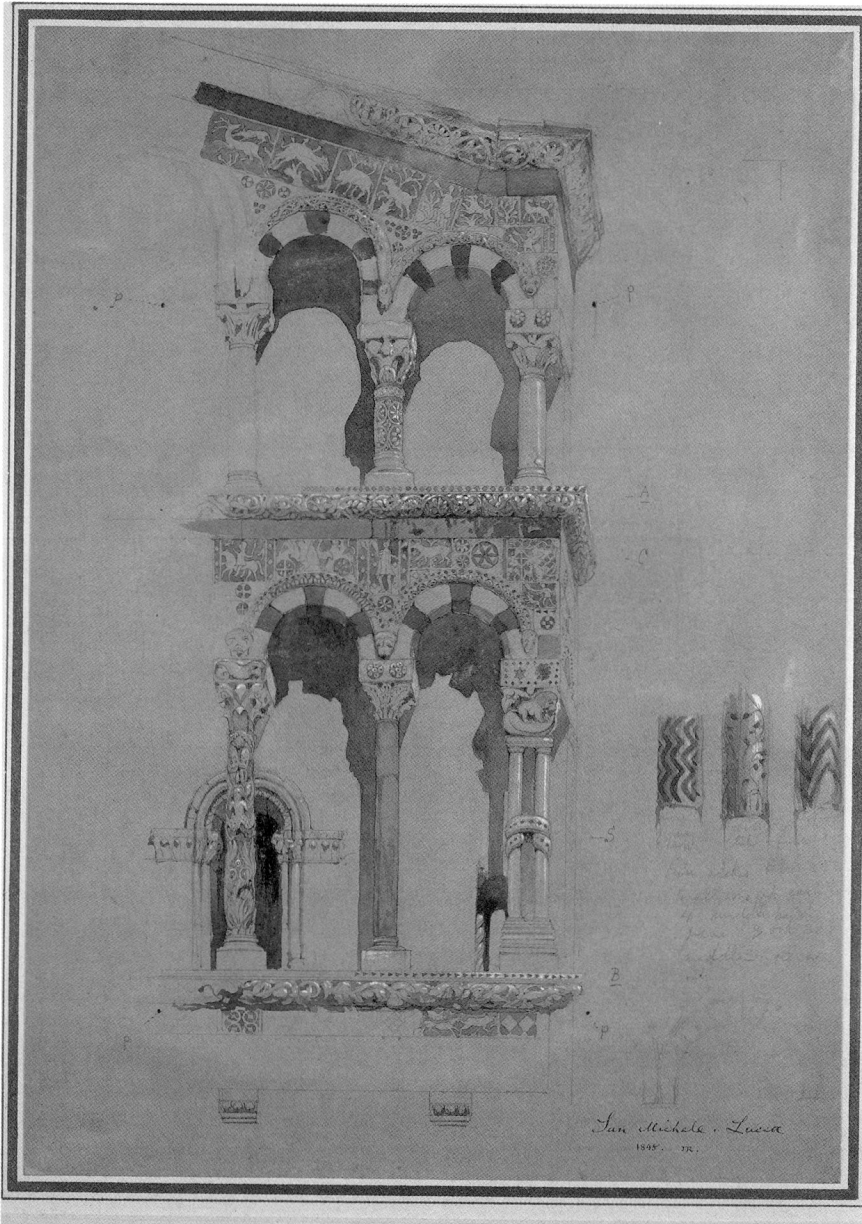

FIGURE 6.6 John Ruskin, *Part of the Façade of the 'destroyed' Church of San Michele in Foro, Lucca, as it appeared in 1845*, watercolour and bodycolour over graphite on grey wove paper, 1845. © Ashmolean Museum, University of Oxford.

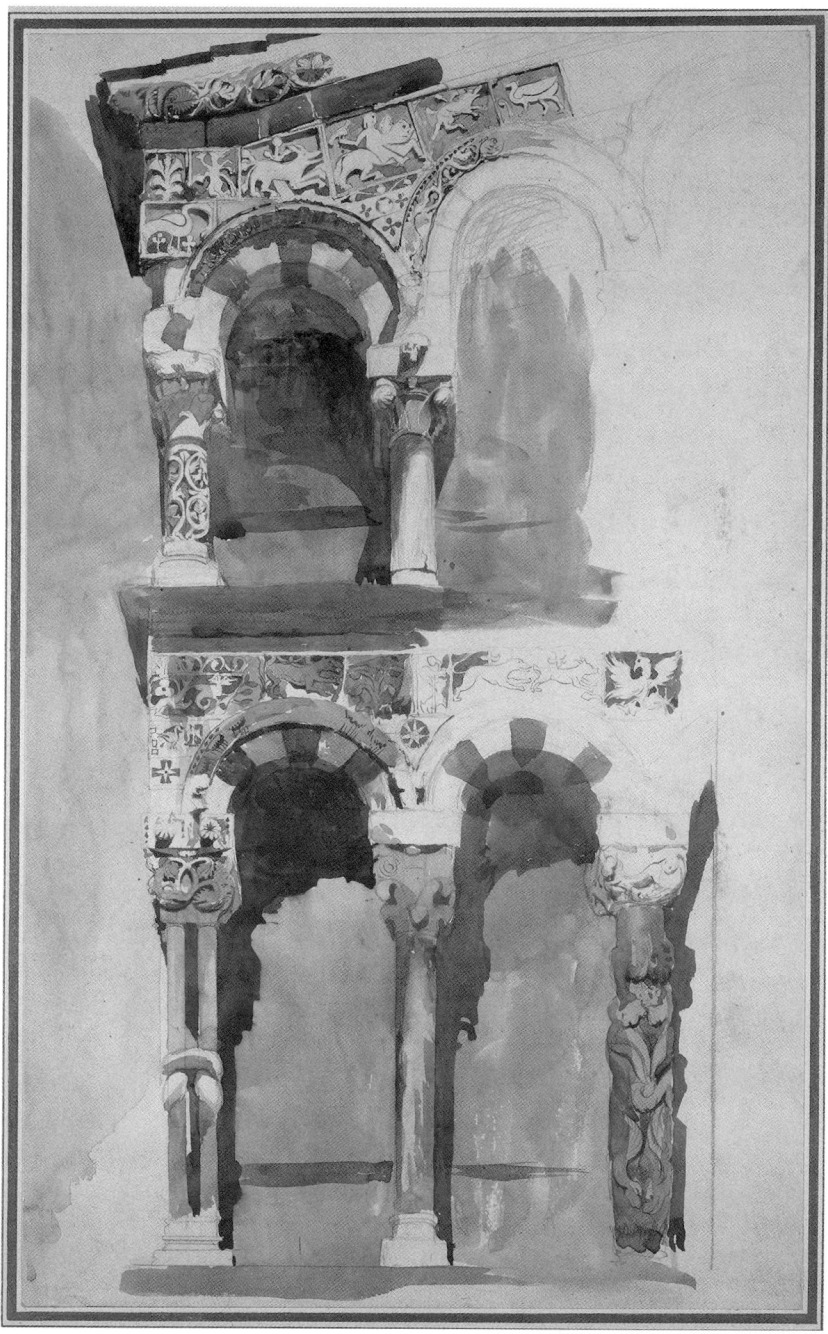

FIGURE 6.7 John Ruskin, *Part of the Façade of the 'destroyed' Church of San Michele in Foro, Lucca, sketched in colour*, watercolour over graphite on wove paper, 1846. © Ashmolean Museum, University of Oxford.

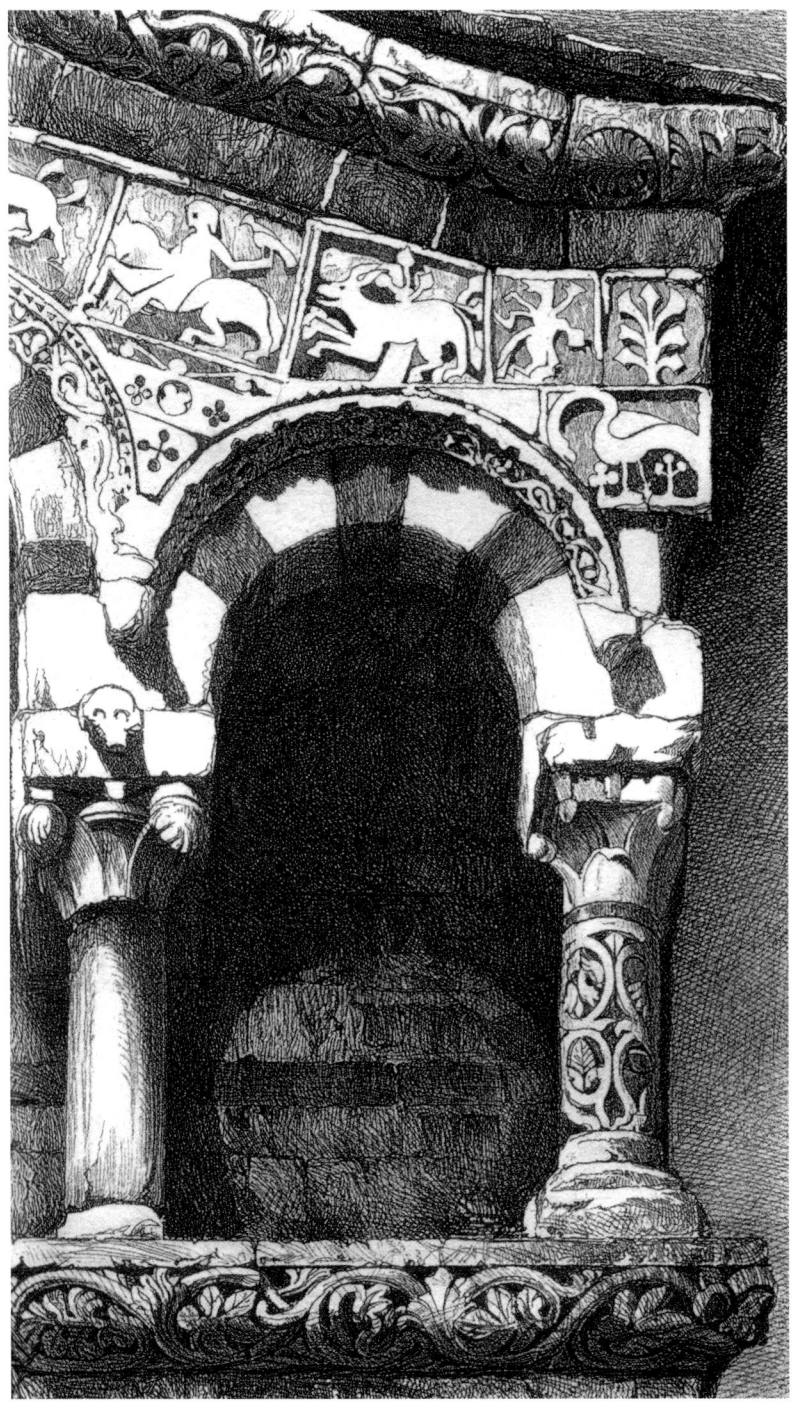

FIGURE 6.8 *The Seven Lamps of Architecture, Plate 6*, detail of San Michele, Lucca.

seventy feet from the ground; and any one who will try the position in which I have had to do some of my work – standing, namely, on a cornice or window sill, holding by one arm round a shaft and hanging over the street (or canal, at Venice), with my sketch-book supported against the wall from which I was drawing, by my breast, so as to leave my right hand free – will not thenceforward wonder that shadows should be occasionally carelessly laid in, or lines drawn with some unsteadiness. But, steady or infirm, the sketches of which those plates in the 'Seven Lamps' are facsimiles, were made from the architecture itself, and represent that architecture with its actual shadows at the time of day at which it was drawn, and with every fissure and line of it as they now exist.[25]

Pointing to Edmund Burke's contention that 'darkness is more productive of sublime ideas than light', Kent Bloomer argues that now in Ruskin 'shadow takes on an independent...multiplicity of meanings'.[26] Forms of shadow seen so independently tend to abstraction, as in the following draft passages for *Seven Lamps*:

The architectural decoration of any space depends of course broadly on the introduction of shade into it, if it be light, and of light if it be shadowed. Given a space of wall to be ornamented within and without the respective necessities are both met by simple penetrations or holes, which, seen from within, are forms of light, and from without are forms of shade. These forms of shade necessary in the actual window, were taken up the early Gothic architects as features of wall decoration: and many surfaces which it was prepared to render interesting were covered with arrangements of starry or circular forms, cut so deep into the stone as in most lights to seem a broad, if not total interior shade. Where it was possible, as in raised screens of stone, these forms were generally cut through, so as to tell as masses of vigorous dark on the light surfaces...the idea being always of dark and beautiful forms placed on a white ground.[27]

These shapes that look like 'stars when seen from within, and like leaves when seen from without' are shown as arrays of abstracted black patterns in Figure 18 of *Stones of Venice* where 'a few of the most common forms are represented, unconfused by exterior mouldings'.[28]

Ruskin's abstract shadows proved to have considerable impact on architectural form-making world-wide. A tympanum from Russell Sturgis's Farnham Hall at Yale University, as illustrated by Bloomer, 'transforms stars into black beacons that are legible from a distance of several hundred feet'.[29] Ruskin's impact on America will be examined later in the chapter. In his near contemporary *A History of the Gothic Revival* of 1872, Charles Eastlake finds Ruskin's influence in the 'star-pierced tympana of the windows' of E. W. Godwin's Northampton Town Hall (1860–5), a work that Godwin himself admitted was 'entirely founded on *The Stones of Venice*'.[30] Reading Ruskin had an immediate impact on Godwin, especially in the punctured zones of shadow found in works such as his St Philip and St James's School, Bristol and the Northampton Town Hall. The 'Lamp of Power' of *Seven Lamps* is again a key defining text wherein Ruskin writes of 'angular and broken lines, vigorous oppositions of light and shadow, and grave, deep, or boldly contrasted colour' linked in association to the 'true and essential sublimity' of 'rocks or mountains, or stormy clouds or waves'.[31]

Parasitical Sublimity

That 'true and essential sublimity' of rocks and mountains lies beyond the horizon of human possibility, so much building in reality occupies the realm of the Picturesque however much it aspires to the sublime – hence Ruskin's definition of Parasitical Sublimity. In *Modern Painters*, when Ruskin compares the outline of 'the gable roof of [an] old French house' to 'the apparent contour of a distant mountain',[32] it can be seen how – in the house's 'angular and broken lines' and, above all, in its 'vigorous oppositions of light and shadow' – the Picturesque vernacular building parasitically draws on the Sublime, especially in the 'wayward umbrae' of its eave shadows (Figure 6.9). As Ruskin defined Parasitical Sublimity earlier in *Modern Painters*: 'The essence of picturesque character has already been defined to be a sublimity not inherent in the nature of the thing but caused by something external to it; as the ruggedness of a cottage roof possesses something of a mountain aspect, not belonging to the cottage as such.'[33] Accordingly, for Landow, the 'picturesque is a reduced form of the sublime … which possesses its sharp oppositions and asymmetry without the large scale necessary to create impressions of grandeur'.[34]

Again it is important to note here how shadow comes to the forefront as the positive figure, not merely as a ground to reveal light. As noted at the beginning of this chapter, Ruskin makes a contrast between the sculpture of the Parthenon and Gothic sculpture; in the Beauty of the former, shadow is not sought in itself, and only those shadows are admitted 'necessary to the explaining of the form', whereas in Gothic work, 'the shadow becomes itself a subject of thought. It is considered as a dark colour, to be arranged in certain agreeable masses; the figures are very frequently made even subordinate to the placing of its divisions: and their costume is enriched at the expense of the forms underneath, in order to increase the complexity of the points of shade'.[35] For Ruskin, in the best work the 'parastitic Picturesque' – or in a related term the 'extraneous sublimity' – is linked to the inherent character of the building, and its age, that aspect in which 'the greatest glory of the building consists'.[36]

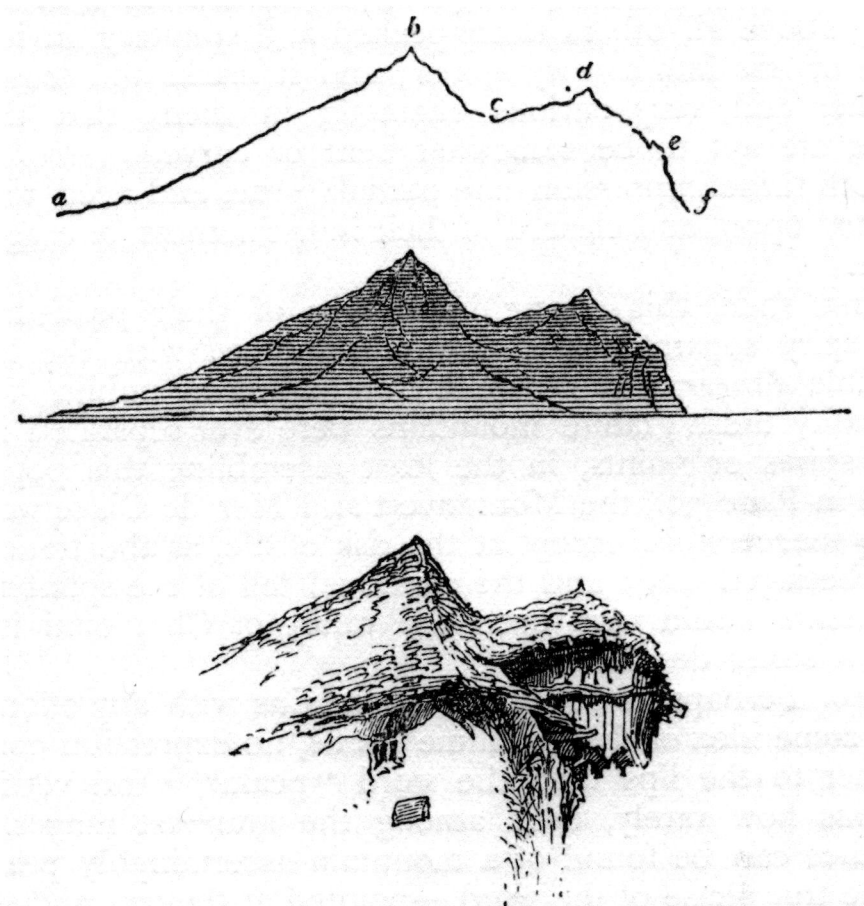

FIGURE 6.9 John Ruskin, Figure 30, *Modern Painters, vol. 4*.

Consider the 'Detail of Notre-Dame, St. Lô' Normandy, in pencil and brown wash, which took Ruskin almost a week to complete in 1848[37] (Figure 6.10). A 'black ... overbitten' detail of this sheet is given as the second plate of *The Seven Lamps* – handed owing to the etching process. This painstaking representation of architecture produced, almost without line, is a working out of the 'shapes of shadows', showing that feeling for shadow as subject Ruskin first learnt from Turner's *Liber Studiorum*. In *The Elements of Drawing* (1857), Ruskin advises the value of 'making memoranda of the shapes of shadows', describing how certain motifs 'become of singular value in consequence of the fantastic shapes of their shadows; for it happens often, in distant effect, that the shadow is by much a more important element than the substance'.[38] In flamboyant architecture like St Lô, writes Ruskin, the carver cuts 'fantastically, – and he goes in for fancy.... The white surface

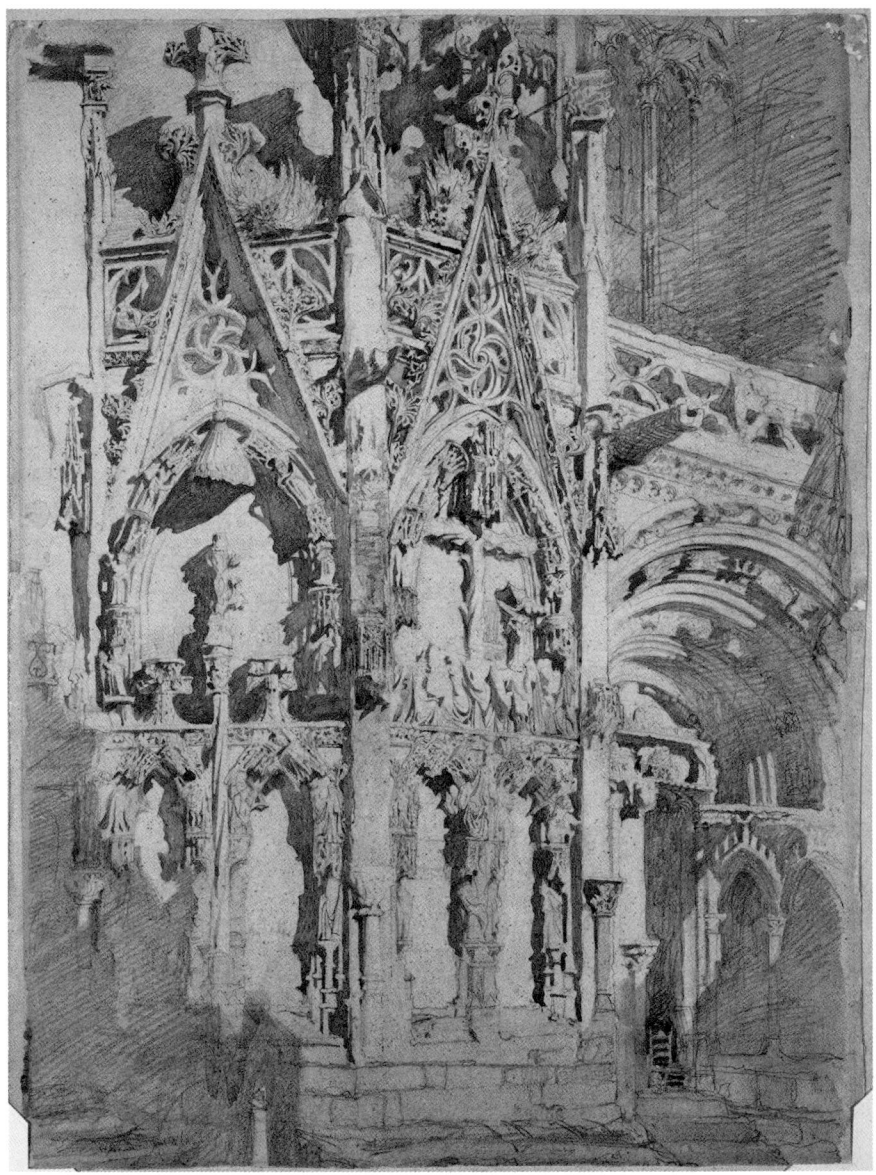

FIGURE 6.10 John Ruskin, *Study of Portal and Carved Pinnacles, Cathedral of St Lô, Normandy*, 1848, graphite, brown ink and brown wash on cream wove paper. Harvard Art Museums/Fogg Museum, Gift of Samuel Sachs. Photo: Imaging Department © President and Fellows of Harvard College.

itself has no preciousness in it, but it becomes piquant when opposed with black shadow'.³⁹ Of course, vibrantly naturalistic architecture such as this St Lô portal, borrows its associations of sublimity not just from the mountains, but also from the wood, the grove, and the cave.⁴⁰

This study has traced many cave symbols from Plato, through Locke's cave metaphor of the mind, to a plethora of cave scapes in Romanticism where one characteristic Sublime image is that of looking from the deeply shadowed cave space to light sources at cave mouth. Turner's Kirkstall is a cave scape of this nature, and San Frediano at Lucca is likewise a cavern space of 'pillared shade'. One of the most lingering images from *Stones of Venice* is that of entering St Mark's: 'There opens before us a vast cave, hewn into the form of a Cross, and divided into shadowy aisles by many pillars.'⁴¹ And Edward Kaufman, exploring the influence of Ruskin's 'Lamp of Power' on mid-Victorian church architecture, stresses the impact of geological imagery on the architectural imaginations of the 1850s and 1860s, characterizing their interiors as 'caves – rock-walled, dark-roofed and dim, with a glitter of coloured marble and semi-precious stones'; churches such as George Edmund Street's St John, Howsham in Humberside, which is lit by those plate traceries which are indeed stars as seen from within.⁴² Recognizing how Pugin himself, in the 1840s, had 'led the way towards a reassessment of breadth, weight and texture' Kaufman argues that it was 'only about 1850 that [mass] came to the forefront of aesthetic discourse as a palpable quality ...' and that 'the crucial text in this transformation was Ruskin's "The Lamp of Power"'.⁴³

Ruskin in America – A thirst for ruins and shadows

Unlike some other Great Victorians, such as Charles Dickens, Ruskin never went to America in person – but his drawings *did* cross the Atlantic. The earlier-mentioned 'Detail of Notre-Dame, St. Lô' (1848) was among a number of drawings Ruskin sent for an exhibition organized by his 'dear friend', Charles Eliot Norton, in Boston and New York in the autumn of 1879 (Norton was named as Harvard Professor of Fine Arts in 1875).⁴⁴ Norton was keen for Ruskin's many American readers to see first-hand 'the quality and range of his artistic powers', readers who had previously only known him through pirated editions, with their 'disgraceful travesties of the noble and exquisite illustrations with which the author's editions of his own works were adorned'.⁴⁵ Summing up Ruskin's impact in 1891, Norton wrote that 'the growth of interest in the Fine Arts ... during the past twenty or thirty years, has been largely due, in England and America, to the influence of Mr Ruskin's writings', seeing them as 'the original source of opinions now widely diffused, and more or less generally accepted'.⁴⁶

Despite America's keen interest in him, Ruskin commonly expressed a dislike of both America's landscape, and its competitive political economy, writing that 'he could not, even for a couple of months, live in a country so miserable as to possess no castles'.[47] Also typical are these remarks in a letter to Norton of 28 December 1856 (from the beginning of their long, forty-year correspondence): 'I can quite understand how, coming from a fresh, pure, and very ugly country like America, there may be a kind of thirst upon you for ruins and shadows: that after the scraped cleanliness & business & fussiness of [America] mildew & mould may be meat & drink to you – and languor the best sort of life – and weeds a bewitchment – (I mean the unnatural sort of weed that only grows on old bricks and mortar and out of cracks in mosaic…).'[48] Norton had written to Ruskin from Rome, and part of the potency of Ruskin's influence in America – as richly provided to gallery-goers in that detail of the Cathedral of St Lô – was to satisfy something of a wider thirst in architecture for 'ruins and shadows', for mass, memory and *gravitas*, to confront the 'fresh, pure' vastness of the land.

America was fertile soil for the reception of Ruskin's ideas, not least through the burgeoning interest in art, and the love of nature evident in the Transcendentalist creed which, though home-grown, was also partly inspired by German philosophy, and by English Romantic writers such as Samuel Taylor Coleridge – a creed expressed in Ralph Waldo Emerson's essay on *Nature* (1836), where Art is 'a nature passed through the alembic of man'.[49] Ruskin's writings legitimized these feelings, for art and nature, by providing a historically validated intellectual structure.[50] So, America embraced Ruskin's texts, and within a decade of the publication of *The Seven Lamps of Architecture* (1849) and *The Stones of Venice* (1851–3), Ruskinian principles had permeated architectural debates.[51] An early and obvious example of Ruskin's influence is P. B. Wight's National Academy of Design in New York (1863–5, demolished), with its direct quotations from the Ruskinian Oxford Museum, and Venice – New Yorkers called it the Doge's Palace. The Academy was praised by Norton in 1866 as 'one of the most original, interesting, and important works of architecture erected during the present generation'.[52] Far more stimulating and thought provoking than this literal translation of Ruskinian principles is another academy – the Brobdingnagian Pennsylvania Academy of the Fine Arts (1872–6) – as realized in Philadelphia by Frank Furness (1839–1912). His Academy looms at the junction of Broad and Cherry Streets in a pugnacious admixture of Anglo-Venetian detail and French pavilion composition. Inspired by Ruskin's 'structural polychromy', Furness collages a dramatically tonal material palette, clashing the pale ashlar sandstones of the entrance, windows and sculptured reliefs against dark panels of red brick and terracotta, and yet darker plinth courses and bastion-like corners of rusticated brownstone (Figure 6.11). In this syntax of incident and emphasis the 'plastic play of light-and-shadow patterns…create parallel visual vibrations'.[53] Furness's father was a well-known Unitarian preacher who had sought to raise the architectural game in Philadelphia,

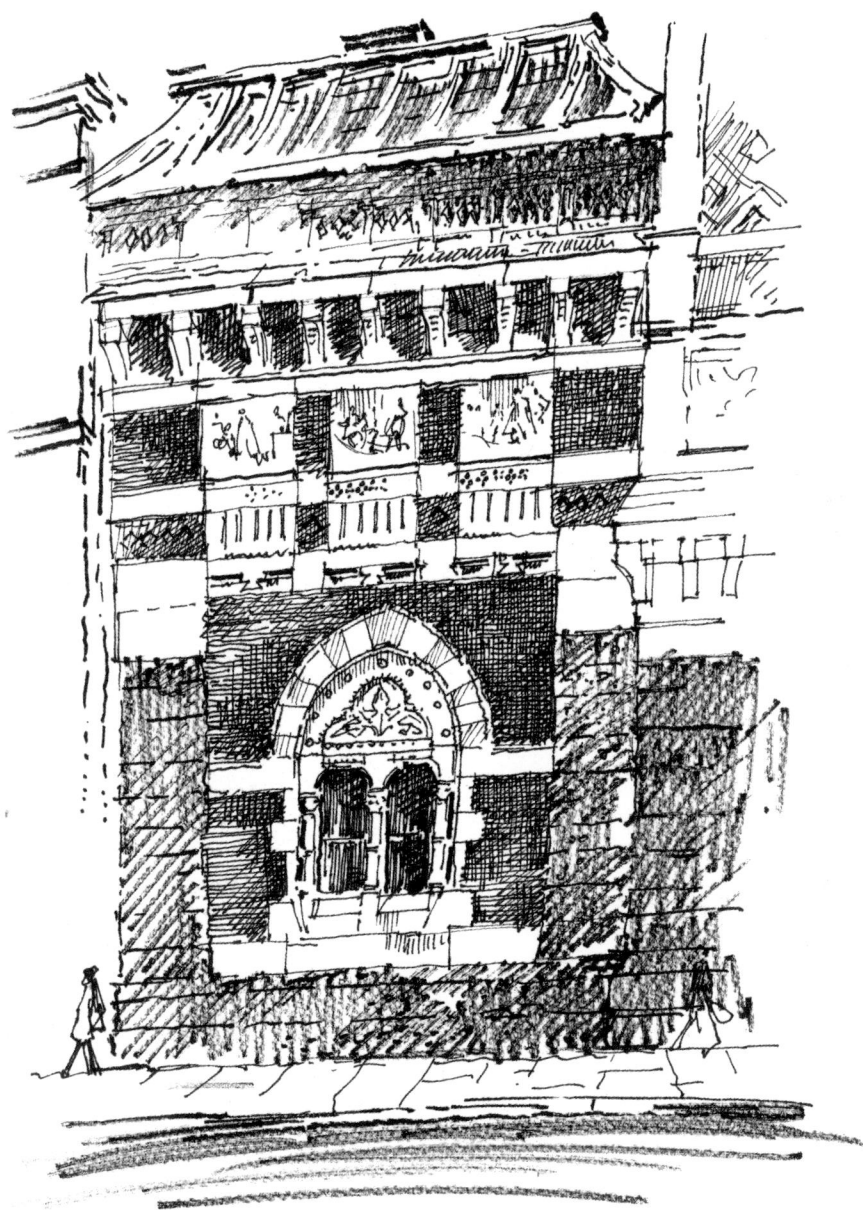

FIGURE 6.11 Frank Furness, Pennsylvania Academy of the Fine Arts (1872–6), detail of façade. Drawing by Stephen Kite.

beyond its Quaker conservatism, when he addressed the Philadelphia meeting of the American Institute of Architects in 1870, sanctioning both Ruskin's distinction of architecture from mere building and his belief that a work of architecture is always 'a great work of public instruction'.[54] The Reverend Furness was also a friend of Emerson, who in his 1841 essay in *The Dial*, 'Thoughts on Art' opined: 'We feel in a noble building, which rhymes well, as we do in hearing a perfect song, that it is spiritually organic, that is, had a necessity in nature for being, was one of the possible forms in the Divine mind, and is now only discovered and executed by the artist, not arbitrarily composed by him.'[55] Here, at one and the same time, Emerson made a vague literary organicism concretely architectural, and provided fertile ground for receiving Ruskin's notion of a responsive naturalized architecture of 'Changefulness'. As George Thomas sums up:

> Furness culminated the nation's first century with a method of working that looked to the problem for the root of the solution. That approach led to making forms represent purpose, in turn opening up the possibility of functional expressionism as an alternative to Beaux-Arts formalism.... Furness's reality-based system became the basis for a flexible and adaptable architecture that spread into the mid-west through Louis Sullivan...ultimately reaching the...Philadelphia school centred around Louis Kahn and Robert Venturi.[56]

Later – in examining Louis Kahn's Richards Medical Research Building and Biology Building at the University of Pennsylvania, Philadelphia (1957–65) – we shall come across an equally dogmatic intensity of thought and expression, noting there, that one thing that connects Kahn to Furness, and explains Furness's muscle, is Ruskin's 'Lamp of Power' (see Chapter 9).

The idea of Louis Sullivan (1856–1924)

There is no more powerful image of the translation of a syntax of energetic shadow to the Midwest of the United States than John Szarkowski's detail of Dankmar Adler and Louis Sullivan's Auditorium Building (1887–9) in Chicago, included by the great photographer in his collection of duotone plates examining *The Idea of Louis Sullivan* (1956, 2000) (Figure 6.12).[57] The man walking briskly along the sidewalk of Congress Parkway presents a spectral figure against the intense shadows of the building's neo-Romanesque arcade, with its rough-hewn granite voussoirs. This 'Idea' – whose origins Sullivan himself traces in his *Autobiography of an Idea* – has significant Philadelphian seeds. The *Autobiography* tells of Sullivan's disenchantments with his brief education in 1872, aged sixteen, at the Massachusetts Institute of Technology, where he found the study and use of the Classical 'Orders' 'rigid, mechanical and inane' in its 'lack of common sense and feeling'.[58] In

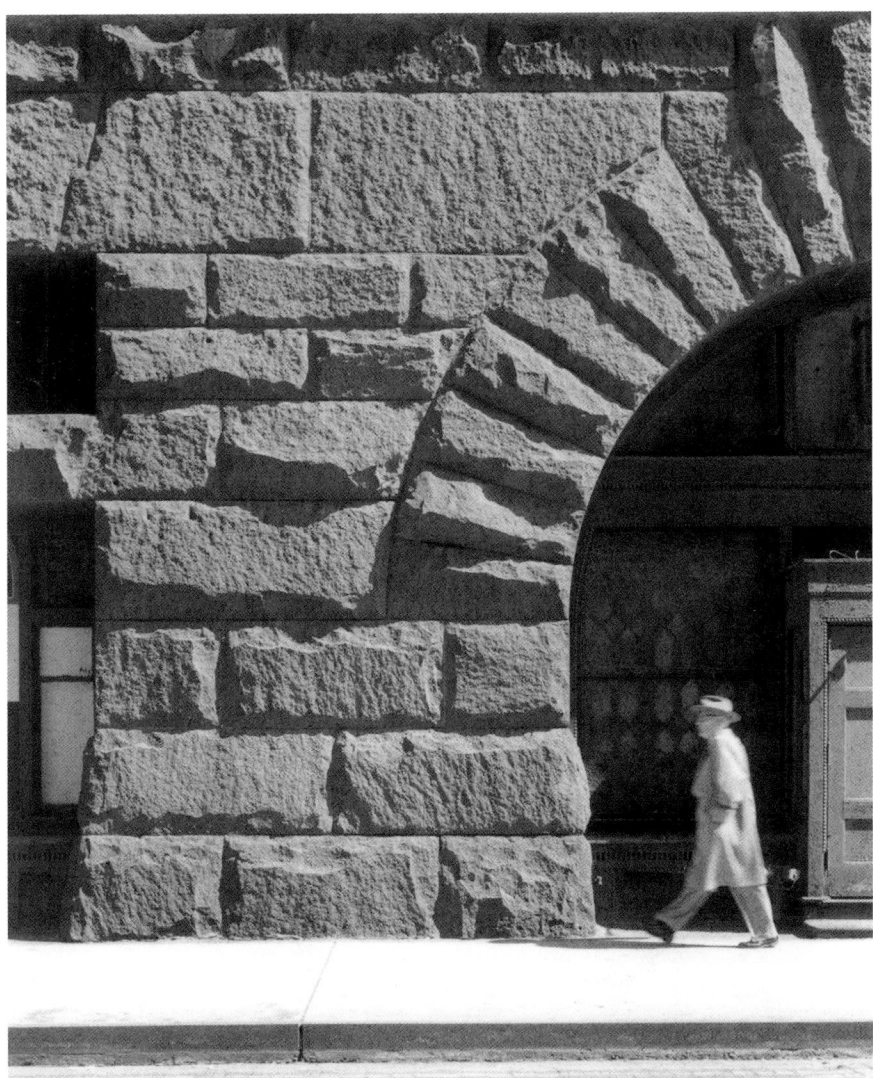

FIGURE 6.12 Adler and Sullivan, The Chicago Auditorium (1887–9). Photograph by John Szarkowski. Pace/MacGill Gallery, New York; The Estate of John Szarkowski.

Boston he was more moved by the neo-Romanesque lithic simplicity of the Brattle Square Church (1869–73) conceived, as he wrote, 'by the mighty [H. H.] Richardson, undoubtedly for Louis's special delight; for was not here a fairy tale indeed'.[59] Then, he spent a critically important half-year in Philadelphia working for Furness, whose Bloomfield H. Moore House (1872–4, demolished) on South Broad Street had 'caught his eye, like a flower by the roadside' on his arrival in the city. He found in its language 'something fresh and fair to him, a human note, as though someone were talking';[60] and he counted it his 'great good fortune' to be taken on by the practice of Furness and Hewitt, and that his first encounter with a practical architect's office was one where 'the atmosphere [was] the free and easy one of a true work shop savouring of the guild where craftsmanship was paramount and personal'.[61] This love of the guild spirit is plain in one of the only two published statements of Sullivan's that directly mention Ruskin, when in 1890 he praises 'that giant in intellect, that noble friend, teacher and toiler for art and the artisan, John Ruskin', in arguing against 'any system of contracting which...could tend to relegate that individual merit, that heretofore triumphant energy of the artisan to obscurity'.[62] In a letter to Claude Bragdon of 1904 Sullivan wrote that his 'real start was made when, as a very young child living out of doors, I received impressions from the shifting aspects of nature so deep, so penetrating that they have persisted to this day'.[63] This short-lived but intense spell in the workaday milieu of Furness's studio gave Sullivan his first practical insights as to how the ideas of Emerson and Ruskin might nurture this innate love of the natural world to generate a penetrating architectural language. Working directly on the drawings for the equally powerful Guarantee Trust and Safe Deposit Building (1873–5) – at a time when the Pennsylvania Academy was also under design – Sullivan absorbed their shared 'Furnessque' features, their clashingly abstracted masses of form and shadow, fierce colour and conventionalized ornamentation; for his part, Furness 'likely encouraged Sullivan to cultivate his Emersonian beliefs using Ruskin's naturalistic aesthetics as a guide'.[64] As Ruskin wrote in the 'Lamp of Power': 'Among the first habits that a young architect should learn, is that of thinking in shadow, not looking at a design in its miserable liny skeleton; but conceiving it as it will be when the dawn lights it, and the dusk leaves it.... Let him cut out the shadows, as men dig wells in unwatered plains.'[65] Some contemporary theoretical context for this sentiment for mass and shadow is provided by the writings on style of an older Philadelphian architect Henry Augustus Sims (1832–75). Sims designed in a modern Gothic and admired the vigorous English work of William Burges and G. E. Street, arguing that the classicism of the *néo grec* was too 'intellectual, severe, and refined' for the American spirit – too lacking in 'chiaro oscuro'. What was needed in a building were 'the heavy vertical shadows of the thirteenth century' and other elements 'to interfere with the flatness of its mouldings on wall surfaces' and to add 'more picturesqueness in its sky-lines than is usually seen'.[66] The impact of Ruskin's 'Lamp of Power' on G. E. Street, and mid-Victorian architecture generally, has been described. Sims also echoes Ruskin here, and the exaggerated metamorphosis of the elements of Furness's PAFA and GTSDP designs meet Ruskin's call in that text for an architecture that is

> broad, dark, and simple. It matters not how clumsy, how common the means are, that get weight and shadow – sloping roof, jutting porch,

projecting balcony, hollow nice, massy gargoyle, frowning parapet; get but gloom and simplicity, and all good things will follow in their place and time; do but design with the owl's eyes first, and you will gain the falcon's afterwards.[67]

For Sullivan, his 'long contemplation of living things' led to the well-known summating dictum of his 'Idea' that '*form follows function*'.[68] Always an organicist belief, not a dryly rational or deterministic one, as he wrote, 'it was not simply a matter of form expressing function, but the vital idea was this: that the function *created* or organized its form' just as in nature 'the oak tree expressed the function oak'.[69] Similarly, in examining *Ruskin and Aesthetic Thought in America*, Roger B. Stein opines that Sullivan's functionalism was

> conceived not merely as a collocation of forms but as an 'idea' related in fundamental ways to the health of the society in which it was to exist. Though removed a generation from Ruskin's direct influence, surely it is not merely fanciful to see the profusion of partly stylized naturalistic decoration which frames like a bower the door of the Schlesinger Mayer (Carson, Pirie, Scott) Building in Chicago or twines around the capitals of the Guaranty (Prudential) Building in Buffalo as Sullivan's revitalized version of the plates of *The Stones of Venice*.[70]

The Guaranty Building

At Buffalo (Western New York State), in the Guaranty (Prudential) Building (1894–5), Sullivan married soaring chords of shadow, sublimity of height and flickering, crystalline detail to produce his most mature skyscraper. In his key essay 'The Tall Office Building Artistically Considered', published in March 1896, just as the Guaranty opened to tenants, he argued:

> We must now heed the imperative voice of emotion. It demands of us, what is the chief characteristic of the tall office building? And at once we answer, it is lofty. This loftiness is to the artist-nature its thrilling aspect.... It must be in turn the dominant chord in his expression of it, the true excitant of his imagination. It must be tall, every inch of it tall.[71]

To emphasize the power of its tallness, he both doubled the cadence of the piers, beyond that required by the structural expression of the steel frame, and deepened them to intensify the chords of cast shadows. As Ruskin had argued, architecture cannot compete with nature in size, but it can in its scale of *apprehension*: 'There are few rocks, even among the Alps, that have a clear vertical fall as high as the choir of Beauvais; and if we secure a good precipice of wall, or a sheer and unbroken flank of tower... we shall feel in them no want of sublimity of size.'⁷² And again, a building 'must have one visible bounding line from top to bottom...and the mass form one grand cliff',⁷³ just as in the sheer Lombardic towers he illustrated in his *Lectures on Architecture and Painting*. For Peter Collins, in this cladding of the Guaranty, Sullivan 'invented a type of terra-cotta panel which, in its appropriateness as well as its beautiful and original detailing, showed the real applicability of Ruskin's notions',⁷⁴ for in its dressing of construction it carries through the logic of Ruskin's theory of incrustation, whereby – as in buildings such as the Baptistery, Florence – an ornamental encrusting of marble conceals the structure, while symbolically indexing it.⁷⁵

Looking closer at the ornament, which vitally fuses real observation of nature with an architectonic abstraction, here is also a lineage running from Furness's ornamentation of the Pennsylvania Academy, into Sullivan's work, and thence into that of Frank Lloyd Wright (who worked on the details of the Auditorium Building).⁷⁶ As in the larger handling of masses, these motifs respect the principle of 'decoration by shadow' as analysed by Ruskin in his plate 'The Acanthus of Torcello' in *Stones of Venice* (plate 2, vol. 2) (Figure 6.13).⁷⁷ Here he draws acanthus leaves from nature, then places below them a spiral acanthus as conventionalized into architectural duty by the carvers of the capitals of Torcello's basilica. A motif which yet retains 'the most graceful freedom of line, separated at the roots by deep drill holes, which tell upon the eye far away like beads of jet'.⁷⁸ The pointillist shadow of these capitals is characterized by 'the sharp, dark, deep penetrations of the chisel into the snowy marble', their 'stalks cut clear so that they might be grasped with the hand, and cast dark shadows, perpetually changing, across the bell of the capital behind them'.⁷⁹ The assertion here in the South of the abstract 'vigorous and simple zigzagged edge' acanthus, is matched by 'the ice spiculae of the North' and a leafage 'crisped and frost-bitten, wrinkled on the edges, and sparkling as if with dew'.⁸⁰ At the Guaranty Building, Sullivan weaves his capitals in complex interlacings that are similarly, vital, branching and spicular (Figure 6.14). Deploring gloomy 'Rembrandtism' as a false manner in painting, Ruskin saw it as 'a noble manner in building' where there should be 'a measure of darkness as great as there is in human life':

> There must be, in this magnificently human art of architecture, some equivalent expression for the trouble and wrath of life, for its sorrow and mystery: and this it can only give by depth or diffusion of gloom, by the frown upon its front, and the shadow of its recess.⁸¹

In Sullivan's agitated mind this tragic quality was stirred by the fact that he was a confessed 'ardent Wagnerite'.⁸² The dark conflicts and forest murmurs of Richard Wagner's Ring Cycle haunt this passage from *Kindergarten Chats* when Sullivan scorns the dead hand of the Beaux-Arts 'arkitek', 'who never made his boughs in the sombre gloom of the primeval

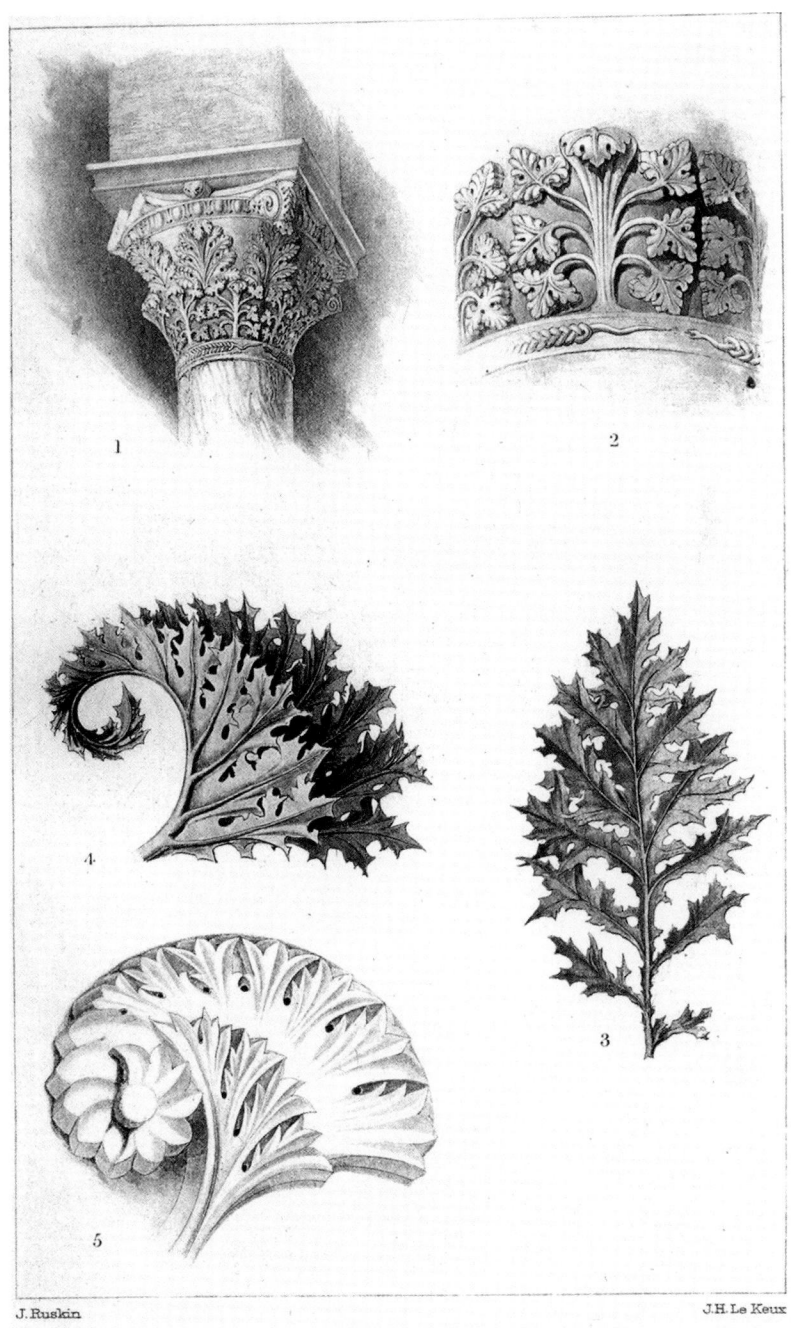

23. The Acanthus of Torcello.

FIGURE 6.13 John Ruskin, 'The Acanthus of Torcello', *Stones of Venice, volume 2, plate 2.*

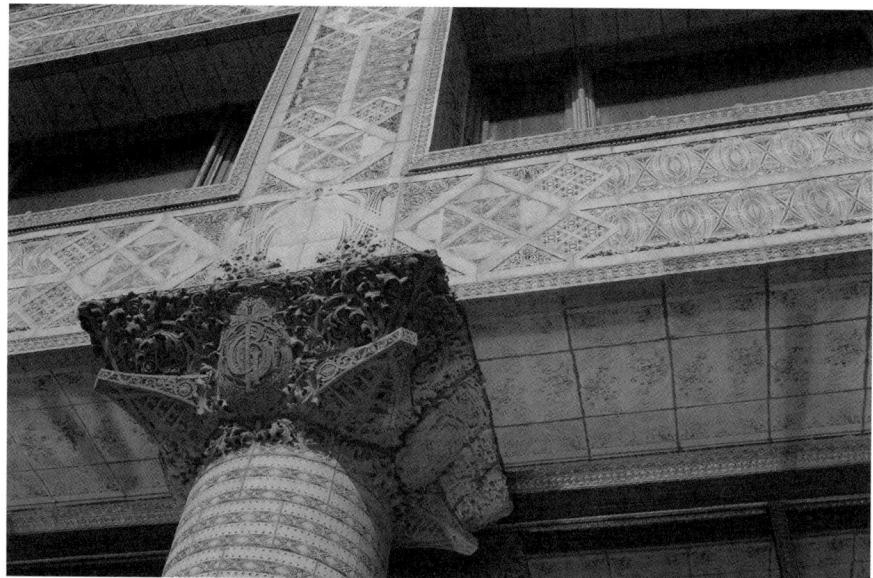

FIGURE 6.14 Sullivan, Guaranty Building, Buffalo, capital detail. Photograph, Stephen Kite.

forest; never saw the opalescent eyes across the waning firelight; ... nor saw the dawn break, pale and white through the filmy branches'.[83] Returning to the Auditorium Building, the effects of 'organizing, upbuilding, unfolding' are also Wagnerian, as Richard Etlin has suggested.[84] As the eye travels up its flanks from the Minnesota granite base – a 'design granitic itself', left with its 'blocks rudely squared'[85] to use Ruskin's words – is to ascend from the darkly primordial Nature of the opening chords of Rhinegold, to where the overlapping archivolts of the upper stories, in their smooth buff-grey Indiana limestone, shape arpeggios of a lighter tonality.

There are threads, then, that link the Venetian lagoon to the shores of Lake Michigan in exploring the ramifications of Ruskin's 'energetic shadows' westwards. Ruskin thought the Ducal Palace of Venice the 'central building of the world', standing, geographically and artistically, at the confluence of Roman currents, the Northern 'glacier stream of the Lombards' and Eastern 'lava stream of the Arab',[86] for Venice can seem a very Eastern city, as well as a European one. Consequently, the next chapter goes East and looks at shadow-making in the cultures of Arabia and Iran.

Notes

1   Cook, E. T., and Wedderburn, Alexander (eds), *The Works of John Ruskin*, vol. 9 (London: George Allen, 1904–13), p. 439, *Stones of Venice, vol. 1*.

Subsequent references in the form, *Ruskin, Works*, 9: 439, *Stones of Venice, vol. 1*.

2   *Ruskin, Works*, 22: 261, *The Eagle's Nest*.
3   *Ruskin, Works*, 8: 238, *Seven Lamps of Architecture*.
4   Warwick, Alexandra, 'Gothic, 1820–1880', in Townshend (ed), *Terror and Wonder: The Gothic Imagination*, pp. 94–123, p. 114.
5   Hill, Rosemary, *God's Architect: Pugin and the Building of Romantic Britain* (London: Allen Lane, 2007), p. 269.
6   See Kite, Stephen, *Building Ruskin's Italy: Watching Architecture* (Farnham: Ashgate, 2012).
7   *Ruskin, Works*, 6: 95, *Modern Painters, vol. 4*.
8   *Ruskin, Works*, 36: 131, *Letters, vol. 1*.
9   'Sketchbook 4. 1846', p. 38.
10 As vividly shown in the black and white, Plate 253, of Arslan, Edoardo, Engel (trans), *Gothic Architecture in Venice*, A. (London: Phaidon Press, 1972).
11 *Ruskin, Works*, 10: 360, *Stones of Venice, vol. 2*.
12 *Ruskin, Works*, 3: 128, 130, *Modern Painters, vol. 1*. See also Landow, George P., *The Aesthetic and Critical Theories of John Ruskin* (Princeton, NJ: Princeton University Press, 1971), pp. 183–4.
13 Spuybroek, Lars, *The Sympathy of Things. Ruskin and the Ecology of Design* (Rotterdam: V2, 2011), p. 222.
14 *Ruskin, Works*, 6: 16, *Modern Painters, vol. 4*.
15 *Ruskin, Works*, 8: 125, *Seven Lamps*.
16 *Ruskin, Works*, 6: 94–5, *Modern Painters, vol. 4*.
17 Walton, Paul H., *The Drawings of John Ruskin* (Oxford: Clarendon Press, 1972), p. 43.
18 *Ruskin, Works*, 35: 340, *Praeterita*.
19 *Ruskin, Works*, 35: 350, *Praeterita*.
20 *Ruskin, Works*, 21: 132, 'The Ruskin Art Collection'.
21 *Ruskin, Works*, 7: 384, *Modern Painters, vol. 5*.
22 *Works*, 9: 432, *Stones of Venice, vol. 1*.
23 *Ruskin, Works*, 8: 125, *Seven Lamps*.
24 *Ruskin, Works*, 8: xlv, *Seven Lamps*.
25 *Ruskin, Works*, 9: 431, *Stones of Venice, vol. 1*.
26 Bloomer, Kent, 'Shadows in Ruskin's Lamp of Power', *Places*, vol. 2, no. 2/4 (1985), pp. 61–6, pp. 63–4. See also the comparative study in Ray Haslam, '"For the Sake of the Subject": Ruskin and the Tradition of Architectural Illustration', in M. Wheeler and N. Whiteley (eds) *The Lamp of Memory. Ruskin, Tradition and Architecture* (Manchester and New York: Manchester University Press, 1992), pp. 138–66.
27 *Ruskin, Works*, 8: 125, *Seven Lamps*.
28 *Ruskin, Works*, 10: 259, 260, *Stones of Venice, vol. 2*.

29 Bloomer, 'Shadows', Fig. 1, pp. 61, 64.
30 Eastlake, Charles L., *A History of the Gothic Revival* (Leicester: Leicester University Press, 1978 [1872]), p. 358. See Reid, Aileen, '"Theoria" in Practice: E. W. Godwin, Ruskin and Art-Architecture', in R. Daniels and G. Brandwood (eds), *Ruskin and Architecture* (Reading: Spire Books, 2003), pp. 278–317, p. 286. Eastlake, *A History of the Gothic Revival*, p. 358.
31 *Ruskin, Works*, 8: 237, *Seven Lamps*.
32 *Ruskin, Works*, 6: 223, *Modern Painters, vol. 4*. Ruskin makes the parallel primarily to illustrate a point about the perspective effects of distant mountains.
33 *Ruskin, Works*, 6: 10, *Modern Painters, vol. 4*.
34 Landow, *Aesthetic and Critical Theories*, p. 224.
35 *Ruskin, Works*, 8: 238, *Seven Lamps*.
36 *Ruskin, Works*, 8: 241, *Seven Lamps*.
37 See Links, J. G., *The Ruskins in Normandy. A Tour in 1848 with Murray's Hand-book* (London: John Murray, 1968), pp. 51–5.
38 *Ruskin, Works*, 15: 105, *Elements of Drawing*.
39 *Ruskin, Works*, 19: 251, *The Flamboyant Architecture of the Valley of the Somme (A Lecture at the Royal Institution, 29 January 1869)*.
40 For example, among Ruskin's mental pictures is Wordsworth's poem *Yew Trees* (1803, published 1815), which Ruskin describes as 'perhaps the most vigorous and solemn bit of forest landscape ever painted', *Ruskin, Works*, 4: 298, *Modern Painters, vol. 2*. As James Twitchell points out in his reading of this poem, the yew is sublime owing to its attributes of 'power and duration', Twitchell, James, *Romantic Horizons. Aspects of the Sublime in English Poetry and Painting, 1770–1850* (Columbia: University of Missouri Press, 1983), p. 69. In the poem Wordsworth writes of: 'Huge trunks!'…'Joined in one solemn and capacious grove'…'Of intertwisted serpentine/Up-coiling…', Wordsworth intones their 'darkness', their 'pillared shade', places where 'ghostly shapes/May meet [even] at noontide' in a 'natural temple' where 'Death [is] the Skeleton/And Time the Shadow….', quoted in Twitchell, *Romantic Horizons*, p. 68. For Twitchell, *Yew Trees* is not really about yew trees as such, but like all imaginative engagements with the Sublime, about the approach to the liminal, 'to the brink of the world beyond "sensible" perception'. Wordsworth's last image in this poem is of 'Glararama's inmost caves', and it is the 'embedded emblem' of that absolute realm of shadow – the cave – that really produces all the images in the poem.
41 *Ruskin, Works*, 10: 88, *Stones of Venice, vol. 2*.
42 Kaufman, Edward N., '"The Weight and Vigour of Their Masses": Mid-Victorian Country Churches and the "Lamp of Power"', in J. D. Hunt and F. M. Holland (eds) *The Ruskin Polygon. Essays on the Imagination of John Ruskin* (Manchester: Manchester University Press, 1982), pp. 95–121, p. 108.
43 Kaufman, 'The Weight and Vigour of Their Masses', p. 97.

44 Listed in the exhibition as: 'Part of the Cathedral of St. Lo, Normandy (1848)'. As noted earlier, a portion of this drawing is engraved in *The Seven Lamps of Architecture*, Plate 2, *Works*, 13: 586.
45 *Ruskin, Works*, 13: 582.
46 Norton in the preface to the (American) 'Brantwood Edition' of *The Two Paths* (1891); *Ruskin, Works*, 16: xxiv.
47 *Ruskin, Works*, 27: 170, *Fors Clavigera vol 1*.
48 Bradley, John Lewis, and Ousby, Ian (eds), *The Correspondence of John Ruskin and Charles Eliot Norton* (Cambridge: Cambridge University Press, 1987), p. 31.
49 The full relevant passage reads:

   The poet, the painter, the sculptor, the musician, the architect seek each to concentrate this radiance of the world on one point, and each in his several work to satisfy the love of beauty which stimulates him to produce. Thus is Art, a nature passed through the alembic of man. Thus in art, does Nature work through the will of a man filled with the beauty of her first works,

   Emerson, Ralph Waldo, *Nature* (Boston: James Munroe, 1836), p. 30.
50 See Stebbins, Theodore E., with Ricci, Susan C., 'Charles Eliot Norton: Ruskin's Friend, Harvard's Sage', in T. E. Stebbins and V. Anderson, *The Last Ruskinians: Charles Eliot Norton, Charles Herbert Moore, and Their Circle* (Cambridge, MA: Harvard University Art Museums, 2007), pp. 12–29, p. 14.
51 Stein, Roger B., *John Ruskin and Aesthetic Thought in America, 1840–1900* (Cambridge, MA: Harvard University Press, 1967), p. 72.
52 Norton, quoted from *North American Review* (1866), in Weingarden, Lauren S., *Louis H. Sullivan and a 19th-Century Poetics of Naturalized Architecture* (Farnham: Ashgate, 2009), p. 85.
53 O'Gorman, James F., *Three American Architects: Richardson, Sullivan, and Wright* (Chicago: University of Chicago Press, 1992), p. 14.
54 Brooks, Michael W., *John Ruskin and Victorian Architecture* (London: Thames and Hudson, 1989), p. 294.
55 York, Jake Adam, *The Architecture of Address: The Monument and Public Speech in American Poetry* (Abingdon, OX: Routledge, 2005), p. 62.
56 Thomas, George E., Cohen, Jeffrey A., Lewis, Michael J., *Frank Furness: The Complete Works* (Princeton, NJ: Princeton Architectural Press, 1996), p. 14.
57 Szarkowski, John, *The Idea of Louis Sullivan* (London: Thames and Hudson, 2000, original work published 1956), p. 39.
58 Sullivan, Louis H., *The Autobiography of an Idea* (New York: Press of the American Institute of Architects, 1924), p. 187.
59 Sullivan, *Autobiography of an Idea*, p. 188.
60 Sullivan, *Autobiography of an Idea*, p. 191; see also Thomas et al., *Furness: Complete Works*, p. 169.
61 Sullivan, *Autobiography of an Idea*, p. 194.

62 Quoted in Weingarden, *Poetics of Naturalized Architecture*, pp. 185–6.
63 Quoted in Szarkowski, *Idea of Louis Sullivan*, p. 19.
64 Weingarden, *Poetics of Naturalized Architecture*, p. 127.
65 *Ruskin, Works*: 8: 117, *Seven Lamps*.
66 Quoted in Thomas et al., *Furness: Complete Works*, p. 93.
67 *Ruskin, Works*, 8: 135, *Seven Lamps*.
68 Sullivan, *Autobiography of an Idea*, p. 262.
69 Sullivan, *Autobiography of an Idea*, p. 294.
70 Stein, *Ruskin and Aesthetic Thought in America*, p. 208.
71 Quoted in Siry, Joseph, 'Adler and Sullivan's Guaranty Building in Buffalo', *Journal of the Society of Architectural Historians*, vol. 55, no. 1 (March 1996), pp. 6–37, p. 24.
72 *Ruskin, Works*, 8: 104, *Seven Lamps*.
73 *Ruskin, Works*, 8: 106, *Seven Lamps*.
74 Collins, Peter, *Changing Ideals in Modern Architecture 1750–1950* (London: Faber and Faber, 1965), p. 115.
75 See Kite, *Building Ruskin's Italy*, p. 150.
76 See analysis of this in Weingarden, *Poetics of Naturalized Architecture*, pp. 134–45.
77 *Ruskin, Works*, 10: 24, *Stones of Venice, vol. 2*.
78 *Ruskin, Works*, 10: 24, *Stones of Venice, vol. 2*.
79 *Ruskin, Works*, 10: 23, *Stones of Venice, vol. 2*.
80 *Ruskin, Works*, 8: 122, *Seven Lamps*.
81 *Ruskin, Works*, 8: 116, *Seven Lamps*.
82 Sullivan, *Autobiography of an Idea*, p. 209.
83 Quoted in Etlin, Richard, 'Louis Sullivan: The Life-Enhancing Symbiosis of Music, Language, Architecture, and Ornament', in Anna-Teresa Tymieniecka (ed), *The Orchestration of the Arts: A Creative Symbiosis of Existential Powers* (Dordrecht: Kluwer Academic, 2000), pp. 165–82, pp. 167, 168.
84 Etlin, 'Sullivan: Symbiosis of Music', p. 169.
85 *Ruskin, Works*, 8: 114, *Seven Lamps*.
86 *Ruskin, Works*, 9: 40, *Stones of Venice, vol. 1*.

7

Shadow Carpets

Patterns and Paradises of the Middle East

Tanizaki's statement from *In Praise of Shadows* (see Chapter 2) as to how 'in making for ourselves a place to live, we first spread a parasol to throw a shadow on the earth' applies forcefully to the stark desert lands of the Middle East, to the arid settings of the Sultanate of Oman and Iran, whose shadow-making is examined in this chapter. In his *Genius Loci: Towards a Phenomenology of Architecture* (1980), Christian Norberg-Schulz identifies three archetypal landscapes with particular patterns of shadow and light: first, the 'romantic Nordic landscape' of central and northern Europe where ever-changing sky patterns reinforce awareness of 'an interminable multitude of different phenomena'[1] – the setting of Lewerentz's, St Peter's Klippan (see Chapter 1); secondly, mediating between South and North lies the 'classical landscape' associated with Greece, whose lucidity of light and shade makes for 'clearly delimited' spaces characterized by 'an intelligible *composition* of distinct elements'[2] thirdly, Norberg-Schulz invokes the 'cosmic landscape' of the semi-arid territories of the Middle East, where he avers 'the complexities of our concrete life-world are reduced to a few simple phenomena', and the 'environment seems to make an absolute and eternal order manifest, a world which is distinguished by permanence and structure'. In confronting the 'embracing vault of the cloudless sky' and the 'infinite extension of the…barren ground', humanity becomes aware of the 'most absolute cosmic properties' of nature.[3] While this cultural study of shadow-making has focused on the first two archetypal landscapes, it would be a major omission not to recognize the shadows of that 'cosmic landscape' which gave birth to the city whose earliest representation is that of Nippur from an Assyrian bas-relief of around 1500 BCE.[4]

Oman's physical setting, in the south-east of the Arabian peninsular conforms to this paradigm of the 'cosmic landscape' in its absolute natural order, the unremitting intensity of light, the framing of the territory by the jagged mountain chains of the Jabal al-Akhdar and the Jabal al-Sharqiya, and the stark confrontation of these mountains with the monotonous extent of the desert. Such challenging habitats encourage settlement within the microworld of the oasis – in Norberg-Schulz's terms 'an intimate place within the cosmic macroworld'. J. C. Wilkinson rightly describes Oman as an arid landscape wherein 'settled man struggles in isolated communities to maintain a precarious foothold'.[5]

A place to live: The tree as shade parasol

At the opposite end of the natural scale to these macro-enclosures of sharp mountains, consider the tree as a shade-making parasol. In Oman's elementally simple traditional architecture the tree, in itself, is a significant architectonic element; there is the palm, the acacia, the mango (*anbah*) and other non-cultivated trees such as the *ghaf* (*Prosopis cineraria*) and the *sidr* (*Zizyphus spinachristi*). Such trees often fulfil the dual requirements of shade and the existential need to feel 'centred' in an arid world. 'In the tree', writes Norberg-Schulz, 'heaven and earth are also united, not only in a spatial sense because the tree rises up from the ground, but because it grows and is "alive".... The tree re-enacts the very process of creation ... the tree *is* the universe, and it is so because it reproduces it and sums it up'.[6] Quranic schools, for example, are found in mosques, in *sablas* (loggias) and at certain times of the year simply in an open space under a tree which thereby makes a place of education, spreading a parasol whose shade circumscribes the lesson circle of Quran recitation (Figure 7.1).[7]

Shawi nomads also commonly appropriate acacia (*samra*) and other trees as dwellings and shelters. These bedu of the hills are semi-settled groups who herd outside the village boundaries; they sometimes hold some agricultural property and in summer move on to the village land where each family seeks the shade of its own tree – called *al-bariza* – around which it encamps and receives guests.[8] In a typical *shawi* tree, from Wadi Hawasina, the natural setting of the tree has been amplified and emphasized by the addition of low stone walls which demarcate the shade zone and define gathering places and hearths. The tree also provides a support for baskets, goatskins and storage platforms (Figures 7.2 and 7.3). In traditional Oman, the tree can be a marketplace too, as was the case in the famous Nizwa goat market – centred on an ancient olive. And larger trees commonly serve as informal *sablas* often delimited by gravel terraces, benches and walls.

Moving up a level in formal and aesthetic realization, the small mosque of Bayt al-Khandaq, from Muslimat, near Nakhl in the interior of

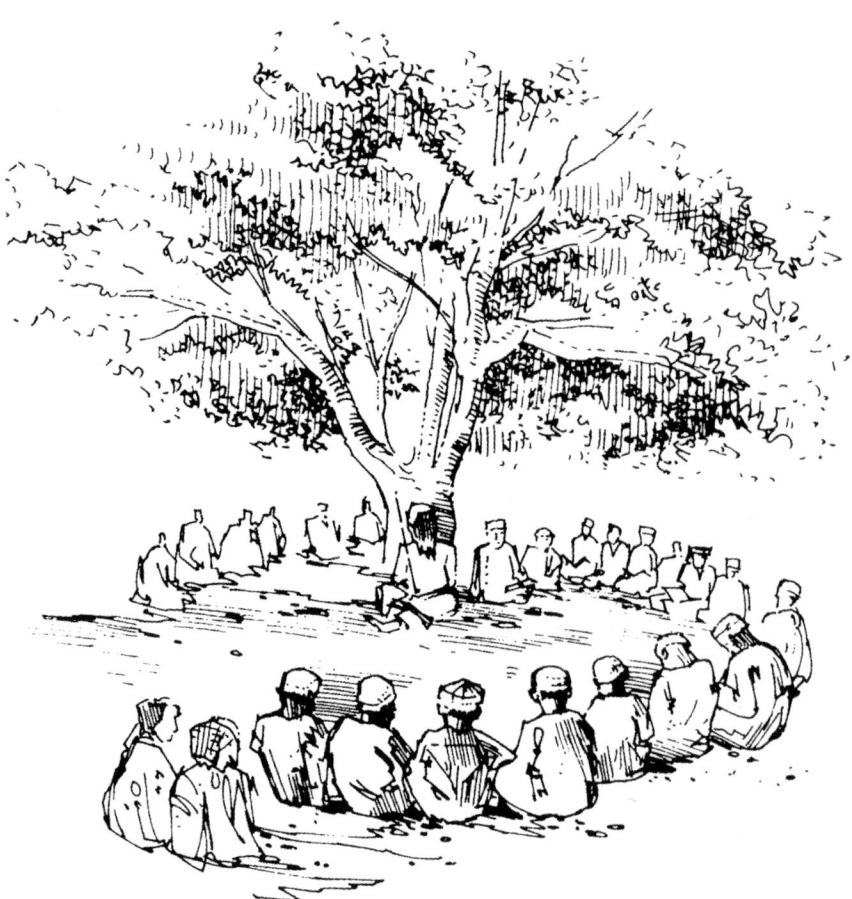

FIGURE 7.1 The lesson circle of the 'one-tree' Quranic school. Drawing by Stephen Kite.

Oman, demonstrates the subtle relationships prevalent in the traditional architecture (Figure 7.4). The building has the absolute simplicity of the traditional Ibadi mosque, reflecting the austere principles of that orientation of Islam. Few external features denote its use and, as is traditional to Ibadism, it has no minaret, just a small-domed cowl (*buma*) to protect the stair access to the roof from where the call to prayers is made, as originally decreed by the Prophet Muhammad.[9] From the ablution areas of the water channel (*falaj*), steps and a natural-cement (*saruj*) pathway lead across the sand up to the raised terrace platform adjoining the plain cuboid of the prayer hall. Again a large shade tree is an intrinsic architectonic element of this gracefully organic composition which describes the movement from the ritual washing at the *falaj* to the place of prayer.

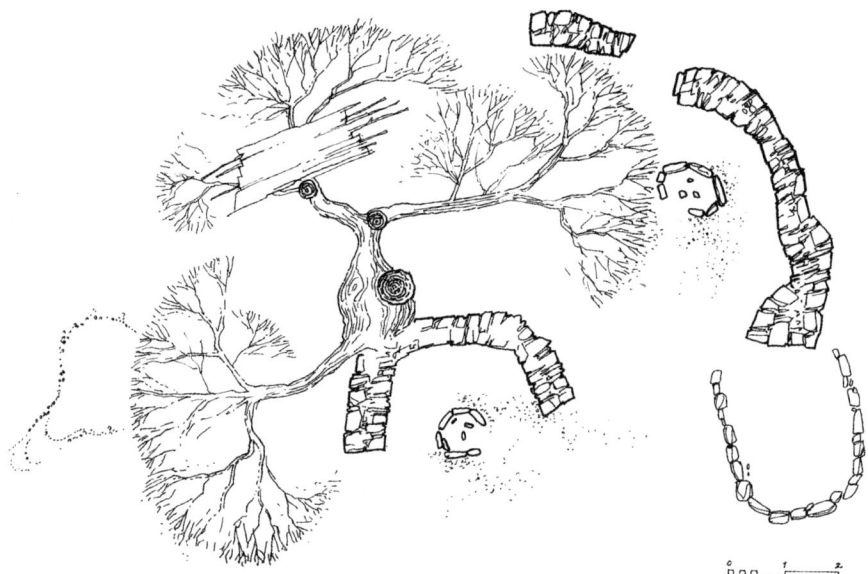

FIGURE 7.2 Sketch plan of *shawi* tree, Wadi al Hawasinah, Oman. Survey and drawing, Stephen Kite.

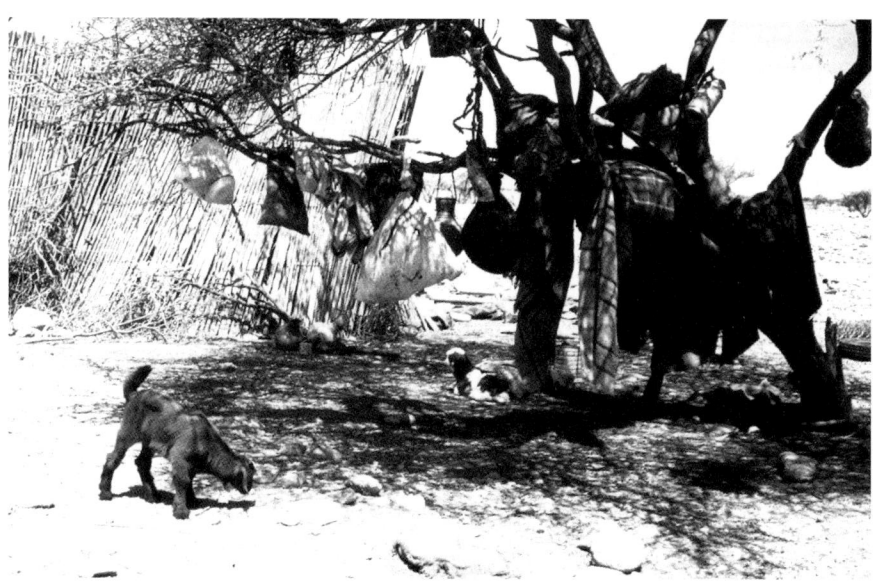

FIGURE 7.3 *Shawi* tree, Wadi al Ma'awil, Oman. Photograph, Stephen Kite.

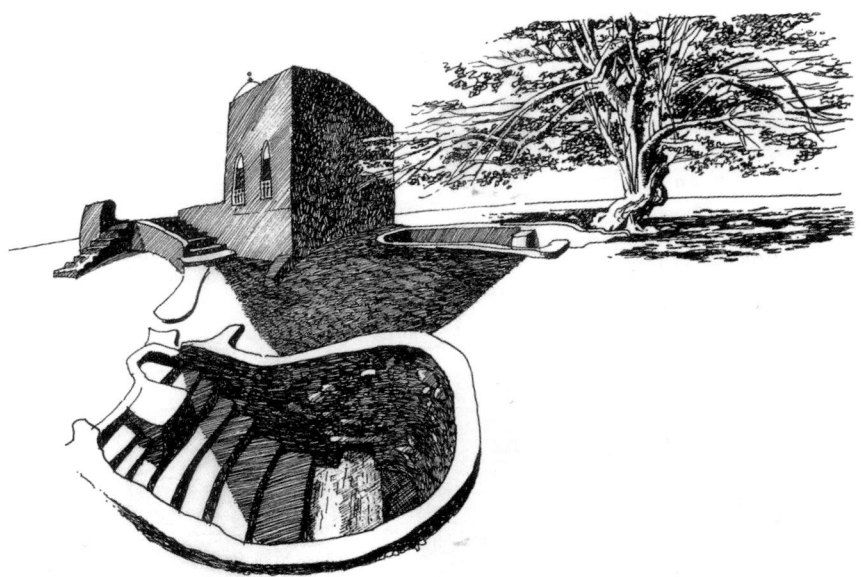

FIGURE 7.4 Mosque Muslimat, Oman. Drawing by Stephen Kite.

Working with shadow in the Islamic City

Has thou not regarded thy Lord, how He has stretched out the shadow? Had he willed, He would have made it still. Then We appointed the sun, to be a guide to it; thereafter We seize it to Ourselves, drawing it gently.[10]

The British architects and urban theorists Alison and Peter Smithson were 'guided by the cyclical nature of shadows' in their Kuwait Urban Study and Mat-Building (1968–72) and Damascus Gate, Jerusalem, projects (1979, 1981–3).[11] This 'working with shadow' is articulated through the theme of 'Holes in Cities' as developed in their writings from 1953, and defined in the Middle East context from 1979. Taking the Mosque of Amr, Fustat, Cairo (641–2 CE, built only a few years after Mohammed death in 632 CE), they describe the lining of the open space of the mosque as made of 'purloined Roman columns supporting palm trunk rafters and palm branch matting':

> This lining casts its turning shadow, acts as time-indicating shadow-dial as each twenty-four hours is apportioned by the Muezzin's call. The hole is filled by the faithful at Friday's prayers; the built-hole and its patterns of occupancy cohere in a way such that there is seemingly no artifice. Indicative shadows manage things; there is almost nothing more to it than a man and his shadow on the sand of the desert.[12]

Accordingly the mosque primordially 'functions in the manner of a grove, allowing the shade to come alive, the shadows to turn, the air to move; communicating a sense of quietude '.[13] Both the poetic and pragmatic aspects of the mosque originate in the Prophet Muhammad's house in Medina where simple portico structures made of palm trunks were erected on the north and south sides of the courtyard in functional response to the need for shaded spaces of prayer and teaching.[14] Certainly the diurnal and annual duties of Islam call for constant attention to the movements of the heavens and of shadow, such as the 'five ritual prayers at times...defined in terms of shadows during the day, by sunset and sunrise, and by twilight phenomena' and which must be made in correct orientation to Mecca.[15] The sayings of the Prophet Muhammad (*hadith*) describe how the angel Gabriel led him to make the *zuhr* prayer – the one between the midday and evening prayer – when the shadow of every object was the same as its length. And the eleventh-century Islamic scientist al-Biruni's *The Exhaustive Treatise on Shadows* remains one of the most significant studies of shadow phenomena.[16]

The great court of the Friday Mosque of Esfahan, Iran is surrounded by a sombre forest of eleventh-century Seljuk brick columns, supporting domes woven of brick in amazing variety; the architect Sir Edwin Lutyens said, 'Do not speak of Persian brickwork but rather of Persian brick magic.'[17] The grove reaches its aesthetic culmination in the north dome known as the Gunbad-i-Kharka of 1088, where 'the subdued bronze colour of the brick, relieved only by inconspicuous dark grey and white carved terra-cotta insets, adds to the solemn impression'.[18] In aerial views this ancient complex reads, not as a building, but as a major shaded 'hole in the city' among the other significant 'holes' of caravanserais and religious schools (*madrasa*) down to the basic constituent cells – the courtyard houses (Figure 7.5). Each of which is a *hortus conclusus* and a Paradise, as derived from the Persian word 'Pairidaeza', which literally means 'surrounded by walls'.[19] In Iran this pre-Islamic love of nature found later expression in the heavenly garden of the Quran, as in the many carpet designs representing a *chahar-bagh* – four gardens quartered by the rivers of Paradise. So the city itself is woven as a continuous shadow carpet, or mat construction, in response to the intense solar radiation of a cloudless hot-dry desert climate, and a cultural context which stresses the sacred inviolability of the private domain. For these reasons dwelling spaces open internally onto the shaded paradise gardens, and the courtyard dwellings are packed tightly together in clusters. Thus, the ratio of the surface envelope of the whole dwelling cluster to the constructed volume is kept low, while the narrow lanes which separate and serve the clusters optimize shade to any exposed walls.

By far the largest void in this fabric is the immense *Maydan Imam* (510 × 165 m) laid out in the seventeenth century by the Safavid Shah Abbas I (1587–1629) as part of his ambitious expansion of the city southwards to the Zayandah River (Figure 7.6). Let us examine the spatial hierarchy

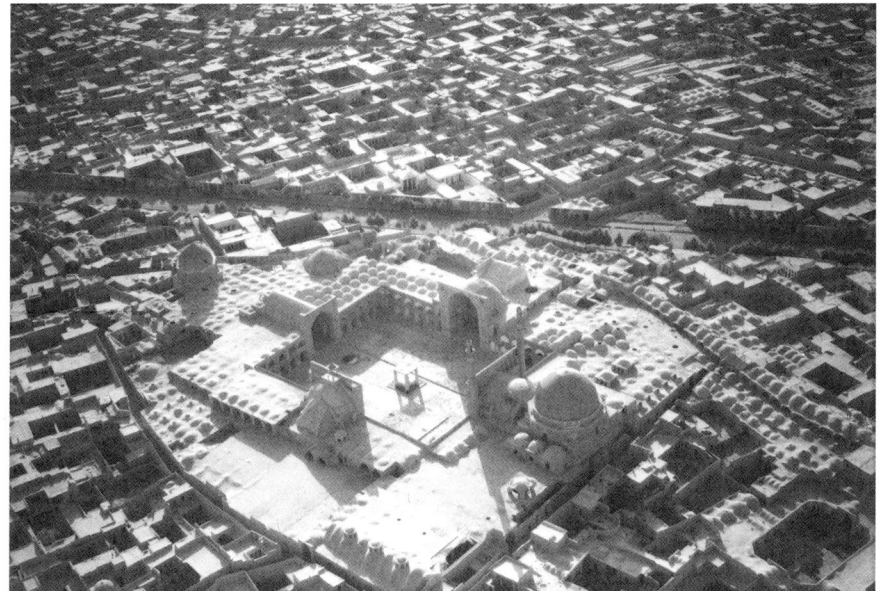

FIGURE 7.5 Aerial survey, Iran, Erich Schmidt, *Isfahan, the Masjid-Jumah or Friday Mosque*. Courtesy of the Oriental Institute of the University of Chicago.

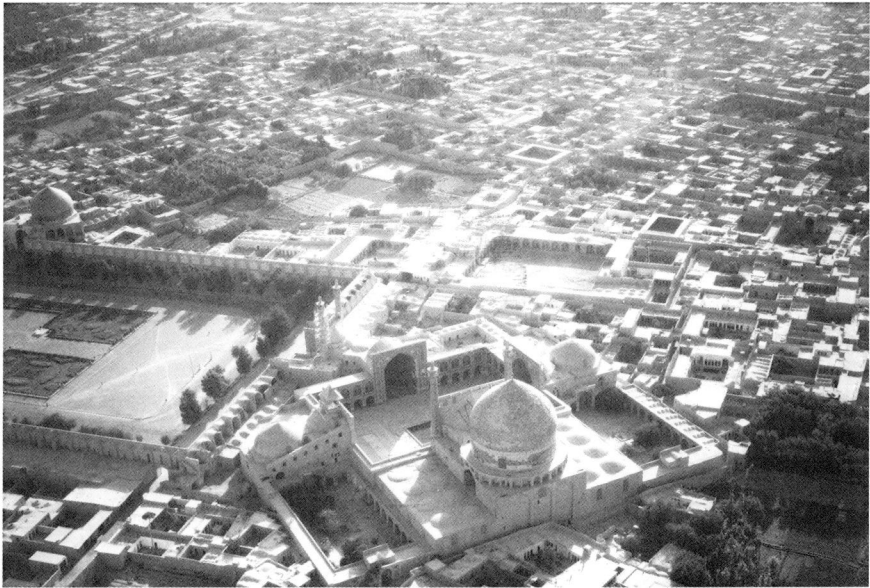

FIGURE 7.6 Aerial survey, Iran, Erich Schmidt, *Isfahan, Capital of the Safavid Kingdom, The Mosque of the Shah [Imam] in the foreground. From altitude of 200 metres on 6 July 1937*. Courtesy of the Oriental Institute of the University of Chicago.

from this, the largest of 'holes', to an intimate court space in the Dardasht quarter of the Friday mosque, to understand the shade patterns of the Islamic city – patterns that are orchestrated as a nesting of thresholds; hence, Stefano Bianca describes an urban system where

> the physical coherence between the various components was based on the graded articulation of a chain of polarities between included and excluded places, that is, between 'inside' and 'outside', or 'private' and 'public'. The courtyard of a house, for instance, was outside with regard to the rooms around it, but inside with regard to the house. The residential alley was outside with respect to the house, but inside with respect to the residential quarter, which was also enclosed by walls and gates.[20]

In this sense Shah Abbas's *maydan* is an 'outside' with respect to the dense tissue of the older city to the north. Its vastness makes for a certain weakness in urban enclosure that is also a strength, for thereby the great themes of the Iranian plateau (and of Norberg-Schulz's 'cosmic landscape') are brought into play – the sky, the great datum of the horizontal and the silhouette. So the *maydan*'s very openness fetches the distinctive purple profile of the distant Kuh-i-Suffeh mountain into the city, in dialogue with the domes of the Masjid-i Imam and the Masjid-i Shaykh Lotfallah, to play against the powerful horizons established by 510 m of double-storey buff brick arcade.

From the 'outside' of the *maydan* the *bazar* is signalled by a great half-octagonal (*nema-hashti*) entrance (Figure 7.7) which leads into the

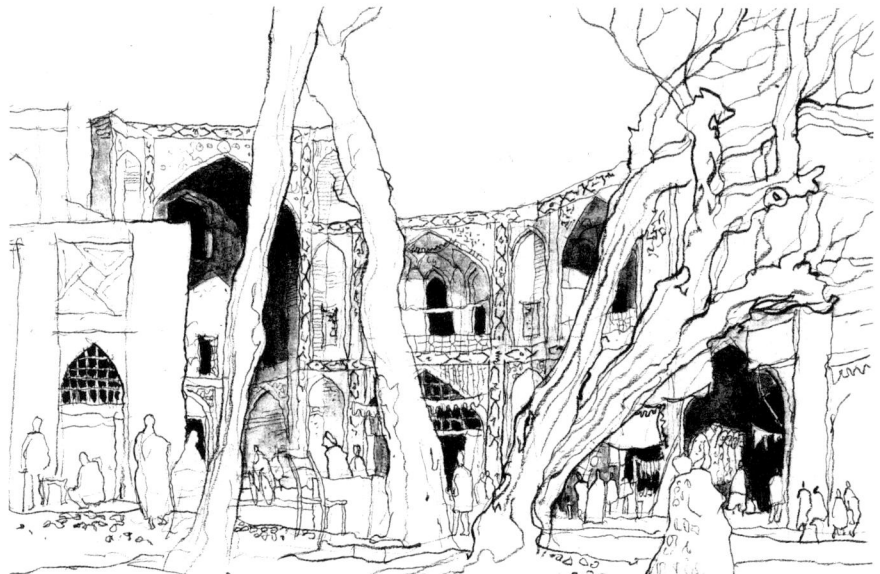

FIGURE 7.7 Entrance to bazar from *Maydan Imam*. Drawing by Stephen Kite.

Qaysariyyih, Shah Abbas's monumentally scaled overture to the primary urban movement system of the *bazar* whose solemn and lofty pulse of brick vaulting leads two kilometres to the Masjid-i Jami (Figure 7.8). From oculi in these brick vaults pencil beams of light penetrate the dusty shadows, to glint on copper, gold and fabric, or the waters of a fountain pool marking a central crossing point (*chahar su*). These intersections signal cross-routes into deeper recesses of the bazar system, or out from the shadows to the dappled light of the *chahar-bagh* of a religious school (*madrasa*) or the bustle of a caravanserai.

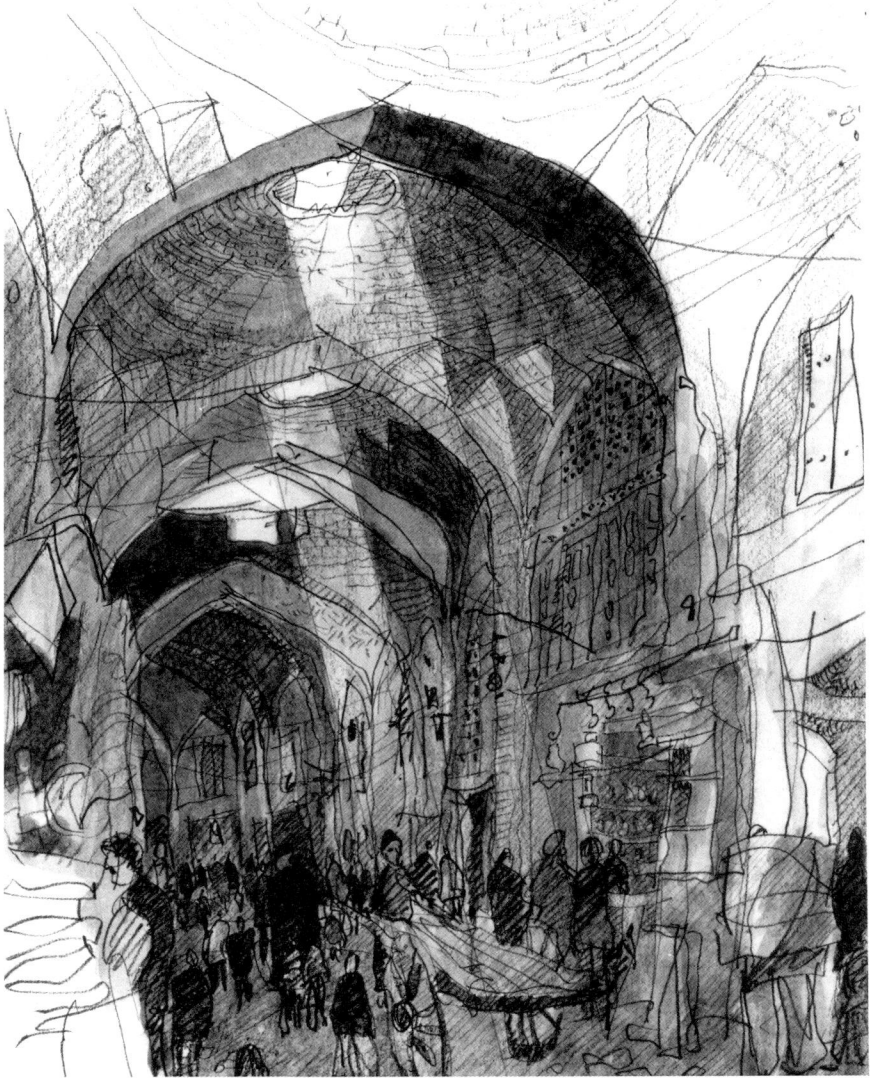

FIGURE 7.8 Qaysariyyih, bazar Esfahan. Drawing by Stephen Kite.

The northern part of this primary *bazar* route marks the eastern boundary of an important quarter; the *mahalla* of Dardasht, the area of the old city lying west and north of the Masjid-i Jami. The Friday Mosque, the vaulted *bazar* and the other principal radial routes to the city gates generate the macro-urban pattern. At the level of a residential quarter, such as Dardasht, these radial routes operate as the apex of a complex hierarchy of movement systems which, with other elements, create the micro-urban pattern of the city. These major ways (*guzars*) are five to six metres wide and, in the hierarchy of the city, they belong both to the quarter and the city as a whole. From the radial routes lead the secondary lanes (*kuchih*) – two to four metres wide – creating a dendritic pattern of organic growth of branching paths feeding the green cells of the individual dwelling courtyards (*khanih*) (Figure 7.9).

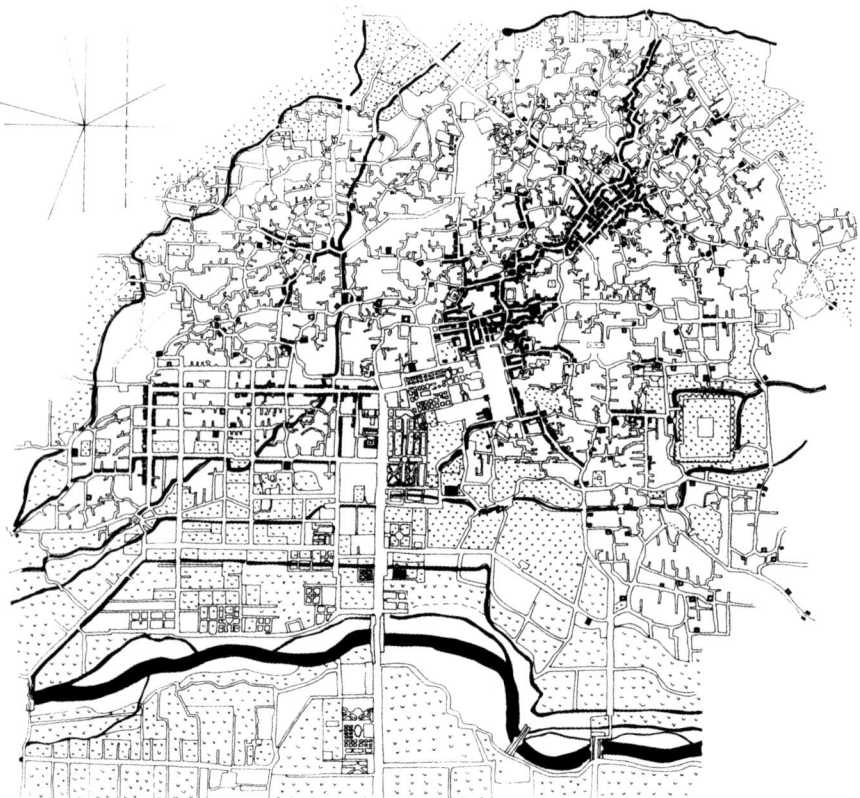

FIGURE 7.9 1919 Map of Esfahan showing the shade system of the bazar leading from the open space of the *Maydan Imam* at centre, north-eastwards to the Friday Mosque at the heart of the older city (from Cantacuzino, Sherban, 'Can Isfahan Survive', *The Architectural Review*, vol. 159, no. 951 (May 1976), pp. 292–300, p. 299).

The cell clusters of dwellings create residential islands, delineated in the 'chain of polarities' by the quarter alleys which are 'outside' to the groups of dwellings they circumscribe, but 'inside' to the quarter as a whole. One such typical 'island' to the west of the Friday Mosque and the main *bazar* in Esfahan contains some seventy to eighty dwellings (some of which are subdivided larger houses). Of these less than 30 per cent are accessed directly of the lanes of the quarter; the great majority are reached via defensive, partially vaulted, dead ends (*bunbast*). In approaching the point of entry to the intimacy of the house itself, the ambient shade deepens in the vaulted spaces of the windowless *bunbasts* to almost total darkness (Figure 7.10). Six principal *bunbast* systems penetrate this characteristic island; originally their

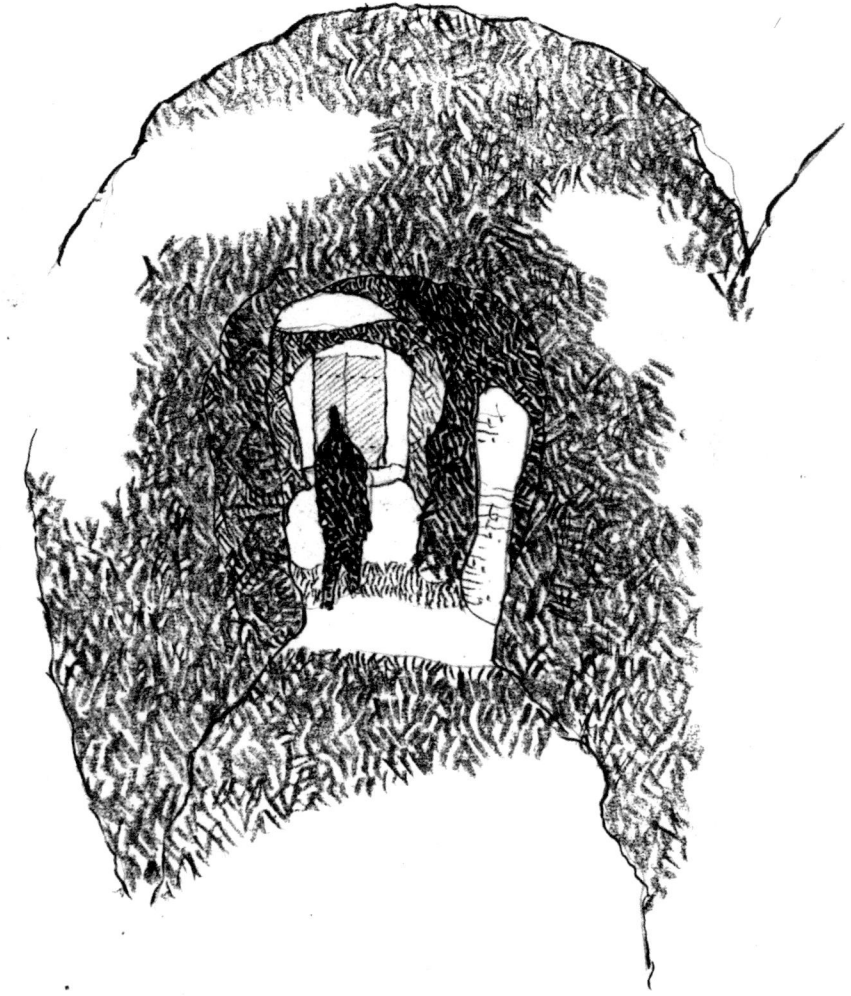

FIGURE 7.10 *Bunbast passage*. Drawing by Stephen Kite.

entrances had strong double gates which would be barred at night, sealing off clusters of up to twenty houses; occasionally a room was provided for a night watchman above the *bunbast* entrance. The southern boundary of this residential island is quite a public one, as it aligns with the radial route to the Dardasht city gate noted; the other perimeter routes serve the quarter alone.

The principal routes threading the residential islands are implanted with public functions necessary to quarter and city life such as shops, workshops, shrines, bath houses, public wells and local mosques. Moments of life in an introverted urban tissue presenting predominantly blank, windowless walls varying in height between seven and ten metres, and protected against winter and spring rains with a dun ochre mud-straw render (*cagale*). Often a small community bazar (*bazarchih*) gathers together these functions, such as one that services our residential island and is also an event on the radial Dardasht gate route (Figure 7.11). Like the main bazar these *bazarchih* announce themselves as vaulted pools of shade under which bakers and butchers gather, and the entrance to a mosque or bathhouse can be found.

So in making a journey from the *Maydan Imam* to a dwelling courtyard in a residential island of the Dardasht quarter, the Iranian city embraces the individual within a hierarchical shade system of up to eight distinctly graded spatial zones, as summarized in the following table:[21]

Circulation system		Nature of shade-space
1 main bazaar route	*bazar*	very public vaulted city space
2 principal street	*Guzar*	public city and quarter space (shaded by walls and vaulted *bazarchih* events)
3 secondary lane	*kuchih*	secondary lane – semi-public quarter space (shaded by walls)
4 dead-end access	*bunbast*	private–public access to house group (part-vaulted)
5 group octagonal space	group *hashti*	semi-private forespace to house group (domed)
6 dwelling octagonal space	private *hashti*	private lobby to house (domed)
7 bent corridor		private space to house (vaulted)
8 courtyard	*khanih*	private courtyard (shaded by walls and garden trees)

Thus, at the end of the examined *bunbast* there is an octagonal space (*hashti – hasht* is 'eight' in Persian) shared by two courtyard houses, which leads into a domed *hashti* private to a single dwelling (Figures 7.12 and 7.13). From this private vestibule *hashti* – which also serves latrines and stores – a bent entrance gives access to the courtyard. The bent entrance has a long provenance in the region as a pre-Islamic defensive device, but what began as

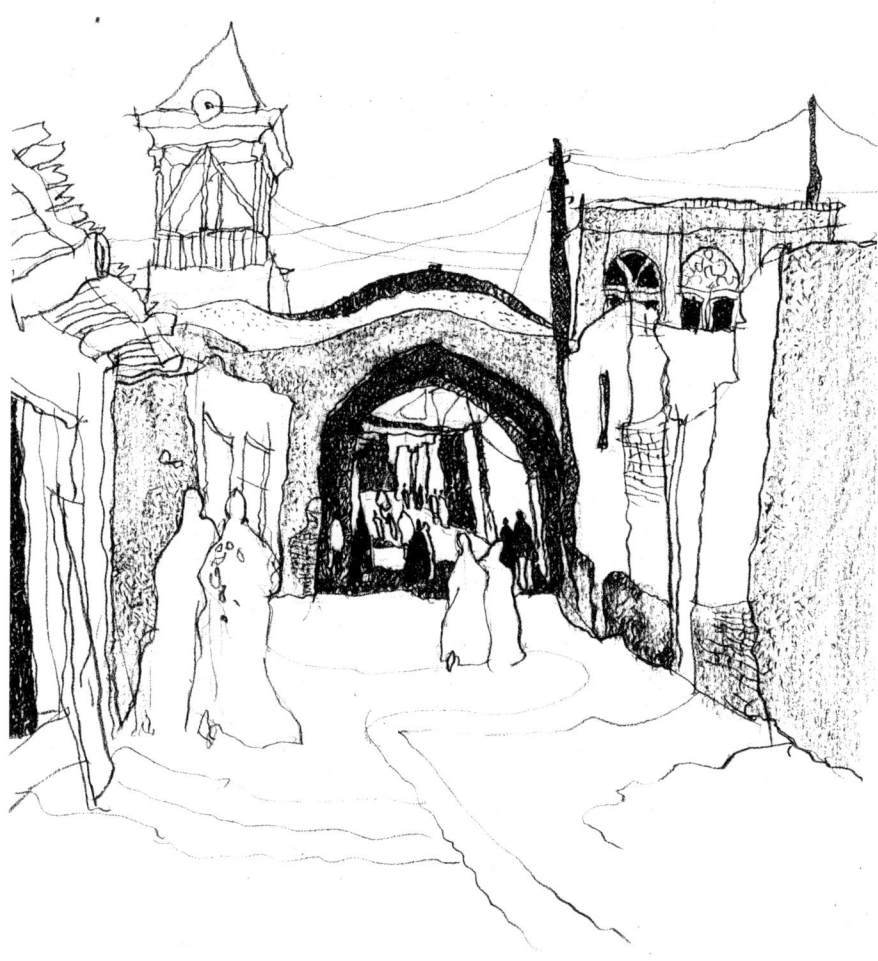

FIGURE 7.11 Small community bazar (*bazarchih*), Dardasht, Esfahan. Drawing by Stephen Kite.

a defensive feature became an important perceptual one in ensuring privacy. The modelling of the section reflects the graded transitions of the entrance sequence: the low tunnel-like approach of the *bunbast*; the domestic pause of the outer and inner *hashtis*; muted tones again in the compressed transition of the bent entrance leading to the vertical release of the courtyard where water and sky are connected by the canopy of trees. This white plastered courtyard with its ornate reception rooms reveals a house of a certain pretension.

In Persian cosmology – in ideas that recall the illusory shadows of Plato's Cave and Louis Kahn's Schopenhauer-inspired 'Treasury of Shadows' (see Chapter 9) – 'darkness is analogous to the phenomenal world'.[22] For the

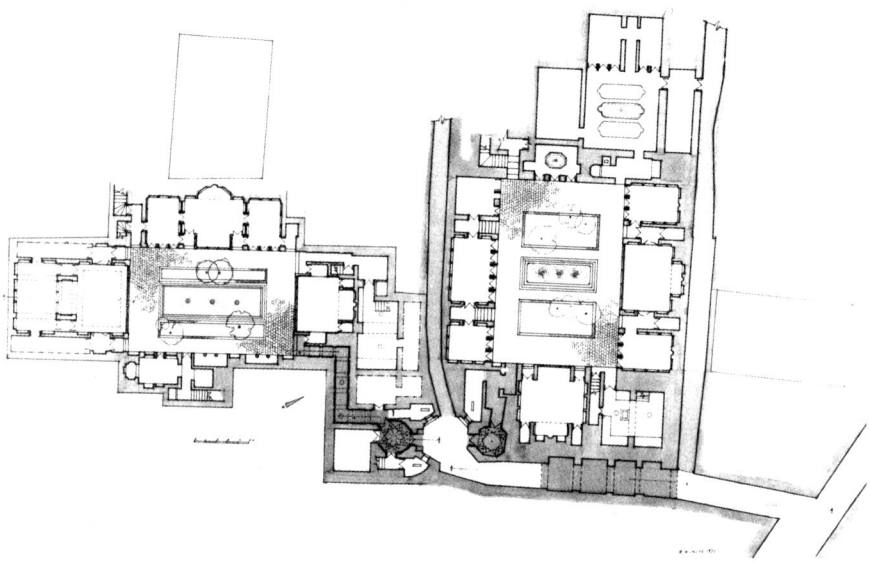

FIGURE 7.12 Plans of courtyard houses, Dardasht. Survey and drawing, Stephen Kite.

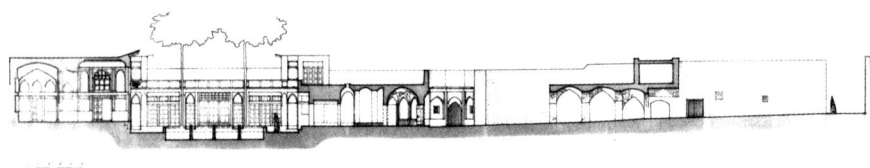

FIGURE 7.13 Section through courtyard house and *bunbast* approach. Survey and drawing, Stephen Kite.

twelfth-century gnostic Ibn Arabi – inspired by the twenty-fifth *sura* of the Quran quoted at the beginning of this section – 'the world is the shadow of the absolute'. Notwithstanding 'the dazzling all pervading light that fills the golden basin of the Persian plateau', it is as darkness compared to the light of the Absolute – of God.[23] The phenomenal forms and details of a building or a city make manifest (*zahir*) that which is hidden (*batin*); as the fifth-century theologian al-Ghazzali states: 'Know that the visible world is to the world invisible as the husk is to the kernel; as the form or body to the spirit; and darkness to light.'[24] Based on ideas such as these, the art and architecture of Islamic Persia is dominated by the system of seven colours (*haft rang*) wherein the first group of three colours are white, black and sandalwood, complemented by the second grouping of four: red, yellow, green and blue – related in turn to to the four elements of Fire, Air, Water Earth.

The *bunbast* entrance to the houses examined earlier lies close to the rear portal of the Masjid-i-Jami. To re-enter the mosque at this point is to be again in the sombre Seljuk forest of columns and domes, where the predominant hues are those of the first group. Sandalwood is the base colour of the earth; it is the floor-plane of the architect, allied to the tonalities of bronze-grey brickwork.[25] To then step into the court with its four giant portals (*iwan*) is to be embraced in a blaze of coloured faience of the second grouping, in coiling arabesque or geometric calligraphy. Blue is the predominant hue, with accents of yellow and green, warmed by dados of pink marble and zones of pink-ochre brickwork. In his twelfth-century poem *Haft Paykar* (The Seven Beauties), the Persian poet Nizami Ganjavi embodies the spirit of the seven colour system as a seven-domed complex, constructed by a master-builder called Shidah, who allots a dome to each of the colours.[26] While blackness has all the negative connotations familiar in the West, there is also a spiritual black, and the *Haft Paykar* tells a journey to perfection through the seven stages of colour to the heaven of the White Dome governed by Venus – but it is a journey that must begin in the Black Dome of Saturn. In a Sufi reading, black is the colour of gnosis. Nizami writes how it is through the black pupils of the eye that we view the world, it is black that is the colour of the hidden (*batin*), and thus there is no colour higher than black:

> There is no better hue than black; ...
> Black hair's a sign of youth; ...
> The eye's black pupil views the world,
> and robes of black are never soiled. ...
> Seven colours 'neath the seven thrones:
> no colour beyond black is known.[27]

Working with shadow at Damascus Gate, Jerusalem

The Smithsons were guided by 'the cyclical nature of shadows' in developing an architectural language for their projects in the Middle East, posited as a pattern of 'holes' and 'edges to holes'. As seen in Esfahan, and many other cities of the region, this is woven as a shadow carpet, in a hierarchical chain of polarities from the largest 'hole' of the *maydan*, through the intermediate religious, civic and commercial structures, down to the key cell unit of the entirety – the Paradise of the house courtyard. This wefting and warping of shadow patterns, inextricably satisfies environmental, experiential and metaphysical needs, as in the *haft rang* scheme. Much of the magic of the pattern arises from the interlock of the formal geometries of the holes, of axes given by the *chahar-bagh*, or the necessary orientation to Mecca, with the branching organic form of the trade routes and street networks.

In Alison and Peter Smithson's project for Damascus Gate, Jerusalem (1979, 1981–3), the consistent orientation of solar panels dictates a strict urban grain that encounters the natural patterns of the 'hole in the city' – north of the Damascus Gate – created by the valley topography, ancient routes and common open ground. At the interference of these two patterns they made the architecture as a communal 'shaded connective lining' – a 'lining-building'.[28] The shadows were examined in detailed studies as in an axonometric of those falling on 21 March (Figure 7.14). The project thus celebrates the discipline of the parallel geometry required by new solar technologies, 'whose shadow periodicity makes new grid rules', meeting the natural order. They saw parallels between the naturalness of the garments of Islam, and its architecture; as they described one perspective view: 'The parallel geometry drops into the form with only minor mutations for the rooflight's meeting with the edge' (Figure 7.15).[29] And summing up:

> The end result of working with shadows allows a vagueness of shape, made more vague by shadow pattern, the shadows retaining for the lining-to-hole that naturalness of periodicity found in a grove of trees:

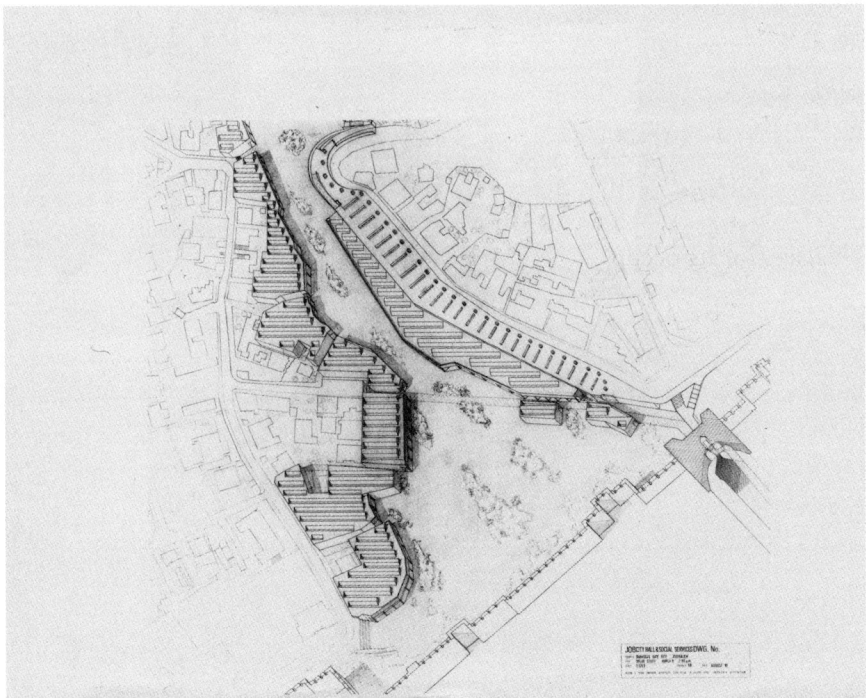

FIGURE 7.14 Alison and Peter Smithson, axonometric of area immediately outside Damascus Gate, Jerusalem. Courtesy of the Frances Loeb Library, Harvard University Graduate School of Design.

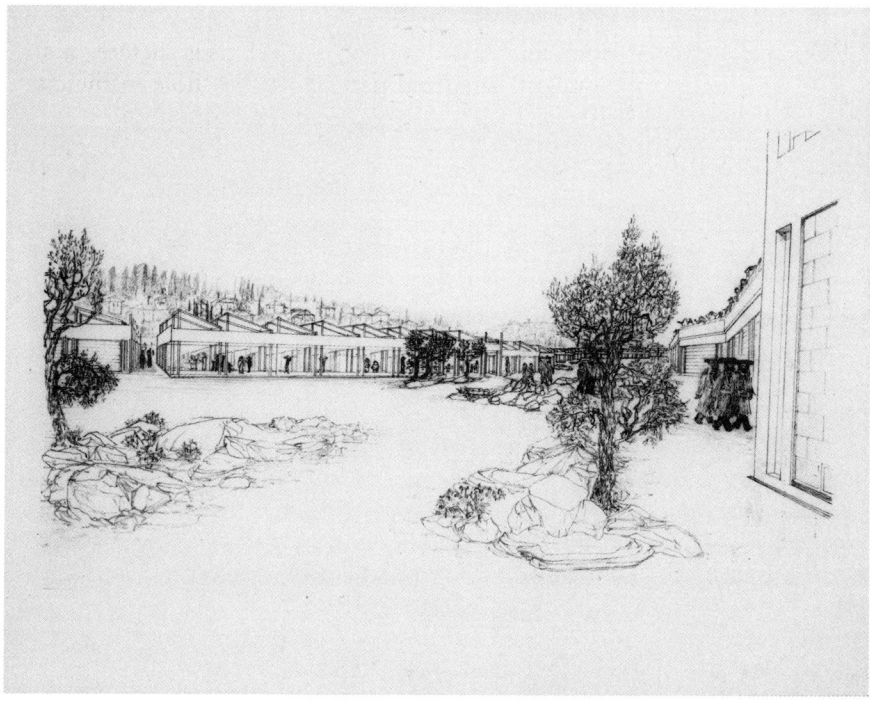

FIGURE 7.15 Alison and Peter Smithson, perspective of Damascus Gate project. Courtesy of the Frances Loeb Library, Harvard University Graduate School of Design.

the lining-building within its context edges comes alive as a solar-directed space for its occupants and their activities.[30]

Notes

1   Norberg-Schulz, Christian, *Genius Loci: Towards a Phenomenology of Architecture* (London: Academy Editions, 1980), p. 42.
2   Norberg-Schulz, *Genius Loci*, p. 45.
3   Norberg-Schulz, *Genius Loci*, p. 45.
4   See Norberg-Schulz, Christian, *Architecture: Presence, Language and Place* (Milano: Skira, 2000), p. 35.
5   Wilkinson, J. C., *Water and Tribal Settlement in South-East Arabia. A Study of the* Aflaj *of Oman* (Oxford: Clarendon Press, 1977), p. 68.
6   Norberg-Schulz, *Genius Loci*, p. 25.
7   See Eickelman, D. F., 'Religious Knowledge in Inner Oman', *Journal of Oman Studies*, vol. 6, Part 1 (1983), pp. 163–72, p. 164.

8   Wilkinson, *Water and Tribal Settlement*, p. 206.
9   For socio-religious background, see Costa, Paolo M., *Historic Mosques and Shrines of Oman* (Oxford: Archaeopress, 2001), p. 34. See also Kite, Stephen, 'The Poetics of Oman's Traditional Architecture: Towards an Aesthetic Interpretation', *The Journal of Oman Studies*, vol. 12 (2002), pp. 133–55.
10 Arberry, Arthur J., *The Koran Interpreted* (London: Oxford University Press, 1964), Sura 25, 45, 46, p. 366.
11 Smithson, Alison and Peter, *The Charged Void: Urbanism* (New York: Monacelli Press, 2005).
12 Smithson, Alison and Peter, 'Working with Shadow: Damascus Gate, Jerusalem', in David Murray (ed.), *VIA 11, Architecture and Shadow* (Philadelphia: University of Pennsylvania, 1990), pp. 76–83, p. 77.
13 Smithson, 'Working with Shadow', p. 79.
14 Bianca, Stefano, *Urban Form in the Arab World: Past and Present* (Zürich: vdf, 2000), pp. 102–4.
15 King, David A., 'A Survey of Medieval Islamic Shadow Schemes for Simple Time-Reckoning', *Oriens*, vol. 32 (1990), pp. 191–249, p. 193.
16 Casati, *Shadows*, see Chapter 9, 'In the Shadow of the Minaret'.
17 Quoted in Pope, Arthur Upham, *Persian Architecture* (London: Thames and Hudson, 1965), p. 145.
18 Pope, *Persian Architecture*, p. 107.
19 Aben, Rob, and de Wit, Saskia, *The Enclosed Garden. History and Development of the Hortus Conclusus and its Reintroduction into the Present-day Urban Landscape* (Rotterdam: 010 Publishers, 2001), p. 32.
20 Bianca, *Urban Form in the Arab World*, pp. 79, 80.
21 Kheirabadi, Masoud, *Iranian Cities: Formation and Development* (Austin: University of Texas Press, 1993), p. 29, identifies six stages in this hierarchy, to which I would also add the internal *hashti* and bent corridor of the dwelling.
22 Ardalan, Nader, 'Colour in Safavid Architecture: The Poetic Diffusion of Light', *Iranian Studies*, vol. 7, no. 1–2 (Winter–Spring 1974), pp. 164–78, p. 167.
23 Ardalan, 'Colour in Safavid Architecture', p. 166.
24 Ardalan, 'Colour in Safavid Architecture', p. 166.
25 See also Ardalan, Nader, and Bakhtiar, Laleh, *The Sense of Unity: The Sufi Tradition in Persian Architecture* (Chicago and London: University of Chicago Press, 1973), 'Colour', pp. 47–55.
26 Hejazi, Mehrdad, and Saradj, Fatemeh Mehdizadeh, *Persian Architectural Heritage: Architecture* (Southampton and Boston: WIT Press, 2014), p. 37.
27 Ganjavi Nizami, *The Haft Paykar: A Medieval Persian Romance*, J. S. Meisami (trans) (Indianapolis, IN: Hackett Publishing, 2015), p. 132.
28 Smithson, 'Working with Shadow', p. 83.
29 Smithson, 'Working with Shadow', p. 81.
30 Smithson, 'Working with Shadow', p. 82.

8

Shadows of the Unconscious

The Venice of Adrian Stokes and Aldo Rossi

This chapter returns to Venice, sometimes looking at buildings of the early Renaissance, sometimes at those of the twentieth century, but consistently through a lens that only became possible in the latter period – that of Freudian psychoanalysis. The focus will be on shadow as a metaphor of the inner worlds of the Unconscious, as read through the psychoanalytic aesthetics of the British art writer Adrian Stokes (1902–72), and the work and ideas of Italian architect and theorist Aldo Rossi (1931–97).

Ruskin has been examined as a great shadow hunter in Venice (Chapter 6), recording the 'vast cave' of St Mark's and keenly watching shadows as they track across arches and capitals. In his own person he also cast a long shadow for the critics who came after him. Here is the young up-and-coming art writer Adrian Stokes writing in explicitly oedipal terms in his diary, in Venice, on 6 May 1925: 'I think Ruskin must have been a eunuch although a great man. He lashes me daily, hurls at me stones of Venice.'[1] Thus Stokes wrote his *Stones of Rimini* in 1934 in clear riposte to *Stones of Venice*, inevitably learning from Ruskin, but strongly carving out his own critical space as an enthusiast of early Renaissance architecture, which period he capitalized as: the Quattro Cento. In a post-Freudian landscape we are alert to 'the oral and the tactile notions that underlie the visual', as Stokes puts it in *Smooth and Rough* (1951), and to 'a hunger of the eyes ... [and the] permeation of the visual sense, as of touch, by the once all-embracing oral impulse'.[2] These oral and haptic feelings drive Ruskin's passion for architecture, whom Stokes – in a footnote to this passage – calls 'the great Victorian depressive genius',[3] while quoting the famous letter Ruskin wrote to his father from Verona in June 1852 wherein he describes his instinct 'to draw and describe the things I love ... like that for eating and drinking. I should like to draw all St Mark's, and all this Verona stone by stone, to eat it all up into my mind, touch by touch'.⁴ Here, it seems that Ruskin – in the evocative English critical tradition, which he shares with Walter Pater – is doing psychoanalytic aesthetics *avant la lettre*. As Stephen Bann contends, it would not be 'too fanciful to imagine that the English aesthetic critics were in some sense working a furrow parallel to Freud's, and … Stokes would have found it only natural to step from one to the other' – pointing out also that Freud had read and valued Pater.⁵ Both Ruskin and Stokes felt the stone and its shadows as alive, and both especially loved the flesh-toned pink marble of Verona, also used throughout Venice, together with the fine-grained milky-white limestones of Istria. In terms of their architectural enthusiasms, Stokes can be bluntly called a 'Classicist' and Ruskin a 'Gothicist'; nonetheless, their interests overlap at the margins, especially in Stokes's favoured Quattro Cento period. Take the example of the Ca' Dario (c. 1487) whose façade is the subject of 'Plate 15' of Stokes's *Venice* of 1945:

> The reader will have felt for himself the interchange between the rows of windows and the wall-space studded with dark circles as if the interior darkness were summed and embossed there, so that *everything* is held on the one level. The second storey balcony is evocative of the same effect, part ironwork showing white stone through the interstices, part white stone embossed with dark marbles.⁶

And, in the very first plate of *Stones of Venice*, on 'Wall-Veil Decoration', Ruskin shows these same 'dark circles' of the Ca' Dario's roundels as an 'incrustation' of porphyry and serpentine. If Ruskin is drawn to this early Renaissance building for its Byzantine affinities, his feeling for Quattrocento architecture will be deepened later by his affection for the art of Vittore Carpaccio and the painted architecture of his narratives.⁷ If the reader does feel this 'interchange between the rows of windows and the wall-space studded with dark circles as if the interior darkness were summed and embossed there', to this point in this book of 1945, even the most attentive would not realize that statements like these are predicated on the work of the Austrian-British Freudian psychoanalyst Melanie Klein (1882–1960). Klein's contribution to psychoanalysis was to examine the roots of the adult world in the inner world of infantile unconscious phantasies, recognizing the role of hate and envy in these early stages, along with love for the mother. Klein herself did not do much to develop a psychoanalytic aesthetic, but in giving a meaningful life and spatiality to the unconscious she created the potential for figures such as Hannah Segal, Marion Milner and Adrian Stokes to do so, as Nicola Glover explains:

> With its focus in the formal, structuring role of our unconscious phantasy life as well as its content, Kleinian theory is well equipped to explore the

artist's relationship to his medium and also the viewer's encounter with the aesthetic object.[8]

Stokes had been interested in Freud from schoolboy days; he was analysed by Melanie Klein for over six years from 1929, and Freudian-Kleinian ideas are latent in a number of his earlier texts. But it is only in the final 'Envoi' section to *Venice* that he fully 'outs' his Kleinian sympathies when he confesses: 'I append the series of abstractions which these volumes have clothed.'[9] His subsequent books will much more explicitly explore the potentials of a Kleinian aesthetics. The following passages come at the end of the 'Envoi':

> Mental as well as physical life is a laying out of strength within, in rivalry, as it were, with the laid-out instantaneous world of space. To project is to distort. From moment to moment we can look upon the truth within only in terms of an outside ramification, taking for our arrangement the exquisite arrangement of space.
>
> We carry with us all the time the certainty of life and death, a relationship parallel to the interdependence of subject and object.... Consciousness is no more of the mind than the surface is of the sea. And just as the surface of the sea lies opposite to the sky and, indeed, is thus defined, so does consciousness lie opposite to the external world. Mental processes, unknown in themselves, obtain entry to consciousness through speech. Symbolic substitution, even before speech, is natural to the infant. The basis of speech is substitution, the basis of all projection. To create is to substitute.[10]

'To create is to substitute'; more so than Freud, Klein's stress on the importance of unconscious phantasy in psychological processes, as evidenced in children's play, was important in encouraging others – Stokes important among them – to develop the study of substitute objects and symbol formation in the creation of art.[11] For Klein, 'the influence of unconscious phantasy on art...and on the activities of every-day life cannot be overrated'.[12] And when Stokes writes of sea surfaces, of consciousness and of mental processes, it calls to mind others who have invoked Venice's 'proximity to the unconscious'.[13] A nearness summoned by the apparently miraculous flotation of its architecture, as described by one sixteenth-century Venetian diplomat: '[The city of Venice], truly a marvel to everyone, was not made by the hands of men, because it is out of reach of human knowledge, but by the word of the heavenly King, above the water...with superb palaces that are simultaneously in the water, earth, and air.'[14] This city is surely also a marvel of colour, the city of those fabulous marbles of the Ca' Dario, or the art of Titian and Tiepolo; so Stokes's *Venice* at first surprises in its strongly tonal depiction of the city:

Venice excels in blackness and whiteness; water brings commerce between them. Italians excel in the use of black and white, white stone and interior darkness. Colour comes between, comes out of them, intensely yet gradually amassed, like a gondola between water and sky.[15]

The black and white derives from the materiality of Venice, especially the remarkable Istrian stone which

bleaches in the light, blackens in the shade, many columns and projections upon Venetian building are most dramatically most intensely light and intensely dark. This darkness that radiates evenly has inspired as well the characteristic chiaroscuro of Venetian painting, the extensive use of dark-coloured discs and circular holes in Venetian architecture, common in all periods.[16]

Consider these alternations of shade and light in a plate from *Venice* of a comparatively humble seventeenth-century house where for Stokes 'the white squares of thick stone surrounding the barred lower windows, in a manner of clear and white arrest, epitomize transaction within' (Figure 8.1).[17]

Stokes's theory of art begins and ends with the short-lived Venetian artist, Giorgione (1478–1510); his Castelfranco *Madonna, Child and Two Saints* is the frontispiece to his second book, *Sunrise in the West* (1927), and he closes *Venice* with an analysis of the *The Tempesta* (c. 1505–6). A detail from this painting (*Venice*, plate 48) shows Giorgione's chiaroscuro, which plays dark approaching storm clouds and trembling trees, against a spectrally lit background of walls and towers, and a foreground of fragmentary columns and arches, typical of the early Renaissance Venice then under construction. Stokes stresses that this is not the Tenebrist chiaroscuro to come – the 'dramatic realism' of Caravaggio for example – rather it is a healing chiaroscuro that allows the full panoply of local colour to unfold between these tonal extremes:

Yet Giorgione had employed chiaroscuro for exactly an opposite effect, for the contemplative, the poetic, pause. That is why his use of chiaroscuro is so enriched by colour.... Not only did he help to make possible the huge achievement of Rembrandt but he enlarged the scope of equal insistence. Venice, as we know, excels in black and white. Colour comes between, uniting them, uniting the vast differences. It is a description also of Giorgione's achievement, a child of Venice.[18]

The images in Venice are by some of the big names in Italian photography such as Alinari and Anderson. In the preface to the first edition written in September 1944, Stokes tells us that the photographs were all taken by Italian firms and that 'some (by Fiorentini) were commissioned when I was last in Venice'.[19] Chapter One of *Venice* organizes the text as a commentary upon

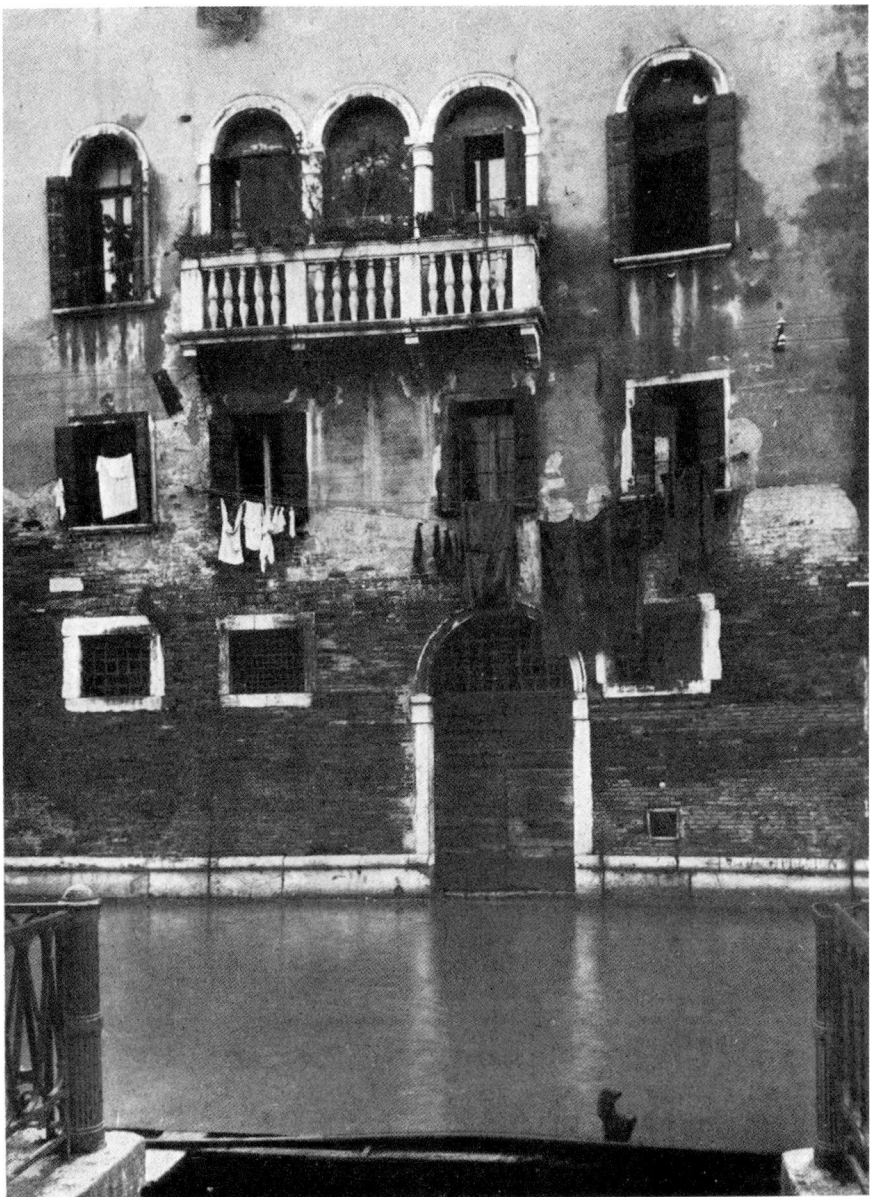

FIGURE 8.1 A house, seventeenth century, from Adrian Stokes, *Venice* (1945), Plate 17. © Estate of Adrian Stokes.

these photographs to explicate Stokes's blackness-and-whiteness thesis. By bringing in accidentals into his argument – such as passing figures, or the folds of a curtain – Stokes reinforces the immediacy of word and image. From the moment of the medium's invention, Venice's dramatic chiaroscuro had drawn photographers, creating 'a whole aesthetic of back-canal photography' that relished liquid reflections lapping dark recesses.[20] Another early enthusiastic commissioner of the photographic process was Ruskin, who oversaw the making of daguerreotypes – probably by the Frenchman Le Cavalier Iller – in Italy in 1846, later acquiring his own daguerreotype equipment. In the images of the French photographic school of the mid-nineteenth century, 'there was not only less concentration on detail but also far greater utilization of opaque shadow'.[21] Ruskin learnt definite lessons in that Power of Shadow, as examined in Chapter 6, from daguerreotypes. When publishing his large-format *Examples of the Architecture of Venice* (1851), he explained how he had 'used the help of the daguerreotype without scruple in completing many of the mezzotinted subjects for the present series'; among 'some of the beautiful effects which the daguerreotype alone can seize' was a 'bold Rembrandtism; that is to say, by the sacrifice of details in the shadow parts, in order that greater depth of tone might be afforded on the lights'.[22] Far removed from wartime Venice (on home guard duties in Carbis Bay, Cornwall), Stokes needed his photographs when writing the book, both practically and emotionally, as records of a treasured city whose fate in the Second World War remained uncertain. The contemplation of these images was also a restorative act, as he wrote in the preface: 'There is an ancient compulsion in the mind whereby it thinks to forge a protector by the very act of taking thought upon an object loved.'[23]

Santa Maria dei Miracoli

Stokes gives three plates and an extended interpretation of this casket-like church: small, but a great mother symbol as a new foundation devoted to the Virgin Mary in response to the nearby discovery of a miracle-working image of her (Pietro Lombardo, and sons Tullio and Amado, 1481–9) (Figure 8.2).[24] Stokes reads the building's propitious apertures and members corporeally:

> Respiration is...suggested by the black space of the open windows beneath. Interior life is dark within these wide connections with the outside world. Like the sense apparatus of the human body, windows bring what is inside in communication with what is without: like consciousness they are the exit upon the external world of the life within. Such, as it were, is the plain physiology of ordinary building of which we are more constantly aware in Venice not only because of the length and darkness of the apertures in the strong light of Italy, but also because they are framed so simply and beautifully by the *liston* of Istrian stone. ...
>
> Much more has been brought upon the surface. Pilasters, with their arch mouldings lying upon the bright marble wall-space, are the inner dark ferment in architectural form upon this marble. ...
>
> Such building, then, is a vast and concrete symbol of inner-outer life.[25]

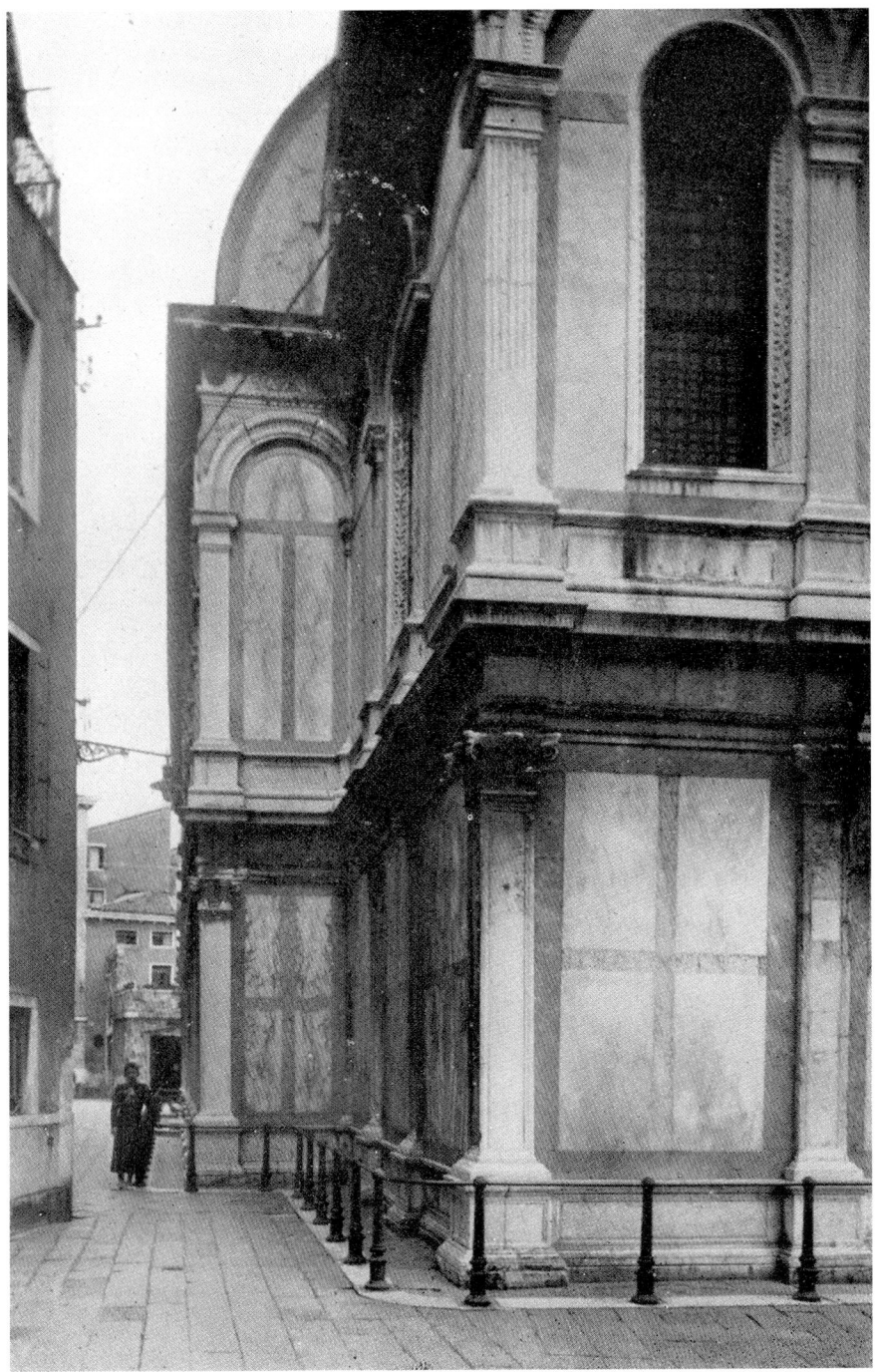

FIGURE 8.2 Santa Maria dei Miracoli, south side, from Adrian Stokes, *Venice* (1945), Plate 12. © Estate of Adrian Stokes.

Though Stokes writes at the Miracoli of 'inner dark ferment', these are restorative shades, for in Venice even 'the darkest windows obtain a kind of radiance from the fact of aperture above the closed waters: their darkness burns slowly and forever over the reflecting element beneath that is partly dark and partly light; just as the white stone sums or solidifies the light part'.[26] Darkness is not always felt as so renewing; in the Sublime it can be a source of terror (see Chapter 4) as in the 'negative sublime' of the last paintings of Mark Rothko (1903–70). Peter Fuller finds 'within the boundaries of his canvases deep black spaces of beckoning nothingness which seem to invite you, the viewer, to annihilate yourself in them'; in the monochromatic paintings Rothko began in 1969, just before his suicide in 1970, the picture spaces have sinisterly flattened into 'something shallow, empty, and murky'.[27] In a trajectory opposed to Rothko's, Fuller gives a case – from a significant early Melanie Klein paper of 1929 – of a healing response to dark blankness. Klein's essay discusses the artist Ruth Kjär, who found it in herself to make masterly portraits of her relatives in response to a 'compelling urge' to heal deep early anxieties and to repair the blank spaces she felt without and within.[28] At the Miracoli, Stokes finds even the 'last of the *inner* darkness ... has squeezed through to be a still and static outward thing'.[29] He explains this squeezing-out of the inner in his paper 'Concerning Art and Metapsychology' (also of 1945): 'A synthesis of inner meaning put outwards to be on its own, as it were, in the open world, always characterizes the work of art.'[30] Here he resists Freud's standpoint of 1911, in 'Formulations on Two Principles of Mental Functioning', that 'the artist is originally a man who turns from reality because he cannot come to terms with the demand for the renunciation of instinctual satisfaction as it is first made, and who then in phantasy-life allows full play to his erotic and ambitious wishes'.[31] Stokes opposed Freud's view of art as reality avoidance, his theory bears a 'faith in substitution', a 'faith in art's form ... in art as an ideal and not as an escape'.[32]

Incrusted caves

As in Soane and Gandy's Sublime imaginings (see Chapter 4), the cave archetype has been a way of reconciling dark inner ferments and outer affirmation. In one sea story Stokes begins the architecture of Venice with the cave:

> Aperture ... existed first, then the skeleton, then the walls that withstand the water. In these terms the ribs are still visible in pilaster, pillar and cornice; they are allowed to project as first defence. The wall lies behind them. And if the remaining apertures suggest caves, then the circular discs, so often in attendance upon Venetian windows, are stones that have been rolled away from these entrances.[33]

This clearly echoes Ruskin's famous passage on 'incrustation' from the *Stones of Venice*:

> The whole early architecture of Venice is architecture of incrustation.... The Venetian habitually incrusted his work with nacre; he built his houses, even the meanest, as if he had been a shell-fish – roughly inside, mother-of-pearl on the surface: he was content, perforce, to gather the clay of the Brenta banks, and bake it into brick for his substance of wall; but he overlaid it with the wealth of ocean, with the most precious foreign marbles. You might fancy early Venice one wilderness of brick, which a petrifying sea had beaten upon till it coated it with marble: at first a dark city – washed white by the sea foam.[34]

Ruskinian themes of rough cave or shell, and smooth incrusting, are reified as the Kleinian-Stokesian unconscious in Stokes's *Smooth and Rough* (1951):

> We partake of an inexhaustible feeding mother (a fine building announces), [such as the Miracoli church above] though we have bitten, torn, dirtied and pinched her, though we thought to have lost her utterly, to have destroyed her utterly in phantasy and act. We are grateful to stone buildings for their stubborn material, hacked and hewed but put together carefully, restored in better shape than those pieces that the infant imagine he had chewed or scattered, for which he searched. Much crude rock stands rearranged; now in the form of apertures, of suffusion at the side of apertures, the bites, the tears, the pinches are miraculously identified with the recipient passages of the body, with sense organs, with features; as well as with the good mother.[35]

A key contribution of Klein's was to give the infant's 'inner world ... the concrete significance of a place, the space where meaning is generated – and the prototype of this space is the child's perception (i.e. phantasies about) the mother's body'.[36] In one of Klein's more accessible papers, 'Our Adult World and its Roots in Infancy' (1959), she stresses the 'sense of persecution' along with the 'capacity to love' in the infant's relationship with the mother – the rough as well as the smooth: 'Love and hate towards the mother are bound up with the very young infant's capacity to project all his emotions on to her, thereby making her into a good as well as dangerous object.'[37] Again, Klein is more positive than Freud in stressing that 'the influence of unconscious phantasy on art, on scientific work, and on the activities of every-day life cannot be overrated', although, as noted, it was left to her followers such as Stokes to develop the aesthetic consequences of these unconscious stimuli. Klein's account of the first three to four months of life – characterized as the paranoid-schizoid position – exhibits 'the tendency of the infantile ego to split impulses and objects', for 'persecutory anxiety reinforces the need to keep separate the loved object from the dangerous one.'[38] Growing integration of the ego at around the fifth and sixth months of life leads to a greater synthesis of the good and bad aspects of the object, to attain the second 'depressive position', so-called because the baby now 'becomes afraid of the harm his destructive impulses and his greed might do, or might have done, to his loved objects.... He experiences feelings of guilt and the urge to preserve these objects and to make reparation to them for harm done'.[39] Klein emphasizes the continuities of these early infantile phantasies and emotions into adult life, in stating that 'nothing that ever existed in the unconscious completely loses its influence on the personality'.[40] Some following aesthetic interpreters, such as Hanna Segal, saw artistic creativity as essentially a resolution of this depressive situation and the aesthetic experience as principally identifying with this process. But Stokes moved from a similar position to the recognition that the artist sought as both an ideal object merged with the self (as in the paranoid-schizoid position) *and* an object perceived as discrete and independent (as in the depressive condition). His foregrounding of the creative possibilities of the paranoid-schizoid position reinforces the earlier points that Stokes posits these shadowy unconscious spaces as creatively 'radiant'. For, although they contain fearful objects of hate and destruction, they also contain objects of goodness, and in these dark spaces, and in creative transactions between the inner and the outer, an integrated personality can be achieved and the good mother restored – as the Miracoli symbolizes.

Aldo Rossi's *Teatro del Mondo*

For Stokes the Miracoli is also boatlike: 'A gondola is made up of curved and rectangular forms. Santa Maria dei Miracoli is the grandest of Venetian vessels. Riding the canal, the capitals along the side just above water level seem to float away from us in perfect line as might a flotilla of swans. The rest of the church, therefore, seems to move towards us.'[41] In common phantasy the buildings of Venice indeed appear to float, but now a real boat building sails into this story, conceived by an architect much concerned with shadows and the unconscious – Aldo Rossi. The 1979 Biennale saw his floating *Teatro del Mondo* towed across the lagoon to the Punta della Dogana, adding its baptistery-like, octagonal-turreted form, to the triumphant setting of the domes of Santa Maria della Salute, and the golden ball and figure of Fortune atop the custom house of the Dogana di Mare. (Rossi's theatre seated an audience of 250 in a volume 9.5 m square on plan, and 11 m high; two attached stair towers served three galleries and the 6 m tall crowning octagon with its pyramidal metal roof) (Figure 8.3). As Rossi says in his *A Scientific Autobiography*, it was moored at 'a place where architecture ended and the world of the imagination began'.[42] Rossi's oneiric *Scientific Autobiography* reads in itself as a map of the unconscious with its

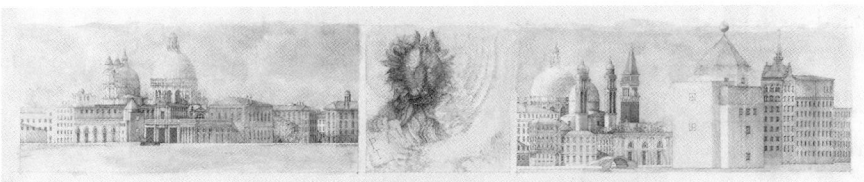

FIGURE 8.3 Aldo Rossi, *Composition with Teatro del Mondo and buildings in Venice* (between 1979 and 1980). Aldo Rossi fonds, Collection Centre Canadien d'Architecture/Canadian Centre for Architecture, Montréal, © Eredi Aldo Rossi, courtesy Fondazione Aldo Rossi.

repetitions and strangely shifting memories, as Vincent Scully finds in his postscript to the book: 'It is not a linear book.... It circles. So everything is dreamlike.... Conscious reasoning is left behind.... It enables [Rossi's] eyes to focus upon the nonrational life of objects that may be said to go on inside the brain of man but is not identical with his reason.'[43] Rossi writes:

> What pleases me above all is that the theatre is a veritable ship, and like a ship, it is subject to the movements of the lagoon, the gentle oscillations, the rising and sinking; so that in the uppermost galleries a few people might experience a slight sea-sickness that proves distracting and is increased by the sight of the water-line, which is visible beyond the windows. I cut these windows according to the level of the lagoon, the Giudecca, and the sky. The shadows from the little crosses of the window mullions stand out against the wood, and these windows make the theatre resemble a house.[44]

In childhood and adolescent memories of the Adriatic, earlier in the text:

> the sea seemed to me a coalescence capable of constructing a mysterious, geometric form made up of every memory and expectation. Perhaps it was really a verse from Alcaeus that led me to architecture when I was in secondary school: 'O seashell/daughter of stone and the whitening sea/ you astonish the minds of children'.... In [these lines] are contained the problem of form, of material, of imagination – that is, of astonishment.[45]

And he returns to Alcaeus's verse when thinking about the theatre:

> Yet *inside* and *outside* are also part of the meaning of theatre, and I rediscovered the other meaning of the seashell, 'daughter of stone and the whitening sea', which Alcaeus had written about, and which perhaps drew me to architecture just as it 'astonishes the minds of children'. Astonishment has a hard crust made of stone and shaped by the sea, like the crust of great constructions of steel, stone, and cement which form the city.[46]

Rossi's invocation of Alcaeus's poetry maps well onto our earlier exploration of the inner and outer transactions of the unconscious, and the incrustation of the petrifying ocean. I do not know if Rossi had read Stokes, but it is certain that he was familiar with *Stones of Venice*, if critical of 'Ruskin's pages of Venice (however beautifully written)' for their 'romantic criticism' and fondness for a picturesque decay associated with the kind of poverty Rossi would 'be delighted to see destroyed'.[47] We shall now probe further into the nature of this inner-outer binary of Rossi's, along with those of shadow and light, the irrational and rational, and the unconscious and conscious.[48]

Analogical architecture and the unconscious

In phantasy, the *Teatro al Mondo* also floats into one of Rossi's 'Analogous' compositions, grouped with two other Venice projects: the entrance gate for the architectural exhibition at the Venice Biennale and a project for a hotel in Cannaregio-West (Figure 8.4). Its arrangement exactly rhymes with Canaletto's capriccio of Venice, from the Parma Museum, which Rossi uses to illustrate the concept of the 'analogical city'; here Palladio's unrealized project for the Rialto bridge is grouped with his Basilica and Palazzo Chiericati transported to the Grand Canal from Vicenza.[49] To further define

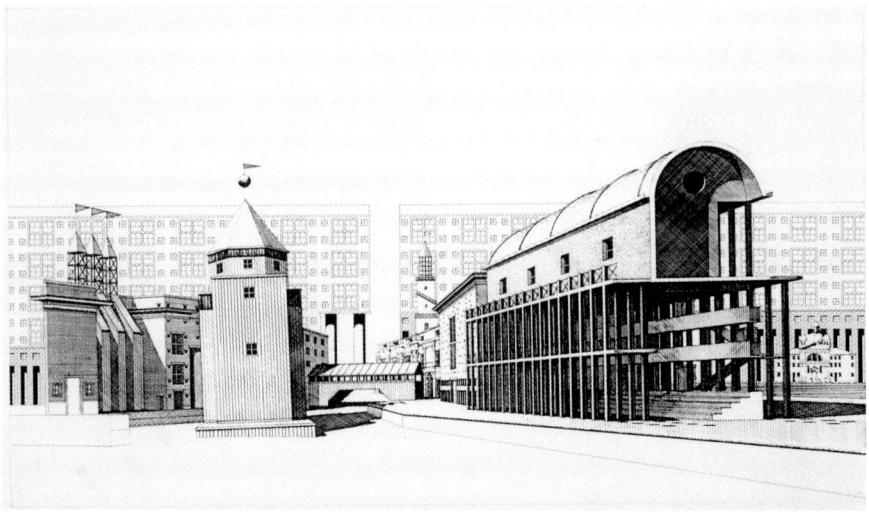

FIGURE 8.4 Aldo Rossi, *'Analogous' composition, with the entrance gate for the Architectural Exhibition at the Venice Biennale, the Teatro del Mondo, and a project for a hotel in Cannaregio-West, Venice, Italy. 1981.* Aldo Rossi fonds, Collection Centre Canadien d'Architecture/Canadian Centre for Architecture, Montréal, © Eredi Aldo Rossi, courtesy Fondazione Aldo Rossi.

the concept of analogy Rossi quotes from a letter of C. G. Jung to Freud of 2 March 1910:

> 'logical' thought is the thought expressed in words, that addresses itself to the outside world as a discourse. The 'analogous' of fantastic thought is sensible, figurative and mute, it is not a discourse but a rumination [on] material of the past, an act of revolt. The logical thought is 'thinking in words'. Analogical thought is archaic, unconscious and practically inexpressible in words.[50]

For that key interpreter of Rossi's unconscious, Peter Eisenman, analogy is the 'shadow of logic', his 'conscious images exist only as a key to their shadow imagery. It is their intrinsic, often unconscious content which confronts the more problematic and perhaps fundamental reality of the extrinsic cultural condition today'.[51] While

> in Rossi's drawings the shadows themselves...take on material solidity. Far from the shadows of neo-classical drawing which throw the actual elements of a building into relief and make their reality sharper, the shadows in Rossi's drawings become another figure. In their highly exaggerated, pitch black shadow they assume a graphic presence that overpowers the actual literal shape of the building. As such they become objects which cannot share the same qualities as the buildings.... They become the negative image of positive reality.[52]

Rossi's shadows represent a cultural condition irrevocably altered by the events of the Second World War, the mass destruction, the Holocaust, and the atomic bomb.[53] He imagines 'photographs of cities during war, sections of apartments, broken toys',[54] and talking of the fragmentary character of certain of his drawings (e.g. *L'Architecture Assasinée*, 1975) declares his belief 'that today we live in a world that cannot be repaired, a world of psychological and human fragments'.[55] In April 1971, Rossi was involved in a serious car accident; in the following summer, and still with pain in his bones, he metaphorized the design of his magnum opus, the Cemetery of San Cataldo at Modena, as a bare skeleton, seeing 'the skeletal structure of the body as a series of fractures to be reassembled' (Figure 8.5).[56] Klein defines this acute sense of fragmentation as 'depressive anxiety', when the ego 'finds itself confronted with the psychic reality that its loved objects are in a state of dissolution – in bits – there is anxiety how to put the bits together in the right way and do away with the bad ones.'[57] Confronted with the unfeasibility of restoring the good whole-object, the art and architecture of modernism has resorted to the collage, composing aspects of the whole-object from fragmented part-objects. So Rossi describes 'analogous' architecture as a 'singular type of collage in which...the ultimate meaning itself remains unknown.'[58] The various projects that

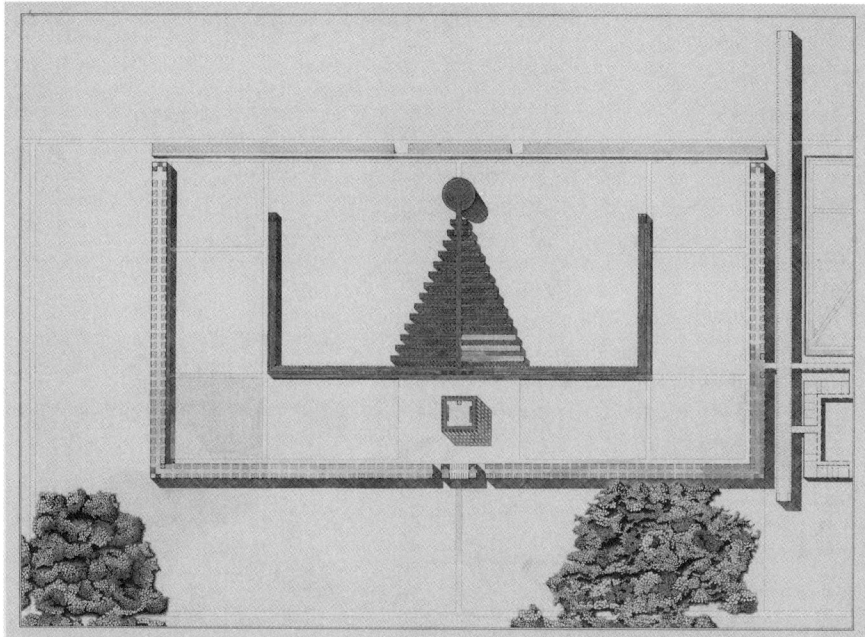

FIGURE 8.5 Aldo Rossi, Gianni Braghieri, *Cimitero di San Cataldo, Modena, Italy: Plan* (between 1971 and 1978). Aldo Rossi fonds, Collection Centre Canadien d'Architecture/Canadian Centre for Architecture, Montréal, © Eredi Aldo Rossi, courtesy Fondazione Aldo Rossi.

compose the analogous drawing of Venice are not shattered to the extremes of *L'Architecture Assasinée*, but they are wilfully displaced, nonetheless, as elements that cannot 'constitute a dialectic:...projected into the infinite as timeless anecdotes'.[59] Stokes's fascinating ruminations on the nature of collage place the moment of cultural fragmentation a whole century earlier than Rossi – to the mid-nineteenth century and the full emergence of the industrial city. His *Invitation in Art* (1965) describes modern art's struggle to 'reach a compromise with our disjointed urban environment, with the illimitable enveloping quality of the startling chaos around us'.[60] This hostile milieu makes whole-object relationships unsustainable, condemning us to 'hypnotic envelopment by part-objects', as in the shadow worlds of the analogous city:

> The employment in collages and assemblages of actual objects points not only to the reiteration of whole-object nature in a void created by the abandonment of representations that truly imitate them, but also to our particular hunger in modern environment for surrounding objects that we may contemplate in their possession of the wholeness and self-sufficiency of which the nude was once the presiding symbol.[61]

Shadows of the in-between

So it is that Rossi's shadows exhibit an extreme melancholy equal to the mood we have seen Boullée describe in his 'Architecture, Essay on Art' when 'on the edge of a wood in the moonlight...the shadows of the trees etched on the ground made a most profound impression'. 'Nature offered itself to [his] gaze in mourning', and he proceeded thereafter to seek a new type of architecture composed of the 'effect of shadows' (Chapter 4). Rossi says how the work of translating this passage on shadows into Italian in 1967 'allowed [him] to understand the complexity of the irrational in architecture'.[62] The paintings of De Chirico are often invoked to read these shadows of Rossi, as when Sheila O'Donnell brackets de Chirico's *The Mystery and Melancholy of a Street* with a view of Rossi's Gallaratese housing noting how the 'elevation drawings [of this project] with their intense shadows...evoke a world of memories and nostalgia, bringing to mind the images of de Chirico' (Figure 8.6).[63] But Rossi himself disavows the de Chirico connections visited on his work, as in this interview of 1990:

> I think that there is an equivocal relationship that most critics find between my work and de Chirico. Certainly there is a de Chirico-like element in my drawings, but I always find it strange that critics fixated on an immediate association with de Chirico. Because the truth is that my

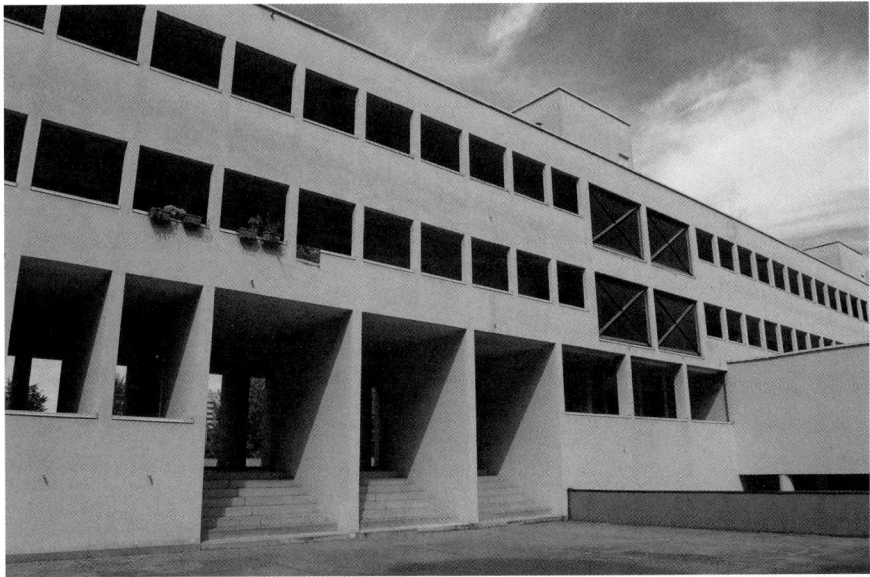

FIGURE 8.6 Gallaratese housing, north Milan, 1969–70. Photograph Stephen Kite.

great influence and love is with Sironi and with Morandi. In fact, what Morandi does with his precise bottles and still lifes is part of what I aim to do in my architecture.[64]

A *Domestic Architecture* (1974) drawing of Rossi's rhymes the shadows of a Giorgio Morandi-like grouping of coffee pot, mug and utensils with those of the elevation of the residential development at Gallaratese, Milan. It illustrates Rossi's feeling for the inner and outer, and his uncannily oneiric mixing of scales. In *A Scientific Autobiography*, he writes of his love for the receptacles of the kitchen as 'miniatures of the fantastic architecture that I would encounter later. Today I still love to draw these large coffeepots, which I liken to brick walls, and which I think of as structures that can be entered'.[65] As Michael Hays points out, 'dimensions are of no importance in analogical thought since the order of the city is cognitively embedded in all architectural types of any scale'.[66] As described in *The Architecture of the City*, a single building such as Diocletian's Palace at Split can come to 'refer *analogically* to the form of a city'.[67]

So if the *Teatro del Mondo* can be imagined as a large kitchen utensil that has found its way into St Mark's Basin, then equally Morandi's still lifes are deeply implicated in his home cityscapes of Bologna, in its famous endless colonnades and in tall medieval towers. The critic Carlo Ludovico Ragghianti says that Morandi's interest in still life is 'wholly architectural, so much so that it should prompt us to think of cathedrals rather than of bottles'.[68] The city of Bologna – as held in the hands of St Petronio from a Lorenzo Costa altarpiece – might be compared with a Morandi *Still Life* of 1956 where the paired bottles echo Bologna's famous medieval twin towers of the Due Torri, soaring above a common urban fabric – represented as three boxes in the still life.[69] In his study, *Morandi's Legacy*, Paul Coldwell describes Bologna as 'an artificial environment where the vertical forms of the towers have a counterpoint in the horizontal colonnades, measuring out the city in units of column and shadow'.[70] The bars of shadow thrown by the pilasters and columns of Bologna's passages syncopate every step Morandi would have made through his city.[71] So on Rossi's suggestion and in more plausibly subtle parallels than with de Chirico, it is fascinating to compare Bologna's colonnades with those at Gallaratese, and then to examine the negative spaces in Morandi's still lifes – those dark alley-like fissures, between his architectonic bottles and boxes, bidding us to the in-betweens of inner and outer. Coldwell says that Morandi's drawings 'tentatively delineate the outline of tree, house and shadow as being of equal value. They deliberately create a jigsaw of positive and negative';[72] patterns striking in some of the *Still Life* watercolours of 1959 where form is entirely described by the negative shadow shapes.[73] To reiterate Eisenman's points, in works like these, Rossi seems to have learnt how shadows might take on 'material solidity' and the 'negative image of positive reality'. As in Bologna, surely shadowed colonnades should invite life:

> In the last few days I saw the first open windows, clothes hanging out to dry in the loggias – the first timid signs of the life it will assume when people move in. I am confident that the spaces reserved for this daily life – the big colonnade, the *ballatoi* – will bring a sharp focus to the dense flow of daily life and the deep popular roots of this residential architecture.[74]

This is Rossi in 1974 on his hopes for the Gallaratese project. But his colonnades are strangely devoid of common life; they belong too much to the analogous city, and are accordingly dislocated spaces where the unconscious inner has made insufficient connection to the outer to establish a viable in-between. Stokes saw the shaded in-betweens of the South as especially desirable spatial realms, as in his essay 'Living in Ticino, 1947–50':

> As I walk under the arcade of Locarno's main square, I see in a clear and liquid shade a café table with a light-blue cloth that touches a stone pier. I think I would be entirely safe there: leaning against the pillar I would be able to partake utterly of every thought: I would be immobile, provided for, as in the womb yet out-of-doors: existence within and existence without would be thinly divided: in the blue tablecloth I would clutch the sky.[75]

'In the womb yet out-of-doors', Stokes progressively stressed the role of the first 'paranoid-schizoid' position in creativity along with the second 'depressive' position, as in his paper 'Form in Art' (1955) where he argued that the infant 'homogeneity associated with idealization (the inexhaustible breast) is harnessed by the work of art to an acute sense of otherness and actuality'.[76] Celebrating his reification of the shadowy in-between, Colin St John Wilson found in Stokes:

> The extraordinary conclusion: that it is uniquely the role of the masterpiece to make possible the *simultaneous* experience of these two polar modes; enjoyment at the same time of intense sensations of being inside and outside, of envelopment and detachment, of oneness and separateness.[77]

The light of low windows

The *Teatro del Mondo* is also corporeal; it is a body that can be entered like the San Carlone colossus at Arona, of which Rossi writes often, where 'the steep ascent through the interior reveals the structure of the work and the welded seams of the huge pieces of sheet metal'.[78] In its internally skeletal structure the *Teatro* is also machine-like, Rossi describes its iron and wood as 'two parallel structures' like the sections of the Byzantine dome of St Mark's. Or like the many festively elaborate *macchine del mondo* precedents, as illustrated in Rossi's book on his Venice theatre, *Teatro del Mondo*.[79] Its controlled modulation of shadows and light make it another kind of *macchina*, a looking machine such as a camera obscura. Musing on his *Teatro* Rossi agrees with those who 'have spoken of the light of Carpaccio in connection with the interior of my theatre', and others who speak of

> a pre-monumental Venice, a Venice not yet white with the stone of Sansovino and Palladio. It is the Venice of Carpaccio, and I see it in the interior light, in the wood, and I am reminded of certain Dutch interiors which evoke ships and are near the sea.[80]

Rossi writes also of Dutch painters who 'cover tables [with Persian carpets] and display their Oriental colours in the light of a low window'.[81] Two pictures that bring together this darkly intimate imagery of South and North are Carpaccio's *Vision of St Augustine* (c. 1502) and Vermeer's *The Astronomer* (1668). They also evoke that camera obscura image of the understanding in Locke's *Essay Concerning Human Understanding* (1690) as a dark closet with little openings (Chapter 3). Here a line from Stokes's *Smooth and Rough* is apposite: 'The candle of reason, brighter, steadier, longer than heretofore, discloses a nearer and more active darkness: we are ringed by emotion.'[82]

There is an allusive pairing of skiagraphic images in Rossi's book on his theatre (*Teatro del Mondo*), in which a section and plan of Vincenzo Scamozzi's Rotonda-like project for the Villa Bardellini (1594) faces Rossi's own sketch sections for his *Teatro*.[83] (Scamozzi had also designed a theatre of the world for the marriage of Dogaressa Morosina Morosini, a floating *macchina* also akin to Palladio's Rotonda.) Scamozzi's villa section is deeply informed by Giordano Bruno's *De Umbris Idearum* (*Shadows of Ideas*, 1582), where Bruno 'points out that men are made opaque by their own corporal darkness and consequently they can see the truth only through the shadow which they are given in the sensitive world'.[84] Accordingly Scamozzi's mystifying tracings and hatchings on plan and section show how shadows will determine the behaviour of the occupants of the villa, making it a kind of inhabitable sundial.[85] In *A Scientific Autobiography*, Rossi remembers Anthony Vidler giving him a copy of Frances Yates's *Theatre of the World*; here and in *The Art of Memory* Yates has exposed the occultly cabbalistic *macchinas* of Bruno and the hermetic tradition which inform the theatres of Palladio and Scamozzi in a magic of revolving Lullian wheels compartmented with signs: 'the images of the stars, closer to reality than the images of the astral forces, the "shadows" intermediary between the ideal world above the stars, and the objects and events in the lower world'.[86] Fearing his dark magic arts the Papal authorities burned Bruno alive as a heretic in the Campo de' Fiori, Rome, in 1600. For Klein, the danger in failing to successfully manage the internal objects of the unconscious, and to successfully negotiate inner and outer, is the psychosis of the damaged individual, lost in inner darkness, in complete denial of the external world.

At the end of the first chapter of his *Venice*, Stokes returns to his Plate 9, a detail of the Torre del'Orologio in the Piazza San Marco, and the gateway to the Merceria (Figure 8.7). For him this photograph is 'the one that is most beautiful' for it is seen to 'exemplify a perfect harmony of inner and outer things'. Stokes says:

> I attribute to the reflections of the piazza, to the street beneath the dark archway, to the stone building, the quality of a visual parable of unconscious, pre-conscious and conscious. For the Quattro Cento building, *by itself* expresses the solution of manifold directions, manifold movements of the spirit as might a vigorous face.[87]

In conclusion – against these more affirmative shadows of the *Teatro del Mondo* – it has to be admitted that Rossi's darks are rarely as radiant as those of Stokes's Quattro Cento palaces. At the same time, Rossi is certainly among those few significant architect-thinkers to have rehabilitated shadow as an operative figure within the architecture of modernism – or rather postmodernism – against prevalent ideologies of transparency and over-illumination. As we have seen his shadows often partake of a sinister, surreal quality – one, in fact, more like de Chirico or the Fascist artist Mario Sironi than like Morandi's more benign influence. Thus, the mourner at Rossi's New Cemetery of San Cataldo at Modena (1971–8) – after passing along the supportive and corporeally humanistic neoclassical colonnades of Cesare Costa's earlier structures (1858–76) – broaches a small door to be 'set adrift in [Rossi's] immense stoa, shadowed and featureless'.[88] And one might add, more or less functionless in any practical sense (Figure 8.8). In making positive figures of what is normally negative, on occasion Rossi's shadows become so materially solid that they take on a spooky life independent of the objects that cast them – becoming in fact part-objects that might be sensed as 'bad'. Reminders, therefore, of nightmarish tales such as that one of the devil who seized Peter Schlemihl's shadow.[89] With all his love for the total integration of the inner and outer represented by such a work of architecture as Mauro Codussi's Torre del' Orologio, Stokes recognized the deconstructed nature of the modern condition and the artist's need to work through collage and the fragment – the condition Rossi articulates in the silence of *his* shadows. Stokes increasingly explored beyond Klein's stress on the role of the 'depressive' existential state in creativity, to understand *The Invitation in Art* (1965) which attracts the artist or architect to plunge into the dark unconscious of oceanic feeling, and to play with depth and with harsh chiaroscuro.[90] Problematizing the collage, we discussed the use, in the post-humanist condition, of whole-objects as fragments – a situation intensified if an object's shadow becomes yet another part-object, as in de Chirico, and often in Rossi. But we have

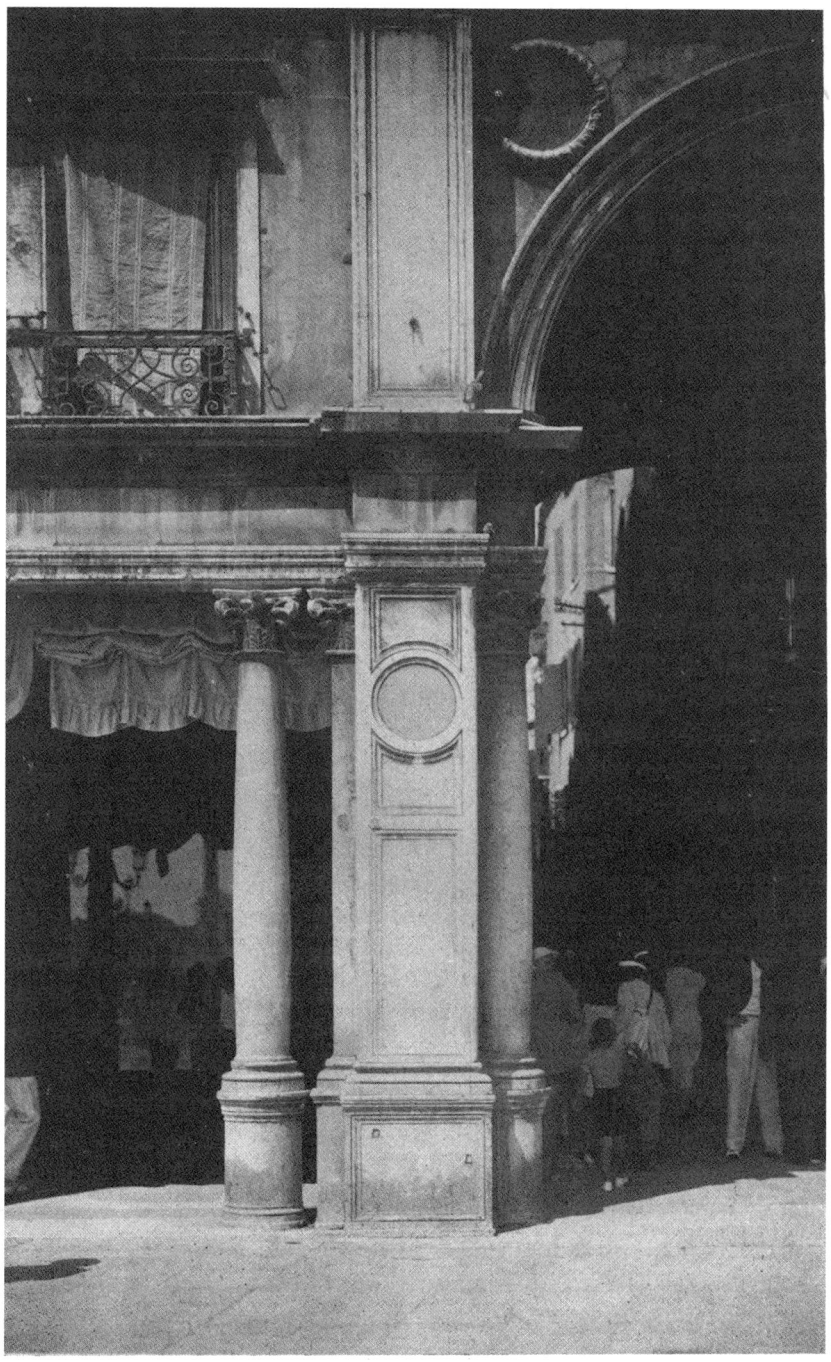

FIGURE 8.7 Detail of clock tower, St Mark's Piazza, Venice, from Adrian Stokes, *Venice* (1945), Plate 9. © Estate of Adrian Stokes.

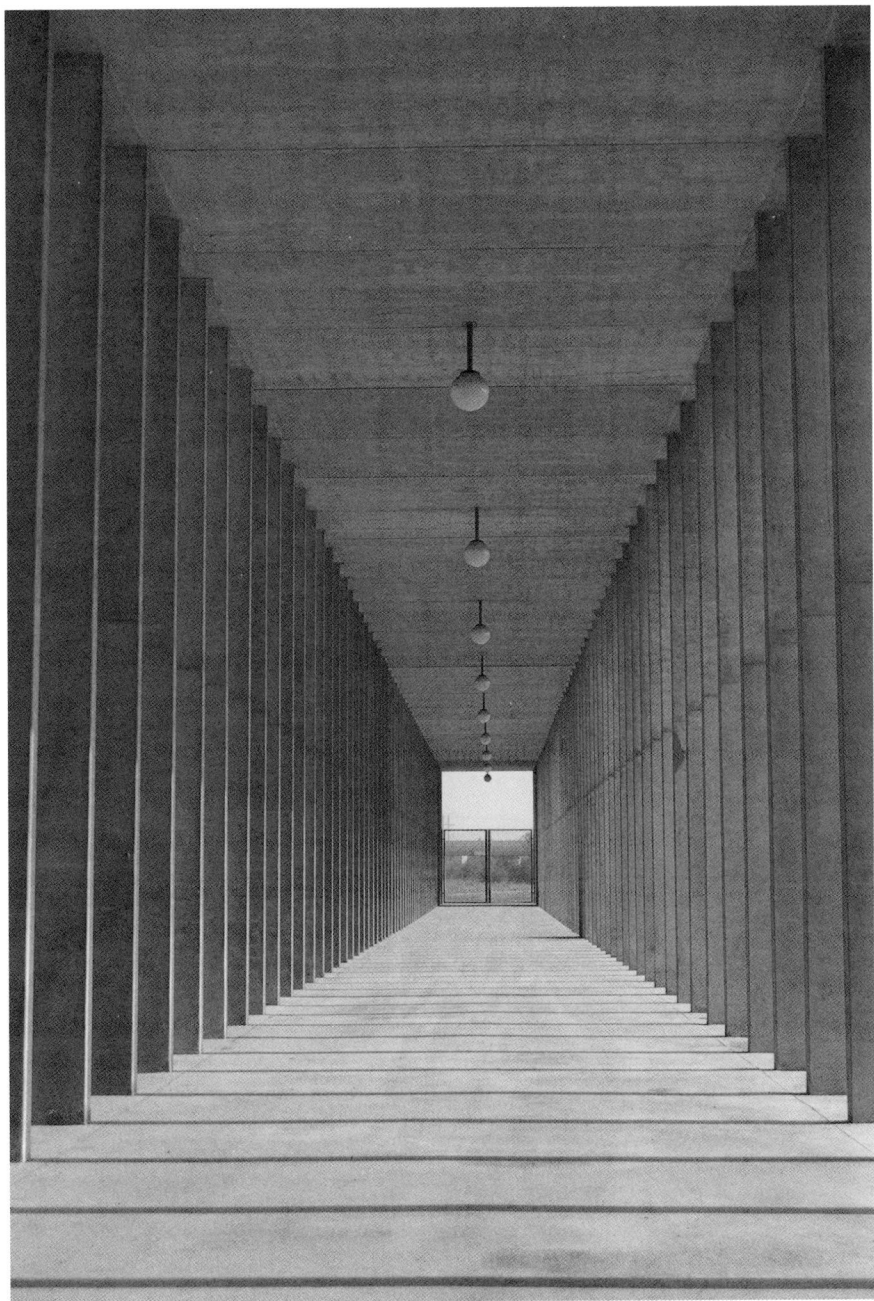

FIGURE 8.8 Stoa, New Cemetery of San Cataldo, Modena, 1971–8. Photograph, Stephen Kite.

also pointed to the enabling darks of Carpaccio's painting of *St Augustine* in the *Scuolo San Giorgio degli Schiavoni* in connection with Rossi. These final words from Stokes's *Venice* speak of the possibility 'to savour the counting house gloom dim with warmed stones' of these *Scuole* of Venice, whose 'great windows of black bottle glass give out upon the sea like portholes'.[91]

Notes

1. Quoted in Read, Richard, *Art and Its Discontents. The Early Life of Adrian Stokes* (Aldershot, Hants.: Ashgate, 2002), p. 35, n. 106. Diary entry of 6 May 1925 from Hotel Savaia e Iolanda, Venice.
2. Gowing, Lawrence (ed), *The Critical Writings of Adrian Stokes* (London: Thames and Hudson, 1978), *vol 2, Smooth and Rough*, p. 243. Subsequent references in the form: *CW Stokes, vol. 2, Smooth and Rough*, p. 243.
3. *CW Stokes, vol. 2, Smooth and Rough*, p. 316, n. 3.
4. Quoted in Kite, Stephen, *Building Ruskin's Italy. Watching Architecture* (Farnham, Surrey: Ashgate, 2012), p. 46.
5. Bann, Stephen, 'Adrian Stokes. English Aesthetic Criticism under the Impact of Psychoanalysis', in E. Timms and N. Segal (eds), *Freud in Exile. Psychoanalysis and Its Vicissitudes* (New Haven, CT and London: Yale University Press, 1988), pp. 134–44. See also Glover, Nicky, *Psychoanalytic Aesthetics. An Introduction to the British School* (London: Karnac, 2009), p. 89.
6. *CW Stokes, vol. 2, Venice*, p. 103.
7. See Kite, *Building Ruskin's Italy*, p. 149.
8. Glover, *Psychoanalytic Aesthetics*, p. 25.
9. *CW Stokes, vol. 2, Venice*, p. 134.
10. *CW Stokes, vol. 2, Venice*, pp. 137, 138.
11. See Glover, *Psychoanalytic Aesthetics*, p. 37.
12. Klein, Melanie, 'Our Adult World and Its Roots in Infancy', in M. Masud and R. Khan (eds), *Melanie Klein. Envy and Gratitude and Other Works* (London: Hogarth Press, 1975), pp. 247–63, p. 251.
13. See Plant, Margaret, *Venice. Fragile City 1797–1997* (New Haven, CT and London: Yale University Press, 2002), p. 339.
14. The Venetian diplomat and ambassador of Rovigo, Giovandomenico Roncale, quoted in Savoy, Daniel, *Venice from the Water. Architecture and Myth in an Early Modern City* (New Haven, CT, and London: Yale University Press, 2012), p. 71.
15. *CW Stokes, vol. 2, Venice*, p. 88.
16. *CW Stokes, vol. 2, Venice*, p. 91 (The adjective 'intensely' light and dark is only in the 1945 edition.)
17. *CW Stokes, vol. 2, Venice*, p. 104.

18 CW Stokes, vol. 2, Venice, p. 131.
19 Stokes, Adrian, Venice (London: Faber and Faber, 1945), p. v, in the Preface to the first edition written in September 1944; the version as published in the Critical Writings omits this information.
20 Plant, Venice. Fragile City 1797–1997, pp. 327–8.
21 Jacobsen, Ken, and Jacobsen, Jenny, Carrying Off the Palaces: John Ruskin's Lost Daguerrotypes (London: Quaritch, 2015), p. 199.
22 Ruskin quoted in Jacobsen and Jacobsen, Carrying Off the Palaces, p. 196.
23 CW Stokes, vol. 2, Venice, p. 87.
24 See Goy, Richard J., Venice. An Architectural Guide (New Haven, CT and London: Yale University Press, 2010), pp. 183–6.
25 CW Stokes, vol. 2, Venice, pp. 98–9.
26 CW Stokes, vol. 2, Venice, p. 91.
27 Fuller, Peter, Art and Psychoanalysis (London: Writers and Readers, 1980), pp. 222–3.
28 Fuller, Art and Psychoanalysis, p. 223. Klein, Melanie, 'Infantile Anxiety-Situations Reflected in a Work of Art and in the Creative Impulse', The International Journal of Psychoanalysis', vol. 10 (1929), pp. 436–43.
29 CW Stokes, vol. 2, Venice, p. 99.
30 Stokes, Adrian, 'Concerning Art and Metapsychology', The International Journal of Psychoanalysis, vol. 26 (1945), pp. 177–9, p. 178.
31 Quoted in Stokes, 'Concerning Art and Metapsychology', p. 179.
32 Deamer, Peggy, 'Adrian Stokes. The Architecture of Phantasy and the Phantasy of Architecture', in J. A. Winer, J. W. Anderson, E. A. Danze (eds), Psychoanalysis and Architecture (Catskill, NY: Mental Health Resources, 2005), pp. 125–37, p. 130.
33 CW Stokes, vol. 2, Venice, p. 91.
34 Ruskin, Works, 9: 323.
35 CW Stokes, vol. 2, Smooth and Rough, p. 241.
36 Glover, Psychoanalytic Aesthetics, p. 62.
37 Klein, 'Our Adult World and Its Roots in Infancy', p. 248.
38 Klein, 'Our Adult World and Its Roots in Infancy', p. 253.
39 Klein, 'Our Adult World and Its Roots in Infancy', p. 255.
40 Klein, 'Our Adult World and Its Roots in Infancy', p. 262.
41 CW Stokes, vol. 2, Venice, p. 100.
42 Rossi, Aldo, A Scientific Autobiography, Lawrence Venuti (trans) (Cambridge, MA: MIT Press, 1981), p. 66.
43 Rossi, A Scientific Autobiography, p. 111.
44 Rossi, A Scientific Autobiography, p. 67.
45 Rossi, A Scientific Autobiography, p. 25.
46 Rossi, A Scientific Autobiography, p. 66.

47 O'Regan, John et al. (eds) *Aldo Rossi. Selected Writings and Projects* (London: Architectural Design, 1983), p. 51.
48 These are just some among many other potential binaries that commentators have discovered in Rossi, see La Marche, Jean, *The Familiar and the Unfamiliar in Twentieth Century Architecture* (Urbana and Chicago: University of Illinois Press, 2003), p. 76.
49 Aldo Rossi, 'An Analogical Architecture', in O'Regan, *Aldo Rossi*, pp. 58–64, p. 59.
50 Quoted in Eisenman, Peter, 'The House of the Dead as the City of Survival', in K. Frampton (ed), *Aldo Rossi in America 1976 to 1979* (New York: The Institute for Architecture and Urban Studies, 1979), pp. 4–15, p. 6. See also the chapter on 'Analogy' in Hays, Michael, *Architecture's Desire. Reading the Late Avant-Garde* (Cambridge, MA: MIT Press, 2010).
51 Eisenman, 'The House of the Dead as the City of Survival', p. 9.
52 Eisenman, 'The House of the Dead as the City of Survival', p. 9.
53 See Eisenman, 'The House of the Dead as the City of Survival', p. 5.
54 Rossi, *A Scientific Autobiography*, p. 8.
55 Jimenez, Carlos, 'Mystic Signs. A Conversation with Aldo Rossi', *Cite*, vol. 24 (Spring 1990), pp. 16, 17, p. 16.
56 O'Regan, *Aldo Rossi. Selected Writings and Projects*, p. 82.
57 Quoted in R. D. Hinshelwood, *A Dictionary of Kleinian Thought* (London: Free Association Books, 1989), p. 145.
58 Rossi, Aldo, 'My Designs and Analogous Architecture', in Frampton, *Rossi in America*, pp. 16–19, p. 19.
59 Rossi, 'My Designs and Analogous Architecture', p. 19.
60 *CW Stokes*, vol. 3, *Invitation in Art*, p. 287.
61 *CW Stokes*, vol. 3, *Reflections on the Nude*, p. 317.
62 Rossi, *A Scientific Autobiography*, p. 52.
63 O'Regan, *Aldo Rossi. Selected Writings and Projects*, p. 10.
64 Jimenez, 'Mystic Signs. A Conversation with Aldo Rossi', p. 17.
65 Rossi, *A Scientific Autobiography*, p. 2.
66 Hays, *Architecture's Desire*, p. 37.
67 Rossi, Aldo, *The Architecture of the City*, D. Ghirardo and J. Ockman (trans) (Cambridge, MA: MIT Press, 1984), p. 174.
68 Quoted in Hustvedt, Siri, 'Not just bottles', *Modern Painters*, vol. 11, no. 4, (Winter 1998), pp. 20–5, p. 22.
69 See Hustvedt, 'Not Just Bottles', p. 22.
70 Coldwell, Paul, *Morandi's Legacy. Influences on British Art* (London: Philip Wilson, 2006), p. 10.
71 For a detailed study and images of these arcades, see Santucci, Andrea, *Il Mirabile Artificio, colonne, archi e capiteli dei portici di Bologna* (Bologona: Gli Inchiostri Associati Editore, 1997–98).

72 Coldwell, *Morandi's Legacy*, p. 17.
73 See Güse, Ernst-Gerhard and Morat, Franz Armin (eds) *Giorgio Morandi. Paintings, Watercolours, Drawings, Etchings* (Munich: Prestel, 1999), plates 57, 58.
74 Rossi quoted in Arnell, Peter and Bickford, Ted, *Aldo Rossi. Buildings and Projects* (New York: Rizzoli, 1985), p. 75.
75 Wollheim, Richard, *The Image in Form. Selected Writings of Adrian Stokes* (Harmondsworth, Middlesex: Penguin Books, 1972), p. 316.
76 Stokes, Adrian, 'Form in Art', in M. Klein, P. Heimann, R. E. Money-Kyrle (eds) *New Directions in Psycho-Analysis. The Significance of Infant Conflict in the Pattern of Adult Behaviour* (London: Tavistock Publications, 1955), pp. 406–20, p. 414.
77 Wilson, Colin St John, 'The Natural Imagination: An Essay on the Experience of Architecture', *Architectural Review*, vol. 185 (1989), pp. 64–70, p. 66.
78 Rossi, *A Scientific Autobiography*, p. 3.
79 Rossi, Aldo, *Teatro del Mondo*, M. Brusatin and A. Prandi (eds) (Venice: Cluva Librería Editrice, 1982).
80 Rossi, *A Scientific Autobiography*, p. 68.
81 Rossi, *A Scientific Autobiography*, p. 69.
82 *CW Stokes*, vol.2, *Smooth and Rough*, p. 234.
83 Rossi, *Teatro del Mondo*, pp. 70, 71.
84 Frascari, Marco, 'A Secret Semotic Skiagraphy: The Corporal Theatre of Meanings in Vincenzo Scamozzi's *Idea* of Architecture', *Via 11 Architecture and Shadow* (University of Pennsylvania: Rizzoli, 1990), pp. 32–51, p. 47.
85 Frascari, 'A Secret Semotic Skiagraphy', p. 44.
86 Yates, Frances A., *The Art of Memory* (London: Pimlico, 1992), p. 220.
87 *CW Stokes*, vol. 2, *Venice*, p. 111.
88 Blundell Jones, Peter, and Canniffe, Eamonn, *Modern Architecture Through Case Studies* (Oxford: Architectural Press, 2007), p. 194.
89 See Stoichita, Victor I., *A Short History of the Shadow* (London: Reaktion, 1997), p. 169.
90 See Glover, *Psychoanalytic Aesthetics*, pp. 96, 97.
91 *CW Stokes*, vol. 2, *Venice*, p. 95.

9

Louis Kahn and the 'Treasury of Shadows'

> *At the threshold, the crossing of silence and light,*
> *lies the sanctuary of art, the only language of man.*
> *It is the treasury of the shadows. Whatever is made of light*
> *casts a shadow. Our work is of shadow; it belongs to light.*[1]

In the Trenton Bath House, New Jersey (1954–8), Louis Kahn created a new beginning for modern architecture by innovating a 'concept of space order' integrated with the 'order of construction' in which the 'hollow columns' – here supporting the pyramidal roofs of the Bath House – 'distinguish the spaces that serve from those being served'.[2] Here he showed a way beyond both *plan-libre* and planar spatial conceptions, with the modern monumentality of his structure space. Equally, he was in the vanguard in confronting 'the denial of the shadow's magic origin' by those exhausted post-Enlightenment polarities of modernism which crudely divided the world into 'good-bad, bright-dark, light-heavy, or transparent-secret', dissolving interior and exterior in the pursuit of evermore brightness to ever greater depths.[3] With biting satire Joseph Roth attacked these 'modernization trends' as early as 1920s Berlin:

> Not even nature affords as much light and air as some of the new dwellings. For a bedroom there is a glass-walled studio. They dine in gyms. Rooms you would have sworn were tennis courts serve them as libraries and music rooms.... They relax after meals on white operating tables. And in the evening concealed fluorescent tubes light the room so evenly that it is no longer illuminated, it is a pool of luminosity.[4]

Kahn clearly learnt from Frank Lloyd Wright, who, despite being the inventor of fluid space, also denounced the 'immense prison of glass facades', and shaped interiors that placed an emphasis, learnt from Japan, 'on a nuanced handling of darkness and effective shadowing' (see Chapter 2).[5] But Kahn only explicitly acknowledged two teachers: 'Every man has a figure in his work who he feels answerable to. I often say to myself, "How'm I doing, Le Corbusier?" You see, Le Corbusier was my teacher. I say Paul Cret was my teacher and Corbusier was my teacher.'[6] It has been said of the later Le Corbusier – as compared to the Euclidian Purism of his earlier work – that he 'revealed himself more as a shaper of shadows who discovered the aesthetic and atmospheric potential of light for modernism and was interested...in the shadows his sculptural facades cast'.[7] The same commentators praise Kahn's 'sophisticated chiaroscuro painting with shadows from which his building volumes derive their plasticity' and also note the qualities of the interiors of his friend Luis Barragán, an architect who 'loved shadow and the semidarkness that models spaces and creates a depth in which contours become blurry and the atmosphere peaceful'.[8] I am emphasizing Kahn as pre-eminent in this turn to shadow in the second half of the twentieth century. In one of his initially unfathomable diagrams Kahn suggestively places the 'treasury of the shadows' on the central axis between 'Silence' and 'Light';[9] as John Lobell explains it, Kahn 'taught us to understand the Order of the Shadow – what lies between idea and reality, between Silence and Light'.[10] To understand Kahn as a shadow-maker it is necessary to explain this Order of Shadow as a theory in his work, and here the links to Schopenhauer's philosophy and architectural aesthetics prove instructive. Closely related is Kahn's conviction that the process of drawing is simultaneously a mode of representation and an act of building in itself. Here we examine how theory, drawing and building come together in two projects rich in their feeling for shadow in dialogue with light, the Rochester Unitarian Church (1959–69) and the Kimbell Art Museum (1966–72).

In one story Kahn's feeling for shadow draws on neoclassical ideas of nature, and in the other it appeals to the romantic traditions of the early nineteenth century. In the neoclassical frame we have encountered Boullées *l'architecture des ombres* of primary volumes, discovered among gloomy forests, within the tragic grandeur of nature (see Chapter 4), while in the romantic context there is all that was found inscribed in the primitive response to nature of Ruskin's 'Lamp of Power' (see Chapter 6). So at Kahn's Salk Institute for Biological Studies (1959–65) the stark cuboids of the perimeter stair towers belong to the world of Boullée or Ledoux, whereas the complex geometries and richer material palette of the courtyard reference romantic and picturesque sources.[11] Kahn had in mind his beloved Philadelphia when he said that 'a city should be a place where a little boy walking through its streets can sense what he someday would like to be' as made visible in the 'commonality' of 'the institutions available'.[12] In the topography of the city the neoclassical acropolis of Philadelphia Museum of Art (1916–28) dominates the north-western corner of William Penn's 1682 grid from its hilltop site beside the Schuykill River. This was under construction in the period of Kahn's last years at high school and the time of his architectural education at the University of Pennsylvania under the École des Beaux-Arts ethos of the École-trained Paul Philippe Cret. Given his French rationalist background, Cret predictably opposed the subjectivism of American Romanticism as crystallized in another prominent embellishment of the city, Kahn's favourite Frank Furness building, the Pennsylvania Academy of Fine Arts (1872–6). While at Philadelphia's Central High School Kahn had been awarded prizes for his artwork by this august institution, and was then offered a scholarship to attend the Academy; by this point, however, he had become so engaged by architecture that he declined the bursary, enrolling instead in the architecture course at the University of Pennsylvania. Examining 'Ruskin in America' (see Chapter 6), Frank Furness's Academy building was seen as a striking fusion of Ruskinian naturalism and the New England transcendentalism of Emerson. The muscular overscaled structure of Furness's stair hall contains not only this vortex of American and English romantic impulses, but also those of the German idealists, among whom Arthur Schopenhauer's (1788–1860) philosophy of art proved to be the most widely influential on artists and architects – including Kahn. To isolate some of these currents: as noted (see Chapter 6), Sullivan's brief tenure in Furness's office in Philadelphia in 1873 gave him his first professional contact with these notions of transcendent naturalism; in *A System of Architectural Ornament* (1924) Sullivan suggests that the seed-germ 'is the real thing; the seat of identity. Within its delicate mechanism lies the will to power: the function of which is to seek and eventually to find its full expression in form'.[13] Then Kahn in a statement of 1955 said: 'Order is a philosophical abstraction. It is that quality, it is the seed element of your design; it's a part which when planted gives you your design.'[14] Both statements, in turn, echo Schopenhauer's *The World as Will and Idea* (1818): 'But only the *will* is *thing in itself*…. It is the innermost essence, the kernel, of every particular thing and also of the whole.'[15]

Kahn's early formative years were steeped in the Emersonian idealism of this political and aesthetic Transcendentalist romanticism known as the 'Progressive Era' (circa 1900–17). Of Kahn's early teachers James Liberty Tadd (1912–14) was a leading voice in this movement within the city, and an 1881 graduate of the Pennsylvania Academy. Kahn was befriended by Tadd in the autumn of 1910 when he was selected to receive supplemental art training in his classes at the Public Industrial Art School of Philadelphia. Tadd's visionary pedagogy fostered a love of the 'Book of Nature' in the student, encouraging direct Ruskin-like observation of natural forms such as shells, plants and animals prior to an analysis of the geometries underlying them. These lessons in looking were supplemented by free Saturday classes in drawing and painting at the Graphic Sketch Club.[16]

Kahn's Beaux-Arts training under Cret was a lesson, not in method, but in the spirit of architecture, and as such it proved its worth. From this system he described three key interrelated attributes: (1) 'the sketch or *esquisse*'

(2) 'the *poché*, the "pocketed" plan' (3) and 'shades and shadows'.[17] Kahn remembers the *esquisse* as the method whereby the student 'would study the problem, be given a period of a few hours in a cubicle (*en loge*) during which he would make a quick sketch of his solution without consultation'. *En loge* Kahn derived no respect for precedent, but learnt to 'revere the sense of beginning' and to recognize that the potency of the sketch 'depended on our intuitive powers'. This 'sense of beginning' will be explored presently through Kahn's lecture at Zurich on 'Silence and Light'. Next attribute is *poché*; in the classical plan, it is that black absence of space which shows 'the generating part of the structure' of wall, pier, or 'articulated wall', and which led to the 'hollow columns' of Trenton Bath House (1954–8): 'I just peeled away the interior of the wall, ate it up, and used the exterior which is the only effective part of the structure anyway. I made the wall a container instead of a solid. That came directly from my training in Beaux-Arts. So did the idea of the service spaces and the spaces served.'[18] This discovery, through classical *poché*, of the hollow column and the hollow wall are vital to the evolution of the 'order of shadow' in Kahn's work. The third attribute is that of 'shades and shadows':

> The Beaux-Arts system included lessons in shades and shadows. These exercises made us aware of light, of shade, of shadow, of reflected light. They gave us an unquestionable feeling of the inseparability of light and building, and the fact that we could construct light. They taught us to differentiate shade from shadow. Today shade and shadow are often confused as the same thing. They aren't.[19]

Silence and light

Over fifty years later Kahn could still demonstrate the ambidextrous skills in drawing on the blackboard which were one of Tadd's unique educational inventions, intended to develop dexterity and tactile awareness – as when he drew leaf forms in his master's studio at the University of Pennsylvania in November 1963.[20] Kahn liked the tactility of blackboards in feeling towards knowledge. He placed them on the external columns of the Salk Institute (1959–65) to prompt the spontaneous creativity of strolling scientists, and the chalkboard was central to his own pedagogy as in the lecture he gave at ETH, Zurich, on 12 February 1969 on 'Silence and Light'. Here there were no projected images, and Kahn illustrated his main points in chalk: 'The drawing is a talk this time', he significantly said.[21] Kahn's teachings were idiosyncratic in their provocative fusion of Socratic dialogue and ambiguous Talmudic utterance.[22] The blackboard goes with the thinking-out-loud hesitancy of his speech, and the tactility of the chalk, as his aphorisms come to light on the dark obscurity of its matt surface – it would be hard to imagine Kahn lecturing to a whiteboard. So the blackboard, in itself, is a metaphor of that mysterious 'treasury of shadows' which, in his 1969 Zurich lecture, he diagrams at the threshold between 'silence' and 'light'.

He opens the talk by saying that he will 'put on the board something of which I thought of only recently what could be a key to my point of view in regard to all works of art including architecture';[23] this is the new concept of 'silence' in relation to light first publically expressed in 1967.[24] An original recording of this talk, made available in 2013 (edited by Alessandro Vassella) with a transcript and photographs of Kahn in the act of drawing-as-talking, brings this important event vividly alive. Kahn begins to build his argument on the rightmost of three blackboards positioned on the podium, writing 'Silence' on the left and – leaving a significant gap – 'Light' to the right. 'Silence', he says, is not meant in the sense of an absence of sound, as 'very, very quiet. It is something which you may say is... Lightless; Darkless. Desire to be; to express'[25] – as he chalks below the heading of 'Silence'. Kahn is a long way from Mexico here, but this sense of a 'lightless' primordial origin seems charged with memories of a visit to the garden of Luis Barragán's Studio House at Tacubaya, in December 1965, when seeking his advice on resolving the cloistered space of the Salk Institute. In a 1968 piece on 'Silence' Kahn essays, the intense experience of finding in a clearing here

> a very large bowl carved out of... dark hard stone filled to overflowing with water.... The black stone is the alchemist. Out of the Odyssey in nature of the stream from the tiniest mountain sources, through the varied grooves of its path in light and shade, [Barragán] selected the darkest place of its dance on the rocks to sense silver of water in a dark bowl and brought it home to contribute to the sense of silence which... prevails in all his house.[26]

Of Barragán's house Kahn has elsewhere written: 'His house is not merely a house but house itself. Its material is traditional, its character eternal.'[27] As in the garden Kahn seems to have sensed the dwelling, as Danièle Pauly has described it, as a fashioning of shadows where 'from the moment one enters, a shadowy atmosphere prevails, acting as a shield against the sunlight'.[28]

Strongly intimated in Kahn's talk of an embryonic, lightless 'desire to be; to express' – and witnessed by the engineer August E. Komendant, who worked with Kahn for eighteen years – is the fact that 'the real part of [Kahn's] philosophy was based upon Schopenhauer: "All living things have an existence of will which dominates their behaviour and actions". Kahn, like Schopenhauer, considered the "existence will" the most important – the driving force for desire.'[29] Other evidence suggests Kahn's mother, Bertha Mendelssohn, 'as his tutor and guide into a Romantic world view based largely upon German literary sources'.[30] Though quite forgotten now, Schopenhauer's aesthetics were a deep influence on the milieu of Kahn's formative years infecting artists of the stature of Mahler, Mann, Proust,

Turgenev, Wagner and so on. His architectural theory is presented in the first volume of *The World as Will and Representation* (first published in 1818) and in greater detail in the second volume of 1844.[31] His conservative, Greek classical 'architectonic idealism' is framed within the three major concepts of his aesthetics: 'the will', the (Platonic) 'Idea' and the pure subject of knowledge. As has been noted, for Schopenhauer 'only the *will* is *thing-in-itself*.... It is the innermost essence, the kernel, of every particular thing and also of the whole. It appears in every blindly acting force of nature.'[32] Again and again he stresses the darkly groping nature of a will which is 'blind impulse', 'blindly urging force' and which objectifies itself from stone, to plant, to animal, to human being, at different levels related by Schopenhauer to Plato's eternal 'Ideas' or unchangeable forms.[33] So Schopenhauer returns us in many ways to Plato's cave, but in Plato the fire projecting the shadows that the prisoners observe is the representative of the Eternal Good, whereas in Schopenhauer if the representations are shadow images of the blind will, 'then they are not shadows of light; they are not even shadows of shadows; they are shadows of this original darkness'.[34] From the unutterable blindness of this 'unmeasurable force' – and with a brightening in the tone of his voice – Kahn turns 'to light, the giver of all presences.... You can say the light, the giver of all presence, is the maker of a material, and the material was made to cast a shadow, and the shadow belongs to the light'.[35]

The contrast reflects Schopenhauer's contention that humanity is both the 'impetuous and dark impulse of willing (indicated by the pole of the genitals as its focal point)' and 'eternal, free, serene subject of pure knowing (indicated by the pole of the brain).... In keeping with this antithesis, the sun is simultaneously the source of *light*, the condition for the most perfect kind of knowledge'.[36] Moreover, Schopenhauer 'is of the opinion that architecture is destined to reveal not only gravity and rigidity, but at the same time the nature of light, which is their very opposite',[37] as directly echoed in Kahn's famous remark 'that the sun was not aware of its wonder until it struck the side of a building'.[38]

In the pregnant gap between 'Silence' and 'Light', Kahn struck next two interrelated arrows to denote 'a kind of ambient threshold', a place of inspiration where the 'Sanctuary of Art' is found, 'Art being the language of man [which]...stems from...the needing, of the desire to be, to express, and the evidence of the promise of the material to do it'.[39] This is that zone of divination where the architect – as in the Beaux-Arts *en loge* process – intuits the *esquisse* in deep reverence for 'the sense of beginning', establishing the 'nature of things' (the nature of a library for example) as if a library had never existed.[40]

In contrast to Plato's equivocal attitude, Schopenhauer accords art an elevated status in his belief that in its pure contemplation we are delivered for a time from the impulses of the will – a neo-mystical notion influenced by the *Upanishads*: 'It is *art*, the work of genius. It repeats the eternal Ideas, apprehended through pure contemplation, the essential and abiding element in all the phenomena of the world.'[41] So far, so good, but despite the many beautiful things Schopenhauer says about architecture he accords it low status in the arts as 'the objectification of the will at the lowest grade of its visibility, where it shows itself as the dumb striving of the mass'.[42] In his chapter 'On the Aesthetics of Architecture', it represents the (Platonic) Idea 'of the lowest grades of nature, that is, gravity, rigidity, and cohesion'.[43] Its theme then is *'support and load'*, an idea clarified in the language of column and entablature of the Greek temple. If discomfited by the low status accorded to architecture here, the neoclassical aspect of Kahn's sensibility empathized with this austerely noble view of architecture, and rejection of wilful form making. For Schopenhauer only music stands apart, for its effect 'is so very much more powerful and penetrating than is that of the other arts, for these others speak only of the shadow, but music of the essence'. Music is not merely a shadow of the Ideas, but a *'copy of the will itself'*.[44] As a talented pianist Kahn took this to heart and made many parallels between the two arts: 'An architect's sense of order is like a composer's sense of music.... It is something underneath and beyond the elements of style':[45] and at Zurich Kahn speaks of how 'nature give us ... the instrument of expression, which we all know as ourselves, which is like giving the instrument upon which the song of the soul can be played'.[46] Finally – in his halting declarative mode of speech – he says: 'The Sanctuary of Art – I'm taking this little lesson to say that it is the treasury of shadows', and so in conclusion to this rightmost of his three boards, writes at bottom-centre: 'treasury of shadows.'[47]

In this neo-Schopenhauerian schema the 'treasury of shadows' resides at the centre, for the primordial shades of 'Silence' (to the left) can only belong to the pre-phenomenal realm of the 'lightless'. Light (to the right), on the other hand, is 'pure knowing' so – apart from the aforesaid special case of music – objects of everyday experience, including the representations of art (and especially such an earthy art as architecture), occupy this illusory territory of the 'treasury of shadows'. However, we are not condemned to illusion for it is the will-less experience of a profound work of architecture that leads us to grasp the idea expressed within it. There are transcendentalist echoes here too; in his great essay on *Nature* (1836) Emerson writes: '[Nature] always speaks of Spirit. It suggests the absolute.... It is a great shadow pointing always to the sun behind us.'[48] For Kahn, if Light is the 'giver of all presences', then the material of building itself is a kind of 'spent light'.[49] One wonders if the students at ETH had the ears to hear all this speaking in parables, and many must have been relieved when Kahn – in addressing the idea of university through the archetypes of Agora and Stoa – enacted some concrete drawing-as-building on the blank central blackboard as he declared: 'The Stoa was made most marvellously. It was made like this....' – the recording recaptures Kahn's staccato as he taps out the Greek Stoa three-line columnar pattern. Here is a 'place of happening'; 'Things grew in it. Shops became. People met to meet there' – then with marked emphasis – 'It's *shaded*'.[50]

Drawing as we build

Hearing Kahn's lecture against the background of Schopenhauer's architectural aesthetics makes his notion of the 'Treasury of Shadows' clearer, but much remains abstract and ungraspable. Kahn offers more help to understanding in the graphic analogy to nineteenth-century book illustration he gave in another lecture published in *Perspecta* of 1982:

> The white piece of paper is the illustration. If I illustrate light, I have a white paper, and that is light. What else can I do? I thought that was the only thing to do. But I realized that I wasn't right at all. When I put a stroke on the paper, a couple of strokes in ink, I realized that the black was where the light was not. And then I really could make a drawing. I would only be discerning as to where I put the black, where the light is not, and this made the picture come out.[51]

Though Kahn did not use slides in the talk, he vividly describes an engraving by the great illustrator George Cruikshank (1792–1878), who was at the summit of his powers in the early Victorian period and is best known for his images to Oliver Twist (Figure 9.1):[52]

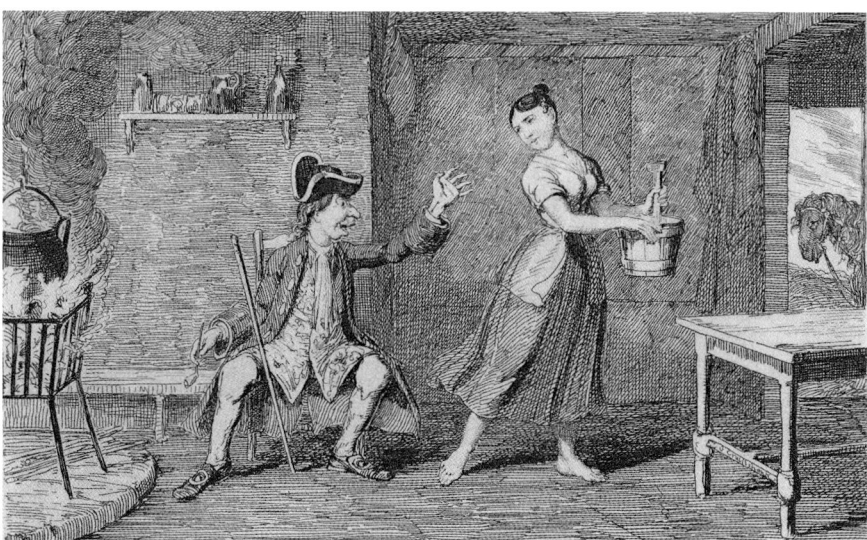

FIGURE 9.1 George Cruikshank, *Jeanie, I say, Jeanie, woman*, etching from Walter Scott, *Waverley Novels, 48 vols.*, *vol. 11* (London: Fisher and Son, 1836–9), facing p. 322.

The drawing is by Cruikshank...an illustrator of great importance to everyone. He made a drawing of a man sitting by a fire with a swaying female sort of next to him. Through a doorway in the night was a horse. The walls were receiving the light from the fire. A fireplace, out of the picture, radiated light, which caught on the folds of the undulating female and on the man sitting on his chair; the horse behind did not receive the light, but just little sparks of it. Every pen was subservient to the sense that where the stroke was, the light was not. And the thing became absolutely luminous. Closer to the fire it was practically white paper, and then it shaded away. It was a beautiful illustration of the realizations of the expressor to find the means of making evident this fact.[53]

Although not specifically named by Kahn, the only drawing by Cruikshank to match this description is from Walter Scott's *The Heart of Midlothian* in a Waverley Novels edition of 1836–9.[54] The well-dressed 'man sitting by a fire' is the comical figure of the Laird of Dumbiedikes, who dotes on Jeanie Deans in his regular visits to her father's bare-walled cottage at St Leonard's, near Edinburgh. She is the 'swaying female' whose *contrapposto* figure twists away to avoid the Laird as he reaches to grasp her shoulder. If further source evidence were needed, Kahn also mentions this drawing in his introductory letter to Richard Saul Wurman and Eugene Feldman's 1973 edition of *The Notebooks and Drawings of Louis I. Kahn* where he confirms it as 'an illustration to the Waverly [sic] Tales' and gives, moreover, a highly abstracted ideogram of the image sufficient to verify the key shadow contours of the seated Laird and Jeanie Dean (Figure 9.2). He adds: 'I noticed [Cruikshank's] lines followed the direction of the source of light. I realized that the stroke of the pen was where the light was not. This was the clue to the illusion.'[55] Cruikshank has been described as 'a major artist' and 'the most versatile genius in the use of line that English art has seen';[56] here firm striations describe the dark framing bareness of cottage walls and floor; his line then becomes fluid and impetuous as it coils up with the smoke from the brazier, twists to shape the Laird's coat and raised arm, and forms the swaying folds of Jeanie's dress in flicks and hatching. As Kahn indicates, in all this treasury of shadow pattern the most luminous moments are the most expressive: the flaming stove, the face and legs of the Laird, and Jeanie's bare arms and feet. Cruikshank poetic line shows a quality of which Kahn has also written, that 'the sheer delight of drawing has its way in the drawing'.[57] After the Cruikshank example of making-through-shadow in a bare cottage, Kahn turns to nobler architecture: 'The column in the Greek Temple is where the light is not', illustrated by a schematic plan and elevation of a Doric colonnade drawn in black, and reminiscent of an immediately following 1951 temple drawing from Luxor where the columns, drawn *contre-jour*, stand as a structure of shadow – of 'spent light' (Figure 9.3).

There is a rich hinterland to Kahn's Cruikshank-inspired musings on shadow and light: the lessons with Tadd and at the Graphic Sketch Club,

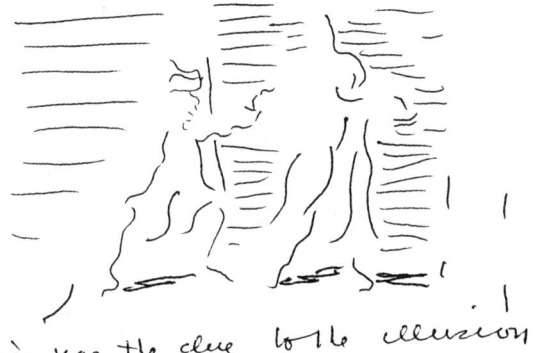

FIGURE 9.2 Louis I. Kahn, introductory letter, p. 3, to Richard Saul Wurman and Eugene Feldman, *The Notebooks and Drawings of Louis I. Kahn* (1973). Louis I. Kahn Collection, The University of Pennsylvania and the Pennsylvania Historical and Museum Commission.

probably with Ruskin's *Elements of Drawing* to hand and its injunction to make 'memoranda of the shapes of shadows'; the Beaux-Arts system which, as he remembered, 'prepared a person to regard drawing of great importance, included lessons in shades and shadows';[58] and then the intimate world of

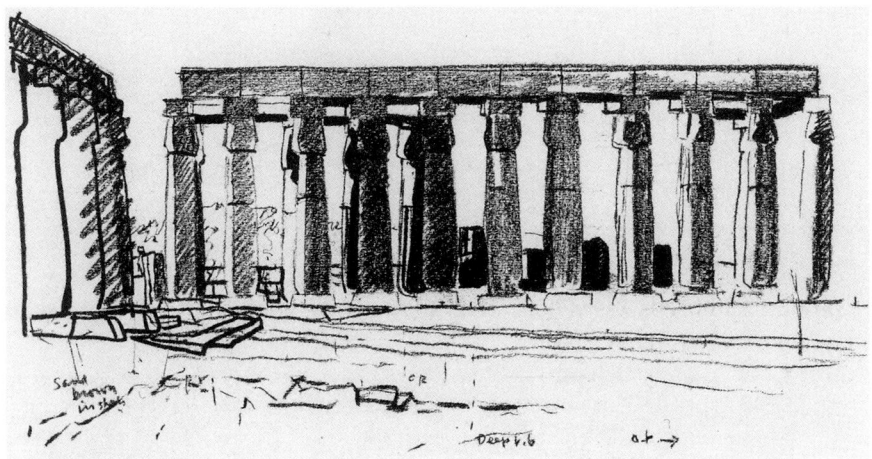

FIGURE 9.3 Louis I. Kahn, Luxor, 1951, plate 8 in Richard Saul Wurman and Eugene Feldman, *The Notebooks and Drawings of Louis I. Kahn* (1973). Louis I. Kahn Collection, The University of Pennsylvania and the Pennsylvania Historical and Museum Commission.

Cruikshank's drawings to Scott and Dickens themselves, that rich visual economy of the print and the illustrated book, of the nineteenth and earlier twentieth centuries, wherein 'the element of darkness was a proclaimed aesthetic property, both formal and iconographic, naturally conveyed in the clouded atmospheres and tonal contrasts of black and white that are inherent in the printed media'[59] of the etching and lithograph. Although Kahn claimed not to be much of a reader, he treasured his books, and the images they contained, as an inspiring resource.[60]

For Kahn's architecture all this portends far more than an art class lesson in drawing shadows as negative shapes, important as these are in reversing figure-ground preconceptions. Kahn decided to become an architect, not an artist, inspired in his final year of high school by the attending the lectures and drawing tasks in architectural history given by William F. Gray. And as an architect and not an artist, Kahn makes the distinction that, unlike the 'painter [who] sketches to paint' the 'architect draws to build'.[61] In one representation of 1969, the threshold between 'silence' and 'light' is drawn as a tremulously fine vertical black line.[62] The foregoing makes clear that, for Kahn, this act of drawing 'the black, where the light is not' is already an act of building, and suggests the depths implied when Kahn insists that we should 'train ourselves to draw as we build, from the bottom up, when we do, stopping our pencil to make a mark at the joints of pouring or erecting'.[63] In Kahn's tectonics, this 'mark' is itself invariably a 'shadow joint', but the whole making of architecture takes place philosophically in the realm of shadows. Kahn relates his own experience of drawing to build through the sketches of Carcassonne he made in 1959:

From the moment I entered the gates, I began to write with drawing, the images which I learned about now presenting themselves to me like realized dreams. I began studiously to memorize in line the proportions and the living details of these great buildings. I spent the whole day in the courts, on the ramparts, and in the towers.... At the close of the day I was inventing shapes and placing buildings.[64]

This was an epochal journey in crystallizing Kahn's sense of mass and shadow, for he went on to visit, and draw, Le Corbusier's chapel at Ronchamp, and the monastery of La Tourette. At Carcassonne, one of his drawings, of a segmentally arched garderobe powerfully carved into the depth of the wall, foreshadows these experiences (Figure 9.4).[65]

In conclusion to this attempt to theorize the 'treasury of shadow', we return to the chthonic lightless realms of 'Silence'. In the diagram with the vertical threshold line the outline of a pyramid floats in the realm of 'Light' on the right; in other versions the pyramid hovers at the centre, above the Shadow Treasury – 'the pyramid echoing silence gives the sun its shadow', says Kahn.[66] A lot can be made of the decisive experiences of 1950–1 when Kahn was able to experience the ancient sites of Italy, Greece and Egypt while spending an academic year at the American Academy in Rome. He drew the stepped pyramid in Saqqara in charcoal as a great looming mass of spent light,[67] and wrote to Anne Tyng that 'the Pyramids are the most wonderful things I have seen so far. No pictures can show you their monumental impact'.[68] Antiquity came alive; that was what struck Vincent Scully in writing the first book on Kahn (1962), wittily pointing out that 'it must have been as if a rather baggy mistress, abandoned in the bread lines, had walked youthful into the room'.[69] The influence of André Malraux's *Voices of Silence* of 1953 helped to deepen and articulate these feelings as Kahn once explained:

By silence I don't mean quiet – but in the sense that Malraux calls his book...*The Voices of Silence* – he means only the feeling you get when you pass the pyramids, you feel that they want to tell you how they were made. Not *how* they were made, but what made them *be*, which means what was the force that *caused* them to be made.... These are the voices of silence.[70]

As a philosopher of art, in *Voices of Silence* Malraux augments his premise of a 'museum without walls' with a magisterial procession of darkly toned heliogravures: fragments of archaic and recent art are brought together in an eternal present in which Cézanne, 'Wei Bodhissattvas...Nava, Khmer and Javanese sculpture and Sung painting...a Romanesque tympanum, a Dance of Siva or the horseman of the Parthenon, all alike express a communion of one kind or another.' They are 'pregnant with the *possible*'[71] and they give

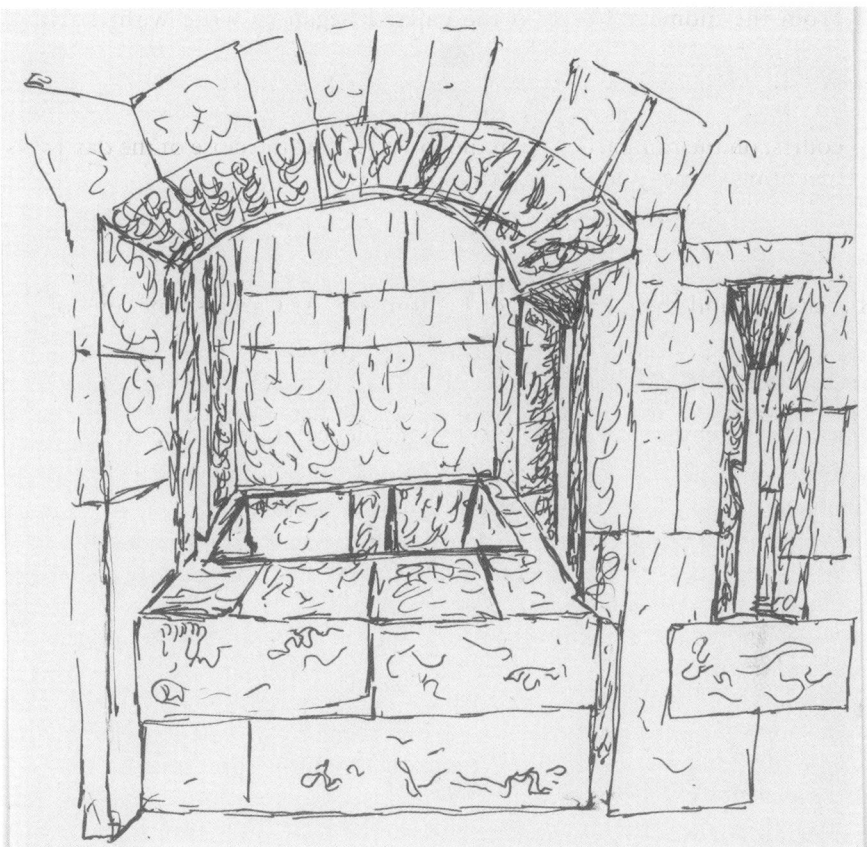

FIGURE 9.4 Louis I. Kahn, Carcassonne study, 1959. Louis I. Kahn Collection, The University of Pennsylvania and the Pennsylvania Historical and Museum Commission.

expression to 'these obscure emotions, the legacy of archaic man'.[72] The way Kahn used books was not as a conventional reader, but he pondered on these astonishing images, and seems to have read at least the final sentences of Malraux's book:

> A man becomes truly Man only when in quest of what is most exalted in him.... In that house of shadows where Rembrandt still plies his brush, all the illustrious Shades, from the artists of the caverns onwards, follow each movement of the trembling hand that is drafting for them a new lease of survival.... And that hand whose waverings in the gloom are watched by ages immemorial is vibrant with one of the loftiest of the secret yet compelling testimonies to the power and the glory of being Man.[73]

The order of shadow

Earlier we noted how Kahn would mentally ask 'How'm I doing, Le Corbusier?' of the great Swiss-French form-giver who had preceded him as a shaper of shadows in the post–Second World War era. On his 1950–1 Mediterranean trips, Kahn had stood under the Paestum-like pilotis of the Unité d'Habitation, then under construction.[74] At the same time the celebrated declaration of *Vers une Architecture* that 'architecture is the masterly, correct and magnificent play of masses brought together in light' holds true for Le Corbusier; shadow-making would increase in his work but still to enhance the perception of light as primary figure. But with the mature Kahn it is different; in the primeval 'lightless' realm of 'Silence' of Schopenhauer, or the *Genesis* of Kahn's Jewish background, when 'the earth was without form, and void; and darkness was upon the face of the deep' we have a place – as Kahn states at Zurich – 'if you go back beyond...in which light and silence were together and maybe are still together';[75] a place before that 'Beginning' of verse 4 of *Genesis* when 'God divided the light from the darkness'. Consequently Kahn insists that 'the shadow *belongs* to the light' in a true linkage. For him – with all his love for light – light and shadow are conjoined as brothers, and indeed there are many moments in his architecture when shadow becomes the predominant figure. Crucial to this heightened sense of the interplay of figure and ground is Kahn's direct exposure – through Josef Albers's art and teaching at Yale – to 'the mythic cradle of [Bauhaus] modernism'[76] and the cognitive processes at the core of its pedagogy. This followed his appointment as a visiting critic at Yale University in the autumn of 1947, and can be seen in the transformation of his painting and sketches of this period which reflect the abstract Bauhaus-inspired studio practice, as remembered by one Yale student, of 'filling space with planes, lines and solids. Our media are cardboard, wire and clay'.[77] In the ink on paper drawings, 'Abstract of Planes and Steps' and 'Abstract of Planes with Landscape Elements, No. 1' of 1948–50, Kahn treats shadows as coequal elements in these playful architectonic compositions. This Albers-like abstract feeling continues strongly in the fine drawings Kahn produces on the above-mentioned 1950–1 Mediterranean trips; one architect who accompanied him recalled that 'the effects of light preoccupied Louis and fascinated him; the deliberateness of the detailed forms; some carved like deep wounds with shadows deepening into reaches'.[78]

Once the shadow significance of the Pyramids is recognized, it can be spotted everywhere in Kahns work. In the first works that brought him international recognition, its form generates the tetrahedral slabs of the Yale Art Gallery (1953) and provides the roofs of the Trenton Bath House (1956), while in his last major completed work – the Center for British Art (1977) also at Yale – the top-lighting is structured as pyramidal geometries.[79] The photographs of the Yale Art Gallery, published in *Perspecta* in 1955, convey the 'illustrious Shades' and the brooding imagery of the 'Musée

Imaginaire' (Museum without Walls) of Malraux's the *Voices of Silence* (1951, 1953): sculptures of diverse periods converse together on plinths with other artworks displayed on the freely aligned 'pogo panels', all gathered together under the dark pyramidal shadows of the raw concrete tetrahedral rib structure, whose enduringly ancient horizon suggests the 'waverings in the gloom' of the 'artists of the caverns onwards' (Figure 9.5).[80] Across the Atlantic, Malraux was an acknowledged inspiration in the Eduardo

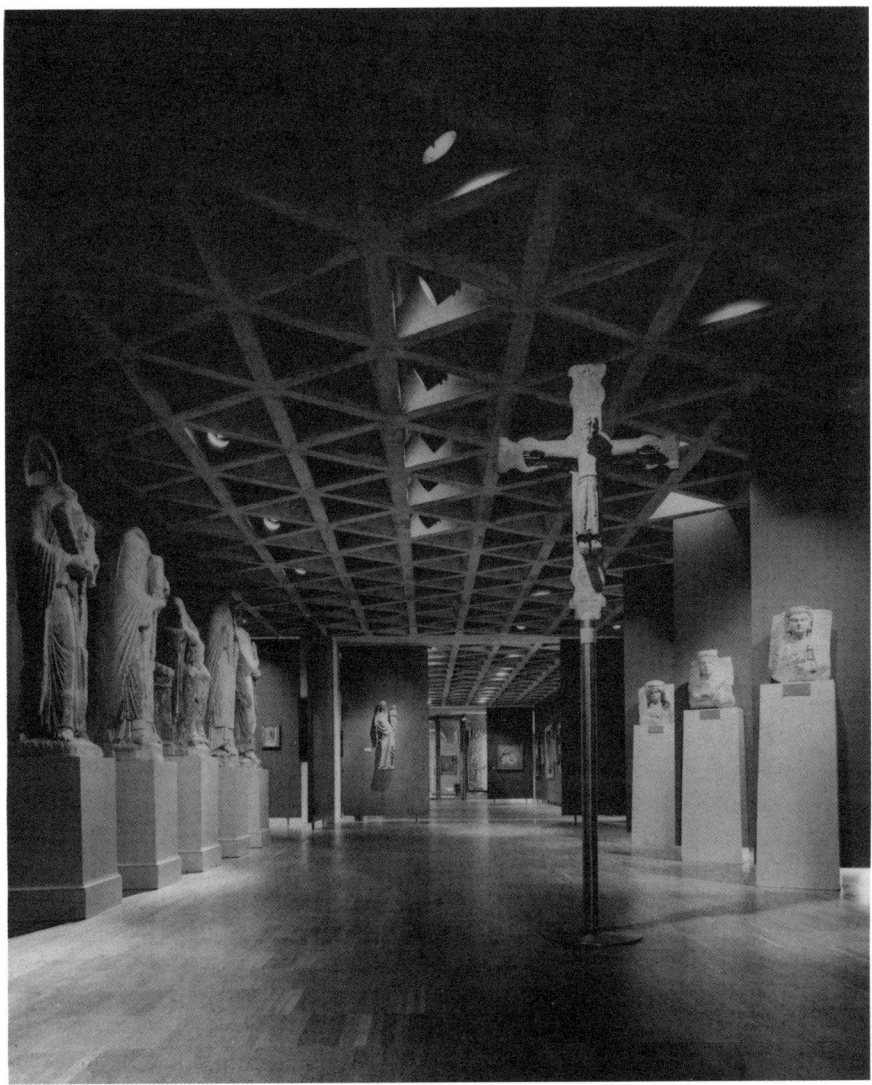

FIGURE 9.5 Louis I. Kahn, interior of Yale University Art Gallery. Photograph, Lionel Freedman. Louis I. Kahn Collection, The University of Pennsylvania and the Pennsylvania Historical and Museum Commission.

Paolozzi and Nigel Henderson exhibition of 'Parallel of Life and Art' held at the Institute of Contemporary Arts, London in 1953, in those not unrelated currents that produced the Brutalist sensibility. Scully immediately realized that there is also a good dose of Miesian elegance and transparency at Yale, as in the 'precise linear detailing of its window walls'.[81] Equally, Scully notes: 'The decision to design the floors as simple open lofts...was related to [Mies's] general practice, as was the clear rectangular envelope in which they were contained.'[82] Pace the Miesian aspects, in retrospect it is easy to see how the awesome structure, the powerful Euclidean 'servant' volume of the stair drum, and the severe brick wall to Chapel Street, of Yale anticipate the monumentality of Kahn's developed language. But nowhere is there much to hint at that radical transformation of the Beaux-Arts *poché* Kahn produces at Trenton Bath House with the hollow column and the hollow wall – inventions vital to his subsequent manipulation of 'shades and shadows'.

The Bath House's composition of four low pyramids, hovering above cubic volumes of rough sand-grey blockwork, planted on suburban greensward at the north-west fringes of Trenton, only slowly discloses its epochal significance. Produced with major inputs from Anne Tyng, Kahn's Greek cross plan orders the four simple components of entrance to basket room, men's and women's dressing rooms and a lounge area (leading via steps to the pool) around an open atrium. All four spaces are deeply shaded by pyramidal roofs (with a square oculus) borne on eight-foot square 'hollow columns' – produced by Kahn's aforementioned eating up of the Beaux-Arts *poché* to make 'the wall a container instead of a solid'.[83] Kahn's 'Order in Architecture' paper, in the 1957 *Perspecta*, identifies here a new 'concept of space order in which the hollow columns supporting the pyramidal roofs distinguish the spaces that serve from those being served'.[84] Accordingly, the hollow columns do their servant work as water closets, stores and, most ingeniously, as the 'wall baffled entries' (the term used on the 1957 *Perspecta* plans) to the dressing rooms. Here, the column is not so much hollowed as *folded* around the dividing panel of blockwork, obviating bothersome doors, and allowing women and men to slip modestly between the atrium and their changing areas. Whether hollowed, folded or layered, the highly articulated wall is present in all its essence at Trenton, containing the potential will-to-shadow in Kahn's subsequent work. A sombre palette underlines this rudimentary sense of beginning wherein 'the shades of gray of the concrete, the black slate and dark wood form an essential chromatic range that later becomes a constant in other works by Kahn'.[85]

There are many shade and shadow refinements: the structural supports of the floating pyramids are centred on the eight-by-eight foot hollow columns, so when the outer walls are pushed to the exterior zone of the hollow columns – as in the wet-dry dressing room areas – this creates a four-foot wide (1.2 m) opening to the sky, admitting light which both washes the internal walls of the dressing rooms, and intensifies the shadow zone of the hovering pyramid. For the fully dry entrance to basket room, the scheme is inverted; the square pyramid oculus is glazed, and the walls are moved to the inner face of the hollow columns. Thus, the columns gain complete muscular expression, externally, as miniature turrets on this entrance aedicule, while the now-overhanging pyramid casts strong shadows on the recessed walls to make an inviting porch at the Bath House's entrance. Kahn further celebrates this moment with a mosaic (expressing the hollow column module) 'where black and orange, angular and semicircular profiles and silhouettes of each structural type play off against one another in ascending registers' (Figure 9.6).[86] Apart from the circle inscribed in the atrium pavement, these mural motifs are the only curves in the building, and confirm the ancient domical origins of the scheme in structures like the St Mark's Venice of Ruskin's description: 'a vast cave, hewn into the form of a cross, and divided into shadowy aisles by many pillars'[87] a building, moreover, with four-pier hollow column structures at the intersections of the cross. Nearer at hand Kahn also knew of the square column cluster, and tartan grids of Wright's Darwin Martin House at Buffalo.[88] Further proof is that Kahn meaningfully called the pyramid roofs of the unrealized Trenton Community Building, 'triangular domes'.[89]

Kahn believed: 'I discovered myself after designing that little concrete-block bath house in Trenton', while recognizing that 'the world discovered me after I designed the Richards towers building'.[90] In the Richards Medical Research Building and Biology Building at the University of Pennsylvania, Philadelphia (1957–65), that indeed made Kahn's international reputation,

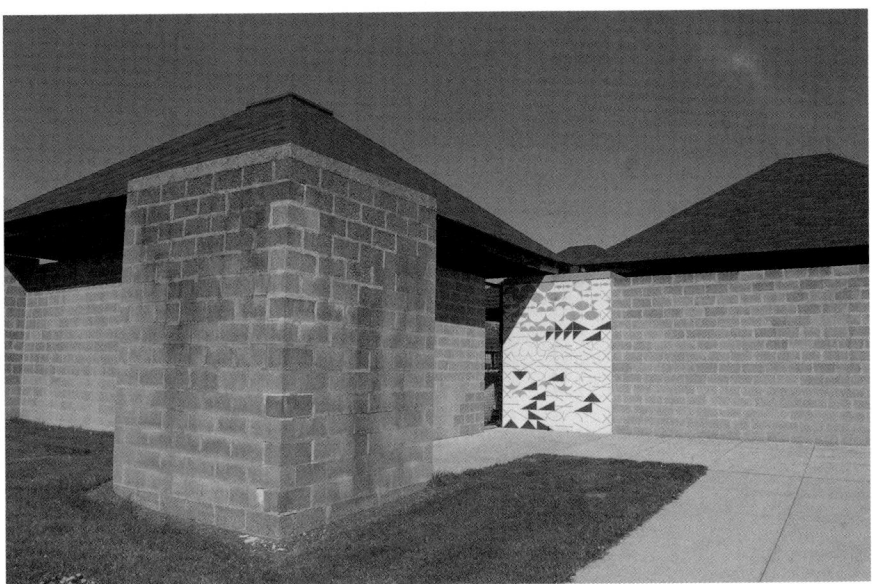

FIGURE 9.6 Louis I. Kahn, Trenton Bath House, mosaic at entrance. Photograph, Stephen Kite.

he dramatically took forward the muscular expression of hollow columns, but did little to develop Trenton's layering and folding of the wall plane. Scully points out that 'Kahn was still refusing to fiddle with the skin when it could not yet be wholly conceived of by him in terms of the structural and spatial order';[91] he therefore held the brick and glass infills of the laboratory studio towers tight to the front plane of the precast cantilevered spandrel beams devised by engineer August Komendant. As a leading apostle of the Machine Age, Reyner Banham worried over the brick monumentalization of the service ducts and stair towers 'and their visual dominance that gives the building its characteristic and fashionable silhouette... that has earned them the affectionately derisive name of "Duct Henge"'.[92] But a year earlier – also in the pages of the *Architectural Review* (February 1961) – William H Jordy expressed the worldwide shock of recognition that this was 'a *real* building.... Real in its tangibility; real in structure and materials; real in the inevitability with which it unfolds from the basic idea of its conception.... It reveals its integrity with a dogmatic earnestness sufficient to have pleased the most ardent Ruskinian'.[93] Indeed, its 'mighty assertion' of the Lamp of Power, and 'rude strength', reminded Scully of Furness[94] (see Chapter 6).

Viewed in spring, through the lightly leafed trees of the small botanical gardens, the south-facing range of the Medical Research Laboratory – together with the somewhat later western phase of the Biological Research Laboratory – extends as a panoply of majestically shadowed towers. Truly a neo-medieval polis of scholars, calling to mind the San Gimignano that partly inspired it – Kahn visited and water-coloured the Italian hill town in 1928.[95] Prominent to the right (east) are the four ventilation shafts of the windowless service tower, modelled as an ABACABA rhythm of towers and major and minor shadow gap recesses. Next come the three shafts which punctuate the laboratory and biology towers facing the park; this westward march of turrets is closed by the final major brick mass of the Biology building's service tower.

So, the external drama of this would-be Italian hill town evidences strong shadow-making, as do Kahn's many crayon and pencil studies on tracing paper for the Richards Building.[96] As for the interior qualities of the laboratory workspaces, when speaking as a participant at the Otterlo, Holland CIAM Conference (Team X) in September 1959, Kahn asserted that in the Medical Research Building he had 'developed characteristics within the studio itself where you can get darkness and light, not by pulling shades, but by simply characterizing the building so that there are natural spaces where darkness exists, and natural places where light exists'.[97] He then goes on to criticize his own Yale Art Gallery for the 'slight conclusion there about order' he had achieved there, and for the (neo-Miesian) universal aspect of its spaces. Whereas if he were to design a gallery now he would aspire to the specificity of a 'realm of spaces' that would *prima facie* limit the freedom of the director, but in truth would offer 'a realm of spaces where one could show things in various aspects'. In an important statement on his evolving sense of the order of shadow he continues:

> I would say that dark spaces are also very essential. But to be true to the argument that an architectural space must have natural light, *I would say that it must be dark, but that there must be an opening big enough, so that light can come in and tell you how dark it really is* – that's how important it is to have natural light in an architectural space'.[98]

But one of the major criticisms of the Richards Building was that it was only by 'pulling shades' that the scientists could control the excessive insolation of their thin-walled studio spaces. Yes, the structuralist plan, and the engaged masses of the servant towers, naturally create places where 'darkness exists' and 'light exists' – as Kahn claimed – but the environmental control is at best episodic. Yet, on the later Biological Research Building the attention is drawn to a much more nuanced 'fiddling with the skin' in the study carrels of the research library housed in the top two floors of their towers. Already in 1957 Kahn had anticipated his volumetric wall-making to come when he mused: 'A man with a book goes to the light. A library begins that way.... The carrel is the niche which could be the beginning of the space order and its structure.'[99] Here Kahn's provision of a generous upper window to light the reading room, and small windows below for the reader in the carrels, begins to actually offer that articulated experience of light and shadow which would grow into one of the most defining aspects of his architecture (Figure 9.7).[100]

Following the 1959 CIAM Otterlo conference, Kahn made efforts to see Le Corbusier's work at Ronchamp and La Tourette in 1959, experiences which catalysed his search for the order of shadow inherent in the thick wall – whether conceived as hollowed niche or folded plane. In a letter to the aspirant landscape architect Harriet Pattison he filled half a page with a drawing of Ronchamp's exterior from the south-east, extolling what he 'found to be a great great work';[101] his sketch seized the building at its maximum plasticity in the mid-morning, early autumn light of September, at a moment when the oversailing roof casts its profile deeply onto the external altar wall, and the whole of the battered south wall is plunged in shadow.[102] At the same mid-morning period he drew two interiors looking east, when a full light strikes the baffles of the south-east brise-lumière and the coupled square aperture enshrining an ancient statue of the Virgin (Figure 9.8). One drawing is sparer, and one more fully worked; both are in the swift, jabbing, pen and ink manner of the aforementioned drawing of the garderobe at Carcassonne, a technique Michael Lewis describes as 'a dancing play of nervous short lines, suggesting surfaces of active, vibrating light'[103] – but surely in this cave nave, also signifying planes of active shadow. Unlike the Mediterranean charcoals and pastels of 1951, these lines are like etchers' marks, subservient – as in Kahn's interpretation of Cruikshank – 'to the sense

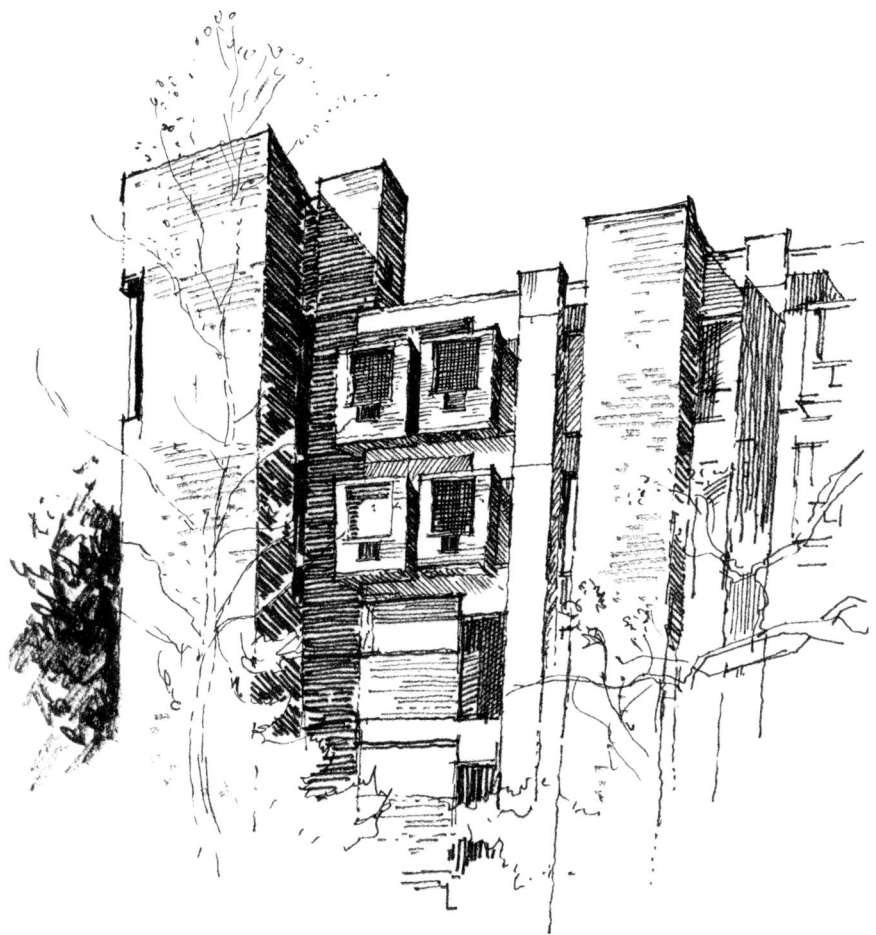

FIGURE 9.7 Detail of library study carrels, Biology Building, University of Pennsylvania, Philadelphia. Drawing by Stephen Kite.

that where the stroke was, the light was not'; Kahn's febrile dashes crowd at Ronchamp's celebrated roof slit – that telling crack where 'light can come in and tell you how dark it really is'. As Le Corbusier wrote in relation to the striking photographs of his own 1957 book on Ronchamp: 'Observez le jeu des ombres, jouez le jeu …' 'Observe the play of shadows, learn the game …. Precise shadows, clear cut or dissolving. Projected shadows, sharp. Projected shadows, precisely delineated, but what enchanting arabesques and frets. Counterpoint and fugue. Great music.'[104] Whereas Le Corbusier's earlier works – such as the Villa Savoye – had been of a 'very general luminosity keyed to the tonalities of purist painting', the vital spaces of these

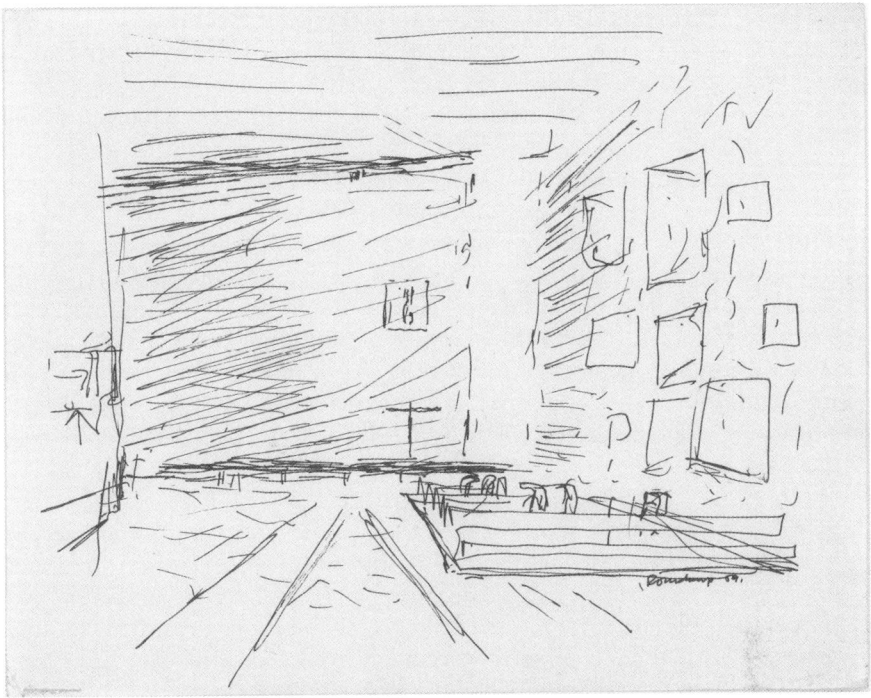

FIGURE 9.8 Louis I. Kahn, interior sketch of Le Corbusier's Ronchamp Chapel, 1959. Louis I. Kahn Collection, The University of Pennsylvania and the Pennsylvania Historical and Museum Commission.

later works are dark and earthy in a 'bolder exploration of how shadow structures luminosity'.[105]

Of even more impact was La Tourette, of which Kahn writes to Pattison: 'The building is a coming together of spaces boldly and even violently meeting each with its own light quality. I felt all humility before this masterpiece of Corbusier's.'[106] George Marcus and William Whitaker's study of *The Houses of Louis Kahn* stresses the impact of this visit, and the almost immediate transfusion of its lessons, first into the modelling of the lighter fabric of the Margaret Esherick House, and thence into the momentous masses and spaces of Rochester Unitarian Church. Other commentators have also recognized how at Rochester Kahn 'conceived the enclosing walls in terms of a perceivable, faceted thickness, infusing his building with a quality of exaggerated mass that was new even to his work', one foreshadowed in the Esherick House, designed just before the Unitarian Church, and 'similarly conceived though less emphatically massive'.[107] In the aggressive collisions that moved Kahn, La Tourette makes us participants in the struggles between dark and light that so absorbed Le Corbusier, linked variously to Gnostic Manichaeism, to the story of Orpheus or the confrontation of Dionysus and Apollo,[108] equatable to Kahn's primordial Silence, Schopenhauer's 'dark impulse of willing' and that 'serene pure knowing' of Light. In her photo-essay, 'Photographing Shadows at La Tourette', Hélène Binet found it a place where 'light and shadow is extremely well articulated' while admitting the elusive nature of shadows which allow them to slip out of the frame: 'Photographing shadows is almost an unnatural thing to do. Framing light is more natural. Shadows are something you have to play with. There is something about the shadow that always escapes you.'[109] Marcus and Whitaker single out the monks' cells at La Tourette as spaces Kahn would particularly have held in his memory when designing Esherick House as a hermetic home for a single woman and a bibliophile.[110] Le Corbusier gives the timber window element of his *cellules* depth in itself – including a full-height ventilation panel as a separate element –related in turn to the deeper embrasure of the balcony brise-soleil.[111] Here is Binet's convincing analysis of these relationships:

> Private life in a cell: Light never comes into the room, but only onto the balcony that is situated at the end of the room. In that balcony space, on the wall that catches shadows, there is a small, square concrete box that is the only ornament in the balcony or the room. It brings you into dialogue with the shadows. It breeds a strong sense of time, and time here is no longer ambiguous. The shadows are very sharp, they become a body. The shadow is a shadow of the box but also of the opening of the balcony: it is a kind of closure; it emphasizes the fact that you are very contained in that room.[112]

So – in contrast to the exposed studios of the Richards Building – the containment by shadow is strongly developed at the Esherick House, thereby realizing the layered potentials of Trenton in a process McCarter aptly describes as 'building shadow and space with folded walls'.[113] The house sits in one of the most bosky parts of the already-leafy Philadelphia model suburb of Chestnut Hill on a site sloping gently south-eastwards to Pastorius Park. It presents a closed frontage to the north-western approach from Sunrise Lane, while on the south-east a rhythm of horizontally opening ventilation panels and fixed glazed planes allows the house to open out fully to the park. An intriguing perspective of the near-final entrance façade design, made by Kahn around May 1960, shows – as he writes on the drawing – a 'House of Dark Stucco, stained natural wood and reveals for windows. The building will not look flat. The deep reveal of windows, entrance alcoves and 2nd floor flower porches will give it an alive look at all times' (Figure 9.9).[114] In contrast to the sand-finished stucco dwelling Kahn actually built, this dark stucco version would have presented a more homogenous volume in which the recesses of the 'keyhole' window to the living room, the entrance, and the bedroom, would have read as darker zones carved into an already solemn mass. Here the brightest planes would have been the upper skins of

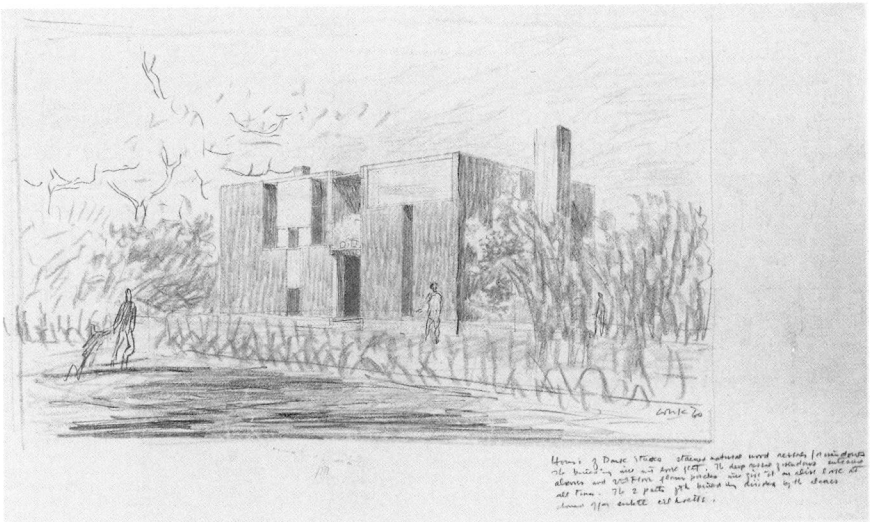

FIGURE 9.9 Louis I. Kahn, perspective view of Margaret Esherick House, Chestnut Hill, Philadelphia (1959–62), c. May 1960. Louis I. Kahn Collection, The University of Pennsylvania and the Pennsylvania Historical and Museum Commission.

glass reflecting the sky – as Kahn's drawing shows. Apart from the laconic gesture of the detached chimney – and the parent cast shadow always shown on Kahn's studies as an integral part of its effect – the south-west wall, as realized, is a bare canvas of light stucco 'additionally ornamented by the play of shadows from surrounding trees'.[115] In each case this involved building of shadow and space achieves magical effects. Take that keyhole window to the right of the entrance which organizes the book wall at the north-west end of the living room as an integral entity of light and ventilation. When the ventilation slot is closed, 'the bookcase becomes a high wall behind which one feels secure'.[116] Shadows cast from the bookcases – from the upper horizontal glazed part of the keyhole – reinforce this feeling of protective enclosure. The vertical ventilation slot is unglazed, so to open its panels is a seasonal act that dramatically admits light, cross-ventilation and a glimpse of nature, into this withdrawn end of the living space.

Kahn had truly invented the, since much emulated, keyhole window at the Tribune Review Publishing Company Building for a local newspaper in Greensburg, Pennsylvania, which he began work on in the autumn of 1958 – perhaps inspired by the play of small and large apertures he had seen in the insulae of Ostia Antica. Though neglected in the Kahn literature, this is a significant transitional project in his evolution of a castellar language of darkness and light. Maybe because the Tribune Review is in fact rather flat as constructed, but never to the extent of the consumerized parody Venturi made of this language, with his stage-flat cut-outs at the Vanna Venturi House (1962–4) – sited just down the lane from the Esherick House. In fact Kahn's earlier studies explore the Tribune Review Building envelope as sturdily modelled arrays of U-plan squared turret volumes. Notably, to the side of one plan sheet he sketches the plan of Ronchamp, apparently as a reminder of how its volumes also arise as if from a bending or folding of walls.[117] He was particularly absorbed with the honorific status of the entrance end walls; one sheet looks forward to the book-wall end of the Esherick House in cutting the keyholes into freestanding U-plan elements distinguished by dark recesses from the adjacent bays. Working in graphite and coloured pencil on white trace, Kahn plays with semicircles over slot windows on the two bays to the left of the entrance – emphasizing the recess in heavy lead – and squat triangles over slots on the right-hand bays (Figure 9.10).[118] The reddish rendering shows a building clad in brick, but as the design moved to its definitive all-concrete phase, all would be superseded in favour of rectilinear keyholes – as at the Esherick dwelling. Nonetheless, the motifs originated here will recur, again and again, in his studies for projects in Luanda, La Jolla and Dacca. Michael Merrill finds a frugal dignity in the Tribune Review which, with its 'pilasters of brick-sized concrete block and filling of full-sized blocks, employs a subtle combination of struck and pointed mortar joints, shadow joints, and strategically placed string courses to tell the story of its tectonics'.[119] The shadow joints are used most strikingly to distinguish the full-size block panels – in which the keyholes are cut – from the adjoining structural pilasters, and the prefabricated concrete beams over (Figure 9.11). The four-inch-wide recess is accented by an insert of Georgia 'white cherokee' marble (replacing the slate envisaged for the brick-clad design). Kahn also used the Georgia marble as a plug to disguise the ends of the pre-stressed beams, seeking the 'introduction of another, more important material' – the 'sharp, precise marble' – to contrast with

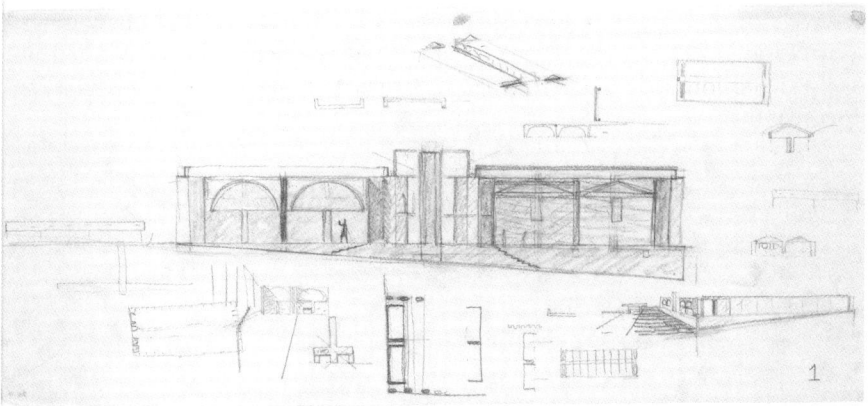

FIGURE 9.10 Louis I. Kahn, early design study of north elevation of the Tribune Review Building, with semi-circular and triangular 'keyhole-window' options. Louis I. Kahn Collection, The University of Pennsylvania and the Pennsylvania Historical and Museum Commission.

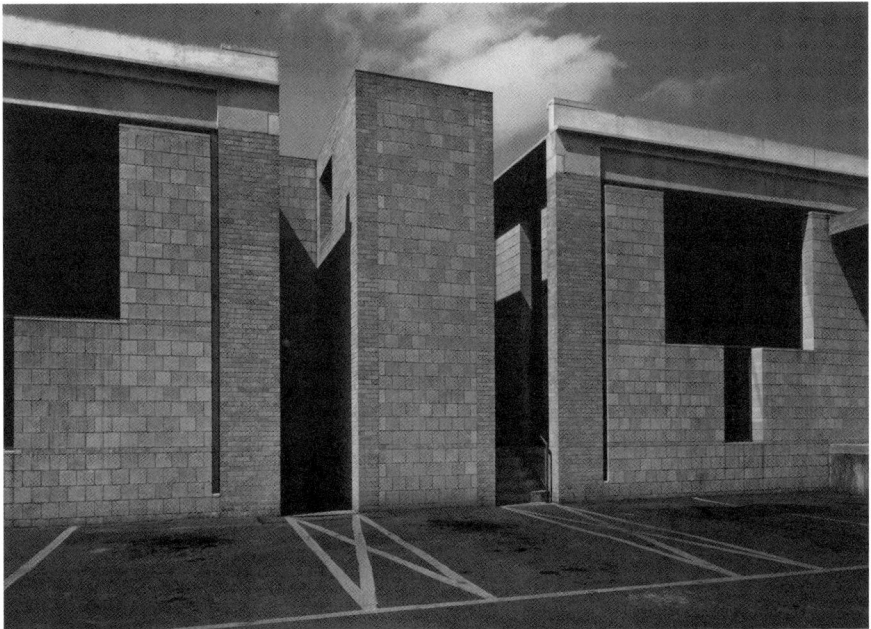

FIGURE 9.11 Louis I. Kahn, south façade detail of the Tribune Review Building. Photograph, John Ebstel. Courtesy Keith de Lellis Gallery, New York.

the predominant grey chromatics of the concrete:[120] thus antedating the National Assembly Building for Bangladesh, where silvery horizontals of marble express the day-work joints, in contrast to the sobriety of the in situ concrete walls.

The shadow recess is a device first associated with the stonework at the Morton and Leonore Weiss House (1947–50), where Kahn insisted on deeply raked joints to give the effect of dry-wall construction, as Ann Tyng explains:

> [It was what] Lou called the 'shadow joint' detail. He became very famous for that. The shadow joint is the idea of separation between materials so that if one has a door jamb in wood against rough stone-work...one actually lets it be separate, with its own straight edge away from the irregular edge of the stone.[121]

In completing the Tribune Review, Kahn has now in his armoury a fully integrated hierarchy of shadow details, from the larger gaps, or dark recesses, that animate the ventilation shafts of the Richards Building, or the Tribune Review wall bay studies, down to the shadow joints – measured in inches, or parts of an inch – of these keyhole blockwork panels. Though we have credited Soane with some early role in this shadow-reveal discovery

(Chapter 4), Tyng is surely correct in attributing to Kahn his modernist fame in the intense use of the detail to tell the story of how a building is made, an architect now accomplished – post Tribune – in 'drawing the black, where the light is not' and in 'stopping [his] pencil to make a mark at the joints of pouring or erecting'. In a debate at the Otterlo 1959 conference Kahn mused upon these discoveries he was making:

> I feel that the beginning of ornament comes with the joint. The way things are made, the way they are put together, the way one thing comes to the other, is the place where ornament begins. It is the glory of the joint which is the beginning of ornament. The more a man knows the joint, the more he wants to show it. The more he wants to show the joint, the more he wants to show the distance. And if he wants to have it show the distance, he wants to exaggerate and caricature things which ordinarily are small.[122]

And internally – as at Esherick House – the upper apertures of the Tribune Review's keyholes establish a horizon of upper diffused light that utilizes the ceilings and walls as reflectors, while allowing the desk-worker a distinctly framed eye-level view within protective shade (Figure 9.12).

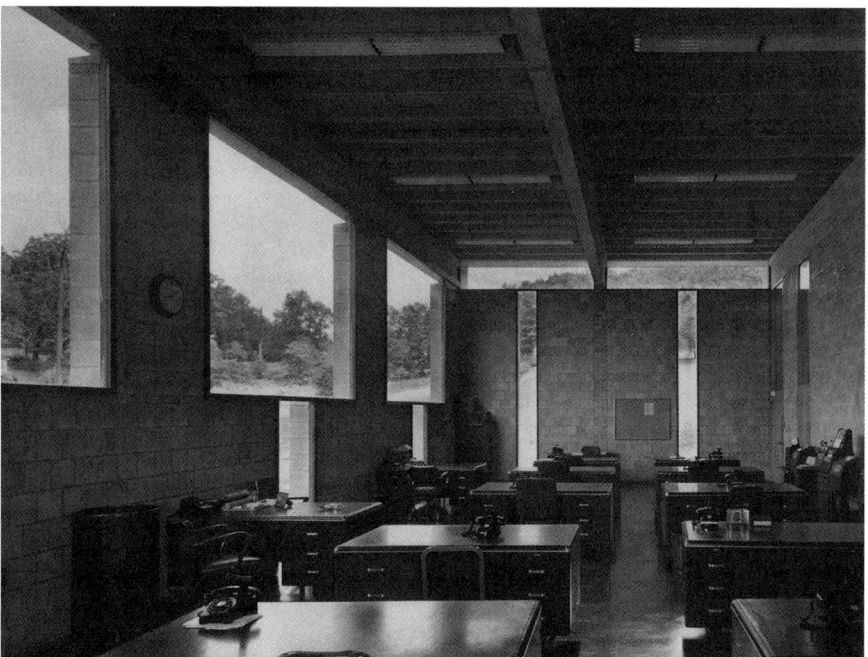

FIGURE 9.12 Louis I. Kahn, ground floor office space of the Tribune Review Building. Photograph, John Ebstel. Courtesy Keith de Lellis Gallery, New York.

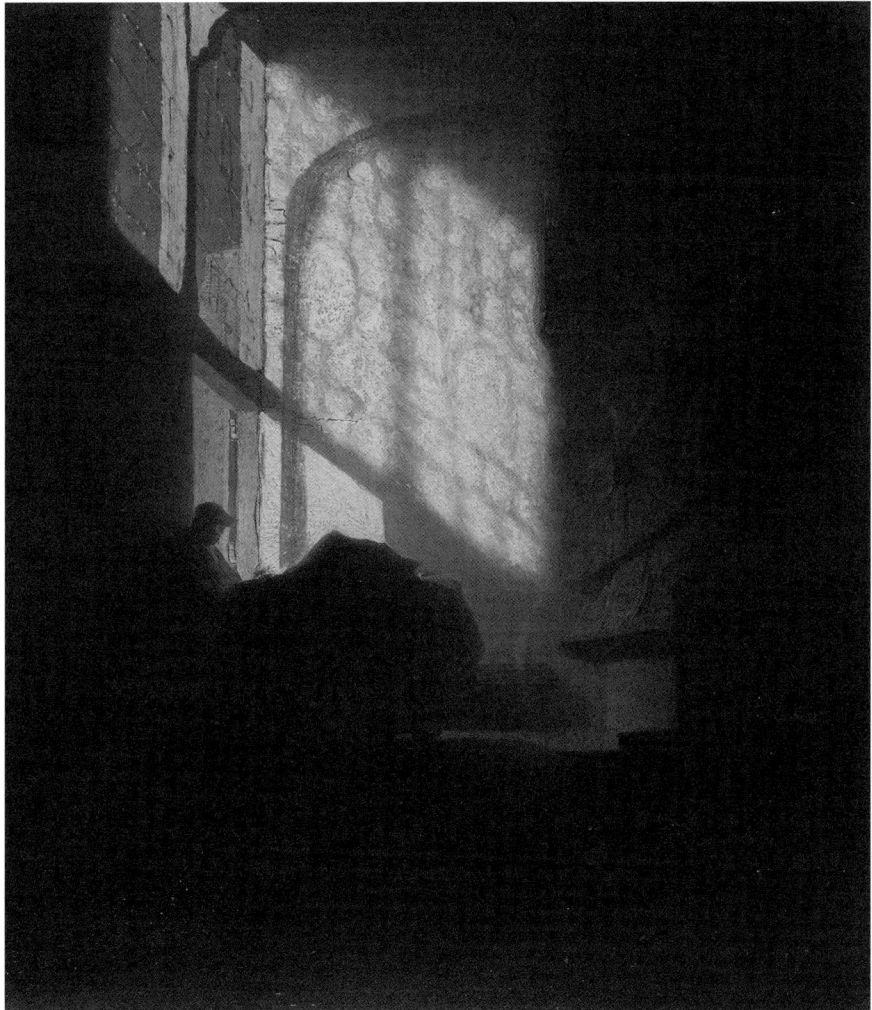

FIGURE 9.13 Follower of Rembrandt, *A man seated reading*, 1628–30. © The National Gallery, London.

Exactly the kind of tonal balance we admire in such seventeenth-century *tenebroso* Dutch interiors as the Rembrandt school's *Man seated reading at a Table in a Lofty Room* (Figure 9.13).[123]

Rochester: Black shadow and white light

In the First Rochester Unitarian Church (1959–63, extension 1959–69), Kahn synthesized the foregoing research into a masterpiece of 'black shadow and white light'. From the entrance courtyard on the north side the churchgoer opens the heavy double doors and enters a low-ceilinged lobby (Figure 9.14). Planted on the concrete block walls here are Kahn's hinged bulletin boards, busy with notices of purposeful church activity. As in Wright's Unity Temple at Oak Park, Chicago, it is then necessary to make a right turn to engage with the axis of the sanctuary. The entrance doors present themselves directly, albeit ambiguously bifurcated by a structural column, and held within an embrasure whose depth defines the width of the ambulatory that serves the church school surrounding the sanctuary – at the same time distancing the worship space from its bustle. Entering the church the scale of the sanctuary is at first withheld by the dark low soffit of the cantilevered choir loft. To proceed further, and to measure its full expansion, is to progress not so much from shadow to light as to a yet-more-awesome darkness as a great keeled concrete cross reveals itself, yawning above and athwart the space. The cross's self-shadows – striated by the board marks of its shuttering – are only deepened by the light Kahn decants into this great room from four light-towers raised between the arms of the cross. Despite this challengingly sombre expression, one miracle of this space is that its character is never louring. On a spring visit I first saw it silent and empty on a bright afternoon – perhaps the best way to initially experience it. The next

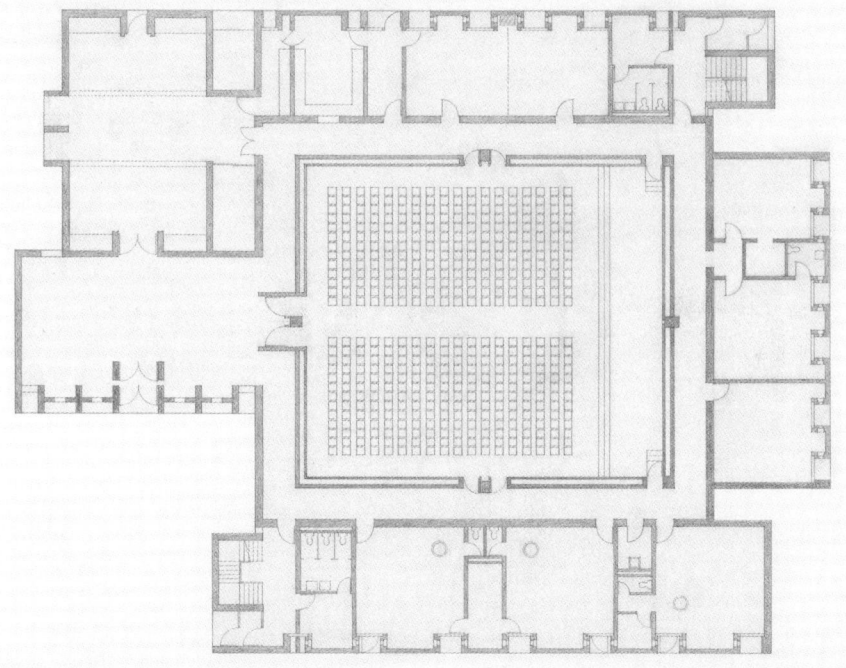

FIGURE 9.14 Rochester, First Unitarian Church, 'Final Plan', c. 1961 (prior to community spaces extension, designed 1965). First Unitarian Church Collection, The Architectural Archives, University of Pennsylvania.

morning dawned drizzly and grey, but I then found the sanctuary abuzz with cheerful musical practice. The instrumentalists gradually dispersed until only a Tuba octet remained whose rehearsals accompanied my own practice of sketching Kahn's shadows (Figure 9.15). The belching of these amusingly beefy instruments seemed not at odds with Kahn and Kommendant's thickset structure – which is also not without its wit. On the first bright afternoon the space was both subdued and luminous – shadow and light

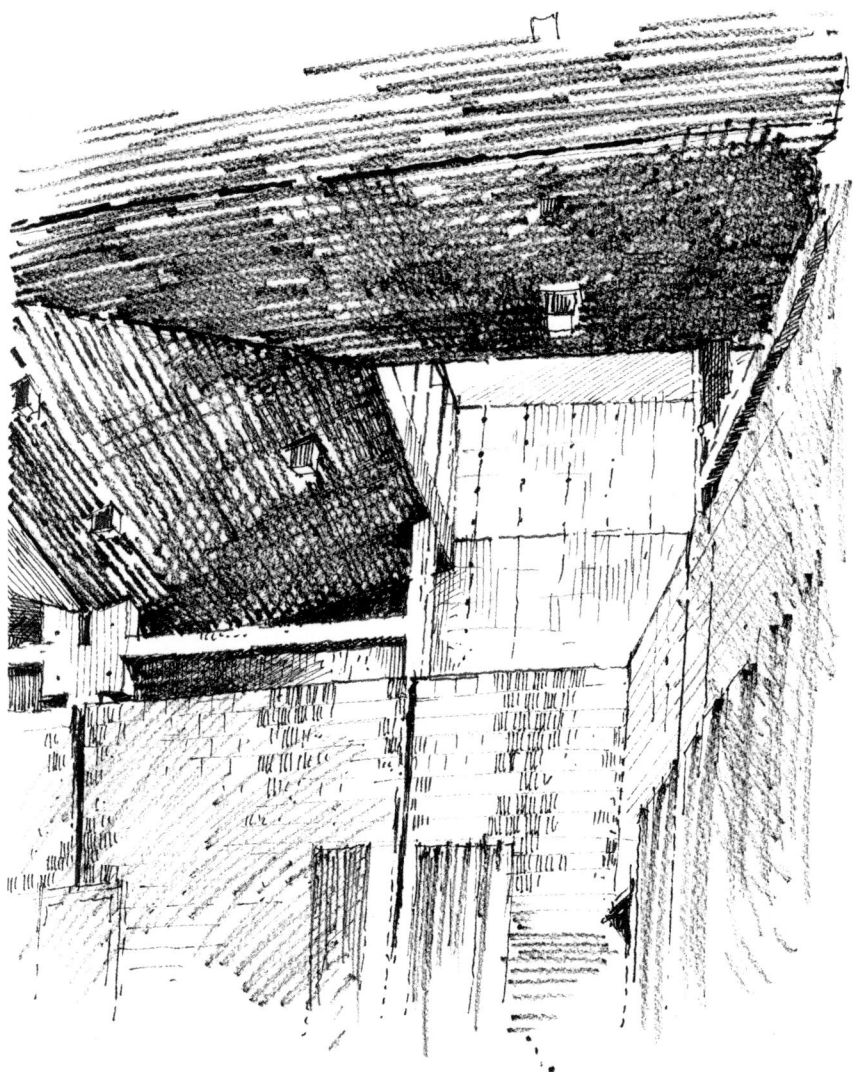

FIGURE 9.15 Rochester, First Unitarian Church, interior of the sanctuary. Drawing by Stephen Kite.

as companions; and even on the second grey day the glint of the burping tubas went with a soft light which Scully has aptly described: 'You can really feel the silence he talked about, thrumming as with the presence of divinity, when the cinder block is washed silver by the light that floods down upon it, while the heavy, heavy slab is lifted overhead.' Scully equates Rochester to the Yale Art Gallery 'as one of Kahn's early essays in the sublime, into whose vast silences all his later work was to move'.[124] Ingeniously, the inverted soffit of these cross-slabs does not bear down or intimidate; it retains its full shadow while diffusing the silver light.

No Christian symbolism is intended by this cross, drawn across a Unitarian setting that places emphasis on 'deeds over creeds', and rejects preordained forms.[125] Its hovering presence is chthonic in its symbolism; for Olivier Marc, 'our body and our psyche both seem to be organized along the lines of an interior cross'; for Norberg-Schulz, the cross, inscribed in square or circle, denotes from prehistory the qualitative 'directions of existential space' – it is also the *cardo* and *decumanus* of the Roman city.[126] All of this is best summed up in Mircea Eliade's authoritative reflections on the symbolism of shadows in archaic religion where he describes the architectural cosmogony of 'the circle or the square built by emanating from a Centre [as] an *imago mundi*. Just as the visible Universe unfolds from a Centre and extends towards the four cardinal points'. At the centre the vertical axis aspires to heaven while 'on the same perpendicular axis at the other extremity is the World of the Dead...or the ideograms of the Shadows'.[127] At the same time the traditional symbolism of the church is inescapably latent – as even in the Greek cross of Trenton Bath House; Hans Sedlmayr describes Byzantine sacred space in equally pre-Christian terms:

> The four parts of the church's interior symbolize the four points of the compass. The interior of the church is the universe. The altar is the paradise, which was shifted to the east.... On the other hand the west is the area of darkness, of horror, of death.... The centre of the church building is the earth.... The four parts of the interior of the church symbolize the four parts of the compass.[128]

Notwithstanding Kahn's equalization of the axes – and despite the reverse in traditional orientation that puts the dais at the west end – we inevitably sense the eastern entrance as a liturgical 'west' as we emerge from under the darkness of the organ loft; moreover, the wall hangings Kahn designed with weaver Jack Lenor Larsen move from duller indigos and violets to the glory of yellow and gold at the liturgical 'east' in the environs of the podium. In writing his 'Volume Zero' at Rochester, Kahn also drew on his knowledge of Ronchamp in the basic schema of a cave space held down by an inverted roof – folded plate in one case, shell in the other –

whose darkness is also told, in part, by the diffused luminosity of encircling light scoops. One intermediate scheme, with 'four umbrellas' and associated columns, even replicates Ronchamp's light slot; a figure is drawn on the section with the line of vision and the note: 'the sight line shows the light strip under the light towers to be visible as a crack of light when eye is far enough back' (Figure 9.16).[129] From experience shadow-makers know that we need some illuminance to see the *deepest* blacks, as experimentally proven in the phenomenon of simultaneous contrast, whereby a lightening background 'blackens' a dark grey square.[130]

Rochester was dedicated in December 1962; six years later Kahn spoke to the students at Rice University School of Architecture:

> I think that it is a time of our sun on trial, of all our institutions on trial. I was brought up when the sunlight was yellow, and the shadow was blue. But I see it clearly as being white light, and black shadow. Yet this is nothing alarming, because I believe that there will come a fresh yellow, and a beautiful blue.[131]

The immediate context of this, as he points out earlier in the talk, had been the turbulent student demonstrations at Berkeley in the 1960s, he had been 'reading in the *New York Times Magazine* of the things that had been going on in California' and he had been through Berkeley and had 'noticed the size of the revolution'.[132] But the condition to which Kahn was responding may be generalized as a broader existential one; how, in times of tremendous dislocation and uncertainty, after two World Wars and the holocaust, is it possible to build with the 'beautiful blue' Impressionist shadows of Kahn's art training – of, for example, Monet's Rouen Cathedral series? Rochester inhabits the same elemental *brut* landscape that had

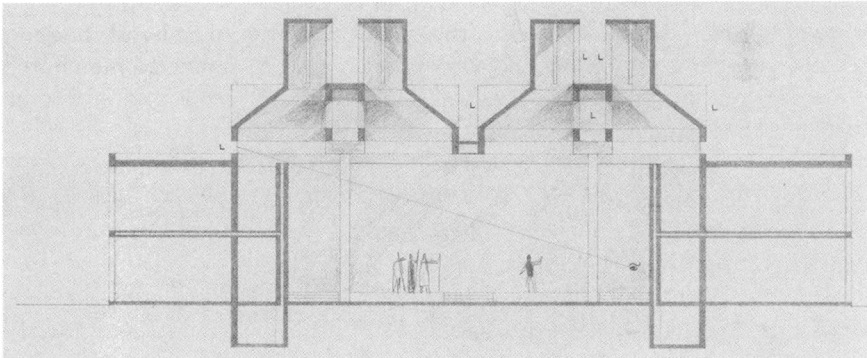

FIGURE 9.16 Rochester, First Unitarian Church, section drawing of intermediate four-column and umbrella-roof design. First Unitarian Church Collection, The Architectural Archives, University of Pennsylvania.

produced the grey chromatics of Trenton, or the primitivity of Yale's 'Museum without Walls', where Michael Cadwell describes an 'architectural chiaroscuro that accents each mark in the concrete's heavy impasto and charges the clerestory triangle with thunderous echoes'.[133] At Rochester we do experience a challenging black shadow and white light – and, at times, even Scully's 'silver', although that silvery quality will not be fully realized until Kahn builds the Kimbell Art Gallery, where he also recovers the possibility of making blue shadows.

At the compositional level, the split entrance and the multiple orientations are among many ambiguities that complexify this moving project. A key move is the interlocking in section of the great room with the ambulatory. Hereness is established by the rough textures, and highly varied greys, of the inner square-faced blockwork wall of the ambulatory, and a numinous thereness by the outer boundary of shuttered pale concrete which rises up to form the light-washed outer walls of the giant light monitors. The job of carrying the mighty cross-vault is shared between the outer walls and almost anthropomorphic head-and-arms armatures of columns embedded in the blockwork; the head-capitals at the centre are marked with vertical nose grooves where they meet the keel. These abstract figures seem to join the congregation in raising a structure that otherwise might seem crushing – in symbolically supporting the burden of existence. Indeed they give the neo-baroque illusion that they are the only structural elements carrying the loads, so crisply do they read against the shadows cast by the vaults as they meet the outer walls (Figure 9.17).

At this time Kahn was still evolving his theory of 'existence will' in dialogue with the 'pure knowing' of light which he would declare fully in the 1969 Swiss lecture on 'Silence and Light' as discussed – with its neo-Platonic aspects as mediated through Schopenhauer. Even so, he had written at this time to Alison and Peter Smithson on 'some ideas about the "existence will"' he was germinating in regard to the formation of contemporary institutions, and Komendant (his engineer on Rochester) remembers Kahn pondering that 'the essence of atmosphere for a church is silence and light. Light and Silence!'[134] Kahn has succeeded here in again bringing architecture back to its roots; in the realm of this dark vibrating cross, he has made concrete a treasury of shadows, mediating between our unfathomable origins, and those towers that shield and mediate the unknowable Light of the Eternal Good.

Shadow falls on castle walls

From Scully (1962) onwards the other Platonic implications of what Kahn calls 'Form and Design' at Rochester have been much debated. Abridging the actual extended client dialogues, it is the story Kahn tells in the 'discussion' in his office in February 1961 recorded in *Perspecta* 7.[135] Kahn

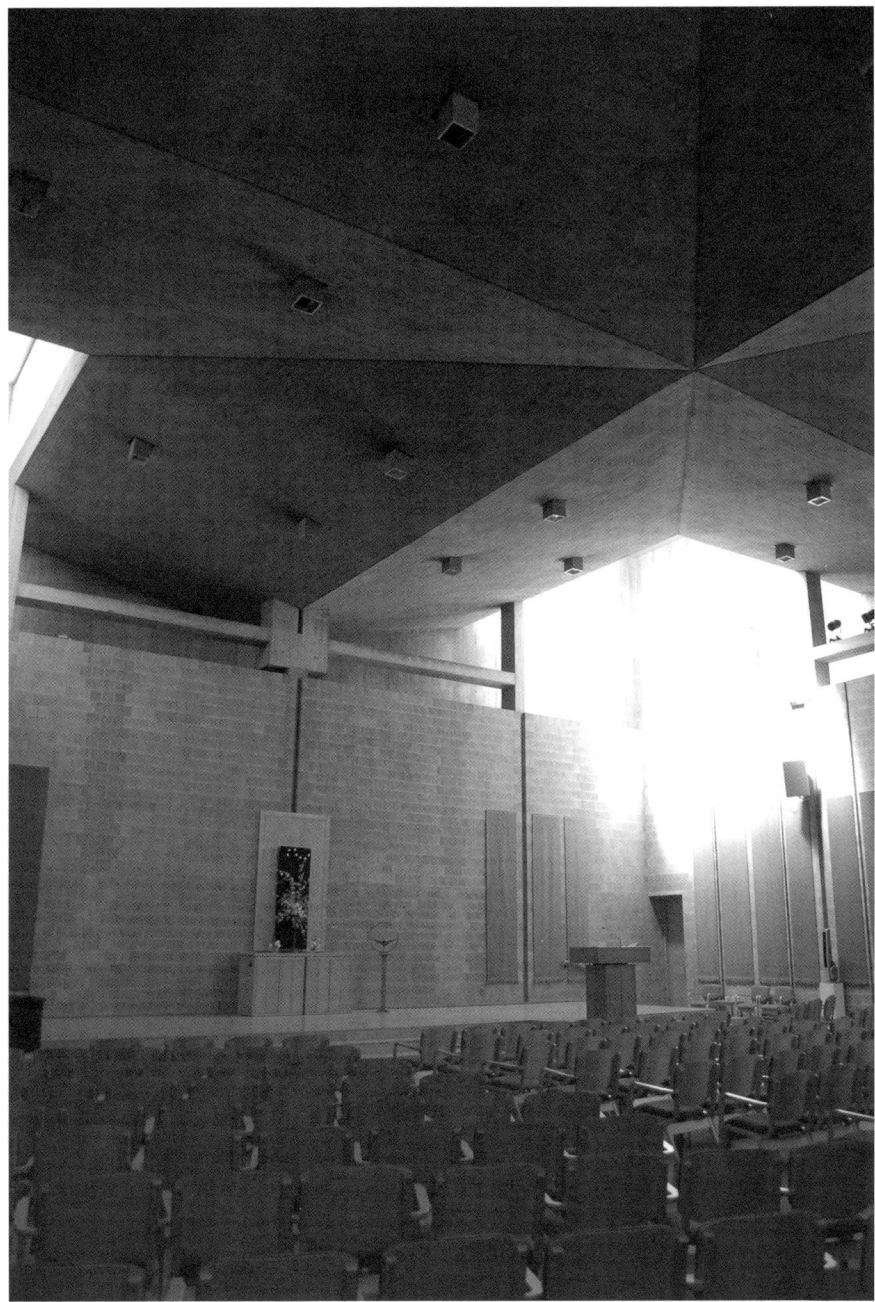

FIGURE 9.17 Rochester, First Unitarian Church, detail of keel vault and column supports. Photograph, Stephen Kite.

first posited a Platonic Idea to the congregation in a 'Form Drawing' which was emphatically 'NOT A DESIGN', with 'a square, the sanctuary, and a circle around the square which was the containment of an ambulatory' and the school around this.[136] His first neo-Renaissance ideal scheme was, as he said, 'almost a literal translation of the form drawing as I would call it: form drawing – that which represented, which presented inseparable parts of what you may call a Unitarian center'.[137] Various budgetary and programme constraints impinged on these early ideas of July 1959–December 1959 until at one point the client insisted that the school must be separated from the sanctuary – a shattering of the idea of the 'Form Diagram' which came as a 'terrible blow' to Kahn. Reluctantly, Kahn diagrammed these elements to test their separation from the sanctuary, but one by one – both functionally and symbolically – the kitchen, the classrooms and so on, found their way back to the original annular clustering. Kahn's nesting here of the great communal room as a treasury of shadows – infiltrated by light from above – within a protective armature of ambulatory and cells, is an instinct that found further expression in many projects such as the Erdman Hall, Bryn Mawr College and the Library, Phillips Exeter Academy. Kahn described these domains in his talk at Otterlo in 1959:

> A chapel, to me, is a space that one can be in, but it must have excess of space around it, so that you don't have to go in. That means, it must have an ambulatory, so that you don't have to go into the chapel; and the ambulatory must have an arcade outside, so that you don't have to go into the ambulatory; and the object outside is a garden.[138]

In moving to the suburbs of Rochester, from its original downtown location, the Unitarian community certainly had plenty of space for gardens and trees on its 2.8-hectare site. Although the obligatory 'arcade outside' is absent, its mediating role is taken by the chiaroscuro of brick walls deeply folded in plan and elevation. The church complex sits mostly on a plateau abutting its suburban boulevards, but the site slopes markedly to the southeast, and from these lawns and woodland gardens it looms up with all the castellar presence that was part of its inspiration (Figure 9.18). Like keeps, the towers of the light monitors peep over a deeply modulated curtain wall of alternating shadow hoods and niches. Drawing the walls of Carcassonne, or pondering the plans of thick-walled castles such as Comlogan in Dumfries, also propelled Kahn's 'conscious fervour to redefine the modernist membrane as a shaper of a *spatial layer* – folding it, capsizing it, doubling it, "wrapping ruins around buildings", and gradually devising a uniquely modern mediating architectural space'.[139] Recalling these castle passions, in a letter of 1973, he wrote: 'The Scottish Castle. Thick, thick walls. Little openings to the enemy. Splayed inwardly to the occupant. A place to read, a place to sew.... Places for the bed, for the stair.... Sunlight. Fairy tale.'[140]

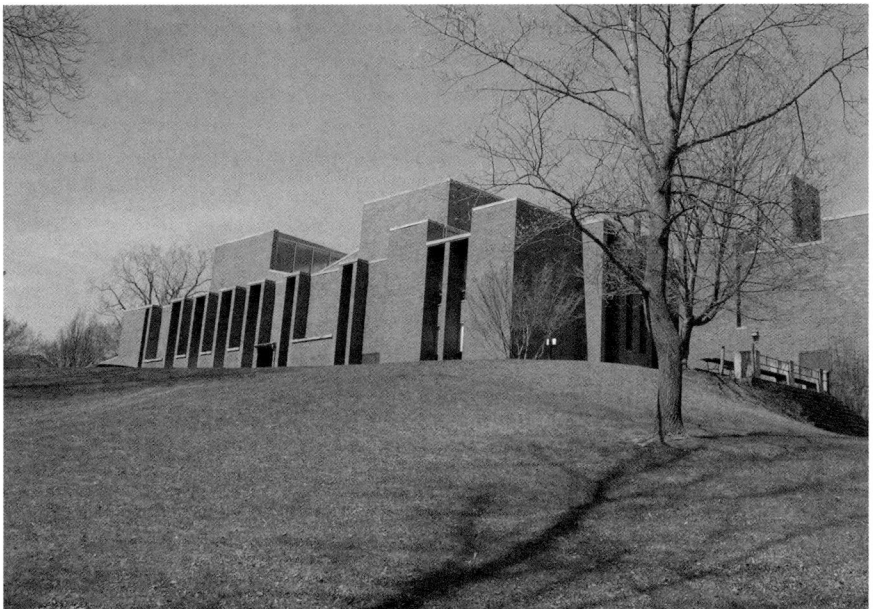

FIGURE 9.18 Rochester, First Unitarian Church, exterior view from south-east. Photograph, Stephen Kite.

A conscious fervour to model in shade and light is palpable in Kahn's vigorous freehand lead drawing of Rochester's main-entrance (north) elevation (Figure 9.19).[141] Within long vertical strokes that establish the overall dark ground tone of the brick monitors and walls, Kahn's tense diagonal marks sculpt deep columns of shade within the light hoods, and against the planes they abut above the window niches. For Sarah Goldhagen, the result is 'a colonnade of shadows that supports neither lintel nor pediment, a kind of negative colonnade'.[142] Certainly, here the 'column is where the light is not' – as the 1950–1 journeys to Egypt and Greece had taught Kahn. Freehand studies like these led to the notable set of tenderly rendered elevations now held by the Museum of Modern Art (MOMA) New York (Figure 9.20). These sheets explore the potential of *chiaroscuro* to simplify monumental forms. In contributing to the overall abstract dynamic the deep shadows are one plastic element among the others – as solid as the planes that produce them. No specific light source is indicated; an ideal light produces the shadows, cast in all cases, conventionally, from the upper left.

At Rochester, Kahn confessed 'a need to reveal', a realization that 'reveals are necessary' to mediate glare as did the traditional Renaissance surround of pediment and columns.[143] There was also 'a desire to have some window seats', and the elaborately folded walls offered ample opportunities to make those intimate places he had discovered in the wall zones of the Scottish castle – 'a place to read, a place to sew' (Figure 9.21). So – in reciprocal play

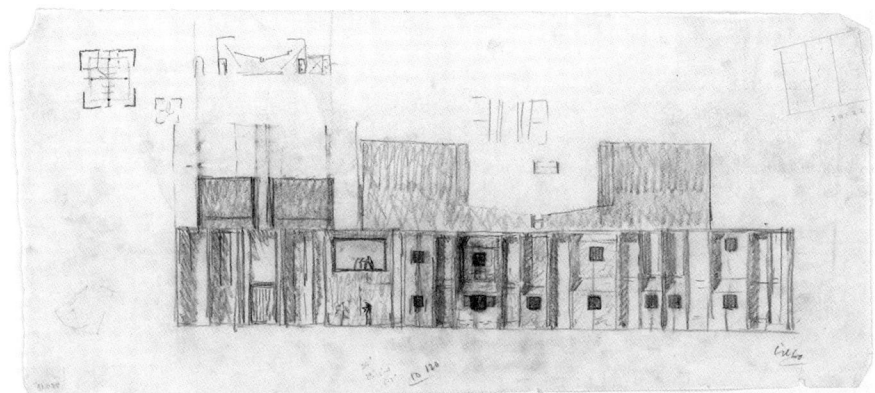

FIGURE 9.19 Rochester, First Unitarian Church, study of entrance (north) elevation. Louis I. Kahn Collection, The University of Pennsylvania and the Pennsylvania Historical and Museum Commission.

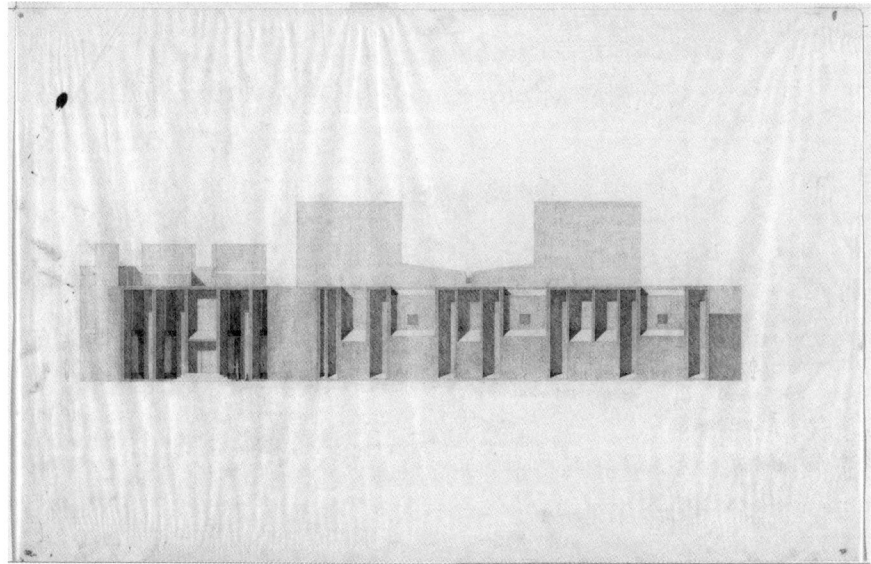

FIGURE 9.20 Rochester, First Unitarian Church, north elevation. © The Museum of Modern Art (MoMA), New York/Scala, Florence.

in plan and section – the hoods that project *out* to shield the windows also shape subdued window seat recesses *within* at ground level; these niches have small openings *to the side* – into the hood zones – to capture gentle light for the task in hand.

Schopenhauer has recorded a pure kind of knowing of the 'beautiful in architecture' within 'the depth of winter' which marries the ideal light and

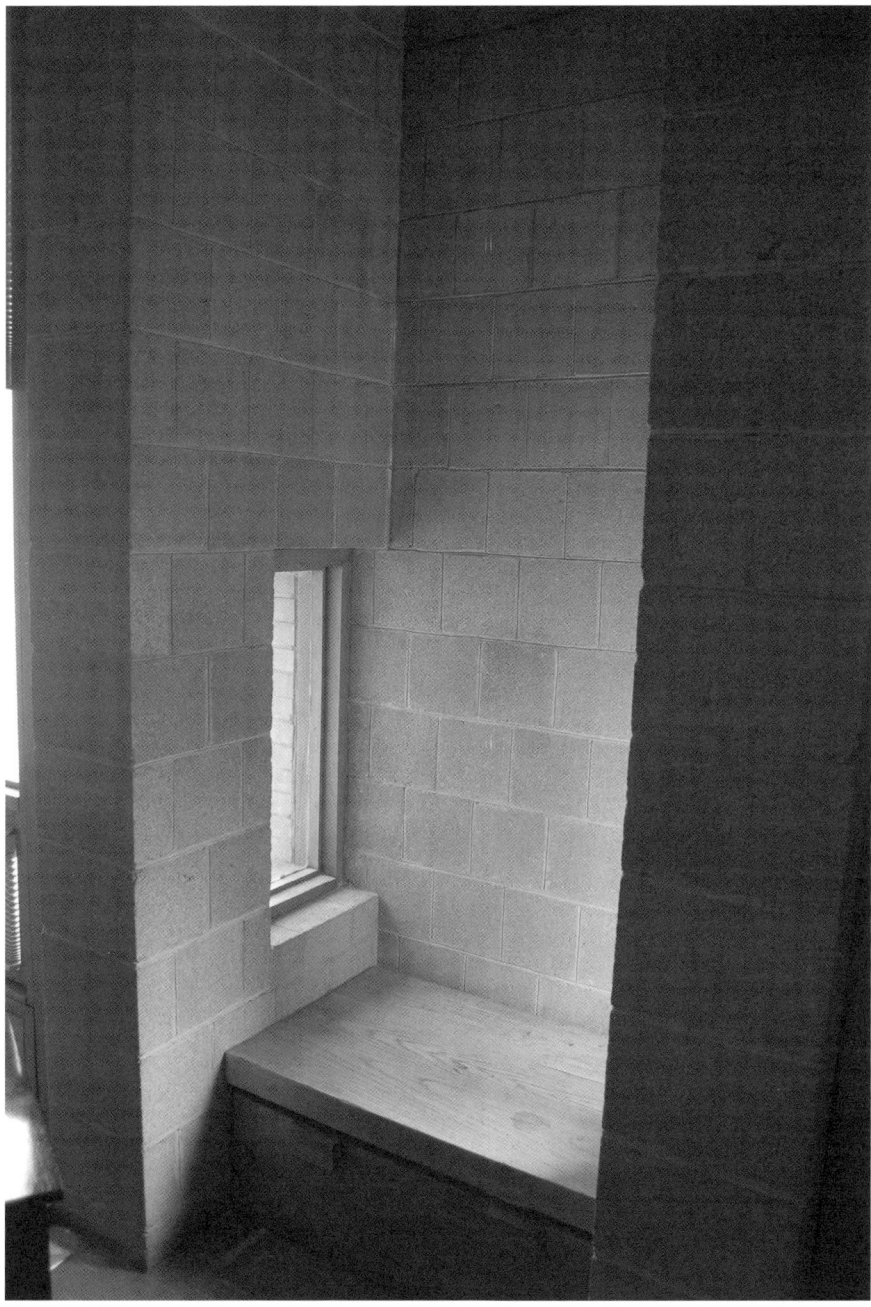

FIGURE 9.21 Rochester, First Unitarian Church, classroom window seat. Photograph, Stephen Kite.

shadow of the MOMA sheets to the setting of the Unitarian Church in wintry Rochester, south of Lake Ontario, where its folded castellar walls often rise from fields of snow.[144] The quality of Schopenhauer's winter light is that it illumines without warming, subduing the dark genital aspect of the will and allowing thereby a state of pure meditation:

> Now if in the depth of winter, when the whole of nature is frozen and stiff, we see the rays of the setting sun reflected by masses of stone, where they illuminate without warming, and are thus favourable only to the purest kind of knowledge, not to the will, then contemplation of the beautiful effect of light on these masses moves us into the state of pure knowing, as all beauty does.[145]

Kimbell – Coloured shadow

Most visitors to the Kimbell Art Museum (1966–72) arrive by vehicle, and enter the building via the stark lower-level car park entrance from the east. But those few who choose to take the magnificent honorific pedestrian approach from the south experience, in succession, three of Kahn's great archetypes of shadow: the standing stone, the stoa and the shaded grove. This gravel walk leads, firstly, to the threshold of the stoa where travertine steps mark a bridge which spans between the plashing of the entrance forecourt pools and a still, sunken grass courtyard which embeds the museum in the landscape. The great sculptor Isamu Noguchi (1904–88) had helped Kahn to this sense he described, of 'the building as a contour; not one contour but an interplay of contours... folding and ... harbouring',[146] through their collaboration on the unrealized Adele Levy Memorial Playground, New York (1961–6). And here in this sunken court, a standing stone is one of the four basalt monoliths Noguchi placed when he made his homage 'Constellation (for Louis Kahn)' in 1980–3. Part untouched and part chiselled and polished – like its fellow stones – it casts its lone memorial shadow onto the plane of smooth grass that extends between a pool and the sheer concrete and travertine-vaulted flanks of the galleries (Figure 9.22). Thus Noguchi alludes to the reverence he shared with Kahn of the archaic wisdom embodied in humankind's 'beginnings' – as in the erection of mysterious menhirs.

Crossing the 'bridge' from the gravel walk, the visitor enters the embracing shade of the hard-paved stoa and escapes the glare and intensity of the Texan sun. In his 1969 Zurich lecture, when Kahn rapped out the supports of the stoa with his chalk, he stressed how the marvel of its making lay in the fact that it is 'no partitions, just columns, just protection.... It's shaded' – but this most rudimentary shaded place has the capacity to become a 'place of happening'.[147] Just four taps of the chalk would have sufficed to indicate the corner columns of this solemn porticus; they alone carry a post-tensioned, cast in situ, reinforced concrete cycloid vault, seven metres wide,

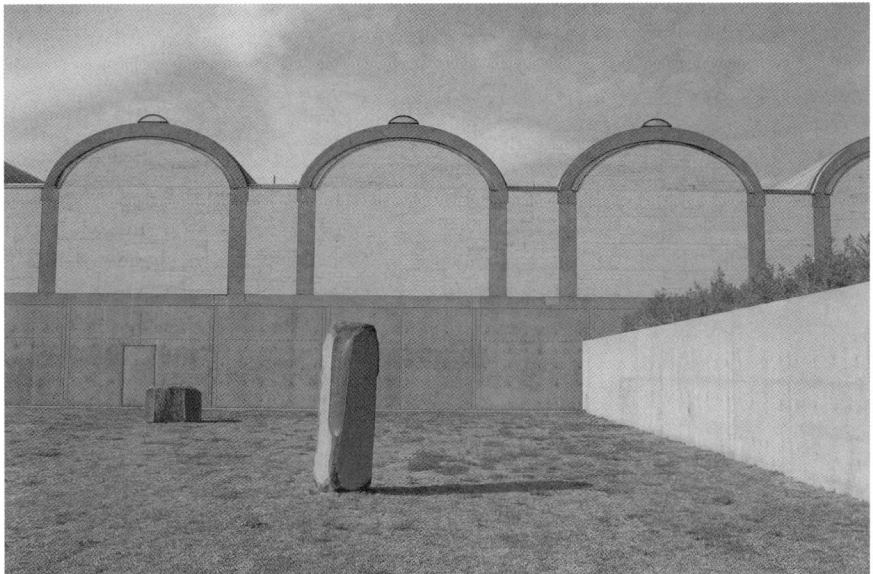

FIGURE 9.22 Isamu Noguchi, *Constellation (for Louis Kahn)*, 1980–3, Kimbell Art Museum, standing stone basalt monolith. Photograph, Stephen Kite.

and a breathtaking thirty metres in its longitudinal span. Not much happens here; for Kahn it is an element that allows the building to say: 'Look, I want to tell you about the way I was made';[148] certainly open to the potential for 'happenings' and being in servitude, but already anticipating that distant time when it will be a ruin, and again free of bondage. Kahn says:

> Because of the open porches, how the building is made is completely clear before you go into it. It is the same realization behind Renaissance buildings, which gave the arcade to the street, though the buildings themselves did not need the arcade for their own purposes. So the porch sits there, made as the interior is made ... a realization of what is architecture. When you look at the building and porch, it is an offering.[149]

So, it is simply a space of promenade, or a place to pause in the shadows on the flanking travertine benches and to enjoy the coolness, intensified by the sounds of the reflecting pools whose cascades the vaults amplify. Presently, this urbane world of the agora debouches the gallerygoer back to nature as, with a sharp tender shock, she/he again feels the crunch of gravel underfoot and enters a shadow grove of close-set Yaupon holly trees. Again Kahn invokes many ancient resonances, such as those pertaining to *Diana Nemorensis* – 'Diana of the Woodland Glade'. Her most famous temple – one celebrated in Sir James Frazer's *The Golden Bough* – was in the Arician grove in the Alban Hills near Rome, on the north side of the still-watered, volcanic crater, Lake Nemi, known as 'Diana's Mirror', *Speculum Dianae*. Immediately related to the temple itself was a small grove of a scale close to that of Kahn's holly grove, some '33 yards in length by 17 yards in breadth, with columns on either side of the pronaos' and 'a retaining wall on the north and east cut into the hillsides' (Figure 9.23).[150] Maybe the story of Diana, the goddess of dark forests and fertility, is in the story of Kahn's Texan 'temple', with its terraced ascent from the specular pools to this mysteriously shadowed and fecund copse, soberly embraced by its own pronaos and stoas.

That sense of building and terrain as a single-moulded entity that Kahn had deepened in his working with Noguchi was confirmed by his relationship with Harriet Pattison, the landscape architect to whom he had enthused about Ronchamp in his letter of 1959. In the early 1950s she had travelled in Europe and 'became mesmerized by Europe's classical gardens, realizing that "these landscapes were 'real' painting"'.[151] Kahn in turn admired Claude Lorraine, who had painted goddess Diana's Lake Nemi, followed by the poetic brushes of many including J. M. W. Turner, John R. Cozens and Richard Wilson. As the principal landscape architect at the Kimbell (working for the Philadelphia practice of George Patton), Pattison argued for a setting that would extend 'the civilized environment of the museum beyond its walls to the limits of the site and in a manner that the structure and landscape will fuse intrinsically'.[152] In a related Heidegger-ian reading Kenneth Frampton has described how Kahn was to 'inscribe the

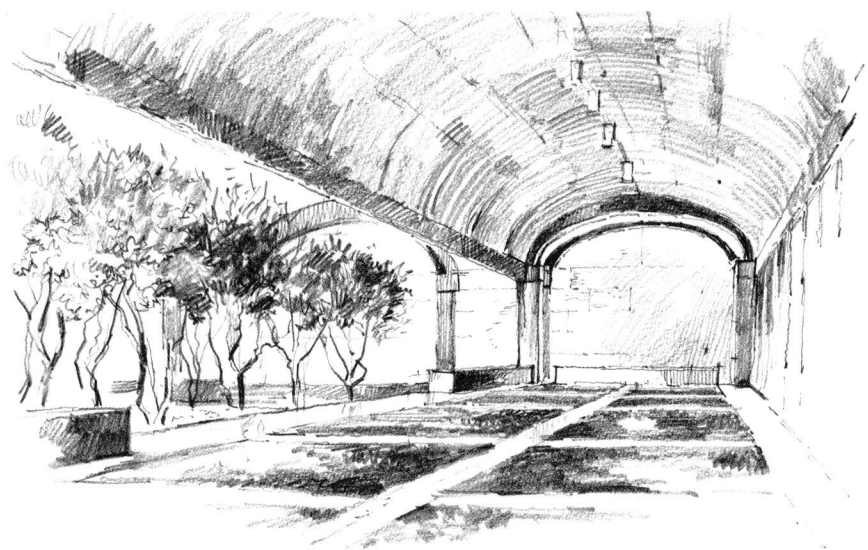

FIGURE 9.23 Pronaos and shadow grove, Kimbell Art Museum. Drawing by Stephen Kite.

Kimbell into its site in such a way as to establish a categoric "clearing" and to endow the precinct with a particular presence'.[153]

This reciprocity of clearing and carving building and landscape as one interpenetrating entity comes across strongly in many of Kahn's studies – in charcoal and graphite on yellow trace – whether in plan, section, elevation or perspective. And it comes across throughout the three key phases of the design development: the initial grandiose 120 metre square plan (March 1967), the second looser 'H' configuration (September–November 1967), to the consolidated 'U' plan of the realized gallery, completed in 1972.[154] The shade trees – in which the 'clearing' seems to be made – are boldly hatched, or drawn with as firm a contour as the building and its spaces.[155] Marshall Meyers (Kahn's associate on the Kimbell) has evocatively described how Kahn's 'chosen drawing tools responded' to his ever-questing dialogue with his team, and his testing of ideas:

> The marks of the vine charcoal barely adhered to the smooth paper, sitting on the hard surface as black dust ready to be brushed away by his hand the moment a better thought arrived. He had invented this technique for himself: vine charcoal on the smooth yellow paper. Drawing and erasing became immediate and as rapid as his thoughts. He would smudge away one idea and follow it with another, leaving only a faint trace of the original sketch. The layers of charcoal left a translucent, animated image of the new ideas superimposed on the ghosts of the old.
>
> He had no reason to save the initial thoughts. No reason to overlay tracing paper on top of paper to record them all: too slow, too wasteful. Then, once he was satisfied and the search was done for the moment, a spray of fixative would seal up the found image with all the thoughts, ghosts, and smudges preserved.[156]

Kahn's choice of this 'archaic drawing material' of charcoal marries with his quest for beginnings; it is 'the charred piece of wood snatched from the primal fire by Apelles', and the willow stick that 'was naturally to hand for the daughter of Butades' in tracing her lover's shadow.[157] And although very friable, he could give the medium longevity by fixing it, as Meyers notes; and even when the carbon deposit of a rejected line is wiped away, 'there is a vibrating ghost mark [which] always reveals the history of its own processes of making'.[158] In some cases Kahn's searching builds up such intensities of black as to obliterate even these histories, as in 'Site plan (study by the court)', where the overlaid scrubbings, dashes and circles look as abstract as a late Rothko.[159] Because of its atavistic overtones, charcoal is the natural tool of such expressive drawing, and Kahn again exploits its tonal and gestural possibilities in two powerful perspectives of the west elevation of the second 'H' plan project he made on 22 September 1967 looking north-east and south-west.[160] These show his instinct towards a lower crouching curve for the vaults, one which Meyers discovered how to

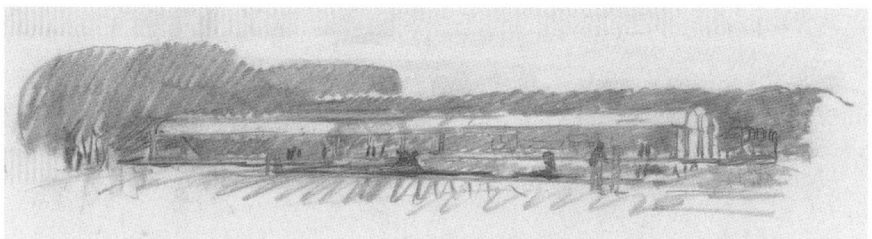

FIGURE 9.24 Louis I. Kahn, *Kimbell Art Museum. Perspective view from southwest*, 22 September 1967. Louis I. Kahn Collection, The University of Pennsylvania and the Pennsylvania Historical and Museum Commission.

generate as a cycloid. Their long horizontals glint out of the strong tonalities of shadowed portico and backdrop tree masses, all hatched in vigorous charcoal diagonals (Figure. 9.24).

From Diana's gravelled grove at the centre of all this labour of earthwork and clearing, the art pilgrim makes an ascent of six broad travertine steps to enter the hard-paved pronaos and regain the earlier sense of civitas. Through revelatory shadow play, Kahn discloses how the Kimbell's *parti* fuses the longitudinals of the great cycloid vault beams with lateral transects. This results in a tripartite organization – centred on the entrance portico, lobby and bookstore – wherein the independence of the vaults is marked by deep shadow recesses three feet (0.9 metre) wide. In *Light Is the Theme* – a booklet made in homage to Kahn and the museum – an image of one of these major transects, adjoining the car park entrance, is coupled with Kahn's aforementioned comments that he 'put the glass between the structure members and the members which are not of structure because the joint is the beginning of ornament.... Ornament is the adoration of the joint'.[161] In the entrance portico this interval becomes a zone of enchantment which allows the strong southern light of Texas to throw the shadow of the portico vault, onto the field of the travertine cladding beyond, in ever-changing skiagraphies (Figure 9.25). In *Deconstructing the Kimbell*, Michael Benedikt includes these recesses among a whole taxonomy of 'ruptures, fissures, slits, omissions, withdrawals, erasures, dis-junctions, "betweens", and separations' governing the 'servant/served economy' of the project.[162] Along with the aforementioned, many of these separations invite shadow play; thus the stairs between the levels within are 'treated as fissures or chasms', and 'the junction of no two materials on the same plane is treated other than with a [shadow] recess'[163] – and then there are the three courtyards. In an address he gave in Boston in November 1967, Kahn singled out these further significant acts of cross-cutting when he spoke of 'an art museum' he was designing in Texas:

> I cut across the vaults, at a right angle, a counterpoint of courts, open to the sky, of calculated dimensions and character, marking them Green

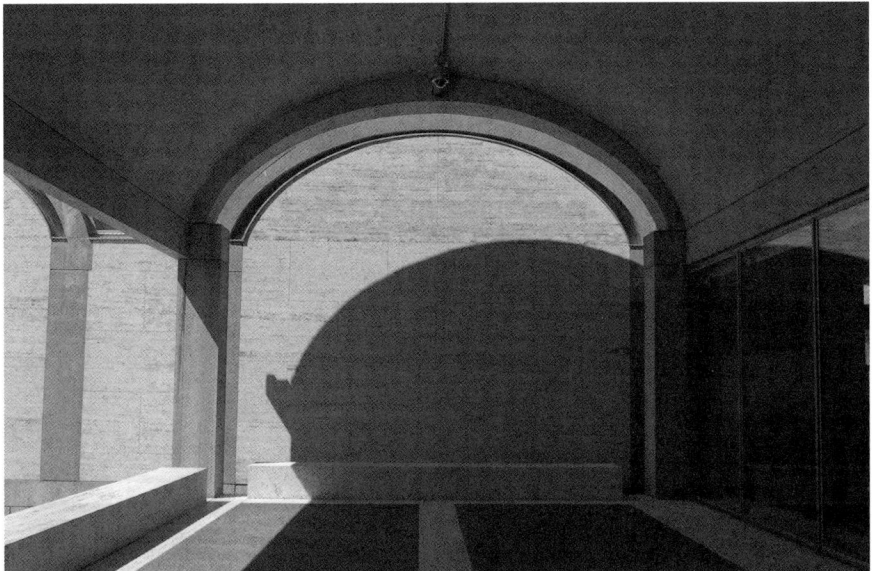

FIGURE 9.25 Shadow play of the portico and vault, Kimbell Art Museum. Photograph, Stephen Kite.

Court, Yellow Court, Blue Court, named for the kind of light that I anticipate their proportions, their foliation, or their sky reflections on surfaces, or on water will give.[164]

These courts are important areas of stasis within the ordered flexibility of much of the rest of the museum, Frampton calls them 'place-forms within the overall matrix that do not change'.[165] And at Boston Kahn goes on to make the point he would make in the following spring of 1968 to the students in Rice, that in a time of social trial the yellow light and blue shadow of his upbringing was inconceivable – only the stark struggle of 'white light, black shadow'.[166] He muses that 'in the present revolt against our institutions and ways, that there is no Wonder' but 'when Wonder is, the light will become a brighter yellow and the shadow a brighter blue'.[167] There are arguably already opportunities for wonder in shadows of these Green, Yellow and Blue courts; the Kahn of 1967 is noticeably in a very different place than at Yale in 1953 or at Rochester in 1959–61; the properties of the lightless, of the treasury of shadows and of light are shifting. Tyng describes how the clear demarcating vertical line, between silence and light, of the 1968 diagram, has become dotted by 1971, to the point that by 1972 he speaks of *silence* and *light* companionably as 'two brothers'.[168] It is worth following this course in Kahn's thinking back briefly to Yale and his last museum, the Yale Center for British Art (1969–74). Here Michael Cadwell has compared the deep blue shadows of the ascetic entrance court to the yellow light of the great drawing room of the library court: 'Looking across the galleries, we see the luminous concrete against its honeyed counterparts in the library court and its darker, shadowed blue brothers in the entry court. Yellow light and blue shadow as we stand in its resolution, a strange concrete luminosity that triggers, perhaps, wonder.'[169]

But we know, in experiencing these 'coloured shadows', that Kahn has told how he was 'raised on Goethe', one of his mother's favourite authors – along with Schiller.[170] Everything in Kahn's sensibility would have attracted him to Goethe's phenomenology of colour rather than Newton's abstract optics. As colours are darker than white and brighter than black, Goethe saw them all as shadowed or dimmed. In his experiments with sunlight, moonlight and candlelight he discovered the phenomenon of complementary hues, whereby shadows cast by an object lit from two different light sources – one red, one white, for example – produces the experience of the complementary opposite of green shadow.[171] Kahn could make his white-walled Philadelphia home sound like a Goethe investigation:

> I have no colour applied on the walls in my home.... Light is mood. The colour of light is very pronounced. We know that a red light will cast a green shadow and a green light will cast a red shadow. A blue light will cast a yellow shadow and a yellow light will cast a blue. It's surprising when a sunset is truly a prevailing red ... you will see an inky green shadow.[172]

In strict terms 'coloured shadows' cannot exist, for 'shadows are privations and so can only be coloured in the parasitic way a void can be coloured';[173] but – as with the earlier discussion of 'filtows' and Soane's *lumière mystérieuse* – too exacting a definition of shadows in architecture risks removing much of the experience itself. In this regard Goethe's interest in what the mind actually experiences has more appeal than excessive fretting over the composition of wavelengths.

Most functional of the three, highly differentiated, Green, Yellow and Blue courts of the Kimbell is the secret conservator's court (Yellow), which is hidden from the galleries and plunges double height to light the lower-level offices and laboratories. The tiny fountain court (Blue) is a charming episode of lateral light among the south galleries, a miniature paradise of the kind depicted in Persian carpets, represented as a walled enclosure against the hostile environs, with undefiled ever-flowing rivers at its heart and shade-trees against the sun – as scorching in Texas as the Iranian desert.[174] Above the source of the fountain's travertine water channel (oriented west-east) stands Antoine Bourdelle's *Penelope* (1909), as patiently still as the Ionic column conjured in the flutings of her cast-bronze dress. Kahn's studies of the fountain's dumb-bell plan of source/channel/pool also show the related idea of flanking travertine bench planters and shade trees.[175] As realized, the slender trunks and branches of the Pin Oak rise and canopy the court, supported on a horizontal grid of fine wire; the Pin Oak is deciduous but provides continual shade as it retains its dead leaves until they are forced off by the new spring foliage.[176] As airborne on her travertine plinth, as Penelope is grounded, the empyrean goddess of Aristide Maillol's bronze *L'Air* (1938) is the presiding deity at the centre of the largest 'Green' north courtyard, a pivotal space between the north-west galleries and the social spaces of the coffee shop and auditorium. *L'Air* is also shielded by a trellis of Pin Oak leaves and thus Kahn closes his major north-south axis with this lyrical vision of femininity, recumbently floating in a bower of dappled shade (Figure 9.26).

The longest fissure in Benedikt's taxonomy of 'ruptures' and 'slits' is the one that slices the cycloid vault along its length and shows that the vault is not a 'vault' at all, but in fact a pair of post-tensioned shells.[177] The vaulted surface brazenly declares its tectonic ambiguity in a construction photo on the very cover of the classic booklet in homage to the Kimbell – *Light Is the Theme* – showing the glaring slash of naked light *before* the veiling reflectors were installed.[178] Here Kahn sought and achieved a mediated quality of light with that 'luminosity of silver' that is only fleetingly experienced at Rochester. But he also knew that rooms for 'paintings and objects that fade should only *most modestly* be given natural light', and perhaps it has not been stressed enough that he wanted these vaulted spaces to have both musical and painterly tonalities 'with *graduating silver*, light to darkness' (Figure 9.27).[179] He also expressed the qualities of the vaults and their light

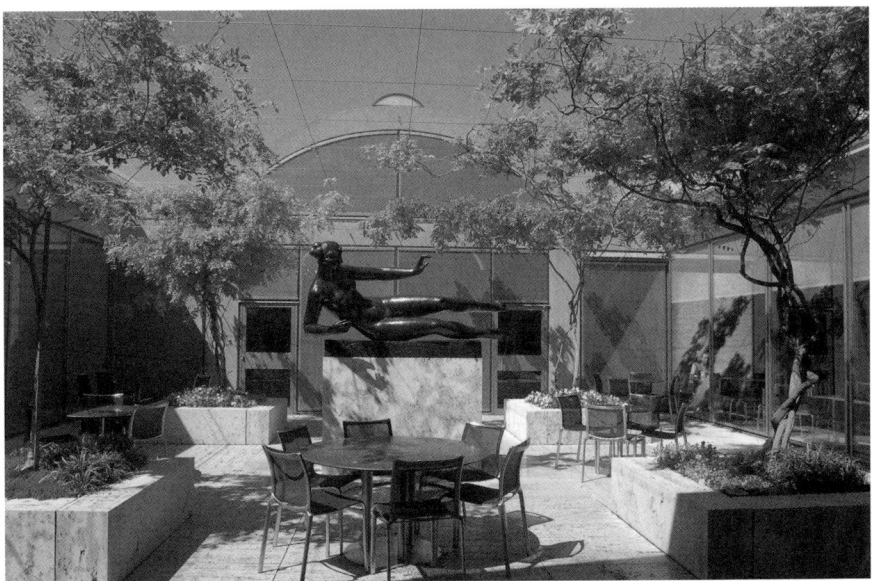

FIGURE 9.26 'Green' north courtyard, and coloured shadows, Kimbell Art Museum. Photograph, Stephen Kite.

as 'a moth spreading its wings';[180] recalling his comment on the enigmatic qualities of the matte stainless steel cladding to the Yale Center for British Art: 'On a grey day it will look like a moth; on a sunny day like a butterfly.'[181] The palazzo-like cube of the Yale Center for British Art is located on the south side of Chapel Street, and therefore is invariably seen mysteriously *contre-jour*; just like the grey-purples of Palazzo Camerlenghi at the Rialto in Venice, as in the oil of that most tonal of painters, Richard

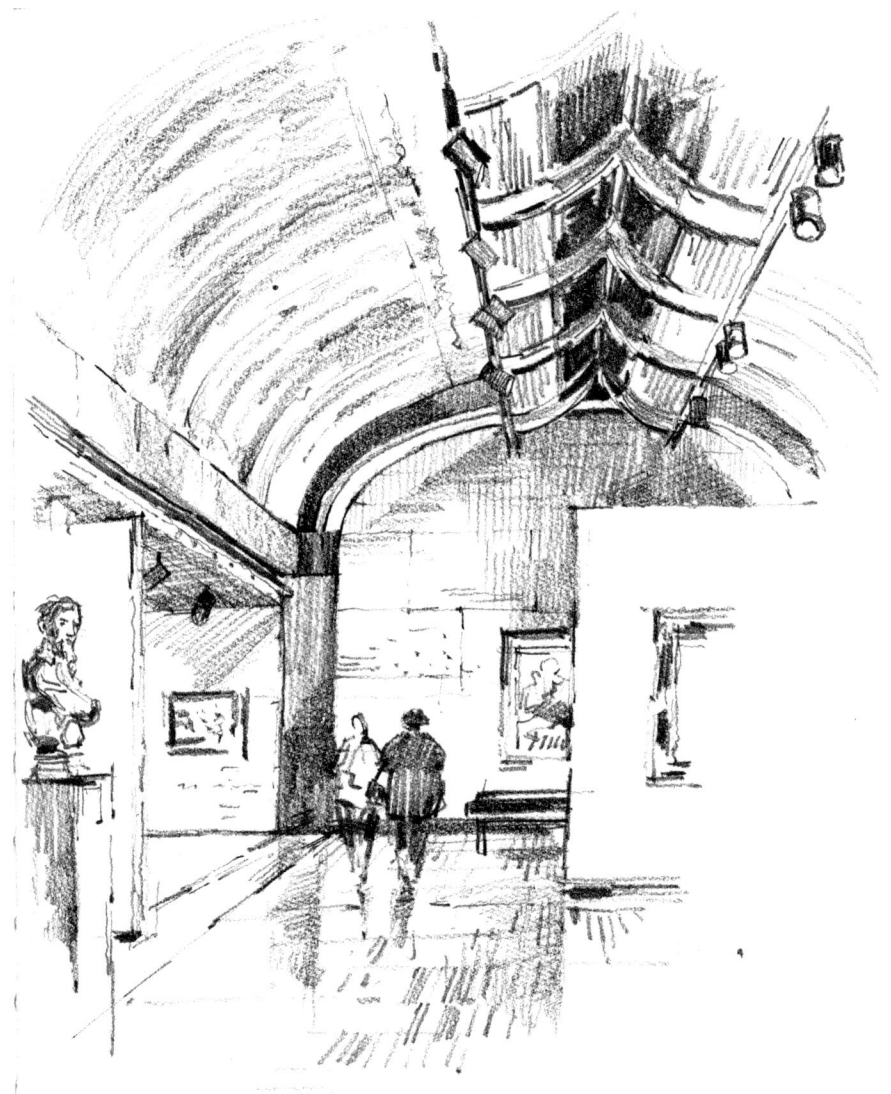

FIGURE 9.27 'Graduating silver, light to darkness', north-west gallery spaces, Kimbell Art Museum. Drawing by Stephen Kite.

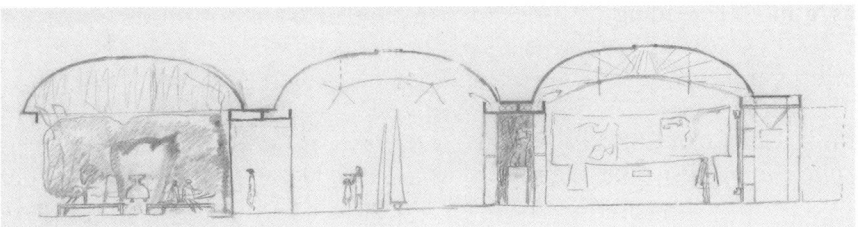

FIGURE 9.28 Louis I. Kahn, *Kimbell Art Museum. Schematic section of galleries*, 22 September 1967. Louis I. Kahn Collection, The University of Pennsylvania and the Pennsylvania Historical and Museum Commission.

Sickert's *Venice, the Rialto Bridge and the Palazzo Camerlenghi* (1895–6) housed in the same Mellon collection. In these very painterly moth-and-butterfly effects of vault and façade, Kahn establishes a subtle scale of melting spatial and tonal variations based on mid-tone penumbras which he can grade up to silver or down to resonant blues. The resemblances between the realized building and the key spatial and tonal concepts are already there in a key presentation section of 22 September 1967, drawn in coloured pencil and charcoal (Figure 9.28). This shows the depressed humanized geometry of the vault before its definition as a cycloid curve, and a tonal spectrum graduating from a couple of luminous main spaces, through a shadowy area with artefacts and benches, to the potential of the 'servant' flat-ceilinged zones – between the vaulted spaces – to be, themselves, darkly intimate display spaces; here Kahn draws a gloomy torso on a plinth (in the built scheme, the system of folded aluminium brackets, linked to free-standing panels, still allows these curatorial potentials).[182] Notwithstanding the human scale of a 'vault, rising not high', Kahn spoke of how his mind remained 'full of Roman greatness', and of a vault that 'etched itself' in his mind. Accordingly a related concept perspective (1967), darkly worked in charcoal, bears the sombre charge of a Piranesi etching, with a vault formed in erratic looping squiggles, the vertical panels in quick vertical strokes, and serried shadows.[183]

Conclusion – 'The lady from Abilene'

And finally in this narrative of incisions, the Kimbell marks the consummation of the shadow joint as manifesting the encounter between materials, as first fully originated in the Tribune Review Building: 'expression', Kahn writes and underlines on an exacting study (August 1969), in red pencil and charcoal, of travertine joints for the panels of the Kimbell's vault ends (Figure 9.29).[184] The joints within the travertine panels themselves are flush, but where they meet the concrete columns, within the portico for example, there is the 'expression' of a shadow recess. Kahn sensed an

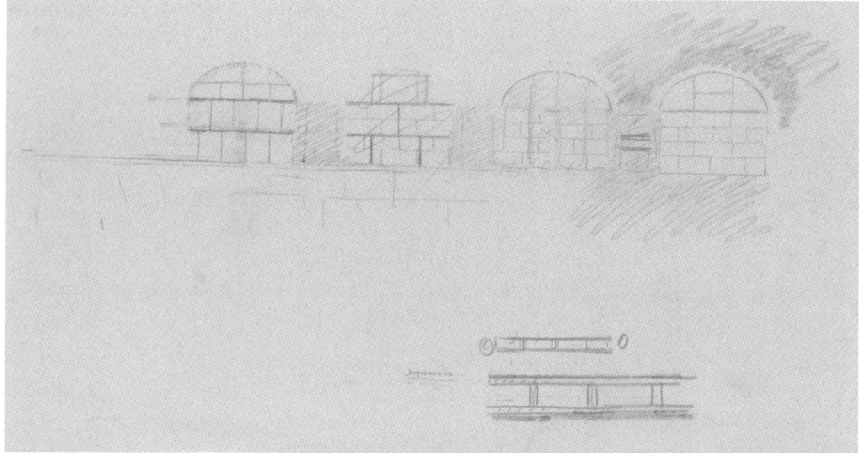

FIGURE 9.29 Louis I. Kahn, *Kimbell Art Museum. Schematic elevations of vault ends, detail of travertine panels*, August 1969. Louis I. Kahn Collection, The University of Pennsylvania and the Pennsylvania Historical and Museum Commission.

identity-in-difference between concrete and travertine: 'Travertine and concrete belong beautifully together because concrete must be taken for whatever irregularities or accidents in the pointing reveal themselves'; with its fossilized pores, 'travertine is very much like concrete – its character is such that they look like the same material'.[185]

For Benedikt this intense valorization – through the shadow-reveal – of 'the difficult-to-achieve flushness of planes' creates within 'a place of considerable serenity and control for the viewing of art'.[186] But Benedikt is also troubled that this same smooth serenity makes the 'actual paintings, especially older ones...seem grotesquely three-dimensional and physical. Often dark in tone, their thick frames hang away from the travertine walls and flush wood panels casting shadows from the incandescent fixtures'.[187] This discordance was not my experience, and, given the broad adulation of the building from the day of its opening in October 1972, it does not seem to have been that of most visitors. Visitors such as that 'lady from Abilene' whom Richard F. Brown (the museum's first director) had in mind when he tried to describe the character of the Kimbell's collection to Kahn.[188] The operative guide for the museum remains an eclectic one of acquiring works of 'definitive excellence' that 'define an artist or type regardless of medium, period, or school of origin', works that are invariably modest in scale – almost domestic.[189] In 'deconstructing' the Kimbell, Benedikt's thesis is to seek out what is normally 'subordinated or suppressed', to valorize 'the thing *and* its shadow'.[190] Now there are certainly plenty of modernist galleries of a different kind of smooth serenity; places where shadows *are* suppressed solely into the reveal, settings where the cast shadows of the Baroque and Rococo frames of intimate artworks *do* loom out oddly in the ways Benedikt suggests at Fort Worth. But among architects, Kahn is acutely aware of the thing *and* its shadow, as I hope to have demonstrated through *inter alia* the standing stone, the stoa, the grove, the colours of the courts and the 'graduating silver, light to darkness' of the ordering vaults themselves. Although the Kimbell is among the most luminous of Kahn's productions, there can be no doubt that even here shadow is fully validated. Notwithstanding his worries over the core issue of the hang of the artworks, Benedikt praises Kahn as 'a man not unaware of how presences become present: through a kind of death, a giving over to absence', a man who embraces fully the central 'absence' of this book: 'If for Kahn light was the maker of presences, it could not operate without material and without shadow.'[191] William Curtis explains Kahn's paradox of absence as an architecture 'full of inversions', of 'masses which suddenly seem weightless...rays of light which reveal the realm of shadows'.[192]

I have presented Kahn as shadow-maker here as the last great master and form-giver in an analogue tradition whereby a building was conceived, developed and detailed entirely through hand drawing. It was a culture that enabled that rich imaginative space between idea and drawing that Kahn characterized as 'Form and Design', a communicative space that recognized the embodied potential of drawing as representation. Given Kahn's instinct towards the ancient world, and his chosen tactile, yet fugitive, medium of charcoal on yellow trace, it was a space that allowed the absence of shadow to become fully present in his work, reciprocally with light. With the end of this long tradition of hand drawing alone, the advent of digital draughting and an architectural production predicated on modelling and performance has tended to collapse the rich representational realms of the analogue era into the narrower expectations of an age of simulation[193] – all of this inevitably presents further challenges to a culture of shadow-making.

Notes

1. Kahn (1971) quoted in Tyng, Alexandra, *Beginnings. Louis I. Kahn's Philosophy of Architecture* (New York: John Wiley, 1984), p. 175.
2. Kahn, Louis I., 'Order in Architecture', *Perspecta*, vol. 4 (1957), pp. 58–63, p. 59.
3. Corrodi, Michelle, and Spechtenhauer, Klaus, *Illuminating. Natural Light in Residential Architecture* (Basel: Birkhäuser, 2008), p. 192.
4. Quoted in Corrodi and Spechtenhauser, *Illuminating*, p. 182.
5. Corrodi and Spechtenhauser, *Illuminating*, p. 192, who also briefly contextualize Kahn's sense of light and shadow in a section on 'Best Of: Eleven Masters of Natural Light', pp. 210–23, 'Louis I. Kahn: Purist Light', p. 216.
6. Quoted in McCarter, Robert, *Louis I. Kahn* (London: Phaidon, 2009), p. 29.

7   Corrodi and Spechtenhauser, *Illuminating*, p. 212.
8   Corrodi and Spechtenhauser, *Illuminating*, pp. 216, 217.
9   Kahn, Louis I., *Silence and Light*, A. Vassella (ed) (Zurich: Park Books, 2013), p. 51.
10 Lobell, John, *Between Silence and Light. Spirit in the Architecture of Louis. I. Kahn* (Boston and London: Shambhala, 2008), p. 70.
11 See Upton, *Architecture in the US*, who makes a neoclassical/romantic contrast between these two aspects of the Salk Institute.
12 Latour, Alessandra (ed), *Louis I. Kahn. Writings, Lectures, Interviews* (New York: Rizzoli, 1991), p. 344.
13 Quoted in Frazer, John, *An Evolutionary Architecture* (London: Architectural Association, 1995), p. 9.
14 Latour, *Kahn. Writings*, p. 63.
15 Schopenhauer, Arthur, *The World as Will and Representation*, 2 vols, vol. 1, E. F. J. Payne (trans) (New York: Dover, 1969), p. 110.
16 See Burton, Joseph A., 'The Aesthetic Education of Louis I. Kahn', *Perspecta*, vol. 28 (1997), pp. 204–17, pp. 205–10; Wiseman, Carter, *Louis. I. Kahn: Beyond Time and Style* (New York: W. W. Norton, 2007), pp. 18–20.
17 Kahn, Louis I., 'Kahn on Beaux-Arts Training', *The Architectural Review*, vol. 155, no. 928 (June 1974), p. 332.
18 Kahn, 'On Beaux-Arts Training', p. 332.
19 Kahn, 'On Beaux-Arts Training', p. 332.
20 See Kries, Mateo; Eisenbrand, Jochen; Von Moos, Stanislaus (eds), *Louis Kahn: The Power of Architecture*, exhibition catalogue (Weil am Rhein: Vitra Design Museum, 2012), p. 27.
21 Kahn, *Silence and Light*, p. 16.
22 See Williamson, James F., 'Louis I. Kahn, Teacher', *Architectural Research Quarterly*, vol. 17, no. 3–4 (December 2013), pp. 313–24, p. 317.
23 Kahn, *Silence and Light*, p. 25.
24 See Tyng, *Beginnings*, p. 132.
25 Kahn, *Silence and Light*, p. 26.
26 Latour, *Kahn. Writings*, p. 232.
27 Latour, *Kahn. Writings*, p. 257.
28 Pauly, Danièle, *Barragán Space and Shadow, Walls and Colour* (Basel: Birkhäuser, 2008), p. 175.
29 Komendant, August E., *18 Years with Architect Louis I. Kahn* (Englewood, NJ: Aloray, 1975), p. 23.
30 Burton, Joseph, 'Notes from Volume Zero: Louis Kahn and the Language of God', *Perspecta*, vol. 20 (1983), pp. 69–90, p. 75.
31 See Korab-Karpowicz, W. Julian, 'Schopenhauer's Theory of Architecture', in B. Vandenabeele (ed), *A Companion to Schopenhauer* (Chichester: Blackwell, 2012), pp. 178–92, p. 178.

32 Schopenhauer, *World as Will and Representation*, vol. 1, p. 110.
33 Schopenhauer, *World as Will and Representation*, vol. 1, pp. 128, 129, Korab-Karpowicz, 'Schopenhauer's Theory of Architecture', p. 180.
34 Desmond, William, 'Schopenhauer's Philosophy of the Dark Origin', in Vandenabeele (ed) *Companion to Schopenhauer*, pp. 89–104, p. 92.
35 Kahn, *Silence and Light*, p. 26.
36 Schopenhauer, *World as Will and Representation*, vol. 1, p. 202.
37 Schopenhauer, *World as Will and Representation*, vol. 1, p. 216.
38 Quoted in Tyng, *Beginnings*, p. 174.
39 Kahn, *Silence and Light*, p. 26.
40 See Kahn, 'On Beaux-Arts Training', p. 332.
41 Schopenhauer, *World as Will and Representation*, vol. 1, p. 184.
42 Schopenhauer, *World as Will and Representation*, vol. 1, p. 255.
43 Schopenhauer, *World as Will and Representation*, vol. 2, p. 414.
44 Schopenhauer, *World as Will and Representation*, vol. 1, p. 257.
45 Quoted in Tyng, *Beginnings*, p. 67.
46 Kahn, *Silence and Light*, p. 27.
47 Kahn, *Silence and Light*, p. 27.
48 Emerson, Ralph Waldo, *Nature* (Boston: James Munroe, 1836), p. 76.
49 Latour, *Kahn. Writings*, p. 248.
50 Kahn, *Silence and Light*, p. 35, Kite's emphasis.
51 Kahn, Louis I., '1973: Brooklyn, New York', *Perspecta*, vol. 19 (1982), pp. 88–100, p. 95.
52 Wakeman, Geoffrey, *Victorian Book Illustration. The Technical Revolution* (Newton Abbot: David and Charles, 1973), p. 23.
53 Kahn, 'Brooklyn, New York', pp. 95, 96.
54 Scott, Walter, *The Heart of Midlothian, Waverley Novels*, 48 vols., vol. 11 (London: Fisher and Son, 1836–9), George Cruikshank image facing p. 322, *Jeanie, I say, Jeanie, woman*.
55 Wurman, Richard Saul, and Feldman, Eugene, *The Notebooks and Drawings of Louis I. Kahn* (Cambridge, MA: MIT Press, 1973, 2nd ed), unpaginated, p. 3 of the letter. Also illustrated in Tyng, *Beginnings*, p. 180.
56 Harvey, John, 'George Cruikshank: A Master of the Poetic Use of Line', in R. L. Patten (ed), *George Cruikshank: A Revaluation* (Princeton, NJ: Princeton University Press, 1992), pp. 129–55, p. 134.
57 Latour, *Kahn. Writings*, p. 258.
58 Meyers, Marshall D., 'Louis Kahn and the Art of Drawing: Some Recollections', in A. Tzonis (ed), *The Louis I. Kahn Archive Personal Drawings*, 7 vols. (New York and London: Garland, 1987), pp. xxv–xxvii, p. xxvi.
59 Parshall, Peter, *The Darker Side of Light: Arts of Privacy, 1850–1900* (Washington, DC: National Gallery of Art, with Lund Humphries, 2009), p. 4.

60 Tyng, *Beginnings*, p. 25.
61 Latour, *Kahn. Writings*, p. 258.
62 Kahn, *Silence and Light*, p. 51.
63 Latour, *Kahn. Writings*, p. 259.
64 Latour, *Kahn. Writings*, p. 258.
65 Louis I. Kahn Collection, The University of Pennsylvania: 945.3.2.
66 Latour, *Kahn. Writings*, p. 232. For this form of the diagram, see, for example, Kahn, *Silence and Light*, p. 27.
67 Kahn, *Silence and Light*, 'Stepped pyramid no 1, Saqqara, Egypt, 1951, Charcoal on paper', p. 30.
68 Quoted in Whitaker, William, 'Chronology', in Kries, Eisenbrand, Von Moos (eds), *Louis Kahn – The Power of Architecture*, pp. 21–8, p. 25.
69 Scully, Jr, Vincent, *Louis I. Kahn* (New York: George Braziller, 1962), p. 18.
70 Latour, *Kahn. Writings*, pp. 308, 309.
71 Malraux, André, *The Voices of Silence*, S. Gilbert (trans) (St Albans, Herts.: Granada Publishing, 1954), p. 635.
72 Malraux, *Voices of Silence*, p. 590.
73 Malraux, *Voices of Silence*, p. 642.
74 See Scully, *Kahn*, p. 18.
75 Kahn, *Silence and Light*, p. 26.
76 Pelkonen, Eeva-Liisa, 'Toward Cognitive Architecture', in Kries, Eisenbrand, Von Moos (eds), *Louis Kahn – The Power of Architecture*, pp. 133–48, p. 134.
77 Quoted in Pelkonen, 'Cognitive Architecture', p. 138, see also Goldhagen, Sarah Williams, *Louis Kahn's Situated Modernism* (New Haven, CT and London: Yale University Press, 2001), p. 52.
78 Joseph Amisano quoted in Goldhagen, *Situated Modernism*, p. 52.
79 See Burton, 'Volume Zero', p. 79.
80 See, for example, Kahn, Louis I., 'Order and Form', *Perspecta*, vol. 3 (1955), pp. 47–63, p. 53, photograph by Louis Glaessman.
81 Scully, *Kahn*, p. 20.
82 Scully, *Kahn*, p. 20.
83 Kahn, 'On Beaux-Arts Training', p. 332.
84 Kahn, 'Order in Architecture', p. 59. The Bath House was also published in the special May 1957 *Architectural Review* surveying the American scene, Kahn, Louis I., 'Genetrix. Personal Contributions to American Architecture. Louis Kahn', *Architectural Review*, vol. 121 (May 1957), pp. 344, 345, p. 345.
85 Gargiani, Roberto, *Louis I. Kahn. Exposed Concrete and Hollow Stones 1949–1959* (Lausanne: EPFL Press, 2014), p. 104.
86 Levine, Neil, 'Kahn's Edge: The Provocative Historicism of the Trenton Jewish Community Centre', in Kries, Eisenbrand, Von Moos (eds), *Louis Kahn –*

The Power of Architecture, pp. 101–14, p. 106, with further discussion of Byzantine, Romanesque precedents.

87 *Ruskin, Works*, 10: 18, *Stones of Venice*, vol. 2.
88 See McCarter, *Kahn*, p. 99.
89 Gargiani, *Exposed Concrete and Hollow Stones*, p. 124.
90 Quoted in McCarter, *Kahn*, p. 122.
91 Scully, *Kahn*, p. 29.
92 Banham, Reyner, 'Louis Kahn. On Trial, the Buttery-Hatch Aesthetic', *Architectural Review*, vol. 131, no. 781 (March 1962), pp. 203–6, p. 204.
93 Jordy, William H., 'Medical Research Building for Pennsylvania University, Philadelphia', *Architectural Review*, vol. 129, no. 768 (February 1961), pp. 98–106.
94 Scully, *Kahn*, p. 30.
95 See Lewis, Michael J., 'Louis Kahn's Art and His Architectural Thought', in Kries, Eisenbrand, Von Moos (eds), *Louis Kahn: The Power of Architecture*, pp. 67–83, fig. 133, p. 81: 'Towers, San Gimignano, Italy, 1928'.
96 See, for example, Wurman and Feldman, *Notebooks and Drawings of Kahn*, figs. 32, 33, 35, 36, 37.
97 Latour, *Kahn. Writings*, p. 92.
98 Latour, *Kahn. Writings*, p. 93, Kite's emphasis.
99 Latour, *Kahn. Writings*, p. 76.
100 See also McCarter, *Kahn*, pp. 120, 122.
101 Letter exhibited in 'Louis Kahn: The Power of Architecture' exhibition, Design Museum, London, 9 July–12 October 2014.
102 See Walker, David, 'Plasticity at Ronchamp: The Interrelationship of Form and Light and Its Plastic Manifestation', *Architectural Research Quarterly*, vol. 16, no. 4 (December 2012), pp. 349–61, for a study of the plastic manifestation of the chapel in varied light conditions.
103 Lewis, 'Kahn's Art', p. 80.
104 Le Corbusier, *Ronchamp* (Stuttgart: Verlag Gerd Hatje, 1957, 1991), pp. 46, 47, translation quoted in Samuel, Flora, *Le Corbusier in Detail* (Oxford: Architectural Press, 2007), p. 73.
105 See Steane, Mary Anne, *The Architecture of Light: Recent Approaches to Designing with Natural Light* (London: Routledge, 2011), p. 9.
106 Quoted in Marcus, George H. and Whitaker, William, *The Houses of Louis Kahn* (New Haven, CT and London: Yale University Press, 2013), p. 63.
107 Brownlee, David B. and De Long, David G., *Louis I. Kahn: In the Realm of Architecture* (New York: Rizzoli, 1991), p. 68.
108 See, for example, Samuel, *Corbusier in Detail*, pp. 73, 74.
109 Binet, Hélène, 'Photographing Shadows at La Tourette', in H. Binet et al. (eds), *The Secret of the Shadow. Light and Shadow in Architecture* (Berlin: Ernst Wasmuth Verlag Tübingen, 2002), pp. 102–25, p. 102.

110 Marcus and Whitaker, *Houses of Louis Kahn*, p. 63.
111 See detail drawings in Samuel, *Corbusier in Detail*, p. 81.
112 Binet, 'Shadows at La Tourette', p. 102.
113 McCarter, *Kahn*, p. 160.
114 Quoted in Marcus and Whitaker, *Houses of Louis Kahn*, p. 174, p. 177, see also fig. 183, p. 175.
115 Eisenbrand, Jochen, 'Between Grid and Pathway: The Houses of Louis Kahn', in Kries, Eisenbrand, Von Moos (eds), *Louis Kahn: The Power of Architecture*, pp. 49–66, p. 61.
116 See analysis in Büttiker, Urs, *Louis I. Kahn. Light and Space* (Basel: Birkhäuser Verlag, 1994), pp. 90–5.
117 See Gargiani, *Exposed Concrete and Hollow Stones*, p. 104, fig. 220, p. 187, Kahn Archive 030.I.C.505.1.
118 Louis I. Kahn Collection, The University of Pennsylvania: 505.10.
119 Merrill, Michael, *Louis Kahn on the Thoughtful Making of Spaces* (Baden: Lars Müller, 2010), p. 100.
120 Gargiani, *Exposed Concrete and Hollow Stones*, p. 101.
121 Quoted in Marcus and Whitaker, *Houses of Louis Kahn*, p. 41.
122 Latour, *Kahn. Writings*, p. 98.
123 See also Gombrich, E. H., *Shadows. The Depiction of Cast Shadows in Western Art* (London: National Gallery Publications, 1995), p. 44.
124 Scully, Vincent, 'Louis I. Kahn and the Ruins of Rome', *Engineering and Science* (Winter 1993), pp. 3–13, p. 9.
125 See Solomon, Susan G., 'Louis Kahn's Buildings for Three Faiths: "Religion...not a religion"', in Kries, Eisenbrand, Von Moos (eds), *Louis Kahn – The Power of Architecture*, pp. 149–63, p. 151.
126 Marc, Olivier, *Psychology of the House* (London: Thames and Hudson, 1977), p. 88; Norberg-Schulz, Christian, *Existence, Space and Architecture* (London: Studio Vista, 1971), pp. 21–2.
127 Eliade, Mircea, *Symbolism, the Sacred, and the Arts*, D. Apostolos-Cappadona (ed) (New York: Crossroad, 1986), p. 112.
128 Quoted in Bollnow, O. F., *Human Space*, C. Shuttleworth (trans), J. Kohlmaier (ed) (London: Hyphen Press, 2011), p. 138.
129 See Kahn, Louis I., 'Kahn. A Discussion Recorded in Mr Kahn's Philadelphia Office in February 1961', *Perspecta*, vol. 7 (1961), pp. 9–28, p. 18.
130 See Sorensen, Roy, *Seeing Dark Things. The Philosophy of Shadows* (Oxford: Oxford University Press, 2008), pp. 212–4.
131 Kahn, Louis I., *Louis I. Kahn. Conversations with Students*, D. Ngo (ed) (Houston, TX: Rice University School of Architecture, 1998, 2nd ed), p. 14.
132 Kahn, *Conversations with Students*, pp. 13–14.
133 Cadwell, Michael, *Strange Details* (Cambridge, MA: MIT Press, 2007), p. 156.

134 Goldhagen, *Situated Modernism*, p. 137; Komendant, *18 Years with Kahn*, p. 35.
135 Kahn, 'Kahn. A Discussion'.
136 Kahn, 'Kahn. A Discussion', pp. 14–15.
137 Kahn, 'Kahn. A Discussion', p. 15.
138 Latour, *Kahn. Writings*, p. 86.
139 Merrill, *Kahn on the Thoughtful Making of Spaces*, p. 164.
140 Quoted in Brownlee and De Long, *In the Realm of Architecture*, p. 107.
141 Louis I. Kahn Collection, The University of Pennsylvania: 525.15
142 Goldhagen, *Situated Modernism*, p. 157.
143 Kahn, 'Kahn. A Discussion', pp. 16–17.
144 See, for example, the three-quarter photograph of the building in snow in Tyng, *Beginnings*, p. 44.
145 Schopenhauer, *World as Will and Representation*, vol. 1, p. 203.
146 Latour, *Kahn. Writings*, p. 205.
147 Quoted in Tyng, *Beginnings*, p. 35.
148 Quoted in Tyng, *Beginnings*, p. 174.
149 Johnson, Nell E. (ed), *Light Is the Theme: Louis I. Kahn and the Kimbell Art Museum* (Fort Worth, TX: Kimbell Art Museum, 2011), p. 28.
150 James, E. O., *From Cave to Cathedral. Temples and Shrines of Prehistoric Classical and Early Christian Times* (London: Thames and Hudson, 1965), p. 291.
151 Quoted in Sauter, Florian, 'Mettre la Nature en Oeuvre', in Kries, Eisenbrand, Von Moos (eds), *Louis Kahn – The Power of Architecture*, pp. 181–201, p. 189.
152 Sauter, 'Mettre la Nature en Oeuvre', p. 189.
153 Frampton, Kenneth, *Studies in Tectonic Culture. The Poetics of Construction in Nineteenth and Twentieth Century Architecture*, J. Cava (ed) (Cambridge, MA: MIT Press, 1995), p. 239.
154 Loud, Patricia Cummings, *The Art Museums of Louis I. Kahn* (Durham and London: Duke University Press, 1989), Chapter 3 'The Kimbell Art Museum', pp. 100–71.
155 For example, see Louis I. Kahn Collection, The University of Pennsylvania and the Pennsylvania Historical and Museum Commission, 730.15.
156 Meyers, Marshall D., 'Louis Kahn and the Art of Drawing: Some Recollections', in A. Tzonis (ed), *The Louis I. Kahn Archive Personal Drawings*, 7 vols. (New York and London: Garland, 1987), pp. xxv–xxvii, p. xxv.
157 Petherbridge, Deanna, *The Primacy of Drawing. Histories and Theories of Practice* (New Haven, CT and London: Yale University Press, 2010), p. 136.
158 Petherbridge, *Primacy of Drawing*, p. 136.
159 Louis I. Kahn Collection, The University of Pennsylvania: 730.30.
160 Louis I. Kahn Collection, The University of Pennsylvania: 730.195; 730.196.

161 Johnson, *Light Is the Theme*, p. 43.
162 Benedikt, Michael, *Deconstructing the Kimbell. An Essay on Meaning and Architecture* (New York: Lumen Books, 1991), p. 68.
163 Benedikt, *Deconstructing the Kimbell*, p. 71.
164 Latour, *Kahn. Writings*, p. 228.
165 Frampton, *Studies in Tectonic Culture*, p. 240.
166 Latour, *Kahn. Writings*, p. 228.
167 Latour, *Kahn. Writings*, p. 229.
168 Tyng, *Beginnings*, pp. 135–7.
169 Cadwell, *Strange Details*, p. 175.
170 McCarter, *Kahn*, p. 14.
171 See Sepper, Dennis L., *Goethe Contra Newton. Polemics and the Project for a New Science of Colour* (Cambridge: Cambridge University Press, 1988), p. 89.
172 Latour, *Kahn. Writings*, p. 295.
173 Sorensen, *Seeing Dark Things*, p. 167.
174 See, for example, Aben, Rob; de Wit, Saskia, *The Enclosed Garden. History and Development of the Hortus Conclusus and Its Reintroduction into the Present-Day Urban Landscape* (Rotterdam: 010 Publishers, 2001), pp. 32, 33.
175 Louis I. Kahn Collection, The University of Pennsylvania: 730.68; 730.69.
176 Millet, Marietta S., *Light Revealing Architecture* (New York: Van Nostrand Reinhold, 1996), p. 163.
177 See Komendant, *18 Years with Kahn*, pp. 122–6.
178 Johnson, *Light Is the Theme*, cover image.
179 Latour, *Kahn. Writings*, p. 228, Kite's emphasis.
180 Benedikt, *Deconstructing the Kimbell*, p. 78.
181 Quoted in Cadwell, *Strange Details*, p. 149.
182 A good contemporary example of this utilization of the 'servant' zone can be seen in *The Architectural Review* of June 1974: Jordy, William H., 'Kimbell Art Museum, Fort Worth, Texas; Library, Philips Exeter Academy, Exeter, New Hampshire', *Architectural Review*, vol. 155, no. 928 (June 1974), pp. 318–42, p. 326.
183 Johnson, *Light Is the Theme*, perspective image and Kahn quote, pp. 32, 33.
184 Louis I. Kahn Collection, The University of Pennsylvania: 730.124; 'Elevation (travertine panels, vault end)' August 1969.
185 Kahn, quoted in Frampton, *Studies in Tectonic Culture*, p. 241.
186 Benedikt, *Deconstructing the Kimbell*, pp. 81, 82.
187 Benedikt, *Deconstructing the Kimbell*, pp. 81, 82.
188 Loud, *Art Museums of Kahn*, pp. 111, 112.

189 Smyth, Megan (ed), *The Kimbell at 40, an Evolving Masterpiece* (Fort Worth, TX: Kimbell Art Museum, 2012), pp. 2, 3.
190 Benedikt, *Deconstructing the Kimbell*, p. 17, Kite's emphasis.
191 Benedikt, *Deconstructing the Kimbell*, p. 93.
192 Curtis, William J. R., 'Louis Kahn, The Space of Ideas', *The Architectural Review*, vol. 232, no. 1389 (November 2012), pp. 78–87, p. 78.
193 See Scheer, David Ross, *The Death of Drawing. Architecture in the Age of Simulation* (New York: Routledge, 2014), *passim*.

10

Shadow Futures

Masses and Veils

A strong intellect will have pleasure in the solemnities of storm and twilight, and in the broken and mysterious lights that gleam among them, rather than in mere brilliancy and glare, while a frivolous mind will dread the shadow and the storm. (John Ruskin, 'The Nature of Gothic', Stones of Venice, vol. 2)[1]

Cultural history needs the long perspective, so the final major study of this book examined Louis Kahn (died 1974) as shadow-maker, distinctive as the last great form-giver in a now-outmoded analogue tradition which conceived, developed and detailed buildings entirely through the medium of hand drawing. Considering recent, present and future shadow-making is a more difficult and speculative task and, by way of conclusion, I want to begin discussion of these questions – and it can be no more than a beginning – by calling upon the still-valid frameworks offered by Gottfried Semper. Semper opens the 'Prolegomena' to his *Style* (*Der Stil*, 1860) with a stark night vision, reflecting the insecurity born of modern knowledge, that human cognition is but a fleeting glimmer within a universe of immense darkness and desolate silence.

> The nocturnal sky shows glimmering nebulae among the splendid miracle of stars – either old extinct systems scattered throughout the universe, cosmic dust taking shape around a nucleus, or a condition in between destruction and regeneration.[2]

Semper analogizes this night vision to 'events on the horizon of art history'; these systems of the universe 'signify a world of art passing into the formless, while suggesting at the same time a new formation in the making'.[3]

To go forward, Semper went back to ethnographic roots, making his model of the Primitive Hut – the 'Caribbean bamboo hut displayed at the Great Exhibition of 1851 in London'– as persuasive as those of Vitruvius and Laugier. For, says Semper, 'it shows all the elements of antique architecture in their pure and most original form: the *hearth* as the centre-point, raised earth as a *terrace* surrounded by posts, the column-supported *roof*, and the mat enclosure as a *spatial termination* or *wall*'.[4] On the basis of these four basic primordial elements of: earthwork, hearth, framework/roof and light enclosing membrane, Semper erects a distinction between the light *tectonics* of the frame, and the heavy *stereotomics* of the earthwork – a tectonic/stereotomic distinction which orders the building crafts into two fundamental processes.[5] These final pages examine shadow futures in the context of this well-known taxonomy – between *masses* and *veils* of shadow – one Semper derived from closely reading the long history of craft and culture, back to its pre-architectural origins.

Shadows of the stereotomic

'The field of stereotomy', writes Semper, 'comprises those arts whose technical challenge is the exploitation of those raw materials that strongly resist crushing and cracking because of their hard, thick, and homogeneous aggregate composition, and thus have significant compressive strength'.[6] From the Greek *stereos* (solid), and *tomia* (to cut), this is the language of load-bearing masonry, of rammed earth and, in our times, of reinforced concrete. Consider some of the champions of shadow of the preceding pages – Hawksmoor, Soane, Rossi, Kahn – and it is clear that one of the first instincts of the shadow-maker is to stress the stereotomic; hence the shock of the new monumentality when Kahn revealed his Richards Medical Research Building, and the dogmatic terribilità of its 'Lamp of Power'. Amid the dinningly harsh 'call for brightness', and the desire of the architectural mainstream to serve the 'undifferentiated frenzy for windows',[7] for ever more transparency and expanses of glass, the shadows of the stereotomic still make an active fringe resistance. As a recent example, the long list of the 2015 Royal Institute of British Architects (RIBA) 'House of the Year' award included a number of dwellings of the *bright=better* school, whose vast sheets of uncurtained glazing were pitted against a few that handled shade and light with more nuance. The chthonic Flint House Buckinghamshire (2014), by Skene Catling de la Peña, took the award; this dwelling makes a geological presence in the landscape with two uneven stepped wedges of stratified knapped flint and chalk, reminiscent of Casa Malaparte, Capri. Flint House even possesses a covert grotto, lined with raw nodules of flint, cut by a rivulet through a corner of the house. Inspired by the bandings of Pisan Romanesque architecture (along with the dressing of marbled 'incrustation') Ruskin had called in *Stones of Venice* for 'wall veils' reflecting the nature of their construction and for 'horizontal bands of colour, or of light and shade', expressive 'of the growth or age of the wall, like the rings in the wood of a tree' and symbolic of the 'alternation of light and darkness' in the human condition.[8] He read this 'alternation of shade with light' in the layers of a wall, or the glinting dentils of a moulding, as metaphysically representing 'the opposition of good and evil, the antagonism of the entire human system...the alternation of labour with rest, the mingling of life with death, or the actual physical fact of the division of light from darkness, and of the falling and rising of night and day'.[9] Inspired in turn by cross-sectional drawings of the geology of the region, The Flint House adopts a sedimentary principle whereby, from base to top:

> the layers of flint and chalk fade through six tonal strata from dark to light. The lower pieces of flint are large and rough hewn....As the flints fade they become more meticulously worked, snapped into smooth square blocks with razor-fine joints. Finally, the misty chalk appears on a different atmospheric layer to the earth and bears a closer kinship with the sky.[10]

Some mocked Kahn for the 'Duct-henge' of his Richards Building, but in his quest for a fundamental understanding of space and order the Benedictine architect Dom Hans van der Laan (1904–91) also studied architecture in its primordial foundations. His *Architectonic Space* (published in English in 1983) presents one of the most coherent theories of form and proportion published within modernism since the Modulor, and concludes with an analysis of Stonehenge as 'an outstanding example of architectonic space'[11] – the stereotomic shadow machine par excellence. Standing within its court of five trilithons, ringed in turn by a wall of thirty stones, Dom van der Laan says 'it is as if here we were present at the birth of architecture'.[12] From such ponderings on the Primitive he derived his Plastic Number, a severely elemental form-bank of blocks, slabs and bars related in geometric progression. The Benedictine talked very rationally of number and ratio, and of the threefold spatial hierarchies leading from the monastic cell, to the court, and thence to the wider domain; but through these geometric relations he sought an architecture sacred in its mood. From his experience as a sacristan, Dom van der Laan understood how liturgical architecture worked as an entirety, from the body of the church, down through its furnishings, to the vestments and communion vessels for which he was responsible.

In the 'haunted beauty' of his masterpiece, the church of the St Benedictusberg Abbey at Vaals, Netherlands (completed 1968), the scholar of Light, Henry Plummer, finds the *pittura metafisica* of the work of the Italian painter Giorgio Morandi – it is a place of 'moody light and long shadows'. Dom van der Laan's 'tenebrous work also points to a timeless source of atmosphere in architecture – beguiling shadows that gather in space and enhance faint light'.[13] Van der Laan conceived his church at Vaals as a threefold organization of slotted elements: the main body of the nave arises between the spaces of the side galleries, which are nested in turn within containing walls. The nave is palely lit from clerestories which run in a contrapuntal rhythm above the openings to the circumscribing galleries (Figure 10.1). Normally in a church such aisle spaces support the clerestories as further sources of filtered light, but these galleries are entirely unlit and present cavernous bodies of shadow between the stern grey columns. In the lower crypt-like church this scheme is reversed; light is gained only from the chapels on one side whose illumination 'casts a dim sacred aura over the unaffected space'.[14] Caroline Voet recognizes sensorial and tangible materialization in the monk's minimal rectilinear vocabulary as, owing to the use of simple materials, 'the focus moves from the building material to matter' itself.[15] At Vaals brick predominates, the mortar joints are flush, and the whole is smeared with a thin layer of lime cement, allowing the bricks still to be read, while intensifying the monolithic space-holding presence of the columns and lintols. Moving through these articulated and roughly textured layers we become sensitized to the different intensities of light which creates a 'pronounced light/dark shadow play' of patterns.[16] It is said that Dom van der Laan emboldened his masons to drink a little more wine at mealtimes to encourage imperfection in the brickwork. In the Benedictine Rule the main meal comes after the midday prayer of Sext followed by a time of rest. As the monks move out from the refectory for a spell of relaxation in the cloister, one senses a natural brotherhood between the measure of their

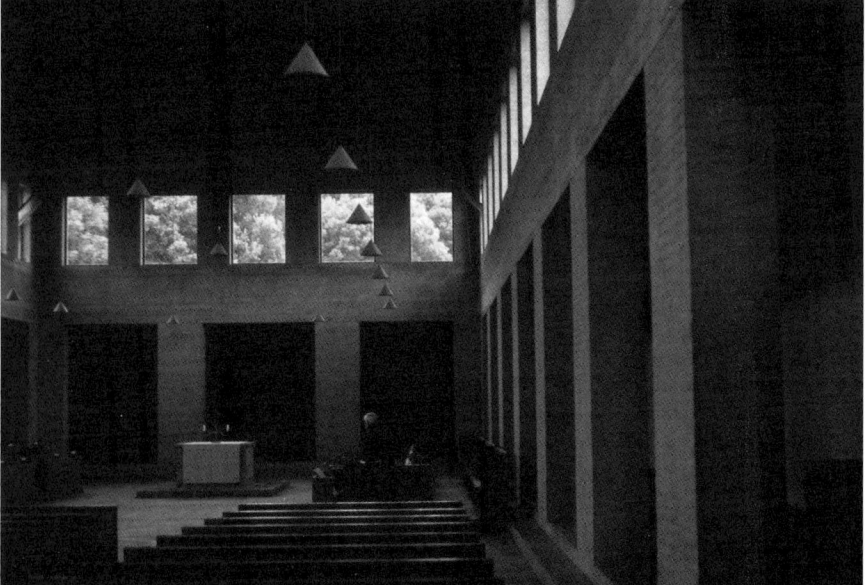

FIGURE 10.1 Dom van der Laan, St Benedictusberg Abbey, Vaals, Netherlands. The church. Photograph, Stephen Kite.

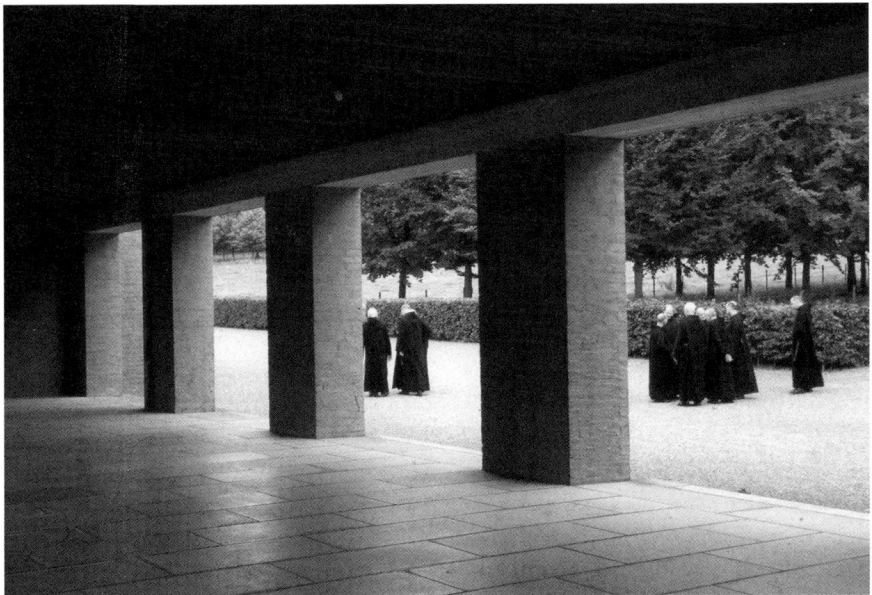

FIGURE 10.2 Dom van der Laan, St Benedictusberg Abbey, Vaals, Netherlands. Cloister. Photograph, Stephen Kite.

dark habits within the garden, and the shadows cast by the sturdy piers of Dom van der Laan's arcade – his architectonic spatializes the Benedictine monastic condition (Figure 10.2).

Zumthor: Hollowing out the darkness

> The first of my favourite ideas is this: to plan the building as a pure mass of shadow then, afterwards, to put in light as if you were hollowing out the darkness, as if the light were a new mass seeping in. (Peter Zumthor, *Atmospheres*, 2006)[17]

Vaals and Dom van der Laan's ideas have had influence on a stereotomic sensibility towards shadow play, even if some acolytes seem attracted more by a surface language of hair-shirt minimalism than the Benedictine's deeply pondered spirituality. But that other Vals – the Swiss village where architect Peter Zumthor created his thermal spa in 1996 – has had greater worldwide resonance in demonstrating what Zumthor points to as the first of his 'favourite ideas': 'to plan the building as a pure mass of shadow then, afterwards, to put in light as if you were hollowing out the darkness.'[18] At *his* Vals, Zumthor recruits shadows made palpable by light admitted through fissures into a potholer's choreography of spaces seemingly carved out of the indigenous gneiss. Here Zumthor writes of 'bright light, darkness, and twilight', of 'standing in shadow and looking into the brightness of a colourful illuminated landscape' and of a natural light that only trickles into the 'mass of shadow' through 'narrow slits or through the gaps we left open between the stone slabs of the ceiling' – 'Stone and water: a love affair', he muses.[19] Writing on 'Stone and Water' in *Stones of Rimini* (1934) Adrian Stokes noticed in Venice how 'Istrian marble blackens in the shade, is snow or salt-white where exposed to the sun. Light and shade are thus recorded, abstracted, intensified, solidified. Matter is dramatized in stone';[20] these are among other fantasies of stone and water we examined in Chapter 8.

Having distinguished shadow and light as thus 'intensified' and 'solidified' at Vals, let us consider these characteristics in two of Zumthor's later projects near and in Cologne – the Chapel in the Fields dedicated to 'Bruder Klaus' (2007), and the Kolumba Diocesan Art Museum (1997–2007). Zumthor ends his *Thinking Architecture* (2006) with a series of meditations on 'Light in the Landscape', which show a sense of light and shadow as comrades, one equal to Kahn's assertion that 'shadow *belongs* to the light'. 'How much light do people need in order to live?' asks Zumthor, 'And how much darkness? ... Are there some things we can experience only in dark, shaded places, in the darkness of night?'[21] He has been inculcated by Tanizaki's praise of shadows, and his imaginings of things without light, or just gently glimmering in the dark recesses of the traditional Japanese home – Tanizaki 'praises shadows. And shadows praise light'.[22] Zumthor urges that even artificial light should accentuate, not cancel out the night, 'as intimate illuminated clearings that we carve out of the darkness'.[23]

The pale ochre menhir of the 'Bruder Klaus' Chapel guards a crest of rising ground, near the hamlet of Wachendorf, thirty miles south of Cologne (Figure 10.3). Approached uphill, across early winter fields, the low sun accentuates the ploughed earth's corrugations. Inside, the cave shaft of the chapel is also deeply furrowed; a legacy of the 112 spruce trees which were raised in a tepee of formwork for its in situ concrete casting of river gravel and local reddish-yellow sand. Between the spruce tree tepee and the external boards, the chapel rose in roughly tamped layers, over twenty-four days to attain its height of twelve metres. At the field's edge the plough surrenders to a margin of grass, and the visitor turns to approach the pewter-toned triangular steel entrance door. Its triangle represents the Trinity as the axis of Nikolaus of Flüe's mysticism (1417–87, 'Bruder Klaus') wherein God emerges from dark innermost depths as Father, Son and Holy Spirit, encompasses creation, and returns to indivisible unity. The Swiss hermit symbolized this cycle in a wheel symbol, and here at Wachendorf his wheel is found of gold-plated brass, glinting among the

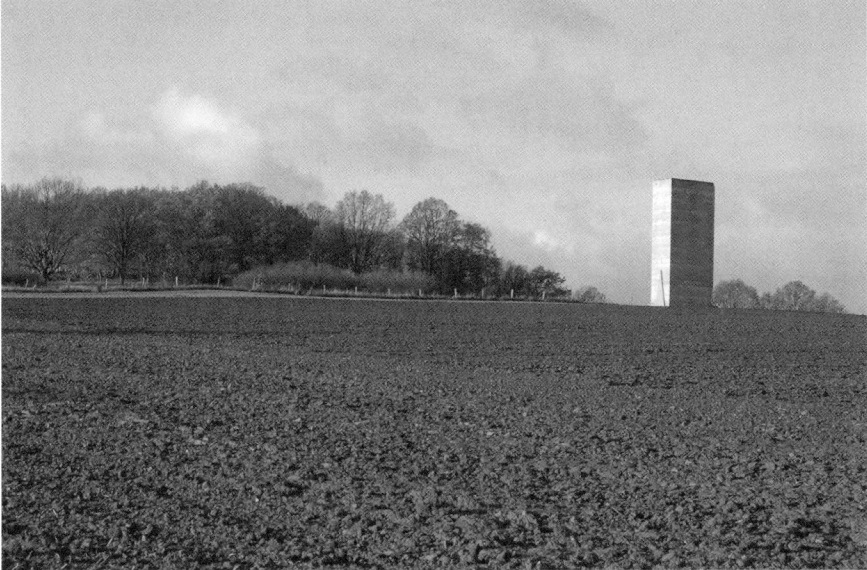

FIGURE 10.3 Peter Zumthor, 'Bruder Klaus' Chapel, Wachendorf, Cologne. Field setting. Photograph, Stephen Kite.

crouching shadows just as the gold of a laquer painting gleams in the darknesses that Tanizaki writes of. It is the only devotional artefact apart from a Giacometti-like impish half-figure of Bruder Klaus himself, made in bronze by the Swiss artist Hans Josephson. The menhir's ostensibly simple form belies its subtle irregular pentagonal plan.[24] The triangular steel door opens on the shortest side of the pentagon, and the pilgrim negotiates a short low curved passage to discover a contemplation bench, there to sit rawly embraced in the concrete whose flutings are like those of an ancient gnarled shaft; like being clasped *inside* one of those primitive columns of Paestum that Piranesi etched (see Chapter 4). But no capital lids this column whose flutes taper steeply upwards to an unglazed tear-drop aperture through which the rain filters down with the light, where it is allowed to puddle in a depression in the tin-lead alloy floor surface (Figure 10.4). This cave column intimates the grotto in other ways, for glinting with Bruder Klaus's Trinitarian wheel are 350 small glass domes made to plug the bolt holes left from the shuttering. These are the only specular elements; the flutes themselves are hacked and blackened from the striking of the spruce tree formwork which was lit like a charcoal kiln to dry the trunks and ease their removal. Even in the consistent sun of a bright winter morning the light percolating into this mass of serious shadow changes constantly; sometimes it is a Stygian realm, sometimes eerily ethereal as if the chapel was lit from within.[25]

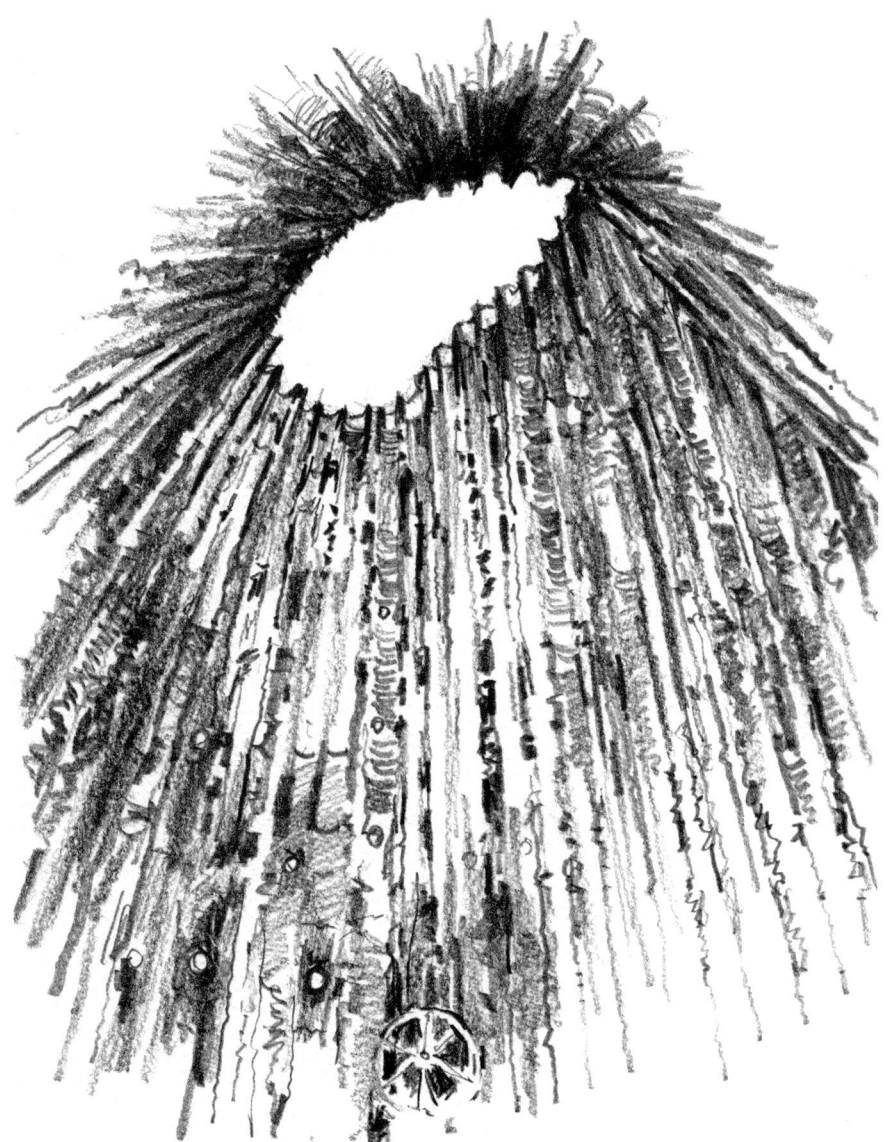

FIGURE 10.4 Peter Zumthor, 'Bruder Klaus' Chapel. Interior looking up to teardrop aperture. Drawing by Stephen Kite.

Healing shadows

The chapel was commissioned for their fields by the Scheidtweiler family at a time when Zumthor was working on the much more complex Kolumba Diocesan Museum in Cologne for which he won the competition in 1997. The Diocesan Museum also has a heart of darkness, for its core space is the crepuscular armarium on the first floor where the greatest church treasures of St Kolumba, such as the reliquaries and monstrances, are displayed. This intense space, lined with black textiles, is the spiritual centre of the Kolumba where the only light comes from the vitrines housing these artefacts: illuminated manuscripts, ivories, enamels and precious jewels.[26] The Armarium is symbolically located directly over the Chapel of the Madonna in the Ruins (1949–57) that Gottfried Böhm built to house a statue of the Virgin that by some miracle survived the devastation Cologne endured in the Second World War; on one night alone – 29 June 1943 – over 90 per cent of the city was destroyed through British (night) and US (day) aerial bombardment. Although Cologne rebuilt many of its destroyed churches St Kolumba's was left as a shell apart from Böhm's new chapel with its Maryan crown – an octagon of concrete fins and stained glass reaching out into the ruins of the Gothic nave.

Given the cramped urban site and the need for a great amount of gallery space, Zumthor's key sectional parti was to sky the body of the museum high above the excavation site over a hypostyle ruin hall. The sudden violence of the bombardment brought abrupt interruption to the story of a place that had witnessed every epoch of Cologne's long history. Beginning as a sacred room in the middle of the first millennium above the footings of an old Roman residence, the fragments of the church site layered the traces of Roman, Frankish, Carolingian, Romanesque, and early and late Gothic eras. Confronted here with remains that presented in acute form our age's enormous dislocation – that condition of irreparable fragmentation Rossi has articulated so forcefully in his texts and drawings (see Chapter 8) – Zumthor opted for the emollient. His is not a Carlo Scarpa-like language that elaborates the fragment, or the junctures of new and old, and in the 1997 text that accompanied his winning design he pointed out that in his project:

> The historical breaks, traceable in the building substance of the location, are not additionally charged and made a theme of as such. In other words, the architectural elements do not consciously heighten the confrontation between old and new. The new underlying building idea is conciliatory and integrative.... It takes in the old, bearing it within. It does not blur any traces nor does it destroy without a need to do so. It rounds out and carries on in the search for its own shape. Thus wounds to the construction are not left gaping, and architectonic means are not used to comment on them. It is rather an as natural as possible treatment of what has come

down to us and been preserved, put into a functional framework of a new building purpose with a meaning of its own.[27]

The healing homogeneity is realized in a fair-faced, light grey-beige Danish brick which gently binds the wounds of the existing fabric and bears directly upon them. The bricks are extremely long and narrow, sometimes over fifty-three centimetres in length, with wide near-flush joints. Around the upper levels of the great twilit hall of the excavation site they are laid in a perforated pattern so that air can pass unmediated – 'filter brickwork' as Zumthor called them. These perforations become briquettes of light which populate the upper reaches of these ancient glooms; sometimes isolated stars, sometimes shimmering nebulae, very like Ruskin's living traceries which are as 'stars when seen from within, and like leaves when seen from without' (see Chapter 6). Against this umbrageous backcloth Zumthor's fourteen daringly slender pilotis carry the large main galleries of the Diocesan collection high above the wreckage of history. They step tenderly around Böhm's Virgin crown chapel, footing themselves adroitly among the successive layers of: Roman residential buildings (second, third century), a Carolingian Hall Church (ninth century), a Romanesque church (eleventh–twelfth century) and a five-aisled Gothic church of c. 1500. As if strung in tension these sinewy columns measure the depths of ancient pits and apses, or the broken arcs of arches as they loom out of the dimness, as seen from the timber footbridge which cranks across the archaeological site (Figure 10.5). Just as when entering a mosque in Istanbul, we must part a heavy leather curtain to access this numinous field of histories from the foyer. Ottoman too is the effect of the hanging conical lights, which 'carve out of the darkness' an intimate lower horizon of illumination – highlighting broken columns and footings – and making the upper zones yet more duskily enigmatic. Like chords, the columns hold in tension all these disparate elements scattered across time; they are certainly presences in the space, but do not thicken it as do the supports of most hypostyle halls. Sketching this moving volume it seemed natural to me to record the pilotis as absences, as much as presences; as Kahn might say they are 'darkless', yet they alone enable the space, and allow the things and the shades to gather about them. Here the soft shadows are themselves active in this integrative work of binding wounds and healing past scars, as in Masaccio's fresco of *St Peter Healing with His Shadow* (1425) in the Brancacci Chapel, Florence – noted in Chapter 1 – where, as the saint passes the cripples crouched by the rusticated walls of the street, his cast shadow alone heals their injuries.[28]

Unsurprisingly, in a study of shadow-making, the focus has been on this great room which is, at the same time, 'outside' the Diocesan Museum proper, but this is not to negate the quality of other memorable places, such as the aforementioned armarium. Using high stair shafts Zumthor connected a variety of cells and looser galleries over three levels, some of which recruit views to the steely spires of Cologne Cathedral. Throughout these internal

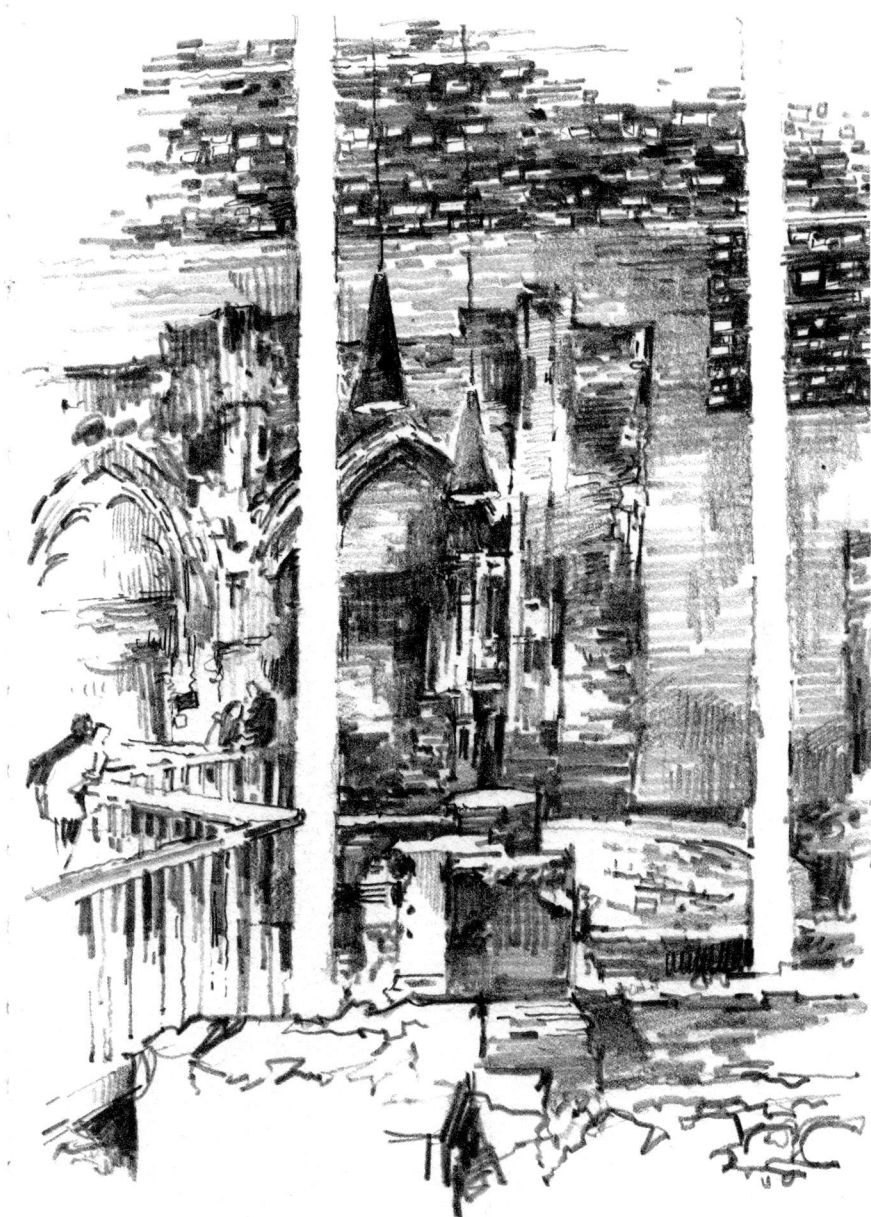

FIGURE 10.5 Peter Zumthor, Kolumba Diocesan Museum, Cologne. Ruin hall. Drawing by Stephen Kite.

passages and levels the Jesuit art-curator Friedhelm Menneckes admires the prevailing penumbral tonality of grey which accords with that of the brickwork:

One thing always remains the same: the warm grey of the walls.... The grey is not that of concrete or a raw cement plaster. The slightly grainy structure makes it different. A hint of 'clay' is what constitutes the charm of its soft, warm effect. Grey is a condition without colour.... Joseph Beuys understood grey in principle as not being a colour, but rather a material substance, as something moving.[29]

In an interview Zumthor has said, 'Joseph Beuys was important for me.... Beuys made art that had to do with the soul, with people's biographies, and with the archaic knowledge that he could detect in things.'[30] Despite the association of Beuys with dessicated and dim materials, such as grey felt and fat, Beuys himself says that, in isolation, 'it's not right to say I'm interested in grey.... Nor am I interested in dirt'. Rather, through the complementary effects Goethe understood, Beuys is 'interested in invoking the whole world of colour in people as counter-image.... A world of light; a clear light-filled ... supersensible, spiritual world'.[31] For this reason Menneckes concludes: 'the walls at *Kolumba* are not really grey.... They steadily break up into all colours and into all dimensions....' – material, spatial and spiritual.[32] The work of Beuys and some of the *Arte Povera* artists impresses Zumthor in anchoring 'an ancient, elemental knowledge about man's use of materials'.[33] When addressing sacred shadows earlier, the primitive archaic qualities of Alberti's Sant' Andrea at Mantua were invoked (see Chapter 3); here Zumthor opines on this building:

A tall portico of light and shadow, single rays of sun on the pilasters. A world of its own, no longer city but not yet the interior of the church. Pigeons are flying high up in shadowy regions where the carved figures and mouldings fade out of sight. I hear but do not see them. Darkness abounds.[34]

There is similar shadow sophistication and a living language of conspicuous mass in some of the work originating from architectural studios of the Republic of Ireland. Sheila O' Donnell and John Tuomey's Student Centre for the London School of Economics (2014) has a 'folded, chamfered, canted and faceted façade' generated by the constraints of rights of light, and sightlines, in this tight warren of streets to the south of Lincoln's Inn Fields. Apart from the origami geometries, the building is not unlike Zumthor's Kolumba in being entirely wrapped in a homogeneous 'permeable blanket' of hand-made brickwork which creates dappled shadow–light patterns within (Figure 10.6).[35] It is a building whose profile is therefore explicitly determined by the kind of anti-shadow codes that governed the skyscrapers of New York in the inter–World Wars period. Casati describes this era of Manhattan as 'a drawing projected from below, from the bottom of the streets, starting with the shapes that the building's shadows *must not* cast. Shadow has determined the profile of the city'.[36] Perhaps this is

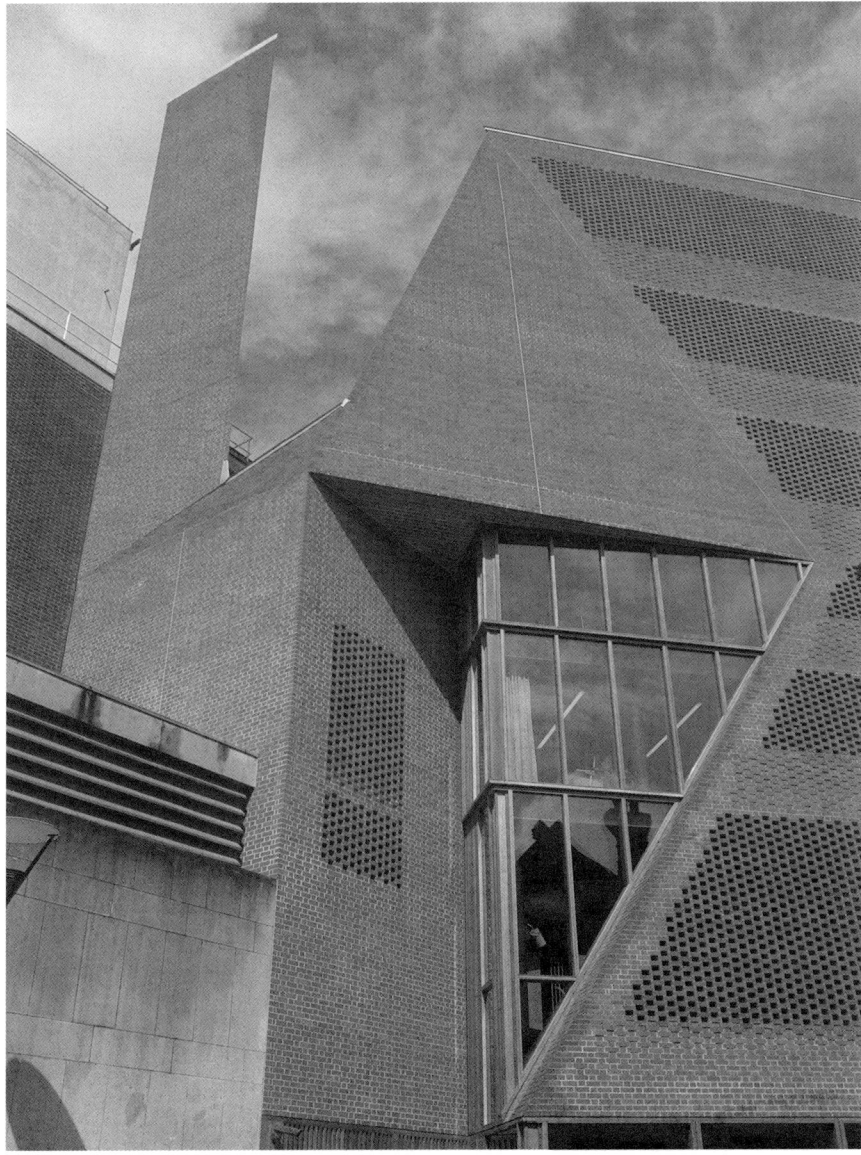

FIGURE 10.6 O' Donnell and Tuomey, Student Centre for the London School of Economics. Photograph, Stephen Kite.

why O'Donnell and Tuomey's LSE building more than passingly evokes the renderings made by the supreme artist of the new American metropolis, Hugh Ferriss (1889–1962), to demonstrate the architectonic potential of the New York 1916 zoning envelope dictates. As the code was intended to allow light and air to penetrate the depths of the city's ever-soaring canyons,

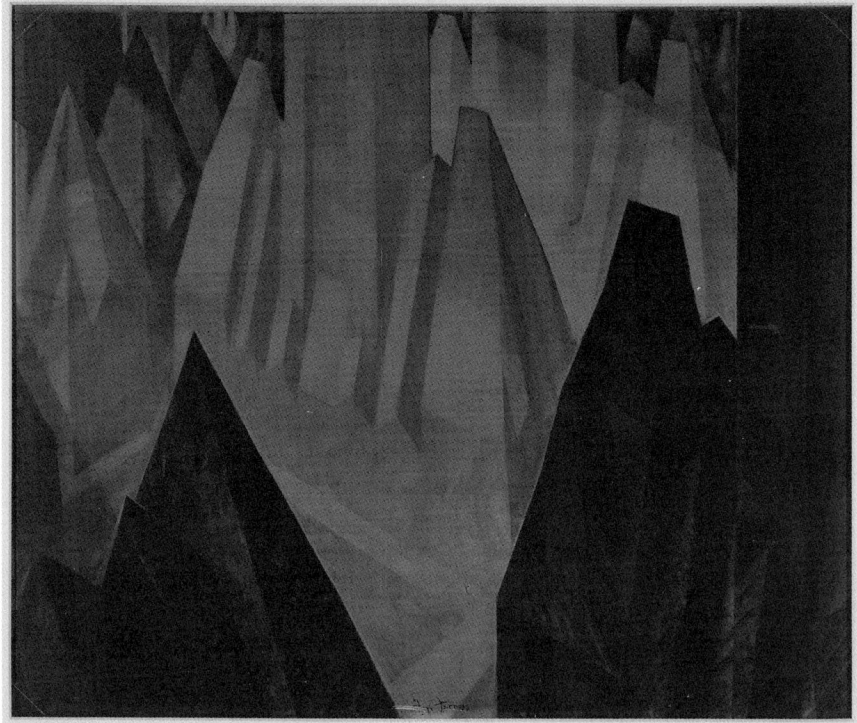

FIGURE 10.7 Hugh Ferriss, Imaginary drawings. Zoning ordinances. Crude Clay for Architects, 1922–4, charcoal pencil on board. Avery Architectural and Fine Arts Library, Columbia University.

it follows that the building envelope *itself* is an absence of light. Delineations of every facet of the code are visible in the influential Ferris series showing the 'Evolution of the Set-Back Building'. Ferris rendered the code envelope, in heavily worked charcoal pencil on board, as a sublime mass of shadow, as sharp and canted as the LSE Student Centre which is carved out of the same primal logic of the London daylighting codes.[37] The chiaroscuro of his artistry has been frequently compared to that of Piranesi. There is similar perspectival drama in another Ferris Zoning Law image – *Crude Clay for Architects* – where New York appears through menacing jagged outcrops like a transcendent panorama of the Rocky Mountains awaiting the architects' sculptural hand (Figure 10.7).[38]

A sun in the north – Australian shadows

As we turn from the stereotomic, with guarded optimism for a limited survival of this tectonic tradition of shadow-making, it has to be acknowledged that the bulk of architectural production now and in the future belongs, not to the *heavy*, but to the *light* – conceptually to the tectonics of Semper's framed bamboo hut with its mat enclosure. Even the handling of the masonry at Kolumba and the LSE Student Centre exhibits aspects of the lightly woven envelope. Semper's *Bekleidung* and Ruskin's wall veil have been appealed to as theoretical anchors amid the yawningly unfathomable potentials of the digital surface wherein architecture, for Lars Spuybroek in his *Textile Tectonics*, 'continues to resemble nothing so much as a drunk rambling down a badly lit street: all directions are possible, but we don't seem to be heading anywhere'.[39] The foregoing chapters have often sought evidence of shadow-making cultures in the act of drawing to building, but these proofs will be harder to discover in the paperless studios of digital design. The digital surface can be 'a profoundly site-less, infinitely thin, and immaterial membrane',[40] and if these 'death of drawing' orientations were pursued to their limits shadows of substance might well disappear along with much materiality.

These vast topics lie outside the scope of a study that has examined shadow-making in a number of cultural contexts ranging geographically from North America, through Europe, the Middle East, to Japan – but all in the northern hemisphere. Yet they can be touched upon in a brief excursion to the southern hemisphere where, for example, the Australian Melbourne-based practice, Ashton Raggatt McDougall (ARM, established 1988), has shown an obsession with 'black shadows and black buildings'.[41] From 1989 to 1991 Howard Raggatt studied in the master of architecture programme at RMIT University, Melbourne, under Leon van Schaik. One studio theme – 'Fringe de Cringe' – used the so-called Australian cultural cringe at its marginal position (vis-à-vis US-European 'centres') as a tactic of resistance, by confronting the authoritative icons head-on. Hence Raggatt made a collage project which rammed the Le Corbusier's Villa Savoye into Rossi's Modena Cemetery, marking the collision point of this *bricolage* with a 'built shadow' of black brick that falls across the junction. This compositional strategy was made in full consciousness of the European shadows of 'Rossi's melancholy and Le Corbusier's *tragic vision*', while recognizing also the 'Australian shadow' which is 'sharp and cast by a sun in the *north*'.[42] Aside from its extraordinary geology and fauna, part of the inescapable strangeness of Australia – for a visitor from the northern hemisphere – must be this existential fact that the shadows are always falling on the 'wrong' side. At the same time Raggatt joked that if for Rossi the built shadow 'seems to provide a sign of the irrevocable and the melancholy', then for Australians – free from the cultural freight of Europe – the shadow also signifies 'merely another beautiful summer day!'[43] In 2002, ARM went on to quote the Villa Savoye directly in the actual construction of the Australian Institute of Aboriginal Studies and Torres Strait Islander Studies (AIATSIS) in Canberra. But this 1:1 doppelganger polemically turns the white European model into a totally black building, in vehement resistance to any clichés as to what a so-called 'Aboriginal architecture' might look like. ARM's is among work emanating from Melbourne that has allowed the city to lay claim to be the centre of architectural experiment in Australia; work that has used digital design methods to take the semiotics of Postmodernism – dosed with veins of Deconstruction – to their (il)logical extremes. If the resulting projects are sometimes weird, they cannot be accused of the dull deracination that characterizes much apolitical Late Modernist architecture. [44]

But it is hardly 'another beautiful summer day' in Melbourne when ARM talk about 'measuring the dark' in their Melbourne Theatre Company project (MTC, 2008) where an 'apparatus' of pipe work is 'pressed and draped across the black mass' of the MTC auditorium giving the anamorphic illusion of a tangle of 3D boxes hanging in a 'galactic dark' – some of the box frames are in fact truly three-dimensional (Figure 10.8). For ARM they owe allegiance to the frames that entrap the screaming *Popes* of Francis Bacon's horrifying series of paintings based on the Velazquez *Portrait of Pope Innocent X* (c. 1650):

> Those lines describe a conceptual space, predestined in the dark, a kind of stage for popes and paralytics, for leaking shadows and fleshy manipulation. It is a shifting contraption, decomposing and recomposing that conceptual demarcation.[45]

Veiling the black box of the auditorium they give the illusion of rooms 'ready to be filled, awaiting occupation', metaphors of the many

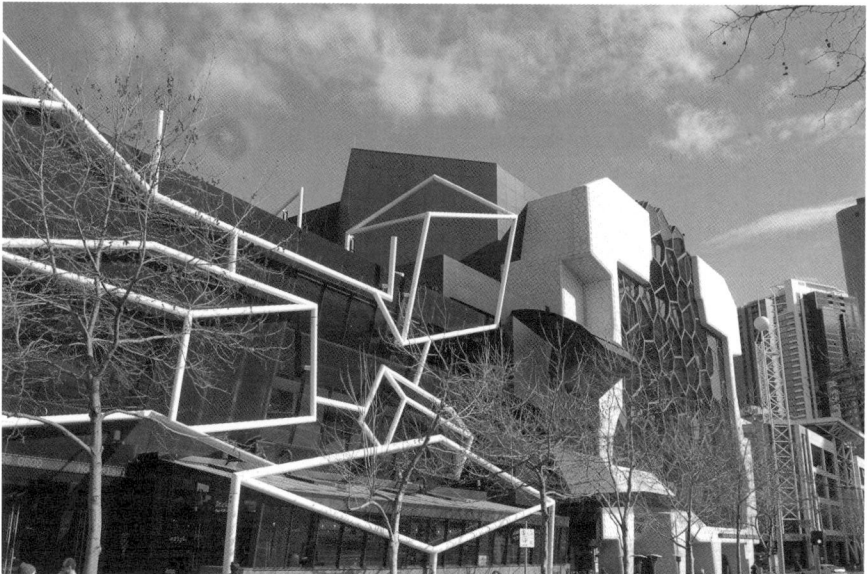

FIGURE 10.8 Ashton Raggatt McDougall (ARM), Melbourne Theatre Company, 2008. Photograph, Stephen Kite.

performances to come, as actors emerge from the shadows to occupy each stage. Doubtless not all the productions at MTC will be as darkly Beckett-ian as these narratives of leaking shadows imply. ARM devise and describe complex layers, such as these frames, in a 'translation' process of total immersion in 3D models 'slicing or sectioning, projecting, shadowing, voxelizing, tracing, pixelating, halftoning and so on'.[46]

The adjoining part of the complex, the Melbourne Recital Centre (MRC), is very different but just as startlingly odd; the 'big black window' to the upper foyer is imaged by ARM as 'almost an orifice, a scream – a seeming confirmation of its emptiness', again like the 'painted screams' of Francis Bacon.[47] The black window is patterned like bubble wrap and its framing unblenchingly simulates the kind of polystyrene packing which is used to protect delicate audio equipment – in this case the exquisite digitally modelled plywood space of the Melbourne Recital Hall. The 'packaging', in turn, extrudes from a sombre box of the local bluestone, in homage to the bluestone cultural bunker of the nearby National Gallery of Victoria (Roy Grounds, 1959–68). Here the critic Charles Jencks finds a High Victorian 'aesthetic of ugliness' wherein 'the outside of the MRC has the kind of discordant and awkward straightforwardness that comes from following functional space, lighting and the image of packaging wherever it will go, as would Butterfield'.[48]

Although William Butterfield never visited Australia, Melbourne has a major monument of his stubbornly strident architecture in the Anglican St Paul's Cathedral he designed for the city in 1878 facing Flinders Street. Outside, and particularly within the nave where bands of blue-grey basalt resonate with courses of ochre limestone, it exhibits that geological stratified 'alternation of shade with light' that Ruskin admired in the aforementioned Pisan Romanesque. Geology, in material and metaphor, and the presence of Butterfield's cathedral, were major determinants in Donald Bates and Peter Davidson's design (LAB Architecture Studio) for Federation Square (1997–2001), intended to give the city a major civic space for the new century, and to reconnect the nineteenth-century central grid to the Yarra River by bridging the rail tracks to the east of Flinders Station. From the gridded city the spatial sequence is initiated by a great parvis that opens up in front of Butterfield's Cathedral; via steps of sandblasted paving this rises and expands to a large 7,500 square metre piazza, around which jostle and cleave the new urban functions of the Australian Centre for the Moving Image (ACMI), the Ian Potter Art Centre, and the headquarters of the television and radio broadcaster SBS, together with the usual complement of visitor centre, restaurants, cafés and shops. Federation Square was considered radical for the turn of the twenty-first century – and well within the zany traditions of post mid-1970s Melbourne – in its forms which the designers variously describe as 'filaments' or 'shards', and in the fractal play of Australian sun and shadow in its tiled skin of zinc, glass and pink local sandstone (Figure 10.9). Some of the deconstructivist aspects have dated

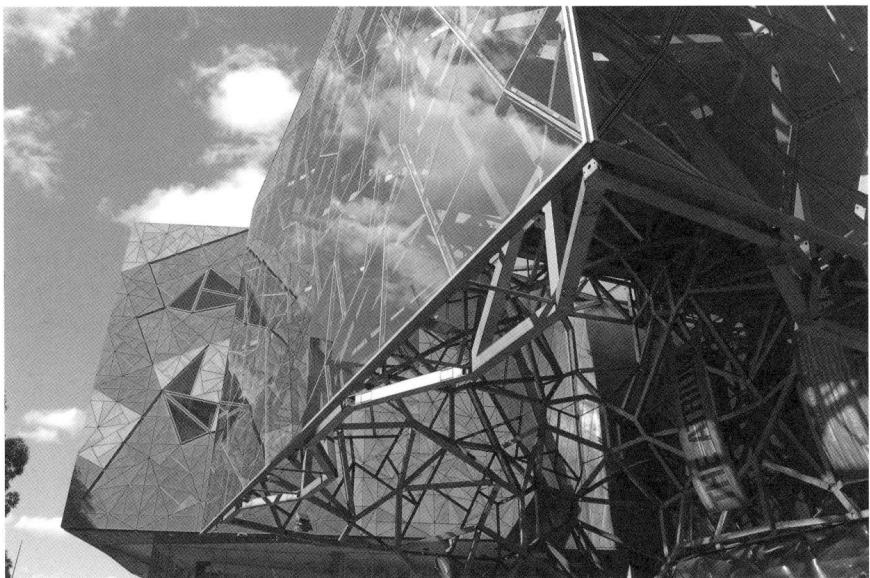

FIGURE 10.9 LAB Architecture Studio, Federation Square, 1997–2001. Photograph, Stephen Kite.

most quickly, particularly those zinc elements – such as the 'shard' on the Cathedral parvis – that quote most directly from Liebeskind's Jewish Museum in Berlin. But if it has already entered history, it is a project that remains of interest, when considering 'shadow futures', as it opened the present century with computing power experiments in fragmented massing and 'surface consciousness' that, for good or ill, are very much with us.

It is easy to see how the jagged irregularity of Federation Square breaks with Melbourne's calm grid, laid out in the 1830s, where major streets 1.5 chain wide (30.84 metres) mesh with much narrower service streets only half a chain in width (10.25 metres) – the basis of Melbourne's renowned network of laneways and arcades. But in the fissures of circulation both within and between the elements of Federation Square, LAB sought more subtle connectivities with these earlier patterns; morphological fractures that also call to mind the dramatic patterns of shadow and light of the gorges and ravines of the Australian interior. The piazza itself rakes like the shelvings of natural topography; here Paul Carter's installation, *Nearamnew*, challenges the visitor to tread slowly while deciphering suppressed Aboriginal memories from 'word-shards' carved into the surface on tablets of stone. Despite their manic busyness of fold and rupture, the façades of Federation Square are composed entirely from one tile shape which can be grouped into fives; these can then be assembled into megapanels, and all this hinging and pleating can, if need be, be laid out flat as a board.[49] Though paper thin, these surfaces again seductively conjure up memories of rock faces, of bright facets of stone counterpoised against jagged, deeply shadowed hollows and clefts. With these, and many subsequent surface experiments, and despite the many references recruited in their support – to nature, to Francis Bacon, or whatever – the anxiety and suspicion remains that we are witnessing an autonomous computer game with, in truth, only specious connections to culture. For Jencks these 'enigmatic shards suggest a new contextualism...the building dissolves the city grid to the north into the parkland to the south using fractal geometries at several scales to do so'.[50] Peter Davey admires the picturesque qualities of the new spaces here but disagrees with Jencks, calling the façades 'anti-human' and 'anti-civic' – they are 'simply frightening, unwelcoming and off-putting to most of us'.[51]

Casting back

Casting back through the veiled passages of this journey the significance of Tanizaki's *In Praise of Shadows* (first English translation 1977) – in allowing shadows themselves to emerge from the shadows as subjects of thought – has been stated a number of times; Zumthor is another case in point. It is strange that it has been left to a novelist to reclaim such a fundamental aspect of architecture against the flood of illuminance. In Chapter 2, we saw how for the influential US architect Charles Moore (1925–93) it came with 'the thrill of a slap for us then to hear praise of shadows and darkness'; us who had been schooled 'in the West [that] our most powerful ally is light' and to heed Kahn's adage that 'the sun never knew how wonderful it was until it fell on the wall of a building' – a narrative that suppresses Kahn's 'Treasury of Shadows'.[52] Moore concluded that Tanizaki's insights into darkness and inhabitation 'could change our lives', and to a modest extent the novelist *did* cause shadow to re-enter the architectural discourse; but on the whole shadow-making has lacked architectural champions to equal Venturi's reclamation of formal *Complexity and Contradiction in Architecture* (1966) or Rossi's reassessment of the *Architecture of the City* (also of 1966) as repository of collective memory. The lightweight permeability of paper screens and woven lattices of bamboo, reeds and timber, of the Japanese vernacular extolled by Tanizaki, readily translates to the perforated and cut surfaces produced by computer numeric controlled (CNC) flat-cutting devices. This rhymes with a cultural sensibility to the calligraphy of shimmering shadows thrown by leaves and branches onto these shoji screens or the textured wall surfaces of temple gardens: 'We find beauty not in the thing itself but in the patterns of shadows, the light and the darkness, that one thing against another creates',[53] says Tanizaki. So, to take a final shadow veil example, the architects of the Sfera Building culture house in Kyoto (Claesson, Koivisto Rune, 2003) drew inspiration from the shadow patterns cast by the trees around the site in developing a veil-like skin for the building of titanium panels perforated in dot matrix patterns of overlapping leaves. In turn, the panels cast gently dappled leaf patterns within, upon the customers who sip from designer bowls in this contemporary evocation of the teahouse (Figure 10.10).[54] Here the shadow veil takes its integral part in a spatial idea, in a desire for ornament and within an environmental strategy of controlling shade, light and air. The way architects use these skins – whether aiming for a similar through-composed authenticity or for a virtual excess of expression divorced from programme – will inevitably make at least some gesture to sustainable environmental performance. There are several ways of apprehending shadow, and if the foregoing pages have concentrated on the experiential, poetic, cultural and tectonic dimensions of shadow-making, this has been in no way to deny the environmental science within, for instance, the *lumière mystérieuse* of Soane's domestic Sublime, or the glare control of Kahn's folded or ruin walls.

The gradual conquest of darkness – at the time of the emergence of the early modern subject – made shadow manipulable and the opposition of darkness and light more contested. The English Baroque church was chosen as a key example of this process. As the ink lines and washes of Hawksmoor's drawings translated to building, shadow became a palpable material in the surfaces and spaces of sacred architecture. The contest between shadow and light only became more acute as the enlightenment project intensified, and the desire for transparent space produced its counter-form in the Burkean Sublime – Soane was among the first to explore its precepts in the domestic realm. These worlds could exist alongside the fashionable shades of the ostensibly dilettante ecstasies of 'gloomth' and 'Gothick', but together they produced powerful cultural formations in the Picturesque and ultimately a seriously archaeological Gothic. In *The Poetry of Architecture,* John Ruskin proposed that 'no man can be an architect, who is not a metaphysician', and went on to transform architecture by imagining shadows of metaphysical power. His nature worship – crossed with the Transcendentalism of America – made for equally powerful shadows in the work of Furness, Sullivan and Wright. As Ruskin's heir, the evocative art writer Adrian Stokes made explicit those aspects of Ruskin's psychologizing of architecture that are Freudian *avant la lettre.* So Stokes's Italian shadows refer to the unconscious in ways that Ruskin intimated but could not describe in those terms, just as do those of Aldo Rossi, as floated across the Venetian lagoon in the Carpaccio-casket of his *Teatro del Mondo*. Venice shares many cultural characteristics with the shadow patterns of the Middle East and Islamic civilization. These were patterns that Louis Kahn understood; he also took the baton from Furness and recuperated treasuries of shadow for modernism along with a recovery of Roman gravitas. As an unstable hole in light, shadows play an ambivalent role in architecture. In episodes such as these I have tried to describe that role, and to urge resistance to the idea that light is all we need.

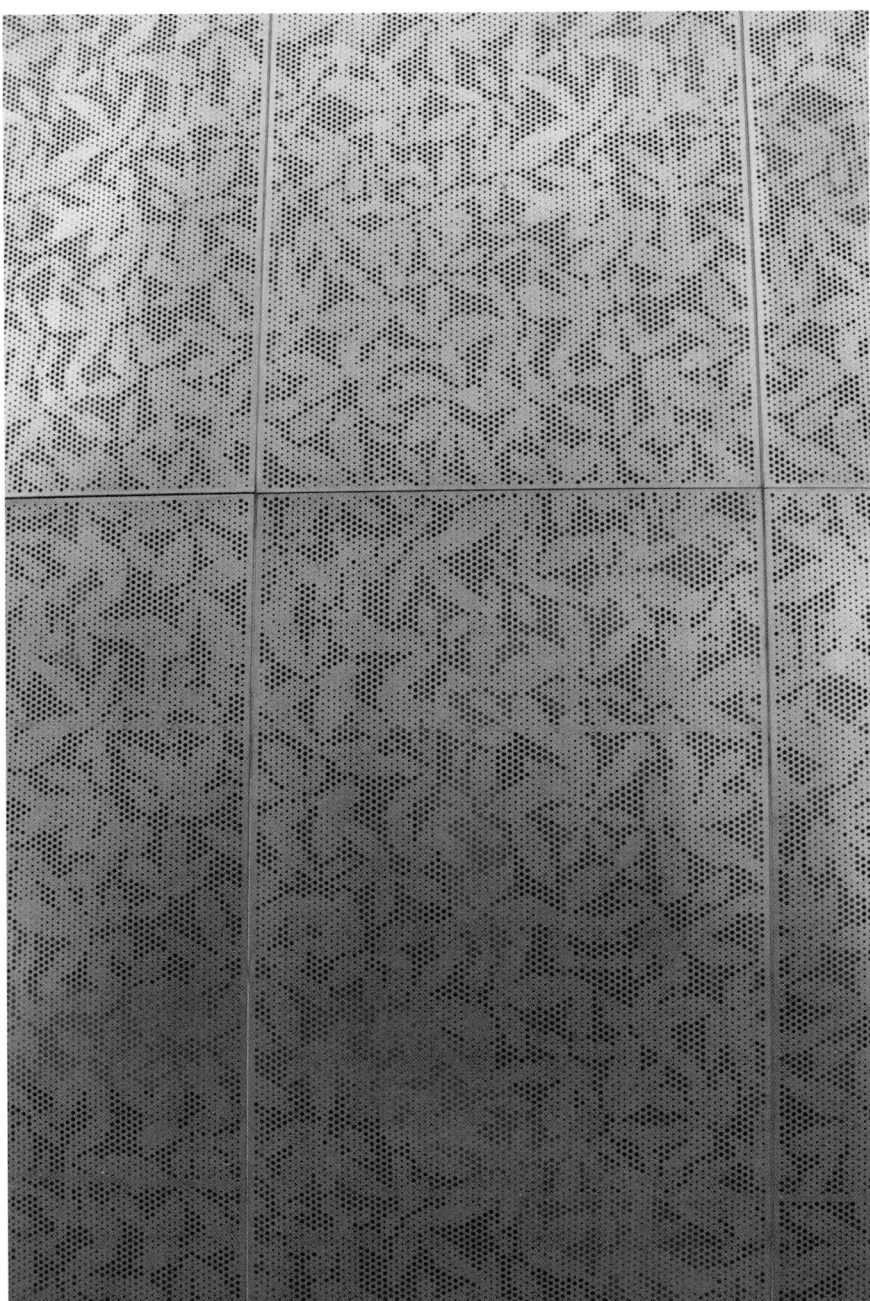

FIGURE 10.10 Claesson, Kovisto Rune, Sfera Building, Kyoto, 2003. Photograph, Stephen Kite.

Notes

1. *Ruskin, Works*, 10: 211, *Stones of Venice, vol. 2*.
2. Semper, Gottfried, *Style in the Technical and Tectonic Arts; or Practical Aesthetics*, H. F. Mallgrave and M. Robinson (trans) (Los Angeles, CA: Getty Publications, 2004), p. 71.
3. Semper, *Style*, p. 71.
4. Semper, *Style*, p. 666.
5. See Frampton, Kenneth, *Studies in Tectonic Culture. The Poetics of Construction in Nineteenth and Twentieth Century Architecture*, J. Cava (ed) (Cambridge, MA: MIT Press, 1995), pp. 1–8.
6. Semper, *Style*, p. 725.
7. Corrodi, Michelle, and Spechtenhauer, Klaus, *Illuminating. Natural Light in Residential Architecture* (Basel: Birkhäuser, 2008), p. 34.
8. Ruskin, *Works*, 9: 347, *Stones of Venice, vol. 1*.
9. Ruskin, *Works*, 9: 306, *Stones of Venice, vol. 1*.
10. Hunter, Will, 'A Raked Progress: The Flint House, Buckinghamshire, England', *The Architectural Review*, vol. 237, no. 1418 (April 2015), pp. 60–71, p. 69.
11. Van der Laan, Dom H., *Architectonic Space*, R. Padovan (trans) (Leiden: E. J. Brill, 1983), p. 204.
12. Quoted in Padovan, Richard, *Dom Hans van der Laan: Modern Primitive* (Amsterdam: Architectura & Natura Press, 1994), p. 167.
13. Plummer, Henry, *The Architecture of Natural Light* (London: Thames and Hudson, 2012), pp. 181, 186.
14. Plummer, *Architecture of Natural Light*, p. 186.
15. Voet, Caroline, 'The Poetics of Order: Dom Hans van der Laan's Architectonic Space', *Architectural Research Quarterly*, vol. 16, no. 2 (2012), pp. 137–54, p. 152.
16. Voet, 'Poetics of Order', p. 152.
17. Zumthor, Peter, *Atmospheres* (Basel: Birkhäuser, 2006), p. 59.
18. Zumthor, *Atmospheres*, p. 59.
19. Durisch, Thomas (ed), *Peter Zumthor 1990–1997: Buildings and Projects Volume 2* (Zurich: Scheidegger & Spiess, 2014), p. 39.
20. Gowing, Lawrence (ed), *The Critical Writings of Adrian Stokes* (London: Thames and Hudson, 1978), *vol. 1, Stones of Rimini*, p. 185.
21. Zumthor, Peter, *Thinking Architecture* (Basel: Birkhäuser, 2006, 2nd ed), p. 90.
22. Zumthor, *Thinking Architecture*, p. 90.
23. Zumthor, *Thinking Architecture*, p. 93.
24. See further images and drawings in Pallister, James, *Sacred Architecture: Contemporary Religious Architecture* (London: Phaidon, 2015), pp. 126–31.
25. The glass dome plugs undoubtedly contribute to this effect.

26 See also Davey, Peter, 'Diocesan Dialogue', *The Architectural Review*, vol. 222, no. 1329 (November 2007), pp. 36–43.
27 Zumthor, Peter, 'The New Building of the Museum for the Archdiocese, Thoughts on the Design', in *Salve* (Prague: Salve, 2011), pp. 139–42, p. 139.
28 Casati, Roberto, *Shadows. Unlocking Their Secrets, from Plato to Our Time* (New York: Vintage Books, 2003), p. 163.
29 Menneckes, Friedhelm, 'The Room of My Breathing: The East Tower at Kolumba', in *Salve* (Prague: Salve, 2011), pp. 66–82, p. 71.
30 Zumthor, Peter, 'If Everything I Planned Had Been Realised, I Would Not Be So Happy Now: Interview with Peter Zumthor', in *Salve* (Prague: Salve, 2011), pp. 122–34, p. 125.
31 Harlan, Volker (ed), *What Is Art: Conversation with Joseph Beuys* (Forest Row: Clairview Books, 2004), p. 98.
32 Menneckes, 'The Room of My Breathing: The East Tower at Kolumba', p. 72.
33 Zumthor, *Thinking Architecture*, p. 8.
34 Zumthor, *Thinking Architecture*, p. 77.
35 O'Donnell, Sheila, and Tuomey, John, *Space for Architecture: The Work of O' Donnell and Tuomey* (London: Artifice, 2014), p. 200.
36 Casati, *Shadows*, p. 17.
37 Ferriss, Hugh, *The Metropolis of Tomorrow* (Princeton, NJ: Princeton Architectural Press, 1986; original work published 1929), p. 73.
38 Ferriss, *The Metropolis of Tomorrow*, p. 83.
39 Spuybroek, Lars (ed), *Textile Tectonics* (Rotterdam: NAi, 2011), p. 7.
40 Pell, Ben, *The Articulate Surface: Ornament and Technology in Contemporary Architecture* (Basel: Birkhäuser, 2010), p. 11.
41 Raggatt, Mark, and Ward, Maitiú (eds), *Mongrel Rapture: The Architecture of Ashton Raggatt McDougall* (Melbourne, Australia: Uro, 2015), p. 1393.
42 Raggatt and Ward, *Mongrel Rapture*, p. 232.
43 Raggatt and Ward, *Mongrel Rapture*, p. 232.
44 I am grateful for conversations with Chris Smith, University of Sydney (Sydney, August 2015), for insights into Australian architectural cultures.
45 Raggatt and Ward, *Mongrel Rapture*, p. 908.
46 Raggatt and Ward, *Mongrel Rapture*, p. 866.
47 Raggatt and Ward, *Mongrel Rapture*, p. 912.
48 Quoted in Raggatt and Ward, *Mongrel Rapture*, p. 1318.
49 Melvin, Jeremy, 'Federation Square, Melbourne', *Architectural Design*, vol. 73, no. 2 (March–April 2003), pp. 103–9.
50 Davey, Peter, 'LAB Experiments. Urban Regeneration, Melbourne, Australia, LAB + Bates Smart', *The Architectural Review*, vol. 214, no. 1275 (May 2003), pp. 55–63, p. 62.
51 Davey, 'LAB Experiments', p. 62.

52 Tanizaki, Junichoro, *In Praise of Shadows*, T. J. Harper and E. G. Seidensticker (trans), (London: Vintage, 2001, original work published 1933–4), pp. 1, 2.
53 Tanizaki, *In Praise of Shadows*, p. 46.
54 Pell, *The Articulate Surface*, p. 49.

BIBLIOGRAPHY

Ackroyd, Peter, *Hawksmoor* (London: Penguin Books, 2010, first published 1985).
Andrews, Malcolm, *The Search for the Picturesque. Landscape Aesthetics and Tourism in Britain, 1760–1800* (Aldershot: Scolar Press, 1989).
Appleton, Jay, *The Experience of Landscape* (Chichester: John Wiley, 1996, revised ed.).
Ardalan, Nader, and Bakhtiar, Laleh, *The Sense of Unity: The Sufi Tradition in Persian Architecture* (Chicago and London: University of Chicago Press, 1973).
Bachelard, Gaston, *The Poetics of Space*, M. Jolas (trans) (New York: Penguin Books, 2014, original work published as *la poetique de l'espace*, 1957).
Baxandall, Michael, *Shadows and Enlightenment* (New Haven, CT and London: Yale University Press, 1995).
Bender, John, *Imagining the Penitentiary. Fiction and the Architecture of Mind in Eighteenth Century England* (Chicago: University of Chicago Press, 1987).
Benedikt, Michael, *Deconstructing the Kimbell. An Essay on Meaning and Architecture* (New York: Lumen Books, 1991).
Bianca, Stefano, *Urban Form in the Arab World: Past and Present* (Zürich: vdf, 2000).
Binet, Hélène, 'Photographing Shadows at La Tourette', in H. Binet et al. (eds), *The Secret of the Shadow. Light and Shadow in Architecture* (Berlin: Ernst Wasmuth Verlag Tübingen, 2002), pp. 102–25.
Bloomer, Kent, 'Shadows in Ruskin's Lamp of Power', *Places*, vol. 2, no. 4 (1985), pp. 61–6.
Blundell Jones, Peter, and Canniffe, Eamonn, *Modern Architecture Through Case Studies* (Oxford: Architectural Press, 2007).
Bollnow, O. F., *Human Space*, C. Shuttleworth (trans), J. Kohlmaier (ed.) (London: Hyphen Press, 2011).
Boullée, E. L., 'Architecture, Essay on Art' (c 1790), in H. Rosenau (ed.), *Boullée and Visionary Architecture* (London: Academy Editions, 1976), pp. 81–116.
Bring, Mitchell, and Wayembergh, Josse, *Japanese Gardens: Design and Meaning* (New York: Mc-Graw Hill, 1981).
Bristow, Ian C., *Architectural Colour in British Interiors 1615–1840* (New Haven, CT and London: Yale University Press, 1996).
Britton, John, *The Union of Architecture, Sculpture and Painting, Exemplified by a Series of Illustrations with Descriptive Accounts of the House and Galleries of John Soane* (London: Longman, 1827).
Brooks, Michael W., *John Ruskin and Victorian Architecture* (London: Thames and Hudson, 1989).
Brownlee, David B., and De Long, David G., *Louis I. Kahn: In the Realm of Architecture* (New York: Rizzoli, 1991).

Burke, Edmund, *A Philosophical Enquiry into the Sublime and Beautiful*, D. Womersley (ed.) (London: Penguin Books, 2004, original work published 1757, 2nd ed. 1759).

Büttiker, Urs, *Louis I. Kahn. Light and Space* (Basel: Birkhäuser Verlag, 1994).

Cadwell, Michael, *Strange Details* (Cambridge, MA: MIT Press, 2007).

Campbell, Gordon, *The Hermit in the Garden. From Imperial Rome to Ornamental Gnome* (Oxford: Oxford University Press, 2013).

Campbell, Malcolm, 'Chiaroscuro and *Non-Finito* in Piranesi's *Prisons*', in David Murray (ed.), *VIA 11, Architecture and Shadow* (Philadelphia, PA: University of Pennsylvania, 1990), pp. 90–101.

Casati, Roberto, *Shadows. Unlocking Their Secrets, from Plato to Our Time* (New York: Vintage Books, 2003).

Chalcraft, Anna, and Viscardi, Judith, *Strawberry Hill. Horace Walpole's Gothic Castle* (London: Frances Lincoln, 2007).

Collins, Peter, *Changing Ideals in Modern Architecture 1750–1950* (London: Faber and Faber, 1965).

Cook, E. T., and Wedderburn, Alexander (eds), *The Works of John Ruskin* (London: George Allen, 1904–13).

Corbusier, Le, *Ronchamp* (Stuttgart: Verlag Gerd Hatje, 1957, 1991).

Corrodi, Michelle, and Spechtenhauer, Klaus, *Illuminating. Natural Light in Residential Architecture* (Basel: Birkhäuser, 2008).

Costa, Paolo M., *Historic Mosques and Shrines of Oman* (Oxford: Archaeopress, 2001).

Crary, Jonathan, *Techniques of the Observer. On Vision and Modernity in the Nineteenth Century* (Cambridge, MA: MIT Press, 1992).

Curl, James Stevens, *Death and Architecture* (Stroud, Gloucestershire: Sutton Publishing, 2002).

Darley, Gillian, *John Soane. An Accidental Romantic* (New Haven, CT and London: Yale University Press, 1999).

Denison, Edward, and Ren, Guang Yu, *The Life of the British Home. An Architectural History* (Chichester: John Wiley, 2012).

Desmond, William, 'Schopenhauer's Philosophy of the Dark Origin', in B. Vandenabeele (ed.), *A Companion to Schopenhauer* (Chichester: Blackwell, 2012), pp. 89–104.

Dillon, Brian, *Ruin Lust. Artists' Fascination with Ruins, from Turner to the Present* (London: Tate Publishing, 2014).

Divitiis, Bianca de, 'New Drawings for the Interiors of the Breakfast Room and Library at Pitzhanger Manor', *Architectural History*, vol. 48 (2005), pp. 163–72.

Dorey, Helen, 'Sir John Soane's Acquistion of the Sarcophagus of Seti I', *Georgian Group Journal*, vol. 1 (1991), pp. 26–35.

Downes, Kerry, *Hawksmoor* (London: Thames and Hudson, 1969).

Downes, Kerry, *Sir Christopher Wren. The Design of St Paul's Cathedral* (London: Trefoil Publications, 1988).

Downes, Kerry, *Vanbrugh* (London: Zwemmer, 1977).

Downes, Kerry, Amery, Colin, and Stamp, Gavin, *St George's Bloomsbury. A Hawksmoor Masterpiece Restored* (London: Scala, 2008).

Du Prey, Pierre de la Ruffinière, *John Soane. The Making of an Architect* (Chicago and London: University of Chicago Press, 1982).

Du Prey, Pierre de la Ruffinière, 'Hawksmoor's "Basilica after the Primitive Christians": Architecture and Theology', *Journal of the Society of Architectural Historians*, vol. 48, no. 1 (March 1989), pp. 38–52.

Du Prey, Pierre de la Ruffinière, *Hawksmoor's London Churches. Architecture and Theology* (Chicago and London: University of Chicago Press, 2000).

Durisch, Thomas (ed.), *Peter Zumthor 1990–1997: Buildings and Projects Volume 2* (Zurich: Scheidegger & Spiess, 2014).

Eastlake, Charles L., *A History of the Gothic Revival* (Leicester: Leicester University Press, 1978 [1872]).

Eisenbrand, Jochen, 'Between Grid and Pathway: The Houses of Louis Kahn', in M. Kries, J. Eisenbrand, and S. Von Moos (eds), *Louis Kahn: The Power of Architecture*, exhibition catalogue (Weil amd Rhein: Vitra Design Museum, 2012), pp. 49–66.

Eisenman, Peter, 'The House of the Dead as the City of Survival', in K. Frampton (ed.), *Aldo Rossi in America 1976 to 1979* (New York: The Institute for Architecture and Urban Studies, 1979), pp. 4–15.

Eliade, Mircea, *Symbolism, the Sacred, and the Arts*, D. Apostolos-Cappadona (ed.) (New York: Crossroad, 1986).

Emerson, Ralph Waldo, *Nature* (Boston: James Munroe, 1836).

Engel, Heinrich, *The Japanese House: A Tradition for Contemporary Architecture* (Rutland, VT and Tokyo: Charles E. Tuttle, 1964).

Evans, Robin, *The Fabrication of Virtue. English Prison Architecture 1750–1840* (Cambridge: Cambridge University Press, 1982).

Evans, Robin, 'Architectural Projection', in David Murray (ed.), *VIA 11, Architecture and Shadow* (Philadelphia, PA: University of Pennsylvania, 1990), pp. 134–9.

Fehn, Sverre, and Fjeld, Per Olave, 'Has a Doll Life', *Perspecta*, vol. 24 (1988), pp. 40–9.

Fernández-Galiano, Luis, *Fire and Memory: On Architecture and Energy*, G. Cariño (trans) (Cambridge, MA: MIT Press, 2000).

Ferriss, Hugh, *The Metropolis of Tomorrow* (Princeton, NJ: Princeton Architectural Press, 1986 original work published 1929).

Feuerstein, Marcia F., 'Illuminating Quality in Architectural Reveals', *Architectural Research Quarterly*, vol. 29, no. 3–4 (2009), pp. 231–9.

Fincham, Kenneth, and Tyacke, Nicholas, *Altar's Restored. The Changing Face of English Religious Worship, 1547–c.1700* (Oxford: Oxford University Press, 2007).

Forty, Adrian, *Words and Buildings. A Vocabulary of Modern Architecture* (New York: Thames and Hudson, 2000).

Foucault, Michel, *Discipline and Punish. The Birth of the Prison*, A. Sheridan (trans) (New York: Vintage Books, 1995, original work published 1975).

Foucault, Michel, 'The Eye of Power', in Colin Gordon (ed.), *Power/Knowledge: Selected Interviews and Other Writings 1972–1977* (New York: Pantheon Books, 1980).

Frampton, Kenneth, *Studies in Tectonic Culture. The Poetics of Construction in Nineteenth and Twentieth Century Architecture*, J. Cava (ed.) (Cambridge, MA: MIT Press, 1995).

Fuller, Peter, *Art and Psychoanalysis* (London: Writers and Readers, 1980).

Gargiani, Roberto, *Louis I. Kahn. Exposed Concrete and Hollow Stones 1949–1959* (Lausanne: EPFL Press, 2014).

Geraghty, Anthony, *The Architectural Drawings of Sir Christopher Wren at All Souls College, Oxford: A Complete Catalogue* (London: Lund Humphries, 2007).
Geraghty, Anthony, 'Nicholas Hawksmoor's Drawing Technique of the 1690s and John Locke's *Essay Concerning Human Understanding*', in Helen Hills (ed.), *Rethinking the Baroque* (Farnham, Surrey: Ashgate, 2011), pp. 125–41.
Gilpin, William, *Observations on the River Wye and Several Parts of South Wales, & c. Relative Chiefly to Picturesque Beauty: Made in the Summer of the Year 1770* (London: Pallas Athene, 2005, first published 1782–3, this edition based on revised fifth edition of 1800).
Glover, Nicky, *Psychoanalytic Aesthetics. An Introduction to the British School* (London: Karnac, 2009).
Goldhagen, Sarah Williams, *Louis Kahn's Situated Modernism* (New Haven, CT and London: Yale University Press, 2001).
Gombrich, E. H., *Shadows. The Depiction of Cast Shadows in Western Art* (London: National Gallery Publications, 1995).
Gowing, Lawrence (ed.), *The Critical Writings of Adrian Stokes* (London: Thames and Hudson, 1978).
Groom, Nick, 'Gothic Antiquity: From the Sack of Rome to *The Castle of Otranto*', in D. Townshend (ed.), *Terror and Wonder: The Gothic Imagination* (London: The British Library, 2014), pp. 38–67.
Harbison, Robert, *Reflections on Baroque* (London: Reaktion, 2000).
Harney, Marion, *Place-Making for the Imagination: Horace Walpole and Strawberry Hill* (Farnham, Surrey: Ashgate, 2013).
Harris, John, 'The Grey Wash Style of the Palladian Office of Works', *The Georgian Group Journal*, vol. 12 (2002), pp. 48–57.
Hart, Vaughan, *Nicholas Hawksmoor. Rebuilding Ancient Wonders* (New Haven, CT and London: Yale University Press, 2002).
Hart, Vaughan, *Sir John Vanbrugh. Storyteller in Stone* (New Haven, CT and London: Yale University Press, 2008).
Haslam, Ray, '"For the Sake of the Subject": Ruskin and the Tradition of Architectural Illustration', in M. Wheeler and N. Whiteley (eds), *The Lamp of Memory. Ruskin, Tradition and Architecture* (Manchester and New York: Manchester University Press, 1992), pp. 138–66.
Hawkes, Dean, *The Environmental Imagination: Technics and Poetics of the Architectural Environment* (Abingdon, Oxon: Routledge, 2008).
Heath, Charles, *Historical and Descriptive Accounts of the Ancient and Present State of Chepstow Castle Including Persfield* (Monmouth: C. Heath, 1801).
Henry Home, Lord Kames, *Elements of Criticism*, vol. 1, Peter Jones (ed.) (Indianapolis, IN: Liberty Fund, 2005, 6th ed., originally published 1785).
Hildebrand, Grant, *The Wright Space: Pattern and Meaning in Frank Lloyd Wright's Houses* (Seattle: University of Washington Press, 1991).
Hildebrand, Grant, *Origins of Architectural Pleasure* (Berkeley: University of California Press, 1999).
Hill, Rosemary, *God's Architect: Pugin and the Building of Romantic Britain* (London: Allen Lane, 2007).
Hills, Helen, 'The Baroque: The Grit in the Oyster of Art History', in Helen Hills (ed.), *Rethinking the Baroque* (Farnham, Surrey: Ashgate, 2011), pp. 11–36.

Jacobsen, Ken, and Jacobsen, Jenny, *Carrying off the Palaces: John Ruskin's Lost Daguerrotypes* (London: Quaritch, 2015).
Jeudwine, Wynne, *Stage Designs* (London: RIBA, 1968).
Johnson, Nell E. (ed.), *Light Is the Theme: Louis I. Kahn and the Kimbell Art Museum* (Fort Worth, TX: Kimbell Art Museum, 2011).
Kahn, Louis I., *Louis I. Kahn. Conversations with Students*, D. Ngo (ed.) (Houston, TX: Rice University School of Architecture, 1998, 2nd ed.).
Kahn, Louis I., *Silence and Light*, A. Vassella (ed.) (Zurich: Park Books, 2013).
Kalman, Harold D., 'Newgate Prison', *Architectural History*, vol. 12 (1969), pp. 50–61, pp. 108–12.
Kaufman, Edward N., '"The Weight and Vigour of Their Masses": Mid-Victorian Country Churches and the "Lamp of Power"', in J. D. Hunt and F. M. Holland (eds), *The Ruskin Polygon. Essays on the Imagination of John Ruskin* (Manchester: Manchester University Press, 1982), pp. 95–121.
Kheirabadi, Masoud, *Iranian Cities: Formation and Development* (Austin: University of Texas Press, 1993).
Kite, Stephen, 'The Poetics of Oman's Traditional Architecture: Towards an Aesthetic Interpretation', *The Journal of Oman Studies*, vol. 12 (2002), pp. 133–55.
Kite, Stephen, *Adrian Stokes: An Architectonic Eye* (London: Legenda, MHRA, Maney, 2009).
Kite, Stephen, *Building Ruskin's Italy: Watching Architecture* (Farnham: Ashgate, 2012).
Klein, Melanie, 'Infantile Anxiety-Situations Reflected in a Work of Art and in the Creative Impulse', *The International Journal of Psychoanalysis*, vol. 10 (1929), pp. 436–43.
Klein, Melanie, 'Our Adult World and Its Roots in Infancy', in M. Masud and R. Khan (eds), *Melanie Klein. Envy and Gratitude and Other Works* (London: Hogarth Press, 1975), pp. 247–63.
Knox, Tim, *Sir John Soane's Museum London* (London: Merrell, 2008), photography by Derry Moore.
Komendant, August E., *18 Years with Architect Louis I. Kahn* (Englewood, NJ: Aloray, 1975).
Korab-Karpowicz, W. Julian, 'Schopenhauer's Theory of Architecture', in B. Vandenabeele (ed.), *A Companion to Schopenhauer* (Chichester, UK: Blackwell, 2012), pp. 178–92.
Koslofsky, Craig, *Evening's Empire. A History of the Night in Early Modern Europe* (Cambridge: Cambridge University Press, 2011).
Kries, Mateo, Eisenbrand, Jochen, and Von Moos, Stanislaus (eds), *Louis Kahn: The Power of Architecture*, exhibition catalogue (Weil am Rhein: Vitra Design Museum, 2012).
Kurokawa, Kisho, *Rediscovering Japanese Space* (New York: Weatherhill, 1988).
Kurokawa, Kisho, 'Shadows, Symbiosis, and a Culture of Wood', in David Murray (ed.), *Via 11. Architecture and Shadow. The Journal of the Graduate School of Fine Arts, University of Pennsylvania* (1990), pp. 26–31.
Landow, George, P., *The Aesthetic and Critical Theories of John Ruskin* (Princeton, NJ: Princeton University Press, 1971).
Latour, Alessandra (ed.), *Louis I. Kahn. Writings, Lectures, Interviews* (New York: Rizzoli, 1991).

Le Camus de Mezières, Nicolas, *The Genius of Architecture, or, The Analogy of That Art with Our Sensations*, Robin Middleton (introduction), David Britt (trans) (Santa Monica, CA: Getty Center for the History of Art and the Humanities, 1992, original work published 1780).

Link, Alex, '"The Capitol of Darkness": Gothic Spatialities in the London of Peter Ackroyd's *Hawksmoor*', *Contemporary Literature*, vol. 45, no. 3 (Autumn 2004), pp. 516–37.

Lobell, John, *Between Silence and Light. Spirit in the Architecture of Louis. I. Kahn* (Boston and London: Shambhala, 2008).

Loud, Patricia Cummings, *The Art Museums of Louis I. Kahn* (Durham and London: Duke University Press, 1989).

Lukacher, Brian, *Joseph Gandy. An Architectural Visionary in Georgian England* (London: Thames and Hudson, 2006).

Macaulay, Rose, *Roloff Beny Interprets in Photographs Pleasure of Ruins*, C. B. Smith (ed.) (London: Thames and Hudson, Book Club Associates, 1977, revised ed.).

Maillet, Arnaud, *The Claude Glass. Use and Meaning of the Black Mirror in Western Art* (New York: Zone Books, 2009).

Malraux, André, *The Voices of Silence*, S. Gilbert (trans) (St Albans, Herts.: Granada Publishing, 1954).

Marc, Olivier, *Psychology of the House* (London: Thames and Hudson, 1977).

Marcus, George H. and Whitaker, William, *The Houses of Louis Kahn* (New Haven and London: Yale University Press, 2013).

McCarter, Robert, *Louis I. Kahn* (London: Phaidon, 2009).

McCarter, Robert, 'The Integrated Ideal: Ordering Principles in Wright's Architecture', in R. McCarter (ed.), *On and By Frank Lloyd Wright: A Primer of Architectural Principles* (London: Phaidon, 2011), pp. 286–337.

McGoodwin, Henry, *Architectural Shades and Shadows* (Washington, DC: The American Institute of Architects Press, 1989, original work published 1904).

Meech, Julia, *Frank Lloyd Wright and the Art of Japan: The Architect's Other Passion* (New York: Japan Society and Harry N. Abrams, 2001).

Melvin, Jeremy, 'Federation Square, Melbourne', *Architectural Design*, vol. 73, no. 2 (March–April 2003), pp. 103–9.

Merrill, Michael, *Louis Kahn on the Thoughtful Making of Spaces* (Baden: Lars Müller, 2010).

Meyers, Marshall D., 'Louis Kahn and the Art of Drawing: Some Recollections', in A. Tzonis (ed.), *The Louis I. Kahn Archive Personal Drawings*, 7 vols (New York and London: Garland, 1987), pp. xxv–xxvii.

Middleton, Robin, 'Soane's Spaces and the Matter of Fragmentation', in Margaret Richardson and Mary Anne Stevens (eds) *John Soane Architect* (London: Royal Academy of Arts, 1999), pp. 26–37.

Millet, Marietta S., *Light Revealing Architecture* (New York: Van Nostrand Reinhold, 1996).

Mitchell, Julian, *The Wye Tour and Its Artists* (Little Logaston, Herefordshire: Logaston Press, 2010).

Norberg-Schulz, Christian, *Genius Loci: Towards a Phenomenology of Architecture* (London: Academy Editions, 1980).

Norberg-Schulz, Christian, *Nightlands. Nordic Building*, T. McQuillan (trans) (Cambridge, MA: MIT Press, 1996).

O'Donnell, Sheila, and Tuomey, John, *Space for Architecture: The Work of O' Donnell and Tuomey* (London: Artifice, 2014).
Oechslin, Werner, 'How the Architect Emerged from the Shadows of the Painter', in H. Binet et al. (eds), *The Secret of the Shadow. Light and Shadow in Architecture* (Berlin: Ernst Wasmuth Verlag Tübingen, 2002), pp. 78–83.
O'Gorman, James F., *Three American Architects: Richardson, Sullivan, and Wright* (Chicago: University of Chicago Press, 1992).
O'Regan, John et al. (eds) *Aldo Rossi. Selected Writings and Projects* (London: Architectural Design, 1983).
Padovan, Richard, *Dom Hans van der Laan: Modern Primitive* (Amsterdam: Architectura & Natura Press, 1994).
Pallasmaa, Juhani, *The Thinking Hand. Existential and Embodied Wisdom in Architecture* (Chichester: Wiley, 2009).
Pallister, James, *Sacred Architecture: Contemporary Religious Architecture* (London: Phaidon, 2015).
Palmer, Bryan D., *Cultures of Darkness. Night Travels in the Histories of Transgression (From Medieval to Modern)* (New York: Monthly Review Press, 2000).
Parry, Graham, *The Arts of the Anglican Counter-Reformation: Glory, Laud and Honour* (Woodbridge: Boydell Press, 2006).
Pauly, Danièle, *Barragán Space and Shadow, Walls and Colour* (Basel: Birkhäuser, 2008).
Pell, Ben, *The Articulate Surface: Ornament and Technology in Contemporary Architecture* (Basel: Birkhäuser, 2010).
Pérez-Gómez, Alberto, and Pelletier, Louise, *Architectural Representation and the Perspective Hinge* (Cambridge, MA: MIT Press, 2000).
Peterken, Susan, *Landscapes of the Wye Tour* (Glasgow: Logaston Press, 2008).
Petherbridge, Deanna, *The Primacy of Drawing. Histories and Theories of Practice* (New Haven and London: Yale University Press, 2010).
Pevsner, Nikolaus, *A History of Building Types* (London: Thames and Hudson, 1976).
Plant, Margaret, *Venice. Fragile City 1797–1997* (New Haven, CT and London: Yale University Press, 2002).
Plummer, Henry, *Light in Japanese Architecture* (Tokyo: Architecture and Urbanism Publishing, 1995).
Plummer, Henry, *The Architecture of Natural Light* (London: Thames and Hudson, 2012).
Pope, Arthur Upham, *Persian Architecture* (London: Thames and Hudson, 1965).
Praz, Mario, 'Introductory Essay', in P. Fairclough (ed.), *Three Gothic Novels: The Castle of Otranto* (Horace Walpole), *Vathek* (William Beckford), *Frankenstein* (Mary Shelley) (Harmondsworth, Middlesex: Penguin Books, 1968).
Raggatt, Mark, and Ward, Maitiú (eds) *Mongrel Rapture: The Architecture of Ashton Raggatt McDougall* (Melbourne: Uro, 2015).
Reed, Arden, 'Signifying Shadows', in David Murray (ed.), *Via 11. Architecture and Shadow. The Journal of the Graduate School of Fine Arts, University of Pennsylvania* (Philadelphia, PA: The Graduate School of Fine Arts, University of Pennsylvania, 1990), pp. 12–25.
Reid, Aileen, '"Theoria" in Practice: E. W. Godwin, Ruskin and Art-Architecture', in R. Daniels and G. Brandwood (eds), *Ruskin and Architecture* (Reading: Spire Books, 2003), pp. 278–317.

Richardson, Margaret, and Stevens, Mary Anne (eds) *John Soane Architect* (London: Royal Academy of Arts, 1999).

Rossi, Aldo, *A Scientific Autobiography*, L. Venuti (trans) (Cambridge, MA: MIT Press, 1981).

Rossi, Aldo, *Teatro del Mondo*, M. Brusatin and A. Prandi (eds) (Venice: Cluva Librería Editrice, 1982).

R. T., *De Templis, a Treatise of Temples Wherein Is Discovered the Ancient Manner of Building, Consecrating, and Adorning of Churches* (London: R. Bishop, Thomas Alchorn, 1638; EEBO Eds., facsimile).

Samuel, Flora, *Le Corbusier in Detail* (Oxford: Architectural Press, 2007).

Scheer, David Ross, *The Death of Drawing. Architecture in the Age of Simulation* (New York: Routledge, 2014).

Schopenhauer, Arthur, *The World as Will and Representation*, 2 vols, E. F. J. Payne (trans) (New York: Dover, 1969).

Scully, Jr, Vincent, *Louis I. Kahn* (New York: George Braziller, 1962).

Semper, Gottfried, *Style in the Technical and Tectonic Arts; or Practical Aesthetics*, H. F. Mallgrave and M. Robinson (trans) (Los Angeles, CA: Getty Publications, 2004).

Sinclair, Iain, *Lud Heat. A Book of the Dead Hamlets – May 1974 to April 1975* (Cheltenham, Glos.: Skylight Press, 2012, first published 1975).

Siry, Joseph, 'Adler and Sullivan's Guaranty Building in Buffalo', *Journal of the Society of Architectural Historians*, vol. 55, no. 1 (March 1996), pp. 6–37.

Smithson, Alison and Peter, 'Working with Shadow: Damascus Gate, Jerusalem', in David Murray (ed.), *VIA 11, Architecture and Shadow* (Philadelphia, PA: University of Pennsylvania, 1990), pp. 76–83.

Smithson, Alison and Peter, *The Charged Void: Urbanism* (New York: Monacelli Press, 2005).

Soane, Sir John, *Description of the House and Museum on the North Side of Lincoln's Inn Fields, the Residence of Sir John Soane* (London: privately printed by Levey, Robson and Franklyn, 1835) (incorporating descriptions by Barbara Hofland).

Soane, Sir John, 'Crude Hints Towards an History of My House in L[incoln's] I[nn] Fields', in *Visions of Ruin. Architectural Fantasies and Designs for Garden Follies with Crude Hints Towards a History of My House by John Soane* (London: Sir John Soane's Museum, 1999).

Solomon, Susan G., 'Louis Kahn's Buildings for Three Faiths: "Religion...not a religion"', in M. Kries, J. Eisenbrand, and S. Von Moos (eds), *Louis Kahn: The Power of Architecture*, exhibition catalogue (Weil am Rhein: Vitra Design Museum, 2012), pp. 149–63.

Sorensen, Roy, *Seeing Dark Things. The Philosophy of Shadows* (Oxford: Oxford University Press, 2008).

Spuybroek, Lars, *The Sympathy of Things. Ruskin and the Ecology of Design* (Rotterdam: V2, 2011).

Spuybroek, Lars (ed.) *Textile Tectonics* (Rotterdam: NAi, 2011).

Steane, Mary Anne, *The Architecture of Light: Recent Approaches to Designing with Natural Light* (London: Routledge, 2011).

Stebbins, Theodore E., with Ricci, Susan C., 'Charles Eliot Norton: Ruskin's Friend, Harvard's Sage', in T. E. Stebbins and V. Anderson (eds), *The Last Ruskinians: Charles Eliot Norton, Charles Herbert Moore, and Their Circle* (Cambridge, MA: Harvard University Art Museums, 2007), pp. 12–29.

Stein, Roger B., *John Ruskin and Aesthetic Thought in America, 1840–1900* (Cambridge, MA: Harvard University Press, 1967).

Stoichita, Victor I., *A Short History of the Shadow* (London: Reaktion Books, 1997).

Sullivan, Louis H., *The Autobiography of an Idea* (New York: Press of the American Institute of Architects, 1924).

Summerson, John, 'Sir John Soane and the Furniture of Death', in John Summerson (ed.), *The Unromantic Castle and Other Essays* (London: Thames and Hudson, 1990), pp. 121–42, originally published in *Architectural Review*, vol. 163, no. 973 (1978), pp. 147–55.

Summerson, John, 'The Vision of J. M. Gandy', in J. Summerson (ed.), *Heavenly Mansions and Other Essays on Architecture* (London: Cresset Press, 1949), pp. 111–34.

Szarkowski, John, *The Idea of Louis Sullivan* (London: Thames and Hudson, 2000, original work published 1956).

Tanizaki, Junichoro, *In Praise of Shadows*, T. J. Harper and E. G. Seidensticker (trans) (London: Vintage, 2001, original work published 1933–4).

Twitchell, James, *Romantic Horizons. Aspects of the Sublime in English Poetry and Painting, 1770–1850* (Columbia: University of Missouri Press, 1983).

Tyng, Alexandra, *Beginnings. Louis I. Kahn's Philosophy of Architecture* (New York: John Wiley, 1984).

Tzonis, Alexander (ed.), *The Louis I. Kahn Archive Personal Drawings*, 7 vols (New York and London: Garland, 1987).

Unwin, Simon, *Analysing Architecture* (Abingdon, Oxon: Routledge, 2014, 4th ed.).

Upton, Dell, *Architecture in the United States* (Oxford: Oxford University Press, 1998).

Vanbrugh, John, 'Mr Van-Brugg's Proposals about Building ye New Churches' (1712), in Caroline van Eck (ed.), *British Architectural Theory 1540–1750* (Aldershot, Hants.: Ashgate, 2003), pp. 136–8.

Van der Laan, Dom H., *Architectonic Space*, R. Padovan (trans) (Leiden: E. J. Brill, 1983).

Van Zanten, David, 'Schooling the Prairie School: Wright's Early Style as a Communicable System', in R. McCarter (ed.), *On and By Frank Lloyd Wright: A Primer of Architectural Principles* (London: Phaidon, 2011), pp. 116–23.

Vidler, Anthony, *The Architectural Uncanny. Essays in the Modern Unhomely* (Cambridge, MA: MIT Press, 1992).

Walker, David, 'Plasticity at Ronchamp: The Interrelationship of Form and Light and Its Plastic Manifestation', *Architectural Research Quarterly*, vol. 16, no. 4 (December 2012), pp. 349–61.

Walker, Robin Noel, *Shoko-Ken. A Late Medieval Daime Sukiya Style Japanese Tea House* (Abingdon, Oxon: Routledge, 2002).

Walpole, Horace, *The Castle of Otranto. A Gothic Story* (London: J. Edwards, 1791, 6th ed.).

Walpole, Horace, *Description of the Villa of Mr Horace Walpole at Strawberry-Hill near Twickenham, Middlesex*, third edition as part of *The Works of Horatio Walpole*, London 1798 (London: Pallas Athene, 2010).

Warwick, Alexandra, 'Gothic, 1820–1880', in D. Townshend (ed), *Terror and Wonder: The Gothic Imagination* (London: The British Library, 2014), pp. 94–123.

Watkin, David, 'Monuments and Mausolea in the Age of Enlightenment', in Giles Waterfield (ed.), *Soane and Death. The Tombs and Monuments of Sir John Soane* (London: Dulwich Picture Gallery, 1996), pp. 9–25.

Watkin, David, *Sir John Soane. Enlightenment Thought and the Royal Academy Lectures* (Cambridge: Cambridge University Press, 1996).

Weingarden, Lauren S., *Louis H. Sullivan and a 19th-Century Poetics of Naturalized Architecture* (Farnham: Ashgate, 2009).

Whateley, Thomas, *Observations on Modern Gardening* (London: T. Payne, 1770, 2nd ed.).

Whittle, Elisabeth, '"All These Inchanting Scenes": Piercefield in the Wye Valley', *Garden History*, vol. 24, no. 1 (Summer 1996), pp. 148–61.

William, Eurwyn, *The Welsh Cottage. Building Traditions of the Rural Poor, 1750–1900* (Aberystwyth: Royal Commission on the Ancient and Historical Monuments of Wales, 2011).

Wilson, Colin St John, *Architectural Reflections. Studies in the Philosophy and Practice of Architecture* (Manchester: Manchester University Press, 2000, 2nd ed.), Chapter 8 'Sigurd Lewerentz. The Sacred Buildings and the Sacred Sites'.

Wilton-Ely, John, *Piranesi, Paestum and Soane* (Munich, London and New York: Prestel, 2013).

Wotton, Henry, *The Elements of Architecture. A Facsimile Reprint of the First Edition (London, 1624)* (Charlottesville: University Press of Virginia, 1968).

Wren, Christopher, 'Letter of Recommendation to a Friend on the Commission for Building Fifty New Churches' (1711), in Caroline van Eck (ed.), *British Architectural Theory 1540–1750* (Aldershot, Hants.: Ashgate, 2003), pp. 131–35.

Wright, Angela, 'Gothic, 1764–1820', in Dale Townshend (ed.), *Terror and Wonder: The Gothic Imagination* (London: The British Library, 2014), pp. 68–93.

Wurman, Richard Saul, and Feldman, Eugene, *The Notebooks and Drawings of Louis I. Kahn* (Cambridge, MA: MIT Press, 1973, 2nd ed.).

Yates, Frances A., *The Art of Memory* (London: Pimlico, 1992).

Zumthor, Peter, *Atmospheres* (Basel: Birkhäuser, 2006).

Zumthor, Peter, *Thinking Architecture* (Basel: Birkhäuser, 2006, 2nd ed.).

Zumthor, Peter, 'The New Building of the Museum for the Archdiocese, Thoughts on the Design', *Salve* (Prague: Salve, 2011), pp. 139–42.

INDEX

Aboriginal architecture 297–8, 300
Ackergem, Ghent 86
Ackroyd, Peter 35, 36, 74, 83
   Hawksmoor 35, 36
Adam, Robert 95, 98, 99, 100, 122 n.88
   Derby House, London 122 n.88
   Kedleston Hall, Derbyshire 95
Addison, Joseph 81, 129
   association 53, 66, 129
   'On the Pleasures of the Imagination' 53, 54
Adler, Dankmar 170, Fig. 6.12. *See also* Sullivan
Albers, Josef 238
Alberti, Leon Battista 47
   De Re Aedificatoria 14
   Sant' Andrea, Mantua 40, 294, Fig. 3.2
   Tempio Malatestiano, Rimini 61
Alcaeus 209–10
Alinari (Fratelli) 202
Andrews, Michael 133
Antigua 138
Apelles 265
Apollo 246
Appleton, Jay 22, 23, 134, 141
ibn-Arabi 194
Arezzo 3
Aroni
   San Carlone colossus 215
Arte Povera 294
Ashton, Raggatt, McDougall (ARM)
   Australian Institute of Aboriginal Studies and Torres Strait Islander Studies (AIATSIS) 297–8
   Melbourne Recital Centre (MRC) 299
   Melbourne Theatre Company (MTC) 298–9, Fig. 10.8

Baalbek 54
Bachelard, Gaston 15, 16, 19–21, 22
Bacon, Francis 299, 301
   Pope Innocent X 298
Banham, Reyner 14, 242
Bann, Stephen 200
Baroque architecture 9, 13, 30, 83, 85, 256, 273, 302, Chapter 3 *passim*
   definition of 35
   representation of 54–64
   sketches and 70
   theatre and 50–4
Barragán, Luis 226
   Studio House, Tacubaya, Mexico 229
Barry, Charles
   Houses of Parliament, London 151
Bataille, Georges 104
Bates, Donald and Davidson, Peter (LAB Architecture Studio)
   Federation Square, Melbourne 299–301, Fig. 10.9
Bath 45, 148 n.47
   Bath Abbey 44, Fig. 3.5
Baudelaire, Charles 19
Baxandall, Michael
   Shadows and Enlightenment 5, 8
Beaux-Arts 8, 170, 174, 227–8, 230, 234, 240
Beckett, Samuel 299
Beckford, William 117, 125
   Fonthill Abbey 145, Fig. 5.11
   Vatheck 125, 127, 136
Belzoni, Giovanni Battista 94, 111–3
Bender, John 84, 88
Benedict of Nursia 285–7, Figs. 10.1, 10.2
Benedikt, Michael 266, 269, 272, 273

Bentham, Jeremy
  Industry-House Establishment 87
  Panopticon 86–8, 92
Bentley, Richard 130
  Frontispiece to Elegy Written in a Country Churchyard 130, Fig. 5.3
  Hall and Staircase at Strawberry Hill Fig. 5.2
Berkeley, University of California 255–6
Berlin 225
  Jewish Museum 300
Beuys, Joseph 294
Bianca, Stefano 188
Bibiena, Ferdinando 51
Bible 7
  Genesis 6, 238
  Psalms 7
Binet, Hélène 246
Bingham, Joseph 40, 68
al-Biruni
  The Exhaustive Treatise on Shadows 186
Blackburn, William 86
Blondel, Jacques-François 47, 89, 92
  Cours d'Architecture 47
Bloomer, Kent 163
Boffrand, Germain 92
  Livre d'Architecture 88–9
Böhm, Gottfried
  Chapel of the Madonna, Kolumba Museum, Cologne 291–2
Bollnow, Otto Friedrich 16
Bologna 214
  Due Torri 214
Boston 167, 267
  Brattle Square Church 171
Boullée, Étienne-Louis, 66, 93, 94, 226
  Architecture, Essay on Art 93–4, 213
  Funerary Monument 66, 93, 94
  The Palace of Justice 93
Bourdelle, Antoine
  Penelope 268
Bragdon, Claude 172
Bramante, Donato 56
Bristol 148 n.47
  Bristol Channel 13
  St. Philip and St. James's School 164
Bristow, Ian 98

Britton, John 111, 113
  The Union of Architecture, Sculpture, and Painting 111
Brown, Lancelot (Capability) 134
Brown, Richard F. 272
Brunelleschi, Filippo 61
Bruno, Giordano
  Shadows of Ideas 216
Brutalism 240
Buffalo, New York State
  Darwin Martin House 32 n.39, 241
  Guaranty (Prudential) Building 173–6, Fig. 6.14
  William R. Heath House 21–2, Fig. 2.5
Burges, William 172
Burke, Edmund 74, 81, 88, 89, 90–1, 93, 94, 99, 112, 130, 163, 302. *See also* sublime
  Philosophical Enquiry into the Sublime and Beautiful 81–3
Bushell, Thomas 125
Butades 6, 265
Butterfield, William
  St. Paul's Cathedral, Melbourne 299
Byzantine architecture 42, 67, 200, 215, 254, 277 n.86

Cadwell, Michael 256, 267
Cairo
  Mosque of Amr 185
camera obscura. *See* shadow
Canaletto 210
Capri
  Casa Malaparte 284
Caravaggio 202
Carbis Bay, Cornwall 204
Cardiff, Wales
  St. Fagans National History Museum 14–15, 16–17, 20–1, Figs. 2.1, 2.2, 2.4
Carpaccio, Vittore 200, 216, 302
  Vision of St. Augustine 216, 220
Carter, Paul
  Nearamnew 300
Casati, Roberto 9, 109, 294
  Shadows 9
Casey, Edward 19
Cast, David 53, 54

Castelfranco 202. *See also* Giorgione
Cézanne, Paul 236
character, *architecture parlante* 66, 88–94, 97, 98, 99, 101, 106, 109, 120 n.39, 164
Charles II 62
Chaucer, Geoffrey 17
Cheere, Sir Henry 74
Chepstow 125, 132, 136, 139, 143, 147 n.27
   Chepstow Castle 136, 145
Chicago. *See also* Sullivan; Wright
   Chicago Auditorium 170, Fig. 6.12
   Columbian World's Fair 23
   Lake Michigan 176
   Robie House 22
   Schlesinger Mayer (Carson, Pirie, Scott) Building 173
   Unity Temple, Oak Park 252
   Wright House and Studio, Oak Park 23
Chirico, Giorgio de 7, 213, 214, 217
   The Mystery and Melancholy of a Street 7, 213
Choando 29–30
Chute, John 130
Claesson, Koivisto, Rune
   Sfera Building, Kyoto 301–2, Fig. 10.10
Claude Glass (Mirror) 133, 144–5, 147 n.27, Fig. 5.10
Clayton and Bell 53
Clérisseau, Charles-Louis 110
Coldwell, Paul 214
Coleridge, Samuel Taylor 168
collage 54, 168, 211–12, 217, 297. *See also* fragmentation
Collins, Peter 174
Cologne. *See also* Zumthor
   'Bruder Klaus' Chapel, Wachendorf 288–90, Figs. 10.3, 10.4
   Cathedral 292
   Kolumba Diocesan Museum 288, 291–4, Fig. 10.5
Comlogan, Dumfies 258
Constantine the Great 42, 47, 95
Copland, Frank
   Section of the Dome area 106, Fig. 4.11

Le Corbusier 226, 236
   Ronchamp Chapel 236, 243–5, Fig. 9.8
   Villa Savoye 244, 297
   La Tourette 236, 245, 246
   Unité d'Habitation, Marseilles 238
   Vers une Architecture 238
Corrodi, Michelle 9
Costa, Cesare 217
Coventry 45
Coxe, William 138, 141
   Historical Tour in Monmouthshire 136, Fig. 5.7
Cozens, John R. 264
Crary, Jonathan 48, 50, 76 n.48, 110
Cret, Paul 226, 227
Cruikshank, George 232–4, 243
   Jeanie, I say, Jeanie, woman 232–4, Fig. 9.1
Curl, James Stevens 65
Curtis, William 273

Dacca
   National Assembly Building 248, 249
daguerrotypes 204
Dance, George 84, 85
   Newgate Prison 84–6, Fig. 4.2
Darley, Gillian 99, 117
Davey, Peter 301
deconstruction 217, 266, 272, 298, 299
Defoe, Daniel 37
Delorme, Philibert 61
Denmark 4, 292
Desprez, Louis-Jean
   Tomb of Agamemnon 95
Diana 263, 264
Dickens, Charles 167, 235
   Oliver Twist 232
Dickinson, William 37
digital design 273, 297, 298, 299
Dionysus 245
Divitiis, Bianca de 97
Downes, Kerry 51, 56, 59, 78 n.76
drawing, representation of shadow 5, 6, 8, 47, 54–64, 67, 70, 90, 92, 95, 98, 110, 122 n.88, 145, 152, 153, 155, 156, 159–63, 165, 167, 185, 211–14, 227, 227–8, 243, 258, 259, 265–6, 273, 283,

294, 297, 302. *See also* Claude Glass; perspectivity; shadow; shadow/camera obscura; shadow/skiagraphy
    drawing-as-building 226, 231, 232–7, 250 (*see also* Kahn)
    engraving, etching, aquatinting 19, 90, 133, 232–4, 243
    wash-shading 56, 62–4
Du Prey, Pierre de la Ruffinière 67, 120 n.54

East Drayton, Nottinghamshire 46
Eastlake, Charles 163
    A History of the Gothic Revival 163
Edinburgh
    St. Leonard's 233
Edward VI 36
Edwards, Edward 96
Egypt 95, 104, 236, 259
    Luxor 233, Fig. 9.3
    Pyramids 53, 236, 238
    Saqqara stepped pyramid 236
    Seti I sarcophagus 104, 112, 117, 124 n.134, 124 n.135, Fig. 4.13
    Valley of the Kings 112
Eisenman, Peter 211, 214
Eliade, Mircea 254
Eliot, Thomas Stearns
    The Love Song of J. Alfred Prufrock 35
    The Waste Land 35
Elizabeth I 36, 43
Emerson, Ralph Waldo 170, 172, 227
    Nature 168, 231
enlightenment reason and shadow 36, 81, 83, 87, 94, 112, 117, 127, 225, 302
Enstone, Oxfordshire 125
Esfahan, Iran 186–95
    Bazars 188–93, Figs. 7.7, 7.8, 7.9, 7.11
    Dardasht quarter 188–94
    Friday Mosque 186, 188, 190, 191, 195, Figs. 7.5, 7.9
    Imam Mosque 188, Fig. 7.6
    Maydan Imam 186, 192, Figs. 7.7, 7.9
    Shaykh Lotfollah Mosque 188
    Zayandah River 186
Etlin, Richard 176
Eumenides 14
Eusebius 40, 42
Evans, Robin 92
Evelyn, John 36, 54

Fehn, Sverre 7, 15
Feldman, Eugene 233, Figs. 9.2, 9.3
Ferris, Hugh
    Zoning ordinances. Crude Clay for Architects 295–6, Fig. 10.7
Feuerstein, Marcia 100, 122 n.95
Florence
    Baptistery 174
    Brancacci Chapel 7, 292
    Casa Vasari 6
Forty, Adrian 89
Foucault, Michel 87–8, 127
    Discipline and Punish 87
    Madness and Civilization 127
fragmentation 57, 85, 95, 98, 110, 113, 125, 130, 136, 202, 211–12, 217, 236, 291, 300. *See also* collage
Frampton, Kenneth 265, 267
Francesca, Piero della
    Restitution of the Cross to Jerusalem, Arezzo 3–4
Francis I 127
Frazer, Sir James
    The Golden Bough 263
Fréart de Chambray, Roland
    A Parallel of the Ancient Architecture with the Modern 54
Freud, Sigmund 199, 200, 201, 207, 211, 302
    'Formulations on Two Principles of Mental Functioning' 206
Fujiwara no Teika 30
Fuller, Peter 206
Furness, Frank 170, 172, 227, 242, 302
    Bloomfield H. Moore House 171
    Guarantee Trust and Safe Deposit Building 172
    Pennsylvania Academy of the Fine Arts 168–70, 174, 227, Fig. 6.11
Furness, William Henry 168, 170

INDEX

Gainsborough, Thomas
  Study of a man sketching, holding a Claude Glass Fig. 5.10
Gandy, Joseph Michael 89–90, 95–6, 110, 206. *See also* Soane
  Architectural visions of early fancy 90
  Bank of England rotunda 100
  Breakfast Room, Pitzhanger Manor 95–6, 98, Fig. 4.5
  Dome area by lamplight 117, Fig. 4.15
  Eight Soane designs for churches 117, Fig. 4.16
  Tomb of Merlin 117
geology and architecture 200, 285, 288, 299. *See also* Ruskin; Stokes
  carving-modelling 60–1
  incrustation 174, 200, 207, 210, 284
  stratification 284–5, 299
Geraghty, Anthony 54, 62
al-Ghazzali 194
Giacometti, Alberti 289
Gibraltar 95
Gilly, Friedrich 100
Gilpin, William 131–3, 136, 138, 145, 147 n.27
  Observations on the River Wye 131, 132, Fig. 5.4
Giorgione 110, 202
  Madonna, Child and Two Saints 202
  The Tempesta 202
Glover, Nicola 200
Godwin, E. W.
  Northampton Town Hall 164
  St. Philip and St. James's School, Bristol 164
Goethe, Johann Wolfgang von 89, 268, 294
Goldhagen, Sarah 259
Gombrich, Ernst 8
Goodrich Castle 132
Gothic architecture 43, 56, 64, 74, 117, 151, 163, 164, 172, 200, 291, 292, Chapter 5 *passim*, Fig. 6.10
  Gothic(k) 125, 127, 130, 145–6, 151, 302, Figs. 5.1, 5.2, 5.11
  Gothic novel 87–8, 125, 127, 136, Fig. 5.6

Gothic Revival 129, 151, 152, 302
Gothic ruin 130, Figs. 5.3, 5.4, 5.5 (*see also* shadow/*ruinenlust*)
Gothic Survival 36
Venetian Gothic 152–4, Figs. 6.1, 6.3
Gray, Thomas 130
  Elegy Written in a Country Churchyard 130, Fig. 5.3
Gray, William F. 235
Greece 6, 41, 42, 45, 63, 67, 81, 90, 92, 95, 98, 100, 101, 117, 181, 230, 231, 233, 236, 240, 254, 259, 284
  Parthenon 151, 164, 236
  Temple of Minerva, Athens 112
  Tower of the Winds, Athens 70
Gregory, John Mack 95
Grelot, Guillaume-Joseph 42
Grounds, Roy
  National Gallery of Victoria, Melbourne 299

Hanging Gardens, Babylon 53
Harbison, Robert 59, 70
Hardouin-Mansart, Jules 62
Hardwick Hall, Derbyshire 43
Harris, John 62
Hart, Vaughan 67
Harvard University 167
Hawkes, Dean 9
Hawksmoor, Nicholas 84, 85, 91, 284, 302, Chapter 3 *passim*. *See also* Vanbrugh; Wren
  All Saint's Church, Northampton 45–6, Fig. 3.6
  Basilica after the Primitive Christians 42
  Bath Abbey (drawing) 44–5, Fig. 3.5
  Blenheim Palace 59, 62, 90
  Castle Howard 59, 62
  Chapell Barr, Nottingham (drawing) 43–4, Fig. 3.4
  Christ Church, Spitalfields, London 59–61, Figs. 3.1, 3.13
  Nottingham Prospect (drawing) 43–4, Fig. 3.3
  St. Anne's Limehouse, London 64–74, Figs. 3.17, 3.19, 3.20, 3.21, 3.22

St. Augustine, Watling St, London 64, Fig. 3.16
St. George in the East, London 64–74, Fig. 3.18
St. George's Bloomsbury, London 48, 50–4, Figs. 3.7, 3.8, 3.9, 3.10
St. John, Horsleydown, London 70
St. Mary, Warwick 56, Fig. 3.11
St. Mary Woolnoth, London 35
St. Paul's Cathedral, London 56–9, Fig. 3.12
Whitehall Palace, London 62, Fig. 3.14
Hays, Michael 214
Heath, Charles 139, 141, 143
Heidegger, Martin 19, 265
Henderson, Nigel 240
Herefordshire, England 132
Hickes, George 40, 42
Hildebrand, Grant 22
Hiorns, Roger 143
Hofland, Barbara 103, 104, 113
Home, Henry (Lord Kames) 99
Homer 149 n.61
Hope, Thomas 97
  Household Furniture and Interior Decoration 97, 98
Horace 5
  Ars Poetica 89
Howard, John 86
Howard, William 67
Humphreys, Richard 132

Iller, Le Cavalier 204
Iran 176, 181, 186, 269. *See also* Esfahan
Istanbul 2, 292
Istria (stone of) 200, 202, 204, 288

Japan 21–3, 226, 288, 297, 301–2
  Kyoto 25, 30
  Daisen-in temple 25–6, Fig. 2.7
  Daitoku-ji Zen temple complex 25–6, 28
  Katsura Palace 29
  Koto-in temple 26–31, Figs. 2.8, 2.9, 2.10, 2.11
  Ryoanji Zen garden 25
  Sfera Building 301–2, Fig. 10.10

Jencks, Charles 299, 301
Jerusalem 3, 4, 42, 185, 195–7
  Solomon's Temple 47
John of the Cross 47, 50
Jones, Inigo
  Banqueting House, London 62
Jordy, William H. 242
Josephson, Hans 289
Jung, Carl 211

Kahn, Louis I. 9, 19, 170, 193, 283, 284, 285, 288, 292, 301, 302, Chapter 9 *passim*
  Abstract of Planes and Steps (drawing) 238
  Abstract of Planes with Landscape Elements, No 1 238
  Adele Levy Memorial Playground, New York 262
  Carcassonne, 1959 (drawing) 235–6, 243, 258, Fig. 9.4
  Erdman Hall, Bryn Mawr College, Philadelphia 258
  Kimbell Art Museum, Fort Worth, Texas 226, 256, 262–73, 280 n.182, Figs. 9.22, 9.23, 9.24, 9.25, 9.26, 9.27, 9.28, 9.29
  Luxor, 1951 (drawing) 233, Fig. 9.3
  Margaret Esherick House, Chestnut Hill, Philadelphia 245–7, 248, 250, Fig. 9.9
  Morton and Leonore Weiss House 249
  National Assembly Building, Dacca 248, 249
  Phillips Exeter Academy, Library, New Hampshire 258
  Richards Medical Research Building and Biology Building, University of Pennsylvania, Philadelphia 170, 241–4, 284, Fig. 9.7
  Rochester, First Unitarian Church 226, 245, 251–62, 267, 269, Figs. 9.14, 9.15, 9.16, 9.17, 9.18, 9.19, 9.20, 9.21
  Ronchamp Chapel, 1959 (drawing) 236, 243–5, Fig. 9.8
  Salk Institute, La Jolla, California 226, 228, 229, 274 n.11

INDEX

San Gimignano (watercolour) 242
'Silence and Light' 225, 226, 228–32, 235–6, 238, 254, 256, 267
Trenton Bath House, New Jersey 225, 228, 238, 240–2, 246, 254, 256, Fig. 9.6
Tribune Review Publishing Company Building, Greensburg, Pennsylvania 247–51, 271, Figs. 9.10, 9.11, 9.12
Yale Center for British Art 238, 267, 270
Yale University Art Gallery 238–40, 242, 254, 256, 267, Fig. 9.5
Kalman, Harold 86
Kaufman, Edward 167
Khan, Adam 143
Kirkstall Abbey 156, 159, 167, Fig. 6.5
Klein, Melanie 200, 201, 206, 207–8, 211, 216–7
 'Our Adult World and its Roots in Infancy' 207
Knight, Richard Payne
 The Landscape 134
Komendant, August E. 229, 242, 256
Koslofsky, Craig 8, 13, 36, 53
Kurokawa, Kisho 25, 30

Laan, Dom Hans van der 285, 287
 Architectonic Space 285
 St. Benedictusberg Abbey, Vaals, Netherlands 285–7, Figs. 10.1, 10.2
Landow, George P. 164
Langley, Batty 47
Larsen, Jack Lenor 254
Laud, William 36, 37, 38, 47
Laugier, Marc-Antoine 284
 Essai sur L'Architecture 91
Lecat, Claude-Nicholas 5
Ledoux, Claude-Nicolas 93, 99, 100, 226
Lerberge, P. Van
 Interior View of Tintern Abbey 134–5, Fig. 5.5
LeRoy, Julien-David 89, 120 n.52
Levine, Jessica 105

Lewerentz, Sigurd 1–5, 10 n.14, 181
 Chapel of the Resurrection, Stockholm 2
 St. Peter's Church, Klippan 1–5, 181, Fig. 1.1
Lewis, Michael 243
Liebeskind, Daniel
 Jewish Museum, Berlin 300
Lobell, John 226
Locarno 215
Locke, John 53, 81, 99, 143, 167
 Essay Concerning Human Understanding 50, 216
Lombardo (Pietro, Tullio, Amado) 204
London 36, 37, Chapter 3 *passim*. See also Hawksmoor; Soane; Wren
 Banqueting House, Whitehall 62
 Central Criminal Court, Old Bailey 84
 daylighting codes 296
 Derby House 122 n.88
 Great Exhibition (1851) 284
 Hawksmoor's London churches (*see* Hawksmoor, Chapter 3 *passim*)
 Houses of Parliament 151
 housing estate (1960s) 143
 Institute of Contemporary Arts (ICA) 240
 light and climate of 36, 61, 62, 84, 104
 Newgate Prison 84–6
 Port of London 37
 River Thames 127, 129, 143
 Royal Academy of Arts 95, 96, 101, 105, 106, 110, 112, 120 n.52
 Soane's London projects (*see* Soane, Chapter 4 *passim*)
 Strawberry Hill, Twickenham 127–30, Fig. 5.2. (*see also* Walpole)
 Student Centre, London School of Economics (LSE) 294–5, 297, Fig. 10.6
 William Saunderson's House, Greenwich 62–4, Fig. 3.15
 Wren's London projects. (*see* Wren)
Longhi, Roberto 4
Longinus
 On the Sublime 81

Lorraine, Claude 110, 111, 129, 133, 144, 145, 147 n.27, 264, Fig. 5.10
  Seaport with the Embarkation of the Queen of Sheba 110
Loutherbourg, Philippe Jacques de
  Coalbrookdale by Night 132
  Eidophusikon 132
Lucca 152, 156, 157–8, 159
  San Frediano 152, 156, 159, 167, Fig. 6.4
  San Michele in Foro 152, 153, 159, Figs. 6.6, 6.7, 6.8
  Santa Maria Foris-Portam 159
Lukacher, Brian 117
Lundy Island 13
Lutyens, Sir Edwin 186

Macaulay, Rose 130
Mahler, Gustav 229
Maillet, Arnaud 50, 145
Maillol, Aristide
  L'Air 269, Fig. 9.26
Malraux, André
  Voices of Silence 236–7, 239
Mann, Horace 129
Mann, Thomas 229
Marc, Olivier 15, 254
Marcus, George 245, 246
Masaccio
  St. Peter Healing the Sick 7, 292
Massachusetts Institute of Technology, Cambridge, MA 170
McCarter, Robert 21, 23, 246
McGoodwin, Henry 8
Mecca 186, 195
Medina 186
Mediterranean 25, 238, 243
Melbourne
  Federation Square 299–301, Fig. 10.9
  Flinders St. 299
  Flinders Station 299
  Melbourne Recital Centre (MRC) 299
  Melbourne Theatre Company (MTC) 298–9
  National Gallery of Victoria 299
  St. Paul's Cathedral 299
  Yarra River 299
Mendelssohn, Bertha (mother of Louis I. Kahn) 229

Menneckes, Friedhelm 293–4
Merlin 117
Merrill, Michael 248
Mexico. *See* Barragán
Meyers, Marshall 265, 266
Mézières, Nicolas Le Camus de 96, 105–6
  The Genius of Architecture 105–6
Middleton, Robin 90, 105, 122 n.88
Mies van der Rohe 240, 242
Milan
  Gallaratese housing 213–4, Fig. 8.6
Milner, Marion 200
Milosz, O. V. de L. 21
Milton, John 130, 138–9
Modena
  San Cataldo Cemetery 211, 217, 297, Figs. 8.5, 8.8
Modulor 285
Monet, Claude
  Rouen Cathedral series 255
Monge, Gaspard 61
Monmouth 132, 139
Moore, Charles 24, 301
Morandi, Giorgio 214, 217, 285
More, Thomas 48
Morris, Robert 134
Morris, Valentine (Colonel) 138
Morris, Valentine 136, 138, 139, 148 n.47
Muhammad 183, 186
Murray, David 8

New York City 167, 294–6
  Adele Levy Memorial Playground 262
  Manhattan 294
  Museum of Modern Art (MOMA) 259, 262
  National Academy of Design 168
  zoning ordinances 295–6, Fig. 10.7
Newton, Sir Isaac 268
Nicholson, Frances
  The Practice of Drawing and Painting from Nature, in Water Colours 145
Nikolaus of Flüe ('Bruder Klaus') 288–90, Figs. 10.3, 10.4
Nippur 181

Nizami Ganjavi
  Haft Paykar 195
Noguchi, Isamu 264
  Adele Levy Memorial Playground, New York 262
  Constellation (for Louis Kahn) 262, Fig. 9.22
nomadic cultures 14, 182, Figs. 7.2, 7.3
Norberg-Schulz, Christian 4, 181, 182, 188, 254
Normandy
  St. Lô 165–7, 168, Fig. 6.10
Northampton 45
  All Saint's Church 45, Fig. 3.6
  Northampton Town Hall 164
Norton, Charles Eliot 167, 168
Nottingham Fig. 3.3
  Chapell Barr 43, Fig. 3.4
  Nottingham Castle 43
  Wollaton Hall 43

Odin 4
O'Donnell, Sheila 213
O'Donnell (Sheila) and Tuomey (John)
  Student Centre, London School of Economics (LSE) 294–5, 297, Fig. 10.6
Oman, Sultanate of 182–5, Fig. 7.1
  Jabal al-Akhdar 182
  Jabal al-Sharqiya 182
  Muslimat 182, Fig. 7.4
  Nakhl 182
  Nizwa 182
  Wadi al Hawasinah Fig. 7.2
  Wadi al Ma'awil Fig. 7.3
ornament 6, 38, 40, 92, 99, 111, 127, 163, 172, 174, 227, 246, 247, 250, 266, 302. *See also* geology; shadow/shadow-gap
Orpheus 245
Otterlo, Holland 242, 243, 250, 258
Ottoman architecture 292
Oxford 45, 46, 156
  Christ Church 156
  Oxford Museum 168

Paestum 89, 90, 112, 238, 289, Fig. 4.3
Palladio, Andrea 47, 216
  Basilica, Vicenza 210
  Palazzo Chiericati, Vicenza 210
  Palazzo Thiene, Vicenza 85
  Rialto Bridge Project, Venice 210
  Villa Rotonda, Vicenza 216
Pallasmaa, Juhani 46
Paolozzi, Eduardo 239–40
Parma 210
Pater, Walter 200
Pattison, Harriet 243, 245, 264
Patton, George 264
Paulson, Ronald 134
Pauly, Danièle 229
Peña, Skene Catling de la
  Flint House, Buckinghamshire 284–5
Pérez-Gómez, Alberto 48, 50
Perrault, Claude
  Louvre, Paris 89
perspectivity 7, 30, 35, 44, 45, 47, 51, 56, 57, 62, 64, 65, 84, 89, 90, 96, 98, 117, 121 n.75, 129, 133, 151, 178 n.32, 196, 246, 265, 266, 271, 296, Figs. 4.5, 4.16, 5.2, 7.15, 9.9, 9.24. *See also* shadow/skiagraphy
Peter, St. 7, 292
Petherbridge, Deanna 6, 119 n.11
Pevsner, Nikolaus 42, 100
Philadelphia, Pennsylvania 170, 171, 172, 226, 227, 264, 268. *See also* Furness; Kahn
  Central High School 227
  Erdman Hall, Bryn Mawr College 258
  Esherick House, Chestnut Hill 246–8, 250, Fig. 9.9
  Pennsylvania Academy of Fine Art 168–70, Fig. 6.11
  Philadelphia Museum of Art 226
  Public Industrial Art School 227
  Richards Medical Research Building and Biology Building 241–3, 246, Fig. 9.7
picturesque 9, 98–9, 104, 111, 112, 125, 130–45, 156, 159, 164, 172, 210, 226, 301, 302. *See also* Gilpin; Ruskin
  lower and noble 154–6, Fig. 6.2
Piercefield (Persfield) House and grounds, Monmouthshire 125, 134, 136–43, 135, 148 n.47, Figs. 5.7, 5.8, 5.9

326   INDEX

Piles, John 100
Piranesi, Giovanni Battista 66, 130, 136, 271, 289, 296, Chapter 4 *passim*
   Carceri 84–6, 111, 136
   Hadrian's Villa, Tivoli 98
   Tempio della Tosse, Tivoli 98
   Vedute di Roma 85, 91
   Vue de Pesto 90–1, Fig. 4.3
Pisa 284, 299
Plato 7, 42, 87, 143, 193, 230. *See also* shadow/caves
   The Republic 7
Pliny the Elder 6, 7, 8
Plummer, Henry 25, 285
Pompeii 99, 117
Pope, Alexander 141, 143, 149 n.61
Postmodernism 217, 298
Pozzo, Andrea 47
   Perspectiva Pictorum et Architectorum 51
Price, Sir Uvedale 155
Prout, Samuel 152, 155, 156
   Kirkstall Abbey 159
psychoanalysis, psychology 5, 9, 14, 15, 19, 36, 50, 81, 82, 87, 88, 135, 146, 254, 302, Chapter 8 *passim. See also* Freud; Klein; Rossi; Stokes
   analogical architecture 193, 210–12, 214, 215 (*see also* Rossi)
   infantile unconscious 200–1, 215, 207–8
   paranoid-schizoid and depressive positions 199, 207–8, 215, 217
   psycho-geography 66
   topoanalysis 19
   unconscious 9, 149 n.61, 302, Chapter 8 *passim*
Pugin, A. W. N. 151, 152, 167
   Houses of Parliament, London 151
   School, Whitwick, Leicestershire 151

R.T. 47, 48
   De Templis 36, 47–8
Radcliffe, Ann 87
Ragghianti, Carlo Ludovico 214
Rembrandt 174, 202, 204, 237, 251, Fig. 9.13

Renaissance architecture 57, 61, 65, 127 (*see also* Baroque)
   Early Renaissance 199, 200, 202, 258, 260, 263, Figs. 8.2, 8.7
   'Quattro Cento' 199, 200, 217 (*see also* Stokes)
Rice University, Houston, Texas 255, 267
Richardson, Charles James
   Upper part of the Breakfast Room 107, Fig. 4.12
   View of part of the Collection of Antiquities 113, Fig. 4.13
Richardson, Henry Hobson 20
   Brattle Square Church, Boston 171
Robert, Hubert
Project for the Transformation of the Louvre 104
Robespierre, Maximilien 93
Rocky Mountains 296
Rococo architecture 64, 272
Romanesque architecture 63, 70, 117, 152, 159, 170, 171, 236, 277 n.86, 284, 292, 299, Figs. 6.6, 6.7, 6.8
Romano, Giulio 85
Rome 37, 59, 61, 85, 90, 92, 134, 168
   Alban Hills 263
   American Academy 236
   Aurelian Wall 65
   Campo de' Fiori 216
   Catacombs 2, 48, 66, 67, 91, 95, 97, 104, 113, 124 n.136
   Colosseum 51, 54, 134
   Hadrian's Villa, Tivoli 98
   Il Gesù 59
   Lake Nemi 264
   Ostia Antica 247
   Pantheon 53, 54
   Tempio della Tosse, Tivoli 98
   Theatre of Marcellus 51
   Tomb of Cecilia Metella 91, 92
   Tomb of Gaius Cestius 65
   Via Appia 91
   Villa Negroni 98
Romney, George 119 n.11
Rosa, Salvator 129
Rosen, Charles 136
Ross-on-Wye 132

Rossi, Aldo 284, 291, 297, 302,
  Chapter 8 *passim*
  Analogous Composition 210, 212,
    Fig. 8.4
  L'Architecture Assasinée 211–2
  The Architecture of the City 214,
    301
  Domestic Architecture 214
  Gallaratese Housing, Milan 213–5,
    Fig. 8.6
  San Cataldo Cemetery, Modena
    211, 217, 297, Figs. 8.5, 8.8
  A Scientific Autobiography 208,
    214, 216
  Teatro del Mondo 208–10, 214,
    215–6, 217, 302, Figs. 8.3, 8.4
Roth, Joseph 225
Rothko, Mark 206, 265
Rouen Cathedral 130, 255
Rowlandson, Thomas 125
  *Tour of Dr Syntax in Search of the
    Picturesque* 125
Royal Institute of British Architects
  (RIBA) 284
Ruskin, John 146, 199, 200, 204, 207,
  210, 227, 241, 242, 292, 297,
  299, 302
  Chapter 6 *passim. See also* geology;
    Gothic; ornament; sublime;
    Turner
  Elements of Drawing 165, 223
  *Examples of the Architecture of
    Venice* 204
  *Lectures on Architecture and
    Painting* 174
  Modern Painters 1, 152, 155, 156,
    159, 164, 178 n.33, n.40,
    Figs. 6.2, 6.9
  Palazzo Contarini-Fasan
    (watercolour) 156, Fig. 6.3
  The Poetry of Architecture 302
  San Frediano, Lucca (watercolour)
    152, 156, 159, 167, Fig. 6.4
  San Michele in Foro, Lucca
    (watercolour, 1845) 152, 153,
    159, Fig. 6.6
  San Michele in Foro, Lucca
    (watercolour, 1846) 152, 153,
    159, Fig. 6.7
  Seven Lamps of Architecture 9,
    151–4, 159, 163–5, 168, 226,
    Fig. 6.8
  Sketchbook 4, 1846 (pocket-book)
    152–4, Fig. 6.1
  St. Lô, Normandy (graphite and
    wash) 165–7, Fig. 6.10
  Stones of Venice 151–4, 159, 163–8,
    173–4, 199–200, 207, 210,
    283–4, Fig. 6.13
Ruskin, John James (father to Ruskin,
  John) 152, 199
Rykwert, Joseph 41

Salisbury Cathedral 42
San Gimignano 242
Sansovino, Jacopo 216
Scamozzi, Bertotti 61
Scamozzi, Vincenzo 216
  Villa Bardellini 216
Scarpa, Carlo 292
Schaik, Leon van 297
Schiller, Friedrich 268
Schopenhauer, Arthur 193, 226–7,
  229–32, 238, 246, 256, 260,
  262
  The World as Will and Idea 227
Schumann-Bacia, Eva 99
Scott, Walter 234
  The Heart of Midlothian 233,
    Fig. 9.1
Scully, Vincent 209, 236, 240, 242,
  254, 256
Sedlmayer, Hans 254
Segal, Hannah 200, 208
Semper, Gottfried 284, 297
  Style 283–4
Sen no Rikyu 28, 29, 30
Serlio, Sebastiano 47
Sestri 152
Severn River 132, 141
shadow
  attached 2, 5, 109
  camera obscura and 48, 50, 53,
    76 n.48, 81, 110, 143, 145, 216
  cast 2, 3, 5, 6, 7, 8, 9, 14, 21, 23,
    30, 35, 56, 61, 62, 64, 96, 109,
    111, 117, 130, 152, 156, 173,
    174, 217, 226, 230, 241, 243,

247, 256, 259, 268, 272, 287, 292, 294, 297, 301, 302
catacombs, crypts and 2, 16, 47–8, 54, 66, 67, 91, 95, 97, 104, 111–7, 124 n.136, n.138, 156, 86, Figs. 3.7, 6.5
caves and 2, 4, 7, 15, 21, 22, 23, 24, 25, 40, 48, 64, 67, 87, 95, 125, 134, 139, 141, 143, 145, 149 n.61, 167, 178 n.40, 193, 199, 206–8, 230, 237, 239, 241, 243, 254, 286, 288, 289, Fig. 5.8
chiaroscuro 35, 57, 61, 67, 111, 112, 117, 129, 134, 152, 153, 156, 172, 202, 203, 217, 226, 256, 258, 259, 296
colour and 19, 30, 98, 109–11, 129, 134, 145, 164, 167, 194–5, 202, 262–71, 285, 294, Fig. 9.26
definitions of 2–3, 5–7, 109, 159–64
filters and 6, 94, 109–11, 145
forests and 2, 4, 23, 87, 90, 93, 138, 141, 174, 176, 178 n.40, 186, 195, 226, 264
gloomth and 9, Chapter 5 *passim*
grottoes and 15, 40, 95, 125, 141–3, 145, 149 n.61, 284, 289, Fig. 5.9
groves and 22, 138, 149 n.61, 167, 178 n.40, 186, 196, 262–4, 266, 273 Fig. 9.23
hearth and 9, 13, 14–18, 20, 21, 22, 24, 32 n.39, 182, 284
hermitages and 125, 129, 141
as holes in light 5
lumière mystérieuse and 96, 105–7, 109–11, 113, 268, 302
mysticism and 13, 47–50, 83, 97, 230, 288
nocturnal culture and 13, 18, 36, 47, 53, 105, 117, 130, 134, 136, 283
penumbra 14, 96, 104, 107, 109, 111, 271, 293
primitive hut and 4, 13, 14, 22, 30, 91, 95, 284
prisons and 7, 225, 230, Chapter 4 *passim*
ruinenlust and 130–6
self-shadows 5, 64, 87, 88, 252

sfumato and 110
shade, *ombra, ombre* 2–3, 6, 14, 26, 28, 53, 57, 58, 64, 89, 100, 106, 107, 109, 111, 122 n.88, 129, 138, 139, 152, 163, 164, 167, 178 n.40, 181, 182–5, 186, 188, 191, 192, 202, 215, 228, 229, 240, 250, 259, 262, 265, 268–9, 284, 285, 288, 299, 302, Fig. 7.9
shading 2, 5, 6, 19, 56, 61, 62, 65, 67, 112, 130
shadow-gap /groove /joint /reveal 99–102, 122 n.95, 235, 242, 248–50, Figs. 4.7, 4.8, 9.11, 9.29, 272
skiagraphy and 8, 61, 216, 266
specular, glinting and 23, 30, 104, 107, 141, 154, 189, 264, 266, 288–9
standing-stones and 7, 262, 273, 288, 289, Fig. 9.22
stoas and 217, 231, 262–4, 273, Fig. 8.8
theatre and 7, 36, 50–4, 96, 112, 113, 117, 208–10, 216, 298, Figs. 8.3, 8.4, 10.8
womb and 15, 16, 215
Shelley, Mary
Frankenstein 127
Shute, John 61
Sickert, Richard
Venice, the Rialto Bridge and the Palazzo Camerlenghi 271
Sims, Henry Augustus 172
Sinclair, Ian 35
Lud Heat 66
Sironi, Mario 214, 217
Smith, Christopher 305 n.44
Smithson, Alison and Peter 185, 195–7, 256
Damascus Gate, Jerusalem 185, 195–7, Figs. 7.14, 7.15
Kuwait Urban Study 185
Soami 25
Soane, Eliza 96
Soane, Sir John 9, 66, 125, 130, 134, 141, 206, 249, 268, 284, 302, Chapter 4 *passim*
Bank of England, London 99–100

Church designs, London 117, Fig. 4.16
Dulwich Picture Gallery 94
Male Penitentiary, London 92–4, Fig. 4.4
Philippe Jacques de Loutherbourg monument, Chiswick 102
Piercefield House, Monmouthshire 134, 139
Pitzhanger Manor, Ealing, London 94–9, 101–2, Figs. 4.5, 4.6, 4.8
13 Lincoln's Inn Fields 102–118, 125, Figs. 4.9, 4.10, 4.11, 4.12, 4.13, 4.14, 4.14, 5.1
Triumphal Bridge 90
Tyringham, Buckinghamshire 100–1, Fig. 4.7
Socrates 228
Sorensen, Roy 9, 107, 109
Spechtenhauser, Klaus 9
Split
   Diocletian's Palace 214
Spuybroek, Lars 155, 297
Stanfield, Clarkson 155, Fig. 6.2
Stein, Roger B. 173
Stella, Claudine Bouzonnet
   La veillée à la ferme pendant l'hiver 18, Fig. 2.3
Sterne, Laurence
   A Sentimental Journey 84
Stoichita, Victor I.
   A Short History of the Shadow 8, 11 n.25
Stokes, Adrian 61, 302, Chapter 8 *passim*
   Art and Science 61
   'Concerning Art and Metapsychology' 206
   Invitation in Art 212, 217
   'Living in Ticino' 215
   Smooth and Rough 199, 207, 216
   Stones of Rimini 60, 199, 288
   Sunrise in the West 202
   Venice 201, 202, 217, 220, 221 n.19, Figs. 8.1, 8.2, 8.7
Stonehenge 285
Stowe, Buckinghamshire 134
Street, George Edmund 172
   St. John's Church, Howsham 167

Sturgis, Russell
   Farnham Hall, Yale University 163
Styx 289
sublime 9, 13, 66, 74, 130, 143, 152, 155, 156, 159, 163, 206, 254, 296, 302, Chapter 4 *passim*
   Burke and 81–3
   caves and 167, 178 n.40, 206–7 (*see also* shadow/caves)
   definition of 81
   industrial 132
   nocturnal 134–6 (*see also* shadow/nocturnal culture)
   parasitical 164–7, Fig. 6.9
   slavery and 148 n.47
Sullivan, Louis 170–6, 227, 302
   Autobiography of an Idea 170
   Chicago Auditorium Building 170–1, 174
   Guaranty Building, Buffalo, NY 173–6, Fig. 6.14
   Kindergarten Chats 174
   A System of Architectural Ornament 227
   'The Tall Office Building Artistically Considered' 173
Summerson, John 94, 95, 96, 102, 112
Suvée, Joseph-Benoit 6
Sweden, 1
Symonds Yat, Wye River 132
Szarkowski, John 170, Fig. 6.12

Tadaoki, Hosokawa 28, 30
Tadd, James Liberty 227, 228, 233
Tanizaki, Junichiro 24, 25, 30, 288, 289, 301
   In Praise of Shadows 8, 24, 181, 301
Team X 242, 243, 250
Teyssot, Georges 105
Thomas, George 170
Thomson, James
   The Seasons 109, 141
Tiepolo, Giovanni Battista 201
Tintern Abbey 130, 131–6, 139, 145, Figs. 5.4, 5.5
Titian 201
Tour, George de la
   The Magdalene with the Smoking Flame 47

Tower of Babel 53
Toyoharu, Utagawa 23
   Festivities in a mansion on the first Rat Day of the year Fig. 2.6
Transcendentalism 168, 227, 231, 302
transparency 88, 104, 105, 112, 136, 217, 240, 284, Fig. 5.6
Trinity (Father, Son and Holy Ghost) 117, 288, Fig. 4.16
Turgenev, Ivan 229
Turner, J. M. W. 109, 110, 111, 112, 152, 155, 156, 264. *See also* Ruskin; Soane
   Crypt of Kirkstall Abbey 156, 159, 167, Fig. 6.5
   Design for Fonthill Abbey Fig. 5.11
   Forum Romanum 110
   Liber Studiorum 152, 156, 165, Figs. 6.2, 6.5
   sublime and 110, 112, 152, 155–6, 159, 167, Figs. 6.2, 6.5 (*see also* sublime)
Tyng, Anne 236, 240, 249–50, 268

Upanishads 230

Vaals, Netherlands
   St. Benedictusberg Abbey 285–7, Figs. 10.1, 10.2
Vals, Switzerland
   thermal spa 287–8
Van Zanten, David 23
Vanbrugh, Sir John 90, 92, Chapter 3 *passim. See also* Hawksmoor, Wren
   Blenheim Palace 59, 62, 90
   Castle Howard 59, 62
   William Saunderson's House, Greenwich 62–4, Fig. 3.15
Vasari, Giorgio 6
Vassella, Alessandro 229
Vaughan, Henry 47
Venice 152, 163, 168, 176, 288, 302, Chapter 8 *passim. See also* Rossi; Ruskin; Stokes
   Biennale 208, 210, Fig. 8.4
   Brenta River 207
   Ca' Dario 200, 201
   Campo St. Angelo 153–4, 156, Fig. 6.1
   Cannaregio 210, Fig. 8.4
   Clock Tower, St. Mark's Piazza 217, Fig. 8.7
   Dogana di Mare 208
   Ducal (Doge's) Palace 168, 176
   Giudecca 209
   House, seventeenth century 202, Fig. 8.1
   Palazzo Camerlenghi 271
   Palazzo Contarini-Fasan 156, Fig. 6.3
   Palazzo Duodo 153
   Palazzo Foscari 153
   Palazzo Gritti 153–4, 156
   Palazzo Priuli 154
   Rialto 271
   Rialto Bridge 210, 271
   Santa Maria dei Miracoli 204–6, 207, 208, Fig. 8.2
   Santa Maria della Salute 208
   Scuolo San Giorgio degli Schiavoni 220
   St. Mark's 167, 199, 200, 215, 241
   Teatro del Mondo 208–10, 214, 215–6, 217, 302, Figs. 8.3, 8.4
   Torcello 174, Fig. 6.13
Venturi, Robert
   Complexity and Contradiction in Architecture 301
   Vanna Venturi House, Chestnut Hill, Philadelphia 247
Vermeer, Johannes
   The Astronomer 50, 83, 216
   The Geographer 50, 83
Verona 199, 200
Vicenza 210. *See also* Palladio
   Basilica 210
   Palazzo Chiericati 210
   Palazzo Thiene 85
   Villa Rotonda 216
Vidler, Anthony 87, 216
Vignola, Giacomo Barozzi da 61
Villar (biographer of Boullée) 93
Vinci, Leonardo da 2, 5, 109
Virgin Mary 243, 291, 292
Vitruvius 47, 284
   De Architectura 14
Voet, Caroline 286

Wagner, Richard 174, 176, 229
  Rhinegold 176
  Ring Cycle 174
Walpole, Horace 9, 117, Chapter 5
    passim
  The Castle of Otranto 125, 127,
    135, 136, Fig. 5.6
  Strawberry Hill, Twickenham
    127–30, Fig. 5.2
Walton, Paul 156
Warwick 45
  St. Mary's Church 56, Fig. 3.11
Warwick, Alexandra 151
Watkin, David 89
Whateley, Thomas 139, 143
  *Observations on Modern
    Gardening* 132
Wheler, George 42
Whitaker, William 245, 246
Wight, P. B.
  *National Academy of Design, New
    York City* 168
Wilkinson, J. C. 182
Wilson, Colin St. John 3, 4, 215
Wilson, Richard 264
Wölfflin, Heinrich 57, 58, 59
  Renaissance and Baroque 57
Wollaton Hall, Nottingham 43
Worcester Cathedral 128, 129
Wordsworth, William
  *Lines written a few miles above
    Tintern Abbey* 134
  Yew Trees 178 n.40
Wotton, Sir Henry 48
  The Elements of Architecture 48
Wren, Sir Christopher 36, 37, 38, 42,
    45, 46, 53, 54, 56, 59, 60, 62,
    64, 85. *See also* Hawksmoor
  St. Augustine, Watling St, London
    64, Fig. 3.16
  St. James's Piccadilly, London 38
  St. Paul's Cathedral, London 36
  Whitehall Palace, London 62,
    Fig. 3.14
Wright, Frank Lloyd 21–5, 174, 225,
    302
  *Avery Coolney House, Springfield,
    Illinois* 22

  Darwin Martin House, Buffalo
    32 n.39, 241
  Imperial Hotel, Tokyo 24
  Robie House, Chicago 22, 23
  Taliesin, Spring Green, Wisconsin
    23, 28
  Unity Temple, Oak Park, Chicago
    252
  William R. Heath House, Buffalo
    21, 22, 23, Fig. 2.5
  *Wright House and Studio, Oak
    Park, Chicago* 23–4
Wright of Derby, Joseph 87
  The Captive, from Sterne 84
  The Prisoner 83, 94, Fig. 4.1
Wurman, Richard Saul 233, Figs. 9.2,
    9.3
Wyatt, James
  *Pelham mausoleum, Brocklesby
    Park, Lincolnshire* 65
  Fonthill Abbey, Wiltshire 145–6,
    Fig. 5.11
Wye River 125, 130–46, 148 n.47,
    Figs. 5,4, 5.8

Yale University. *See also* Kahn
  Farnham Hall 168
  Yale Center for British Art 268, 271
  Yale University Art Gallery 238–9,
    240, 242, 254, 256, 268, Fig. 9.5
Yates, Francis 216
Yorkshire Sculpture Park, Wakefield
    143

Zen temples and gardens. *See* Japan/
    Kyoto
Zoroaster 42
Zumthor, Peter 287–94, 301
  'Bruder Klaus' Chapel, Wachendorf,
    Cologne 288–90, Figs. 10.3, 10.4
  *Kolumba Diocesan Museum,
    Cologne* 288, 291–4, Fig. 10.5
  Thinking Architecture 288
  Vals thermal spa 287–8
Zurich
  Swiss Federal Institute of
    Technology (ETHZ) 228–9, 231,
    238, 262